Risk Ratios

Short-Term Liquidity Risk

$$\text{Current Ratio} = \frac{\text{Current Assets}}{\text{Current Liabilities}}$$

$$\text{Quick Ratio} = \frac{\text{Quick Assets}}{\text{Current Liabilities}}$$

$$\text{Operating Cash Flow to Current Liabilities Ratio} = \frac{\text{Cash Flow from Operations}}{\text{Average Current Liabilities}}$$

$$\text{Accounts Receivable Turnover} = \frac{\text{Sales}}{\text{Average Accounts Receivable}}$$

$$\text{Days Receivable Outstanding} = \frac{365}{\text{Accounts Receivable Turnover}}$$

$$\text{Inventory Turnover} = \frac{\text{Cost of Goods Sold}}{\text{Average Inventories}}$$

$$\text{Days Inventory Outstanding} = \frac{365}{\text{Inventory Turnover}}$$

$$\text{Accounts Payable Turnover} = \frac{\text{Purchases}}{\text{Average Accounts Payable}}$$

$$\text{Days Payable Outstanding} = \frac{365}{\text{Accounts Payable Turnover}}$$

$$\text{Operating Cash Flow to Cash Interest Costs Ratio} = \frac{\text{(Cash Flow from Operations + Cash Outflow for Interest + Cash Outflow for Income Taxes)}}{\text{Cash Outflow for Interest}}$$

Long-Term Solvency Risk

$$\text{Long-Term Debt Ratio} = \frac{\text{Long-Term Debt}}{\text{Long-Term Debt + Shareholders' Equity}}$$

$$\text{Debt-Equity Ratio} = \frac{\text{Long-Term Debt}}{\text{Shareholders' Equity}}$$

$$\text{Long-Term Debt to Assets Ratio} = \frac{\text{Long-Term Debt}}{\text{Total Assets (Equities)}}$$

$$\text{Interest Coverage Ratio} = \frac{\text{(Net Income + Interest Expense + Income Tax Expense)}}{\text{Interest Expense}}$$

$$\text{Operating Cash Flow to Total Liabilities Ratio} = \frac{\text{Cash Flow from Operations}}{\text{Average Total Liabilities}}$$

$$\text{Operating Cash Flow to Capital Expenditures Ratio} = \frac{\text{Cash Flow from Operations}}{\text{Capital Expenditures}}$$

Financial Statement Analysis
A Strategic Perspective

Second Edition

Financial Statement Analysis
A Strategic Perspective

Second Edition

Clyde P. Stickney
The Signal Companies Professor of Management
Amos Tuck School of Business Administration
Dartmouth College

The Dryden Press
Harcourt Brace College Publishers
Fort Worth   Philadelphia   San Diego
New York   Orlando   Austin   San Antonio
Toronto   Montreal   London   Sydney   Tokyo

Editor in Chief: Robert A. Pawlik
Acquisitions Editor: Tim Vertovec
Assistant Project Editor: Cathy Spitzenberger
Book Designer: Jeanette Barber
Production Manager: Jacqui Parker
Art Program: Academy Artworks, Inc.

Address for Editorial Correspondence
The Dryden Press, 301 Commerce Street, Suite 3700, Fort Worth, TX 76102

Address for Orders
The Dryden Press, 6277 Sea Harbor Drive, Orlando, FL 32887
1-800-782-4479, or 1-800-433-0001 (in Florida)

Copyrights and Acknowledgements
The author wishes to thank the following for permission to reprint the mater-
ial listed:
AMERICAN ACCOUNTING ASSOCIATION for Tanaguchi Corporation—Part A on
pp. 297–307 and Tanaguchi Corporation—Part B on pp. 427–430.
JAMES A. LARGAY III for W.T. Grant Company on pp. 72–93.

ISBN: 0-03-096594-2
Library of Congress Catalog Card Number: 92-74067
Printed in the United States of America

4 5 6 7 8 9 0 1   067   9 8 7 6 5 4

The Dryden Press

To my students,
with thanks for permitting me to take the journey with you

The Dryden Press Series in Accounting

Introductory

Bischoff
Introduction to College Accounting
Second Edition

Principles

Hanson, Hamre, and Walgenbach
Principles of Accounting
Sixth Edition

Hillman, Kochanek, and Norgaard
Principles of Accounting
Sixth Edition

Computerized

Bischoff and Wanlass
The Computer Connection
Second Edition

Brigham and Knechel
Financial Accounting Using Lotus 1-2-3

Wanlass
Computer Resource Guide: Principles of Accounting
Fourth Edition

Yasuda and Wanlass
The Real Time Advantage

Financial

Backer, Elgers, and Asebrook
Financial Accounting: Concepts and Practices

Beirne and Dauderis
Financial Accounting: An Introducion to Decision Making

Hanson, Hamre, and Walgenbach
Financial Accounting
Seventh Edition

Hoskin and Hughes
Financial Accounting Cases

Kochanek, Hillman, and Norgaard
Financial Accounting
Second Edition

Stickney, Weil, and Davidson
Financial Accounting: An Introduction to Concepts, Methods, and Uses
Sixth Edition

Managerial

Ketz, Campbell, and Baxendale
Management Accounting

Maher, Stickney, Weil, and Davidson
Managerial Accounting: An Introduction to Concepts, Methods, and Uses
Fourth Edition

Intermediate

Williams, Stanga, and Holder
Intermediate Accounting
Fourth Edition

Advanced

Huefner and Largay
Advanced Financial Accounting
Third Edition

Pahler and Mori
Advanced Accounting
Fourth Edition

Financial Statement Analysis

Stickney
Financial Statement Analysis: A Strategic Perspective
Second Edition

Auditing

Guy, Alderman, and Winters
Auditing
Third Edition

Theory

Belkaoui
Accounting Theory
Third Edition

Bloom and Elgers
Accounting Theory & Policy: A Reader
Second Edition

Taxation

Everett, Raabe, and Fortin
Income Tax Fundamentals

Sommerfeld, Madeo, Anderson, and Jackson
Concepts of Taxation

Reference

Miller and Bailey
HBJ Miller GAAS Guide
College Edition

Williams and Miller
HBJ Miller GAAP Guide
College Edition

The HBJ College Outline Series includes these fine study aids:

Campbell, Grierson, and Taylor
Principles of Accounting I
Revised Edition

Emery
Principles of Accounting II

Emery
Intermediate Accounting I
Second Edition

Emery
Intermediate Accounting II

Frigo
Cost Accounting

PREFACE

The effective analysis of a set of financial statements requires an understanding of (1) the economic characteristics and current conditions of a firm's businesses, (2) the particular strategies the firm selects to compete in each of these businesses, and (3) the accounting principles and procedures underlying the firms financial statements. Equipped with these three essential building blocks, the analyst can assess the success of the strategies as measured by profitability, relative to the level of risk incurred. This three-fold approach to financial statement analysis elevates it from one involving the mechanical calculation of a long list of financial statement ratios to one where the analyst has an opportunity to integrate concepts from economics, business strategy, accounting, and other business disciplines. This synthesizing experience rewards the student both intellectually and practically.

The premise of this book is that students learn financial statement analysis most effectively by performing the analyses on actual companies. The text portion of the book sets out the important concepts and analytical tools and demonstrates their application using the financial statements of Coca Cola and Pepsi. Each chapter contains a set of short- and intermediate-length problems based, for the most part, on financial data of publicly held companies. Most chapters also contain case studies. Nine industry analysis cases appear after Chapter 10 that permit the student to apply these concepts and tools in a variety of industry settings. A financial statement analysis package (FSAP) that runs on either an IBM PC or Apple Macintosh microcomputer with Lotus 1 2-3 or Excel is available to aid in the analytical tasks.

Overview of Text

Chapter 1 describes the various settings in which an analyst might perform a financial statement analysis (for example, equity investment, credit extension, antitrust investigation) to emphasize the need to specify the purpose of the analysis before selecting the analytical tools. The chapter presents a structural framework for assessing industry economics and business strategies. It also reviews the purpose and content of each of the three principal financial statements, including those of non-U.S. companies appearing in a different format.

Chapter 2 reviews the statement of cash flows and presents a model for relating the cash flows from operating, investing, and financing activities to a firm's position in its product life cycle. The chapter demonstrates procedures for preparing the statement of cash flows when the firm either provides a funds flow statement (common outside of the United States) or provides no funds flow information.

Chapters 3 through 5 provide a review of various generally accepted accounting principles. Chapter 3 considers revenue recognition, inventory cost-flow assumption, and accounting for fixed assets and intangibles. Chapter 4 focuses on leases, retirement benefits, income taxes, reserves, and off-balance-sheet obligations. Chapter 5 discusses corporate acquisitions, investments in securities and consolidations, foreign currency translation, and segment reporting. We discuss each topic from the viewpoint of a financial analyst who is interested in interpreting the disclosures in the financial statements and notes. We consider each topic more or less independently of the others, so the instructor can choose which, if any, topics will be covered. Even if previous courses have exposed students to the accounting for each of these topics, they may find it helpful to take a "user" perspective and further develop their interpretive skills.

Chapter 6 discusses data issues that the student should address before embarking on a financial statement analysis, including the use of originally reported versus restated data (from acquisitions and divestitures), the effect of alternative accounting principles, and the impact of different reporting periods. The chapter closes by considering the use of average industry ratios as a basis for comparison.

Chapters 7 and 8 discuss the analysis of profitability. Chapter 7 explores the rate of return on assets (ROA). We disaggregate ROA into profit margin and assets turnover components, using the disaggregation to study the strategic positioning of a firm. We draw relevant concepts for interpreting the profit-margin/assets-turnover mix from the economics (economies of scale, marginal rate of substitution) and business strategy (product differentiation, low cost leadership) literatures. We obtain further insight into the behavior of ROA, profit margin, and assets turnover at a level-three (individual expense percentages and individual asset turnovers) and a level-four (segment data) depth of analysis. Thus, this chapter presents a four-level framework for analyzing the profitability of operations.

Chapter 8 explores the rate of return on common shareholders' equity (ROCE). Unlike ROA, ROCE explicitly considers the return and risk implications for a firm that takes on additional financial leverage. This chapter considers the characteristics of firms that tend to have the highest financial leverage (degree of capital intensity, cash generating ability of operations, variability of earnings, and need to take anti-takeover defenses). The chapter also considers the calculation and interpretation of earnings per share and price-earnings ratios.

Chapter 9 focuses on the analysis of risk, with emphasis on the role of information from the statement of cash flows in assessing the short-and long-term cash-generating ability of an enterprise. We relate firm-specific analysis of risk to systematic, or market, risk as measured by beta.

Chapter 10 describes and illustrates the procedures for preparing pro forma financial statements and using these projections in the valuation of companies. The financial statement relationships and analytical frameworks discussed in the preceding nine chapters form the basis for making these projections. We illustrate the procedures for preparing pro forma financial statements using data for Pepsi.

Overview of Cases

The cases fall into two groups: chapter-end cases and industry analysis cases. The W.T. Grant Company case (Case 2.1) demonstrates how poor management of working capital absorbs cash flows and can lead a firm into bankruptcy. The Arizona Land Development case (Case 3.1) shows the effects of alternative income recognition methods on the balance sheet, income statement, and statement of cash flows and requires students to select the appropriate income recognition method. The Fisher Corporation case (Case 5.1) illustrates the relation between financing strategy and the method of accounting for a corporate acquisition and requires students to trade off these two factors in structuring an acquisition. The Tanaguchi Corporation—Part A (Case 6.1) explores differences in U.S. and Japanese financial reporting and asks the student to develop an approach for neutralizing the effects of such differences. The Fly-By-Night International Group case (Case 9.13 involves bankruptcy prediction and raises ethical questions about dealings between a firm and its chief executive officer who is also its major shareholder. The Kroger Company case (Case 9.2) examines the financial performance of a company prior and subsequent to a major restructuring. The Tanaguchi Corporation—Part B case (Case 9.3) compares financial ratios of U.S. and Japanese machine tool companies to identify economic, institutional, strategic, and cultural reasons for differences in their performance. The Holmes Corporation case (Case 10.1) involves the valuation of a leveraged buyout candidate; the Rodriguez Home Center case (Case 10.2) involves the valuation of a small family-owned business; and the Revco case (Case 10.3) involves valuation in a fraudulent conveyance case.

The industry analysis cases should be assigned after completing the first nine chapters. These cases permit the student to integrate the industry economics, business strategies, and financial statement analysis for three firms in the same industry. These cases parallel the discussion of Coke and Pepsi in Chapters 1 through 9.

The industry analysis cases fall into four groups: consumer products, services, technology companies, and capital intensive companies. The key factors for success in each of these industry groups are different; the financial statement analysis performed will also differ as a consequence.

The consumer products cases (athletic footwear, consumer goods retailing) build on the discussion of Coke and Pepsi in the text and present opportunities for studying strategic tradeoffs between product differentiation (brand recognition, niche positioning) and low cost leadership (volume focus). Thus, the cases demonstrate effectively the usefulness of analyzing profit margins and assets turnovers.

The service industries (marketing services, commercial banking) present a uniquely challenging analytical task in that their most important asset, their employees, does not appear on the balance sheet. In addition, the financial statements of commercial banks are materially different from those of industrial companies, providing the analyst with an opportunity to apply accounting concepts to perhaps unfamiliar settings. These are also industries that are experiencing significant change at the current time as a result of mergers and deregulation. The marketing services industry case includes two non-U.S. companies.

The technology industries (the two pharmaceutical industry cases and the engineering workstation segment of the computer industry) provide the challenge of analyzing companies that have high front-end research and development costs, significant opportunities for economies of scale, relatively short product life cycles, and extensive foreign operations. The second pharmaceutical industry case includes two non-U.S. companies.

The capital-intensive industries (forest products and airlines) illustrate the importance of capacity utilization and the potential economies-of-scale benefits. Changes in regulation in recent years are causing major restructuring in these industries that surface when performing financial statement analysis.

Most instructors will probably find that assigning three to five industry analysis cases is sufficient to cement understanding and integration of material in the first nine chapters. Perhaps the instructor might use one case from each of the four groups. The cases include the case narrative and the amounts taken from the balance sheet, income statement, and statement of cash flows for the years 1987 to 1991. The instructor can teach these cases using only this set of materials.

The instructor has several additional options however:

1. Photocopy the full financial statements and notes for 1991 for each firm analyzed in the cases. The *Instructor's Manual* includes these financial statements and notes.

2. Obtain for free from The Dryden Press a financial statement analysis package (FSAP) for either IBM or Apple Macintosh and data files for the companies being analyzed. This option permits the students to integrate financial statement analysis with the financial analysis software.

3. Obtain copies of annual reports for 1991 and later years directly from the companies. By using the "Move" command in FSAP, the student can eliminate one year of data and add the most recent year's data. This option permits analysis of the most recent financial information about each company.

Significant Changes Made in this Edition

Users of the first edition of *Financial Statement Analysis* will find the following major changes In the second edition.

1. The second edition adds a new chapter (Chapter 2) on the statement of cash flows, including an expanded discussion of the cash flow characteristics of various types of businesses.

2. Chapters 3 through 5 include an expanded discussion of alternative accounting principles, with new material on off-balance-sheet commitments, health care commitments, and reserves.

3. Cases appear at the end of most chapters, with new cases added on income recognition (Case 3.1), U.S. and Japanese reporting (Cases 6.1 and 9.3), risk analysis (Cases 9.1 and 9.2), and valuation (Cases 10.2 and 10.3). New industry analysis cases appear for the athletic footwear industry, international pharmaceutical industry, and international marketing services industry.

4. Research findings applicable to most topics now appear throughout the book. The objective has been to obtain a balance between integrating the research findings without overemphasizing research methodology.

5. The second edition contains a significant amount of new text, problem, and case materials relevant to analyzing non-U.S. companies.

6. Chapter 10 includes an expanded discussion of valuation and its link to financial statement analysis. The chapter includes two new valuation cases in addition to the Holmes case included in the first edition.

7. The financial statements of Coke and Pepsi replace those of Campbell and Heinz used throughout the first edition.

8. The text, problems, cases, and the *Instructor's Manual* have been written in active voice to enhance readability.

Overview of the Ancillary Package

A financial statement analysis package (FSAP) is available as a free master disk to all adopters of the text. The package performs various analytical tasks (common size and trend statements, ratio computations) and displays the results both numerically and graphically. By altering data files for the companies in the cases (also included on the software disk), students can study the impact of the capitalization of operating leases, the conversion from LIFO to FIFO, and similar adjustments of reported data. Using FSAP to perform the tedious number crunching frees time and energy that the analyst can devote to the important interpretive task. Appendix C contains a user manual for FSAP as well as output for Coke and Pepsi.

An *Instructor's Manual* is also available to adopting professors. It contains suggestions for using this textbook, solutions to problems, teaching notes to cases, and the complete financial statements and notes for each company in the industry analysis cases. This latter section has been designed so that it can be photocopied for distribution to students.

Acknowledgments

Many people provided invaluable assistance in the preparation of this book and I wish to acknowledge their help in a formal manner here.

The following professional colleagues have assisted in the development of this edition by critically reviewing this edition or its predecessor or by responding to a user survey:

M. J. Abdolmohammadi, Bentley College

John Anderson, Syracuse University

Randy P. Beatty, Southern Methodist University

Joe Bylinski, University of North Carolina at Chapel Hill

John Cook, College of Wooster

Ben Copeland, University of North Texas

John A. Elliott, Cornell University

Marc J. Epstein, Yeshiva University

Laverne E. Gebhard, University of Wisconsin

P. R. Grierson, Slippery Rock University

Raymond D. King, University of Oregon

C. Jevons Lee, Tulane University

Janet H. Marler, Cornell University

Bruce Miller, University of California, Los Angeles

Bruce R. Neumann, University of Colorado

Larry M. Prober, Rider College

Edward Schwan, Susquehanna University

David Smith, Claremont-McKenna College

Gregory Waymire, Emory University

Peter R. Wilson, Duke University

Harold Wyman, Florida International University

The following individuals at The Dryden Press contributed to the development, production, and marketing of this edition: Jeanette Barber, Kevin Cottingim, Joan Harlan, Elizabeth Hayes, Jacqui Parker, Cathy Spitzenberger, Leigh Tedford, and Tim Vertovec.

The following former students or colleagues worked on the financial analysis software, helping to keep it both up-to-date with changing technology and increasingly user friendly: Mike Cleary, David Crowley, Cuong Do, Chris Duncan, Joanne Farrar, Jack Huisman, Larry Kaufmann, Dan Longnecker Mark Boughter, and particularly Susan Hardy.

The following individuals worked hard helping to prepare the manuscript: Mary Hill, Peg McGann, Suzanne Sweet, Lori Cantin, and particularly Tammy Stebbins. Their efforts and patience are very much appreciated.

The following individuals provided major assistance with this revision: Dawn M. Hargrave, Hanan S. Miron, and Ellyn Zeve.

My own thinking about accounting and financial statement analysis has been influenced over the years by four colleagues, coauthors, and friends: Paul R. Brown (New York University), Sidney Davidson (University of Chicago), Tom Selling (Securities and Exchange Commission), and Roman Weil (University of Chicago).

Finally, I wish to acknowledge the role played by former students in my financial statement analysis course at the Amos Tuck School of Business Administration, Dartmouth College. Learning is a mutual endeavor, and you have certainly been challenging and encouraging partners. This book is dedicated to each of you with thanks.

Clyde P. Stickney

Contents

Chapter 3 Generally Accepted Accounting Principles: Income Recognition and Asset Valuation 95

Chapter 4 Generally Accepted Accounting Principles: Liability Recognition and Related Expenses 143

Overview of Financial Reporting and Financial Statement Analysis

Analyzing a set of financial statements involves using ratios of key financial variables and other analytical tools to gain insight into the operating performance (profitability) and financial health (risk) of a firm. This textbook discusses the underlying rationale for important financial statement ratios and illustrates their usefulness in analyzing financial statements, using as examples the financial statements of the Coca-Cola Company (Coke) and Pepsico, Inc. (Pepsi). Appendix A and Appendix B, respectively, at the end of the book include the financial statements and notes for Coke and Pepsi.

The easiest job facing the analyst is calculating the financial statement ratios. In fact, the availability of computerized databases and financial analysis packages permits the analyst to do much of the *analytical* work "on line." The real challenge is *interpreting* the resulting analyses. Such interpretations require the analyst to (1) specify the purpose of the analysis, (2) identify the economics and current conditions facing the business, and (3) understand the important concepts and principles underlying the financial statements used in computing the financial ratios.

Before embarking on a study of the tools of financial statement analysis, we will identify the settings in which an analyst might perform a financial statement analysis. The purpose or objective of the analysis drives the analytical tools used. We will also review the purpose and content of the three principal financial statements included in corporate annual reports and relate them to the principal business activities of a firm. These are the primary objectives of this chapter.

Objectives of Financial Statement Analysis

The first question usually raised in analyzing a set of financial statements is: What do I look for? The answer to this question depends on the reason for, or objective of, the analysis. This section describes the more common purposes for analyzing financial statements and suggests the most important factors to examine in each case.

Equity Investment.   Perhaps the most frequently encountered reason for analyzing financial statements is to aid in decisions to acquire, retain, or sell an equity, or ownership, interest in a firm. The investor's primary interest is usually the expected return from the investment relative to the risks involved. Being risk averse, most investors will not assume greater risks unless the return anticipated from the investment compensates for the additional risk.

Equity investors receive their return in the form of dividends plus changes in the market price of their shares (that is, capital gains and losses). This return, in turn, relates to the ability of a firm to operate profitably. The investor analyzes the past operating performance of a firm as a basis for projecting future operating performance and the likely return from the equity investment.

The risks underlying an equity investment involve economywide factors, such as recessions, inflation, and unemployment; industry factors, such as increased competition, changes in technology, and availability of raw materials; and firm-specific factors, such as quality of management, existence of patents, and customer goodwill. Each of these dimensions of risk usually has financial consequences, affecting the ability of a firm to generate cash. A firm that is experiencing financial difficulty or even bankruptcy will be unable to generate needed amounts of cash at the right times to finance ongoing operations. Most analyses of risk involve a study of the experience of a firm in generating cash in the past and a projection of its continuing ability to do so.

Credit Extension.   Lenders of funds to a firm receive their return in the form of interest. They also have a right to have the principal amount repaid either periodically or at maturity. Loans may cover relatively short periods, such as six months to two years, as is common with loans from commercial banks, or extend to twenty years or more, as is common for corporate bonds.

Short-term credit analysis focuses on the ability of a firm to pay the interest and repay the principal at maturity. Given the time frame involved, the analyst examines the short-term cash-generating ability of the firm. Investors in a firm's corporate bonds have similar concerns, but the longer time period until maturity necessitates a more thorough examination of the long-run viability of the entity. Long-term credit analysis requires a closer look at the ability of the firm to remain profitable and to repay short-term and intermediate-term debt as it comes due.

Supplier Health.   A firm that depends on a supplier for a key raw material will want to be sure that the supplier is a healthy and viable entity. Given the ongoing relationship that is likely to exist, the analysis of the financial statements of that supplier will examine its profitability, financial condition, and ability to generate needed cash to sustain operations and to meet debt obligations as they come due. Knowing the profitability of the supplier may also help the firm in negotiating purchase discounts.

Customer Health.   A firm that extends credit to its customers will want to be sure that the customers can pay the receivables when they are due. The factor analyzed in this case is the cash-generating ability of the customer. The type of analysis performed depends on whether the customer is an individual or another business firm and on the size and term to maturity of the credit arrangement.

Employer Health.   Whether the employer is a viable entity and can maintain employment relationships in the future are interests of employees and labor unions. The profitability of the employer in relation to competitors is also of interest. Their analysis will therefore examine the firm's profitability, financial condition and cash-generating ability.

Antitrust Regulation.   Government antitrust regulators study the profitability of enterprises relative to their competitors to assess whether such firms have earned unreasonable (monopoly) returns in the past or might generate such returns in the future if regulators allow them to merge with another company. These regulators study the financial health of target companies in some mergers to determine if the "failing company doctrine" justifies a merger that would otherwise be disallowed because of its impact on competition in an industry.

Internal Operations Analysis.   Firms analyze the operating performance of their business segments or divisions as a basis for performance evaluation, planning and budgeting, or alteration of business unit strategy.

Competitor Analysis.   Firms examine the profitability of competitors to ascertain market shares and profit margins. This information may aid a firm in pricing, product mix, and similar decisions.

Audit Tests and Going Concern Judgments by Auditors.   Auditors must make judgments regarding the nature and extent of audit tests they will perform on clients' accounts. Auditors typically perform an analytical review of the financial statements to identify significant changes in financial statement relationships relative to prior years in making these judgments. The independent accountant must also make a judgment regarding whether a firm is a going concern in order to render an opinion on a client's financial statements. The independent accountant assesses the profitability, financial condition, and cash-generating ability of the enterprise in making these judgments.

Legal Judgment.   Courts often use lost profits as a measure of damages arising from injurious acts. The historical profitability of a firm often serves as a base for estimating the amount of the damage award. A more recent use of financial statements in legal judgments relates to cases involving fraudulent conveyance. Equity holders who sell their shares in a leveraged buyout transaction indirectly take assets out of a firm. The underlying assumption made in such transactions is that the assets remaining in the firm after the buyout are sufficient to cover creditors' claims (that is, that the firm is solvent). Subsequent evidence sometimes indicates that remaining assets are insufficient to satisfy creditors' claims and that the firm was in fact insolvent at the time of the leveraged buyout. Creditors have sued various participants in the buyout (equity holders, investment bankers, attorneys) claiming that a fraudulent conveyance of the firm's assets occurred. Courts examine the value of a firm's assets relative to the value of creditors' claims in assessing whether a fraudulent conveyance occurred.

Valuation of Acquisition Candidate.   Analysis of the financial statements of a target company assists in determining the price to be paid and the impact of the acquisition on postmerger financial statements of the new, combined enterprise.

The numerous settings in which financial statement analysis plays a role suggest that the type of analysis performed depends on the purpose of the analysis. In some cases, profitability is of primary concern. *Profitability* is of primary concern in antitrust regulation, internal operations analysis, competitor analysis, and damage award valuations by courts. Chapters 7 and 8 discuss tools for analyzing profitability. Short-term cash-generating ability, or *liquidity risk analysis*, is of primary concern to banks in lending to businesses for working capital needs and to individuals for auto and other short-term loans. Short-term cash-generating ability is also of concern to business firms in extending credit to customers for purchases made on account. The first half of Chapter 9 discusses liquidity risk analysis. Long-term cash-generating ability, or *solvency risk analysis*, is the concern of investors who wish to acquire the long-term bonds of a company and to independent auditors who must make going concern judgments regarding their client firms. The second half of Chapter 9 discusses solvency risk analysis. Both profitability and risk (liquidity and solvency) are of interest in many settings. Most investment decisions, for example, involve comparisons of expected return with the level of risk. Those comparisons utilize the full set of analytical tools. Because the factors of concern and the analytical tools used differ depending on the setting for the financial statement analysis, the analyst should clearly specify the purpose of the analysis at the outset.

Role of Financial Statement Analysis in an Efficient Capital Market

There are differing views as to the benefits of analyzing a set of financial statements. One view is that the stock market is efficient in reacting to published information about a firm. That is, market participants react intelligently and quickly to information they receive, so that market prices continually reflect underlying economic values. One implication of an efficient capital market is that financial statement users cannot routinely analyze financial statements to find "undervalued" or "overvalued" securities. The market quickly impounds new information in security prices.

Empirical research examining the effect of new information on security returns generally uses a statistical regression model that filters out the effects of economywide, or marketwide, phenomena. The researcher begins by regressing a particular firm's security returns (the sum of dividends plus changes in the market price of common shares divided by the market price at the beginning of the period) on an index of returns for all shares in the market. The researcher uses either a daily, weekly, or monthly return series for some period that excludes the period of release of the new information being studied. A regression equation of the following form results:

$$\frac{\text{Firm Specific}}{\text{Rate of Return}} = a + B\left(\frac{\text{Marketwide}}{\text{Rate of Return}}\right) + \text{residual.}$$

The B, or beta coefficient, measures the covariability of a firm's returns with that of the market. As Chapter 9 discusses more fully, analysts use beta as a measure of systematic, or market, risk. The a, or alpha coefficient, and the residual measure firm-specific elements of return. The regression that generates the alpha and beta coefficients has positive and negative residuals for individual firms but a zero residual using ordinary least squares regression techniques for all firms combined (that is, positive and negative residuals net to zero). The coefficients from this regression serve as a basis for generating expected firm-specific rates of return in future periods. The underlying assumption is that the return-generating process is constant (that is, the alpha and beta coefficients do not change). The release of new (unexpected) information about a firm to the market should cause the actual rate of return to deviate from the expected rate of return. The differential return gets captured in the residual. Thus, the researcher can study the behavior of the residual around the time of release of new information to ascertain whether the market reacts quickly and intelligently to the information.

A significant portion of the research on efficient capital markets uses recently released financial statement data as the new item of information. Most of these studies use earnings for this purpose. Because a firm's return-generating process, as captured in the alpha and beta coefficients in the regression, implicitly incorporates an expectation about the level of earnings (as well as other factors), the researcher examines the correlation between *unexpected* earnings and firm-specific return residuals. High correlations for a particular item of information when studied across a large number of firms suggest that the market reacts to that information. The direction and speed of that reaction indicate the degree of market efficiency with respect to the information. Later chapters discuss the results of many of the research studies linking financial statement data and market rates of return.

Opponents of the view that capital markets are efficient point to the market crash in October 1987 and the sharp increases in the market prices of potential merger buyout candidates as evidence that the stock market does not always price securities efficiently. They further point out that empirical research on capital market efficiency focuses on average aggregate market reactions to information, which does not preclude the possibility that the market might misprice shares of individual firms. As a consequence, the analyst can study the financial statements and other information of firms to identify misvalued securities. Opponents further note that various empirical studies on capital market efficiency often generate conflicting results. It is seldom clear whether the conflicting results emanate from flaws in the research design (for example, misspecifying the return-generating process), data problems, or market inefficiencies.

Even if we accept the notion of capital market efficiency, financial statement analysis still has a role to play. Someone, presumably sophisticated financial analysts, must perform the analysis if the market is to react appropriately to new information. Analysts perform the analysis, however, soon after firms release the information and market prices respond accordingly. Also, financial statement analysis serves a role in settings other than capital markets. The previous section described numerous such situations. In most of these cases, a particular firm or other entity performs the analysis rather than the many buyers and sellers involved in the capital market settings.

The strength of the research findings on capital market efficiency during the 1970s and 1980s led many academics to downplay the benefits of financial statement analysis. Several research studies, for example, found that current market prices were better predictors of future earnings than were current earnings predictors of future stock prices. The implication of this research is that analysts learn very little of value in analyzing financial statements that the market has not already reflected in security prices. This situation placed academics at odds with securities analysts who made their living identifying undervalued or overvalued securities and making buy/sell recommendations to customers. Recent academic research has demonstrated anew the benefits of performing "fundamental analysis" using information from the financial statements. Two studies by Ou and Penman showed that financial statements contain useful information for distinguishing permanent and transitory components of past earnings.[1] This information enhances predictions of future earnings and stock price changes. Whether these two widely acclaimed research studies will lead to a new stream of research linking financial statement information and stock prices remains uncertain.

Overview of Business Activities

Financial statements serve as "score sheets" of a firm's business activities. That is, accounting is a system for measuring the results of a firm's business transactions and summarizing them in a form that interested parties can understand. Enhanced understanding results from relating these financial statements to the busi-

---

[1] Jane A. Ou and Stephen H. Penman, "Financial Statement Analysis and the Prediction of Stock Returns," *Journal of Accounting and Economics* (November 1989), pp. 295—329; and "Accounting Measurement, Price-Earnings Ratio, and the Information Content of Security Prices," *Journal of Accounting Research—Supplement 1989* (1989), pp. 111–144.

Figure 1.1
Summary of Business Activities

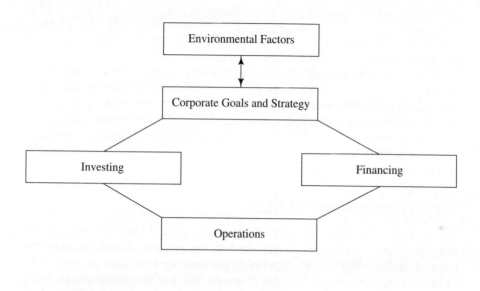

ness activities they attempt to portray. Figure 1.1 summarizes the business activities discussed in this section.

Environmental Factors

The economic characteristics and current conditions in the industries in which a firm participates are critical factors to consider when interpreting the results of financial statement analysis. Some of the questions an analyst is likely to address are:

1. What is the competitive market (output) profile of the industry? Are there few competitors with well-differentiated products or many competitors with similar, commodity-like products? Is foreign competition a factor of concern?

2. What is the production (input) profile of the industry? Is it labor intensive or capital intensive? Is it unionized or not? Are there constraints on the availability of raw materials or labor?

3. How important is technological change? Are products mature with few technological innovations or do new products continually emerge to shorten the life cycle of existing products?

4. What are the growth characteristics of the industry? Is the industry growing rapidly, holding stable, or declining?

5. What is the regulatory status? Are there barriers to entry, such as licenses or patents? Is the antitrust environment encouraging or discouraging mergers in the industry?

6. How sensitive is the industry to demographic changes or trends (aging of the population, two-income families)?

7. How sensitive is the industry to macroeconomic forces such as inflation or deflation, changes in interest rates, unemployment, and business cycles?

Coke derives over 80 percent of its revenues from soft drinks, with the remainder coming from consumer food products. Pepsi is more diversified, with approximately equal portions of sales derived from soft drinks, consumer foods, and restaurants. Exhibit 1.1 summarizes the more important economic characteristics and current conditions in these industries.

Corporate Goals and Strategy

The *goals* of a firm are the targets, or end results, toward which a firm directs its energies. A firm's managers serve as agents for owners in striving to increase the value of the firm. The relative importance of other corporate goals, such as maintenance of a contented work force or supportive community relations, varies among firms.

The *strategies* of a firm are the means for achieving the goals. Firms adopt company-level strategies and also specific product strategies. At a company level, firms must decide whether to operate primarily in one industry (for example, soft drinks) or whether to pursue a diversified strategy. Coke operates almost exclusively in soft drinks, whereas Pepsi conducts operations in soft drinks, consumer foods, and restaurants. Firms must also decide whether they intend to operate primarily in the domestic market or whether foreign operations will make up a significant part of their activities. The geographical business segment data for Coke and Pepsi indicate the following for Year 8:

	Sales Mix		Income Mix		Asset Mix	
	Domestic	**Foreign**	**Domestic**	**Foreign**	**Domestic**	**Foreign**
Coke............	39%	61%	20%	80%	39%	61%
Pepsi............	79%	21%	83%	17%	72%	28%

Coke's foreign operations dominate its activities, whereas Pepsi has a smaller foreign involvement.

The business strategy literature uses several schemes for classifying product-level strategies. One such scheme classifies products along a continuum from product differentiation to low-cost leadership. In a product differentiation strategy, a firm attempts to identify a specific market need and to develop a unique product (good or service) to meet that need. For example, a firm might base its product differentiation on technological or other inherent product advantages, a

Exhibit 1.1
**Summary of Economic Characteristics and Current Conditions
in the Soft Drink, Consumer Foods, and Restaurant Industries**

	Soft Drinks	**Consumer Foods**	**Restaurants**
Competitive Profile	Small number of direct competitors but larger number of competitors with substitute products. Established brand names create customer loyalty.	Many competitors with similar products but established brand names create customer loyalty.	Intensive competition in a highly saturated market with similar product offerings; some opportunities for brand recognition.
Production Profile	Production process is of moderate capital intensity. Quality control is important.	Production process is of moderate capital intensity. Quality control is critical.	Capital-intensive restaurant facilities combine with labor-intensive rendering of services. Quality control is critical.
Technological Change	Not significant.	Not significant, although some recent advances in packaging.	Not significant, although some recent advances in information accumulation and dissemination.
Growth Profile	Mature market in the U.S. but growth opportunities abroad.	Mature market in the U.S. but significant growth opportunities abroad.	Mature market in the U.S. but growth opportunities abroad.
Regulatory Attitude	Not an issue despite Coke and Pepsi's dominance in the industry.	Increased pressure on accurate labeling and advertising of products.	Not an issue.
Sensitivity to Demographic Changes	Aging of population could negatively impact demand in future years.	Two-income families increase the need for speed and convenience in meal preparation. Price is somewhat less important.	Two-income families increase the demand for restaurant foods.
Sensitivity to Macroeconomic Trends	Not particularly sensitive due to low relative price of product.	Not particularly sensitive because everyone has to eat.	Somewhat sensitive to recessionary conditions.

reputation for consistent quality, the availability in multiple sizes or colors, or similar characteristics. The aim is to build customer loyalty and generate attractive profit margins. The low-cost leadership strategy aims more to compete on the basis of low prices and low profit margins. The objective is to keep costs to a minimum (through quantity purchases, lean administrative organizations, attainment of economies of scale, and so on) and position products to underprice the competition.

Few firms actually pursue one of these strategies to the exclusion of the other. Most firms, for instance, attempt to develop customer loyalty for their products while maintaining control over their costs. When comparing firms, we should understand the relative emphasis each firm places on product differentiation versus low-cost leadership. Later chapters use this overview of the strategies of Coke and Pepsi and the environmental assessment of their principal businesses to aid in interpreting the financial statement analysis.

The narrative portion of a firm's annual report often describes, at least in general terms, the strategies it pursues. Firms commonly structure this narrative around their principal business segments, describing the products, current conditions, and financial performance of each segment.

Financing

A firm obtains financing for its business activities from creditors and owners. Short-term creditors, such as banks, suppliers, employees, and governmental units, provide financing for receivables, inventories, and operating expenses. Long-term creditors, purchasers of a firm's bonds and lessors, usually provide financing for property, plant, and equipment. Owners provide financing directly through capital contributions or indirectly by permitting firms to retain earnings rather than distribute dividends. The term structure of a firm's assets usually dictates the amount of its short-term versus long-term financing. Retailers, with heavy investments in receivables and inventories, tend to rely on short-term financing. Electric utilities use a preponderance of long-term financing for their large investments in plant assets. Firms base their decisions on the mix of long-term financing obtained from creditors versus owners on such factors as the firm's attitude toward risk (debt is more risky than equity because of the fixed interest and principal payments), its tax position (interest payments are tax deductible; dividend payments are not), and its ability to benefit from financial leverage. Chapter 8 describes and illustrates financial leverage.

Investing

A firm must invest the funds obtained from financing. It can use the funds to finance receivables or to acquire inventories, property, plant and equipment, securities of other firms, patents, licenses, or other contractual rights, or simply leave it as cash. The nature of a firm's businesses usually determines the particular investments made.

Operations

A firm obtains financing and invests in various resources to generate a profit. That is, it strives to sell its goods and services for a higher price than the cost of the investments made in those goods and services, including the cost of any financing. Through operations, a firm accomplishes a primary goal of business activities: increasing the value of the firm and thereby the wealth of its owners.

Principal Financial Statements

Business firms typically prepare three principal financial statements:

1. Balance sheet.

2. Income statement.

3. Statement of cash flows.

These financial statements report the results of financing, investing, and operating activities and serve as a basis for assessing the success of corporate strategies. This section presents a brief overview of the purpose and content of each of these three financial statements.

Generally accepted accounting principles, or GAAP, determine the valuation and measurement methods underlying financial statements. Official rule-making bodies set these principles. The Securities and Exchange Commission (SEC), an agency of the federal government, has the legal authority to specify acceptable accounting principles in the United States. The SEC has, for the most part, delegated the responsibility for setting GAAP to private-sector bodies within the accounting profession. Since 1973, that rule-making body has been the Financial Accounting Standards Board (FASB). The FASB specifies acceptable accounting principles only after receiving extensive comments from various preparers and users of financial statements.

The process followed in countries outside of the United States in setting accounting principles varies widely. In some countries, the amounts reported for financial and tax reporting closely conform. In these cases, legislative arms of the government play a major role in setting acceptable accounting principles. Other countries employ a model similar to that of the United States where financial and tax reporting methods differ and the accounting profession plays a major role in establishing GAAP.

The International Accounting Standards Committee, or IASC, strives to reduce diversity in accounting principles across countries and to encourage greater standardization. The IASC, established in 1973, comprises members from approximately 70 countries. Its pronouncements have no enforceability of their own. Rather, the representatives to the IASC pledge their best efforts in establishing the pronouncements of the IASC as GAAP within their countries.

Most references to GAAP in this book refer to accounting standards in the United States, although we point out instances where practices abroad differ from those in the United States.

Balance Sheet—Measuring Financial Position

The balance sheet, or statement of financial position, presents a snapshot of the resources of a firm (assets) and the claims on those resources (liabilities and shareholders' equity) as of a specific time. The assets portion of the balance sheet reports the effects of a firm's past investment decisions. The liabilities and shareholders' equity portion of the balance sheet reports the effects of a firm's past financing decisions.

The balance sheet derives its name from the fact that it shows the following balance or equality:

$$\text{Assets} = \text{Liabilities} + \text{Shareholders' Equity.}$$

That is, a firm's assets or resources are in balance with, or equal to, the claims on those assets by creditors and owners. The balance sheet views resources from two perspectives: a listing of the specific forms in which a firm holds the resources (such as, cash, inventory, equipment) and a listing of the persons or entities that provided the funds to obtain the assets and therefore have claims on them (such as, suppliers, employees, governments, shareholders). Thus, the balance sheet portrays the equality of investing (assets) and financing (liabilities plus shareholders' equity) activities.

The format of the balance sheet in some countries differs from that in the United States. In Germany and France, for example, property, plant and equipment, and other noncurrent assets appear first, followed by current assets. On the financing side, shareholders' equity appears first, followed by noncurrent liabilities and current liabilities. This format maintains the balance between investing and financing but presents accounts in the opposite sequence to that common in the United States. In the United Kingdom, the balance sheet equation takes the following form:

$$\begin{array}{c} \text{Noncurrent} \\ \text{Assets} \end{array} + \left(\begin{array}{c} \text{Current} \\ \text{Assets} \end{array} - \begin{array}{c} \text{Current} \\ \text{Liabilities} \end{array} \right) - \begin{array}{c} \text{Noncurrent} \\ \text{Liabilities} \end{array} = \begin{array}{c} \text{Shareholders'} \\ \text{Equity.} \end{array}$$

This format takes a shareholder's perspective by reporting the assets available for shareholders after subtracting claims by creditors. Financial analysts can easily rearrange the components of published balance sheets to whatever format they consider most informative.

Assets—Recognition, Valuation, and Classification.   Which resources of a firm does it recognize as assets? At what amount does the firm report these assets? How does it classify these assets within the assets portion of the balance sheet? GAAP determines responses to these questions.

Assets are resources that have the potential for providing a firm with future economic benefits: the ability to generate future cash inflows or to reduce future cash outflows. Firms recognize as assets those resources (1) for which a firm has acquired rights to their future use as a result of a past transaction or exchange and (2) for which the firm can measure, or quantify, the future benefits with a reasonable degree of precision.[2] Resources that firms do not normally recognize as assets because of failure to meet one or both of the above criteria include purchase orders received from customers, employment contracts with corporate officers, and a quality reputation with employees, customers, or citizens of the community.

Assets on the balance sheet are either *monetary* or *nonmonetary*. Monetary assets include cash and claims to a fixed amount of cash receivable in the future. The latter includes accounts and notes receivable and investments in bonds. The balance sheet reports monetary assets at the amount of cash the firm expects to receive in the future. If the date or dates of receipt extend beyond one year, the firm reports the monetary asset at the present value of the future cash flows (using a discount rate appropriate to the claim at the time it initially arose). Nonmonetary assets include inventories, plant, equipment, and other assets that do not represent a claim to a fixed amount of cash. A firm could report nonmonetary assets at the amount initially paid to acquire them (historical cost), the amount required currently to acquire them (current replacement cost), the amount for which the firm could currently sell them (current realizable value), or the present value of the amounts the firm expects to receive in the future from selling or using the assets (present value of future cash flows). GAAP generally requires the reporting of nonmonetary assets on the balance sheet at their historical cost amounts because this valuation is usually more objective and verifiable than other possible valuation bases. GAAP in some countries, such as the United Kingdom and France, permits periodic revaluations of property, plant, and equipment to current values.

The classification of assets within the balance sheet varies widely in published annual reports. The principal asset categories are the following:

Current Assets.   Current assets include cash and other assets that a firm expects to sell or consume during the normal operating cycle of a business, usually within one year. Cash, accounts receivable, inventories, and prepayments are the most common current assets.

Property, Plant, and Equipment.   This category includes the tangible, long-lived assets used in a firm's operations over a period of years and generally not acquired for resale. Property, plant, and equipment include land, buildings, machinery, automobiles, furniture, fixtures, computers, and other equipment.

Investments.   Included in this category are long-term investments in the debt or equity securities of other entities. If a firm makes such investments for short-term purposes, it classifies them under current assets.

---

[2] Financial Accounting Standards Board, *Statement of Financial Accounting Concepts No. 6*, "Elements of Financial Statements," (1985), para. 25.

Intangibles.   Intangibles include rights established by law or contract to the future use of property. Patents, trademarks, and franchises are intangible assets. The most troublesome questions of asset recognition revolve around which rights satisfy the criteria for an asset. For example, should firms recognize the value of a brand name as an intangible asset? Intangibles also include goodwill, which arises when one firm acquires another firm and pays an amount that exceeds the market value of the identifiable net assets. GAAP defines the excess as goodwill.

Liabilities—Recognition, Valuation, and Classification.   A liability represents a firm's obligation to make payments of cash, goods, or services in a reasonably definite amount at a reasonably definite future time for benefits or services received in the past.[3] Liabilities include obligations to financial institutions, suppliers, employees, and governments. Most troublesome questions regarding liability recognition relate to unexecuted contracts. GAAP does not recognize labor union agreements, purchase order commitments, and some lease agreements as liabilities because firms will receive the benefits from these items in the future instead of having received them in the past. Notes to the financial statements disclose material, unexecuted contracts, and other contingent claims.

Most liabilities are monetary, requiring payments of fixed amounts of cash. GAAP reports those due within one year at the amount of cash the firm expects to pay to discharge the obligation. If the payment dates extend beyond one year, then GAAP states the liability at the present value of the required future cash flows (discounted at an interest rate appropriate to the obligation when it initially arose). Some liabilities, such as warranties, require the delivery of goods or services instead of the payment of cash. The balance sheet states these liabilities at the expected future cost of these goods or services.

Published balance sheets classify liabilities in various ways. Virtually all firms use a current liabilities category, which includes obligations expected to be settled within one year. Balance sheets report the remaining liabilities in a section labeled as noncurrent liabilities or long-term debt.

Shareholders' Equity Valuation and Disclosure.   The shareholders' equity in a firm is a residual interest or claim. That is, the owners have a claim on all assets not required to meet the claims of creditors. The valuation of assets and liabilities in the balance sheet therefore determines the valuation of total shareholders' equity.

Balance sheets separate the total shareholders' equity into amounts initially contributed by shareholders for an interest in a firm (that is, preferred stock or common stock) and the amount of net income a firm subsequently realizes in excess of dividends declared (that is, retained earnings).

---

[3] *Ibid.,* para. 35.

Common Size Balance Sheets. One useful analytical tool for gaining insight about the structure of a firm's assets, liabilities, and shareholders' equity is a common size balance sheet. Exhibit 1.2 presents common size balance sheets for Coke and Pepsi for December 31, Year 7 and Year 8. Note that the common size balance sheet expresses each amount as a percentage of total assets or total liabilities plus shareholders' equity. Observe the following:

1. Receivables and inventories comprise a smaller proportion of Pepsi's total assets than of Coke's, reflecting Pepsi's greater involvement in restaurants (where sales are for cash and inventory turnover is higher than for soft drinks and consumer foods).

2. Investments represent a higher proportion of total assets for Coke than for Pepsi. Coke maintains a minority ownership position in its bottling operations whereas Pepsi owns most of its bottling operations.

3. Property, plant, and equipment make up a higher proportion of total assets for Pepsi than for Coke, reflecting the greater capital intensity of Pepsi's restaurant operations.

4. Intangible assets, principally goodwill, comprise a significantly higher percentage of total assets for Pepsi than for Coke, reflecting Pepsi's acquisition of restaurant chains (Pizza Hut, Taco Bell, Kentucky Fried Chicken).

5. Total current assets and total current liabilities represent approximately the same proportion of total assets and total liabilities plus shareholders' equity, respectively, indicating that these firms use short-term financing to finance short-term assets.

6. The long-term debt percentages for Pepsi significantly exceed those for Coke, reflecting Pepsi's need to finance capital-intensive restaurant operations and corporate acquisitions.

7. The retained earnings percentages of Coke exceeds those of Pepsi, due in part to Coke's higher profitability (analyzed more fully in later chapters).

8. The treasury stock percentages for Coke exceed those of Pepsi because Coke has followed a strategy of reacquiring its common shares on the market in recent years.

Analysts should interpret common size financial statements carefully because the percentages for individual accounts are not independent of the amounts for other accounts. For example, Pepsi's goodwill arising from acquisitions comprises a larger proportion of its total assets, leaving a smaller proportion for other assets. The fact that Pepsi's percentages for current assets are smaller than those for Coke does not *necessarily* mean that Pepsi needs less receivables or inventories for its operations.

Percentage Change Balance Sheets. A useful analytical tool for gaining insights about changes in the amount and structure of a firm's assets, liabilities, and

Exhibit 1.2
Common Size Balance Sheets for Coke and Pepsi

	Coke		Pepsi	
	Year 7	Year 8	Year 7	Year 8
Assets				
Cash and Marketable Securities	14%	16%	10%	11%
Accounts Receivable	10	10	8	8
Inventories	10	11	4	3
Other Current Assets	10	8	2	2
Total Current Assets	44%	45%	24%	24%
Investments	29	26	6	9
Property, Plant, and Equipment	24	26	34	33
Intangible and Other Assets	3	3	36	34
Total Assets	100%	100%	100%	100%
Liabilities and Shareholders' Equity				
Accounts Payable	17%	17%	7%	7%
Short-Term Borrowing	17	21	6	9
Other Current Liabilities	10	8	11	12
Total Current Liabilities	44%	46%	24%	28%
Long-Term Debt	7	6	40	32
Other Noncurrent Liabilities	7	7	10	11
Total Liabilities	58%	59%	74%	71%
Preferred Stock	3%	1%	—	—
Common Stock	10	9	2%	2%
Retained Earnings	68	69	27	30
Treasury Stock	(39)	(38)	(3)	(3)
Total Shareholders' Equity	42%	41%	26%	29%
Total Liabilities and Shareholders' Equity	100%	100%	100%	100%

shareholders' equity is a percentage change balance sheet. Exhibit 1.3 presents percentage change balance sheets for Coke and Pepsi for December 31, Year 7 and Year 8. It also shows the compound annual growth rate in various balance sheet accounts for the five years ending December 31, Year 8. Observe the following:

1. Pepsi's total assets grew more rapidly than Coke's during each of the last two years as well as over the last five years. The higher growth evidences itself in most of Pepsi's individual assets. Pepsi's largest growth item during the period is goodwill (included in other assets) arising from acquisitions.

2. Pepsi financed this growth with both debt and shareholders' equity.

3. Coke reduced its long-term debt during the period but increased its short-term borrowing. It also issued new shares of common stock at approximately the same pace that it repurchased treasury stock. The common stock issues

Exhibit 1.3
Percentage Change Balance Sheet for Coke and Pepsi

	Coke			Pepsi		
	Year 7	Year 8	Five-Year Compound Annual Growth Rate	Year 7	Year 8	Five-Year Compound Annual Growth Rate
Assets						
Cash and Marketable Securities ..	(4.0%)	26.3%	11.5%	(5.2%)	18.4%	14.7%
Accounts Receivable	4.7%	16.0%	1.2%	26.7%	14.1%	16.9%
Inventories	1.3%	24.5%	1.5%	23.3%	7.3%	9.0%
Current Assets	11.1%	15.0%	6.9%	8.8%	15.0%	7.9%
Investments	1.5%	2.0%	12.5%	17.6%	55.1%	45.4%
Property, Plant, and Equipment	13.3%	14.9%	4.7%	17.4%	14.8%	18.6%
Accumulated Depreciation	10.8%	9.9%	4.4%	22.4%	21.5%	21.1%
Intangibles and Other Assets	307.0%	18.5%	(16.4%)	112.0%	6.8%	86.1%
Total Assets	11.2%	12.0%	6.1%	35.9%	13.3%	23.9%
Liabilities						
Accounts Payable	28.3%	13.6%	7.3%	19.8%	5.8%	12.4%
Short-Term Borrowing	5.1%	33.0%	34.9%	(40.3%)	87.9%	36.4%
Current Liabilities	27.5%	12.4%	16.5%	(4.7%)	29.2%	21.0%
Long-Term Debt	(27.9%)	(2.4%)	(14.3%)	128.8%	(7.8%)	37.0%
Total Liabilities	16.8%	13.2%	6.7%	40.9%	8.9%	24.9%
Shareholders' Equity						
Common Stock	.5%	.2%	43.5%	.0%	180.0%	22.9%
Retained Earnings	28.1%	14.8%	15.8%	19.5%	19.5%	18.2%
Treasury Stock	56.4%	9.5%	42.5%	(3.5%)	24.2%	5.4%
Total Shareholders' Equity	4.2%	10.4%	5.3%	23.1%	26.0%	21.7%

occurred early in the five-year period whereas the stock repurchases occurred late in the period.

As with the common size balance sheet, the analyst should interpret percentage change balance sheets cautiously. A large percentage change in one year for a particular item (such as, other assets for Coke in Year 7) may simply reflect a relatively small amount from the previous year that serves as a base. Also, a large percentage change for a particular item may not be significant if that item represents a small proportion of total assets or total liabilities plus shareholders' equity. Note, for example, that intangible and other assets for Coke represent only 3 percent of total assets in Year 7 and Year 8 (refer to Exhibit 1.2). Thus, the large percentage change for other assets in Year 7 and over the last five years plays only a minor role in explaining the changes in total assets.

Income Statement—Measuring Operating Performance

The total assets of a firm change over time because of investing and financing activities. For instance, a firm may issue common stock for cash, acquire a building by assuming a mortgage for part of the purchase price, or issue common stock in exchange for convertible bonds. These investing and financing activities affect the amount and structure of a firm's assets and equities.

The total assets of a firm also change over time because of operating activities. A firm sells goods or services to customers for a larger amount than the cost to the firm of acquiring or producing the goods and services. Creditors and owners provide capital to a firm with the expectation that the firm will use the capital to generate a profit and provide an adequate return to the suppliers of capital. The second principal financial statement, the income statement, provides information about the operating performance of a firm for some particular time period.

Net income equals revenues and gains minus expenses and losses. Revenues measure the inflows of net assets (that is, assets less liabilities) from selling goods and providing services. Expenses measure the outflows of net assets that a firm uses, or consumes, in the process of generating revenues. As a measure of operating performance, revenues reflect the services rendered by a firm and expenses indicate the efforts required or expended. Gains and losses arise from sales of assets or settlements of liabilities that are only peripherally related to a firm's primary operating activities (for example, sale of a building, early extinguishment of long-term debt). These gains and losses arise when a firm receives or pays a different amount than the amount at which the accounting records state the asset or liability.

Accrual Basis of Accounting.   Figure 1.2 depicts the operating, or earnings, process for a manufacturing firm. Net income from this series of activities equals the amount of cash received from customers minus the amount of cash paid for raw materials, labor, and the services of production facilities.

If the entire operating process occurred within one accounting period, few difficulties would arise in measuring operating performance. Net income would equal cash inflows minus cash outflows. However, a firm acquires raw materials in one accounting period and uses them in several future accounting periods. It acquires plant and equipment in one accounting period and uses them during many accounting periods. A firm often sells goods or services in an earlier period than when it receives cash from customers.

Under a cash basis of accounting, a firm recognizes revenue when it receives cash from customers and recognizes expenses when it pays cash to suppliers, employees, and other providers of goods and services. Because a firm's operating process usually extends over several accounting periods, the cash basis of accounting provides a poor matching of revenues and expenses, and therefore a poor measure of operating performance for specific periods of time. To overcome this deficiency of the cash basis, GAAP requires that firms use the accrual basis of accounting in measuring operating performance.

Figure 1.2
Operating Process for a Manufacturing Firm

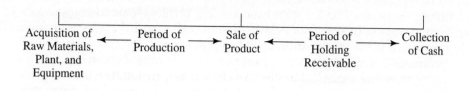

Under the accrual basis of accounting, a firm recognizes revenue when it performs all, or a substantial portion, of the services it expects to perform and receives either cash or a receivable subject to reasonably objective measurement. Most firms recognize revenue at the time they sell goods or render services. They match expenses with the associated revenues. For example, the cost of manufacturing a product remains on the balance sheet as an asset until the time of sale. At the time of sale, the firm recognizes revenue in the amount of the cash it expects to collect. It recognizes the cost of manufacturing the product as a matching expense. When a firm cannot easily link costs with a particular revenue, it recognizes an expense in the period when it consumes services in operations (for example, the corporate president's salary). The accrual basis of accounting focuses on the acquisition and use of economic resources in operations and not necessarily on their associated cash flows. The accrual basis provides a better measure of operating performance because it matches more accurately inputs with outputs.

Classification and Format within the Income Statement.   The future earnings stream of an asset or collection of assets is often the basis for investment valuation models. Analysts form predictions of the future earnings, or net income, of a firm by studying the past trend of earnings. Inaccurate projections from past data can occur if net income includes unusual or nonrecurring amounts. To provide more useful information for prediction, GAAP requires that the income statement include some or all of the following sections or categories, depending on the nature of the firm's income for the period:

1. Income from continuing operations.

2. Income, gains, and losses from discontinued operations.

3. Extraordinary gains and losses.

4. Adjustments for changes in accounting principles.

The first section reports the revenues and expenses of activities in which a firm anticipates an ongoing involvement. A firm that intends to remain in a line of business (for example, soft drinks) but decides to sell or close down some bottling operations would report any income, gain, or loss from such an action under "continuing operations." On the other hand, if a firm decides to terminate its involvement in a line of business (for example, restaurants), it would report the income, gain, or loss in the second section of the income statement labeled "discontinued operations."

"Extraordinary gains and losses" arise from events that are (1) unusual, given the nature of a firm's activities, (2) nonrecurring, and (3) material in amount. Corporate annual reports rarely disclose such items (except for tax benefits of net operating tax loss carryforwards and gains or losses on early debt retirements, both of which firms must report as extraordinary items). Many firms in recent years have reported "restructuring charges" in their income statements. Such charges reflect the cost of inventories, fixed assets, intangibles, or other assets that the firm does not expect to recover from future revenues. These charges also reflect future cash flows to settle obligations that the firm had not previously recognized as a liability. Because restructuring charges do not usually satisfy the criteria for "discontinued operations" or for "extraordinary gains and losses," firms report these charges in the continuing operations section of the income statement. Such charges usually appear, however, on a separate line to distinguish them clearly.

When firms change their methods of accounting, GAAP generally requires them to report the cumulative difference between the income reported under the old and new methods in a separate section of the income statement.

The majority of income statements include only the first section. Firms add the other sections as needed. Note, for instance, that the income statements for Coke and Pepsi in Appendices A and B, respectively, contain sections for continuing and discontinued operations.

The continuing operations section of the income statement commonly appears in one of two formats. A *single step* format lists and sums all revenues, lists and sums all expenses, and then derives net income in a single mathematical calculation. A *multiple step* format groups similar kinds of revenues and expenses and computes several subtotals before deriving net income. The income statement of Pepsi in Appendix B illustrates the single step format, although Pepsi adds one additional step to report the effect of income taxes. The income statement of Coke in Appendix A appears in a multiple step format, with subtotals for gross profit, income from continuing operations before income taxes, income from continuing operations, and net income.

Firms also vary in their reporting of expenses. Most firms in the United States report expenses by their function: cost of goods sold for manufacturing, selling expenses for marketing, administrative expenses for administrative management, and interest expense for financing. Other firms report expenses by their nature: raw materials, compensation, advertising, and research and development. The income statements of firms in countries outside of the United States typically contain sections for continuing operations and extraordinary items (if any). These income statements commonly report expenses by their nature rather than by their function.

Common Size Income Statements.   Common size income statements provide useful insights about the profitability of firms. Most common size income statements express expenses and net income as a percentage of sales. Exhibit 1.4 presents common size income statements for Coke and Pepsi. Note the following:

1. Coke's higher percentages for other revenues reflect its share of the earnings of its minority-owned bottling operations (appears as "equity income" on Coke's income statement).

2. Coke's lower percentages for cost of goods sold reflect either more efficient manufacturing operations, a greater ability to obtain premium prices for its products relative to Pepsi, or a different product mix. The difference in the cost of goods sold percentages for the two firms accounts for most of Coke's superior profitability.

3. Coke's higher percentages for income tax expense to sales occur because of Coke's higher percentages for income before taxes to sales. Both firms have average tax rates between 30 and 35 percent of net income before income taxes.

Percentage Change Income Statements.   A percentage change income statement, such as that shown in Exhibit 1.5 for Coke and Pepsi, provides insights about the rate of growth of operations. Consistent with the picture portrayed in the percentage change balance sheet, Pepsi's operations (sales, income

Exhibit 1.4
Common Size Income Statements for Coke and Pepsi

	Coke			Pepsi		
	Year 6	Year 7	Year 8	Year 6	Year 7	Year 8
Sales	100%	100%	100%	100%	100%	100%
Other Revenues	2	4	3	1	1	1
Cost of Goods Sold	(44)	(43)	(41)	(48)	(49)	(48)
Selling and Administrative						
Expenses	(36)	(37)	(40)	(41)	(39)	(40)
Interest Expense	(3)	(4)	(2)	(3)	(4)	(4)
Income Before Income Taxes ..	19%	20%	20%	9%	9%	9%
Income Tax Expense	(6)	(7)	(6)	(3)	(3)	(3)
Income from Continuing						
Operations	13%	13%	14%	6%	6%	6%
Discontinued Operations	—	6	—	—	—	—[a]
Net Income	13%	19%	14%	6%	6%	6%

[a]Amount rounds to zero.

Exhibit 1.5
Percentage Change Income Statements for Coke and Pepsi

	Coke			Pepsi		
	Year 7	Year 8	Five-Year Compound Annual Growth Rate	Year 7	Year 8	Five-Year Compound Annual Growth Rate
Assets						
Sales	7.5%	14.2%	4.2%	17.2%	16.8%	17.7%
Cost of Goods Sold	5.2%	8.1%	(2.4%)	19.4%	15.3%	23.2%
Selling and Administrative						
Expenses	10.2%	21.7%	10.9%	11.1%	16.0%	10.0%
Interest Expense	33.3%	(25.3%)	5.5%	76.8%	13.0%	27.2%
Income Tax Expense	6.5%	10.7%	2.3%	19.7%	28.5%	27.0%
Income from Continuing						
Operations	14.2%	15.8%	10.3%	18.2%	21.1%	24.2%

from continuing operations) grew more rapidly than Coke's during each of the last two years as well as over the last five years. Coke's income growth occurred largely because cost of goods sold increased less rapidly than sales. Pepsi's income growth, particularly prior to Year 8, occurred because selling and administrative expenses did not increase as rapidly as sales revenue. Perhaps Pepsi realized economies of scale in the marketing of its wide offering of consumer foods products.

Statement of Cash Flows

The third principal financial statement is the statement of cash flows. This statement reports for a period of time the net cash flow (inflows minus outflows) from three of the principal business activities depicted in Figure 1.1: operating, investing, and financing.

Rationale for the Statement of Cash Flows. Profitable firms, especially those growing rapidly, sometimes find themselves strapped for cash and unable to pay suppliers, employees, and other creditors. This occurs for two principal reasons:

1. The timing of cash receipts from customers does not necessarily coincide with the recognition of revenue, and the timing of cash expenditures to suppliers, employees, and other creditors does not necessarily coincide with the recognition of expenses under the accrual basis of accounting. In the usual case, cash expenditures precede the recognition of expenses, and cash receipts occur after the recognition of revenue. Thus, a firm might have posi-

tive net income for a period but the cash outflow for operations exceeds the cash inflow.

2. The firm may retire outstanding debt or acquire new plant and equipment at a time when there is insufficient cash available.

In many cases, a profitable firm finding itself short of cash can obtain the needed funds from either short- or long-term creditors or from owners. The firm must repay the borrowed funds from creditors with interest. Owners may require that the firm pay periodic dividends as an inducement to invest in the firm. Eventually, the firm must generate cash internally from operations if it is to survive. Cash flows are the connecting link between investing, financing, and operating activities. They permit each of these three principal business activities to continue functioning smoothly and effectively.

Classification of Cash Flows. The statement of cash flows reports the net amount of cash flow from a firm's operating, investing, and financing activities. It also shows the principal inflows and outflows of cash from each of these three activities. Figure 1.3 presents the major types of cash flows, which the following sections describe.

Operating. Selling goods and providing services are among the most important ways of generating cash for a financially healthy company. When assessed over several years, cash flow from operations indicates the extent to which operating activities have generated more cash than they have used. The firm can use excess cash from operations for dividends, acquisition of buildings and equipment, repayment of long-term debt, and other investing and financing activities.

Investing. The acquisition of noncurrent assets, particularly property, plant, and equipment, usually represents a major ongoing use of cash. Firms must replace such assets as they wear out and acquire additional noncurrent assets if they are to grow. Firms obtain a portion of the cash needed to acquire noncurrent assets from sales of existing noncurrent assets. However, such cash inflows are seldom sufficient to cover the cost of new acquisitions.

Financing. A firm obtains cash from short- and long-term borrowing and from issuing capital stock. It uses cash to pay dividends to shareholders, to repay short- or long-term borrowing, and to reacquire shares of outstanding capital stock. The amount of cash flow from these financing activities is the third major component reported in the statement of cash flows.

Firms sometimes engage in investing and financing transactions that do not directly involve cash. For example, a firm may acquire a building by assuming a mortgage obligation. It might also exchange a tract of land for equipment. The firm might issue common stock upon conversion of long-term debt. Firms disclose these transactions in a supplementary schedule or note to the statement of

Figure 1.3
Components of the Statement of Cash Flows

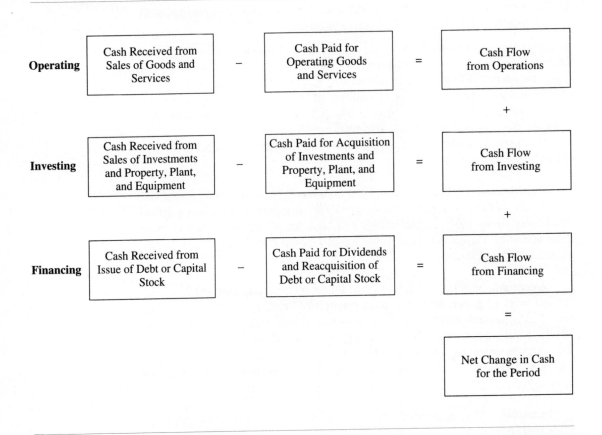

cash flows in a way that clearly indicates that they are investing and financing transactions that do not affect cash.

The statement of cash flows is not a required financial statement in many countries around the world. Common practice in Europe is to present a statement of sources and uses of funds, where "funds" are defined as current assets minus current liabilities, or working capital. Chapter 2 describes and illustrates analytical procedures for preparing a statement of cash flows. It also demonstrates the conversion of a statement of sources and uses of funds into a statement of cash flows.

Figure 1.4 summarizes the principal business activities and principal financial statements. The five business activities might be viewed as interconnected cogwheels. Cash flows reported in the statement of cash flows tie these activities together and keep them running smoothly.

It might be helpful at this point to study the financial statements and notes for Coke and Pepsi presented in Appendix A and Appendix B respectively. We make reference to these financial statements throughout the book.

Figure 1.4
Summary of Principal Business Activities and Financial Statements

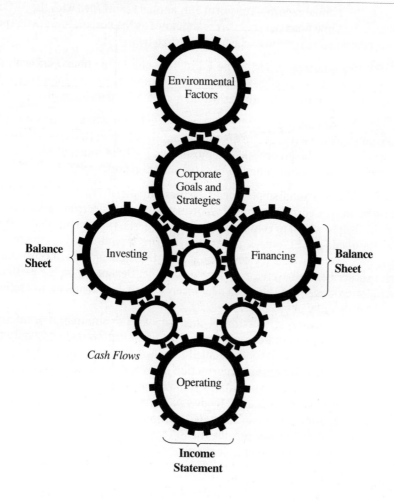

Sources of Financial Statement Information

Firms in the United States with publicly traded bonds or capital stock outstanding typically make available the following financial statements:

1. Annual report to shareholders—The "glossy" annual report includes balance sheets for the most recent two years and income statements and statements of cash flows for the most recent three years, along with various notes and supporting schedules. The annual report also includes a letter from the firm's chairman of the board or chief executive officer summarizing the activities of

the most recent year and a discussion by management of the firm's operations, financial position, and liquidity.

2. Form 10K annual report—The Form 10K annual report filed with the SEC includes the same financial statements and notes as the corporate annual report plus additional supporting schedules required by the SEC.

3. Form 10Q quarterly report—The Form 10Q quarterly report filed with the SEC includes condensed balance sheet and income statement information for the most recent three months, as well as comparative data for earlier quarters.

4. Prospectus or registration statement—Firms intending to issue new bonds or capital stock file a prospectus that describes the offering (the amount and intended uses of the proceeds). The prospectus includes much of the financial statement information found in the 10K annual report.

Most firms will send single copies of these financial reports to anyone requesting them. The corporate annual report usually lists the person or department within the firm to whom to communicate such requests. Documents filed with the SEC are available at SEC offices, generally requiring a photocopying charge. Disclosure, Inc., provides for a fee copies of each of these documents. Most business libraries subscribe to the services of Disclosure, Inc. Depending on the particular subscription arrangement, libraries may receive these documents on microfiche, on optical disk, or by photocopy.

Several information services firms offer databases or summaries of information extracted from corporate annual reports. Compustat, owned by Standard & Poor's, offers on-line databases of detailed financial statement items. Lotus One Source, a comprehensive on-line information source about firms (products, divisions, officers, analyst reports), contains summary financial statements. Standard & Poor's *Corporation Records* and Moody's *Industrial Manual* and other industry manuals provide summary financial statement information. Most of the sources listed in this paragraph do not provide the full text of notes to the financial statements that the original documents contain.

Summary

When performing financial statement analysis, many analysts have a tendency to want to "get cranking," that is, to start calculating a long list of financial statement ratios. This chapter has discussed several important preliminary steps that analysts should take:

1. Identify the purpose or objective of the analysis. This will better focus the particular analyses performed and analytical tools used.

2. Gain an understanding of the economics and current conditions of the industries in which a firm operates and the firm's particular strategies for competing in these industries. This step will aid in the interpretive process.

A third preliminary step is to study the financial statements to gain an understanding of the accounting methods used, account classification scheme followed, and other data issues that might affect the comparability of the financial statement amounts over time or across firms. Chapters 3 through 5 describe several of the more important alternative accounting principles that firms use in preparing financial statements. Chapter 6 considers other data issues, including retroactively restated financial statements, account classification differences, and reporting period differences. Students who have studied GAAP at an "intermediate principles" level can skip Chapters 3 through 5 and move directly to Chapter 6 at this point.

Perhaps the least challenging aspect of financial statement analysis is the calculation of financial statement ratios. An analysis package referred to as Financial Statement Analysis Package, or FSAP, is available to adopters from the publisher. FSAP runs on either an IBM or Apple personal computer. Appendix C includes a user manual for FSAP. It also presents the output of FSAP for Coke and Pepsi.

Problems

1.1 *Ratio Detective Exercise.* Effective financial statement analysis requires an understanding of a firm's economic characteristics. The relations between various financial statement items provide evidence of many of these economic characteristics. Exhibit 1.6 presents common size condensed financial statement information for firms in 13 different industries. These common size balance sheets and income statements express various items as a percentage of total revenues (that is, the statements divide all amounts by total revenues for the year). The 13 companies shown (all corporations except the professional basketball franchise) represent the following industries:

1. Advertising agency
2. Aerospace manufacturer (significant government contracts)
3. Beer brewery
4. Computer manufacturer
5. Department store chain
6. Distiller of hard liquor
7. Electric utility
8. Finance company (also involved in leasing)
9. Grocery store chain
10. Life insurance company
11. Pharmaceutical company
12. Professional basketball franchise (a partnership)
13. Steel manufacturer

Use whatever clues that you can to match the companies in Exhibit 1.6 with the industries listed above.

Exhibit 1.6
Data for Ratio Detective Exercise

	Company Numbers				
	(1)	(2)	(3)	(4)	(5)
Balance Sheet at End of Year					
Cash and Marketable Securities	.7%	19.1%	9.0%	.9%	11.9%
Current Receivables	.2	4.5	16.3	4.9	15.2
Inventories	7.5	—	11.9	5.6	13.2
Property, Plant, and Equipment					
Cost	17.0	.8	42.9	79.4	54.0
Accumulated Depreciation	(5.5)	(.7)	(21.0)	(21.7)	(26.9)
Net	11.5	.1	21.9	57.7	27.1
Other Assets	1.4	23.2	12.5	6.9	8.7
Total Assets	21.3%	46.9%	71.6%	76.0%	76.1%
Current Liabilities	7.8%	21.0%	32.7%	13.2%	22.3%
Long-Term Debt	3.6	—	6.3	14.7	8.7
Other Noncurrent Liabilities	1.4	15.6	5.5	14.2	4.9
Owners' Equity	8.5	10.3	27.1	33.9	40.2
Total Equities	21.3%	46.9%	71.6%	76.0%	76.1%
Income Statement for Year					
Sales	100.0%	100.0%	100.0%	100.0%	100.0%
Cost of Goods Sold (Excluding					
Depreciation) or Operating					
Expenses[a]	76.9	61.8	74.8	62.0	71.1
Depreciation	1.4	.1	4.1	3.6	6.8
Interest	.4	1.9	.7	.8	.5
Advertising and Promotion	3.6	.5	—	8.0	—
Research and Development	—	—	3.5	—	7.7
Income Taxes	1.1	—	4.5	5.5	2.8
All Other Items (Net)	15.5	(.7)	7.2	13.4	6.5
Total Expenses	98.9%	63.6%	94.8%	93.3%	95.4%
Net Income	1.1%	36.4%	5.2%	6.7%	4.6%
Cash Flow from Operations/					
Capital Expenditures	1.22	—	2.95	1.17	1.09

[a]Represents operating expenses for the following companies: advertising agency, finance company, life insurance company, professional basketball franchise.

1.2 *Interpreting Common Size Financial Statements.* R. V. Suppliers manufactures "Kaps," a relatively low-cost camping unit attached to a pickup truck. Most units consist of an aluminum frame and a fiberglass skin. The firm experienced a 59 percent increase in sales between Year 4 and Year 5 as a result of heightened interest in camping and other outdoor activities. However, fears of conflict in the Middle East beginning early in Year 6 led potential buyers to shun pickup trucks in preference for more energy-efficient small domestic and foreign automobiles, re-

(6)	(7)	(8)	(9)	(10)	(11)	(12)	(13)
1.6%	4.4%	22.7%	5.1%	14.4%	245.6%	1.0%	25.2%
36.2	13.5	21.3	13.2	70.6	11.9	7.8	562.5
14.4	21.7	13.0	10.5	7.5	—	11.4	—
37.5	25.3	65.9	162.5	18.4	3.6	398.4	70.8
(12.0)	(11.8)	(27.4)	(80.5)	(9.3)	(1.8)	(109.6)	(21.4)
25.5	13.5	38.5	82.0	9.1	1.8	288.8	49.4
2.2	31.8	16.7	4.0	22.1	51.9	8.7	57.5
79.9%	84.9%	112.2%	114.8%	123.7%	311.2%	317.7%	694.6%
35.1%	15.3%	43.6%	12.5%	87.1%	203.9%	30.4%	437.5%
11.6	17.4	3.3	18.0	4.3	21.4	126.0	196.1
6.8	10.8	12.9	5.0	7.8	8.4	23.1	12.2
26.4	41.4	52.4	79.3	24.5	77.5	138.2	48.8
79.9%	84.9%	112.2%	114.8%	123.7%	311.2%	317.7%	694.6%
100.0%	100.0%	100.0%	100.0%	100.0%	100.0%	100.0%	100.0%
72.1	46.5	26.6	86.1	89.6	86.6	57.8	21.8
2.6	2.0	4.2	6.6	2.6	.9	10.2	14.8
1.3	2.0	1.1	1.8	1.2	3.4	10.1	47.3
3.3	11.2	4.0	—	—	—	—	—
—	—	11.2	—	—	—	—	—
2.9	6.6	9.9	(4.1)	3.9	2.5	8.2	7.0
13.5	23.5	25.1	6.4	(1.3)	(1.2)	(5.5)	—
95.7%	91.8%	82.1%	96.8%	96.0%	92.2%	80.8%	90.9%
4.3%	8.2%	17.9%	3.2%	4.0%	7.8%	19.2%	9.1%
1.09	5.20	5.20	1.36	3.06	44.80	.95	.80

sulting in a sales decrease between Year 5 and Year 6. Exhibit 1.7 presents common size balance sheets as of December 31, Years 4, 5, and 6. Exhibit 1.8 presents common size income statements for Years 4, 5, and 6. Exhibit 1.9 presents comparative statements of cash flows in dollars for Years 5 and 6.

    a. What is the likely explanation for the increased common size percentage for property, plant, and equipment between December 31, Year 4, and December 31, Year 5?

Exhibit 1.7
R. V. Suppliers
Common Size Balance Sheets

	December 31		
	Year 4	**Year 5**	**Year 6**
Assets			
Cash	10.6%	5.1%	2.7%
Accounts Receivable	21.9	23.8	12.5
Inventories	41.0	36.6	41.9
Prepayments	3.6	3.1	5.5
Total Current Assets	77.1%	68.6%	62.6%
Property, Plant, and Equipment (Net)	22.9	31.4	37.4
Total Assets	100.0%	100.0%	100.0%
Liabilities and Shareholders' Equity			
Notes Payable	7.6%	6.5%	15.7%
Accounts Payable	24.0	22.8	9.0
Other Current Liabilities	7.6	5.9	2.3
Total Current Liabilities	39.2%	35.2%	27.0%
Long-Term Debt	11.5	22.2	28.4
Total Liabilities	50.7%	57.4%	55.4%
Common Stock	22.3%	12.6%	15.2%
Retained Earnings	27.0	30.0	29.4
Total Shareholders' Equity	49.3%	42.6%	44.6%
Total Liabilities and Shareholders' Equity	100.0%	100.0%	100.0%

b. The statement of cash flows indicates that inventories increased $31.6 million between December 31, Year 4, and December 31, Year 5. Why then did the common size percentage for inventories decline from 41.0 percent to 36.6 percent?

c. What is the likely explanation for the shift in the common size percentages for long-term debt and common stock between December 31, Year 4, and December 31, Year 5?

d. What is the likely explanation for the increased common size percentage for property, plant and equipment between December 31, Year 5, and December 31, Year 6?

e. What is the likely explanation for the increase in the common size percentage for notes payable between December 31, Year 5, and December 31, Year 6?

f. What is the likely explanation for the decreased common size percentage for net income between Year 4 and Year 5?

g. What is the likely explanation for the decreased common size percentage for net income between Year 5 and Year 6?

Exhibit 1.8
R. V. Suppliers
Common Size Income Statements

| | For the Year Ended December 31 | | |
	Year 4	Year 5	Year 6
Sales	100.0%	100.0%	100.0%
Cost of Goods Sold	(71.9)	(74.2)	(85.1)
Selling and Administrative Expense	(12.4)	(12.7)	(18.3)
Interest Expense	(.9)	(1.1)	(4.0)
Income Tax Expense	(4.6)	(3.8)	2.0
Net Income	10.2%	8.2%	(5.4%)

1.3 *Relations between Net Income and Cash Flows.* The ABC Company started the year in fine shape. The firm made widgets—just what the customer wanted. It made them for $0.75 each and sold them for $1.00. The ABC Company kept an inventory equal to shipments of the past 30 days, paid its bills promptly, and collected cash from customers within 30 days after the sale. The sales manager predicted a steady increase of 500 widgets each month beginning in February. It looked like a great year, and it began that way.

January 1   Cash, $875; receivables, $1,000; inventory, $750.

January   In January, ABC Company sold 1,000 widgets costing $750 on account for $1,000. It collected receivables outstanding at the beginning of the month. Production equaled 1,000 units at a total cost of $750. Net income for the month was $250. The books at the end of January showed:

February 1   Cash, $1,125; receivables, $1,000; inventory $750.

February   This month's sales jumped, as predicted, to 1,500 units. With a corresponding stepup in production to maintain the 30-day inventory, ABC Company made 2,000 units at a cost of $1,500. It collected all receivables from January sales. Net income so far, $625. Now the books looked like this:

March 1   Cash, $625; receivables, $1,500; inventory, $1,125.

March   March sales were even better—2,000 units. Collections, on time; production, to adhere to the inventory policy, 2,500 units; operating results for the month, net income of $500; net income to date $1,125. The books:

April 1   Cash, $250; receivables, $2,000; inventory, $1,500.

April   In April, sales jumped another 500 units to 2,500, and the manager of ABC Company patted the sales manager on the back.

Exhibit 1.9
R. V. Suppliers
Comparative Statements of Cash Flows
(amounts in millions)

	For the Year Ended December 31	
	Year 5	Year 6
Operations		
Net Income (Loss)	$ 34.6	$ (13.4)
Plus Depreciation Expense	4.8	7.6
(Increase) Decrease in Accounts Receivable	(26.8)	31.4
(Increase) Decrease in Inventories	(31.6)	4.6
(Increase) Decrease in Prepayments	(2.6)	(3.2)
Increase (Decrease) in Accounts Payable	21.8	(36.0)
Increase (Decrease) in Other Current Liabilities	3.8	(9.4)
Cash Flow from Operations	$ 4.0	$ (18.4)
Investing		
Acquisition of Property, Plant, and Equipment	$ (48.0)	$ (6.4)
Financing		
Increase in Notes Payable	$ 5.3	$ 15.0
Increase in Long-Term Debt	36.7	3.0
Cash Flow from Financing	$ 42.0	$ 18.0
Change in Cash	$ (2.0)	$ (6.8)

Customers were paying right on time. ABC Company pushed production to 3,000 units, and the month's business netted $625 for a net income to date of $1,750. The manager of ABC Company took off for Miami. Suddenly a phone call came from the treasurer: "Come home! We need money!"

May 1   Cash, $0; receivables, $2,500; inventory, $1,875.

a. Prepare an analysis that explains what happened to ABC Company. (Hint: Compute the amount of cash receipts and cash disbursements for each month during the period January 1 to May 1.)

b. How can a firm show increasing net income but a decreasing amount of cash?

c. What insights does this problem provide about the need for all three financial statements—balance sheet, income statement, and statement of cash flows?

1.4 Financial Statement Format and Terminology for a British Company. Exhibit 1.10 presents a consolidated balance sheet, Exhibit 1.11 presents a statement of consolidated profit and loss account, and Exhibit 1.12 presents a statement of

Exhibit 1.10
Grand Metropolitan Consolidated Balance Sheet at September 30

	Year 7		Year 6	
	£m	£m	£m	£m
Fixed Assets				
Intangible Assets		**2,317**		2,652
Tangible Assets		**3,756**		3,839
Investments		**214**		144
		6,287		6,635
Current Assets				
Stocks	**1,349**		1,269	
Debtors	**1,541**		1,451	
Cash at Bank and in Hand	**243**		215	
	3,133		2,935	
Creditors—Due within One Year				
Borrowings	**(206)**		(362)	
Other Creditors	**(2,343)**		(2,316)	
	(2,549)		(2,678)	
Net Current Assets		**584**		257
Total Assets Less Current Liabilities		**6,871**		6,892
Creditors—Due after More Than One Year				
Borrowings	**(2,925)**		(3,494)	
Other Creditors	**(191)**		(231)	
	(3,116)		(3,725)	
Provisions for Liabilities and Charges		**(328)**		(325)
		3,427		2,842
Capital and Reserves				
Called Up Share Capital		**508**		506
Reserves				
Share Premium Account	**451**		436	
Revaluation Reserve	**(940)**		(944)	
Associates' Reserves	**17**		10	
Profit and Loss Account	**3,365**		2,802	
		2,893		2,304
		3,401		2,810
Minority Interests		**26**		32
		3,427		2,842

Exhibit 1.11
**Grand Metropolitan Consolidated Profit and Loss Account
for the Year Ended September 30**

	Year 7	Year 6
	£m	£m
Turnover	9,394	9,298
Operating Costs	(8,335)	(8,349)
	1,059	949
Income from Interests in Associates	23	18
Trading Profit	1,082	967
Profit on Sale of Property	79	80
Net Exceptional Items	(3)	(35)
Interest	(239)	(280)
Profit on Ordinary Activities before Taxation	919	732
Taxation on Profit on Ordinary Activities	(279)	(216)
Profit on Ordinary Activities after Taxation	640	516
Minority Interests and Preference Dividends	(6)	(8)
Profit before Extraordinary Items	634	508
Extraordinary Items	435	560
Profit for the Financial Year	1,069	1,068
Ordinary Dividends	(198)	(167)
Transferred to Reserves	871	901

sources and application of funds for Grand Metropolitan, a British consumer foods firm. Identify the major differences in financial statement format and terminology used by Grand Metropolitan relative to that commonly encountered in financial reporting in the United States.

1.5 *Financial Statement Format and Terminology for a German Company.* Exhibit 1.13 presents a balance sheet, Exhibit 1.14 presents a statement of income, and Exhibit 1.15 presents a statement of sources and application of funds for Bayerische Motore Werke (BMW), a German automobile manufacturer. Identify the major differences in financial statement format and terminology used by BMW relative to that commonly encountered in financial reporting in the United States.

1.6 *Understanding Efficient Capital Markets Research Methodology.* Jim Seward, chief financial officer of Victoria Corporation, recently attended an alumni seminar at the business school where he received his MBA. A finance professor teaching at the seminar described the results of recent research on the efficiency

Exhibit 1.12

Grand Metropolitan Sources and Application of Funds for the Year Ended September 30

	Year 7	Year 6
	£m	£m
Funds Generated		
Group Profit before Taxation	919	732
Adjustments for Items Not Involving Cash Movement:		
Depreciation	216	190
Profit on Sale of Property	(79)	(80)
Other Items	(7)	—
	1,049	842
Sales of Fixed Assets and Investments	838	1,619
Share Issues, less Expenses	17	492
	1,904	2,953
Funds Applied		
Investments:		
Intangible Fixed Assets	—	1,853
Tangible Fixed Assets	513	1,341
Associates and Other Fixed Asset Investments	117	127
Goodwill	321	1,909
	951	5,230
Increase (Decrease) in Working Capital:		
Stocks	80	508
Debtors	206	627
Creditors and Provisions	12	(1,270)
	1,249	5,095
Exchange Adjustments	(483)	357
Tax Paid	218	262
Dividends Paid	167	129
	1,151	5,843
Decrease/(Increase) in Net Borrowings	753	(2,890)
Movements in Net Borrowings		
Borrowings —Due within One Year	(156)	175
—Due wfter More Than One Year	(569)	2,792
Cash at Bank and in Hand	(28)	(77)
Net Movement Shown Above	(753)	2,890

of capital markets. Jim was impressed by the obvious rigor of the research and the fervor with which the finance professor expounded on the wisdom of the marketplace in pricing a firm's securities. Jim felt that he remembered enough from the statistical regression course that he took as part of the MBA program that he would try out some of the efficient market ideas using data for Victoria Corporation.

Exhibit 1.13
BMW AG Balance Sheet

	31.12. Year 4	31.12. Year 3
	DM thousand	DM thousand
Assets		
Intangible Assets	14,111	10,470
Tangible Fixed Assets	3,467,347	3,462,998
Financial Assets	537,634	490,754
Fixed Assets	**4,019,092**	**3,964,222**
Inventories	1,040,237	1,020,581
Trade Receivables	286,466	239,044
Receivables from Subsidiaries	1,162,120	1,004,712
Other Receivables and Miscellaneous Assets.......	897,235	602,931
Receivables and Miscellaneous Assets	2,345,821	1,846,687
Marketable Securities	756,497	735,173
Liquid Funds	1,201,650	1,056,032
Current Assets	**5,344,205**	**4,658,473**
Prepaid Expenses	620	2,989
	9,363,917	**8,625,684**
Shareholders' Equity and Liabilities		
Subscribed Capital	750,000	750,000
Capital Reserve	590,357	590,357
Profit Reserves	1,925,679	1,738,179
Net Income Available for Distribution	187,500	187,500
Shareholders' Equity	**3,453,536**	**3,266,036**
Special Reserves	—	21,900
Registered Dividend Right Certificates	**106,921**	**87,714**
Pension Fund Provisions	983,706	890,970
Other Provisions	3,456,041	2,976,963
Provisions	**4,439,747**	**3,867,933**
Due to Banks	66,010	149,974
Trade Payables	1,040,896	955,173
Liabilities to Subsidiaries	12,227	2,468
Other Liabilities	244,580	274,486
Liabilities	**1,363,713**	**1,382,101**
	9,363,917	**8,625,684**

Exhibit 1.14
BMW AG Statement of Income for the Year Ended December 31

	Year 4	Year 3
	DM thousand	DM thousand
Net Sales	19,883,653	17,656,718
Increase in Product Inventories and Other Company-Produced Additions to Tangible Fixed Assets	115,180	91,203
Total Value of Production	**19,998,833**	**17,747,921**
Other Operating Income	498,049	344,510
Expenditure on Materials	(11,880,879)	(10,260,329)
Expenditure on Personnel	(4,000,186)	(3,586,372)
Depreciation on Intangible Assets and on Fixed Assets	(1,231,031)	(1,145,622)
Other Operating Expenditures	(2,638,471)	(2,459,803)
Income from Investment in Subsidiaries and Associated Companies	131,750	172,696
Interest Income	112,421	113,018
Income from Normal Business	990,486	926,019
Taxes on Income and Profits	(545,098)	(484,252)
Other Taxes	(70,388)	(66,767)
Net Income	**375,000**	**375,000**

Victoria Corporation, a publicly held firm traded on the over-the-counter market, manufactures optical scanning disks. For many years, Victoria Corporation used a first-in, first-out cost-flow assumption for inventories and cost of goods sold. It recently switched to a last-in, first-out cost-flow assumption. Jim is interested in how the market reacted to this change in accounting method.

To study this question, Jim obtained weekly closing prices for Victoria Corporation's common stock for the three-year period ending three months prior to the announcement of the accounting method change. This announcement was part of the firm's first-quarter earnings report. He then computed the weekly market rate of return for Victoria Corporation's common stock by dividing the change in market price (Friday closing price of the week minus Friday closing price of the preceding week) plus any dividends for which the record date occurred during the week by the market price at the end of the preceding week. This step resulted in a series of 156 weekly rates of return for Victoria Corporation. He also computed similar weekly rates of return using the Standard & Poor's 500 stock price index to measure marketwide price changes. Jim then regressed Victoria Corporation's rates of returns on the market-indexed rates of return. He obtained the following results:

Exhibit 1.15
BMW AG Sources and Application of Funds for Year 4

Application of Funds	DM thousand	Sources of Funds	DM thousand
Investment in Intangible Assets and Tangible Fixed Assets	1,254,934	Transfer to Profit Reserves from Net Income	187,500
Investment in Financial Assets	57,108	Increase in Liabilities in Registered Dividend Right Certificates	19,207
Reversal of Special Reserves	21,900	Transfer to Pension Fund Provisions	92,736
Change in Long-Term Liabilities	55,443	Transfer to Other Long-Term Provisions	28,000
		Depreciation and Retirement of Tangible Fixed Assets	1,246,944
		Depreciation and Retirement of Financial Assets	10,228
Long-Term	**1,389,385**	**Long-Term**	**1,584,615**
Increase in Inventories	19,656	Increase in Other Provisions	451,078
Increase in Trade Receivables	47,422	Increase in Trade Payables	85,723
Change in Receivables and Trade Payables to Subsidiaries	147,649	Net Income Available for Distribution	187,500
Change in Other Receivables, Miscellaneous Assets, and Prepaid Expenses	291,935		
Increase in Marketable Securities and Liquid Funds	166,942		
Decrease in Other Short-Term Liabilities	58,427		
Distribution for the Previous Year	187,500		
Short-Term	**919,531**	**Short-Term**	**724,301**
	2,308,916		**2,308,916**

$$\begin{array}{c} \text{Victoria Corporation's} \\ \text{Market Rate} \\ \text{of Return} \end{array} = .02 + 1.2 \left(\begin{array}{c} \text{Market Index} \\ \text{Rate of} \\ \text{Return} \end{array} \right).$$

Statistical tests of significance revealed that both coefficients were significantly different from zero.

Jim was now ready to study the market's reaction to the announced change in cost-flow assumption for inventories. He computed an *expected* market rate of return for Victoria Corporation for each week during the three months preceding the announcement and each week during the three months after the announcement. He based the calculation of this expected rate of return on weekly changes in the Standard & Poor's 500 stock price index and the alpha and beta coefficients in the regression shown above. He then compared those rates of return to the *actual* rates of return for Victoria Corporation for these same weekly periods. The difference between expected and actual rates of return Jim interpreted to reflect the effect of new information about Victoria Corporation coming to the market.

    a. Assume that actual rates of return closely parallel expected rates of return for the three months preceding and the three months succeeding the announcement of a change in accounting method for inventories. Would it be appropriate to conclude that the market reacted irrationally to this accounting change (that is, it accepted the reported earnings numbers as reported with no apparent consideration given to the different cost-flow assumption)? Elaborate.

    b. Assume that actual rates of return equaled expected rates of return for the 13 weeks prior to the announcement but that actual rates of return exceeded those expected for the 13 weeks after the announcement (most of the excess return occurred in the first few weeks after the announcement). Would it be appropriate to conclude that the market reacted rationally to the accounting change? Elaborate.

Income Flows versus Cash Flows: Key Relations in Understanding the Dynamics of a Business

2

The income statement reports the revenues and expenses of a firm during a particular period using the principles of the accrual basis of accounting. The objective in preparing an income statement is to obtain a measure of operating performance that matches a firm's outputs (revenues) with associated inputs (expenses). Chapter 1 pointed out that a firm's cash flows will not precisely track, or mirror, its income flows[1] because (1) cash receipts from customers do not necessarily occur in the same period that a firm recognizes revenues and cash expenditures to employees, suppliers, and governments do not necessarily occur in the same period that a firm recognizes expenses, and (2) cash inflows and outflows occur relating to investing and financing activities that do not flow directly through the income statement. The statement of cash flows reports the relation between income flows and cash flows from operations. It also reports the cash-flow effects of investing and financing activities. An understanding of the relation between income flows and cash flows is a critical ingredient in analyzing both the profitability and financial health of a business.

This chapter explores the statement of cash flows in greater depth than the overview presented in Chapter 1. We will look at the relation between income flows and cash flow from operations for various types of business and at the relation between the cash flows from operating, investing, and financing activities for firms in various stages of their life cycles. We will also describe and illustrate procedures for preparing the statement of cash flows using information from the balance sheet and income statement, as well as procedures for converting a statement of sources and uses of funds, commonly found in countries outside of the United States, into a statement of cash flows.

---

[1] This chapter uses income flows to mean net income and not revenues.

Income Flows, Cash Flows, and Life-Cycle Relations

Interpreting the statement of cash flows requires an understanding of two relations:

1. The relation between net income and cash flow from operations.

2. The relation among the net cash flows from operating, investing, and financing activities.

Net Income and Cash Flow from Operations

The first section of the statement of cash flows reconciles net income with cash flow from operations. This reconciliation involves two types of adjustments. First, certain revenues and expenses relate to changes in noncurrent asset or noncurrent liability accounts and have cash-flow effects that differ from their income effect. As an example, depreciation expense reduces net property, plant and equipment and net income. The addback of depreciation expense to net income eliminates the effect of depreciation since it does not use cash flow for operations. Chapter 5 points out that a firm holding an investment of 20 percent to 50 percent in another entity uses the equity method to account for the investment (a noncurrent asset). The investor recognizes its share of the investee's earnings each period, increasing the investment account and net income. It reduces the investment account for dividends received. Thus, net income reflects the investor's share of earnings, not the cash received. The statement of cash flows usually shows a subtraction from net income for the excess of the investor's share of the investee's earnings in excess of dividends received. Other examples of revenues and expenses that relate to changes in noncurrent asset or noncurrent liability accounts include amortization of intangible assets, deferred income taxes, amortization of premium or discount on bonds, and minority interest in the earnings of consolidated subsidiaries. Later chapters discuss each of these items more fully. Published statements of cash flows sometimes report a subtotal after adjusting net income for the above items and label the subtotal "working capital from operations."

The second type of adjustment to reconcile net income to cash flow from operations involves changes in operating current asset and current liability accounts. For example, an increase in accounts receivable indicates that the firm did not collect as much cash from customers as suggested by the amount of sales revenue included in net income. A subtraction from net income for the increase in accounts receivable converts accrual basis revenues to cash receipts from customers. Similar adjustments for changes in inventories, prepayments, accounts payable, and other operating current liabilities convert accrual basis income amounts to their associated cash flow amounts.

A study of the relation between net income and various measures of operating cash flows revealed (1) a high correlation between net income and working capital from operations, and (2) a low correlation between net income and cash flow from operations and between working capital from operations and cash flow from operations.[2] The primary difference between net income and working capital from operations for most firms is the addback for depreciation expense. If a firm's income growth tracks its additions to property, plant, and equipment, we would expect a high correlation between net income and working capital flow from operations. The low correlation between these two measures and cash flow from operations suggests that changes in operating working capital accounts do not track changes in net income. The next section uses the product life-cycle concept to explain further the behavior of working capital accounts as a firm grows, matures, and declines.

Relation between Cash Flows from Operating, Investing, and Financing Activities

A helpful framework for understanding more fully the relation between income flows and cash flows is the product life-cycle concept from marketing and microeconomics. Individual products (goods or services) move through four more or less identifiable phases: introduction, growth, maturity, and decline, as the top panel of Figure 2.1 depicts. The length of these phases and the steepness of the revenue curve vary by the type of product. Although it is generally difficult to pinpoint the precise location of a product on its life-cycle curve at any particular time, it is usually possible to identify its phase and whether it is in the early or later portion of that phase.

The middle panel of Figure 2.1 shows the trend of net income over the product life cycle. Net losses usually occur in the introduction and early growth phases as revenues do not cover the cost of designing and launching new products. Net income peaks during the maturity phase and then begins its decline.

The lower panel of Figure 2.1 shows the cash flows from operating, investing, and financing activities during the four life-cycle phases. During the introduction and early growth phases, negative cash flow from operations results from the cash outflows needed to launch the product. Negative cash flow from investing activities also occurs during these early phases to build productive capacity. The relative size of this negative cash flow for investing activities depends on the degree of capital intensity of the business. Firms must obtain the cash needed for operating and investing activities during these early phases from external sources (debt and shareholders' equity).

As the growth phase accelerates, operations become profitable and begin to generate cash. However, firms must use the cash generated to finance accounts receivable and build inventories for expected higher sales levels in the future. Thus, net income usually turns positive earlier than cash flow from operations. The

[2]Robert M. Bowen, David Burgstahler, and Lane A. Daley, "Evidence on the Relationship Between Earnings and Various Measures of Cash Flow," *Accounting Review* (October, 1986), pp. 713–725.

Figure 2.1
Relation of Income Flows and Cash Flows from Operations, Investing and Financing at Various Stages of Product Life Cycle

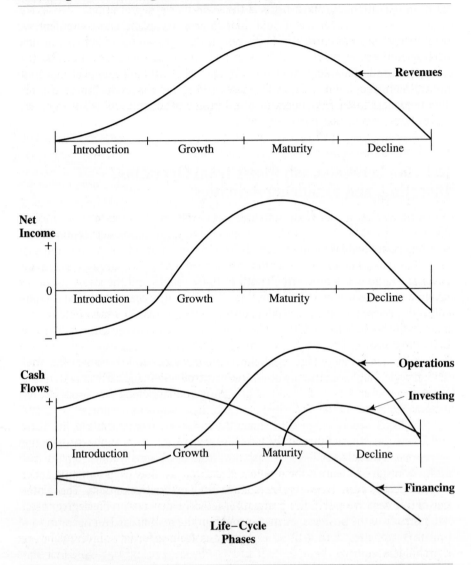

extent of the negative cash flow from investing activities depends on the rate of growth and the degree of capital intensity. As in the introduction phase, firms obtain most of the cash needed during the growth phase from external sources. (A multiproduct firm can use cash generated from products in the maturity phase of their life cycles to finance products in the introduction and growth phases and therefore does not need as much external financing.)

As products move through the maturity phase, the cash-flow pattern changes dramatically. Operations become a net provider of cash, both because of market acceptance of the product and a leveling off of working capital needs. Also, with revenues leveling off, firms invest to maintain rather than to increase productive capacity. During the later stages of the maturity phase, net cash flows from investing activities may even turn positive as cash inflows from sales of unneeded plant assets exceed new investments. Firms can use the excess cash flow from operations and to a lesser extent from the sale of investments to repay debt incurred during the introduction and growth phases and to pay dividends. During the decline phase, cash flow from operations and investing activities tail off as sales decrease. Firms repay their remaining debt.

The product life-cycle model discussed above provides helpful insights about the relation between sales, net income, and cash flows from operating, investing, and financing activities for a single product. Few business firms, however, rely on a single product; most have a range of products at different stages of their life cycles. Furthermore, the statement of cash flows reports amounts for a firm as a whole and not for each product. If the life-cycle concept is to assist in interpreting published statements of cash flows, the analyst needs a multiproduct view.

The analyst obtains such a multiproduct view by aggregating the positioning of each of a firm's products in their respective life cycles into a reading on the average life-cycle positioning of the firm. For example, the average positioning of a firm in technology-driven industries (biotechnology, pharmaceuticals, computers) is probably in the growth phase. Although such firms will have some products fresh off the drawing board and other products in their decline phase because of the emergence of new technologies, most of these firms' products are in their high growth phase. Most consumer foods companies have an average life-cycle positioning in the maturity phase. Branded consumer foods products can remain in their maturity phase for many years with proper product quality control and promotion (consider, for instance, Coke and Pepsi). Such companies continually bring new products to the market and eliminate products that do not meet consumer acceptance, but their average positioning is probably in the maturity phase. Certain industries in the United States, such as textiles and steel, are probably in the early decline phase because of foreign competition and outdated technology. Some companies in these industries have built technologically advanced production facilities to compete more effectively on a worldwide basis and essentially reentered the maturity phase. Other firms have diversified into more growth-oriented industries.

Exhibits 2.1 to 2.5 present statements of cash flows for firms in five different industries to illustrate the point that a firm's phase in its aggregate product life-cycle affects the interpretation of its statement of cash flows. Exhibit 2.1 shows a statement of cash flows for Sun Microsystems, a designer and manufacturer of computer workstations for use in scientific, engineering, and similar applications. Sun Microsystems is in the growth phase of its life cycle. Note that net income increased rapidly over the five years. Its cash flow from operations was either negative or only marginally positive relative to net income. The rapid growth required Sun Microsystems to carry accounts receivable and invest in inventories. Although suppliers provided some of the needed cash to finance these current assets, such

Exhibit 2.1
Sun Microsystems Statement of Cash Flows
(amounts in millions)

	Year 4	Year 5	Year 6	Year 7	Year 8
Operations					
Net Income	$ 3	$9	$ 12	$ 36	$ 66
Depreciation	1	4	6	25	51
Working Capital Provided by Operations ... $	4	$13	$ 18	$ 61	$ 117
(Inc.) Decr. in Receivables	−9	−5	−24	−58	−117
(Inc.) Decr. in Inventories	−8	−8	−21	−32	−77
(Inc.) Decr. in Other Current Assets	−1	−1	−18	−31	−30
Inc. (Decr.) Accounts Payable-Trade	4	4	21	33	58
Inc. (Decr.) in Other Current Liabilities	2	9	6	35	52
Cash Flow from Operations .... $	−8	$ 12	$ −18	$ 8	$ 3
Investing					
Fixed Assets Acquired .... $	−5	$ −15	$ −36	$ −76	$−117
Other Investing Transactions	0	−2	−2	−23	−32
Cash Flow from Investing .... $	−5	$ −17	$ −38	$ −99	$−149
Financing					
Incr. Short-Term Borrowing .... $	1	$ 3	$ 11	$ 21	$ 0
Incr. Long-Term Borrowing	3	5	1	121	0
Issue of Capital Stock	11	21	47	96	63
Decr. Short-Term Borrowing	0	0	0	0	−6
Decr. Long-Term Borrowing	0	−1	−2	0	0
Other Financing Transactions	0	3	3	0	0
Cash Flow from Financing .... $	15	$ 31	$ 60	$ 238	$ 57
Change in Cash .... $	2	$ 26	$ 4	$ 147	$ −89

financing was not sufficient. The relatively high proportion of depreciation expense to net income (over 50 percent for most years) is a clue that the firm is relatively capital intensive. The rapid increase in capital expenditures to acquire fixed assets reported among the investing activities provides further evidence of its capital intensity. To finance the negative cash flows from operating and investing activities, Sun Microsystems obtained cash by issuing debt and capital stock. Firms commonly issue debt when they use the proceeds to acquire physical assets, such as property, plant, and equipment. When firms need funds to finance ongoing research and development of products, they often issue common stock. The absence of physical assets to serve as collateral for such investments and the desire by investors to take an equity position to benefit from the upside potential of new technological breakthroughs explain the use of common stock in these instances.

Exhibit 2.2 presents a statement of cash flows for Wal-Mart, a rapidly growing discount store chain. Wal-Mart's net income increased rapidly during the five-year period, but so did its cash flow from operations. Wal-Mart either sells for cash or

Exhibit 2.2
**Wal-Mart Statement of Cash Flows
(amounts in millions)**

	Year 5	Year 6	Year 7	Year 8	Year 9
Operations					
Net Income	$ 271	$ 327	$ 450	$ 628	$ 837
Depreciation	67	90	124	166	214
Other Addbacks	9	18	7	0	1
Other Subtractions	0	0	0	−1	0
Working Capital Provided by					
Operations.	$ 347	$ 435	$ 581	$ 793	$1,052
(Inc.) Decr. in Receivables	−6	−12	−33	−6	−31
(Inc.) Decr. in Inventories	−368	−284	−643	−575	−700
(Inc.) Decr. in Other Current Assets	−77	−12	−8	0	−6
Inc. (Decr.) Accounts Payable—Trade	161	287	229	127	290
Inc. (Decr.) in Other Current					
Liabilities	22	16	139	120	129
Cash Flow from Operations.	$ 79	$ 430	$ 265	$ 459	$ 734
Investing					
Fixed Assets Acquired	$−322	$−513	$−675	$−757	$ −797
Other Investing Transactions	148	−160	−4	−51	9
Cash Flow from Investing	$−174	$−673	$−679	$−808	$ −788
Financing					
Incr. Short-Term Borrowing	$ 0	$ 0	$ 0	$ 104	$ 0
Incr. Long-Term Borrowing	129	298	460	194	248
Issue of Capital Stock	6	5	6	7	4
Decr. Short-Term Borrowing	0	0	0	0	−85
Decr. Long-Term Borrowing	−16	−12	−13	−42	−21
Acquisition of Capital Stock	−1	−1	0	0	0
Dividends	−30	−40	−48	−68	−91
Cash Flow from Financing	$ 88	$ 250	$ 405	$ 195	$ 55
Change in Cash	$ −7	$ 7	$ −9	$−154	$ 1

uses bank credit cards, so it does not need to carry heavy investments in receivables. It used suppliers to finance part of its increasing investments in inventories. The remaining cash needed for inventories came from operating cash flows. Wal-Mart realizes one of the highest profit margins in its industry. Because it receives cash at approximately the time of sale, it generates cash flow commensurate with its attractive profit margins. Wal-Mart's positive cash flow from operations, however, was not sufficient to fully finance the rapid expansion of stores and buildup of fixed assets. It relied primarily on long-term borrowing to make up the difference.

Exhibit 2.3 shows the statement of cash flows for Merck and Company, a pharmaceutical company. Merck, like Sun Microsystems and Wal-Mart, experienced rapid growth in net income. Its cash flow from operations also increased rapidly.

Exhibit 2.3
Merck and Company Statement of Cash Flows
(amounts in millions)

	Year 4	Year 5	Year 6	Year 7	Year 8
Operations					
Net Income	$ 493	$ 540	$ 676	$ 906	$1,207
Depreciation and Amort.	162	182	194	210	205
Other Addbacks	130	86	37	0	0
Other Subtractions	0	0	0	−66	−245
Working Capital Provided by Operations	$ 785	$ 808	$ 907	$1,050	$1,167
(Inc.) Decr. in Receivables	−102	−53	−42	−170	−106
(Inc.) Decr. in Inventories	0	22	−35	−80	−14
(Inc.) Decr. in Other Cash	29	−1	0	0	0
Inc. (Decr.) Accounts Payable—Trade	78	81	98	144	−77
Inc. (Decr.) in Other Current Liabilities	−49	152	166	379	417
Cash Flow from Operations	$ 741	$1,009	$1,094	$1,322	$1,387
Investing					
Fixed Assets Sold	$ 0	$ 92	$ 0	$ 0	$ 0
Fixed Assets Acquired	−274	−238	−211	−254	−373
Other Invest. Transact.	119	−278	−126	−206	262
Cash Flow from Investing	$−155	$ −424	$ −337	$ −460	$ −111
Financing					
Incr. Short-Term Borrowing	$ 38	$ 0	$ 43	$ 478	$ 0
Incr. Long-Term Borrowing	0	0	0	0	1,997
Issue of Capital Stock	2	18	25	21	30
Decr. Short-Term Borrowing	0	−79	0	0	−392
Decr. Long-Term Borrowing	−206	−8	−3	0	−1,991
Acquisition of Capital Stock	−164	−242	−500	−1,000	0
Dividends	−224	−235	−278	−335	−505
Other Financing Trans.	0	0	0	0	31
Cash Flow from Financing	$−554	$ −546	$ −713	$ −836	$ −830
Change in Cash	$ 32	$ 39	$ 44	$ 27	$ 446

Merck has used its suppliers and other creditors to finance its working capital needs so that cash flow from operations approximately equals net income plus depreciation. Merck's cash flow from operations was more than sufficient to finance capital expenditures on fixed assets and investments. It used the excess to pay dividends and reacquire capital stock. The reacquisition of common stock had the effect of increasing the price of its stock and increasing the proportion of debt in its capital structure. Such actions made Merck a less attractive candidate for an un-

Exhibit 2.4
Delta Airlines Statement of Cash Flows
(amounts in millions)

	Year 4	Year 5	Year 6	Year 7	Year 8
Operations					
Net Income	$ 176	$ 259	$ 47	$ 264	$ 307
Depreciation and Amort.	347	350	364	278	354
Other Addbacks	53	124	0	200	44
Other Subtractions	0	−1	−62	−229	−158
Working Capital Provided by Operations	$ 576	$ 732	$ 349	$ 513	$ 547
(Inc.) Decr. in Receivables	−95	−71	53	−95	−18
(Inc.) Decr. in Inventories	0	0	0	0	0
(Inc.) Decr. in Other Current Assets	79	−22	3	−2	−63
Inc. (Decr.) Accounts Payable—Trade	74	32	−7	22	103
Inc. (Decr.) in Other Current Liabilities	58	54	−206	112	107
Cash Flow from Operations	$ 692	$ 725	$ 192	$ 550	$ 676
Investing					
Fixed Assets Sold	$ 37	$ 67	$ 28	$ 44	$ 70
Fixed Assets Acquired	−484	−682	−601	−1,225	−1,331
Investments Acquired	0	0	−38	−17	−6
Other Investing Transactions	185	8	0	−162	0
Cash Flow from Investing	$−262	$−607	$−611	$−1,360	$−1,267
Financing					
Incr. Short-Term Borrowing	$ 14	$ 2	$ 0	$ 0	$ 0
Incr. Long-Term Borrowing	0	512	668	1,810	1,399
Issue of Capital Stock	0	7	1	1	1
Decr. Short-Term Borrowing	−12	0	0	0	0
Decr. Long-Term Borrowing	−430	−607	−186	−638	−308
Dividends	−24	−28	−40	−44	−58
Cash Flow from Financing	$−452	$−114	$ 443	$ 1,129	$ 1,034
Change in Cash	$ −22	$ 4	$ 24	$ 319	$ 443

friendly takeover by another firm. Merck's large new debt issue in Year 8 simply refinanced a debt issue coming due.

Exhibit 2.4 presents a statement of cash flows for Delta Airlines. Cash flow from operations significantly exceeds net income in each year because of the add-back of depreciation expense to net income. Depreciation is an expense that does not use cash. The cash outflow occurred when Delta acquired its fixed assets. The relation between net income and cash flow from operations for Delta is typical of capital-intensive firms. During Year 4 and Year 5, Delta's cash flow from opera-

Exhibit 2.5
Interpublic Group Statement of Cash Flows
(amounts in millions)

	Year 4	Year 5	Year 6	Year 7	Year 8
Operations					
Net Income	$ 33	$ 37	$ 41	$ 49	$ 60
Depreciation and Amortization	13	13	16	21	25
Other Addbacks	13	13	7	14	24
Other Subtractions	–2	0	–11	–12	–13
Working Capital Provided by Operations	$ 57	$ 63	$ 53	$ 72	$ 96
(Inc.) Decr. in Receivables	–20	–63	–126	–129	–214
(Inc.) Decr. in Inventories	0	0	0	0	0
(Inc.) Decr. in Other Current Assets	0	–1	–4	–1	–7
Inc. (Decr.) Accounts Payable—Trade	–22	46	157	142	152
Inc. (Decr.) in Other Current Liabilities	18	11	–7	22	64
Cash Flow from Operations	$ 33	$ 56	$ 73	$ 106	$ 91
Investing					
Fixed Assets Sold	$ 0	$ 0	$ 0	$ 3	$ 7
Fixed Assets Acquired	–12	–17	–17	–21	–44
Investments Acquired	–4	–8	–3	–6	–7
Other Investing Transactions	–23	–45	3	–7	–73
Cash Flow from Investing	$ –39	$ –70	$ –17	$ –31	$ –117
Financing					
Incr. Short-Term Borrowing	$ 19	$ 0	$ 10	$ 0	$ 17
Incr. Long-Term Borrowing	0	0	18	2	27
Issue of Capital Stock	2	2	3	3	3
Decr. Short-Term Borrowing	0	–8	0	–15	0
Decr. Long-Term Borrowing	–3	–3	–3	–8	–5
Acquisition of Capital Stock	0	0	–6	–22	–2
Dividends	–11	–12	–13	–14	–17
Cash Flow from Financing	$ 7	$ –21	$ 9	$ –54	$ 23
Change in Cash	$ 1	$ –35	$ 65	$ 21	$ –3

tions exceeded capital expenditures and Delta repaid long-term borrowing. Delta's net income dropped sharply in Year 6. However, because one of its major expenses, depreciation, did not require a cash outflow, cash flow from operations again exceeded net income. Despite the decline in net income and cash flow from operations, Delta essentially maintained its capital expenditures in Year 6. It used long-term debt to finance these acquisitions. Net income and cash flow from operations rebounded in Year 7 and Year 8. Delta dramatically increased its capital expenditures in those years, however, requiring external financing. Note that Delta (and other airlines) tend to use debt rather than equity financing for their fixed asset acquisitions. Debt is usually a less costly source of capital than equity. The assets acquired serve as collateral for the borrowing. Also, some of this financing comes in the form of capital leases (discussed in Chapter 4) in which the lessor, not Delta, takes advantage of income tax deductions for depreciation. Airlines tend to operate at a net loss for income tax purposes because of the low profit margins in this highly competitive industry and the use of accelerated depreciation methods. Delta leases certain equipment rather than purchasing it, allowing the lessor to claim the tax benefits and hopefully passing some of these benefits to Delta by way of lower lease payments.

Finally, Exhibit 2.5 presents a statement of cash flows for Interpublic Group, an advertising agency. Depreciation represents a less significant addback for Interpublic, a service firm, than for Delta. The primary source of variation between net income and cash flow from operations is management of working capital, particularly accounts receivable and accounts payable. An advertising agency serves as a conduit between clients wishing to place advertisements (giving rise to an accounts receivable for the agency) and the various media in which they place advertisements (giving rise to an accounts payable). Interpublic manages its position so that the receivables and payables do not closely offset each year, resulting in a varying relationship between net income and cash flow from operations. Because of the low level of capital intensity of an advertising agency, cash flow from operations is more than sufficient to finance capital expenditures. In most years cash flow from operations was also sufficient to finance acquisitions of other advertising agencies (included in the "other investing activities" line). Interpublic uses the excess cash to pay dividends.

These five statements of cash flows present typical patterns for firms in different types of industries and in different stages of their product life cycles. They also illustrate some of the interpretations that an analyst can make about the economic characteristics and performance of an entity by studying its statement of cash flows.

Preparing the Statement of Cash Flows

Publicly held firms in the United States typically include a statement of cash flows in their published financial statements each period. Smaller, privately held firms often prepare just a balance sheet and an income statement. Firms outside of the United States only infrequently include a statement of cash flows in their published statements. If they include a "funds flow" statement, they report it in a sources and uses format (instead of classifying items as related to operations, investing, and financing activities) and define "funds" differently than cash. This section illustrates a procedure for preparing a statement of cash flows using information from the balance sheet and income statement. It also illustrates the conversion of a statement of sources and uses of funds into a statement of cash flows. The resulting statement merely approximates the amounts that the statement of cash flows would report if the analyst had full access to a firm's accounting records. However, the estimated amounts should approximate the actual amounts closely enough for the analyst to make meaningful interpretations.

Algebraic Formulation

We know from the accounting equation that:

$$\text{Assets} = \text{Liabilities} + \text{Shareholders' Equity.}$$

This equality holds for balance sheets at the beginning and end of each period. If we subtract the amounts from the balance sheet at the beginning of the period from the corresponding amounts from the balance sheet at the end of the period, we obtain the following equality for changes (Δ) in balance sheet amounts:

$$\Delta \text{ Assets} = \Delta \text{ Liabilities} + \Delta \text{ Shareholders' Equity.}$$

We can now expand the change in assets as follows:

$$\Delta \text{ Cash} + \Delta \text{ Noncash Assets} = \Delta \text{ Liabilities} + \Delta \text{ Shareholders' Equity.}$$

Rearranging terms:

$$\Delta \text{ Cash} = \Delta \text{ Liabilities} + \Delta \text{ Shareholders' Equity} - \Delta \text{ Noncash Assets.}$$

The statement of cash flows explains the reasons for the change in cash during a period. We can see that the change in cash equals the change in all other (noncash) balance sheet amounts.

For this example we will use data from Exhibit 2.6, which shows the comparative balance sheet of Logue Shoe Stores for the years ending December 31, Year 5, Year 6, and Year 7. The balance sheets at the end of Year 5 and Year 6 report the following equalities:

	Cash	+	Noncash Assets	=	Liabilities	+	Shareholders' Equity
Year 5	$13,698	+	$132,136	=	$105,394	+	$40,440
Year 6	$12,595	+	$129,511	=	$85,032	+	$57,074

Subtracting the amounts at the end of Year 5 from the amounts at the end of Year 6, we obtain:

$$\Delta \text{ Cash} \quad + \quad \Delta \text{ Noncash Assets} \quad = \quad \Delta \text{ Liabilities} \quad + \quad \Delta \text{ Shareholders' Equity.}$$
$$-\$1,103 \quad + \quad (-\$2,625) \quad = \quad -\$20,362 \quad + \quad \$16,634$$

Rearranging terms we get:

$$\Delta \text{ Cash} \quad = \quad \Delta \text{ Liabilities} \quad + \quad \Delta \text{ Shareholders' Equity} \quad - \quad \Delta \text{ Noncash Assets.}$$
$$-\$1,103 \quad = \quad -\$20,362 \quad + \quad \$16,634 \quad - \quad (-\$2,625)$$

Exhibit 2.6
Logue Shoe Stores—Balance Sheet

	December 31, Year 5	December 31, Year 6	December 31, Year 7
Assets			
Cash	$ 13,698	$ 12,595	$ 5,815
Accounts Receivable	1,876	1,978	1,816
Inventories	98,824	106,022	123,636
Other Current Assets	3,591	—	1,560
Total Current Assets	$117,989	$120,595	$132,827
Property, Plant, and Equipment (Cost)	$ 63,634	$ 65,285	$ 64,455
Less Accumulated Depreciation	(37,973)	(45,958)	(54,617)
Net Property, Plant, and Equipment	$ 25,661	$ 19,327	$ 9,838
Other Assets	2,184	2,184	2,184
Total Assets	$145,834	$142,106	$144,849
Liabilities and Shareholders' Equity			
Accounts Payable	$ 21,768	$ 15,642	$ 13,954
Notes Payable	—	—	10,814
Current Portion of Long-Term Debt	18,256	10,997	7,288
Other Current Liabilities	4,353	6,912	5,489
Total Current Liabilities	$ 44,377	$ 33,551	$ 37,545
Long-Term Debt	61,017	51,481	43,788
Total Liabilities	$105,394	$ 85,032	$ 81,333
Common Stock	$ 1,000	$ 1,000	$ 1,000
Additional Paid-in Capital	124,000	124,000	124,000
Retained Earnings	(84,560)	(67,926)	(61,484)
Total Shareholders' Equity	$ 40,440	$ 57,074	$ 63,516
Total Liabilities and Shareholders' Equity	$145,834	$142,106	$144,849

Classifying Changes in Noncash Balance Sheet Accounts

The statement of cash flows classifies the reasons for the change in cash as being either operating, investing, or financing activities. The remaining task then is to classify the change in each noncash balance sheet account (right-hand side of the equation above) into one of these three categories. The analyst injects approximations into the preparation of the statement of cash flows at this step. Some of the changes in balance sheet accounts unambiguously fit into one of the three categories (for example, the change in common stock is a financing transaction). However, some balance sheet changes (for example, retained earnings) result from the netting of several changes, some of which relate to operations (net income) and some of which relate to investing or financing (dividends) activities. The analyst should use whatever information that the financial statements and notes provide about changes in balance sheet accounts to classify the net change each period.

Exhibit 2.7 shows a worksheet for preparing a statement of cash flows. The exhibit classifies the changes in the noncash balance sheet accounts. We will discuss the worksheet line by line.

(1) Accounts Receivable: Cash collections from customers during a period equal sales for the period plus accounts receivable at the beginning of the period minus accounts receivable at the end of the period. Thus, the change in accounts receivable clearly relates to operations. Line (16) shows net income as a source of cash from operations. Net income includes sales revenue. The amount for sales revenue included in the amount on line (16) plus or minus the change in accounts receivable on line (1) results in the amount of cash received from customers.

(2) Inventories: Purchases of inventory during a period equal cost of goods sold for the period plus inventories at the end of the period minus inventories at the beginning of the period. Line (16) includes cost of goods sold as an expense in measuring net income. The change in inventories on line (2) coupled with cost of goods sold included in the amount on line (16) results in the amount of purchases for the period. The presumption at this point is that the firm made a cash outflow equal to the amount of purchases. If the firm does not pay cash for all of these purchases, then accounts payable changes. We adjust for the change in accounts payable on line (8), discussed later.

(3) Other Current Assets: This balance sheet account typically includes prepayments for various operating costs. Unless the financial statements and notes present information to the contrary, the presumption is that the change in Other Current Assets relates to operations.

(4) Investments in Securities: This account can change for the following possible reasons:

Source of Change	Classification in Statement of Cash Flows
Acquisition of New Investments	Investing
Recognition of Income Using Equity Method	Operations
Receipt of Dividend from Investee	Operations
Sale of Investments	Investing

If the balance sheet and income statement provide information that permits the disaggregation of the net change in Investments in Securities into these components, then the analyst can make appropriate classifications of the components. Absent such information, we classify the change in the account as an investing activity.

(5) Property, Plant, and Equipment: We classify purchases and sales of fixed assets as investing activities.

(6) Accumulated Depreciation: The amount of depreciation recognized each period reduces net income but does not use cash. Thus, we classify depreciation as an operating item with a positive sign on line (6). When we add the amount for depreciation included under operations on line (6) to depreciation expense included as a negative element in net income on line (16), we eliminate the effect of depreciation from the Operations column. This treatment is appropriate since depreciation is not a cash flow (ignoring income tax consequences).

Exhibit 2.7
Worksheet for Preparation of Statement of Cash Flows

	Balance Sheet Changes	Operations	Investing	Financing
(Inc.) Decr. in Assets				
(1) Accounts Receivable		x		
(2) Inventories		x		
(3) Other Current Assets		x		
(4) Investments in Securities			x	
Property, Plant, and Equipment				
(5) Cost			x	
(6) Accumulated Depreciation		x		
(7) Other Assets			x	
Inc. (Decr.) in Equities				
(8) Accounts Payable		x		
(9) Notes Payable				x
(10) Current Portion of Long-Term Debt ..				x
(11) Other Current Liabilities		x		
(12) Long-Term Debt				x
(13) Deferred Income Taxes		x		
(14) Other Noncurrent Liabilities				x
(15) Common Stock				x
(15) Additional Paid-in Capital				x
(16) Retained Earnings	x (net income)			x (dividends)
(17) Treasury Stock				x
(18) Cash				

(7) **Other Assets:** Other Assets on the balance sheet include patents, copyrights, goodwill, and similar assets. Unless the financial statements and notes provide contrary information, the presumption is that the changes in these accounts are investing activities.

(8) **Accounts Payable:** The cash outflow for purchases equals purchases during the period plus accounts payable at the beginning of the period minus accounts payable at the end of the period. We derived the amount for purchases of the period as part of the calculations in line (2) for inventories. The adjustment on line (8) for the change in accounts payable converts purchases to cash payments on purchases and, like inventories, is an operating transaction.

(9) **Notes Payable:** This account is generally used when a firm engages in short-term borrowing from a bank or other financial institution. GAAP in the United States classifies such borrowing as a financing activity on the statement of cash flows, even though the firm might use the proceeds to finance accounts receivable, inventories, or other working capital needs.

(10) **Current Portion of Long-Term Debt:** The change in the current portion of long-term debt during a period equals (a) the reclassification of long-term debt from a noncurrent liability to a current liability (that is, debt that the firm expects to repay within one year as of the end-of-the-period balance sheet) minus

(b) long-term debt actually repaid during the period. The latter amount represents the cash outflow from this financing transaction. We consider the amount arising from the reclassification in connection with line (12) below.

(11) Other Current Liabilities: Firms generally use this account for obligations related to goods and services used in operations other than purchases of inventories. Thus, we classify the change as an operating activity.

(12) Long-Term Debt: This account changes for the following reasons:

Issuance of new long-term debt
Reclassification of long-term debt from a noncurrent to a current liability
Early retirement of long-term debt
Conversion of long-term debt to preferred or common stock

These items are clearly financing transactions but they do not all affect cash. The issuance of new debt and early retirement of old debt do affect cash flows. The reclassification of long-term debt included in the amount on line (12) offsets the corresponding amount included in the change on line (10), and they effectively cancel each other out. This is appropriate because the reclassification does not affect cash flows. Likewise, any portion of the change in long-term debt on line (12) due to a conversion of debt into capital stock offsets a similar change on line (15). The analyst enters reclassifications and conversions of debt, such as those described above, on the *worksheet* for the preparation of a statement of cash flows since such transactions help explain changes in balance sheet accounts. However, these transactions do not appear on the formal statement of cash flows because they do not involve actual cash flows.

(13) Deferred Income Taxes: Income taxes currently payable equal income tax expense [included as a negative element of net income on line (16)] plus or minus the change in deferred taxes during the period. Thus, we classify the change in line (13) as an operating activity.

(14) Other Noncurrent Liabilities: This account includes unfunded pension obligations, long-term deposits received, and other miscellaneous long-term liabilities. Absent information to the contrary, we classify the change as a financing activity.

(15) Common Stock and Additional Paid-in Capital: These accounts change when a firm issues new stock or repurchases and retires outstanding stock. We classify these transactions as financing activities.

(16) Retained Earnings: Retained earnings increase by the amount of net income and decrease for dividends each period. We classify net income as an operating activity and dividends as a financing activity.

(17) Treasury Stock: We classify repurchases of a firm's outstanding capital stock as a financing activity.

Illustration of Preparation Procedure

We will illustrate the procedure for preparing the statement of cash flows using the data for Logue Shoe Stores in Exhibit 2.6. Net income was $16,634 for Year 6 and $6,442 for Year 7. Exhibit 2.8 presents the worksheet for Year 6. The first col-

Exhibit 2.8
Worksheet for Statement of Cash Flows for Logue Shoe Stores
Year 6

	Balance Sheet Changes	Operations	Investing	Financing
(Inc.) Decr. in Assets				
Accounts Receivable	$ (102)	$(102)		
Inventories	(7,198)	(7,198)		
Other Current Assets	3,591	3,591		
Property, Plant, and Equipment	(1,651)		$(1,651)	
Accumulated Depreciation	7,985	7,985		
Other Assets	—			
Inc. (Decr.) in Equities				
Accounts Payable	$(6,126)	$(6,126)		
Notes Payable	—			—
Current Portion of Long-Term Debt	(7,259)			$(7,259)
Other Current Liabilities	2,559	2,559		
Long-Term Debt	(9,536)			(9,536)
Common Stock	—			—
Additional Paid-in Capital	—		—	—
Retained Earnings	16,634	16,634		
Cash	$(1,103)	$17,343	$(1,651)	$(16,795)

umn shows the change in each noncash balance sheet account that nets to the $1,103 decrease in cash for the period. We should observe particular caution with the direction of the change. Recall from the earlier equation:

$$\Delta \text{ Cash} = \Delta \text{ Liabilities} + \Delta \text{ Shareholders' Equity} - \Delta \text{ Noncash Assets.}$$

Increase	=	Increase		
Decrease	=	Decrease		
Increase	=		Increase	
Decrease	=		Decrease	
Decrease	=			Increase
Increase	=			Decrease

Thus, changes in liabilities and shareholders' equity have the same directional effect on cash, whereas changes in noncash assets have just the opposite directional effect.

We classify the change in each account as an operating, investing, or financing activity. Observe the following for Year 6:

1. Operating activities were a net source of cash for the period. The firm used the cash derived from operations to repay long-term debt.

2. Inventories increased substantially during the period, while accounts payable decreased. The two events reduced operating cash flows.

3. Compared to the level of depreciation during the year, capital expenditures on new property, plant, and equipment were small.

Exhibit 2.9 presents a worksheet for Year 7. The preparation procedure is identical to that in Exhibit 2.8. Note in this case that operations were a net user of cash. This is due primarily to a substantial increase in inventories. Long-term debt was again redeemed in Year 7, but it appears that the firm used short-term bank borrowing to finance the redemption.

The negative cash flow from operations coupled with the use of short-term debt to redeem long-term debt suggests an increase in short-term liquidity risk. Exhibit 2.10 presents the statement of cash flows for Logue Shoe Stores for Year 6 and Year 7 using the amounts taken from the worksheets in Exhibits 2.8 and 2.9.

Converting a Funds Flow Statement into a Statement of Cash Flows

Converting a statement of sources and uses of funds into a statement of cash flows requires two actions:

1. Converting the definition of "funds" a firm used in the sources and uses of funds statement into a cash and cash equivalents definition.

2. Reclassifying the sources and uses into an operations, investing, and financing format.

Exhibit 2.11 presents a sources and uses of funds statement (called here a statement of changes in financial position) for Mazda Motor Corporation, a Japanese automobile manufacturer. Mazda defines funds as working capital (that is, current assets minus current liabilities). The top portion of Exhibit 2.11 shows the sources and uses of working capital that net to the ¥ 7,945 million increase for Year 6. The lower portion of Exhibit 2.11 shows the changes in individual current asset and current liability accounts that net to the ¥ 7,945 million increase in working capital explained in the top portion.

The statement of cash flows defines funds as cash and cash equivalents. Thus, we wish to account for the ¥ 69,334 million decrease in cash and time deposits. To do this, we classify the change in each noncash balance sheet account as either an operating, investing, or financing activity. Exhibit 2.12 presents a statement of cash flows for Mazda. Most items are easy to classify into one of these three categories. The following discussion elaborates on a few items.

Provision for Employee Retirements, Net.   Japanese GAAP requires firms to provide annually as a charge against net income a portion of the estimated cost of employee retirement benefits that the firms will pay later to employees. Japanese firms rarely set aside funds equal to the expense each period. Rather, such firms pay the benefits out of their cash account when employees retire. Thus, the actual

Exhibit 2.9
Worksheet for Statement of Cash Flows for Logue Shoe Stores
Year 7

	Balance Sheet Changes	Operations	Investing	Financing
(Inc.) Decr. in Assets				
Accounts Receivable	$ 162	$ 162		
Inventories	(17,614)	(17,614)		
Other Current Assets	(1,560)	(1,560)		
Property, Plant, and Equipment	830		$ 830	
Accumulated Depreciation	8,659	8,659		
Other Assets	—			
Inc. (Decr.) in Equities				
Accounts Payable	$ (1,688)	$ (1,688)		
Notes Payable	10,814			$10,814
Current Portion of Long-Term Debt	(3,709)			(3,709)
Other Current Liabilities	(1,423)	(1,423)		
Long-Term Debt	(7,693)			(7,693)
Common Stock	—			—
Additional Paid-in Capital	—		—	—
Retained Earnings	6,442	6,442		
Cash	$ (6,780)	$ (7,022)	$ 830	$ (588)

cash outflow during the year to retired employees seldom equals the provision for employee retirements. Mazda shows an addition to net income for this item, suggesting that the provision for Year 5 and Year 6 exceeded the cash outflow.

Increase in Trade Receivables, Inventories, and Other Current Assets.   Increases in operating current asset accounts use cash and require a subtraction from net income in computing cash flow from operations. The subtraction for the increase in accounts receivable indicates that cash flow from operations did not increase by the full amount of sales revenue included in net income. The subtraction for the increase in inventories indicates that Mazda used more cash to acquire inventory than the amount of cost of goods sold subtracted in computing net income.

Changes in Operating Current Liability Accounts.   Some current liability accounts (for example, Accrued Income Taxes, Accrued Expenses) relate to operating activities, whereas other accounts (Short-Term Bank Loans, Long-Term Debt Due within One Year) relate to financing activities. Unless the notes provide information to the contrary, we classify changes in Other Current Liabilities (as well as Other Current Assets) as operating activities.

The analyst should use particular caution when entering changes in current liability accounts on a statement of cash flows worksheet. Firms follow different

Exhibit 2.10
Statement of Cash Flows for Logue Shoe Stores

	Year 6	Year 7
Operations		
Net Income	$ 16,634	$ 6,442
Depreciation	7,985	8,659
(Inc.) Decr. in Accounts Receivable	(102)	162
(Inc.) Decr. in Inventories	(7,198)	(17,614)
(Inc.) Decr. in Other Current Assets	3,591	(1,560)
Inc. (Decr.) in Accounts Payable	(6,126)	(1,688)
Inc. (Decr.) in Other Current Liabilities	2,559	(1,423)
Cash Flow from Operations	$ 17,343	$ (7,022)
Investing		
Sale (Acquisition) of Property, Plant, and Equipment.........	$ (1,651)	$ 830
Financing		
Increase in Notes Payable	—	$ 10,814
Repayment of Long-Term Debt	$(16,795)	$(11,402)
Cash Flow from Financing	$(16,795)	$ (588)
Net Change in Cash	$ (1,103)	$ (6,780)

practices with respect to their use of parentheses in their published statements. Mazda shows the effect of the change in individual current liability accounts on *total current liabilities*. Thus, trade notes and accounts payable increased current liabilities by ¥ 42,233 million during Year 6. Mazda's statement of changes in financial position reports this increase as a positive amount. Because increases in current liabilities increase cash (that is, delay the time when the firm must pay cash), they appear as a positive amount as well in the statement of cash flows in Exhibit 2.12.

Other firms report changes in current liabilities in terms of their effect on working capital. Because increases in current liabilities reduce working capital, the published statement reports these items with parentheses, indicating a negative change. The proper treatment still adds increases in operating current liability accounts to net income in computing cash flow from operations. In this case, therefore, the analyst changes the directional sign from that reported in the published statement of sources and uses of funds. When doubt exists as to the direction of the change, the analyst should examine the comparative balance sheet.

Changes in Marketable Securities.   Firms with temporarily excess cash not needed in operations invest in government or other marketable securities to generate a return. These firms sell the securities when they need cash. Classifying changes in marketable securities as an operating activity seems appropriate. However, GAAP in the United States classifies purchases and sales of marketable

Exhibit 2.11
Mazda Motor Corporation
Consolidated Statement of Changes in Financial Position
(amounts in millions of yen)

	Year Ended March 31	
	Year 6	**Year 5**
Source		
Net Income	¥ 23,438	¥ 17,064
Charges to Income Not Requiring Current Outlay of Working Capital		
Depreciation	73,070	30,445
Provision for Employees' Retirement Benefits, Net	1,916	503
Working Capital Provided from Operations	98,424	48,012
Increase in Long-Term Debt	31,075	110,775
Common Stock Issued upon Conversion of Convertible Bonds and Notes	29,600	9,452
Disposal of Book Value of Property, Plant, and Equipment	6,813	1,997
Other, Net	10,045	1,801
	¥ 175,957	¥ 172,037
Application		
Additions to Property, Plant, and Equipment	71,626	49,089
Increase in Investments and Other Assets	46,503	11,394
Decrease in Long-Term Debt	24,542	30,248
Cash Dividends Paid	6,921	4,016
Conversion of Convertible Bonds and Notes	18,420	6,331
	168,012	101,078
Increase in Working Capital	¥ 7,945	¥ 70,959
Changes in Components of Working Capital		
Increase (Decrease) in Current Assets		
Cash and Time Deposits	¥ (69,334)	¥ 59,002
Marketable Securities	6,718	2,388
Trade Notes and Accounts Receivable	73,399	11,926
Inventories	14,873	19,033
Other Current Assets	7,203	4,048
	¥ 32,859	¥ 96,397
Increase (Decrease) in Current Liabilities		
Short-Term Bank Loans	3,744	13,653
Long-Term Debt Due within One Year	(46,097)	16,476
Trade Notes and Accounts Payable	42,233	(2,717)
Accrued Income Taxes	(908)	(2,019)
Accrued Expenses	16,774	(3,329)
Other Current Liabilities	9,168	3,374
	24,914	25,438
Increase in Working Capital	¥ 7,945	¥ 70,959

Exhibit 2.12
Mazda Motor Corporation
Statement of Cash Flows
(amounts in millions of yen)

	Year Ended March 31	
	Year 6	Year 5
Operations		
Net Income	¥ 23,438	¥ 17,064
Depreciation	73,070	30,445
Provision for Employee Retirements, Net	1,916	503
Loss on Conversion of Bonds and Notes	11,180	3,121
(Increase) Decrease in Trade Notes and Accounts Receivable	(73,399)	(11,926)
(Increase) Decrease in Inventories	(14,873)	(19,033)
(Increase) Decrease in Other Current Assets	(7,203)	(4,048)
Increase (Decrease) in Trade Notes and Accounts Payable	42,233	(2,717)
Increase (Decrease) in Accrued Income Taxes	(908)	(2,019)
Increase (Decrease) in Accrued Expenses	16,774	(3,329)
Increase (Decrease) in Other Current Liabilities	9,168	3,374
Cash Flow from Operations	¥ 81,396	¥ 11,435
Investing		
Disposal of Property, Plant, and Equipment	¥ 6,813	¥ 1,997
Additions to Property, Plant, and Equipment	(71,626)	(49,089)
Increase in Investments and Other Assets	(46,503)	(11,394)
(Increase) Decrease in Marketable Securities	(6,718)	(2,388)
Cash Flow from Investing	¥ (118,034)	¥ (60,874)
Financing		
Increase (Decrease) in Short-Term Bank Loans	¥ 3,744	¥ 13,653
Increase in Long-Term Debt	31,075	110,775
Decrease in Long-Term Debt	(24,542)	(30,248)
Increase (Decrease) in Long-Term Debt Due within One Year	(46,097)	16,476
Dividends	(6,921)	(4,016)
Other, Net	10,045	1,801
Cash Flow from Financing	¥ 32,696	¥ 108,441
Change in Cash	¥ (69,334)	¥ 59,002

securities as investing activities. GAAP stipulates this classification perhaps to provide consistency with the classification of changes in short-term borrowing, discussed next.

Changes in Short-Term Bank Loans.   Firms temporarily needing cash for operations often obtain bank loans. They usually repay the loans soon thereafter with cash generated from operations. Bank loans are also sometimes a substitute for supplier financing. As with marketable securities, classifying changes in bank loans as an operating activity seems appropriate. GAAP in the United States, however, classifies changes in short-term bank loans as a financing activity. Accounting standard-setters in the United States apparently desired to keep cash flow from operating a measure of cash flows directly relating to dealings with customers, suppliers, employees, and others. Obtaining a bank loan should not increase operating cash flow, nor should acquiring marketable securities use operating cash flow.

Changes in Long-Term Debt.   The analyst should aggregate the lines "decrease in long-term debt" and "increase (decrease) in long-term debt due within one year" to obtain the cash outflow for debt retirement during the year. During Year 6, Mazda transferred ¥ 24,542 million from long-term debt to the current liability account, Long-Term Debt Due within One Year. The latter account decreased by ¥ 46,097 million net during the year. Thus, Mazda repaid debt totaling ¥ 70,639 million as shown in the first column below:

Analysis of Changes in the Account, Long-Term Debt Due within One Year (in millions)	Year Ended March 31, Year 6	Year Ended March 31, Year 5
Increases in Account: Transfer from Long-Term Debt Account	¥ 24,542	¥ 30,248
Decreases in Account: Long-Term Debt Repaid	(70,639)	(13,722)
Increase (Decrease) in Account During the Year	¥ (46,097)	¥ 16,476

During Year 5, Mazda transferred ¥ 30,248 million from long-term debt to the current liability account. Because the latter account increased by ¥ 16,476 million net, Mazda repaid long-term debt totaling ¥ 13,772 million during the year (see the second column above).

Debt Conversion Transactions.   When a firm's creditors convert convertible bonds into common stock, GAAP in the United States accounts for the transaction by transferring an amount equal to the book value of the bonds from long-term debt to common shareholders' equity accounts. The firm recognizes no gain or loss on the conversion. Because no cash inflow or outflow occurs, the entity cannot report the conversion on the statement of cash flows. Mazda reports bond conversions on its statement of changes in financial position on two lines: common stock issued upon conversion of bonds and notes (a source) and bonds and notes converted (a use). The firm reports a larger amount for the common stock issued than for the bonds converted, suggesting that it recognized a loss upon conversion. The loss reduced net income in the operations section of the statement of cash flows. The following summarizes Mazda's reporting for Year 6 (in millions of yen):

	Year Ended March 31, Year 6
Operations	
Net Income: Loss on Conversion of Bonds	¥ (11,180)
Cash Flow from Operations	¥ (11,180)
Financing	
Common Stock Issued upon Conversion of Bonds and Notes	29,600
Conversion of Bonds and Notes	(18,420)
Cash Flow from Financing	¥ 11,180
Net Effect on Cash Flows	¥ 0

Consistency with reporting practices in the United States requires an addback to net income in the amount of the loss and elimination of the two lines for the conversion of bonds and notes into common stock. This restatement results in reporting the transaction as having no effect on either net cash flow or on any of the three component activities of the statement of cash flows.

Other Net.   Firms usually aggregate funds flow items that are immaterial in amount into an "other, net" line. The analyst usually cannot determine the portion of this single-line item that relates to operating, investing, and financing activities. The analyst should select a classification rule for such items and follow it consistently across firms and across years. We treat such items as financing activities in Exhibit 2.12.

Summary

Compared to the balance sheet and income statement, the statement of cash flows is a relatively new statement. The Financial Accounting Standards Board issued its most recent comprehensive standard on the statement of cash flows in 1987, although GAAP in the United States has required some form of "funds flow" statement since the late 1960s. When firms outside of the United States issue funds flow statements, they typically define "funds" more broadly than cash (usually either cash plus marketable securities and short-term borrowing or net working capital).

The statement of cash flows will likely increase in usefulness during the next several years for the following reasons:

1. Analysts will understand better the types of information that this statement presents and the kinds of interpretations that are appropriate.

2. Analysts will increasingly recognize that cash flows do not necessarily track income flows. A firm with a healthy income statement is not necessarily financially healthy. Cash requirements to service debt may outstrip the ability of operations to generate cash.

Exhibit 2.13
The H. J. Heinz Company
Statement of Cash Flows
(amounts in millions)

	Year 4	Year 5	Year 6	Year 7	Year 8
Operations					
Net Income	$ 339	$ 386	$ 440	$ 504	$ 568
Depreciation	110	133	148	169	196
Other Addbacks	68	44	65	38	38
Other Subtractions	0	0	(45)	(32)	(53)
Working Capital from Operations	$ 517	$ 563	$ 608	$ 679	$ 749
(Inc.) Decr. in Accounts Receivable	(18)	(39)	(70)	(105)	(36)
(Inc.) Decr. in Inventories	(29)	(39)	(134)	(87)	38
(Inc.) Decr. in Prepayments	(35)	(22)	(14)	18	(1)
Inc. (Decr.) in Accounts Payable	9	64	25	47	34
Inc. (Decr.) in Other Current Liabilities	64	(9)	1	(24)	(10)
Cash Flow from Operations	$ 508	$ 518	$ 416	$ 528	$ 774
Investing					
Fixed Assets Acquired	$ (179)	$ (214)	$ (323)	$ (355)	$ (345)
Investments Acquired	(287)	(300)	(53)	(13)	(142)
Cash Flow from Investing	$ (466)	$ (514)	$ (376)	$ (368)	$ (487)
Financing					
Increase in Short-Term Borrowing	$ 51	$ 0	$ 49	$ 88	$ 42
Increase in Long-Term Borrowing	328	73	227	231	5
Issue of Capital Stock	15	39	30	60	101
Decrease in Short-Term Borrowing	0	(7)	0	0	0
Decrease in Long-Term Borrowing	(43)	(107)	(34)	(28)	(95)
Acquisition of Capital Stock	(236)	(124)	(98)	(280)	(68)
Dividends	(132)	(155)	(178)	(208)	(239)
Other	0	0	(9)	0	(8)
Cash Flow from Financing	$ (17)	$ (281)	$ (13)	$ (137)	$ (262)
Change in Cash	$ 25	$ (277)	$ 27	$ 23	$ 25

3. Differences in accounting principles have less of an impact on the statement of cash flows than on the balance sheet and income statement. Such differences in accounting principles between countries are a major issue as capital markets become more integrated across countries.

Problems

2.1 *Interpreting the Statement of Cash Flows.* The H. J. Heinz Company (Heinz) manufactures a wide range of consumer foods products in the United States and abroad. Exhibit 2.13 presents a statement of cash flows for Heinz for Year 4 to Year

Exhibit 2.14
Inland Steel Industries
Statement of Cash Flows
(amounts in millions)

	Year 4	Year 5	Year 6	Year 7	Year 8
Operations					
Net Income	$ 19.3	$ 145.0	$ 262.1	$ 119.7	$ (20.6)
Depreciation and Amortization	124.0	123.4	134.8	131.2	119.7
Other Addbacks	12.7	12.2	107.6	56.3	16.6
Other Subtractions	(64.8)	(18.3)	(22.3)	(31.0)	(33.6)
Working Capital Provided by Operations	$ 91.2	$ 262.3	$ 482.2	$ 276.2	$ 82.1
(Inc.) Decr. in Receivables	(15.9)	(26.8)	33.6	10.3	47.6
(Inc.) Decr. in Inventories	82.2	(25.3)	(66.4)	2.9	39.9
(Inc.) Decr. in Other Current Assets	(3.7)	(27.4)	35.9	(16.3)	(1.2)
Inc. (Decr.) Accounts Payable—Trade	(33.1)	15.7	4.8	(3.4)	60.2
Inc. (Decr.) in Other Current Liabilities	8.4	(29.4)	41.7	(29.5)	(39.4)
Cash Flow from Operations	$ 129.1	$ 169.1	$ 531.8	$ 240.2	$ 189.2
Investing					
Fixed Assets Sold	$ 152.2	$ 39.3	$ 2.6	$ 7.7	$ 19.5
Fixed Assets Acquired	(119.2)	(126.9)	(136.5)	(196.5)	(261.1)
Investments in Joint Steel-Making Ventures	(95.8)	(10.5)	(123.0)	(58.3)	(49.8)
Cash Flow from Investing	$ (62.8)	$ (98.1)	$(256.9)	$(247.1)	$(291.4)
Financing					
Increase in Long-Term Borrowing	$ 68.6	$ 24.5	$ 1.3	$ 3.1	$ 146.9
Issue of Capital Stock	85.2	180.3	—	185.0	—
Decrease in Short-Term Borrowing	(76.6)	—	(14.2)	(13.3)	—
Decrease in Long-Term Borrowing	(39.1)	(192.1)	(32.3)	(32.8)	(25.6)
Acquisition of Capital Stock	—	—	(64.7)	(144.1)	(126.5)
Dividends	(7.8)	(12.0)	(40.8)	(58.9)	(71.7)
Cash Flow from Financing	$ 30.3	$ .7	$(150.7)	$ (61.0)	$ (76.9)
Net Change in Cash	$ 96.6	$ 71.7	$ 124.2	$ (67.9)	$(179.1)

8. Discuss the relation between net income and cash flow from operations and the pattern of cash flows from operating, investing, and financing activities for the firm over the five-year period.

2.2 *Interpreting the Statement of Cash Flows.* Inland Steel Industries manufactures steel used in the automotive, construction, heavy equipment, appliance, and similar industries. Exhibit 2.14 presents a statement of cash flows for Inland Steel Industries for Year 4 to Year 8. Discuss the relation between net income and cash flow from operations and the pattern of cash flows from operating, investing, and financing activities for this firm over the five-year period.

Exhibit 2.15
GTI, Inc.
Balance Sheets
(amounts in thousands)

	December 31		
	Year 7	Year 8	Year 9
Assets			
Cash	$ 430	$ 475	$ 367
Accounts Receivable	3,768	3,936	2,545
Inventories	2,334	2,966	2,094
Prepayments	116	270	122
Total Current Assets	$ 6,648	$ 7,647	$ 5,128
Property, Plant, and Equipment (Net)	3,806	4,598	4,027
Other Assets	193	559	456
Total Assets	$10,647	$12,804	$ 9,611
Liabilities and Shareholders' Equity			
Accounts Payable	$ 1,578	$ 809	$ 796
Notes Payable to Banks	11	231	2,413
Other Current Liabilities	1,076	777	695
Total Current Liabilities	$ 2,665	$ 1,817	$ 3,904
Long-Term Debt	2,353	4,692	2,084
Deferred Income Taxes	126	89	113
Total Liabilities	$ 5,144	$ 6,598	$ 6,101
Preferred Stock	$ —	$ 289	$ 289
Common Stock	83	85	85
Additional Paid-in Capital	4,385	4,392	4,395
Retained Earnings	1,035	1,440	(1,259)
Total Shareholders' Equity	$ 5,503	$ 6,206	$ 3,510
Total Liabilities and Shareholders' Equity	$10,647	$12,804	$ 9,611

2.3 *Preparing a Statement of Cash Flows from Balance Sheets and Income Statements.* GTI, Inc., manufactures parts, components, and processing equipment for
electronics and semiconductor applications for the communication, computer,
automotive, and appliance industries. Its sales tend to be cyclical since the sales of
most of its customers are cyclical. Exhibit 2.15 presents balance sheets for GTI as
of December 31, Year 7 through Year 9 and Exhibit 2.16 presents income statements for Year 8 and Year 9.

   a. Prepare a worksheet for the preparation of a statement of cash flows for
       GTI, Inc. for Year 8 and Year 9. Follow the format in Exhibit 2.7 in the
       text. Footnotes to the firm's financial statements reveal the following
       (amounts in thousands):

       (1) Depreciation expense was $641 thousand in Year 8 and $625 thousand
       in Year 9.

       (2) Other assets represent patents. Patent amortization was $25 thou-
       sand in Year 8 and $40 thousand in Year 9.

Exhibit 2.16
GTI, Inc.
Income Statements
(amounts in thousands)

	Year 8	Year 9
Sales	$ 22,833	$ 11,960
Cost of Goods Sold	(16,518)	(11,030)
Selling and Administrative Expenses	(4,849)	(3,496)
Interest Expense	(459)	(452)
Income Tax Expense	(590)	328
Net Income	$ 417	$ (2,690)
Dividends on Preferred Stock	(12)	(9)
Net Income Available to Common	$ 405	$ (2,699)

Exhibit 2.17
Oji Paper Company Balance Sheets
(amounts in millions of yen)

	March 31:			
	Year 4	**Year 5**	**Year 6**	**Year 7**
Assets				
Cash	¥ 26,727	¥ 29,662	¥ 21,656	¥ 19,526
Accounts and Notes Receivable—Trade	91,788	104,143	96,645	97,304
Inventories	44,708	48,713	50,840	44,187
Prepayments	6,413	3,520	3,900	3,194
Total Current Assets	¥ 169,636	¥ 186,038	¥ 173,041	¥ 164,211
Investments	56,637	58,861	58,539	60,605
Property, Plant, and Equipment	360,572	369,978	423,009	442,422
Less Accumulated Depreciation	(225,746)	(229,790)	(243,181)	(263,007)
Total Assets	¥ 361,099	¥ 385,087	¥ 411,408	¥ 404,231
Liabilities and Shareholders' Equity				
Accounts and Notes Payable—Trade	¥ 50,935	¥ 64,149	¥ 52,267	¥ 43,627
Notes Payable to Banks	81,255	84,127	77,699	81,299
Current Portion of Long-Term Debt	3,620	3,800	3,240	3,250
Other Current Liabilities	32,311	35,486	34,325	34,733
Total Current Liabilities	¥ 168,121	¥ 187,562	¥ 167,531	¥ 162,909
Long-Term Debt	72,725	64,399	93,777	76,289
Employee Retirement Benefits	17,824	17,275	17,376	18,862
Total Liabilities	¥ 258,670	¥ 269,236	¥ 278,684	¥ 258,060
Common Stock	¥ 26,197	¥ 26,198	¥ 28,682	¥ 31,245
Additional Paid-in Capital	27,312	27,314	29,578	32,142
Retained Earnings	48,920	62,339	74,464	82,784
Total Shareholders' Equity	¥ 102,429	¥ 115,851	¥ 132,724	¥ 146,171
Total Liabilities and Shareholders' Equity	¥ 361,099	¥ 385,087	¥ 411,408	¥ 404,231

Exhibit 2.18
**Oji Paper Company Income Statements
amounts in millions of yen)**

| | Year Ended March 31 | | |
	Year 5	Year 6	Year 7
Sales	¥ 374,233	¥ 375,856	¥ 363,490
Other Revenues	7,218	9,109	5,314
Total Revenues	¥ 381,451	¥ 384,965	¥ 368,804
Cost of Goods Sold	(274,109)	(282,361)	(263,840)
Selling and Administrative Expenses	(62,298)	(64,748)	(69,693)
Interest Expense	(11,135)	(10,442)	(9,358)
Income Tax Expense	(16,800)	(11,200)	(13,700)
Net Income	¥ 17,109	¥ 16,214	¥ 12,213

(3) Changes in deferred income taxes are operating transactions.

b. Discuss the relation between net income and cash flow from operations and the pattern of cash flows from operating, investing, and financing activities for Year 8 and Year 9.

2.4 *Preparing a Statement of Cash Flows from Balance Sheets and Income Statements.* Oji Paper Company is the largest forest products company in Japan. Exhibit 2.17 presents the firm's balance sheets for the years ended March 31, Year 4 to Year 7 and Exhibit 2.18 presents the firm's income statements for the years ended March 31, Year 5 to Year 7.

a. Prepare a worksheet for the preparation of a statement of cash flows for Oji Paper Company for each of the years ending March 31, Year 5 to Year 7. Follow the format of Exhibit 2.7 in the text. Footnotes to the firm's financial statements indicate the following:

(1) The changes in the Investments account relate to earnings and dividends of associated companies, both of which the statement of cash flows classifies as operating activities.

(2) The changes in the Employee Retirement Benefits account relate to provisions made for retirement benefits net of payments made to retired employees, both of which the statement of cash flows classifies as operating activities.

b. Discuss the pattern of cash flows from operating, investing and financing activities for Year 5, Year 6, and Year 7, indicating the stage in the firm's life cycle suggested by the pattern.

2.5 *Converting a Funds Flow Statement into a Statement of Cash Flows.* Exhibit 1.12 (part of Problem 1.4 on page 35) presents a statement of sources and uses of funds for Grand Metropolitan, a British food processing company. This funds

Exhibit 2.19
Mitsukoshi, Ltd.
Statement of Changes in Financial Position
(amounts in millions of yen)

	Year 8	Year 9
Sources of Funds		
Operations:		
Net Income	¥ 4,220	¥ 5,932
Charges (Credits) to Income Not Requiring Funds		
Depreciation and Amortization	4,928	6,020
Provision for Severance Indemnities, less		
Payments	283	255
Loss on Disposal of Equipment	623	1,041
Other, Net	(74)	5
Working Capital from Operations	¥ 9,980	¥ 13,253
Proceeds from Sale of Convertible Bonds	40,000	—
Increase in Common Stock upon Conversion of Bonds	—	14,408
Total Sources	¥ 49,980	¥ 27,661
Uses of Funds:		
Additions to Property, Plant, and Equipment	9,541	20,860
Increase in Investments in Securities	1,045	1,880
Increase in Investments in Affiliated Companies	1,979	2,384
Increase in Leaseholds and Deposits	1,088	831
Reduction in Convertible Bonds upon Conversion	—	14,408
Dividends	2,651	2,651
Other	(172)	1,940
Total Uses	¥ 16,132	¥ 44,954
Increase (Decrease) in Working Capital	¥ 33,848	¥ (17,293)
Analysis of Changes in Working Capital		
Increase (Decrease) in Current Assets		
Cash	¥ 37,374	¥ (13,008)
Marketable Securities	761	(91)
Notes and Accounts Receivable	4,673	5,780
Inventories	(1,648)	611
Other Current Assets	2,142	3,939
Total	¥ 43,302	¥ (2,769)
(Increase) Decrease in Current Liabilities:		
Notes and Accounts Payable	(3,171)	(5,139)
Accrued Income Taxes	(1,306)	(932)
Other Current Liabilities	(4,977)	(8,453)
	¥ (9,454)	¥ (14,524)
Increase (Decrease) in Working Capital	¥ 33,848	¥ (17,293)

statement uses cash net of short- and long-term borrowing as the definition of funds.

a. Prepare a worksheet similar to Exhibit 2.7 in the chapter for a statement of cash flows for Year 6 and Year 7. Treat exchange adjustments as relating to operating activities.

b. Discuss the change in the pattern of cash flows from operating, investing, and financing activities between Year 6 and Year 7.

2.6 *Converting a Funds Flow Statement into a Statement of Cash Flows.* Exhibit 2.19 presents a statement of changes in financial position for Mitsukoshi, Ltd., a Japanese department store chain for Year 8 and Year 9.

a. Prepare a worksheet similar to Exhibit 2.7 in the chapter for a statement of cash flows for Year 8 and Year 9. Classify "other uses of funds, net" as a financing activity.

b. Discuss the relation between net income and cash flow from operations and the pattern of cash flows from operating, investing, and financing activities for each year.

Case 2.1:
W. T. Grant Company*

At the time that it filed for bankruptcy in October 1975, W. T. Grant (Grant) was the 17th largest retailer in the United States, with almost 1,200 stores, over 82,000 employees, and sales of $1.7 billion. It had paid dividends consistently since 1906. The collapse of Grant came largely as a surprise to the capital markets, particularly to the banks that provided short-term working capital loans. Grant had altered its business strategy in the mid-1960s to transform itself from an urban discount store chain to a suburban housegoods store chain. Its failure serves as a classic study of poor implementation of what seemed like a sound business strategy. What happened to Grant, and why, are questions that, with some analysis, can be answered. On the other hand, why the symptoms of Grant's prolonged illness were not diagnosed and treated earlier is difficult to understand.

THE STRATEGIC SHIFT

Prior to the mid-1960s, Grant built its reputation on sales of low-priced softgoods (clothing, linens, sewing fabrics). It placed its stores in large, urban locations, and appealed primarily to lower income consumers.

The mid-1960s marked the beginning, however, of urban unrest and a movement to the suburbs. To service the needs of these new homeowners, suburban shopping centers experienced rapid growth. Sears led the way in this movement, establishing itself as the anchor store in many of the more upscale locations. Montgomery Ward and J. C. Penney followed suit. At this time, Sears held a dominant market share in the middle-income consumer market. It saw an opportunity, however, to move its product line more upscale to compete with the established department stores (Macy's, Marshall Field), which had not yet begun their movement to the suburbs. To implement this new strategy, Sears introduced its Sears Best line of products.

The outward population movement to the suburbs and increased competition from growing discount chains such as K Mart caused Grant to alter its strategy as well. One aspect of this strategic shift was rapid expansion of new stores into suburban shopping centers. Between 1963 and 1973, Grant opened 612 new stores and expanded 91 others. It concentrated most of that expansion in the 1969–1973 period when it opened 369 new stores, 15 on one particularly busy day. Because Grant's reputation had been built on sales to lower-income consumers, it was often unable to locate its new stores in the choicest shopping centers. Louis C. Lustenberger, President of Grant from 1959 to 1968, started the expansion

---

*Copyright 1979, 1991 by James A. Largay III and Clyde P. Stickney.

program, although later, as a director, he became concerned over dimensions of the growth and the problems it generated. After Mr. Lustenberger stepped down, the pace of expansion accelerated under the leadership of Chairman Edward Staley and President Richard W. Mayer.

A second aspect of Grant's strategy involved a change in its product line. Grant perceived a vacuum in the middle-income consumer market when Sears moved more upscale. Grant introduced a higher-quality, medium-priced line of products into its new shopping center stores to fill this vacuum. In addition, it added furniture and private-brand appliances to its product line and implemented a credit card system. With much of the movement to the suburbs representing middle-income consumers, Grant attempted to position itself as a primary supplier to outfit the new homes being constructed.

To implement this new strategy, Grant chose a decentralized organizational structure. Each store manager controlled credit extension and credit terms. At most stores, Grant permitted customers 36 months to pay for their purchases; the minimum monthly payment was $1, regardless of their total purchases. Bad debt expenses averaged 1.2 percent of sales each year until fiscal 1975, when a provision of $155.7 million was made. Local store managers also made inventory and pricing decisions. Merchandise was acquired either from regional Grant warehouses or ordered directly from the manufacturer. At this time Grant did not have an information system in place that permitted one store to check the availability of a needed product from another store. Compensation of employees was considered among the most generous in the industry, with most employees owning shares of Grant's common stock acquired under employee stock option plans. Compensation of store managers included salary plus stated percentages of the store's sales and profits.

To finance the expansion of receivables and inventory, Grant used commercial paper, bank loans, and trade credit. To finance the expansion of store space, Grant entered into leasing arrangements. Because Grant was liquidated before the Financial Accounting Standards Board issued *Statement of Financial Accounting Standards No. 13* requiring the capitalization of capital leases on the balance sheet and the disclosure of information on operating leases in the notes to the financial statements, it did not disclose its long-term leasing arrangements. Property, plant, and equipment reported on its balance sheet consisted mostly of store fixtures. Grant's long-term debt included debentures totaling $200 million issued in 1971 and 1973. Based on per-square-foot rental rates at the time, Grant's disclosures of total square footage of space, and an 8 percent discount rate, the estimated present values of Grant's leases are as follows (in 000s):

January 31	Present Value of Lease Commitments	January 31	Present Value of Lease Commitments
1966	$ 394,291	1971	$ 496,041
1967	$ 400,090	1972	$ 626,052
1968	$ 393,566	1973	$ 708,666
1969	$ 457,111	1974	$ 805,785
1970	$ 486,837	1975	$ 821,565

ADVANCE AND RETREAT— THE ATTEMPT TO SAVE GRANT

By 1974, it became clear that Grant's problems were not of a short-term operating nature. In the spring of 1974, both Moody's and Standard & Poor's eliminated their credit rating for Grant's commercial paper. Banks entered the picture in a big way in the summer of 1974. To provide financing, a group of 143 banks agreed to offer lines of credit totaling $525 million. Grant obtained a short-term loan of $600 million in September, 1974, with three New York money center banks absorbing approximately $230 million of the total. These three banks also loaned $50 million out of a total of $100 million provided to Grant's finance subsidiary.

Support of the banks during the summer of 1974 was accompanied by a top management change. Messrs. Staley and Mayer stepped down in the spring and were replaced in August 1974 by James G. Kendrick, brought in from Zeller's, Ltd., Grant's Canadian subsidiary. As chief executive officer, Mr. Kendrick moved to cut Grant's losses. He slashed payroll significantly, closed 126 unprofitable stores and phased out the big-ticket furniture and appliance lines. New store space brought on line in 1975 was 75 percent less than in 1974.

The positive effects of these moves could not overcome the disastrous events of early 1975. In January, Grant defaulted on about $75 million in interest payments and, in February, results of operations for the year ended January 31, 1975, were released. Grant reported a loss of $177 million, with substantial losses from credit operations accounting for 60 percent of the total.

The banks now assumed a more active role in what was becoming a struggle to save Grant. Robert H. Anderson, a vice president of Sears, was offered a lucrative $2.5 million contract, decided to accept the challenge to turn the company around, and joined Grant as its new president in April 1975. Mr. Kendrick remained as chairman of the board. The banks holding 90 percent of Grant's debt extended their loans from June 2, 1975, to March 31, 1976. The balance of about $56 million was repaid on June 2. A major problem confronting Mr. Anderson was to maintain the continued flow of merchandise into Grant stores. Suppliers became skeptical of Grant's ability to pay for merchandise and, in August 1975, the banks agreed to subordinate $300 million of debt to the suppliers' claims for merchandise shipped. With the approach of the Christmas shopping season, the need for merchandise became critical. Despite the banks' subordination of their claims to those of suppliers and the intensive cultivation of suppliers by Mr. Anderson, Grant did not receive sufficient quantities of merchandise in the stores.

During this period, Grant reported a $111.3 million net loss for the six months ended on July 31, 1975. Sales had declined 15 percent from the comparable period in 1974. Mr. Kendrick observed that a return to profitability before the fourth quarter was unlikely.

On October 2, 1975, Grant filed a Chapter XI bankruptcy petition. The rehabilitation effort was formally underway and the protection provided by Chapter XI permitted a continuation of the reorganization and rehabilitation activities for the next four months. On February 6, 1976, after store closings and liquidations of inventories had generated $320 million in cash, the creditors committee overseeing the bankruptcy voted for liquidation, and W. T. Grant ceased to exist.

FINANCIAL STATEMENTS FOR GRANT

Two changes in accounting principles affect Grant's financial statements. Prior to fiscal 1970, Grant accounted for the investment in its wholly owned finance subsidiary using the equity method. Beginning with the year ending January 31, 1970, Grant consolidated the finance subsidiary. Prior to fiscal 1975, Grant recorded the total finance charge on credit sales as income in the year of the sale. Accounts receivable therefore included the full amount to be received from customers, not the present value of such amount. Beginning with the fiscal year ending January 31, 1975, Grant recognized finance charges on credit sales over the life of the installment contract.

Exhibit 1 presents comparative balance sheets and Exhibit 2 presents statements of income and retained earnings for Grant based on the amounts as originally reported for each year. Exhibits 3, 4, and 5 present balance sheets, income statements, and statements of cash flows respectively based on revised amounts reflecting retroactive restatement for the two changes in accounting principles discussed above. These latter statements consolidate the finance subsidiary for all years. Grant provided the necessary data to restate for the change in income recognition of finance charges for the 1971 to 1975 fiscal years only. Exhibit 6 presents selected other data for Grant, the variety chain store industry, and the aggregate economy.

REQUIRED

Using the narrative information and the financial data provided in Exhibits 1 through 6, your mission is to apply tools of financial analysis to determine the major causes of Grant's financial problems. If you had been performing this analysis contemporaneously with the release of publicly reported information, when would you have become skeptical of the ability of Grant to continue as a viable going concern? To assist in this analysis, Exhibits 7, 8, and 9 present selected ratio and growth rate information based on the following assumptions:

Exhibit 7: Based on the amounts as originally reported for each year (Exhibits 1 and 2).

Exhibit 8: Based on the amounts as retroactively restated for changes in accounting principles (Exhibits 3, 4, and 5).

Exhibit 9: Same as Exhibit 8, except assets and liabilities reflect the capitalization of leases using the amounts presented in the case.

Exhibit 1

W. T. GRANT COMPANY
Comparative Balance Sheets
(as originally reported, amounts in thousands)

January 31	1966	1967	1968	1969
ASSETS				
Cash and Marketable Securities	$ 22,559	$ 37,507	$ 25,047	$ 28,460
Accounts Receivable[c]	110,943	110,305	133,406	154,829
Inventories	151,365	174,631	183,722	208,623
Other Current Assets	—	—	—	—
Total Current Assets	$ 284,867	$ 322,443	$ 342,175	$ 391,912
Investments	38,419	40,800	56,609	62,854
Property, Plant, and Equipment (Net)	40,367	48,071	47,572	49,213
Other Assets	1,222	1,664	1,980	2,157
Total Assets	$ 364,875	$ 412,978	$ 448,336	$ 506,136
EQUITIES				
Short-Term Debt	$ —	$ —	$ 300	$ 180
Accounts Payable—Trade	58,252	75,885	79,673	102,080
Current Deferred Taxes	37,590	47,248	57,518	64,113
Total Current Liabilities	$ 95,842	$ 123,133	$ 137,491	$ 166,373
Long-Term Debt	70,000	70,000	62,622	43,251
Noncurrent Deferred Taxes	6,269	7,034	7,551	7,941
Other Long-Term Liabilities	4,784	4,949	4,858	5,519
Total Liabilities	$ 176,895	$ 205,116	$ 212,522	$ 223,084
Preferred Stock	$ 15,000	$ 15,000	$ 14,750	$ 13,250
Common Stock	15,375	15,636	16,191	17,318
Additional Paid-in Capital	25,543	27,977	37,428	59,945
Retained Earnings	132,062	149,249	167,445	192,539
Total	$ 187,980	$ 207,862	$ 235,814	$ 283,052
Less Cost of Treasury Stock	—	—	—	—
Total Stockholders' Equity	$ 187,980	$ 207,862	$ 235,814	$ 283,052
Total Equities	$ 364,875	$ 412,978	$ 448,336	$ 506,136

[a]In the year ending January 31, 1970, W. T. Grant changed its consolidation policy and commenced consolidating its wholly owned finance subsidiary.

[b]In the year ending January 31, 1975, W. T. Grant changed its method of recognizing finance income on installment sales. In prior years, Grant recognized all finance income in the year of the sale. Beginning in the 1975 fiscal period, it recognized finance income over the time the installment receivable was outstanding.

[c]Accounts receivable comprises the following:

	1966	1967	1968	1969
Customer Installment Receivables...............	$ 114,470	$ 114,928	$ 140,507	$ 162,219
Less Allowances for Uncollectible Accounts .	(7,065)	(9,383)	(11,307)	(13,074)
Unearned Credit Insurance	—	—	—	—
Unearned Finance Income	—	—	—	—
Net..	$ 107,405	$ 105,545	$ 129,200	$ 149,145
Other Receivables	3,538	4,760	4,206	5,684
Total Receivables	$ 110,943	$ 110,305	$ 133,406	$ 154,829

	1970[a]	1971	1972	1973	1974	1975[b]
	$ 32,977	$ 34,009	$ 49,851	$ 30,943	$ 45,951	$ 79,642
	368,267	419,731	477,324	542,751	598,799	431,201
	222,128	260,492	298,676	399,533	450,637	407,357
	5,037	5,246	5,378	6,649	7,299	6,581
	$ 628,409	$ 719,478	$ 831,229	$ 979,876	$1,102,686	$ 924,781
	20,694	23,936	32,367	35,581	44,251	49,764
	55,311	61,832	77,173	91,420	100,984	101,932
	2,381	2,678	3,901	3,821	5,063	5,790
	$ 706,795	$ 807,924	$ 944,670	$1,110,698	$1,252,984	$1,082,267
	$ 182,132	$ 246,420	$ 237,741	$ 390,034	$ 453,097	$ 600,695
	104,144	118,091	124,990	112,896	104,883	147,211
	80,443	94,785	112,846	130,137	132,085	2,000
	$ 366,719	$ 459,296	$ 475,577	$ 633,067	$ 690,065	$ 749,906
	35,402	32,301	128,432	126,672	220,336	216,341
	8,286	8,518	9,664	11,926	14,649	—
	5,700	5,773	5,252	4,694	4,196	2,183
	$ 416,107	$ 505,888	$ 618,925	$ 776,359	$ 929,246	$ 968,430
	$ 11,450	$ 9,600	$ 9,053	$ 8,600	$ 7,465	$ 7,465
	17,883	18,180	18,529	18,588	18,599	18,599
	71,555	78,116	85,195	86,146	85,909	83,914
	211,679	230,435	244,508	261,154	248,461	37,674
	$ 312,567	$ 336,331	$ 357,285	$ 374,488	$ 360,434	$ 147,652
	(21,879)	(34,295)	(31,540)	(40,149)	(36,696)	(33,815)
	$ 290,688	$ 302,036	$ 325,745	$ 334,339	$ 323,738	$ 113,837
	$ 706,795	$ 807,924	$ 944,670	$1,110,698	$1,252,984	$1,082,267

	1970	1971	1972	1973	1974	1975
	$ 381,757	$ 433,730	$ 493,859	$ 556,091	$ 602,305	$ 518,387
	(15,270)	(15,527)	(15,750)	(15,770)	(18,067)	(79,510)
	(5,774)	(9,553)	(12,413)	(8,768)	(4,923)	(1,386)
	—	—	—	—	—	(37,523)
	$ 360,713	$ 408,650	$ 465,696	$ 531,553	$ 579,315	$ 399,968
	7,554	11,081	11,628	11,198	19,484	31,233
	$ 368,267	$ 419,731	$ 477,324	$ 542,751	$ 598,799	$ 431,201

Exhibit 2
W.T. GRANT COMPANY
Statements of Income and Retained Earnings
(as originally reported, amounts in thousands)

Year Ended January 31	1967	1968	1969
Sales	$ 920,797	$ 979,458	$ 1,096,152
Concessions	2,249	2,786	3,425
Equity in Earnings	2,072	2,987	3,537
Finance Charges	—	—	—
Other Income	1,049	2,010	2,205
Total Revenues	$ 926,167	$ 987,241	$ 1,105,319
Cost of Goods Sold	$ 631,585	$ 669,560	$ 741,181
Selling, General, and Administration	233,134	253,561	287,883
Interest	4,970	4,907	4,360
Taxes: Current	13,541	17,530	25,600
Deferred	11,659	9,120	8,400
Total Expenses	$ 894,889	$ 954,678	$ 1,067,424
Net Income	$ 31,278	$ 32,563	$ 37,895
Dividends	$ (14,091)	$ (14,367)	$ (17,686)
Change in Accounting Principles			
Consolidation of Finance Sub	—	—	4,885
Recognition of Financing Chgs	$ —	$ —	$ —
Change in Retained Earnings	$ 17,187	$ 18,196	$ 25,094
Retained Earnings—Beg. of Period	132,062	149,249	167,445
Retained Earnings—End of Period	$ 149,249	$ 167,445	$ 192,539

1970	1971	1972	1973	1974	1975
$ 1,210,918	$ 1,254,131	$ 1,374,811	$ 1,644,747	$ 1,849,802	$ 1,761,952
3,748	4,986	3,439	3,753	3,971	4,238
2,084	2,777	2,383	5,116	4,651	3,086
—	—	—	—	—	91,141
2,864	2,874	3,102	1,188	3,063	3,376
$ 1,219,614	$ 1,264,768	$ 1,383,735	$ 1,654,804	$ 1,861,487	$ 1,863,793
$ 817,671	$ 843,192	$ 931,237	$ 1,125,261	$ 1,282,945	$ 1,303,267
307,215	330,325	374,334	444,879	491,287	769,253
14,919	18,874	16,452	21,127	78,040	86,079
24,900	21,140	13,487	9,588	(6,021)	(19,439)
13,100	11,660	13,013	16,162	6,807	(98,027)
$ 1,177,805	$ 1,225,191	$ 1,348,523	$ 1,617,017	$ 1,853,058	$ 2,041,133
$ 41,809	$ 39,577	$ 35,212	$ 37,787	$ 8,429	$ (177,340)
$ (19,737)	$ (20,821)	$ (21,139)	$ (21,141)	$ (21,122)	$ (4,457)
(2,932)					
$ —	$ —	$ —	$ —	$ —	$ (28,990)
$ 19,140	$ 18,756	$ 14,073	$ 16,646	$ (12,693)	$ (210,787)
192,539	211,679	230,435	244,508	261,154	248,461
$ 211,679	$ 230,435	$ 244,508	$ 261,154	$ 248,461	$ 37,674

Exhibit 3
W. T. GRANT COMPANY
Comparative Balance Sheets
(as retroactively reported for changes in accounting principles, amounts in thousands)

January 31	1966	1967	1968	1969
ASSETS				
Cash and Marketable Securities	$ 22,638	$ 39,040	$ 25,141	$ 25,639
Accounts Receivable[c]	172,706	230,427	272,450	312,776
Inventories	151,365	174,631	183,722	208,623
Other Current Assets	3,630	4,079	3,982	4,402
Total Current Assets	$ 350,339	$ 448,177	$ 485,295	$ 551,440
Investments	13,405	14,791	16,754	18,581
Property, Plant, and Equipment (Net)	40,372	48,076	47,578	49,931
Other Assets	1,222	1,664	1,980	2,157
Total Assets	$ 405,338	$ 512,708	$ 551,607	$ 622,109
EQUITIES				
Short-Term Debt	$ 37,314	$ 97,647	$ 99,230	$ 118,125
Accounts Payable	58,252	75,885	79,673	102,080
Current Deferred Taxes	36,574	44,667	56,545	65,073
Total Current Liabilities	$ 132,140	$ 218,199	$ 235,448	$ 285,278
Long-Term Debt	70,000	70,000	62,622	43,251
Noncurrent Deferred Taxes	6,269	7,034	7,551	7,941
Other Long-Term Liabilities	4,785	5,159	5,288	5,519
Total Liabilities	$ 213,194	$ 300,392	$ 310,909	$ 341,989
Preferred Stock	$ 15,000	$ 15,000	$ 14,750	$ 13,250
Common Stock	15,375	15,636	16,191	17,318
Additional Paid-in Capital	25,543	27,977	37,428	59,945
Retained Earnings	136,226	153,703	172,329	189,607
Total	$ 192,144	$ 212,316	$ 240,698	$ 280,120
Less Cost of Treasury Stock	—	—	—	—
Total Stockholders' Equity	$ 192,144	$ 212,316	$ 240,698	$ 280,120
Total Equities	$ 405,338	$ 512,708	$ 551,607	$ 622,109

[a]See Note a to Exhibit 1.
[b]See Note b to Exhibit 1.
[c]Accounts receivable comprises the following:

	1966	1967	1968	1969
Customer Installment Receivables		NOT DISCLOSED ON A FULLY		
Less Allowances for Uncollectible Accounts				
Unearned Credit Insurance		CONSOLIDATED BASIS		
Unearned Finance Income				
Net		WITH FINANCE SUBSIDIARY		
Other Receivables				
Total Receivables	$ 172,706	$ 230,427	$ 272,450	$ 312,776

1970[a]	1971	1972	1973	1974	1975[b]
$ 32,977	$ 34,009	$ 49,851	$ 30,943	$ 45,951	$ 79,642
368,267	358,428	408,301	468,582	540,802	431,201
222,128	260,492	298,676	399,533	450,637	407,357
5,037	5,246	5,378	6,649	7,299	6,581
$ 628,409	$ 658,175	$ 762,206	$ 905,707	$ 1,044,689	$ 924,781
20,694	23,936	32,367	35,581	44,251	49,764
55,311	61,832	77,173	91,420	100,984	101,932
2,381	2,678	3,901	3,821	5,063	5,790
$ 706,795	$ 746,621	$ 875,647	$ 1,036,529	$ 1,194,987	$ 1,082,267
$ 182,132	$ 246,420	$ 237,741	$ 390,034	$ 453,097	$ 600,695
104,144	118,091	124,990	112,896	104,883	147,211
80,443	58,536	72,464	87,431	103,078	2,000
$ 366,719	$ 423,047	$ 435,195	$ 590,361	$ 661,058	$ 749,906
35,402	32,301	128,432	126,672	220,336	216,341
8,286	8,518	9,664	11,926	14,649	—
5,700	5,773	5,252	4,694	4,196	2,183
$ 416,107	$ 469,639	$ 578,543	$ 733,653	$ 900,239	$ 968,430
$ 11,450	$ 9,600	$ 9,053	$ 8,600	$ 7,465	$ 7,465
17,883	18,180	18,529	18,588	18,599	18,599
71,555	78,116	85,195	86,146	85,909	83,914
211,679	205,381	215,867	229,691	219,471	37,674
$ 312,567	$ 311,277	$ 328,644	$ 343,025	$ 331,444	$ 147,652
(21,879)	(34,295)	(31,540)	(40,149)	(36,696)	(33,815)
$ 290,688	$ 276,982	$ 297,104	$ 302,876	$ 294,748	$ 113,837
$ 706,795	$ 746,621	$ 875,647	$ 1,036,529	$ 1,194,987	$ 1,082,267

1970	1971	1972	1973	1974	1975
$ 381,757	$ 433,730	$ 493,859	$ 556,091	$ 602,305	$ 518,387
(15,270)	(15,527)	(15,750)	(15,770)	(18,067)	(79,510)
(5,774)	(9,553)	(12,413)	(8,768)	(4,923)	(1,386)
—	(61,303)	(69,023)	(74,169)	(57,997)	(37,523)
$ 360,713	$ 347,347	$ 396,073	$ 457,384	$ 521,318	$ 399,968
7,554	11,081	11,628	11,198	19,484	31,233
$ 368,267	$ 358,428	$ 408,301	$ 468,582	$ 540,802	$ 431,201

Exhibit 4

W. T. GRANT COMPANY
Statements of Income and Retained Earnings
(as retroactively revised for changes in accounting principles, amounts in thousands)

Year Ended January 31	1967	1968	1969
Sales	$ 920,797	$ 979,458	$ 1,096,152
Concessions	2,249	2,786	3,425
Equity in Earnings	1,073	1,503	1,761
Finance Charges	—	—	—
Other Income	1,315	2,038	2,525
Total Revenues	$ 925,434	$ 985,785	$ 1,103,311
Cost of Goods Sold	$ 631,585	$ 669,560	$ 741,181
Selling, General & Administration	229,130	247,093	278,031
Interest	7,319	8,549	9,636
Taxes: Current	14,463	18,470	27,880
Deferred	11,369	9,120	8,400
Total Expenses	$ 893,866	$ 952,792	$ 1,065,128
Net Income	$ 31,568	$ 32,993	$ 38,183
Dividends	$ (14,091)	$ (14,367)	$ (17,686)
Change in Accounting Principles			
Consolidation of Finance Sub.	—	—	(3,219)
Recognition of Financing Chgs.	$ —	$ —	$ —
Change in Retained Earnings	$ 17,477	$ 18,626	$ 17,278
Retained Earnings—Beg. of Period	136,226	153,703	172,329
Retained Earnings—End of Period	$ 153,703	$ 172,329	$ 189,607

1970	1971	1972	1973	1974	1975
$ 1,210,918	$ 1,254,131	$ 1,374,811	$ 1,644,747	$ 1,849,802	$ 1,761,952
3,748	4,986	3,439	3,753	3,971	4,238
2,084	2,777	2,383	5,116	4,651	3,086
—	63,194	66,567	84,817	114,920	91,141
2,864	2,874	3,102	1,188	3,063	3,376
$ 1,219,614	$ 1,327,962	$ 1,450,302	$ 1,739,621	$ 1,976,407	$ 1,863,793
$ 817,671	$ 843,192	$ 931,237	$ 1,125,261	$ 1,282,945	$ 1,303,267
307,215	396,877	445,244	532,604	601,231	769,253
14,919	18,874	16,452	21,127	78,040	86,079
24,900	22,866	13,579	11,256	(6,021)	(19,439)
13,100	9,738	12,165	14,408	9,310	(98,027)
$ 1,177,805	$ 1,291,547	$ 1,418,677	$ 1,704,656	$ 1,965,505	$ 2,041,133
$ 41,809	$ 36,415	$ 31,625	$ 34,965	$ 10,902	$ (177,340)
$ (19,737)	$ (20,821)	$ (21,139)	$ (21,141)	$ (21,122)	$ (4,457)
$ —	$ (21,892)	$ —	$ —	$ —	$ —
$ 22,072	$ (6,298)	$ 10,486	$ 13,824	$ (10,220)	$ (181,797)
189,607	211,679	205,381	215,867	229,691	219,471
$ 211,679	$ 205,381	$ 215,867	$ 229,691	$ 219,471	$ 37,674

Exhibit 5
W. T. GRANT COMPANY
Statements of Cash Flows
(as retroactively revised for changes in accounting principles, amounts in thousands)

	1967	1968	1969
Operations			
Net Income	$ 31,568	$ 32,993	$ 38,183
Depreciation	7,524	8,203	8,388
Other	66	(856)	(1,140)
(Inc.) Decr. in Receivables	(57,721)	(42,023)	(40,326)
(Inc.) Decr. in Inventories	(23,266)	(9,091)	(24,901)
(Inc.) Decr. in Prepayments	(449)	97	(420)
Inc. (Decr.) in Accounts Payable	17,633	3,788	22,407
Inc. (Decr.) in Other Cur. Liab.	8,093	11,878	8,528
Cash Flow from Operations	$ (16,552)	$ 4,989	$ 10,719
Investing			
Acquistion of Property, Plant, and Equipment	$ (15,257)	$ (7,763)	$ (10,626)
Acquisition of Investments	(269)	(418)	(35)
Cash Flow from Investing	$ (15,526)	$ (8,181)	$ (10,661)
Financing			
Inc. (Decr.) in Short-Term Borrowing	$ 60,333	$ 1,583	$ 18,895
Inc. (Decr.) in Long-Term Borrowing	—	(1,500)	(1,500)
Inc. (Decr.) in Capital Stock	2,695	3,958	844
Dividends	(14,091)	(14,367)	(17,686)
Cash Flow from Financing	$ 48,937	$ (10,326)	$ 553
Other	$ (457)	$ (381)	$ (113)
Change in Cash	$ 16,402	$ (13,899)	$ 498

1970	1971	1972	1973	1974	1975
$ 41,809	$ 36,415	$ 31,625	$ 34,965	$ 10,902	$ (177,340)
8,972	9,619	10,577	12,004	13,579	14,587
(1,559)	(2,470)	(1,758)	(1,699)	(1,345)	(16,993)
(55,491)	(11,981)	(49,873)	(60,281)	(72,220)	109,601
(13,505)	(38,364)	(38,184)	(100,857)	(51,104)	43,280
(635)	(209)	(132)	(1,271)	(650)	718
2,064	13,947	6,899	(12,094)	(8,013)	42,328
15,370	(21,907)	13,928	14,967	15,647	(101,078)
$ (2,975)	$ (14,950)	$ (26,918)	$(114,266)	$ (93,204)	$ (84,897)
$ (14,352)	$ (16,141)	$ (25,918)	$ (26,251)	$ (23,143)	$ (15,535)
—	(436)	(5,951)	(2,216)	(5,700)	(5,282)
$ (14,352)	$ (16,577)	$ (31,869)	$ (28,467)	$ (28,843)	$ (20,817)
$ 64,007	$ 64,288	$ (8,679)	$ 152,293	$ 63,063	$ 147,598
(1,687)	(1,538)	98,385	(1,584)	93,926	(3,995)
(17,860)	(8,954)	7,407	(8,227)	1,833	886
(19,737)	(20,821)	(21,139)	(21,141)	(21,122)	(4,457)
$ 24,723	$ 32,975	$ 75,974	$ 121,341	$ 137,700	$ 140,032
$ (58)	$ (416)	$ (1,345)	$ 2,484	$ (645)	$ (627)
$ 7,338	$ 1,032	$ 15,842	$ (18,908)	$ 15,008	$ 33,691

Exhibit 6
W. T. GRANT COMPANY
Other Data
(amounts in thousands, except per share)

December 31:	1965	1966	1967	1968
W.T. Grant Co.				
Sales (millions of dollars)[a]	$ 839.7	$ 920.8	$ 975.5	$ 1,096.1
Number of Stores	1,088	1,104	1,086	1,092
Store Area (thousands of square feet)[a]	———————— DATA NOT AVAILABLE ————————			
Dividends per Share[a]	$ .80	$ 1.10	$ 1.10	$ 1.30
Stock Price — High	$ 31-$\frac{1}{8}$	$ 35-$\frac{1}{8}$	$ 37-$\frac{3}{8}$	$ 45-$\frac{1}{8}$
— Low	$ 18	$ 20-$\frac{1}{2}$	$ 20-$\frac{3}{4}$	$ 30
— Close (12/31)	$ 31-$\frac{1}{8}$	$ 20-$\frac{3}{4}$	$ 34-$\frac{3}{8}$	$ 42-$\frac{5}{8}$
Variety Chain Store Industry				
Sales (millions of dollars)	$ 5,320.0	$ 5,727.0	$ 6,078.0	$ 6,152.0
Standard & Poor's Variety				
Chain Stock Price Index — High	31.0	31.2	38.4	53.6
— Low	24.3	22.4	22.3	34.7
— Close (12/31)	31.0	22.4	37.8	50.5
Aggregate Economy				
Gross National Product (billions of dollars)	$ 684.9	$ 747.6	$ 789.7	$ 865.7
Average Bank Short-Term Lending Rate	4.99%	5.69%	5.99%	6.68%
Standard & Poor's 500				
Stock Price Index — High	92.6	94.1	97.6	108.4
— Low	81.6	73.2	80.4	87.7
— Close (12/31)	92.4	80.3	96.5	103.9

[a]These amounts are for the fiscal year ending January 31 of year after the year indicated in the column. For example, sales for W. T. Grant of $839.7 in the 1965 column are for the fiscal year ending January 31, 1966.

1969	1970	1971	1972	1973	1974
$ 1,210.9	$ 1,254.1	$ 1,374.8	$ 1,644.7	$ 1,849.8	$ 1,762.0
1,095	1,116	1,168	1,208	1,189	1,152
	38,157	44,718	50,619	53,719	54,770
$ 1.40	$ 1.40	$ 1.50	$ 1.50	$ 1.50	$ .30
$ 59	$ 52	$ 70-$5/8$	$ 48-$3/4$	$ 44-$3/8$	$ 12
$ 39-$1/4$	$ 26-$7/8$	$ 41-$7/8$	$ 38-$3/4$	$ 9-$7/8$	$ 1-$1/2$
$ 47	$ 47-$1/8$	$ 47-$3/4$	$ 43-$7/8$	$ 10-$7/8$	$ 1-$7/8$
$ 6,426.0	$ 6,959.0	$ 6,972.0	$ 7,498.0	$ 8,212.0	$ 8,714.0
66.1	61.4	92.2	107.4	107.3	73.7
48.8	40.9	60.2	82.1	60.0	39.0
59.6	60.4	88.0	106.8	66.2	41.9
$ 932.1	$ 1,075.3	$ 1,107.5	$ 1,171.1	$ 1,233.4	$ 1,210.0
8.21%	8.48%	6.32%	5.82%	8.30%	11.28%
106.2	93.5	104.8	119.1	120.2	99.8
89.2	69.3	90.2	101.7	92.2	62.3
92.1	92.2	102.1	118.1	97.6	68.6

Exhibit 7

W. T. GRANT COMPANY
Financial Ratios and Growth Rates Based on Amounts as Originally Reported

Financial Ratios	1967	1968	1969
Profitability Analysis			
Profit Margin	3.7%	3.6%	3.7%
Assets Turnover	2.4	2.3	2.3
Return on Assets	8.7%	8.2%	8.4%
Return on Common Shareholders' Equity	16.8%	15.5%	15.2%
Operating Performance			
Cost of Goods Sold/Sales	68.6%	68.4%	67.6%
Sell. & Admin. Exp./Sales	25.3%	25.9%	26.3%
Asset Turnovers			
Accounts Receivable	8.3	8.0	7.6
Inventory	3.9	3.7	3.8
Fixed Asset	20.8	20.5	22.7
Short-Term Liquidity Risk			
Current Ratio	2.62	2.49	2.36
Quick Ratio	1.20	1.15	1.10
Days Receivables	44	45	48
Days Inventory	94	98	97
Days Payables	37	42	43
Operating Cash Flow/Current Liabilities	(15.1%)	3.8%	7.1%
Long-Term Solvency Risk			
Liabilities/Assets	49.7%	47.4%	44.1%
LT Debt/Assets	17.0%	14.0%	8.5%
Operating Cash Flow/Liabilities	(8.7%)	2.4%	4.9%
Interest Coverage	12.4	13.1	17.5

Growth Rates		1968	1969
Accounts Receivable		20.9%	16.1%
Inventories		5.2%	13.6%
Fixed Assets		(1.0%)	3.4%
Total Assets		8.6%	12.9%
Accounts Payable		5.0%	28.1%
Bank Loans		—	(40.0%)
Long-Term Debt		(10.5%)	(30.9%)
Shareholders' Equity		13.4%	20.0%
Sales		6.4%	11.9%
Cost of Goods Sold		6.0%	10.7%
Sell. and Admin. Expense		8.8%	13.5%
Net Income		4.1%	16.4%

1970	1971	1972	1973	1974	1975
4.1%	3.9%	3.2%	3.0%	2.6%	(7.5%)
2.0	1.7	1.6	1.6	1.6	1.5
8.2%	6.5%	5.0%	4.7%	4.1%	(11.4%)
15.1%	13.7%	11.4%	11.7%	2.5%	(84.1%)
67.5%	67.2%	67.7%	68.4%	69.4%	74.0%
25.4%	26.3%	27.2%	27.0%	26.6%	43.7%
4.6	3.2	3.1	3.2	3.2	3.4
3.8	3.5	3.3	3.2	3.0	3.0
23.2	21.4	19.8	19.5	19.2	17.4
1.71	1.57	1.75	1.55	1.60	1.23
1.09	.99	1.11	.91	.93	.68
79	115	119	113	113	107
96	104	110	113	121	120
45	46	46	35	30	37
(1.1%)	(3.6%)	(5.8%)	(20.6%)	(14.1%)	(11.8%)
58.9%	62.6%	65.5%	69.9%	74.2%	85.9%
5.0%	4.0%	13.6%	11.4%	17.6%	20.0%
(.9%)	(3.2%)	(4.8%)	(16.4%)	(10.9%)	(9.0%)
6.4	4.8	4.8	4.0	1.1	(2.4)

1970	1971	1972	1973	1974	1975
137.9%	14.0%	13.7%	13.7%	10.3%	(28.0%)
6.5%	17.3%	14.7%	33.8%	12.8%	(9.6%)
12.4%	11.8%	24.8%	18.5%	10.5%	.9%
39.6%	14.3%	17.0%	17.6%	12.8%	(13.6%)
2.0%	13.4%	5.8%	(9.7%)	(7.1%)	40.4%
N/A	35.3%	(3.5%)	64.1%	16.2%	32.6%
(18.1%)	(8.8%)	297.6%	(1.4%)	73.9%	(1.8%)
2.7%	3.9%	7.8%	2.6%	(3.2%)	(64.8%)
10.5%	3.6%	9.6%	19.6%	12.5%	(4.7%)
10.3%	3.1%	10.4%	20.8%	14.0%	1.6%
6.7%	7.5%	13.3%	18.8%	10.4%	56.6%
10.3%	(5.3%)	(11.0%)	7.3%	(77.7%)	(2203.9%)

Exhibit 8
W. T. GRANT COMPANY
Financial Ratios and Growth Rates Based on Amounts Retroactively Restated for Changes in Accounting Principles (Leases Not Capitalized)

Financial Ratios	1967	1968	1969
Profitability Analysis			
Profit Margin	3.8%	3.8%	3.9%
Assets Turnover	2.0	1.8	1.9
Return on Assets	7.7%	7.0%	7.4%
Return on Common Shareholders' Equity	16.6%	15.3%	15.3%
Operating Performance			
Cost of Goods Sold/Sales	68.6%	68.4%	67.6%
Sell. & Admin. Exp./Sales	24.9%	25.2%	25.4%
Asset Turnovers			
Accounts Receivable	4.6	3.9	3.7
Inventory	3.9	3.7	3.8
Fixed Asset	20.8	20.5	22.5
Short-Term Liquidity Risk			
Current Ratio	2.05	2.06	1.93
Quick Ratio	1.23	1.26	1.19
Days Receivables	80	94	97
Days Inventory	94	98	97
Days Payables	37	42	43
Operating Cash Flow/Current Liabilities	(9.4%)	2.2%	4.1%
Long-Term Solvency Risk			
Liabilities/Assets	58.6%	56.4%	55.0%
LT Debt/Assets	13.7%	11.4%	7.0%
Operating Cash Flow/Liabilities	(6.4%)	1.6%	3.3%
Interest Coverage	8.8	8.1	8.7

Growth Rates	1968	1969
Accounts Receivable	18.2%	14.8%
Inventories	5.2%	13.6%
Fixed Assets	(1.0%)	4.9%
Total Assets	7.6%	12.8%
Accounts Payable	5.0%	28.1%
Bank Loans	1.6%	19.0%
Long-Term Debt	(10.5%)	(30.9%)
Shareholders' Equity	13.4%	16.4%
Sales	6.4%	11.9%
Cost of Goods Sold	6.0%	10.7%
Sell. and Admin. Expense	7.8%	12.5%
Net Income	4.5%	15.7%

1970	1971	1972	1973	1974	1975
4.1%	3.7%	2.9%	2.8%	2.8%	(7.5%)
1.8	1.7	1.7	1.7	1.7	1.5
7.5%	6.4%	5.0%	4.8%	4.6%	(11.6%)
15.1%	13.2%	11.3%	11.9%	3.6%	(90.2%)
67.5%	67.2%	67.7%	68.4%	69.4%	74.0%
25.4%	31.6%	32.4%	32.4%	32.5%	43.7%
3.6	3.5	3.6	3.8	3.7	3.6
3.8	3.5	3.3	3.2	3.0	3.0
23.0	21.4	19.8	19.5	19.2	17.4
1.71	1.56	1.75	1.53	1.58	1.23
1.09	.93	1.05	.85	.89	.68
103	106	102	97	100	101
96	104	110	113	121	120
45	46	46	35	30	37
(.9%)	(3.8%)	(6.3%)	(22.3%)	(14.9%)	(12.0%)
58.9%	62.9%	66.1%	70.8%	75.3%	89.5%
5.0%	4.3%	14.7%	12.2%	18.4%	20.0%
(.8%)	(3.4%)	(5.1%)	(17.4%)	(11.4%)	(9.1%)
6.4	4.7	4.5	3.9	1.2	(2.4)

1970	1971	1972	1973	1974	1975
17.7%	(2.7%)	13.9%	14.8%	15.4%	(20.3%)
6.5%	17.3%	14.7%	33.8%	12.8%	(9.6%)
10.8%	11.8%	24.8%	18.5%	10.5%	.9%
13.6%	5.6%	17.3%	18.4%	15.3%	(9.4%)
2.0%	13.4%	5.8%	(9.7%)	(7.1%)	40.4%
54.2%	35.3%	(3.5%)	64.1%	16.2%	32.6%
(18.1%)	(8.8%)	297.6%	(1.4%)	73.9%	(1.8%)
3.8%	(4.7%)	7.3%	1.9%	(2.7%)	(61.4%)
10.5%	3.6%	9.6%	19.6%	12.5%	(4.7%)
10.3%	3.1%	10.4%	20.8%	14.0%	1.6%
10.5%	29.2%	12.2%	19.6%	12.9%	27.9%
9.5%	(12.9%)	(13.2%)	10.6%	(68.8%)	(1726.7%)

Exhibit 9
W. T. GRANT COMPANY
Financial Ratios and Growth Rates Based on Amounts Retroactively Restated for Changes in Accounting Principles (Leases Capitalized)

Financial Ratios	1967	1968	1969
Profitability Analysis			
Profit Margin...	3.8%	3.8%	3.9%
Assets Turnover...	1.1	1.1	1.1
Return on Assets	4.1%	4.0%	4.3%
Return on Common Shareholders' Equity	16.6%	15.3%	15.3%
Operating Performance			
Cost of Goods Sold/Sales	68.6%	68.4%	67.6%
Sell. and Admin. Exp./Sales	24.9%	25.2%	25.4%
Asset Turnovers			
Accounts Receivable	4.6	3.9	3.7
Inventory	3.9	3.7	3.8
Fixed Asset	2.1	2.2	2.3
Short-Term Liquidity Risk			
Current Ratio	2.05	2.06	1.93
Quick Ratio	1.23	1.26	1.19
Days Receivables	80	94	97
Days Inventory	94	98	97
Days Payables	37	42	43
Operating Cash Flow/Current Liabilities	(9.4%)	2.2%	4.1%
Long-Term Solvency Risk			
Liabilities/Assets	76.7%	74.5%	74.0%
LT Debt/Assets	51.5%	48.3%	46.4%
Operating Cash Flow/Liabilities	(2.5%)	.7%	1.4%
Interest Coverage	8.8	8.1	8.7

Growth Rates		1968	1969
Accounts Receivable		18.2%	14.8%
Inventories		5.2%	13.6%
Fixed Assets		1.6%	14.9%
Total Assets		3.5%	14.2%
Accounts Payable		5.0%	28.1%
Bank Loans		1.6%	19.0%
Long-Term Debt		(3.0%)	9.7%
Shareholders' Equity		13.4%	16.4%
Sales		6.4%	11.9%
Cost of Goods Sold		6.0%	10.7%
Sell. and Admin. Expense		7.8%	12.5%
Net Income		4.5%	15.7%

1970	1971	1972	1973	1974	1975
4.1%	3.7%	2.9%	2.8%	2.8%	(7.5%)
1.1	1.0	1.0	1.0	1.0	.9
4.4%	3.8%	2.9%	2.8%	2.7%	(6.8%)
15.1%	13.2%	11.3%	11.9%	3.6%	(90.2%)
67.5%	67.2%	67.7%	68.4%	69.4%	74.0%
25.4%	31.6%	32.4%	32.4%	32.5%	43.7%
3.6	3.5	3.6	3.8	3.7	3.6
3.8	3.5	3.3	3.2	3.0	3.0
2.3	2.3	2.2	2.2	2.2	1.9
1.71	1.56	1.75	1.53	1.58	1.23
1.09	.93	1.05	.85	.89	.68
103	106	102	97	100	101
96	104	110	113	121	120
45	46	46	35	30	37
(.9%)	(3.8%)	(6.3%)	(22.3%)	(14.9%)	(12.0%)
75.6%	77.7%	80.2%	82.6%	85.3%	94.0%
43.8%	42.5%	50.2%	47.9%	51.3%	54.5%
(.3%)	(1.6%)	(2.5%)	(8.6%)	(5.9%)	(4.9%)
6.4	4.7	4.5	3.9	1.2	(2.4)

1970	1971	1972	1973	1974	1975
17.7%	(2.7%)	13.9%	14.8%	15.4%	(20.3%)
6.5%	17.3%	14.7%	33.8%	12.8%	(9.6%)
6.9%	2.9%	26.1%	13.8%	13.3%	1.8%
10.6%	4.1%	20.8%	16.2%	14.6%	(4.8%)
2.0%	13.4%	5.8%	(9.7%)	(7.1%)	40.4%
54.2%	35.3%	(3.5%)	64.1%	16.2%	32.6%
4.4%	1.2%	42.8%	10.7%	22.8%	1.1%
3.8%	(4.7%)	7.3%	1.9%	(2.7%)	(61.4%)
10.5%	3.6%	9.6%	19.6%	12.5%	(4.7%)
10.3%	3.1%	10.4%	20.8%	14.0%	1.6%
10.5%	29.2%	12.2%	19.6%	12.9%	27.9%
9.5%	(12.9%)	(13.2%)	10.6%	(68.8%)	(1726.7%)

Generally Accepted Accounting Principles: Income Recognition and Asset Valuation

The particular accounting principles, or methods, that a firm selects from the set of alternative methods deemed acceptable by the accounting profession (that is, GAAP) can significantly impact its financial statements and affect the appropriateness of interpretations made. This chapter and the next two describe several alternative accounting methods commonly encountered in corporate annual reports. This chapter examines income recognition, inventory cost-flow assumptions, and depreciable and intangible asset accounting. The focus is on GAAP in the United States, although the chapter notes differences between those used in the United States and other countries. It begins with a discussion of reporting strategies a firm might pursue in selecting its accounting principles.

Reporting Strategies and the Selection of Accounting Principles

Numerous research studies during the last three decades have examined the following questions: Why do firms select particular accounting principles rather than alternative, generally accepted methods? And do the particular methods selected make any difference to the users of financial statements? Researchers have addressed these questions by examining particular selection decisions (for example, FIFO versus LIFO for inventories, straight-line versus accelerated methods for depreciable assets), rather than the aggregate effect of all accounting principles chosen by firms.

The literature suggests three reporting strategies that might motivate firms' selection decisions: profit maximization, conservatism, and income smoothing. Each of these reporting strategies focuses on the income effect of alternative accounting principles rather than on their balance sheet effect. Chapter 1 pointed out that income over long enough time periods equals cash inflows less cash outflows from operating and investing activities. Thus, the total income under each of these reporting strategies is the same, only the timing of the income recognition differs.

1.   Profit maximization: Firms might select those accounting principles that maximize cumulative reported earnings. Such firms would likely use the percentage-of-completion method for long-term contracts, a first-in, first-out (FIFO) cost-flow assumption for inventories, and the straight-line depreciation method for depreciable assets (later sections of this chapter discuss each of these accounting principles). Management might select this reporting strategy with the intent of placing the firm in the most favorable light before shareholders. Also, management might maximize its compensation if the firm ties bonuses or other compensation to reported earnings. The shareholders of a publicly held firm are too numerous and detached from the firm to monitor its day-to-day operations. The shareholders therefore hire managers as their agents to conduct and monitor these operations. Shareholders must implement incentive schemes to ensure that managers act in the best interests of shareholders. A bonus-based compensation scheme tied to earnings might serve as such an incentive arrangement. Increased earnings beyond those already anticipated by the market should increase stock prices and thereby reward shareholders. Increased earnings should also increase management's compensation. Thus, properly designed incentive schemes help both shareholders and management. Note that the firm could base the bonus arrangement on objectives other than maximizing earnings, such as maximizing cash flow or rates of return on assets or shareholders' equity.[1] Note also that the profit maximization strategy focuses on reported earnings to shareholders and not the profit maximization dictum of microeconomics. The latter uses economic values, not accounting values, in measuring net income.

2.   Conservatism: Firms might also select those accounting principles that minimize cumulative reported earnings. Such firms would likely use the completed-contract method for long-term contracts, a last-in, first-out (LIFO) cost-flow assumption for inventories, and an accelerated depreciation method for depreciable assets. Minimizing cumulative taxable income usually results in the smallest present value of tax payments to governmental bodies. Some firms might pursue the same reporting strategy in preparing financial statements for shareholders. Such an action eliminates the need to keep two sets of books, one for tax reporting and one for financial reporting. Management might wish to portray a conservative, controlled image to shareholders, perhaps thereby reducing the risk that future earnings levels will disappoint shareholders. In some countries (France, Germany, Japan), tax reporting rules heavily influence financial reporting to banks and shareholders. Regulators may even require conformity between tax and financial reporting methods (as is the case in the United States with LIFO). In these cases, firms adopt conservatism as a reporting strategy.

---

[1] A rich literature on agency theory has developed during the last decade. For a summary of its principal concepts, see Ross L. Watts and Jerold L. Zimmerman, *Positive Accounting Theory* (Englewood Cliffs, NJ: Prentice-Hall, 1986).

3. Income smoothing: Chapter 1 discussed briefly the relation between earnings and stock prices. Later chapters develop this relation more fully. There is evidence to suggest, however, that changes in earnings correlate with changes in stock prices. We might expect, therefore, that a firm with wide fluctuations in its reported earnings would also experience wide fluctuations in its stock prices. Analysts often view fluctuations in stock prices as an indicator of risk. Increased risk should lead to a higher cost of funds. The rationale for an income smoothing strategy is that firms can reduce market-perceived risk by selecting accounting methods that smooth reported earnings. Such firms would probably use the percentage-of-completion method rather than the completed-contract method for long-term contracts and a LIFO cost-flow assumption for inventories (a later section of this chapter discusses why LIFO generally results in smoother earnings over time than FIFO or weighted average). Firms would select either the straight-line or an accelerated depreciation method to smooth earnings depending on whether maintenance and other costs of maintaining depreciable assets are level over the life of the assets (straight-line method used) or whether such costs increase with age (an accelerated depreciation method used). Note that the income smoothing reporting strategy focuses on net income, not necessarily on individual revenues and expenses. Note also that firms can accomplish income smoothing in ways other than by their selection of accounting principles. For example, firms can time their expenditures on maintenance, advertising, research and development, and similar costs to smooth earnings.[2]

Income Recognition

Figure 3.1 depicts the operating process for a typical manufacturing firm. The *amount* of income from operating activities is equal to the difference between the cash a firm ultimately receives from customers and the cash it pays to suppliers, employees, and others to manufacture and sell a product. To obtain an appropriate matching of revenues (outputs) and expenses (inputs) in the income statement, firms use the accrual basis, rather than the cash basis, of accounting.

Using the accrual basis, however, does not settle the question of *when* firms recognize revenues (and matching expenses). Firms could recognize revenues (1) during the period of production, (2) at the completion of production, (3) at the time of sale, (4) during the period while receivables are outstanding, or (5) at the time of cash collection.

Criteria for Revenue Recognition

GAAP requires the recognition of revenue under the accrual basis of accounting when a firm:

---

[2] For a summary of the principal concepts underlying income smoothing, see Joshua Ronen and S. Sadan, *Smoothing Income Numbers: Objectives, Means, and Implications* (Reading, MA: Addison-Wesley, 1981). Also, see Brett Trueman and Sheridan Titman, "An Explanation for Accounting Income Smoothing," *Journal of Accounting Research* (Supplement, 1988), pp. 127–139.

Figure 3.1
Operating Process for a Manufacturing Firm

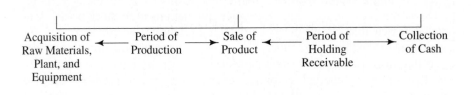

1. Has provided all, or a substantial portion, of the services to be performed.

2. Has received either cash, a receivable, or some other asset susceptible to reasonably precise measurement.

A firm incurs costs as it performs services. To justify revenue recognition, a firm needs to have performed sufficient services so that it can measure or estimate the total costs it expects to incur. Such measurement of total costs permits an appropriate matching of expenses with revenues.

The benefit that a firm obtains from providing services is the cash or cash-equivalent value of other consideration it expects to receive. To justify revenue recognition, a firm needs to have a reasonably precise measurement of the amount of this expected benefit. Receiving cash provides such measurement. Receiving other assets may also provide such measurement if the firm can ascertain the cash-equivalent value of these assets in a reasonably reliable manner.

Most firms recognize revenues at the time of sale (delivery). At this time, the firm transfers the goods to a buyer or performs the required services. Its obligation for future services, such as for warranties, is either insignificant or, if significant, is subject to reasonably precise measurement. An exchange between an independent buyer and seller provides an objective measure of the amount of revenue. If the firm makes the sale on account, its past experience and assessment of the credit standing of customers provide a basis for predicting the amount of cash it will collect. Thus, the firm usually meets the criteria for revenue recognition at the time of sale.

Criteria for Expense Recognition

GAAP requires the recognition of expenses under the accrual basis of accounting as follows:

1. Costs directly associated with revenues become expenses in the period when a firm recognizes the revenues.

2. Costs not directly associated with revenues become expenses in the period when a firm consumes the services or benefits of the costs in operations.

Most of the costs of manufacturing and selling a product closely relate to particular revenues. The firm matches expense recognition with revenue recognition for such items. Other costs—such as insurance and property taxes on administrative facilities, salaries of corporate officers, and depreciation on computer equipment—bear only an indirect relation to revenues generated during the period. Such costs become expenses in the period in which the firm consumes the benefits of insurance, governmental, administrative, and computer services. Accountants refer to such costs as *period expenses*.

Although most firms recognize revenues and expenses at the time of sale, the analyst should assess whether this timing of income recognition is appropriate in particular cases. The next section illustrates some of the issues that the analyst should address.

Application of Revenue and Expense Recognition Criteria

This section illustrates the application of the criteria for revenue and expense recognition for various types of businesses.

Example 1. Paramount Communications produces movies. It incurs production costs in filming the movies, advertising costs in promoting them, and royalty costs for the principal actors and actresses, producers, directors, and others. Paramount Communications generates revenues from movie theaters based on the number of tickets sold. It may also generate revenues from video sales and the sale of residual rights to the movies to television or cable networks or to foreign licensees. The amount of revenues generated from video sales and the sale of residual movie rights depends in part on the success of the films in their initial theater run.

The movie studio can easily measure the amount of revenues from theater ticket sales and recognize it as sales occur. The amount of revenues that a film will generate from video sales and the sale of residual rights is highly uncertain as of the time of the movie's initial release. The criteria for the recognition of revenue are therefore not met until sales of videos and residual rights occur in later periods. The movie studio can easily match royalty expenses with revenues because the royalty amount is usually a percentage of the revenues. The principal income recognition issue for movie studios is, how much of the costs of filming and promoting the movie should the studio match with theater ticket revenues and how much should it leave on the balance sheet as an asset to match with revenues from video sales and residual rights in later periods? The revenue patterns of previous movies may provide a basis for projecting the likely total revenues from new releases. Also, we would expect that the movie studio considered revenue projections in establishing the cost budget for the movie. The analyst examining the financial statements of a movie studio should study carefully the profit margin on movies reported in the income statement and the amount of deferred production costs appearing on the balance sheet.

Example 2.   Columbia Records runs periodic promotions to enlist subscribers into their tape or compact disc-of-the-month programs. For a nominal fee, new subscribers receive a set of tapes or compact discs and promise to purchase a certain minimum number of such items over some future period of time. The firm sends out cards each month with the list of tapes or compact discs available for that month. Subscribers return the cards if they wish to purchase one of the selections. Similar arrangements apply to book-of-the-month and craft-of-the-month programs.

The principal income measurement issue in these settings is the timing of revenue recognition. Should these firms recognize the revenues from selling the required minimum number of tapes or compact discs when customers commit to such purchases upon subscription? Or should these firms recognize a portion of the revenues each month when they send out the cards? The return rate from customers desiring to purchase the tape or compact disc selection is relatively low each month. If the return rate were highly predictable, such as 20 percent or 30 percent, then the firms could simply recognize revenue for that portion of customer orders. The return rate, however, is not only low but unpredictable. The selections for one month may have a 20 percent customer order rate while the next month's selections may experience a 50 percent customer demand rate. Furthermore, several months might elapse before the size of customer orders becomes clear. These firms do not meet the criteria for revenue recognition either at the time customers subscribe or at the time the firm sends out cards each month because the amount of cash that the firm will ultimately receive and its date of receipt are not measurable with sufficient precision. Such firms should delay revenue recognition until they ship products to customers.

Additional income recognition issues arise with respect to the initial promotional offer. Should the firm recognize the costs of the promotional tapes or compact discs as an expense in the period when the customer subscribes to the program or should it spread such costs over the future periods when the customer purchases the additional items required by the program? Firms that defer such costs report a deferred asset, such as Deferred Subscription Costs, on their balance sheets.

Example 3.   Automotive and appliance manufacturers typically provide warranty or maintenance services for products sold. Some companies include such services automatically in the sale of their products; the selling price includes a charge for the automobile or appliance and its related warranty. Other companies provide a very limited warranty with the product and sell a more comprehensive warranty or maintenance agreement separately. Customers can decide whether or not to purchase the extended protection. This protection may cover a period of three to five years.

These firms typically receive cash for both the product sold and any related warranty at the time they sell the main product. Thus, little uncertainty exists regarding the amount of revenue. The principal income recognition issue regards the amount of expense to match against the revenue. These firms must provide future services, the cost of which the firms will not know for certain for several years. If these firms will perform only minimal future services or can predict the costs of such services with a reasonably high degree of precision, then such firms can recognize the warranty revenue in the period when they sell the main product. Such firms would also recognize an estimated warranty expense to match against such revenues. A Warranty Liability account appears on the balance sheet reflecting the expected costs of future warranty claims. If these firms must provide substantial future services or if the cost of the future services is highly uncertain, then they should delay the recognition of warranty revenue. A Warranty Advances account appears among liabilities for such firms. These firms recognize warranty revenue and warranty expense each period as time passes and customers make warranty claims.

Example 4.   Metropolitan Life Insurance Company sells life insurance policies to customers. The firm receives premium payments each year and invests the cash in stocks, bonds, real estate, and other income-producing assets. The premiums received from customers plus the income from investments over the life of insured individuals provide the funds to pay the required death benefits.

Life insurance companies receive cash from premiums and from investments each period. They invest in readily marketable securities for the most part, so that they can measure the changes in the market value of their investments. Measuring the amount of revenue each period while the life insurance policy is outstanding presents few difficulties. The only issue on the revenue side is whether these firms should recognize as revenue the unrealized gains and losses from changes in the market value of investments. Common practice in the insurance industry is to recognize such gains and losses each year in computing net income.

There is usually little question about the total expense on a life insurance policy. Other than administrative costs, the only expense is the face value of the policy. The income recognition issue is, how much of this total cost life insurance companies should recognize as an expense each year to match against premium and investment revenues? The objective is to spread these costs over the life of the insured. Determining the length of this period and the pattern of expense recognition requires actuarial calculations of expected life, investment returns, and similar factors. Note that allocation of an equal portion of the total cost to each year of expected life will not necessarily provide an appropriate matching of revenues and expenses. Although insurance premiums typically remain level over the contract period, investment revenues increase over time as premiums and investment returns accumulate. Life insurance companies increase a liability each period, often called Policyholder Reserves, for the amount of expense recognized. They reduce this account when they pay insurance claims. An analyst examining the financial statements of a life insurance company should study carefully the amount shown for Policyholder Reserves and the change in this account each year. Such an assessment provides information about both the adequacy of investments to cover potential claims and the amount of net income each period.

These four examples illustrate situations where firms in certain industries do not necessarily meet the criteria for revenue and expense recognition at the time of sale. An underlying theme in each instance is uncertainty—uncertainty about the amount of cash that the firm will ultimately receive and uncertainty about the amount of cash it will ultimately expend. Analysts sometimes use the concept of *quality of earnings* to refer to how well reported earnings amounts reflect cash flows ultimately received or paid. Earnings amounts that require significant estimations of future cash flows, as in the four examples discussed above, are of lower quality than the earnings of firms that do not require such estimations (consider, for instance, a service business where earnings and cash flows closely coincide). In addition to the selection of accounting principles (such as the timing of income recognition), the application of accounting principles (such as the depreciable lives used for plant and equipment) and managerial discretion in timing costs (such as maintenance, advertising, and research and development) affect earnings quality. The lower the quality of earnings, the higher is the *potential* for a firm to manage reported earnings and possibly mislead investors.[3] The analyst assesses earnings quality subjectively rather than measuring it in a precise manner.

The next section explores more fully the financial statements impact of recognizing income either earlier than the time of sale (a common practice among long-term contractors) or later than the time of sale (a common practice when firms sell goods on an installment payment basis and experience high uncertainty regarding the collectibility of cash).

Income Recognition for Long-Term Contractors

The operating process for a long-term contractor (for example, building contractor, shipbuilder) differs from that of a manufacturing firm (depicted in Figure 3.1) in three important respects:

1. The period of construction (or production) may span several accounting periods.

2. Contractors identify customers and agree upon a contract price in advance (or at least in the early stages of construction).

3. Customers often make periodic payments of portions of the contract price as work progresses.

Long-term contractors often satisfy the criteria for the recognition of revenue during the period of construction. The existence of a contract indicates that the contractor has identified a buyer and agreed upon a price. The contractor either collects cash in advance or concludes, based on an assessment of the customer's credit standing, that it will receive cash equal to the contract price after completion of construction. Although the contract may obligate the contractor to per-

---

[3] For an excellent discussion of earnings management, see Katherine Schipper, "Earnings Management," *Accounting Horizons* (December 1989), pp. 91–102.

form substantial future services, the contractor should be able to estimate the cost of these services with reasonable precision. In agreeing to a contract price, the firm must have some confidence in the estimates of the total costs it will incur on the contract.

When contractors meet the criteria for revenue recognition as construction progresses, they usually recognize revenue during the period of construction using the *percentage-of-completion method*. Under the percentage-of-completion method, contractors recognize a portion of the total contract price, based on the degree of completion of the work during the period, as revenue for the period. They base this proportion either on engineers' or architects' estimates of the degree of completion or on the ratio of costs incurred to date to the total expected costs for the contract. The actual schedule of cash collections is *not* significant for the revenue recognition process when contractors use the percentage-of-completion method. Even if a contractor expects to collect the entire contract price at the completion of construction, it will still use the percentage-of-completion method as long as it can make reasonable estimates as construction progresses of the amount of cash it will collect and of the costs it will incur.

As contractors recognize portions of the contract price as revenues, they recognize corresponding proportions of the total estimated costs of the contract as expenses. The percentage-of-completion method, following the principles of the accrual basis of accounting, matches expenses with related revenues.

Example 5. To illustrate the percentage-of-completion method, assume that a firm agrees to construct a bridge for $5,000,000. Estimated costs are as follows: Year 1, $1,500,000; Year 2, $2,000,000; and Year 3, $500,000. Thus, the expected gross margin from the contract is $1,000,000 (= $5,000,000 − $1,500,000 − $2,000,000 − $500,000). Assuming that the contractor bases the degree of completion on the percentage of total costs incurred to date and that it incurs actual costs as anticipated, revenue and expense from the contract are as follows:

Year	Degree of Completion	Revenue	Expense	Gross Margin
1	$1,500,000/$4,000,000 = 37.5%	$1,875,000	$1,500,000	$ 375,000
2	$2,000,000/$4,000,000 = 50.0%	2,500,000	2,000,000	500,000
3	$ 500,000/$4,000,000 = 12.5%	625,000	500,000	125,000
		$5,000,000	$4,000,000	$1,000,000

Actual costs on contracts seldom coincide precisely with expectations. As new information on expected total costs becomes available, contractors must adjust reported income on the contract. They make the adjustment to reported income of the current and future periods rather than retroactively restating income of prior periods.

Example 6. Refer to Example 5. Assume now that actual costs incurred in Year 2 for the contract were $2,200,000 instead of $2,000,000 and that total expected costs on the contract are now $4,200,000. Revenue, expense, and gross margin from the contract are as follows:

Year	Cumulative Degree of Completion		Revenue	Expense	Gross Margin
1	$1,500,000/$4,000,000 =	37.5%	$1,875,000	$1,500,000	$375,000
2	$3,700,000/$4,200,000 =	88.1%	2,530,000[a]	2,200,000	330,000
3	$4,200,000/$4,200,000 =	100.0%	595,000[b]	500,000	95,000
			$5,000,000	$4,200,000	$800,000

[a]$(.881 \times \$5,000,000) - \$1,875,000 = \$2,530,000$
[b]$\$5,000,000 - \$1,875,000 - \$2,530,000 = \$595,000$

Example 7. If it appears that the contractor will ultimately realize a loss upon completion of a contract, the contractor must recognize the loss in full as soon as it becomes evident. For instance, if at the end of Year 2 the contractor expects to realize a loss of $200,000 on the contract, it must recognize a loss of $575,000 in Year 2. The $575,000 amount offsets the income of $375,000 recognized in Year 1 plus a loss of $200,000 anticipated on the overall contract.

Contractors report actual contract costs on the balance sheet in a Contracts in Process account. This account includes not only accumulated costs to date but any income or loss recognized on the contract. Exhibit 3.1 shows the Contracts in Process account for the bridge contract. If the contractor periodically billed the customer for portions of the contract price, it would report the amount billed as a subtraction from the amount in the Contracts in Process account.

Some long-term contractors postpone the recognition of revenue until they complete the construction project. Such firms use the *completed-contract method* of recognizing revenue. If the firm in the previous example had used the completed-contract method, it would have recognized no revenue or expense from the contract during Year 1 or Year 2. It would recognize contract revenue of $5,000,000 and contract expenses of $4,200,000 in Year 3. Note that total income is $800,000 under both the percentage-of-completion and completed-contract methods, equal to cash inflows of $5,000,000 less cash outflows of $4,200,000. If the contractor anticipates a loss on a contract, it recognizes the loss as soon as the loss becomes evident, even if the contract is incomplete.

The Contracts in Process account under the completed-contract method shows a balance of $1,500,000 on December 31, Year 1, the accumulated costs to date. This account shows a balance on December 31, Year 2, of $3,500,000 under Example 5, $3,700,000 under Example 6, and $3,500,000 under Example 7. These amounts reflect accumulated costs to date minus, in Example 7, the estimated loss on the contract. These amounts are less than the amounts shown in the Contracts in Process account for Examples 5 and 6 under the percentage-of-completion method (see Exhibit 3.1) by the amount of accumulated income recognized under the latter method. Accelerating the recognition of income under the percentage-of-completion method increases both assets and net income (part of retained earnings). Thus, income recognition and asset valuation closely interrelate.

In some cases contractors use the completed-contract method because the contracts are of such short duration (such as a few months) that earnings reported with the percentage-of-completion method and the completed-contract method are not significantly different. In these cases the lower costs of implementing the

Exhibit 3.1
Calculation of Balance in Contracts in Process Account Using the Percentage-of-Completion Method

	Accumulated Costs	Accumulated Income	Amount in Contracts in Process Account
Example 5 (Profit = $1,000,000)			
During Year 1	$1,500,000	$ 375,000	$1,875,000
Balance, December 31, Year 1	$1,500,000	$ 375,000	$1,875,000
During Year 2	2,000,000	500,000	2,500,000
Balance, December 31, Year 2	$3,500,000	$ 875,000	$4,375,000
During Year 3	500,000	125,000	625,000
Completion of Contract during Year 3	(4,000,000)	(1,000,000)	(5,000,000)
Balance, December 31, Year 3	$ -0-	$ -0-	$ -0-
Example 6 (Profit = $800,000)			
During Year 1	$1,500,000	$ 375,000	$1,875,000
Balance, December 31, Year 1	$1,500,000	$ 375,000	$1,875,000
During Year 2	2,200,000	330,000	2,530,000
Balance, December 31, Year 2	$3,700,000	$ 705,000	$4,405,000
During Year 3	500,000	95,000	595,000
Completion of Contract during Year 3	(4,200,000)	(800,000)	(5,000,000)
Balance, December 31, Year 3	$ -0-	$ -0-	$ -0-
Example 7 (Loss = $200,000)			
During Year 1	$1,500,000	$ 375,000	$1,875,000
Balance, December 31, Year 1	$1,500,000	$ 375,000	$1,875,000
During Year 2	2,200,000	(575,000)	1,625,000
Balance, December 31, Year 2	$3,700,000	$(200,000)	$3,500,000
During Year 3	1,500,000	—	1,500,000
Completion of Contract during Year 3	(5,200,000)	200,000	(5,000,000)
Balance, December 31, Year 3	$ -0-	$ -0-	$ -0-

completed-contract method explain its use. Contractors also use the completed-contract method in situations when they have not obtained a specific buyer during the construction phase, as is sometimes the case in the construction of residential housing. These cases require future selling efforts. Substantial uncertainty may exist regarding the ultimate contract price and the amount of cash that the contractor will receive.

The primary reason why a contractor would not use the percentage-of-completion method when a contract exists is that there is substantial uncertainty regarding the total costs it will incur in completing the project. If the contractor cannot estimate the total costs, it will be unable to estimate the percentage of total costs incurred as of a given date and thereby the percentage of services already rendered. It will also be unable to estimate the total income from the contract.

Contractors must use the percentage-of-completion method for income tax purposes. Although most firms would prefer to use the completed-contract method for tax purposes, thereby delaying the recognition of income and payment of income taxes, the Internal Revenue Code does not permit it.

A statement of the International Accounting Standards Committee (IASC) provides only for the percentage-of-completion method. Wide variation exists, however, among member countries with respect to implementing this IASC standard. For example, Canada, France, Germany, Japan, and the United States permit both methods, the United Kingdom and the Netherlands allow only the percentage-of-completion method, and Austria allows only the completed-contract method.

Income Recognition When Cash Collectibility Is Uncertain

Occasionally, estimating the amount of cash or cash-equivalent value of other assets that a firm will receive from customers is difficult. This may occur because the future financial condition of the customer is highly uncertain or because the customer may have the right to return the items purchased, thereby avoiding the obligation to make cash payments. This uncertainty regarding future cash flows may prevent the selling firm from measuring at the time of sale the present value of the cash it will receive. It will therefore recognize income at the time it collects cash using either the installment method or the cost-recovery-first method. Unlike the cash method of accounting, these income recognition methods attempt to match expenses with associated revenues.

Installment Method.   Under the *installment method*, a firm recognizes revenue as it collects portions of the selling price in cash. At the same time, it recognizes corresponding portions of the cost of the good or service sold as an expense. For example, assume that a firm sells for $100 merchandise costing $60. The buyer agrees to pay (ignoring interest) $20 each month for five months. The firm recognizes revenue of $20 each month as it receives cash. Likewise, it recognizes cost of goods sold of $12 (= $20/$100 × $60) each month. By the end of five months, the firm recognizes total income of $40 [= 5 × ($20 − $12)].

Land development companies, which typically sell undeveloped land and promise to develop it over several future years, sometimes use the installment method. The buyer makes a nominal down payment and agrees to pay the remainder of the purchase price in installments over 10, 20, or more years. In these cases, future development of the land is a significant aspect of the earnings process. Also, substantial uncertainty often exists as to the ultimate collectibility of the installment notes, particularly those not due until several years in the future. The customer can always elect to stop making payments, losing the right to own the land.

Cost-Recovery-First Method.   When firms experience substantial uncertainty about cash collection, they can also use the *cost-recovery-first method* of income recognition. The cost-recovery-first method matches the costs of generating revenues dollar for dollar with cash receipts until the firm recovers all such costs. Revenues equal expenses in each period until full cost recovery occurs. Only when cumulative cash receipts exceed total costs will a firm show profit (that is, revenue without any matching expense) in the income statement.

To illustrate the cost-recovery-first method, refer to the previous example relating to the sale of merchandise for $100. During the first three months, the firm would recognize revenue of $20 and expense of $20. By the end of the third month, cumulative cash receipts of $60 exactly equal the cost of the merchandise sold. During the fourth and fifth months, the firm would recognize revenue of $20 each month but without an offsetting expense. For the five months as a whole, total income is again $40 (equal to cash inflow of $100 less cash outflow of $60) but the income recognition pattern differs from that of the installment method.

Comprehensive Illustration of Income Recognition Methods for Installment Sales. Digital Equipment Corporation (DEC) sold a computer costing $16,000,000 to the City of Boston for $20,000,000 on January 1, Year 1. The City of Boston agreed to make annual payments of $5,548,195 on December 31, Year 1, to December 31, Year 5 (five payments in total). The top panel of Exhibit 3.2 shows an amortization table for the note receivable underlying this transaction. The five payments of $5,548,195 each when discounted at 12 percent have a present value equal to the $20,000,000 selling price. Thus, 12 percent is the interest rate implicit in the note. Column (2) shows the interest revenue that DEC recognizes each year from providing financing services to the City of Boston (that is, permitting the city to delay payment of the $20,000,000 selling price).

The middle panel shows the revenue and expense that DEC recognizes under three income recognition methods. Columns (6) and (7) assume DEC recognizes income from the sale of the computer at the time of sale. Such immediate recognition rests on the premise that the City of Boston will pay the amounts due under the note with a high probability.

If substantial uncertainty exists regarding cash collectibility of the note, then DEC should use either the installment or cost-recovery-first method. Columns (8) and (9) show the amounts for the installment method. Revenues in column (8) represent collections of the $20,000,000 principal amount of the note (that is, the portion of each cash payment made by the city that does not represent interest). Column (9) shows the expense each year, which represents 80 percent (= $16,000,000/$20,000,000) of the revenue recognized. Columns (10) and (11) show the amounts for the cost-recovery-first method. Note that DEC recognizes no income until Year 5, when cumulative cash receipts exceed the $16,000,000 cost of manufacturing the computer. Note also that total cash inflows of $27,740,973 (column 3) equal total revenue [sales revenue (columns 6, 8, and 10) plus interest revenue (column 12) and total cash outflows of $16,000,000 equal total expense (columns 7, 9, and 11].

The lower panel of Exhibit 3.2 shows the amounts that DEC reports on its balance sheet for each of the three income recognition methods. Recognizing income at the time of sale results in the largest cumulative income through the first four years and the largest assets. Recognizing income using the installment method results in the next largest cumulative income and the next largest assets. The cost-

Exhibit 3.2
Illustration of Income Recognition Methods from Installment Sales

Amortization Schedule for Note Receivable

Year	Note Receivable January 1 (1)	Interest Revenue at 12 Percent (2)	Cash Payment Received (3)	Repayment of Principal (4)	Note Receivable, December 31 (5)
1	$20,000,000	$2,400,000	$ 5,548,195	$ 3,148,195	$16,851,865
2	16,851,865	2,022,217	5,548,195	3,525,978	13,325,827
3	13,325,827	1,599,099	5,548,195	3,949,096	9,376,731
4	9,376,731	1,125,208	5,548,195	4,422,987	4,953,744
5	4,953,744	594,449	5,548,193	4,953,744	-0-
		$7,740,973	$27,740,973	$20,000,000	

Column (2) = .12 × column (1)
Column (3) = given
Column (4) = column (3) − column (2)
Column (5) = column (1) − column (4)

Income Recognition from Sale of Computer

	Time of Sale		Installment Method		Cost-Recovery-First Method		All Three Methods
Year	(6) Revenue	(7) Expense	(8) Revenue	(9) Expense	(10) Revenue	(11) Expense	(12) Interest Revenue
1	$20,000,000	$16,000,000	$ 3,148,195	$ 2,518,556	$ 3,148,195	$ 3,148,195	$2,400,000
2	—	—	3,525,978	2,820,782	3,525,978	3,525,978	2,022,217
3	—	—	3,949,096	3,159,277	3,949,096	3,949,096	1,599,099
4	—	—	4,422,987	3,538,390	4,422,987	4,422,987	1,125,208
5	—	—	4,953,744	3,962,995	4,953,744	953,744	594,449
	$20,000,000	$16,000,000	$20,000,000	$16,000,000	$20,000,000	$16,000,000	$7,740,973

Column (8) = column (4)
Column (9) = .80 × column (8)
Column (12) = column (2)

Column (10) = column (4)
Column (11) = column (10) until cumulative revenues = $16,000,000

Exhibit 3.2
Illustration of Income Recognition Methods from Installment Sales (*continued*)

Notes Receivable-Net Reported on Balance Sheet

Income Recognition	Time of Sale	Installment Method			Cost-Recovery-First Method		
	(13) Notes Receivable	(14) Notes Receivable	(15) Less Deferred Gross Margin	(16) Notes Receivable Net	(17) Notes Receivable	(18) Less Deferred Gross Margin	(19) Notes Receivable Net
January 1, Year 1	$20,000,000	$20,000,000	$4,000,000	$16,000,000	$20,000,000	$4,000,000	$16,000,000
December 31, Year 1	16,851,865	16,851,865	3,370,361	13,481,504	16,851,865	4,000,000	12,851,865
December 31, Year 2	13,325,827	13,325,827	2,665,165	10,660,662	13,325,827	4,000,000	9,325,827
December 31, Year 3	9,376,731	9,376,731	1,875,346	7,501,385	9,376,731	4,000,000	5,376,731
December 31, Year 4	4,953,744	4,953,744	990,749	3,962,995	4,953,744	4,000,000	953,744
December 31, Year 5	—	—	—	—	—	—	—

Column (13), column (14), column (17) = column (1).
Column (15) = $4,000,000 minus cumulative income recognized = column (8) – column (9) for the current and prior years.
   For example, $3,370,361 = $4,000,000 – ($3,148,195 – $2,518,556).
Column (16) = column (14) – column (15).
Column (18) = $4,000,000 minus cumulative income recognized = column (10) – column (11) for the current and prior years.
Column (19) = column (17) – column (18).

recovery-first method results in the smallest cumulative income and the smallest assets. The differences in assets equal the differences in cumulative income recognized. Thus, we see again that asset valuation closely relates to income recognition. Notice also that at the end of five years, cumulative income and assets are identical for all three income recognition methods.

Use of Installment and Cost-Recovery-First Methods.   GAAP permits firms to use the installment method and the cost-recovery-first method only when substantial uncertainty exists about cash collection. For most sales of goods and services, past experience and an assessment of the credit standing of customers provide a sufficient basis for estimating the amount of cash firms will receive. GAAP does not permit firms to use the installment method and the cost-recovery-first method in these cases for financial reporting. These firms must generally recognize revenue at the time of sale.

Income tax laws allow the installment method for income tax reporting under some circumstances, even when no uncertainty exists regarding cash collections. Manufacturing firms selling on extended payment plans often use the installment method for income tax reporting (while recognizing revenue at the time of sale for financial reporting). Firms use the cost-recovery-first method for tax reporting only in special circumstances, such as for pension benefits received.

Disclosure of Income Recognition Method

The notes to the financial statements include a note on the accounting policies that a firm follows. If a firm recognizes a significant amount of income at times other than the time of sale, this note will indicate the methods followed. The notes on accounting policies for Coke and Pepsi do not include information on income recognition, implying that both firms recognize income at the time of sale.

Inventory Cost-Flow Assumption

Firms selling relatively high dollar-valued items, such as automobiles, trailers, and real estate, can ascertain from the accounting records the specific cost of the items sold. They recognize this amount as an expense, cost of goods sold, and match it against sales revenue in measuring net income.

In most cases, firms cannot specifically identify the cost of items sold. Inventory items are sufficiently similar and their unit costs sufficiently small that firms cannot justify economically the cost of designing an accounting system to keep track of specific unit costs. To measure cost of goods sold in these cases, firms must make some assumption about the *flow of costs* (not the flow of units, since firms usually sell the oldest goods first). GAAP permits three cost-flow assumptions:

1. First-in, first-out (FIFO).

2. Weighted average.

3. Last-in, first-out (LIFO).

FIFO assigns the cost of the earliest purchases to the units sold and the cost of the most recent purchases to ending inventory. LIFO assigns the cost of the most recent purchases to the cost of goods sold and the earliest purchases to inventory. Weighted average assigns the average cost of all units available for sale during the period (units in beginning inventory plus units purchased) to both units sold and units in ending inventory. Figure 3.2 depicts these relations graphically, assuming that a firm purchases units evenly over the year.

FIFO

FIFO results in balance sheet amounts for ending inventory that are closest to current replacement cost. The cost of goods sold tends to be somewhat out of date, however, because FIFO charges to expense the earlier prices of beginning inventory and the earliest purchases during the year. When prices are rising, FIFO leads to the highest reported net income of the three methods, and when prices fall it leads to the smallest.

LIFO

LIFO results in amounts for cost of goods sold that closely approximate current costs. Balance sheet amounts, however, can contain the cost of acquisitions made many years previously. Consider the diagram in Figure 3.3 that shows purchases, LIFO ending inventory, and LIFO cost of goods sold over several periods for a firm. During each of the first four periods, the firm purchases more units than it sells. Thus, the physical units in ending inventory grow each year. The firm assigns costs to the units in inventory at the end of Year 1 based on the earliest purchases in Year 1. We refer to the costs assigned to these units as the base LIFO layer (denoted with the letter *a* in Figure 3.3). LIFO prices the units in inventory at the end of Year 2 in two layers. Units equal to those on hand at the end of Year 1 carry unit costs based on purchase prices paid at the beginning of Year 1. Units *added* to ending inventory during Year 2 carry unit costs based on purchase prices paid at the

Figure 3.2
Cost-Flow Assumptions

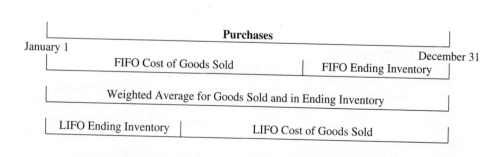

Figure 3.3
Illustration of LIFO Ending Inventory Layers

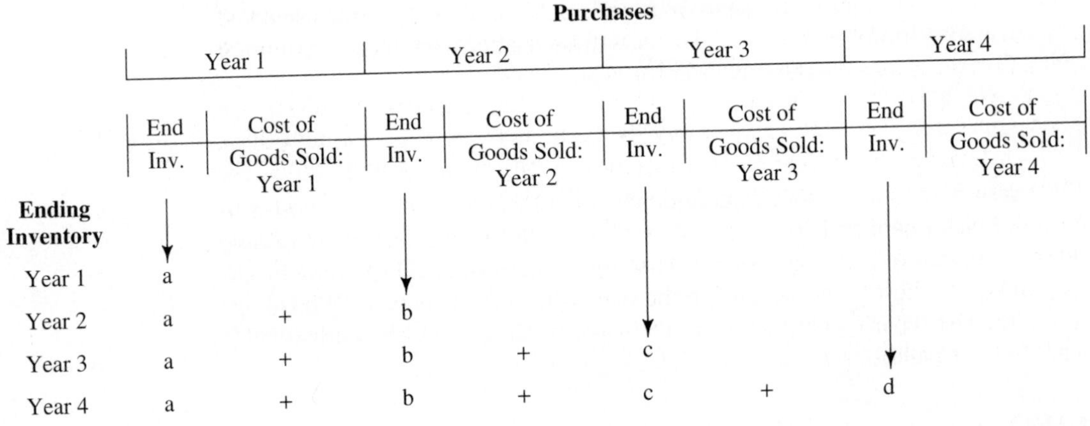

beginning of Year 2 (denoted with the letter *b* in Figure 3.3). The balance sheet at the end of Year 2 states the inventory at the sum of the costs assigned to these two layers. Note that LIFO does not assume that the actual physical flow of units sold will track a LIFO assumption. LIFO is a *cost-flow*, or cost-assignment, method and not a means of capturing the physical movement of goods.

As the quantity of units in ending inventory continues to increase in Year 3 and Year 4, the firm adds new LIFO layers. At the end of Year 4, LIFO assigns costs to ending inventory based on purchases made at the beginning of Year 1, Year 2, Year 3, and Year 4. Thus, the longer a firm remains on LIFO, the more its ending inventory valuation will differ from current replacement costs.

During periods of rising prices, LIFO generally results in the highest cost of goods sold and the lowest net income of the three cost-flow assumptions. It is for this reason that firms usually prefer LIFO for income tax purposes. If a firm chooses a LIFO cost-flow assumption for tax purposes, the income tax law requires the firm to use LIFO for financial reporting to shareholders.

LIFO Liquidation

One exception to the generalization that LIFO produces the lowest net income during periods of rising prices can occur when a firm sells more units during a period than it purchases, referred to as a LIFO layer liquidation. In this case, LIFO assigns the cost of all of the current period's purchases plus the costs assigned to the most recent LIFO layers to the cost of goods sold. For instance, assume that sales exceeded purchases in Year 5 in the example above. The firm assigns the cost of all of Year 5's purchases to the units sold. LIFO then assigns the cost of Year 4's LIFO layer (reflecting purchase prices at the beginning of Year 4) to the excess units sold, then assigns Year 3's LIFO layer (reflecting purchase prices at the beginning of Year 3) to any remaining excess units, and so on until it has assigned a unit cost to all units sold. Because LIFO assigns older, lower costs to a portion of the units sold, LIFO cost of goods sold may not exceed FIFO cost of goods sold, despite experiencing rising prices during the current period.

When firms experience LIFO liquidations, two cash-flow effects likely occur. First, firms delay purchasing inventory items, thereby delaying a cash outflow. Second, firms increase their taxable income and the required cash outflow for taxes. Researchers have examined the effect of LIFO liquidations on abnormal stock price behavior at the time firms disclose such liquidations. No abnormal stock price reaction was observed in these studies when those firms' tax positions (for example, availability of net operating loss carryforwards) were ignored. However, when this tax position was considered, low tax-paying firms had a higher abnormal price reaction to a LIFO liquidation than other firms.[4]

Characteristics of LIFO Adopters

Researchers have examined the characteristics of firms that do and do not adopt LIFO. Although these research studies do not always show consistent results, the following factors appear related to the decision to adopt LIFO[5]:

1. Direction and rate of factor price changes for inventory items: Firms experiencing rapidly increasing factor prices for raw materials, labor, or other product costs obtain greater tax benefits from LIFO than firms that experience smaller factor price increases or that experience price decreases.

2. Variability in the rate of inventory growth: LIFO adopters show more variable rates of inventory growth before adopting LIFO than firms that remain on FIFO. The variability of inventory growth declines after adopting LIFO. Because LIFO tends to match more recent inventory costs with sales than does FIFO or weighted average (these methods use costs that are six to fifteen months old relative to current replacement costs), LIFO tends to result in less variability in the gross margin percentage over the business cycle. Firms with variable rates of inventory growth (perhaps because of cyclicality in their industry) can more easily accomplish an income smoothing reporting objective than if they use FIFO or average cost.

3. Tax savings opportunities: LIFO adopters tend not to have tax loss carryforwards available to offset future taxable income. These firms instead adopt LIFO to

---

[4] Thomas L. Stober, "The Incremental Information Content of Financial Statement Disclosures: The Case of LIFO Inventory Liquidations," *Journal of Accounting Research* (Supplement, 1986), pp. 138–160. Sen Yo Tse, "LIFO Liquidations," *Journal of Accounting Research* (Spring 1990), pp. 229–238.

[5] For a review of these studies, see Frederick W. Lindahl, "Dynamic Analysis of Inventory Accounting Choice," *Journal of Accounting Research* (Autumn 1989), pp. 201–226; and Nicholas Dopuch and Morton Pincus, "Evidence on the Choice of Inventory Accounting Methods: LIFO versus FIFO," *Journal of Accounting Research* (Spring 1988), pp. 28–59.

provide future tax savings. LIFO adopters also realize larger tax savings in the year of adoption than in the surrounding years, suggesting that the decision is in part motivated by tax rather than financial reporting considerations.

4. Industry membership: Firms in certain industries are more likely to adopt LIFO than firms in other industries. Since firms in a particular industry face similar factor price changes and variability in their inventory growth rates, we would expect similar choices of cost-flow assumptions.

5. Asset size: Larger firms are more likely to adopt LIFO than smaller firms. LIFO increases record-keeping costs, relative to FIFO, both in the year of adoption and in subsequent years. Larger firms realize larger amounts of tax savings than smaller firms to absorb the adoption and ongoing record-keeping costs of LIFO.

One hypothesis examined in this research is the relation between LIFO adoption and managerial compensation. Because LIFO usually results in lower earnings, we would expect that managerial compensation of LIFO adopters would either be less than compensation of non-LIFO adopters or else include a lower component of compensation based on earnings. Studies have found no difference in managerial compensation of LIFO and non-LIFO adopters, although adopters had a smaller earnings component to their compensation.

Weighted Average

The weighted average cost-flow assumption falls between the other two in its effects on the balance sheet and the income statement. It is, however, much more like FIFO than like LIFO in its effects on the balance sheet. When inventory turns over rapidly, purchases during the current period receive a heavy weight in the weighted average unit cost. The weighted average assumption therefore reflects current prices almost as much as FIFO.

Conversion from LIFO to FIFO

No cost-flow assumption based on historical cost can simultaneously report current cost data in both the income statement and the balance sheet. If a firm reports current costs in the income statement under LIFO, its balance sheet amount for ending inventory contains some very old costs. The out-of-date LIFO inventory valuation provides potentially misleading information to users of financial statements. Consequently, the Securities and Exchange Commission requires firms using LIFO to disclose in notes to the financial statements the amounts by which LIFO inventories are less than if the firm had reported inventories at FIFO or current cost. Analysts sometimes refer to the difference in ending inventory valuation between LIFO and FIFO or current cost as the LIFO reserve. From this disclosure, it is possible to restate a LIFO firm's income to a FIFO basis. In this way, the analyst can place firms using LIFO on a basis more comparable to firms using FIFO.

Refer to the financial statements of Coke and Pepsi in Appendix A and Appendix B, respectively. Note 1 to Coke's financial statements indicates that it uses a combination of FIFO, LIFO, and average cost-flow assumptions for inventories

Exhibit 3.3

Restatement of Inventories and Cost of Goods Sold for Differences in Cost-Flow Assumptions (amounts in thousands)

Coke—Restatement to a Combination of FIFO and Average Cost

	FIFO/LIFO/ Average Cost	Excess of Current Cost over LIFO Cost	FIFO/Average Cost
Beginning Inventory	$ 789,077[a]	$ 34,000[e]	$ 823,077
Purchases	4,402,086[d]		4,402,086
Available	$5,191,163[c]		$5,225,163
Less Ending Inventory	(982,313)[a]	(42,000)[e]	(1,024,313)
Cost of Goods Sold	$4,208,850[b]	$ (8,000)	$4,200,850

[a]As reported in the balance sheet.
[b]As reported in the income statement.
[c]$5,191,163 = $4,208,850 + $982,313.
[d]$4,402,086 = $5,191,163 – $789,077.
[e]As reported in Note 1 to Coke's financial statements.

Pepsi—Restatement to a Combination of FIFO and Average Cost

	FIFO/LIFO/ Average Cost	Excess of Current Cost over LIFO Cost	FIFO/Average Cost
Beginning Inventory	$ 546.1[a]	$ 15.5	$ 561.6
Purchases	8,649.6[d]		8,649.6
Available	$9,195.7[c]		$9,211.2
Less Ending Inventory	(585.8)[a]	(14.9)	(600.7)
Cost of Goods Sold	$8,609.9[b]	$ .6	$8,610.5

[a]As reported in the balance sheet.
[b]As reported in the income statement.
[c]$9,195.7 = $8,609.9 + $585.8.
[d]$8,649.6 = $9,195.7 – $546.1.
[e]As reported in Pepsi's Notes on inventories.

and cost of goods sold. This note also indicates that the current cost of inventories exceeds their LIFO amounts by $34 million at the end of Year 7 and $42 million at the end of Year 8. The top panel of Exhibit 3.3 shows the conversion of Coke's inventories and cost of goods sold from a combination of three cost-flow assumptions to a combination of FIFO and average costs. Because reporting standards do not require the disclosure of the excess of current cost over average cost of inventories, it is not possible to restate inventories and cost of goods sold fully to a FIFO basis. As we would expect during a period of increasing prices, cost of goods sold on a FIFO/average cost basis is lower than when a firm uses LIFO for a portion of its inventories. Coke's gross margin percentage (sales minus cost of goods sold divided by sales) on a combination of FIFO, LIFO, and average costs is 58.9 percent [= ($10,236,350 – $4,208,850)/$10,236,350] and on a combination of FIFO and average cost is 59.0 percent [= ($10,236,350 – $4,200,850)/$10,236,350]. Thus, Coke's use of LIFO for a portion of its inventories had virtually no effect on measures of its operating profitability.

Pepsi indicates in Note 5 on inventories that it also uses a combination of FIFO, LIFO, and average costs. The lower panel of Exhibit 3.3 shows the conversion of Pepsi's inventories and cost of goods sold to a combination of FIFO and average costs. The excess of current cost over LIFO cost was less at the end of Year 8 than at the beginning, suggesting either that prices decreased during Year 8 for the inventories valued at LIFO cost or that Pepsi dipped into its LIFO layers during the year. As with Coke, the restatement had virtually no effect on cost of goods sold and gross margin.

The conversion procedure illustrated in Exhibit 3.3 is especially useful when comparing U.S. firms and non-U.S. firms. Most industrialized countries do not permit the use of LIFO for financial reporting. One important exception is Japan, but even in Japan most firms use specific identification or average costs rather than LIFO. Thus, the analyst should restate inventories and cost of goods sold for U.S. firms using LIFO to make them more comparable to cost-flow assumptions used outside of the United States.

Stock Price Reaction to Changes in Inventory Cost-Flow Assumption

The required conformity of tax and financial reporting for firms choosing a LIFO cost-flow assumption provides fertile ground for researchers studying the efficiency of capital markets. LIFO saves taxes and therefore cash flows. A switch to LIFO should result in a positive stock price reaction if capital markets react intelligently to information about the switch. The switch also results in lower reported earnings to shareholders. A negative stock price reaction suggests an inefficient stock market that fails to examine the underlying economic effects of accounting principles decisions.

Numerous research studies[6] have examined this question, some observing positive price reactions and others observing negative price reactions at the time of the switch. Refinements to the research methodology to provide for different earnings expectation models, tax positions, and other factors have not yet resulted in a definitive answer to the question about the intelligence of the market's reaction. Recent research studies have examined the characteristics of firms that remain on FIFO versus firms that switch to LIFO (see discussion above) in an attempt to sort out these conflicting results.

Accounting for Fixed Assets

Virtually all firms report some amount of property, plant, and equipment on their balance sheets. The higher the degree of capital intensity of a firm, the higher will be the proportion of total assets represented by property, plant, and equipment.

---

[6] See Dopuch and Pincus, "Choice of Inventory Accounting Methods," for a summary of this research.

Among the questions analysts should raise about property, plant, and equipment are the following:

1. At what amount does the balance sheet report gross property, plant, and equipment?

2. Over what useful lives does the firm depreciate its plant and equipment?

3. What depreciation method does the firm use to write off the cost of property, plant, and equipment?

The sections below consider each of these questions.

Asset Valuation

Fixed assets by their nature have useful lives that extend over several years. Consequently, the extent to which the amounts reported on the balance sheet for fixed assets reflect current replacement costs versus historical costs becomes a concern both in judging the profitability of operations and in valuing a company.

Generally accepted accounting principles in the United States and virtually all other countries require the valuation of fixed assets at historical costs. Exceptions include Great Britain and the Netherlands, where GAAP in those countries permit periodic revaluations to current replacement cost. Accounting's use of historical cost valuations rests on the notion that such amounts are more objectively measurable than current market values of fixed assets. Difficulties encountered in determining current market values include (1) the absence of active markets for many used fixed assets, particularly those specific to a particular firm's needs, (2) the need to identify comparable assets currently available in the market to value assets in place, and (3) the need to make assumptions about the effect of technological and other improvements in using the prices of new assets currently available on the market in the valuation process.

The disclosures of property, plant, and equipment on the balance sheet or in the notes permit the analyst to estimate the relative age of depreciable assets and get some sense of the extent to which historical costs reflect outdated valuations. Appendix A and Appendix B, respectively, disclose the following information for Coke and Pepsi at the end of Year 8:

	Coke	Pepsi
Depreciable Assets (excluding land)	$3,638.7	$8,192.3
Accumulated Depreciation	(1,400.2)	(3,266.8)
Net Depreciable Assets	$2,238.5	$4,925.5
Depreciation Expense	$ 236.0	$ 686.0

Both companies use the straight-line depreciation method. At the end of Year 8, Coke's depreciable assets were 5.9 years old on average (= $1,400.2/$236.0) and Pepsi's were 4.8 years old on average (= $3,266.8/$686.0). Pepsi's somewhat newer assets reflect its heavy acquisition activity in recent years. Given relatively low inflation rates in the United States in recent years, the historical costs' values shown on Coke's and Pepsi's balance sheets are probably not significantly out of date.

A different picture emerges in the steel industry. At the end of a recent year, Bethlehem Steel's depreciable assets were 16.3 years old and Inland Steel's depreciable assets were 20.1 years old. These amounts represent average ages of such assets. Thus, the historical cost amounts likely differ significantly from their current market value. Ascertaining the current market value of such assets is particularly difficult because new steel-making facilities currently available on the market are far superior technologically.

A second issue related to the amount shown for the gross amount of fixed assets is the treatment of expenditures to add to or improve existing plant and equipment. GAAP stipulates that firms should capitalize (that is, add to the asset's cost) expenditures which increase the service potential (either in quantity or quality) of an asset beyond that originally anticipated. Firms should expense immediately those expenditures that merely maintain the originally expected service potential. A firm's capitalization versus expense policy with respect to such expenditures affects its reported earnings and provides management with some flexibility to manage earnings. Unfortunately, firms do not provide sufficient information to permit the analyst to assess the quality of earnings with respect to such expenditures. Examples of typical disclosures include the following:

Bristol-Myers Squibb: Expenditures for additions, renewals, and betterments are capitalized at cost.

Georgia-Pacific: Replacements of major units of property are capitalized and the related properties are retired. Replacements of minor units of property and repair and maintenance costs are charged to expense as incurred.

American Airlines: Maintenance and repair costs for owned and leased equipment and property are charged to operating costs as incurred.

Depreciable Life

Depreciation is a process of allocating the historical cost of depreciable assets to the periods of their use in a reasonably systematic manner. One factor in this depreciation process is the expected useful life. Both physical wear and tear and technological obsolescence affect this life. Firms make estimates of this expected total life, a process that again offers management an opportunity to manage reported earnings.

The disclosures firms make about depreciable lives are usually not very helpful to the analyst in assessing a firm's aggressiveness in lengthening depreciable lives to increase earnings. Consider the following typical disclosures:

American Airlines: The depreciable lives used for the principal asset classifications are as follows:

Jet aircraft: 6–20 years

Commuter aircraft: 5–15 years

Major parts and assemblies: life of equipment

Buildings and improvements: 10–30 years

Other equipment: 3–15 years

Delta Airlines: Flight equipment is depreciated over a 15-year period from dates placed in service. Ground property and equipment are depreciated over their estimated service lives, which range from 3 to 30 years.

United Airlines: Estimated useful lives range from 5 to 15 years for flight equipment and 3 to 32 years for other property and equipment.

Because most firms in the United States use the straight-line depreciation method, the analyst can measure the average total life of depreciable assets by dividing average depreciable assets (gross) by depreciation expense for the year. The calculations for Coke and Pepsi are as follows:

	Coke	Pepsi
Depreciable Assets (Gross)		
December 31, Year 7	$3,148.2	$7,116.4
December 31, Year 8	3,638.7	8,192.3
Average Depreciable Assets (Gross) for Year 8	$3,393.5	$7,654.4
Depreciation Expense, Year 8	$ 236.0	$ 686.0
Average Total Depreciable Life	14.4 years	11.2 years

This difference is somewhat surprising given the following components of depreciable assets:

	Coke		Pepsi	
Average Buildings and Improvements	$1,005.1	29.6%	$3,248.3	42.4%
Average Equipment	2,388.4	70.4	4,406.1	57.6
Average Depreciable Assets	$3,393.5	100.0%	$7,654.4	100.0%

We would expect Coke, with its higher proportion of equipment, to have a smaller average total life. It is difficult to conclude, however, whether Coke uses unusually long lives or Pepsi uses unusually short lives.

Depreciation Method

The third factor in the calculation of depreciation (in addition to the historical cost and expected useful life of depreciable assets) is the depreciation method. GAAP permits firms to write off assets evenly over their useful lives (straight-line method) or to write off larger amounts during the early years and smaller amounts in later years (accelerated depreciation methods). Note that total depreciation over an asset's life cannot exceed historical costs (unless firms revalue such assets to current market values). Thus, straight-line and accelerated depreciation methods differ only in the timing of depreciation expense, not in its total amount over time.

Virtually all firms in the United States use the straight-line method for financial reporting. They use accelerated depreciation methods for tax reporting based on depreciable lives specified in the income tax law. These lives are usually shorter than the depreciable lives firms use for financial reporting.

GAAP in most countries outside of the United States also permit both accelerated and straight-line depreciation methods. In countries where tax laws heavily influence financial reporting (Germany, France, Japan), most firms use accelerated depreciation methods for both financial and tax reporting. Thus, comparisons of U.S. firms with those of some other countries require the analyst to assess the effects of different depreciation methods. The analyst must either restate reported U.S. amounts to an accelerated basis or convert reported amounts for other countries to a straight-line basis.

One technique to place U.S. firms on an accelerated basis uses information in the deferred tax notes on depreciation timing differences. Pepsi, for example, reports in its note on income taxes that it provided $34.5 million of deferred tax expense during Year 8 for depreciation timing differences. These timing differences relate to differences in both depreciable lives and depreciation methods. The analyst can approximate the difference between financial and tax depreciation by dividing $34.5 million by the statutory tax rate of 34 percent. The result is a $101.5 million ($34.5/.34) difference. Financial reporting depreciation was $686 million; accelerated tax depreciation is therefore $787.5 million (= $686 + $101.5). Pepsi's net income using accelerated depreciation for Year 8 is as follows:

Reported Net Income from Continuing Operations, Year 8	$1,090.6
Plus Depreciation Expense on Straight-Line Basis (net of taxes); (1 − .34)($686.0)	452.8
Less Depreciation Expense on Accelerated Basis (net of taxes); (1 − .34)($787.5)	(519.8)
Restated Net Income from Continuing Operations, Year 8	$1,023.6

Restating the balance sheet to an accelerated depreciation basis requires information on the cumulative amount of deferred taxes provided for depreciation timing differences. Firms in the United States do not normally disclose the portions of the Deferred Tax Liability on the balance sheet related to depreciation and other individual timing differences. Thus, extending the procedure illustrated above from the income statement to the balance sheet is difficult.

A research study comparing U.S. and Japanese financial statements developed a methodology for converting both income statement and balance sheet amounts from straight-line to double-declining balance depreciation (an accelerated method).[7] The two items of information needed to make the conversion are (1) the average total life of depreciable assets, and (2) the growth rate of depreciable assets. We illustrated above the procedure for measuring the average total life: divide gross depreciable assets by straight-line depreciation expense for the year. This amounts to 11.2 years for Pepsi. The analyst can estimate the growth rate of depreciable assets by measuring the growth rate in depreciation expense over some

---

[7] Paul R. Brown, Virginia E. Soybel, and Clyde P. Stickney, "Achieving Comparability between U.S. and Japanese Financial Statement Data," *Japan and the World Economy*, 1993.

recent period. Pepsi's depreciation expenses for the last five years are as follows (in millions):

Year 4	$487	Year 7	$610
Year 5	$526	Year 8	$686
Year 6	$566		

Depreciation expense increased at a compound annual rate of 8.9 percent during this period.

Exhibit 3.4 shows the relation between straight-line and double-declining balance depreciation amounts, with the top panel showing amounts for depreciation expense and the lower panel showing amounts for depreciable assets on the balance sheet. The amounts shown in Exhibit 3.4 result from a simulation in which assets with various total depreciable lives grow at specified rates until the simulation attains an equilibrium position. This equilibrium occurs after one complete replacement cycle.

The top panel of Exhibit 3.4 indicates that for an 11.2-year average life and 8.9 percent growth rate in depreciable assets, depreciation expense on a double-declining balance depreciation method is approximately 10 percent of gross plant and equipment. We noted earlier that Pepsi's average gross depreciable assets for Year 8 were $7,654.4 million. This suggests double-declining balance depreciation of $765.4 million. This amount compares to $787.5 million depreciation computed using deferred taxes provided for depreciation timing differences. The tax depreciation expense amount should exceed that calculated using Exhibit 3.4 because the tax amount uses a shorter depreciable life.

The lower panel of Exhibit 3.4 indicates that accumulated depreciation should represent approximately 53.8 percent of gross plant and equipment on a declining-balance depreciation method. Pepsi's reported depreciable assets using straight-line depreciation and its restated depreciable assets to reflect declining-balance depreciation are the following:

	As Reported (Straight-Line)	As Restated (Double-Declining Balance)
Buildings and Improvements	$3,173.7	$3,173.7
Capital Leases	265.4	265.4
Machinery and Equipment	4,753.2	4,753.2
Total	$8,192.3	$8,192.3
Accumulated Depreciation	(3,266.8)	(4,407.5)
Depreciable Assets—Net	$4,925.5	$3,784.8

Accounting for Intangible Assets

Intangible assets include patents, copyrights, trademarks, trade names, franchise rights, customer lists, goodwill, and similar items. Two characteristics distinguish intangible assets: their intangibility (that is, lack of physical characteristics) and their multiple-period useful life. GAAP in the United States accounts for intangible assets as follows:

Exhibit 3.4
Factors for Conversion from Straight-Line to Double-Declining Balance Depreciation Given Selected Average Lives and Growth Rates

Double-Declining Balance Depreciation Expense/Gross Plant and Equipment

Average Life (years)	Growth Rate					
	5%	6%	7%	8%	9%	10%
5	0.22043	0.22162	0.22280	0.22398	0.22515	0.22632
6	0.17325	0.17454	0.17584	0.17712	0.17840	0.17967
7	0.15590	0.15701	0.15812	0.15923	0.16033	0.16143
8	0.13108	0.13228	0.13348	0.13468	0.13587	0.13706
9	0.12102	0.12210	0.12318	0.12425	0.12532	0.12638
10	0.10579	0.10695	0.10810	0.10925	0.11039	0.11153
11	0.09921	0.10027	0.10133	0.10238	0.10343	0.10447
12	0.08895	0.09008	0.09120	0.09231	0.09342	0.09453
13	0.08439	0.08534	0.08638	0.08743	0.08846	0.08949
14	0.07693	0.07803	0.07913	0.08023	0.08131	0.08239
15	0.07345	0.07449	0.07552	0.07655	0.07758	0.07859

Double-Declining Balance Accumulated Depreciation/Gross Plant and Equipment

Average Life (years)	Growth Rate					
	5%	6%	7%	8%	9%	10%
5	0.55484	0.55557	0.55626	0.55690	0.55749	0.55804
6	0.55078	0.55088	0.55092	0.55091	0.55084	0.55073
7	0.56036	0.55958	0.55874	0.55785	0.55689	0.55589
8	0.55343	0.55202	0.55054	0.54899	0.54739	0.54573
9	0.55957	0.55723	0.55481	0.55233	0.54980	0.54721
10	0.55209	0.54912	0.54608	0.54298	0.53981	0.53659
11	0.55606	0.55213	0.54814	0.54408	0.53998	0.53583
12	0.54866	0.54412	0.53952	0.53485	0.53014	0.52539
13	0.55114	0.54564	0.54008	0.53446	0.52882	0.52315
14	0.54400	0.53790	0.53174	0.52555	0.51932	0.51308
15	0.54541	0.53835	0.53124	0.52411	0.51697	0.50985

1. Firms expense in the period incurred the cost of developing intangibles. The rationale for immediate expensing of such costs is the difficulty in ascertaining whether a particular expenditure results in a future benefit (that is, an asset) or not (an expense). Accountants provide more conservative measures of earnings by expensing such costs immediately. Thus, Coke and Pepsi spend millions of dollars each year promoting their names and products. The names "Coke" and "Pepsi" represent one of the most valuable "assets" of these firms. Yet, GAAP does not permit these firms to recognize an asset for the expenditures made to develop and maintain these trade names.

2. Firms recognize as an asset expenditures made to acquire intangible assets from others. In this case the firm makes an expenditure on a specifically identifiable intangible asset. The existence of an external market transaction provides evidence of the value of the intangible asset. The acquiring firm must consider the future benefits of the intangible to at least equal the price paid. Financial statement preparers and users have criticized the differing treatment of internally developed versus externally purchased intangibles. They point out that internally developed intangibles also result from external market exchanges (payments to advertising agencies for promotion services, payments to employees for research and development services). Supporters of GAAP point out that the market exchange in the case of externally acquired intangibles validates the existence of a "completed asset," whereas the market exchange in the case of internally developed intangibles validates only that the firm has made an expenditure. It does not validate the existence and value of future benefits.

3. Firms must amortize intangible assets over their expected useful lives. If the firm cannot estimate the useful life, then GAAP permits a maximum amortization period of 40 years. Common practice uses straight-line amortization.

The most common setting in which intangibles arise is in corporate acquisitions. As Chapter 5 discusses more fully, acquiring firms must allocate the purchase price to the assets acquired and liabilities assumed when purchasing another entity. Acquiring firms usually allocate the purchase price to identifiable, tangible assets (inventories, land, equipment) first. They then allocate any excess purchase price to identifiable, intangible assets such as patents, customer lists, or trade names, with the remainder allocated to goodwill. Goodwill is a residual and effectively represents all intangibles that are not specifically identifiable.

Firms seldom disclose much information about their intangible assets. For instance, Coke shows Goodwill and Other Intangible Assets on its balance sheet. Coke's Note 1 on accounting policies states only that it values these intangibles at cost and amortizes them on a straight-line basis over estimated periods of benefit (not exceeding 40 years). Coke gives no information about the type of intangibles included. Pepsi lists a similar account on its balance sheet but its note on accounting policies indicates that the largest portion of this asset represents "the value of Pepsi-Cola franchise rights reacquired in the acquisition of franchised domestic soft drink bottling operations." Pepsi's remaining disclosures are similar to Coke's.

The income tax law in the United States follows GAAP as described above with one important exception: firms cannot amortize goodwill and other intangibles that have an indefinite useful life.

GAAP in countries outside of the United States likewise require amortization of goodwill, but the amortization period is usually less than 40 years. Some of these countries have a shorter amortization period because of the close conformity of tax and financial reporting (for example, France, Germany, Japan).

Summary

The centralizing concept for the various GAAP discussed in this chapter (income recognition, inventory cost-flow assumption, depreciable asset, and intangible asset accounting) is the link between income recognition and asset valuation. The recognition of revenue usually coincides with an increase in assets (usually cash or a receivable). The recognition of expense usually coincides with a decrease in assets (cash, inventories, depreciable, or intangible assets) or an increase in liabilities (which will require a decrease in assets in a later period). Thus, the income statement and balance sheet closely interrelate.

Problems

3.1 *Income Recognition for Various Types of Businesses.* Discuss when each of the following types of businesses is likely to recognize revenues and expenses.

    a. A savings and loan association lending money for home mortgages.

    b. A seller of trading stamps to food stores; food store customers can redeem the stamps for various household products.

    c. A travel agency that books hotels, transportation, and similar services for customers and earns a commission from the providers of these services.

    d. A major league baseball team that sells season tickets before the season begins and signs multiyear contracts with players. These contracts typically defer the payment of a significant portion of the compensation provided by the contract until the player retires.

    e. A firm that manufactures and sells limited edition figurines. The firm agrees to repurchase the figurines at any time during the 20 years after sale if the market value of the figurine does not increase by at least 10 percent annually.

    f. A producer of fine whiskey that ages 12 years before sale.

    g. A timber-growing firm that contracts to sell all timber in a particular tract when it reaches 20 years of age. Each year it harvests another tract. The price per board foot of timber equals the market price when the customer signs the purchase contract plus 10 percent for each year until harvest.

    h. An airline that provides transportation services to customers. Each flight grants frequent-flier miles to customers. Customers earn a free flight when they accumulate sufficient frequent-flier miles.

3.2 *Income Recognition on Long-Term Contracts.* Curtiss Construction Company, Inc., entered into a firm fixed-price contract with Axelrod Associates on July 1, Year 1, to construct a four-story office building. Curtiss estimated that it would take between two and three years to complete the project. The total contract price for construction of the building is $4,000,000. Curtiss appropriately accounts for this contract under the percentage-of-completion method in its financial statements. It deemed the building substantially completed on December 31, Year 3. It made delivery to the customer on January 2, Year 4. Accumulated contract costs incurred, estimated costs to complete the contract, and accumulated billings to Axelrod under the contract were as follows:

	At December 31, Year 1	At December 31, Year 2	At December 31, Year 3
Cumulative Contract Costs Incurred	$ 350,000	$2,500,000	$4,250,000
Estimated Costs to Complete the Contract	$3,150,000	$1,700,000	—
Cumulative Billings to Axelrod	$ 720,000	$2,160,000	$3,600,000

a. Prepare schedules to compute the sales revenue and cost of goods sold that Curtiss would report as a result of this contract for the years ended December 31, Year 1, Year 2, and Year 3. Ignore income taxes.

b. Prepare schedules to compute the amount Curtiss would show on its balance sheet as "cost plus income from uncompleted contract in excess of related billings" or "billings on uncompleted contract in excess of related costs and income" at December 31, Year 1, Year 2, and Year 3. Ignore income taxes.

3.3 *Income Recognition on Long-Term Contracts.* Douglas Corporation provides long-term contract services for both government and commercial customers. It uses the percentage-of-completion revenue recognition method on government contracts and the completed-contract method on commercial contracts. Information relating to Year 4 and Year 5, its first two years of operations, appears below.

Contract	Contract Price	Costs Incurred in Year 4	Estimated Cost to Complete as of Dec. 31, Year 4	Costs Incurred in Year 5	Estimated Cost to Complete as of Dec. 31, Year 5
A	$100	$ 25	$ 50	$ 30	$ 25
B	$200	$120	$ 60	$ 40	$ 50
C	$300	$140	$185	$ 85	$110
D	$400	$225	$125	$110	-0-

Contracts A and B are government contracts and Contracts C and D are commercial contracts.

a. Compute the amount of sales revenue and cost of goods sold recognized during Year 4 and Year 5 for each of these contracts.

b. Compute the amount shown in the Contracts in Process account on the balance sheet at the end of Year 4 and Year 5 for each of these contracts.

3.4 *Income Recognition at Time of Sale and Time of Cash Collection.* Keyes Manufacturing Corporation sold a tract of land to Lilley Company on January 1, Year 5. Keyes carried the land on its books at $21,617. Lilley gave Keyes a $45,000 noninterest-bearing note payable in three equal installments on December 31, Year 5,

Year 6, and Year 7. Keyes determines that 12 percent is a reasonable lending rate to Lilley as of this date. The present value of the $45,000 note on January 1, Year 5, discounted at 12 percent is $36,027. Keyes will recognize any gain or loss from the sale at the time of sale for financial reporting and as it collects cash using the installment method for tax reporting. Keyes will recognize interest revenue as it accrues over the term of the note for both financial and tax reporting. The income tax rate is 34 percent.

a. Complete the amortization schedule below for this note.

Year	Balance, January 1	Interest at 12% on January 1 Balance	Cash Received On December 31	Balance, December 31
5	$36,027			
6				
7				-0-

b. Compute the amount of income before taxes and the amount of taxable income that Keyes will recognize for each of Years 5, 6, and 7.

Income before Taxes	Year 5	Year 6	Year 7
Gain on Sale of Land	_____	_____	_____
Interest Revenue.................	_____	_____	_____
Total	_____	_____	_____

Taxable Income			
Gain on Sale of Land	_____	_____	_____
Interest Revenue.................	_____	_____	_____
Total	_____	_____	_____

c. Compute the amount of income tax expense, disaggregated into the portions currently payable and deferred, relating to the sale of the land for each of Year 5, Year 6, and Year 7.

Income Tax Expense:	Year 5	Year 6	Year 7
Current	_____	_____	_____
Deferred	_____	_____	_____
Total	_____	_____	_____

3.5 *Income Recognition When Cash Receipts Vary in Uncertainty.* Standard Manufacturing Company sold an electrical generator costing $9,000,000 to Chicago General Hospital for $10,000,000 on January 1, Year 4. Chicago General paid $2,000,000 down and signed an $8,000,000 promissory note for the balance of the purchase price. The note is payable at the rate of $2,000,000 per year on December 31 of each of the next four years, with the first payment due on December 31, Year 4. In addition, Chicago General must make interest payments at the rate of 8 percent per year on the unpaid balance on December 31 of each year.

a. Complete the following amortization schedule for this note:

Year	Balance, January 1	Interest at 8% on January 1 Balance	Cash Received On December 31	Balance, December 31
4	$8,000,000			
5				
6				
7				-0-

b. Assume for this part that the cash collectibility of the note is highly certain. Compute the amount of revenue, expense, and gross margin recognized from the sale of the generator and related promissory note on (1) January 1, Year 4, (2) December 31, Year 4, and (3) December 31, Year 5.

c. Assume for this part that the hospital is experiencing severe financial difficulty and that the collectibility of the note is therefore highly uncertain. Because of this uncertainty, Standard Manufacturing intends to recognize income from the sale of the generator using the installment method. Compute the amount of revenue, expense, and gross margin recognized from sale of the generator and related promissory note on (1) January 1, Year 4, (2) December 31, Year 4, and (3) December 31, Year 5.

d. Compute the total amount of income that Standard Manufacturing Company will recognize over the four-year period under the assumption in part *(b)* and under the assumption in part *(c)*.

3.6 *Effects of Cost-Flow Assumption on Reported Gross Margin.* Selected information regarding the inventories and cost of goods sold of Westwood Electrical Supply for Year 5 and Year 6 appears below:

Income Statement	Year 6	Year 5
Sales	$17,287	$14,296
Cost of Goods Sold	13,134	11,080
Gross Margin	$ 4,153	$ 3,216

	December 31		
Balance Sheet	Year 6	Year 5	Year 4
Inventories	$1,186	$1,473	$1,258

Notes to the Financial Statements

Westwood Electrical Supply uses a last-in, first-out (LIFO) cost-flow assumption for inventories and cost of goods sold. Inventories on a first-in, first-out (FIFO) cost-flow assumption would have exceeded the amounts reported on a LIFO basis by $376 at the end of Year 6, $497 at the end of Year 5, and $338 at the end of Year 4.

a. Compute the amount of cost of goods sold and gross margin on a FIFO basis for Year 5 and Year 6.

b. Compute the gross margin percentage (that is, gross margin as a percent of sales) for Year 5 and Year 6 on a LIFO and on a FIFO basis.

c. During periods of rising prices, LIFO generally results in a higher cost of goods sold and lower gross margin than FIFO. Why does this generalization not describe accurately the experience of Westwood Electrical Supply?

3.7 *Effects of Cost-Flow Assumptions on Reported Income.* Exhibit 3.5 shows data for the General Electric (GE) Company's inventories for a period of years (1) under the LIFO assumption actually used and (2) under FIFO if GE had used it for inventories.

a. Compute the pretax income for Years 2 through 6, assuming that GE had used a FIFO cost-flow assumption.
b. Calculate the percentage change in pretax income for each of the Years 3 through 6 under both LIFO and FIFO (that is, the increase in pretax income in Year 3 relative to Year 2, the increase in pretax income in Year 4 relative to Year 3, and so on).
c. Calculate the percentage change in pretax income between Year 2 and Year 6 (that is, the five-year period taken as a whole) under both LIFO and FIFO.
d. Did the quantity of items in inventory increase or decrease during each of the Years 3 through 6? How can you tell?
e. Did the acquisition cost of items in inventory increase or decrease during each of the Years 3 through 6? How can you tell?

Exhibit 3.5
General Electric Company (amounts in millions)

End of Year	LIFO Ending Inventory	FIFO Ending Inventory
1	$1,611.7	$1,884.5
2	1,759.0	2,063.1
3	1,986.2	2,415.9
4	2,257.0	3,040.7
5	2,202.9	3,166.6
6	2,354.4	3,515.2

For the Year	Pretax Operating Income Using LIFO
2	$ 897.2
3	1,011.6
4	1,000.7
5	1,174.0
6	1,627.5

End of Year	Current Assets	Current Liabilities
2	$3,979.3	$2,869.7
3	4,485.4	3,492.4
4	5,222.6	3,879.5
5	5,750.4	4,163.0
6	6,685.0	4,604.9

f. Assume for this part that the inventory value under LIFO of $1,611.7 at the end of Year 1 is the initial LIFO layer. We might view this layer as the bottom layer on a cake. Construct a figure showing the addition or subtraction of LIFO layers for each of the Years 2 through 6.

g. Exhibit 3.5 shows the current assets and current liabilities of the General Electric Company at the end of Years 2 through 6 using a LIFO cost-flow assumption. Compute GE's current ratio (current assets/current liabilities) for each year using the data given.

h. Recompute GE's current ratio for each year using a FIFO cost-flow assumption. Assume an income tax rate of 34 percent and that GE pays all taxes in cash at the end of each year.

3.8 *Comparing LIFO and FIFO with Declines in Inventory Quantities.* The LIFO Company and the FIFO Company both manufacture paper and cardboard products. Prices of timber, paper pulp, and finished paper products have generally increased by about 5 percent per year through the *start of this year*. Inventory data for the beginning and end of the year appear below:

	Inventory Amounts	
	January 1	**December 31**
LIFO Company Inventory (last-in, first out; historical cost)	$19,695,000	$15,870,000
FIFO Company Inventory (first-in, first out; lower of cost or market)	$46,284,000	$38,250,000

Income statements for the two companies for the year ending December 31 appear below:

	LIFO Company	**FIFO Company**
Sales	$57,000,000	$129,000,000
Expenses		
Cost of Goods Sold	$44,580,000	$108,000,000
Depreciation	5,400,000	12,000,000
General Expenses	2,220,000	5,400,000
Income Taxes (40 percent of pretax income)	1,920,000	1,440,000
Total Expenses	$54,120,000	$126,840,000
Net Income	$ 2,880,000	$ 2,160,000

a. Assuming that the prices for timber, paper pulp, and finished paper remained unchanged during the year, how do the two companies' respective inventory choices affect the interpretation of their financial statements for the year?

b. How would the answer to part (*a*) differ if prices at the end of the year were lower than at the beginning of the year?

c. How would the answer to part (*a*) differ if prices at the end of the year were higher than at the beginning of the year?

Exhibit 3.6
Wilson Company
Layers of Year 10 Year-End Inventory

Year Acquired	Purchase Price per Pound	Year 10 Year-End Inventory Pounds	Cost
Year 1	$30	2,000	$60,000
Year 6	46	200	9,200
Year 7	48	400	19,200
Year 10	52	1,400	72,800
		4,000	$161,200

3.9 *LIFO Layers Influence Purchasing Behavior and Provide Opportunity for Income Manipulation.* The Wilson Company sells chemical compounds made from expensium. The company has used a LIFO inventory flow assumption for many years. The inventory of expensium on December 31, Year 10, consisted of 4,000 pounds from Year 1 through Year 10 at prices ranging from $30 to $52 per pound. Exhibit 3.6 shows the layers of Year 10 ending inventory.

Expensium costs $62 per pound during Year 11, but the purchasing agent expects its price to fall back to $52 per pound in Year 12. Sales for Year 11 require 7,000 pounds of expensium. Wilson Company wants to carry a stock of 4,000 pounds of inventory. The purchasing agent suggests that the company should allow the inventory of expensium to decrease from 4,000 to 600 pounds by the end of Year 11 and then replenish it to the desired level of 4,000 pounds early in Year 12.

The controller argues against such a policy. If the firm allows inventories to decrease to 600 pounds, it will report extraordinarily low cost of goods sold (because the firm will consume the older LIFO layers) and extraordinarily high income taxes. He suggests that the firm plan Year 11 purchases to maintain an end-of-year inventory of 4,000 pounds.

Assume that sales for Year 11 do require 7,000 pounds of expensium, that the prices for Year 11 are as forecast, and that the income tax rate for Wilson Company is 34 percent.

    a. Calculate the cost of goods sold and end-of-year LIFO inventory for Year 11 assuming that the firm follows the controller's advice and inventory at the end of Year 11 is 4,000 pounds.

    b. Calculate the cost of goods sold and end-of-year LIFO inventory for Year 11 assuming that the firm follows the purchasing agent's advice and inventory at the end of Year 11 is 600 pounds.

    c. Assuming that the firm follows the controller's, not the purchasing agent's, advice, calculate the tax savings for Year 11 and the extra cash costs for inventory.

d. What should Wilson Company do?

e. Management of Wilson Company wants to know what discretion it has to vary income for Year 11 by planning its purchases of expensium. If the firm follows the controller's policy, aftertax income for Year 11 will be $50,000. What is the range of income after taxes that the firm can achieve by the purposeful management of expensium purchases?

3.10 *Interpreting Financial Statement Data for Depreciable Assets.* Exhibit 3.7 presents selected financial statement data for three chemical companies: Ethyl Corporation, Monsanto, and Olin Corporation.

a. Compute the average total depreciable life of assets in use for each firm during Year 5.

b. Compute the average age to date of depreciable assets in use for each firm at the end of Year 5.

c. Compute the amount of depreciation expense recognized for tax purposes for each firm for Year 5 using the amount of deferred taxes provided for depreciation timing differences.

d. Compute the amount of net income for Year 5 for each firm assuming depreciation expense for financial reporting equals the amount computed in part (c) for tax reporting.

e. Using Exhibit 3.4 in the text, estimate the amount of depreciation expense for Year 5 for each firm on a double-declining balance depreciation method.

Exhibit 3.7

Selected Financial Statement Data on Depreciable Assets for Three Chemical Companies (amounts in millions)

	Ethyl Corporation	Monsanto Corporation	Olin Corporation
Depreciable Assets at Cost			
December 31, Year 4	$1,096	$6,470	$1,944
December 31, Year 5	1,187	7,033	2,051
Accumulated Depreciation			
December 31, Year 4	607	3,764	1,388
December 31, Year 5	657	4,128	1,468
Net Income, Year 5	232	546	84
Depreciation Expense, Year 5	89	504	116
Compound Annual Growth Rate in Depreciation Expense,			
Year 1 to Year 5	12.0%	2.6%	.4%
Deferred Tax Expense for Depreciation Timing Difference, Year 5	6	28	19
Income Tax Rate	34%	34%	34%
Depreciation Method for Financial Reporting	Straight-Line	Straight-Line	Straight-Line
Depreciation Method for Tax Reporting	Accelerated	Accelerated	Accelerated

f. What factors might explain the difference in average total life and average age of depreciable assets for Olin Corporation relative to the other two firms?

g. Given your response to part (*f*), what factors might explain Olin Corporation's relatively larger deferred taxes provided for depreciation timing differences for Year 5?

3.11 *Interpreting Financial Statement Data for Depreciable Assets.* Exhibit 3.8 presents selected financial statement data for May Department Stores (department stores), The Limited (specialty stores), and Wal-Mart (discount stores).

a. Compute the average total depreciable assets in use for each firm during Year 5.

b. Compute the average age to date of depreciable assets in use for each firm at the end of Year 5.

c. Compute the amount of depreciation expense recognized for tax purposes for each firm for Year 5 using the amount of deferred taxes provided for depreciation timing differences.

d. Compute the amount of net income for Year 5 for each firm assuming depreciation expense for financial reporting equals the amount computed in part (*c*) for tax reporting.

e. What factors might explain the difference in average total life of The Limited's depreciable assets relative to those for the other two firms?

f. Refer to your analysis in part (*d*). Why are the net income amounts in part (*c*) only 5 to 10 percent less than the reported net income amounts instead of some higher amount, given the rates of growth in depreciable assets?

Exhibit 3.8
Selected Financial Statement Data on Depreciable Assets for Three Retailers (amounts in millions)

	May Department Stores	The Limited	Wal-Mart
Depreciable Assets at Cost			
December 31, Year 4	$3,736	$1,691	$3,838
December 31, Year 5	4,180	2,048	5,163
Accumulated Depreciation			
December 31, Year 4	1,070	519	972
December 31, Year 5	1,195	653	1,265
Net Income, Year 5	500	398	1,291
Depreciation Expense, Year 5..................	294	184	345
Compound Annual Growth Rate in Depreciation Expense			
Year 1 to Year 5	10.1%	17.4%	29.2%
Deferred Tax Expense for Depreciation Timing Differences, Year 5	11	19	44
Tax Rate	34%	34%	34%
Depreciation Method for Financial Reporting	Straight-Line	Straight-Line	Straight-Line
Depreciation Method for Tax Reporting	Accelerated	Accelerated	Accelerated

Case 3.1:
Arizona Land Development Company

Joan Locker and Bill Dasher organized the Arizona Land Development Company (ALDC) on January 2, Year 1. They contributed land with a market value of $300,000 and cash of $100,000 for all of the common stock of the corporation. The land served as the initial inventory of property sold to customers.

ALDC sells undeveloped land, primarily to individuals approaching retirement. Within a period of nine years from the date of sale, ALDC promises to develop the land so that it is suitable for the construction of residential housing. ALDC makes all sales on an installment basis. Customers pay 10 percent of the selling price at the time of sale and remit the remainder in equal installments over the next nine years.

ALDC estimates that development costs will equal 50 percent of the selling price of the land and that development work will take nine years to complete from the date of sale. Actual development costs have coincided with expectations. The firm incurs 10 percent of the development costs at the time of sale and incurs the remainder evenly over the next nine years.

ALDC remained a privately held firm for its first six years. Exhibits 1 through 3 present the firm's income statement, balance sheet, and statement of cash flows, respectively, for Year 1 to Year 6. ALDC recognizes income from sales of undeveloped land at the time of sale. The amount shown for sales each year in Exhibit 1 represents the gross amount ALDC ultimately expects to collect from customers for land sold in that year. The amount shown for estimated development costs each year is the gross amount ALDC expects ultimately to disburse to develop land sold in that year. The firm treats selling expenses as a period expense. It is subject to a 34 percent income tax rate. ALDC uses the installment method of income recognition for income tax purposes.

ALDC contemplates making its initial public offering of common stock early in Year 7. The firm asks you to assess whether its income recognition method, as reflected in Exhibits 1 to 3, accurately reflects its operating performance and financial position. To assist you, the firm has prepared financial statements following three other income recognition methods as described next.

Income Recognition at Time of Sale but with Discounting of Future Cash Flows to Their Present Value.   Exhibits 4 to 6 present the financial statements following this income recognition method. This method discounts future cash inflows from customers and future cash outflows for development work to their present values. The gross profit recognized at the time of sale equals the present value of cash inflows net of the present value of cash outflows. One might view this gross profit as the current cash-equivalent value of the gross profit that the firm will ultimately realize over the nine-year period. This method reports the increase in the present value of cash inflows as time passes as interest revenue each year and the increase in the present value of cash outflows as interest expense. Thus, this income recognition method results in reporting two types of income: a gross profit from the selling of land and interest from delayed cash flows. The computations of present values underlying the financial statements in Exhibits 4 to 6 rest on the following assumptions:

1. ALDC makes all sales on January 1 of each year. It receives 10 percent of the gross selling price at the time of sale and also pays 10 percent of the gross development costs immediately.

2. The firm receives 10 percent of the gross selling price from customers and pays 10 percent of the gross development costs on December 31 of each year, beginning with the year of sale.

3. The interest rates used in discounting are as follows:

Sales in	Interest Rate
Year 1	12%
Year 2	12%
Year 3	15%
Year 4	15%
Year 5	12%
Year 6	12%

Income Recognition Using the Installment Method—with Discounting of Cash Flows.   Exhibits 7 to 9 present the financial statements following this income recognition method. ALDC uses this income recognition method for tax reporting.

Income Recognition Using the Percentage-of-Completion Method.   Exhibits 10 to 12 present the financial statements following this income recognition method. The presumption underlying this method is that ALDC is primarily a developer of real estate and that its income should reflect its development activity, not its sales activity. The difference between the contract price and the total estimated costs of the land and development work represents the total income from development of the land. The percentage-of-completion method uses actual costs incurred to date as a percentage of estimated total costs to determine the degree of completion each period. Multiplying this percentage times the contract price yields sales revenue each year. Multiplying this percentage times the total expected costs yields cost of goods sold.

REQUIRED

a. For each of the four income recognition methods illustrated in Exhibits 1 through 12, show the supporting calculations for each of the following items for Year 2:
   (1) Sales Revenue for Year 2.
   (2) Cost of Goods Sold for Year 2.

(3) Gross Profit for Year 2.

(4) Notes Receivable on December 31, Year 2 under the first three income recognition methods and the Contracts in Process account on December 31, Year 2 under the fourth income recognition method.

(5) Estimated Development Costs Liability on December 31, Year 2 under the first three income recognition methods and the Progress Billings account on December 31, Year 2 under the fourth income recognition method.

b. Evaluate each of the four income recognition methods described in the case relative to the criteria for revenue and expense recognition. Which method do you think best portrays the operating performance and financial position of ALDC? Discuss your reasoning.

c. Which income recognition method is ALDC likely to prefer in reporting to shareholders?

d. Why did ALDC choose the installment method for tax reporting?

e. With respect to maximizing cumulative reported earnings, the four income recognition methods rank order as follows:

1. Income Recognition at Time of Sale—No Discounting of Cash Flows
2. Income Recognition at Time of Sale—with Discounting of Cash Flows
3. Income Recognition Using the Percentage-of-Completion Method
4. Income Recognition Using the Installment Method—with Discounting of Cash Flows

What is the reason behind this rank ordering?

Exhibit 1

Arizona Land Development Company Income Statements
Income Recognition at Time of Sale—No Discounting of Cash Flows

	Year 1	Year 2	Year 3	Year 4	Year 5	Year 6
Sales	$650,000	$900,000	$1,500,000	$2,500,000	$1,200,000	$400,000
Less:						
Cost of Land Inventory Sold	(65,000)	(90,000)	(150,000)	(250,000)	(120,000)	(40,000)
Estimated Development Costs	(325,000)	(450,000)	(750,000)	(1,250,000)	(600,000)	(200,000)
Gross Profit	$260,000	$360,000	$ 600,000	$1,000,000	$ 480,000	$160,000
Selling Expenses	(65,000)	(90,000)	(150,000)	(250,000)	(120,000)	(40,000)
Net Income before Taxes	$195,000	$270,000	$450,000	$ 750,000	$ 360,000	$120,000
Income Taxes						
Current	—	—	(9,778)	(26,091)	(73,009)	(94,902)
Deferred	(66,300)	(91,800)	(143,222)	(228,909)	(49,391)	54,102
Net Income	$128,700	$178,200	$ 297,000	$ 495,000	$ 237,600	$ 79,200

Exhibit 2
Balance Sheets
Income Recognition at Time of Sale—No Discounting of Cash Flows

	Year 1	Year 2	Year 3	Year 4	Year 5	Year 6
Assets						
Cash	$ 100,000	$ 132,500	$ 100,222	$ 126,631	$ 131,122	$ 273,720
Notes Receivable	520,000	1,175,000	2,220,000	3,915,000	4,320,000	3,965,000
Land Inventory	235,000	145,000	95,000	45,000	125,000	185,000
Total Assets	$ 855,000	$1,452,500	$2,415,222	$4,086,631	$4,576,122	$4,423,720
Liabilities and Shareholders' Equity						
Estimated Development Cost Liability	$ 260,000	$ 587,500	$1,110,000	$1,957,500	$2,160,000	$1,982,500
Deferred Income Taxes	66,300	158,100	301,322	530,231	579,622	525,520
Common Stock	400,000	400,000	400,000	500,000	500,000	500,000
Retained Earnings	128,700	306,900	603,900	1,098,900	1,336,500	1,415,700
Total Liabilities and Shareholders' Equity	$ 855,000	$1,452,500	$2,415,222	$4,086,631	$4,576,122	$4,423,720

f. The difference in cumulative reported earnings between any two income recognition methods equals (1) the difference in Notes Receivable or Contracts in Process (net) minus (2) the difference in the Estimated Development Cost Liability minus (3) the difference in the Deferred Income Taxes Liability. What is the rationale behind this relation?

g. Why is the amount shown on the income statement for "current" income taxes the same in each year for all four income recognition methods but the amount of total income tax expenses (current plus deferred) in each year different across income recognition methods?

h. Given that net income each year differs across the four income recognition methods, why is the amount of cash provided by operations the same? Under what conditions would a firm report different amounts of cash flow from operations for different income recognition methods?

Exhibit 3

Arizona Land Development Company Statements of Cash Flows
Income Recognition at Time of Sale—No Discounting of Cash Flows

	Year 1	Year 2	Year 3	Year 4	Year 5	Year 6
Operations						
Net Income	$128,700	$178,200	$ 297,000	$ 495,000	$237,600	$ 79,200
(Inc.) Decr. in Notes Receivable	(520,000)	(655,000)	(1,045,000)	(1,695,000)	(405,000)	355,000
(Inc.) Decr. in Land Inventory	65,000	90,000	50,000	50,000	(80,000)	(60,000)
Inc. (Decr.) in Estimated Development Cost Liability	260,000	327,500	522,500	847,500	202,500	(177,500)
Inc. (Decr.) in Deferred Income Taxes	66,300	91,800	143,222	228,909	49,391	(54,102)
Cash Flow from Operations	$ 0	$ 32,500	$ (32,278)	$ (73,591)	$ 4,491	$142,598
Financing						
Common Stock Issued	—	—	—	100,000	—	—
Change in Cash	$ 0	$ 32,500	$ (32,278)	$ 26,409	$ 4,491	$ 142,598

Exhibit 4

Arizona Land Development Company Income Statements
Income Recognition at Time of Sale—With Discounting of Cash Flows

	Year 1	Year 2	Year 3	Year 4	Year 5	Year 6
Sales	$411,336[a]	$569,543	$865,737	$1,442,895	$759,390	$253,130
Less						
Cost of Land Inventory Sold	(65,000)	(90,000)	(150,000)	(250,000)	(120,000)	(40,000)
Estimated Development Costs	(205,668)[b]	(284,771)	(432,869)	(721,448)	(379,695)	(126,565)
Gross Profit	$140,668	$194,772	$282,868	$ 471,447	$259,695	$ 86,565
Selling Expenses	(65,000)	(90,000)	(150,000)	(250,000)	(120,000)	(40,000)
Interest Revenue	41,560[c]	96,293	196,609	361,257	411,130	400,899
Interest Expense	(20,780)[d]	(48,147)	(98,304)	(180,628)	(205,566)	(200,449)
Net Income before Taxes	$ 96,448	$152,918	$231,173	$ 402,076	$345,259	$247,015
Income Taxes						
Current	—	—	(9,778)	(26,091)	(73,009)	(94,902)
Deferred	(32,792)	(51,992)	(68,821)	(110,615)	(44,379)	10,917
Net Income	$ 63,656	$100,926	$152,574	$ 265,370	$227,871	$163,030

[a]Represents the present value of $65,000 received on January 1, Year 1, plus the present value of a series of $65,000 cash inflows on December 31, Year 1 to Year 9, discounted at 12 percent.
[b]Represents the present value of $32,500 paid on January 1, Year 1, plus the present value of a series of $32,500 cash outflows on December 31, Year 1 to Year 9, discounted at 12 percent.
[c].12($411,336 – $65,000) = $41,560.
[d].12($205,668 – $32,500) = $20,780.

Exhibit 5

Arizona Land Development Company Balance Sheets
Income Recognition at Time of Sale—With Discounting of Cash Flows

	Year 1	Year 2	Year 3	Year 4	Year 5	Year 6
Assets						
Cash	$100,000	$ 132,500	$ 100,222	$ 126,631	$ 131,122	$ 273,720
Notes Receivable	322,896[a]	743,732	1,351,078	2,350,230	2,725,750	2,624,779
Land Inventory	235,000	145,000	95,000	45,000	125,000	185,000
Total Assets	$657,896	$1,021,232	$1,546,300	$2,521,861	$2,981,872	$3,083,499
Liabilities and Shareholders' Equity						
Estimated Development Cost Liablity	$161,448[b]	$ 371,866	$ 675,539	$1,175,115	$1,362,876	$1,312,390
Deferred Income Taxes ...	32,792	84,784	153,605	264,220	308,599	297,682
Common Stock	400,000	400,000	400,000	500,000	500,000	500,000
Retained Earnings	63,656	164,582	317,156	582,526	810,397	973,427
Total Liabilities and Shareholders' Equity ...	$657,896	$1,021,232	$1,546,300	$2,521,861	$2,981,872	$3,083,499

[a]$411,336 − $65,000 + $41,560 − $65,000 = $322,896 (see Notes a and c to Exhibit 4).
[b]$205,668 − $32,500 + $20,780 − $32,500 = $161,448 (see Notes b and d to Exhibit 4).

Exhibit 6

Arizona Land Development Company Statements of Cash Flows
Income Recognition at Time of Sale—With Discounting of Cash Flows

	Year 1	Year 2	Year 3	Year 4	Year 5	Year 6
Operations						
Net Income	$ 63,656	$100,926	$ 152,574	$ 265,370	$227,871	$163,030
(Inc.) Decr. in Notes Receivable	(322,896)	(420,836)	(607,346)	(999,152)	(375,520)	100,971
(Inc.) Decr. in Land Inventory	65,000	90,000	50,000	50,000	(80,000)	(60,000)
Inc. (Decr.) in Estimated Development Cost Liability	161,448	210,418	303,673	499,576	187,761	(50,486)
Inc. (Decr.) in Deferred Income Taxes	32,792	51,992	68,821	110,615	44,379	(10,917)
Cash Flow from Operations $	0	$ 32,500	$ (32,278)	$ (73,591)	$ 4,491	$142,598
Financing						
Common Stock Issued				100,000		
Change in Cash	$ 0	$ 32,500	$ (32,278)	$ 26,409	$ 4,491	$142,598

Exhibit 7

Arizona Land Development Company Income Statements
Income Recognition Using Installment Method—with Discounting of Cash Flows

	Year 1	Year 2	Year 3	Year 4	Year 5	Year 6
Sales Revenue	$88,440[a]	$148,707	$249,802	$427,243	$377,706	$347,017
Cost of Goods Sold	(58,195)[a]	(97,852)	(164,374)	(281,133)	(248,537)	(228,343)
Gross Profit	$30,245[a]	$50,855	$85,428	$146,110	$129,169	$118,674
Selling Expenses	(65,000)	(90,000)	(150,000)	(250,000)	(120,000)	(40,000)
Interest Revenue	41,560[b]	96,293	196,609	361,257	411,130	400,899
Interest Expense	(20,780)[c]	(48,147)	(98,304)	(180,628)	(205,566)	(200,449)
Net Income before Taxes	$(13,975)	$9,001	$33,733	$76,739	$214,733	$279,124
Income Taxes						
Current	—[d]	—[d]	(9,778)[d]	(26,091)	(73,009)	(94,902)
Deferred	—	—	—	—	—	—
Net Income	$(13,975)	$9,001	$23,955	$50,648	$141,724	$184,22

[a]Exhibit 4 indicates that the total gross profit from land sold in Year 1 is $140,668. The present value of the amounts that ALDC will receive from customers is $411,336 (see Exhibit 4). Thus, for each dollar of the $411,336 collected, the firm recognizes 34.2 cents (= $140,668/$411,336) of gross profit. During Year 1, ALDC collects $130,000 from sales of land made in Year 1 ($65,000 on January 1 and $65,000 on December 31). However, only $23,440 (= $65,000 – $41,560) of the December 31 payment represents payment of a portion of the $411,336 selling price. The remainder ($41,560) represents interest. Thus, the gross profit recognized in Year 1 is $30,245 [.342($65,000 + $23,440)].

[b]See Note c to Exhibit 4.

[c]See Note d to Exhibit 4.

[d]ALDC carries forward the $13,975 loss in Year 1 to offset net income before taxes in future years ($9,001 in Year 2 and $4,974 in Year 3).

Exhibit 8
Arizona Land Development Company Balance Sheets
Income Recognition Using Installment Method—with Discounting of Cash Flows

	Year 1	Year 2	Year 3	Year 4	Year 5	Year 6
Assets						
Cash	$100,000	$132,500	$ 100,222	$ 126,631	$ 131,122	$ 273,720
Notes Receivable	212,473[a]	489,392	899,298	1,573,113	1,818,107	1,749,245
Land Inventory	235,000	145,000	95,000	45,000	125,000	185,000
Total Assets	$547,473	$766,892	$1,094,520	$1,744,744	$2,074,229	$2,207,965
Liabilities and Shareholders' Equity						
Estimated Development Cost Liability	$161,448[b]	$371,866	$ 675,539	$1,175,115	$1,362,876	$1,312,390
Deferred Income Taxes	—	—	—	500,000	500,000	500,000
Common Stock	400,000	400,000	400,000	500,000	500,000	500,000
Retained Earnings	(13,975)	(4,974)	18,981	69,629	211,353	395,575
Total Liabilities and Shareholders' Equity	$547,473	$766,892	$1,094,520	$1,744,744	$2,074,229	$2,207,965

[a]The derivation of this amount is as follows:

	Notes Receivable Gross	Deferred Gross Profit	Notes Receivable Net
January 1, Year 1	$411,336	$140,668	$270,668
Less Cash Received, January 1, Year 1	(65,000)	—	(65,000)
Plus Interest Revenue, Year 1	41,560	—	41,560
Less Cash Received, December 31, Year 1	(65,000)	—	(65,000)
Gross Profit Recognized, Year 1	—	(30,245)	30,245
Totals	$322,896	$110,423	$212,473

[b]See Note b to Exhibit 5.

Exhibit 9

Arizona Land Development Company Statements of Cash Flows
Income Recognition Using Installment Method—with Discounting of Cash Flows

	Year 1	Year 2	Year 3	Year 4	Year 5	Year 6
Operations						
Net Income (Loss)	$(13,975)	$ 9,001	$ 23,955	$ 50,648	$141,724	$184,222
(Inc.) Decr. in Notes Receivable	(212,473)	(276,919)	(409,906)	(673,815)	(244,994)	68,862
(Inc.) Decr. in Land Inventory	65,000	90,000	50,000	50,000	(80,000)	(60,000)
Inc. (Decr.) in Estimated Development Cost Liability	161,448	210,418	303,673	499,576	187,761	(50,486)
Inc. (Decr.) in Deferred Income Taxes	—	—	—	—	—	—
Cash Flow from Operations	$0	$ 32,500	$(32,278)	$(73,591)	$ 4,491	$142,598
Financing						
Common Stock Issued	—	—	—	100,000	—	—
Change in Cash	$ 0	$ 32,500	$(32,278)	$ 26,409	$ 4,491	$ 142,598

Exhibit 10

Arizona Land Development Company Income Statements
Income Recognition Using Percentage-of-Completion Method

	Year 1	Year 2	Year 3	Year 4	Year 5	Year 6
Sales	$216,667[a]	$354,167	$629,167	$1,087,500	$862,500	$695,833
Cost of Goods Sold	(130,000)[a]	(212,500)	(377,500)	(652,500)	(517,500)	(417,500)
Gross Profit	$ 86,667[a]	$141,667	$251,667	$ 435,000	$345,000	$278,333
Selling Expenses	(65,000)	(90,000)	(150,000)	(250,000)	(120,000)	(40,000)
Net Income before Taxes	$ 21,667	$51,667	$101,667	$ 185,000	$225,000	$238,333
Income Taxes						
Current	—	—	(9,778)	(26,091)	(73,009)	(94,902)
Deferred	(7,367)	(17,567)	(24,789)	(36,809)	(3,491)	13,869
Net Income	$ 14,300	$ 34,100	$ 67,100	$ 122,100	$148,500	$ 157,300

[a]Land sold under contract in Year 1 had a contract price of $650,000 and estimated contract cost of $390,000 (= $65,000 + $325,000) (see Exhibit 1). ALDC incurred development costs of $130,000 (= $65,000 for land + $32,500 on January 1, Year 1 + $32,500 on December 31, Year 1) during Year 1. Thus, the percentage of completion as of the end of Year 1 is 33.3 percent (= $130,000/$390,000). Sales are 33.3 percent of $650,000 and cost of goods sold is 33.3 percent of $390,000.

Exhibit 11
Arizona Land Development Company Balance Sheets
Income Recognition Using Percentage-of-Completion Method

	Year 1	Year 2	Year 3	Year 4	Year 5	Year 6
Assets						
Cash	$100,000	$132,500	$ 100,222	$ 126,631	$ 131,122	$ 273,720
Contracts in Process	216,667[a]	570,834	1,200,001	2,287,501	3,150,001	3,845,834
Less Progress Billings	(130,000)[b]	(375,000)	(830,000)	(1,635,000)	(2,430,000)	(3,185,000)
Contracts in Process (net)	$ 86,667	$195,834	$ 370,001	$ 652,501	$ 720,001	$ 660,834
Land Inventory	235,000	145,000	95,000	45,000	125,000	185,000
Total Assets	$421,667	$473,334	$ 565,223	$ 824,132	$ 976,123	$1,119,554
Liabilities and Shareholders' Equity						
Deferred Income Taxes	$ 7,367	$ 24,934	$ 49,723	$ 86,532	$ 90,023	$ 76,154
Common Stock	400,000	400,000	400,000	500,000	500,000	500,000
Retained Earnings	14,300	48,400	115,500	237,600	386,100	543,400
Total Liabilities and Shareholders' Equity	$421,667	$473,334	$ 565,223	$ 824,132	$ 976,123	$1,119,554

[a]Accumulated costs of $130,000 + gross profit recognized in Year 1 of $86,667 (see Note a to Exhibit 10).
[b]Down payment of $65,000 received on January 1, Year 1, plus $65,000 installment payment received on December 31, Year 1.

Exhibit 12
Arizona Land Development Company Statements of Cash Flows
Income Recognition Using Percentage-of-Completion Method

	Year 1	Year 2	Year 3	Year 4	Year 5	Year 6
Operations						
Net Income	$ 14,300	$ 34,100	$ 67,100	$ 122,100	$ 148,500	$ 157,300
(Inc.) Decr. in Contracts in Process	(216,667)	(354,167)	(629,167)	(1,087,500)	(862,500)	(695,833)
Inc. (Decr.) in Progress Billings	130,000	245,000	455,000	805,000	795,000	755,000
(Inc.) Decr. in Land Inventory	65,000	90,000	50,000	50,000	(80,000)	(60,000)
Inc. (Decr.) in Deferred Income Taxes	7,367	17,567	24,789	36,809	3,491	(13,869)
Cash Flow from Operations	$ 0	$ 32,500	$ (32,278)	$ (73,591)	$ 4,491	$ 142,598
Financing						
Common Stock Issued	—	—	—	100,000	—	—
Change in Cash	$ 0	$ 32,500	$ (32,278)	$ 26,409	$ 4,491	$ 142,598

Generally Accepted Accounting Principles: Liability Recognition and Related Expenses

4

The recognition and measurement of liabilities affect the analysis of financial statements in two important ways:

1. Profitability analysis: Firms use, or consume, various goods and services during a period in generating revenues for which they may not make cash payments until future periods. Also, firms promise to provide goods or perform services in the future related to revenues recognized during the current period (for example, under warranty plans). The cost of the goods and services that the firm has already consumed or will consume in the future is an expense of the current period. Effective analysis of profitability requires that the analyst assess whether the firm has measured these expenses properly.

2. Risk analysis: The amount shown on the balance sheet for liabilities indicates the present value of the cash or other assets that the firm will need to discharge obligations coming due within the next year (current liabilities) and after one year (noncurrent liabilities). A firm with inadequate resources to satisfy these obligations runs the risk of insolvency or even bankruptcy. Effective analysis of risk requires the analyst to assess whether the firm has recognized and measured its liabilities properly. Recognition issues are particularly important because many firms engage in transactions that create financial risk but do not recognize a liability for such risks on the balance sheet. In fact, GAAP stipulates that the firm not recognize a liability in some cases.

This chapter discusses the concept of an accounting liability and illustrates its application to several financial reporting issues, including leases, pensions, deferred taxes, and reserves. The chapter emphasizes GAAP in the United States, but notes significant differences in accounting principles used in other countries.

Concept of an Accounting Liability

Accounting recognizes an obligation as a liability if it satisfies three criteria[1]:

1. The obligation involves a probable future sacrifice of resources—a future transfer of cash, goods, or services or the foregoing of a future cash receipt—at a specified or determinable date. The firm can measure with reasonable precision the cash-equivalent value of the resources needed to satisfy the obligation.

2. The firm has little or no discretion to avoid the transfer.

3. The transaction or event giving rise to the obligation has already occurred.

Application of Criteria for Liability Recognition

The criteria for liability recognition may appear straightforward and subject to unambiguous interpretation. Unfortunately, this is not so. Various obligations of an enterprise fall along a continuum with respect to how well they satisfy these criteria. Exhibit 4.1 classifies obligations into six groups. The following sections discuss each of these groups.

Obligations with Fixed Payment Dates and Amounts. The obligations that most clearly satisfy the liability recognition criteria are those with fixed payment due dates and amounts (usually set by contract). Most obligations arising from borrowing arrangements fall into this category. A firm receives the benefit of having funds available for its use. The borrowing agreement specifies the timing and amount of interest and principal payments.

Obligations with Fixed Payment Amounts but Estimated Payment Dates. Most current liabilities fall into this category. Either oral agreements, written agreements, or legal statutes fix the amounts payable to suppliers, employees, and governmental agencies. Firms normally settle these obligations within a few months after incurring them. The firm can estimate the settlement date, although not precisely, with sufficient accuracy to warrant recognizing a liability.

Obligations with Estimated Payment Dates and Amounts. Obligations in this group require estimation because the firm cannot identify the specific future recipients of cash, goods, or services at the time the obligation becomes a liability. In addition, the firm cannot compute precisely the amount of resources it will transfer in the future. For example, when a firm sells products under a warranty agree-

---

[1]Financial Accounting Standards Board, *Statement of Financial Accounting Concepts No. 6,* "Elements of Financial Statements," (1985), par. 36.

Exhibit 4.1
Classification of Accounting Liabilities by Degree of Certitude

Obligations with Fixed Payment Dates and Amounts	Obligations with with Fixed Payment Amounts but Estimated Payment Dates	Obligations for Which the Firm Must Estimate Both Timing and Amount of Payment	Obligations Arising from Advances from Customers on Unexecuted Contracts and Agreements	Obligations under Mutually Unexecuted Contracts	Contingent Obligations
Notes Payable Interest Payable Bonds Payable	Accounts Payable Salaries Payable Taxes Payable	Warranties Payable	Rental Fees Received in Advance Subscription Fees Received in Advance	Purchase Commitments Employment Commitments	Unsettled Lawsuits[a] Financial Instruments with Off-Balance Sheet Risk[a]

Most Certain ⟵――――――――――――――――――――――――――――――⟶ Least Certain

⟵―――――― Recognized as Accounting Liabilities ―――――⟶ ⟵―― Not Generally Recognized as ――⟶ Accounting Liabilities

[a]If a firm meets certain criteria for a loss contingency, it recognizes this obligation as a liability. See the discussion later in this chapter.

ment, it promises to replace defective parts or perform certain repair services for a specified period of time. At the time of sale, the firm can neither identify the specific customers who will receive warranty benefits nor ascertain the amounts of their claims. Past experience, however, often provides the necessary information for estimating the likely proportion of customers who will make claims and the probable average amount of their claims. As long as the firm can estimate the probable amount of the obligation, it satisfies the first criterion for a liability. The selling price of goods sold under warranty includes an explicit or implicit charge for the warranty services. Thus, the receipt of cash or the right to receive cash in the sales transaction benefits the firm and creates the warranty liability.

Obligations Arising from Advances from Customers on Unexecuted Contracts and Agreements. A firm sometimes receives cash from customers in advance for goods or services it will provide in a future period. For instance, a rental firm may receive cash in advance of the rental period on rental property. A magazine publisher may receive subscription fees in advance of the subscription period. Organizations and associations may receive membership dues prior to the membership period. These firms could recognize revenue upon the receipt of cash, as with the sale of products under warranty plans. In the case of advances from customers, however, all of the required transfer of resources (goods or services) will occur in the future. Revenue recognition generally requires that the firm deliver the goods or provide the services. Thus, the receipt of cash in advance creates a liability equal to the cash received. The firm might conceivably recognize a liability equal to the expected cost of delivering the promised goods or services, but doing so would result in recognizing the profit from the transaction before substantial performance had occurred.

Obligations under Mutually Unexecuted Contracts. Mutually unexecuted contracts arise when two entities agree to make a transfer of resources but *neither* entity has yet made a transfer. For example, a firm may agree to supply its customers with specified amounts of merchandise over the next two years. Or a firm may agree to pay its president a certain sum as compensation over the next five years. A bank may agree to provide lines of credit to its business customers in the event that these firms need funds in the future. Because neither party has transferred resources, no accounting liability arises. This category of obligation, called executory contracts, differs from the preceding two, where the contracts or agreements are partially completed. With warranty agreements, a firm receives cash but has not fulfilled its warranty obligation. With rental, subscription, and membership fees, a firm receives cash but has not provided the required goods or services. Firms generally do not recognize obligations under mutually unexecuted contracts as accounting liabilities. If the amounts involved are material, the firm must disclose the nature of the obligation and its amount in the notes to the financial statements.

Contingent Obligations. An event whose outcome today is unknown may create an obligation for the future transfer of resources. For instance, a firm may be a defendant in a lawsuit, the outcome of which depends on the results of legal proceedings. The obligation is *contingent* on future events.

Contingent obligations may or may not give rise to accounting liabilities. GAAP requires firms to recognize an estimated loss from a contingency (called a *loss contingency*) only if both of the following conditions are met:

1. Information available prior to the issuance of the financial statements indicates that it is probable that an asset has been impaired or that a liability has been incurred.

2. The firm can estimate the amount of the loss with reasonable precision.[2]

The first criterion for recognition of a loss contingency rests on the probability, or likelihood, that an asset has been impaired or a liability has been incurred. GAAP does not provide clear guidance as to what probability cutoff defines *likely* or *probable*. The FASB has stated that "*probable* is used with its usual general meaning, rather than in a specific accounting or technical sense, and refers to that which

---

[2]Financial Accounting Standards Board, *Statement of Financial Accounting Standards No. 5,* "Accounting for Contingencies," (1975), para. 8.

can be expected or believed on the basis of available evidence or logic but is neither certain or proved."[3]

The second criterion requires reasonable estimation of the amount of the loss. Again, GAAP does not define "reasonably estimated" in any precise terms. Instead, if the firm can narrow the amount of the loss to a reasonable range, however large, GAAP presumes that the firm has achieved sufficient precision to justify recognition of a liability. The amount of the loss is the most likely estimate within the range. If no amount within the range is more likely than any other, then the firm should use the amount at the lower end of the range.

GAAP refers to obligations meeting both of these two criteria as "loss contingencies." One example suggested by the FASB relates to a toy manufacturer that sold toys later found to present a safety hazard. The toy manufacturer concludes that the likelihood of having to pay damages is high. The firm meets the second criterion if experience or other information enables the manufacturer to make a reasonable estimate of the loss. The toy manufacturer recognizes a loss and a liability in this case.

Controversial Issues in Liability Recognition

Most obligations discussed in the preceding sections clearly were or were not liabilities. Recently, firms have structured innovative financing arrangements in ways that may not satisfy the criteria for the recognition of a liability. A principal aim of such arrangements is to reduce the amount shown as liabilities on the balance sheet. The proportion of debt in a firm's capital structure affects its perceived level of risk and therefore its cost of obtaining funds. Other things being equal, firms prefer to obtain funds without showing a liability on the balance sheet in the hope that future lenders will ignore such financing in setting interest rates. Although there is little empirical evidence to support the notion that lenders ignore such financing in assessing a firm's risk, some firms *act* as if lenders do overlook such borrowing.

Firms may accomplish this objective by issuing securities that have both debt and equity characteristics (referred to as *hybrid securities*) but classifying them only as equity on the balance sheet. As an example, some firms issue preferred stock that is subject to mandatory redemption after some period of time by the issuing firm. Such stock probably has more debt than equity characteristics. Firms also issue preferred stock that is subject to a call option by the issuing firm. The firm sets out provisions in the preferred stock agreement that make exercise of the call option highly probable. This preferred stock also has more debt than equity characteristics. On the other hand, some firms issue debt securities that have more equity than debt characteristics. For instance, firms might issue bonds that are convertible into common stock. The firm sets out provisions in the debt instrument that make conversion into common stock highly probable. Or, the firm

---

[3]Financial Accounting Standards Board, *Statement of Financial Accounting Concepts No. 6,* "Elements of Financial Statements," (1985), para. 35 (Note 21).

might issue debt with interest payments tied to the firm's operating performance or dividend yield. (Firms treat these equity-like securities as debt to obtain a tax deduction for "interest expense.") Although accounting attempts to classify all financial instruments as either a liability or a shareholders' equity, the securities of most firms range along a continuum from pure debt to pure equity. The accountant's dividing line is not always clear-cut. The analyst should study the notes to the financial statements to assess whether the firm's classification of hybrid securities as debt versus equity seems reasonable.

Another means of reducing the amount shown as liabilities on the balance sheet is to structure a borrowing arrangement so that the firm does not recognize an obligation (referred to as *off-balance-sheet financing*). The following sections describe several off-balance-sheet financing arrangements. In several cases, the Financial Accounting Standards Board has issued a reporting standard setting out more clearly how firms are to treat such transactions for financial reporting purposes.

A general theme runs throughout the various off-balance-sheet financing arrangements: When firms leave liabilities off the balance sheet, they maintain the balance sheet equation either by reducing an existing asset or by not recognizing a newly acquired "asset."

Sale of Receivables with Recourse. Firms sometimes sell their accounts receivable with recourse as a means of obtaining short-term financing. If collections from customers are not sufficient to repay the amount borrowed plus interest, then the firm must pay the difference.

The question arises as to whether the recourse provision creates an accounting liability. Some argue that the arrangement is similar to a collateralized loan. The firm should leave the receivables on the books and recognize a liability in the amount of the cash received. Others argue that the firm has sold an asset; it should recognize a liability only if it is *probable* that collections from customers will be insufficient and the firm will be required to repay some portion of the amount received.

The FASB has ruled that firms should recognize transfers of receivables with recourse as sales if (1) the selling firm surrenders control of the future economic benefits and risks (for example, credit risk, interest-rate risk) of the receivables; (2) the buying firm cannot require the selling firm to repurchase the receivables except as set out in the recourse provisions; and (3) the selling firm can estimate any probable future obligation with reasonable accuracy.[4]

The principal refinement to the concept of an accounting liability brought out by *Statement No. 77* relates to identifying the party involved in the transaction that enjoys the economic benefits or sustains the economic risk of the *assets* (receivables in this case). If the selling (borrowing) firm controls the economic benefits/risks, then the transaction is a collateralized loan. If the arrangement transfers these benefits/risks to the buying (lending) firm, then the transaction is a sale.

---

[4]Financial Accounting Standards Board, *Statement of Financial Accounting Standards No. 77*, "Reporting for Transfers of Receivables with Recourse," (1983), para. 5

Product Financing Arrangements. Product financing arrangements occur when a firm (sponsor):

1. Sells inventory to another entity and, in a related transaction, agrees to re-purchase the inventory at specified prices over specified times.

2. Arranges for another entity to purchase inventory items on the firm's behalf and, in a related transaction, agrees to purchase the inventory items from the other entity.

The first arrangement is similar to the sale of receivables with recourse except that greater certainty exists that the inventory transaction will require a future cash outflow. The second arrangement is structured to appear as a purchase commitment (recall that GAAP views purchase commitments as mutually unexecuted contracts, with a liability not normally recognized). In this case, however, the sponsoring firm usually creates the entity purchasing the inventory for the sole purpose of acquiring the inventory. The sponsoring firm usually guarantees the debt incurred by the other entity in acquiring the inventory. The other entity is often set up as a trust.

FASB *Statement No. 49* provides that firms recognize product financing arrangements as liabilities if they meet two conditions:

1. The arrangement requires the sponsoring firm to purchase the inventory, substantially identical inventory, or processed goods of which the inventory is a component, at specified prices.

2. The payments made to the other entity cover all acquisition, holding, and financing costs.[5]

The second criterion suggests that the sponsoring firm recognize a liability whenever it incurs the economic risks (changing costs, interest rates) of purchasing and holding inventory, even though it may not physically control the inventory or have a legal obligation to the supplier of the inventory. Thus, as with sales of receivables with recourse, a firm recognizes a liability when it incurs the economic risks of the asset involved. It also recognizes an asset of equal amount, usually inventory.

Research and Development Financing Arrangements. When a firm borrows funds to carry out research and development work, it recognizes a liability at the time of borrowing and recognizes expenses as it incurs research and development costs. Firms have engaged in an innovative means of financing aimed at both keeping liabilities off the balance sheet and effectively excluding research and development expenses from the income statement. The arrangements vary somewhat but generally operate as follows:

---

[5]Financial Accounting Standards Board, *Statement of Financial Accounting Standards No. 49*, "Accounting for Product Financing Arrangements," (1981), para. 5.

1. The sponsoring firm contributes either preliminary development work or rights to future products to a partnership for a general interest in the partnership. It obtains limited partners (often corporate directors or officers) who contribute cash for their partnership interests.

2. The sponsoring firm conducts research and development work for the partnership for a fee. The sponsoring firm usually performs the research and development work on a best-efforts basis, with no guarantee of success. The sponsoring firm recognizes amounts received from the partnership for research and development services as revenues. The amount of revenue generally equals or exceeds the research and development costs it incurs.

3. The rights to any resulting products usually reside in the partnership. However, the partnership agreement usually constrains the returns and risks of the limited partners. The sponsoring firm can often acquire the limited partners' interests in the partnership if extremely valuable products emerge. On the other hand, the sponsoring firm may have to guarantee certain minimum royalty payments to the partnership or agree to purchase the partnership's rights to the product.

In arrangements like this, the sponsoring firm obtains financing for its research and development work without having to recognize a liability.

FASB *Statement No. 68* establishes criteria for when firms must recognize such financing arrangements as liabilities.[6] The sponsoring firm recognizes a liability:

1. If the contractual agreement requires the sponsoring firm to repay any of the funds provided by the other parties regardless of the outcome of the research and development work.

2. If surrounding conditions indicate that the sponsoring firm bears the risk of failure of the research and development work, even though the contractual agreement does not obligate it to repay the other parties. For example, if a sponsoring firm must make minimum royalty payments to the partnership or acquire the partnership's interest in any product, then the sponsoring firm bears the risk of the research and development work.

As with the two off-balance-sheet financing arrangements discussed previously, firms recognize liabilities when they bear the risk associated with the asset or product involved in the financing.[7]

---

[6]Financial Accounting Standards Board, *Statement of Financial Accounting Standards No. 68*, "Research and Development Arrangements," (1982).

[7]A study of firms that conduct their research and development through limited partnerships found that the stock market appears to consider the call option that firms have on research findings in the valuation of the firm. The author calls for improved disclosure of these arrangements instead of recognition of a liability in the balance sheet. See Terry Shevlin, "The Valuation of R&D Firms with R&D Limited Partnerships," *Accounting Review* (January 1991), pp. 1–21.

Take-or-Pay or Throughput Contracts. A take-or-pay contract is an agreement in which a purchaser agrees to pay specified amounts periodically to a seller for products or services. A throughput contract is similar to a take-or-pay contract except that the "product" purchased is transportation or processing services.

To understand the rationale for such arrangements, consider the following case. Suppose that two petroleum companies are in need of additional refining capacity. If either company builds a refinery, it will record an asset and any related financing on its balance sheet. Suppose instead that the two companies form a joint venture to construct a refinery. The joint venture, an entity separate from the two petroleum companies, obtains financing and constructs the refinery. In order to secure financing for the joint venture, the two petroleum companies sign take-or-pay contracts agreeing to make certain payments to the joint venture each period for refining services. The payments are sufficient to cover all operating and financing costs of the refinery. The joint owners must make the payments even if they acquire no refinery services. The economic substance of this arrangement is that each petroleum company owns half of the refinery and is obligated to the extent of half of the financing. The legal status of the arrangement is that the two firms have signed noncancelable purchase commitments.

The FASB has not yet issued a reporting standard setting out when firms must recognize take-or-pay and throughput contracts as liabilities. FASB *Statement No. 47* requires firms to disclose such commitments in the notes. Given the Board's pronouncements on other off-balance-sheet financing arrangements discussed above, we might predict that GAAP will soon require the recognition of take-or-pay and throughput contracts as liabilities.

Summary of Off-Balance-Sheet Financing. The conventional accounting model based on historical cost is exchange- or transaction-oriented. Accounting recognizes events when an exchange takes place. The criteria for liability recognition discussed earlier in this chapter illustrate this exchange orientation. Accounting recognizes liabilities when a firm incurs an obligation to sacrifice resources in the future for benefits already received. GAAP has typically not recognized mutually unexecuted contracts as liabilities because the parties have merely exchanged promises to perform in the future. GAAP also does not generally require the recognition of contingent obligations as liabilities because some future event must occur to establish the existence of a liability.

The evolving concept of an accounting liability recognizes that exchanges of promises can have economic substance even though a legal obligation to pay does not immediately arise. When a firm enjoys the economic benefits and/or incurs the economic risks from an asset, the firm should recognize the asset and its related financing.

The FASB has examined the topic of off-balance-sheet financing for several years. Issues concerning the recognition and measurement of the obligations arising from transactions such as those described above are currently under consideration. In the meantime, the FASB requires firms to disclose in the notes information about material off-balance-sheet commitments or contingencies.

Furthermore, firms must disclose certain information about financial instruments that contain off-balance-sheet risk or concentrations of credit risk. Firms already recognize some of these financial instruments as liabilities, such as futures contracts. Other financial instruments, such as financial guarantees and standby letters of credit, do not appear among liabilities unless payment is highly likely. Each of these financial instruments is subject to the risk that one party to the financial instrument will fail to perform as stipulated by contract. Also, changes in market prices (for example, interest rates) may result in a substantial shift in value from one party to the other party and affect the willingness of the negatively affected party to perform as required. The FASB refers to these risks as "off-balance-sheet risks" because they arise from events that are external to the firm and not under its control. Firms holding financial instruments with material off-balance-sheet risks must disclose the following information about the financial instrument[8]:

1. The face, contract, or notional principal amount.

2. The terms of the instruments and a discussion of their credit and market risk, cash requirements, and related accounting policies.

3. The *accounting loss* the entity would incur if any party to the financial instrument failed completely to perform according to the terms of the contract and the collateral or other security, if any, for the amount due proved to be of no value to the entity.

4. The entity's policy for requiring collateral or other security on financial instruments it accepts and a description of collateral on instruments presently held.

Illustrations of these disclosures appear in Coke's Notes 4, 7, and 8 and in Pepsi's Notes 8 and 13.

The analyst should view these disclosures as a first attempt by the FASB to require more information about off-balance-sheet obligations and off-balance-sheet risks. The disclosures assume a worst case scenario regarding possible losses and financial risks. It is unlikely that firms will ultimately incur obligations or liabilities equal to the face or principal amount disclosed.

The next three sections of this chapter discuss more fully three particularly controversial liability recognition topics: leases, retirement benefits, and deferred income taxes. A final section considers the accounting for reserves.

Leases

Many firms acquire rights to use assets through long-term leases. A company might, for example, agree to lease an office suite for five years or an entire building for 40 years, promising to pay a fixed periodic fee for the duration of the lease. Leasing provides benefits to lessees such as the following:

---

[8]Financial Accounting Standards Board, *Statement of Financial Accounting Standards No. 105*, "Disclosure of Information about Financial Instruments with Off-Balance-Sheet Risk and Financial Instruments with Concentrations of Credit Risk," (1990), para. 17 and 18.

1. Ability to shift the tax benefits of depreciation and other deductions from a lessee that has little or no taxable income (such as an airline) to a lessor that has substantial taxable income. The lessee expects the lessor to share some of the benefits of these tax deductions by requiring lower lease payments.

2. Flexibility to change capacity as needed without having to purchase or sell assets.

3. Ability to reduce the risk of technological obsolescence, relative to outright ownership, by maintaining the flexibility to shift to technologically more advanced assets.

4. Ability to finance the "acquisition" of an asset using lessor financing when alternative sources of financing are unavailable.

These potential benefits of leasing to lessees do not come without a cost. When the lessor assumes the risks of ownership, it will require the lessee to make larger lease payments than if the lessee incurs these risks. The party bearing the risks is a matter of negotiation between lessor and lessee.

Promising to make an irrevocable series of lease payments commits the firm just as surely as a bond indenture or mortgage, and the accounting is similar in many cases. This section examines two methods of accounting for long-term leases: the operating lease method and the capital lease method. The illustrations show the accounting by the lessee, the user of the leased asset. A later section discusses the accounting for the lessor, the owner of the asset.

To illustrate these two methods, suppose that Myers Company wants to acquire a computer that has a three-year life and costs $45,000. Assume that Myers Company must pay 15 percent per year to borrow money for three years. The computer manufacturer is willing to sell the equipment for $45,000 or to lease it for three years. Myers Company is responsible for property taxes, maintenance, and repairs of the computer whether it leases or purchases the computer.

Assume that Myers Company signs the lease on January 1, Year 1, and must make payments on the lease on December 31, Year 1, Year 2, and Year 3. (In practice, lessees usually make lease payments in advance, but the assumption of end-of-the-year payments simplifies the computations.) Compound interest computations show that each lease payment must be $19,709. (The present value of an annuity of $1 paid at the end of this year and each of the next two years is $2.28323 when the interest rate is 15 percent per year. Because the lease payments must have a present value equal to the current cash purchase price of $45,000, each payment must be $45,000/2.28323 = $19,709.)

Operating Lease Method

In an *operating lease*, the owner, or lessor, transfers only the rights to use the property to the lessee for specified periods of time. At the end of the lease period, the lessee returns the property to the lessor. For instance, car rental companies lease cars by the day or week on an operating basis. In leasing arrangements where the lessee neither assumes the risks nor enjoys the rewards of ownership, the

Exhibit 4.2

Amortization Schedule for $45,000 Lease Liability, Repaid in Three Annual Installments of $19,709 Each, Interest Rate 15 Percent, Compounded Annually

Year (1)	Lease Liability, Start of Year (2)	Interest Expense for Year (3)	Payment (4)	Portion of Payment Reducing Lease Liability (5)	Lease Liability, End of Year (6)
1	$45,000	$6,750	$19,709	$12,959	$32,041
2	32,041	4,806	19,709	14,903	17,138
3	17,138	2,571	19,709	17,138	0

Column (2) = column (6), previous period.
Column (3) = .15 × column (2).
Column (4) is given.
Column (5) = column (4) – column (3).
Column (6) = column (2) – column (5).

lessee treats the lease as an operating lease. Accounting gives no recognition to the signing of an operating lease (that is, the lessee reports neither the leased asset nor a lease liability on its balance sheet). The lessee recognizes rent expense in measuring net income each year. Myers Company recognizes rent expense of $19,709 each year if it accounts for the computer lease using the operating lease method.

Capital Lease Method

In leasing arrangements where the lessee assumes the risks and enjoys rewards of ownership, the arrangement is a form of borrowing and GAAP treats such leases as *capital leases*. This treatment recognizes the signing of the lease as the simultaneous acquisition of a long-term asset and the incurring of a long-term liability for lease payments. At the time the lessee signs the lease, it records both the leased asset and the lease liability on its books at the present value of the liability, $45,000 in this example.

Lessees recognize two expense items each year on capital leases. First, the lessee must amortize the leased asset over its useful life. Assuming that Myers Company uses straight-line depreciation, it recognizes depreciation expense of $15,000 (= $45,000/3) each year. Second, the lease payment made each year is part interest expense on the lease liability and part reduction in the liability itself. Exhibit 4.2 shows the amortization schedule for this liability. Column (3) shows the amount of interest expense.

Notice that, in the capital lease method, the total expense over the three years is $59,127, comprising $45,000 (= $15,000 + $15,000 + $15,000) for depreciation expense and $14,127 (= $6,750 + $4,806 + $2,571) for interest expense. This total expense is exactly the same as that recognized under the operating lease method described previously ($19,709 × 3 = $59,127). The capital lease method recognizes expenses sooner than does the operating lease method, as Exhibit 4.3 summarizes.

Exhibit 4.3

Comparison of Expense Recognized under Operating and Capital Lease Methods

Year	Operating Lease Method	Capital Lease Method
		Expense Recognized Each Year under
1	$19,709	$21,750 (= $15,000 + $ 6,750)
2	19,709	19,806 (= 15,000 + 4,806)
3	19,709	17,571 (= 15,000 + 2,571)
Total	$59,127[a]	$59,127 (= $45,000[b] + $14,127[c])

[a]Rent expense.
[b]Depreciation expense.
[c]Interest expense.

But, over sufficiently long time periods, total expense equals the cash expenditure. One difference between the operating lease method and the capital lease method is the *timing* of the expense recognition. The other difference is that the capital lease method recognizes both the asset and the liability on the balance sheet.

Choosing the Accounting Method

When a lessee treats a lease as a capital lease it increases both an asset account and a liability account, thereby increasing total liabilities and making the company appear more risky. Given a choice, most managements prefer not to show the asset and a related liability on the balance sheet. These managements prefer an operating lease to either an installment purchase or a capital lease, where both the asset and liability appear on the balance sheet. Many managements also prefer to recognize expenses later rather than sooner for financial reporting. These preferences have led managements to structure asset acquisitions so that the financing takes the form of an operating lease, thereby achieving off-balance-sheet financing.

Conditions Requiring Capital Lease Accounting.   FASB *Statement No. 13* provides detailed rules of accounting for long-term leases. The lessor and lessee must account for a lease as a capital lease if it meets any one of four conditions.[9] A lease is a capital lease (1) if it extends for at least 75 percent of the asset's life, or (2) if it transfers ownership to the lessee at the end of the lease term, or (3) if it seems likely that the lessor will transfer ownership to the lessee because of a "bargain purchase" option. A bargain purchase option gives the lessee the right to purchase the asset for a price less than the expected fair market value of the asset when the lessee exercises its option. These three conditions are relatively easy to avoid in lease contracts if a firm prefers to treat a lease as an operating lease rather than a capital lease.

---

[9]Financial Accounting Standards Board, *Statement of Financial Accounting Standards No. 13*, "Accounting for Leases," (1976), para. 7.

The most difficult of the four conditions to avoid compares the contractual minimum lease payments discounted at an "appropriate" market interest rate with 90 percent of the fair market value of the asset at the time the lessee signs the lease. (The interest rate used must reflect the creditworthiness of the lessee.) (4) If the present value of the contractual minimum lease payments equals or exceeds 90 percent of the fair market value of the asset at the time of signing, the lease is a capital lease. Many lessors do not wish to lease assets where they have more than 10 percent of the asset's value at risk. The lease therefore transfers the major risks and rewards of ownership from the lessor (landlord) to the lessee. In economic substance, the lessee has acquired an asset, and has agreed to pay for it under a long-term contract, which the lessee recognizes as a liability.

Most countries outside of the United States also set out criteria for distinguishing operating and capital leases (France and Japan are major exceptions where all leases are operating leases). The particular criteria differ somewhat from those described above but attempt to identify the party enjoying the rewards or bearing the risks of ownership.

Effects on Lessor

The lessor (landlord) generally uses the same criteria for classifying a lease as a capital lease or an operating lease as does the lessee (tenant). At the time of the signing of a capital lease, the lessor recognizes revenue in an amount equal to the present value of all future cash flows ($45,000 in the Myers Company lease) and recognizes expense (analogous to cost of goods sold) in an amount equal to the book value of the leased asset. The difference between the revenue and expense is the lessor's gross margin from the "sale" of the asset. The lessor records the lease receivable like any other long-term receivable at the present value of the future cash flows. It recognizes interest revenue over the term of the lease in amounts that closely mirror interest expense by the lessee. Lessors tend to prefer capital lease accounting for financial reporting, because it enables them to recognize income at the time of signing. Under the operating lease method, the lessor recognizes rent revenue in the same amounts as the lessee recognizes rent expense.

Lease Accounting for Tax Purposes

An earlier section indicated that one of the benefits of leasing is that it permits the user of the property (the lessee) to shift the tax benefits of depreciation, interest, and other deductions to the lessor in the expectation of lowering the required lease payments. To achieve this benefit, the lease must satisfy the criteria for an operating lease for tax purposes. These criteria differ somewhat from those GAAP uses to classify leases for financial reporting. The five criteria for operating leases for tax reporting are:

1. Use of the property at the end of the lease term by someone other than the lessee is commercially feasible.

2. The lease does not have a bargain purchase option.

3. The lessor has a minimum 20 percent of its capital at risk.

4. The lessor has a positive cash flow and profit from the lease independent of tax benefits.

5. The lessee does not have an investment in the lease and has not lent any of the purchase price to the lessor.

These criteria attempt to identify the party to the lease that enjoys the rewards and bears the risks of ownership. Because the financial and tax reporting criteria for leases differ, lessors and lessees may treat particular leases one way for financial reporting and another way for tax reporting.

Converting Operating Leases to Capital Leases

Given the preference of lessees to structure leases as operating leases and the thin line that distinguishes operating and capital leases, the analyst may wish to restate the financial statements of lessees to convert all operating leases into capital leases. Such a restatement provides a more conservative measure of total liabilities. To illustrate the procedure followed, refer to Pepsi's Note 7 on leases in Appendix B. Column (2) below shows Pepsi's commitments on noncancelable operating leases net of sublease revenues (amounts in millions):

Year (1)	Reported Lease Commitments (2)	Present Value Factor at 10%	Present Value
9	$171.0	.90909	$155.5
10	$153.1	.82645	126.5
11	$136.9	.75131	102.9
12	$123.5	.68301	84.4
13	$115.9	.62092	72.0
After 13	$553.7	.49443	273.8
			$815.1

The analyst must express the lease commitments in terms of present value. The discount rate that the analyst uses is the lessee's incremental borrowing rate for secured debt with similar terms as the leasing arrangement. We assume a 10 percent rate in this case. To select a present value factor for payments after Year 13, we need to know the years and amounts in which Pepsi will pay the $553.7 million. If we presume that the $115.9 million payment in Year 13 will continue, then Pepsi will pay the $553.7 million over 4.78 years (= $553.7/$115.9), or an average 2.39 years after Year 13. The calculation above uses the present value factor for 7.39 years (that is, Pepsi will pay the $553.7 million at the rate of $115.9 million at the end of Year 14, $115.9 million at the end of Year 15, $115.9 million at the end of Year 16, $115.9 million at the end of Year 17, and $90.1 million at the end of Year 18; the elapsed time for Pepsi to pay the *average* dollar in this $553.7 million aggregate amount is at Year 15.39, which is 7.39 years from the beginning of Year 9). The analyst adds the $815.1 million lease amount to property, plant, and equipment and to long-term debt on the December 31, Year 8, balance sheet.

Similar calculations at the end of Year 7 (calculation not shown) result in a capital lease of $780.2 million and an average remaining life of 9.8 years.

The analyst could also convert the income statement for Year 8 from the operating to the capital lease method (amounts in millions):

Operating Lease Method (as reported)

Lease Expense (see note on leases):	
Noncontingent Rents	$245.7
Contingent Rents	16.5
	$262.2

Capital Lease Method (as restated)

Depreciation Expense ($780.2/9.8)	$ 79.6
Interest Expense (.10 × $780.2)	78.0
Contingent Rents	16.5
	$174.1
Decrease in Reported Expenses	$ 88.1

If the average lease is in the first half of its life, total expenses under the capital lease method tend to exceed total expense under the operating lease method. If the average lease is in the last half of its life, total expenses under the capital lease method tend to be less than under the operating lease method. The two expense amounts are approximately equal at the midlife point (see Exhibit 4.3). In general, balance sheet restatements are more significant than income statement restatements. Consequently, the analyst can usually ignore restatements of the income statement.[10]

Retirement Benefits

Employers typically provide two types of benefits to retired employees: pension benefits and health-care benefits. GAAP, both in the United States and most other countries, requires that the employer recognize the cost of these benefits as an expense while the employees work rather than when they receive the benefits during retirement. Estimating the cost of the benefits requires assumptions about employee turnover, future compensation and health-care costs, interest rates, and other factors. Because the employer will not know the actual costs of these benefits until many years elapse, estimating their costs while the employees work involves imprecision.

---

[10]For an alternative procedure for converting operating into capital leases, see Eugene A. Imhoff, Jr., Robert C. Lipe, and David W. Wright, "Operating Leases: Impact of Constructive Capitalization," *Accounting Horizons* (March 1991), pp. 51–63. In this study the authors found that capitalizing operating leases decreased the rate of return on assets 34 percent for high lease firms and 10 percent for low lease firms and increased the debt to equity ratio 191 percent for high lease firms and 47 percent for low lease firms.

A further issue relates to the pattern for recognizing the costs as an expense. Should the employer recognize an equal amount each year over the employee's working years? Or, should the amount increase over time as compensation levels increase? Recent FASB pronouncements on pension and health-care benefits further complicate the question of the timing of expense recognition. These pronouncements do not require immediate recognition of an expense and a liability for benefits already earned by employees at the time firms adopt these new reporting standards. Instead, the costs of benefits already earned become expenses in future periods. One consequence of this reporting procedure is that the amount that firms show as pension or health-care liabilities on the balance sheet may understate the economic liability at the time. This section discusses the accounting issues related to pensions and health-care benefits.

Pensions

Pension plans work as follows:

1. Employers agree to provide certain pension benefits to employees. The arrangement may take the form of either a defined contribution plan or a defined benefit plan. Under a defined contribution plan, the employer agrees to contribute a certain amount to a pension fund each period (usually based on a percentage of employees' compensation), without specifying the benefits employees will receive during retirement. The amounts employees eventually receive depend on the performance of the pension fund. Under a defined benefit plan, the employer agrees to make pension payments to employees during retirement based on wages earned and number of years of employment. The plan does not specify the amounts the employer will contribute to the pension fund. The employer must make contributions to the fund such that those amounts plus earnings from pension investments are sufficient to make the promised payments.

2. Employers periodically contribute cash to a pension trust. The trustee, or administrator, of the trust invests the cash received from the employer in stocks, bonds, and other investments. The assets in the pension trust accumulate each period from both employer contributions and income from investments. These assets appear on the balance sheet of the pension trust and not on the employer's balance sheet.

3. The employer satisfies its obligation under a defined contribution plan once it makes periodic contributions to the pension trust. The employer's obligation under a defined benefit plan increases each period from two factors. First, employees' services during the period usually give them rights to increased benefits. Most defined benefit plans measure the pension benefit employees will ultimately receive using the number of working years and their highest compensation levels (usually an average of their last several years of compensation before retirement). Employees earn increased benefits each period as they work an additional period at a higher compensation level. Second, the employer's obligation increases each period because time passes and the remaining time until employees begin receiving their pensions decreases. Thus, the present value of the pension obligation increases.

4. The pension trust makes pension payments to retired employees using assets in the pension fund. The employer's obligation under a defined benefit plan decreases by the amount paid.

The balance sheet of a defined benefit pension fund changes each period as follows :

Pension Fund Assets

	Assets at Beginning of Period
±	Actual Earnings on Investments
+	Contributions Received from the Employer
−	Payments to Retirees
=	Assets at End of Period

Pension Fund Liabilities

	Liabilities at Beginning of Period
+	Increase in Liabilities from Employee Services
+	Increase in Liabilities Due to Passage of Time
±	Actuarial Gains and Losses Due to Changes in Assumptions
−	Payments to Retirees
=	Liabilities at End of Period

If a firm contributes cash to the pension fund equal to the increase in pension liabilities from current employee services, earns a return on pension investments exactly equal to the discount rate used in computing the present value of pension liabilities, and experiences employee turnover, compensation increases, and other factors exactly as assumed in computing pension liabilities, then pension assets will equal pension liabilities each period.

Few firms experience this precise matching of pension assets and pension liabilities. Actual investment returns, employee turnover rates, and compensation cost increases seldom occur as expected. In addition, firms adopt or sweeten pension benefit plans, giving employees credit for services rendered prior to adoption or sweetening, but do not immediately contribute cash to the pension fund equal to the newly created liability. Thus, most firms find that pension assets do not equal pension liabilities. Pension disclosures permit the analyst to assess the degree to which a firm has an over- or underfunded pension plan. These disclosures also permit an assessment of the performance of the pension fund during the period.

Obligations under Defined Benefit Plans. Financial Accounting Standards Board *Statement No. 87* requires firms to disclose certain information about defined benefit pension plans in the notes to the financial statements.[11] Refer to

---

[11] Financial Accounting Standards Board, *Statement of Financial Accounting Standards No. 87*, "Employer's Accounting for Pensions," (1985).

Pepsi's Note 11 on retirement plans in Appendix B. Pepsi reports the funded status of the plan as follows (amounts in millions):

	December 31, Year 7	December 31, Year 8
Actuarial present value of benefit obligations		
Vested	$ (449.0)	$ (549.9)
Nonvested	(75.0)	(90.8)
Accumulated benefit obligation	(524.0)	(640.7)
Effect of projected future salary increases	(92.1)	(101.9)
Projected benefit obligation	$ (616.1)	$ (742.6)
Plan assets at market value	869.8	985.7
Projected benefit obligation (in excess of) or		
less than plan assets	253.7	243.1
Unrecognized net loss	(104.0)	(84.6)
Unrecognized prior service cost	26.2	42.4
Unrecognized net assets at July 29, Year 5	(167.1)	(148.1)
Prepaid pension asset	$ 8.8	$ 52.8

Interpreting these disclosures requires several definitions:

Accumulated benefit obligation: The present value of amounts the employer expects to pay to retired employees (taking into consideration actuarial assumptions concerning employee turnover and mortality) based on employees' service to date and current-year compensation levels. The accumulated benefit obligation indicates the present value of the benefits earned to date excluding any future salary increases that will serve as the base for computing the pension payment and excluding future years of service prior to retirement. Vested benefits usually comprise the largest portion of the accumulated benefit obligation, meaning that employees will not lose the right to their pension benefit if they leave the employer prior to retirement. Employees lose nonvested benefits if they terminate employment prior to vesting. Most nonvested benefits vest after an employee works for five to ten years.

Projected benefit obligation: The actuarial present value of amounts the employer expects to pay to retired employees based on employees' service to date but using the expected future salaries that will serve as the base for computing the pension payment. The difference between the accumulated and projected benefit obligation is the effect of future salary increases. Consequently, the projected benefit obligation exceeds the accumulated benefit obligation. The projected benefit obligation is also closer in amount to what we might view as an economic measure of the pension obligation: the present value of amounts the employer expects to pay to employees during retirement based on total expected years of service (past and future) and expected future salaries. FASB *Statement No. 87* does not require disclosure of the economic obligation.

The required disclosures show the relationship between the market value of pension fund assets and the projected benefit obligation at each valuation date. The pension plan of Pepsi is overfunded as of the end of Year 8 by $243.1 million. There are several implications of an overfunded pension plan:

1. Pepsi can reclaim the excess assets for corporate uses. The amount reclaimed becomes immediately subject to income taxes. Corporate raiders have sometimes used excess pension assets to help finance a leveraged buyout of a firm.

2. Pepsi can discontinue contributions to the pension fund until such time as the assets in the pension fund equal the projected benefit obligation.

3. Pepsi can continue its historical pattern of funding on the presumption that the overfunded status is due to temporary market appreciation that could easily reverse in the future.

Although we might argue that an excess of pension fund assets over the projected benefit obligation represents an asset to a firm, FASB *Statement No. 87* does not permit firms to recognize this resource on the balance sheet.

In like manner, we might view an excess of the projected benefit obligation over pension fund assets as a liability that firms should report on the balance sheet. Refer to Note 12 to Coke's financial statements in Appendix A. Coke has certain U.S. pension plans for which the projected benefit obligation exceeds the assets in the pension fund by $49.619 million at the end of Year 7 and $64.892 million at the end of Year 8. The FASB, responding to criticisms that the measurement of the projected benefit obligation requires subjective projections of future salary increases, stipulates instead that firms show an excess of the *accumulated* benefit obligation over pension fund assets on the balance sheet as a liability. Note that Coke has an accumulated benefit obligation of $43.391 million at the end of Year 7 for certain U.S. plans but no assets in its pension fund related to this obligation. Coke includes $43.391 million in "Other Liabilities" on its balance sheet. It reports similar amounts for Year 8. Because the accumulated benefit obligation is smaller than the projected benefit obligation, only a few firms report a liability for underfunded benefits by this measure.

The only asset or liability that will normally appear on the balance sheet occurs when the amount recognized as pension expense differs from the amount of cash contributed to the pension fund. This asset or liability is a relatively small amount compared to the aggregate pension assets and obligations. Note, for example, that Pepsi has a Prepaid Pension Asset of $52.8 million at the end of Year 8 included among its assets. For reasons discussed below, Pepsi has contributed more to its pension fund than it has recognized as an expense, resulting in a Prepaid Pension Asset on the balance sheet.

An analyst assessing the risk of a firm faces the question as to whether an underfunded projected benefit obligation represents a liability. The argument for recognizing this obligation as a liability is that it represents a closer measure of the economic obligation than does the underfunded accumulated benefit obligation[12] and that including it among liabilities provides a more conservative basis for assessing risk. The argument for including only the underfunded accumulated

---

[12] Thomas I. Selling and Clyde P. Stickney, "Accounting Measures of Unfunded Pension Liabilities and the Expected Present Value of Future Pension Cash Flows," *Journal of Accounting and Public Policy* (April 1987), pp. 267–285.

benefit obligation among liabilities (already included) is that the accumulated benefit obligation comes closer to measuring the firm's legal obligation as of the date of the balance sheet.

Measurement of Pension Expense. Firms must calculate net pension expense each year based on the projected benefit cost method, which means that actuarial calculations use accumulated service to date and projected future salaries. Exhibit 4.4 summarizes the seven elements comprising net pension expense.

Pepsi discloses these seven components of pension expense on five lines [Pepsi combines items 4, 6, and 7 on the line, Deferred gain (loss)], as follows (amounts in millions):

	Year 6	Year 7	Year 8
Service cost-benefits earned during the year........	$ 24.8	$ 32.0	$ 48.1
Interest cost on projected benefit obligation	40.0	47.1	63.3
Actual return on plan assets	(86.1)	(154.6)	(27.0)
Deferred gain	23.5	89.9	(55.9)
Amortization of net transition gain	_(19.0)_	_(19.0)_	_(19.0)_
Net pension expense	$ (16.8)	$ (4.6)	$ 9.5

Note the following aspects about net pension expense:

1. The effect of combining the third and fourth components of pension expense is that pension expense decreases by the *expected* return on pension assets each period. The disclosure of this expected return appears in two steps: (a) the actual return plus or minus (b) the difference between the actual and the expected return. This method of disclosure permits the financial statement user to assess the actual performance of the pension fund during the period but smooths out the effect of unexpected gains and losses by including them as part of the amortization of actuarial gains and losses (seventh component of pension expense). Pepsi's actual return on investments during Year 6 and Year 7 exceeded expectations. Pepsi deferred a portion of this return each year. The actual return during Year 8 was less than expectations, so Pepsi deferred the shortfall. Pepsi's disclosure practice of combining items 4, 6, and 7 of pension expense on the line, deferred gain, makes it difficult to disaggregate the portion of the net amount due to differences between the actual and expected rates of return on pension assets (line 4) and amortization of deferred amounts from prior years (lines 6 and 7).

2. In addition to amortization of actuarial gains and losses, amortization of any net pension asset or net pension liability when the firm adopts FASB *Statement No. 87* affects pension expense. The objective in amortizing this item is to smooth its effect on pension expense.

3. The seven components of pension expense may net to a pension expense (Year 8 for Pepsi) or a pension credit (Years 6 and 7 for Pepsi).

Relation of Pension Expense to Pension Funding. The amount that a firm recognizes as pension expense each period will not necessarily equal the amount

Exhibit 4.4
Components of Pension Expense

	Effect on Pension Expense	
	Debit (Increase)	Credit (Decrease)
1. Service Cost—the increase in the projected benefit obligation because employees worked an additional year	X	
2. Interest Cost—the increase in the projected benefit obligation because of the passage of time	X	
3. Actual Return on Plan Assets—the change in the market value of plan assets due to interest, dividends, and changes in the market value of investments		X
4. Difference between Actual Return and Expected Return on Plan Assets		
Actual Return > Expected Return	X	
Actual Return < Expected Return		X
5. Amortization of net pension asset (pension fund assets exceed projected benefit obligation) or net pension liability (pension fund assets are less than projected benefit obligation) as of the date of initial adoption of *Statement No. 87*. The firm amortizes the net asset or net liability straight-line over the average remaining service life of employees.		
Net Pension Liability	X	
Net Pension Asset		X
6. Amortization of increases in the projected benefit obligation that arise because the firm sweetens the pension benefit formula and gives employees credit for their prior service under the sweetened benefit arrangement. The amortization period is generally the average remaining service life of employees, although a shorter period may be required if an employer regularly sweetens its pension plan.	X	
7. Amortization of gains and losses because actual experience differs from actuarial assumptions (e.g., salary, interest rate, turnover, mortality, asset returns).		
Actuarial Loss	X	
Actuarial Gain		X

the firm contributes to its pension fund. The firm measures the amount for pension expense in accordance with the provisions of FASB *Statement No. 87*. The amount the firm contributes to its pension fund relies on actuaries' recommendations concerning the needed level of funding plus decisions by the firm regarding investments of its financial resources. For example, a firm with a significantly overfunded pension plan might delay additional contributions for a few years and use the cash for other corporate purposes. In this case, the firm recognizes pension expense each year but does not contribute cash to the pension fund. Alternatively, a firm might contribute more than the amount of pension expense. Earnings on pension investments are not subject to income taxation, whereas earnings on cash left within a firm are subject to taxation. Within prescribed limits, firms can make excess pension contributions and delay or avoid taxes on investment earnings.

When a firm recognizes more pension expense than it contributes to the pension fund, a pension liability appears on the balance sheet. When pension expense is less than pension funding, a pension asset appears on the balance sheet. Pepsi, for instance, reports a Prepaid Pension Asset of $8.8 million at the end of Year 7 and $52.8 million at the end of Year 8, suggesting that it has funded pensions faster than it has recognized pension expense. Note that this pension asset or pension liability on the balance sheet bears no necessary relation to the more important measure of the status of a pension plan: the difference between the total assets in the pension fund and the projected benefit obligation. The latter are much larger amounts.

Refer now to Note 12 to the financial statements of Coke in Appendix A. The combined assets in Coke's pension plans at the end of Year 8 of $732.358 million (= $508.267 + $.811 + $160.945 + $62.335) are less than the projected benefit obligation of $733.098 million (= $424.118 + $65.703 + $129.435 + $113.842) by $.740 million (= $732.358 − $733.098), whereas pension assets exceeded the projected benefit obligation by $117.415 million at the end of Year 7. The switch from an overfunded to an underfunded plan during Year 8 is due in part to poor investment performance. Investments were expected to earn approximately $67.042 million [= (.095 × (.529.067))+(.08 × ($207.806 + $1.961))]. Actual returns on investments were only $12.932 million (= 9.121 + $3.811). Thus, the investment performance fell $54.110 million (= $67.042 − $12.932) short of expectations. In addition, Coke increased its actuarial assumption for compensation increases for foreign plans during Year 8, thereby increasing the projected benefit obligation.

Health-Care Obligations

In addition to pensions, most employers provide health-care benefits to retired employees. This benefit may take the form of a fixed dollar amount to cover part or all of the cost of health insurance (analogous to the defined contribution type of pension plan) or the benefit may specify the level of health care provided (analogous to the defined benefit type of pension plan).

The accounting issues related to the health-care obligation are similar to those discussed previously for pensions. The employer must recognize the cost of the health-care benefit over the employees' years of service. The employer may or may not set aside funds to cover the cost of the health-care benefit. Health insurance expense each period includes an amount for current service plus interest on the health-care insurance obligation at the beginning of the period. Expected earnings on investments in a health-care benefits fund, if any, reduce health-care expense. The employer defers and then amortizes actuarial gains and losses due to changes in employee turnover, health-care costs, interest rates, and similar factors. The major difference between the accounting for pensions and the accounting for health-care benefits is that firms need not report an excess of the accumulated health-care benefits obligation over assets in a health-care benefits fund as a liability on the balance sheet.[13] Firms must report this amount in the notes to the financial statements. During the deliberation process on the health-care benefits reporting standard, business firms exerted pressure on the FASB not to require recognition of the underfunded accumulated health-care benefits obligation. These business firms argued that the amount of this obligation was both large, relative to other liabilities and shareholders' equity, and uncertain, because of uncertainties regarding future health-care inflation rates. Some firms indicated that they would eliminate health-care retirement benefits if the FASB required recognition of the liability. As a compromise, the FASB requires firms to recognize the obligation piecemeal over employees' working years.

Analysts' concerns with the health-care obligation are similar to those for pensions. Should the analyst add the health-care obligation to liabilities in assessing risk? How reasonable are the firm's assumptions regarding health-care cost increases, discount rates, and amortization periods? Is the health-care fund, if any, generating returns consistent with the expected rate of return? The FASB delayed the effective date of *Statement No. 106* until 1993, so many firms will not report information on their health-care benefits obligation until that time.

Income Taxes

Firms often select different methods of accounting for financial and income tax reporting. The total amount of revenue or expense recognized over the life of an asset or other item is the same for the two purposes. However, the *timing* of their recognition may differ. For example, the total depreciation for both financial and tax reporting over an asset's life is its acquisition cost. In the early years, tax depreciation for an asset using an accelerated method exceeds depreciation recognized for financial reporting using the straight-line method, so that taxable income is less than financial statement income before taxes. In later years, depreciation for tax reporting is less than that for financial reporting, so that taxable income exceeds income before taxes.

The use of different accounting methods for financial and tax reporting creates a problem in measuring income tax expense each period:

1. Should income tax expense equal the income taxes payable based on the current period's taxable income?

2. Should income tax expense equal the income taxes that the firm will ultimately pay based on both the current period's taxable income and on taxable incomes of future periods when temporary, or timing, differences reverse?

---

[13] The accumulated health-care benefit obligation incorporates health-care costs expected when employees receive benefits and is therefore more similar to the projected benefit pension obligation than to the accumulated benefit pension obligation. See Financial Accounting Standards Board, *Statement of Financial Accounting Standards No. 106*, "Employer's Accounting for Postretirement Benefits Other than Pensions," (1990).

Exhibit 4.5
Illustration of Deferred Tax Accounting

	First Year		Second Year	
	Tax Return	**Financial Reporting**	**Tax Return**	**Financial Reporting**
Income before Depreciation and Taxes	$100,000	$100,000	$100,000	$100,000
Depreciation Expense	(70,000)	(50,000)	(30,000)	(50,000)
Income before Taxes	$ 30,000	$ 50,000	$ 70,000	$ 50,000
Income Taxes Payable Currently (at 34%)	$ 10,200		$ 23,800	
Income Tax Expense				
On Taxable Income	$ (10,200)		$ (23,800)	
On Financial Reporting Income		(17,000)		(17,000)
Net Income	$ 19,800	$ 33,000	$ 46,200	$ 33,000

Under the second approach, revenues and expenses recognized for financial reporting rather than the amounts recognized for tax reporting determine the amount of income tax expense.

Illustration of Deferred Tax Accounting

To illustrate, refer to Exhibit 4.5. A firm has $100,000 of income before depreciation and taxes for financial and tax reporting for Year 1 and Year 2. The only difference between financial and tax reporting amounts is depreciation on a $100,000 machine with a two-year life. Depreciation for tax purposes is $70,000 in Year 1 and $30,000 in Year 2. Depreciation for financial reporting is $50,000 each year. Over the two-year period, the firm will pay $34,000 (= $10,200 + $23,800) of income taxes. Because *total* tax expense must equal cash paid out, the firm must recognize $34,000 as expense over the two years in measuring net income for financial reporting. FASB *Statement No. 109* requires that firms measure income tax expense using the methods of accounting followed for financial reporting (the second approach described above).[14] In this case, income tax expense is $17,000 each year. The rationale for this approach is that it better matches income tax expense with income before taxes reported in the financial statements. Note that income before taxes is $50,000 each year. The $17,000 of income tax expense in the first year comprises $10,200 of taxes payable immediately and $6,800 [= .34($70,000 - $50,000)] of taxes that the firm will pay in the second year when the timing difference reverses. Under the approach required by GAAP, income tax expense tracks income before taxes for financial reporting rather than taxable income.

---

[14]Financial Accounting Standards Board, *Statement of Financial Accounting Standards No. 109,* "Accounting for Income Taxes," (1992).

Because income tax expense of $17,000 in the first year exceeds income taxes payable of $10,200, a Deferred Tax Liability of $6,800 emerges. This liability represents the income tax the firm expects to pay when the timing difference reverses in the second year. If income tax laws provided for a change in tax rates in the second year, the firm would base the Deferred Tax Liability on the new rate.

In the second year, income tax expense of $17,000 is less than income taxes payable. The $23,800 of taxes paid comprises $17,000 payable on financial reporting income before taxes of the second year plus $6,800 of deferred taxes previously recognized on the first year's income.

Interpreting Income Tax Disclosures

The notes to the financial statements contain useful information for understanding a firm's income tax position. For this illustration refer to Note 13 to the financial statements of Coke in Appendix A. Income tax expense for Year 8 is $632.532 million (this agrees with the amount shown on the income statement). This $632.532 million comprises $662.786 million of currently payable taxes net of $30.254 million deferred. The amount shown in the income tax note for "Income Taxes—Current" is the required cash flow. Income before taxes for financial reporting was less than taxable income in Year 8, so Coke experienced a $30.254 million reversal of deferred taxes. This $30.254 million decreased the Deferred Tax Liability account on the balance sheet. Just the opposite relation between income for financial and tax reporting occurred in Year 7 and Year 6. Income before taxes exceeded taxable income, increasing deferred tax expense and the Deferred Tax Liability account.

One of the items disclosed in the income tax note is the components of deferred tax expense for the period. The $30.254 million for Year 8 includes income taxes on timing differences for depreciation, employee compensation, and certain capital transactions. Most firms (for example, see Pepsi's Note 10 on income taxes in Appendix B) disclose the amount of deferred taxes relating to each timing difference. Coke's omission of such detail probably occurs because the amounts for individual timing differences are immaterial.

The income tax note also shows a reconciliation between (1) income taxes at the statutory tax rate on income before taxes and (2) income tax expense. The statutory tax rate was 34 percent in each year. The effective tax rate (= income tax expense/income before taxes) was less than the statutory rate each year, primarily because of lower foreign tax rates and equity in earnings of affiliates on which Coke does not pay taxes.

The tax reconciliation includes the tax effects of any *permanent differences* between financial reporting pretax income and taxable income. For example, firms must amortize goodwill arising from a corporate acquisition (see Chapter 5) for financial reporting but cannot amortize it for tax reporting. Thus, a permanent difference between financial and tax reporting arises. Firms need not provide income tax expense for permanent differences.

Refer now to Pepsi's Note 10 on income taxes in Appendix B. Deferred income tax expense increased income tax expense in each of the last three years, indicating that income before taxes for financial reporting exceeded taxable income. However, income for financial reporting must have been less than taxable income for Year 6 within certain states because there is a net credit of $2.7 million to deferred tax expense. Pepsi provided deferred taxes for timing differences relating to depreciation of property, plant, and equipment and amortization of intangibles (principally franchise rights). The reconciliation of the statutory tax rate with the effective tax rate is similar to that of Coke. The major reconciling item for Pepsi relates to lower tax rates in Puerto Rico and Ireland.

Is the Deferred Tax Liability Really a Liability?

Considerable controversy has surrounded the accounting for deferred income taxes for decades, particularly with respect to whether the Deferred Income Tax Liability account is really a liability. Proponents of the required accounting point out that timing differences eventually reverse. When they do, taxable income will likely exceed income before taxes for financial reporting and the firm's cash payment for taxes will exceed income tax expense. Thus, a future cash outflow in the amount of the Deferred Tax Liability will occur.

Opponents point out that, for a growing firm, timing differences originating in a period will exceed timing differences reversing in the period, so that the Deferred Tax Liability account continually increases. Opponents therefore argue that net timing differences never require future cash flows. They further point out that the Deferred Tax Liability account does not represent a legal obligation of a firm. If the firm became bankrupt, it would not owe the amount in the Deferred Tax Liability account to governmental bodies. The firm pays the required taxes to governmental bodies each year based on its taxable income. The amount in the Deferred Tax Liability account arises only because accountants attempt to smooth income tax expense so that it matches income before taxes for financial reporting.

The analyst obtains a more conservative measure of liabilities by leaving the Deferred Income Tax Liability account on the balance sheet as a liability. An alternative approach involves studying the behavior of deferred income taxes during recent years. If the Deferred Tax Liability account has increased continually, the analyst might eliminate it from liabilities and add it to retained earnings. This treatment presumes that the firm should not have provided deferred taxes to begin with. If the Deferred Tax Liability account increases in some years and decreases in other years, then the analyst can leave the account among liabilities.

The treatment of deferred taxes assumes even greater importance when comparing U.S. firms with non-U.S. firms. Firms in France, Germany, and Japan use similar accounting methods for financial and tax reporting so that the issue of deferred tax accounting does not arise. Firms in Great Britain provide deferred taxes for timing differences only when a high probability exists that a liability will become due. Deferred tax accounting in Canada closely mirrors U.S. reporting practices.

Understanding Reserves in the Financial Statements

Chapters 3 and 4 emphasized two important concepts underlying the financial statements:

1. Income over long-enough time periods equals cash inflows minus cash outflows from operating and investing activities.

2. Because accountants prepare financial statements for discrete periods of time shorter than the life of a firm, the recognition of revenues does not necessarily coincide with the receipt of cash and the recognition of expenses does not necessarily coincide with the disbursement of cash.

Assets such as inventories, investments, property, plant, equipment, and intangibles result from past cash outflows. The costs of these assets become expenses in future periods when the firm uses the services of these assets in operations or through sale. Liabilities such as salaries payable, interest payable, taxes payable, and pensions payable reflect the cost of services already received by a firm. They generally require a future cash outflow. Thus, most asset and liability accounts result from efforts to match revenues with expenses for discrete periods of time.

Because revenues must ultimately equal the total cash inflows and expenses must ultimately equal the total cash outflows from operating and investing activities, firms in the long run cannot alter the total *amount* of revenues and expenses. In the short run, however, firms can only estimate ultimate cash flows. In addition, the accountant allocates benefits received in the form of revenues and services consumed in the form of expenses to discrete accounting periods with some degree of imprecision. As an earlier section of Chapter 3 discussed, management may have incentives to shift revenues or expenses between accounting periods to accomplish certain reporting objectives. Audits by the firm's independent accountants, taxing authorities, or government regulators serve as a control mechanism on management's behavior.

The analyst should develop a sensitivity to financial reporting areas where firms enjoy flexibility in measuring revenues, expenses, assets and liabilities. The last two chapters have discussed reporting areas that allow management to select from among alternative GAAP to influence reported earnings (for example, FIFO versus LIFO). These chapters have also discussed reporting areas that require estimates in applying accounting principles (for example, useful lives for depreciable assets, future salary increases for pensions). Management's potential for influencing reported earnings correlates directly with the role or significance of estimates in applying accounting principles.

In the United States, all revenues, gains, expenses, and losses from operating and investing activities eventually flow through the income statement. The analyst can study the time series pattern of earnings to assess the extent to which firms attempt to shift income through time. In some countries outside of the United States, certain income items do not flow through the income statement but instead increase or decrease a shareholders' equity account directly. In addition, common practice in certain countries permits liberal shifting of income between accounting periods to either minimize income taxes or smooth earnings. The accounting mechanism used to accomplish these reporting results is called a *reserve*. This section discusses briefly the nature and use of reserves.

Nature of a Reserve Account

As the sections below discuss, reserve accounts may appear on the balance sheet as a deduction from an asset, as a liability, or as a component of shareholders' equity. They may appear for a limited period of time or may represent a permanent account. Reserve accounts may shift earnings between periods or may not affect earnings in any period. These multiple uses of reserve accounts and the implication that firms have set aside assets equal to the reserve result in considerable confusion among financial statement users. In the United States, using the term "reserve" in the title of an account is generally unacceptable. When firms use an account that functions similarly to a reserve, U.S. firms must use more descriptive terminology. Reserve accounts commonly appear in the financial statements of non-U.S. firms.

Use of Reserve Accounts

This section illustrates some of the ways firms inside and outside the United States use reserve accounts and the issues they raise for analysts.

1. **Matching Expenses with Associated Revenues.** The recognition of an expense during the current period could result in an increase in a reserve account. The reserve account might appear on the balance sheet as a reduction in an asset. For instance, firms might provide for bad debt expense and increase the account Reserve for Bad Debts (U.S. firms use the account Allowance for Uncollectible Accounts). This reserve account appears as a subtraction from Accounts Receivable on the balance sheet. Likewise, firms might recognize depreciation expense and increase the account Reserve for Depreciation (U.S. firms use the account Accumulated Depreciation). The reserve account appears as a reduction from fixed assets on the balance sheet.

Alternatively, the reserve account might appear as a liability on the balance sheet. For example, a firm might provide for warranty expense or pension expense and increase the accounts Reserve for Warranties (Estimated Warranty Obligation for U.S. firms) or Reserve for Retirement Benefits (Retirement Obligation for U.S. firms). When used properly, these reserve accounts serve the same functions as the corresponding accounts U.S. firms use: to permit appropriate matching of revenues and expenses and appropriate valuation of assets and liabilities. Of course, firms in both the United States and other countries can misuse these accounts (that is, under- or overstating the provisions each year) to shift earnings between periods. In addition to searching for situations where such shifting has occurred, the analyst's main concern with these reserves is understanding the nature of the reserve account in each case. There is usually an analogous account used in the United States that helps the analyst in this interpretation.

2. Keeping Expenses Out of the Income Statement. A practice in some countries is to create a reserve account by reducing the Retained Earnings account. For example, a firm might create a Reserve for Price Increases account or a Reserve for Contingencies account. These accounts appear among the shareholders' equity accounts and may carry a title such as Retained Earnings Appropriated for Price Increases or Retained Earnings Appropriated for Contingencies. When firms later experience the price increase or contingency, they charge the cost against the reserve account rather than include it among expenses. These costs therefore bypass the income statement and usually result in an overstatement of earnings. Note that this use of reserves does not misstate total shareholders' equity because all of the affected accounts (Retained Earnings, reserve accounts, expense accounts) are components of shareholders' equity. Thus, the analyst's primary concern with these reserves is interpreting net income as a measure of operating performance. The analyst can study the shareholders' equity portion of the balance sheet to ascertain whether firms have used a reserve account to avoid sending legitimate expenses through the income statement.

3. Revaluing Assets but Delaying Income Recognition Effect. Firms might use reserves in situations where they revalue assets but do not desire the income effect of the revaluation to affect income of the current period. Chapter 5 points out that firms in the United States account for long-term investments in equity securities using the lower of cost or market valuation method. When market value is less than acquisition costs, U.S. firms write down the investment account. GAAP in the United States does not require the immediate recognition of this decrease in market value in measuring income. Instead, these firms increase an account titled Unrealized Loss in Market Value of Investments and include it as a negative element among shareholders' equity accounts. When the firm sells the securities, it eliminates the unrealized loss account and recognizes a realized loss in measuring net income. Another example of this use of the reserve account relates to foreign currency translation (discussed in Chapter 5). U.S. firms with foreign operations usually translate the financial statements of their foreign entities into U.S. dollars each period using the exchange rate at the end of the period. Changes in the exchange rate cause an unrealized foreign currency gain or loss. Firms do not recognize this gain or loss in measuring income each period but instead use a shareholders' equity account titled Unrealized Foreign Currency Adjustment (see the balance sheets of Coke in Appendix A and Pepsi in Appendix B). When the firm disposes of the foreign unit, it eliminates the unrealized foreign currency adjustment account and recognizes a gain or loss on disposal. U.S. firms could use titles such as Reserve for Price Declines in Investments or Reserves for Foreign Currency Gains and Losses, as is common practice in some countries, but U.S. GAAP requires a more descriptive title.

GAAP in the United Kingdom permits periodic revaluations of fixed assets and intangible assets to their current market value. The increased valuation of assets that usually occurs leads to an increase in a revaluation reserve account included among shareholders' equity. Depreciation or amortization of the revalued assets may appear fully on the income statement each period as an expense or may be split between the income statement (depreciation or amortization based on acquisition cost) and a reduction in the revaluation reserve (depreciation or amortization based on the excess of current market value over acquisition cost).

The analyst's concern with this type of reserve is the appropriateness of revaluing the asset and delaying recognition of its income effect. Note that total shareholders' equity is the same regardless of whether the unrealized gain or loss affects net income immediately or whether it affects another shareholders' equity account and later affects net income. This use of reserves does affect net income of the current period. The analyst may wish to restate reported net income of the current period to incorporate changes in these reserves.

4. Permanently Reclassifying Retained Earnings. Local laws or practices may dictate that firms transfer an amount from retained earnings, which is available for dividends, to a more permanent account that is not available for dividends. U.S. firms typically "capitalize" a portion of retained earnings when they issue a stock dividend. Several countries outside of the United States require firms to report a certain amount of legal capital on the balance sheet. Such firms reduce retained earnings each period and increase an account titled Legal Capital or Legal Reserve. The implication of such disclosures is that assets equal to the amount of this legal capital are not available for dividends. This use of reserves has no effect on net income of the current or future periods.

Summary of Reserves

The quality of disclosures regarding reserves varies considerably across countries. Analysts will often encounter difficulties attempting to understand, much less adjust for, the effect of changes in reserves. An awareness of the ways that firms might use reserve accounts should help the analyst in knowing the kinds of questions to raise when studying the financial statements. Until greater standardization occurs across countries in the use of reserves, the analyst must recognize the lack of comparability of net income and balance sheet amounts and perhaps the increased importance of a statement of cash flows.

Summary

This chapter has explored various reporting areas where expense measurement and liability recognition interact. These reporting areas therefore affect both profitability analysis and risk analysis. The desire of many firms to keep debt off the balance sheet, with the hope of lowering their cost of financing, should put the analyst on guard for the existence of unreported liabilities. The lack of physical existence of liabilities (unlike most assets) increases the difficulties experienced by both the independent auditor and the analyst in identifying the existence of unreported liabilities. This chapter described some of the areas that the analyst should consider when engaging in this search.

Problems

4.1 *Achieving Off-Balance-Sheet Financing (adapted from materials by R. Dieter, D. Landsittel, J. Stewart, and A. Wyatt).* Brion Company wishes to raise $50 million cash but, for various reasons, does not wish to do so in a way that results in a newly recorded liability. It is sufficiently solvent and profitable that its bank is willing to lend up to $50 million at the prime interest rate. Brion Company's financial executives have devised six different plans, described as follows:

1. **Transfer of Receivables with Recourse:** Brion Company will transfer to Credit Company its long-term accounts receivable, which call for payments over the next two years. Credit Company will pay an amount equal to the present value of the receivables less an allowance for uncollectibles as well as a discount because it is paying now but will collect cash later. Brion Company must repurchase from Credit Company at face value any receivables that become uncollectible in excess of the allowance. In addition, Brion Company may repurchase any of the receivables not yet due at face value less a discount specified by formula and based on the prime rate at the time of the initial transfer. (This option permits Brion Company to benefit if an unexpected drop in interest rates occurs after the transfer.) The accounting issue is whether the transfer is a sale (where Brion Company increases Cash, reduces Accounts Receivable, and recognizes expense or loss on transfer) or whether the transfer is merely a loan collateralized by the receivables (where Brion Company increases Cash and increases Notes Payable at the time of transfer).

2. **Product Financing Arrangement:** Brion Company will transfer inventory to Credit Company, which will store the inventory in a public warehouse. Credit Company may use the inventory as collateral for its own borrowings, the proceeds of which credit company will use to pay Brion Company. Brion Company will pay storage costs and will repurchase all the inventory within the next four years at contractually fixed prices plus interest accrued for the time elapsed between the transfer and later repurchase. The accounting issue is whether the inventory is sold to Credit Company, with later repurchases treated as new acquisitions for Brion's inventory, or whether the transaction is merely a loan, with the inventory remaining on Brion's balance sheet.

3. **Throughput Contract:** Brion Company wants a branch line of a railroad built from the main rail line to carry raw material directly to its own plant. It could, of course, borrow the funds and build the branch line itself. Instead, it will sign an agreement with the railroad to ship specified amounts of material each month for ten years. Even if it does not ship the specified amounts of material, it will pay the agreed shipping costs. The railroad will take the contract to its bank and, using it as collateral, borrow the funds to build the branch line. The accounting issue is whether Brion Company would increase an asset for future rail services and in-

crease a liability for payments to the railroad. The alternative is to make no accounting entry except when Brion makes payments to the railroad.

4. Construction Joint Venture: Brion Company and Mission Company will jointly build a plant to manufacture chemicals both need in their own production processes. Each will contribute $5 million to the project, called Chemical. Chemical will borrow another $40 million from a bank, with Brion, only, guaranteeing the debt. Brion and Mission are each to contribute equally to future operating expenses and debt service payments of Chemical, but, in return for its guaranteeing the debt, Brion will have an option to purchase Mission's interest for $20 million four years hence. The accounting issue is whether Brion Company should recognize a liability for the funds borrowed by Chemical. Because of the debt guarantee, debt service payments will ultimately be Brion Company's responsibility. Alternatively, the debt guarantee is a commitment merely to be disclosed in the notes to Brion Company's financial statements.

5. Research and Development Partnership: Brion Company will contribute a laboratory and preliminary findings about a potentially profitable gene-splicing discovery to a partnership, called Venture. Venture will raise funds by selling the remaining interest in the partnership to outside investors for $2 million and borrowing $48 million from a bank with Brion Company guaranteeing the debt. Although Venture will operate under the management of Brion Company, it will be free to sell the results of its further discoveries and development efforts to anyone, including Brion Company. Brion Company is not obligated to purchase any of Venture's output. The accounting issue is whether Brion Company would recognize the liability. (Would it make any difference if Brion Company has either the *option* to purchase or an *obligation* to purchase the results of Venture's work?)

6. Hotel Financing: Brion Company owns and operates a profitable hotel. It could use the hotel as collateral for a conventional mortgage loan. Instead, it considers selling the hotel to a partnership for $50 million cash. The partnership will sell ownership interests to outside investors for $5 million and borrow $45 million from a bank on a conventional mortgage loan, using the hotel as collateral. Brion Company guarantees the debt. The accounting issue is whether Brion Company would record the liability for the guaranteed debt of the partnership.

Consider each of these proposed arrangements (a) from the viewpoint of the auditor who must decide whether the transaction will result in a liability to be recorded or whether footnote disclosure will suffice and (b) from the viewpoint of an investment banker who must assess the financing structure of Brion Company in order to make a competitive bid on a proposed new underwriting of Brion company's common shares.

4.2 *Applying Capital Lease Criteria.* McRobin Corporation manufactures industrial equipment. Model CCX is produced at a cost of $70,000 and is sold for $90,000. On January 1, Year 4, McRobin Corporation agrees to lease a Model CCX machine to MacDonald Corporation for the five-year period beginning on that date. The parties set the annual rental payments at $15,000 per year, payable in advance on January 1 of each year, with the first rental payment due on January 1, Year 4. In addition, MacDonald Corporation must make rental payments equal to 5 percent of its sales; the payments are payable on January 1 of the next year. MacDonald Corporation expects sales of at least $100,000 each year over the five-year period of the lease. At the end of the five-year rental period, the machine reverts to McRobin Corporation, which intends to rent it to another party for the remainder of its expected total eight-year life. McRobin expects the salvage value at the end of five years to be approximately $37,200. However, because salvage values are uncertain, McRobin Corporation requires that MacDonald Corporation guarantee a minimum salvage value of $23,000. That is, if the salvage value is less than $23,000, MacDonald Corporation must pay the difference to McRobin Corporation at the end of five years. The interest rate appropriate for computing the present value of the minimum lease payments is 8 percent. Use the straight-line depreciation method throughout the problem.

a. Should McRobin Corporation and MacDonald Corporation treat this lease as an operating lease or as a capital lease for financial reporting? Show supporting computations for your response.

b. Assume for this part that the lease qualifies as an operating lease for financial reporting. Compute the amount of rent revenue that McRobin Corporation recognizes and the amount of rent expense that MacDonald Corporation recognizes for Year 4. Sales of MacDonald Corporation were $105,000 for the year.

c. Assume for the remainder of this problem that the lease qualifies as a capital lease for financial reporting. Sales of MacDonald Corporation were $105,000 for Year 4. Compute the amount of revenue and expense that McRobin Corporation recognizes from this lease during Year 4. Generally accepted accounting principles require that McRobin Corporation (the lessor) set up a lease receivable equal to the cash selling price (that is, $90,000) at the signing of the lease.

d. Repeat part (c) for MacDonald Corporation.

e. Assume that McRobin Corporation and MacDonald Corporation treat this lease as an operating lease for income tax purposes but as a capital lease for financial reporting. Also assume a 34 percent income tax rate. Compute the amount of deferred taxes that McRobin Corporation and MacDonald Corporation would recognize for Year 4. Indicate whether the deferred taxes provided for timing differences increase or decrease income tax expense for the year.

4.3 *Effect of Capitalizing Operating Leases on Balance Sheet Ratios.* Some retailing companies own their own stores or acquire their premises under capital leases. Other retailing companies acquire the use of store facilities under operating leases, contracting to make future payments. An analyst comparing the capital structure risks of retailing companies may wish to make adjustments to reported financial statement data to put all firms on a comparable basis.

Certain data from the financial statements of J.C. Penney and Sears Roebuck merchandising group appear below (amounts in millions):

	J.C. Penney	Sears
Balance Sheet as of End of Year 3		
Current Liabilities	$2,070	$2,181
Long-Term Debt	1,384	188
Shareholders' Equity	3,228	4,318
Total	$6,682	$6,687
Minimum Payments under Operating Leases		
Year 4	$ 195	$ 212
Year 5	186	181
Year 6	172	138
Year 7	167	110
Year 8	158	89
After Year 8	1,890	540
Total	$2,768	$1,270

a. Compute the present value of operating lease obligations using a 12 percent discount rate for J.C. Penney and Sears at the end of Year 3. Assume that all cash flows occur at the end of each year.

b. Compute each of the following ratios for J.C. Penney and Sears as of the end of Year 3 using the amounts as originally reported in their balance sheets for the year.

$$\text{Debt-Equity Ratio} = \text{Total Liabilities}/(\text{Total Liabilities} + \text{Shareholders' Equity})$$

$$\text{Long-Term Debt Ratio} = \text{Long-Term Debt}/(\text{Long-Term Debt} + \text{Shareholders' Equity})$$

c. Repeat part (**b**) but assume that these firms capitalize operating leases.

d. Comment on the results from parts (**b**)and (**c**).

4.4 *Analyzing Lease Disclosures for Lessee.* Short Island Railroad regularly leases railcars needed in its operations. Information taken from the financial statements and notes for Year 7 relating to these leases appears below:

Balance Sheet	December 31, Year 6	December 31, Year 7
Property Rights under Capital Leases (net of accumulated amortization)	$287,900	$289,712
Capitalized Lease Obligation	$313,344	$341,004

Notes to the Financial Statements

Leases: Minimum lease payments under capital leases as of December 31, Year 6 and Year 7, appear below:

Lease Payments on December 31 of:	December 31, Year 6	December 31, Year 7
Year 7	$ 32,600	—
Year 8	41,900	$ 45,900
Year 9	47,200	52,400
Year 10	48,300	54,700
Year 11	49,100	55,600
After Year 11	241,700	275,300
Total	$460,800	$483,900
Less Discount	(147,456)	(142,896)
Present Value	$313,344	$341,004

Short Island Railroad signed new capital leases on December 31, Year 7, and properly recorded them in the accounts. The average interest rate for all capitalized leases is 7 percent.

   a.   Compute the amount of the following for Year 7:
   (1) Interest expense for Year 7.
   (2) Present value of new leases capitalized during Year 7.
   (3) Depreciation expense for Year 7.

   b.   Assume that Short Island Railroad treated these leases as operating leases for income tax purposes. Using an income tax rate of 34 percent, compute the amount of deferred taxes that the company would recognize for Year 7. Indicate whether the deferred taxes provided for timing differences increase or decrease income tax expense for the year.

4.5 *Financial Statement Effects of Operating versus Capital Leases.* Swift Airlines regularly leases airplanes and ground equipment in its operations. Information taken from its financial statements and notes for Year 8 relating to leases appears below:

Balance Sheet	December 31, Year 7	December 31, Year 8
Property Rights under Capital Leases (net of accumulated amortization)	$400,000	$421,220
Capitalized Lease Obligation	$399,875	$449,531

Notes to the Financial Statements

Leases: Minimum lease payments under *capital leases* as of December 31, Year 7 and Year 8 appear below (assume all cash flows occur at the end of each year):

Lease Payments on December 31 of:	December 31, Year 7	December 31, Year 8
Year 8	$ 75,800	—
Year 9	80,000	$ 86,000
Year 10	85,000	89,000
Year 11	90,000	94,000
Year 12	90,000	98,000
After Year 12	289,200	441,020
Total	$710,000	$808,020
Less Discount	(310,125)	(358,489)
Present Value	$399,875	$449,531

Swift Airlines entered into new capital leases having a present value of $70,000 on December 31, Year 8, and properly recorded these leases in the accounts. These were the only new capital leases recorded for Year 8.

Minimum lease payments under *operating leases* as of December 31, Year 7 and Year 8, appear below:

Lease Payments on December 31 of:	December 31, Year 7	December 31, Year 8
Year 8	$28,900	—
Year 9	32,770	$34,270
Year 10	43,990	45,660
Year 11	41,660	44,370
Year 12	40,220	43,980
After Year 12	246,900	263,980

a. Complete the following analyses relating to capital leases for Year 8:

Property Rights under Capital Leases, December 31, Year 7 ....
New Capital Leases Entered into during Year 8 ....
Amortization of Property Rights for Year 8 ....
Property Rights under Capital Leases, December 31, Year 8 ....
Capitalized Lease Obligation, December 31, Year 7 ....
Increase in Capitalized Lease Obligation for Interest during Year 8 ....
New Capitalized Lease Obligations Entered into during Year 8 ....
Cash Payments under Capital Leases during Year 8 ....
Capitalized Lease Obligation, December 31, Year 8 ....

b. Compute the average interest rate for leases capitalized as of December 31, Year 7.

c. Determine the amount that Swift Airlines would have reported as rent expense for Year 8 if it had treated all capital leases as operating leases.

d. Determine the amount reported as rent expense for Year 8 for all operating leases.

e. Compute the present value of commitments under operating leases on December 31, Year 7 and Year 8, assuming that 12 percent is an appropriate discount rate.

f. Assume that Swift Airlines capitalized all operating leases using the amounts computed in part (e). Complete the following analysis for Year 8:

Capitalized Value of Operating Leases, December 31, Year 7 ....
Increase in Capitalized Value for Interest during Year 8 ....
New Operating Leases Capitalized during Year 8 ....
Cash Payments under Capitalized Operating Leases during Year 8 ....
Capitalized Value of Operating Leases, December 31, Year 8 ....

g. For income tax purposes, Swift Airlines accounts for *all* of its leases as operating leases. Swift is subject to a 34 percent income tax rate and it expects this rate to continue for the foreseeable future. Compute the amount of deferred income taxes that Swift Airlines would recognize for Year 8 relating to its leased assets. Be sure to indicate whether the deferred taxes provided for timing differences increase or decrease income tax expense.

4.6 *Financial Statement Effects of Operating versus Capital Leases.* Delta Airlines leases aircraft used in its operations. Information taken from its financial statements and notes for Year 3 and Year 4 appears below (amounts in thousands):

Balance Sheet	December 31, Year 3	December 31, Year 4
Property Rights under Capital Leases (net of accumulated depreciation)	$122,270	$101,928
Capitalized Lease Obligation	$157,587	$146,785

Notes to the Financial Statements

Leases: Minimum lease payments under *capital leases* as of December 31, Year 3 and Year 4 are (assume all cash flows occur at the end of each year):

Lease Payments on December 31 of:	December 31, Year 3	December 31, Year 4
Year 4	$ 24,436	—
Year 5	24,415	$ 24,415
Year 6	24,722	24,722
Year 7	19,708	19,708
Year 8	20,565	20,565
After Year 8	126,969	126,969
Total	$240,815	$216,379
Less Discount	(83,228)	(69,594)
Present Value	$157,587	$146,785

Minimum lease payments under operating leases as of December 31, Year 3 and Year 4 appear below:

Lease Payments on December 31 of:	December 31, Year 3	December 31, Year 4
Year 4	$ 503,607	—
Year 5	483,890	$ 533,891
Year 6	472,682	533,106
Year 7	467,082	523,391
Year 8	460,086	515,457
After Year 8	6,586,151	7,497,676
Total	$8,973,498	$9,603,521

a. Complete the following analyses relating to capital leases for Year 4:

Property Rights under Capital Leases, December 31, Year 3 ....
New Capital Leases Entered into during Year 4 ....
Amortization of Property Rights for Year 4 ....
Property Rights under Capital Leases, December 31, Year 4 ....

Capitalized Lease Obligation, December 31, Year 3 ....
Increase in Capitalized Lease Obligation for Interest During Year 4 ....
New Capitalized Lease Obligations Entered into during Year 4 ....
Cash Payments under Capital Leases during Year 4 ....
Capitalized Lease Obligation, December 31, Year 4 ....

    b. Compute the average interest rate for leases capitalized as of December 31, Year 4.

    c. Determine the amount that Delta would have reported as rent expense for Year 4 if it had treated all capital leases as operating leases.

    d. Determine the amount reported as rent expense for Year 4 for all operating leases.

    e. Compute the present value of commitments under operating leases on December 31, Year 3 and Year 4, assuming that 10 percent is an appropriate discount rate.

    f. Assume that Delta had capitalized all operating leases using the amounts computed in part *e*. Complete the following analysis for Year 4:

Capitalized Value of Operating Leases, December 31, Year 3 ....
Increase in Capitalized Value for Interest during Year 4 ....
New Operating Leases Capitalized during Year 4 ....
Cash Payments under Capitalized Operating Leases during Year 4 ....
Capitalized Value of Operating Leases, December 31, Year 4.......................

    g. Assume that Delta Airlines treats *all* of its leases as operating leases for tax purposes. The income tax rate is 34 percent and Delta expects this rate to continue into the foreseeable future. Compute the amount of deferred income taxes that Delta Airlines will recognize for Year 4. Indicate whether the deferred taxes that Delta Airlines provides for lease timing differences increase or decrease income tax expense.

4.7 *Analyzing and Interpreting Pension Disclosures.* The notes to the financial statements of Stanadyne Corporation for Year 5 reveal the following:

Pensions

The Company adopted the provisions of FASB *Statement No. 87* on January 1, Year 5. Pension expense was $318,000 in Year 5, $6,000,000 in Year 4, and $6,500,000 in Year 3. The Company's contributions to the pension fund were $8,100,000 in Year 5, $6,000,000 in Year 4, and $6,500,000 in Year 3.

    Significant assumptions used in measuring pension expense and related pension obligations were:

	As of January 1, Year 5	As of December 31, Year 5
Discount Rate	11.00%	10.25%
Increase in Compensation Levels	6.10%	6.10%
Long-Term Rate of Return on Assets	7.50%	7.50%

Pension expense for Year 5 comprises the following (amounts in thousands):

Service Cost	$ 1,863
Interest Cost on Projected Benefit Obligation	7,453
Net Amortization and Deferral	30,008
	$ 39,324
Less Actual Return on Pension Assets	(39,006)
Net Pension Expense	$ 318

The funded status of the plan and the amounts recognized in the balance sheet as of January 1 and December 31, Year 5 appear below (amounts in thousands):

	January 1, Year 5	December 31, Year 5
Accumulated Benefit Obligation (including $52,220 and $79,085 of vested benefits)	$62,526	$ 82,487
Projected Benefit Obligation	$67,758	$ 87,628
Plan Assets at Market Value	95,399	135,755
Plan Assets Greater Than Projected Benefit Obligation	$27,641	$ 48,127
Unrecognized Net Asset on January 1, Year 5 Being Amortized over 15 Years	(27,641)	(25,798)
Unrecognized Net Gain from Past Experience Different from That Assumed	—	(14,547)
Prepaid Pension Asset	—	$ 7,782

a. Complete the following analyses of the pension fund for Year 5:

Pension Fund Assets

Balance, January 1, Year 5	
Earnings on Pension Investments	
Contributions Received from Employer	
Payments to Retired Employees	_____
Balance, December 31, Year 5	_____

Projected Benefit Obligation

Balance, January 1, Year 5	
Interest Cost	
Service Cost	
Increase due to Change in Actuarial Assumptions	
Payments to Retired Employees	_____
Balance, December 31, Year 5	_____

Pension Expense

Interest Cost	
Service Cost	
Actual Return on Pension Investments	
Excess of Actual Return over Expected Return on Pension Investments	
Amortization of Net Pension Asset upon Adoption of *Statement No. 87*	
Amortization of Actuarial Loss	_____
Net Pension Expense	_____

b. Why did pension expense for Year 5 decrease so significantly relative to the amounts for Year 3 and Year 4?

c. Why does a pension asset of $7,782 appear on the December 31, Year 5, balance sheet?

d. Assuming that Stanadyne made its pension fund contribution on December 31, Year 5, compute the actual rate of return earned on pension fund investments during Year 5. What factors should the analyst consider in evaluating the performance of the pension fund manager for Year 5?

e. What factor appears to explain the significant increase in the projected benefit obligation during Year 5 arising from changes in actuarial assumptions?

4.8 *Analyzing and Interpreting Pension Disclosures.* Texas Instruments adopted the provisions of FASB *Statement No. 87* for its pension plan on January 1, Year 6. The company has a defined benefit plan covering all of its employees, with pension benefits based on years of service and the highest five years of compensation during each employee's working life. The company funds the minimum amount required by ERISA each year; that minimum is zero for an overfunded plan. Plan assets consist primarily of common stock, U.S. government obligations, commercial paper, and real estate.

Pension expense for Year 6 includes the following components (amounts in millions):

Service Cost		$ 37.3
Interest Cost on Projected Benefit Obligation		46.1
Actual Return on Plan Assets	$(188.2)	
Deferred Portion of Above	124.6	(63.6)
Amortization of Net Asset on January 1, Year 6		(19.3)
Pension Expense		$ .5

The funded status of the plan on December 31, Year 6 appears below (amounts in millions):

Actuarial Present Value of		
Vested Benefit Obligation	$(216.5)	
Accumulated Benefit Obligation	(261.9)	
Projected Benefit Obligation		$ (531.1)
Plan Assets at Market Value		778.8
Excess of Assets over Projected Benefit Obligation		$ 247.7
Unrecognized Net Asset on January 1, Year 6		(288.2)
Unrecognized Actuarial Loss (Net)		40.0
Pension Liability on Balance Sheet on December 31, Year 6		$ (.5)

Assumptions underlying the pension plan for Year 6 were as follows:

	January 1, Year 6	December 31, Year 6
Return on Assets	9.0%	9.0%
Discount Rate for Projected Benefit Obligation	9.5%	9.0%
Long-Term Salary Progression	8.5%	8.5%

The effect of the adoption of *Statement No. 87* was a reduction in pension expense of $52.9 million in Year 6. Pension expense was $56.9 million in Year 5 and

$51.0 million in Year 4. Pension payments to retired employees totaled $116.1 million in Year 6.

a. Prepare an analysis of changes in pension fund assets for Year 6. (Note: You must work backwards from the amount of pension fund assets at the end of Year 6.)

b. Prepare an analysis of changes in the projected benefit obligation for Year 6.

c. Why does a pension liability of $.5 million appear on the December 31, Year 6, balance sheet if Texas Instruments has an overfunded pension plan?

d. The excess of plan assets over the projected benefit obligation decreased between the beginning and end of Year 6, yet the actual return on pension fund investments exceeded expectations. Explain this apparent paradox.

4.9 *Analyzing and Interpreting Pension Disclosures.* The notes to the financial statements of Exxon Corporation for Year 6 revealed the following:

Pensions

Exxon adopted the provision of FASB *Statement No. 87* for the year ending December 31, Year 6. Pension expense was $520 million, $328 million, and $(93) million for Year 4, Year 5, and Year 6, respectively.

Pension expense for Year 6 comprises the following (amounts in millions):

Benefits Earned during the Year		$ 115
Interest Accrued on Benefits Earned in Prior Years		328
Return on Assets—Actual	$(984)	
—Less Deferred Gain	543	(441)
Amortization of Net Gain on January 1, Year 6		(95)
Net Negative Pension Expense for the Year		$ (93)

The pension obligation comprises the following:

	January 1, Year 6	December 31, Year 6
Accumulated Benefit Obligation		
Vested	$2,773	$2,949
Nonvested	136	179
Total	$2,909	$3,128
Additional Amounts Relating to Future		
Salary Increases	719	899
Projected Benefit Obligation	$3,628	$4,027
Assets Available for Benefits	4,926	5,608
Assets in Excess of Projected Benefit Obligation	$1,298	$1,581
Consisting of		
Unrecognized Net Asset upon Adoption of		
Statement No. 87	1,298	1,203
Unrecognized Net Gain from Favorable		
Actuarial Experience Since Adoption of		
Statement No. 87	—	378

a. Compute the actual rate of return earned on pension fund investments during Year 6.

b. Compute the expected rate of return on pension fund investments for Year 6.

c. Compute the average interest rate used in computing the projected benefit obligation during Year 6.

d. Calculate the number of years over which Exxon is amortizing the unrecognized net asset at date of initial adoption of *Statement No. 87*.

e. Determine the amounts of the component elements that make up the $378 million unrecognized net gain from favorable actuarial experience to the maximum extent permitted by the disclosures.

f. The accumulated benefit obligation increased 7.53 percent during Year 6 while the projected benefit obligation increased 11 percent. What is the likely explanation for this difference in the rates of increase?

4.10 *Analyzing and Interpreting Pension Disclosures.* Whirlpool Corporation adopted the provisions of *Statement No. 87* on January 1, Year 6. Assumptions used in measuring pension expense for Year 6 and Year 7 include 8.5 percent for both the discount rate and the expected rate of return on plan assets and 5 percent to 7 percent for compensation level increases.

Pension expense for Year 6 and Year 7 includes the following components (amounts in millions):

	Year 6	Year 7
Service Cost-Benefits Earned during the Year	$ 17.5	$ 19.1
Interest Cost on Projected Benefit Obligation	44.1	48.6
Actual Return on Plan Assets	(94.7)	(29.3)
Net Amortization and Deferral	39.7	(27.4)
Net Pension Expense	$ 6.6	$ 11.0

The funded status of the pension plan appears below (amounts in millions):

	December 31	
	Year 6	Year 7
Projected Benefit Obligation	$556.2	$576.0
Less Plan Assets at Market Value	663.8	692.5
Plan Assets in Excess of Projected Benefit Obligation	$107.6	$116.5
Unrecognized Net Asset on Adoption of *Statement No. 87*	(62.2)	(58.0)
Unrecognized Net Experience Gain	(22.9)	(59.9)
Unrecognized Prior Service Cost	—	13.8
Net Pension Assets Included in Prepaid Expenses	$ 22.5	$ 12.4

a. Whirlpool reported no pension asset or pension liability on its balance sheet on January 1, Year 6, when it adopted the provisions of *Statement No. 87*. Compute the amount contributed by Whirlpool to its pension fund during Year 6 and Year 7. (Hint: To compute these amounts, you must use the amounts for pension expense each year and the net pension asset included on the balance sheet at the end of each year.)

b. Prepare an analysis of changes in pension fund assets for each of the Years 6 and 7. Pension fund assets totaled $585.2 million on January 1, Year 6.

c. Prepare an analysis of changes in the projected benefit obligation for each of the Years 6 and 7.

d. Why did the "net amortization" component of pension expense change from a positive amount in Year 6 to a negative amount in Year 7?

4.11 *Analyzing and Interpreting Pension Disclosures.* Ford Motor Company reports the following information relating to its U.S. pension plans for Year 3 and Year 4 (amounts in millions):

Components of Pension Expense	Year 3	Year 4
Current Service	$ 295.7	$ 326.0
Interest on Projected Benefit Obligation	1,195.2	1,283.9
Actual Return on Pension Assets	(3,308.5)	(258.4)
Other[a]	2,224.0	(1,000.6)
Net Pension Expense	$ 406.4	$ 350.9

[a]Includes amortization of the initial difference between assets and obligations at adoption of SFAS No. 87, amortization of plan amendments after adoption and amortization or deferral of gains and losses resulting from actual experience in the current period and changes in assumptions for future periods.

Exhibit 4.6 shows the year-end status on U.S. pension plans.

a. Complete the following analyses of the combined pension funds for Year 4:

Pension Fund Assets

Balance, January 1, Year 4	
Earnings on Pension Investments	
Contributions Received from Employer	400.3
Payments to Retired Employees (Plug)	
Balance, December 31, Year 4	

Projected Benefit Obligation

Balance, January 1, Year 4	
Interest Cost	
Service Cost	
Increase Due to Change in Actuarial Assumptions (Plug)	
Payments to Retired Employees (from above)	
Balance, December 31, Year 4	

b. Compute the amount of return expected for Year 4 on pension fund assets. How well did the pension fund perform during Year 4 relative to this expectation?

c. What factors might explain the increase in the projected benefit obligation related to changes in actuarial assumptions?

d. Compute the amount of the excess of the accumulated benefit obligation over plan assets at the end of Year 3 and Year 4 for plans where this is a

Exhibit 4.6
Pension Information for Ford Motor Company (in millions)

	Year 3			Year 4		
	Assets Exceed Accum. Benefits	Accum. Benefits Exceed Assets	Combined	Assets Exceed Accum. Benefits	Accum. Benefits Exceed Assets	Combined
Actuarial present value of						
Vested Benefits	$ 6,436.4	$6,196.4	$12,632.8	$ 6,135.4	$ 6,935.1	$13,070.5
Accumulated Benefits	7,081.4	7,551.1	14,632.5	6,751.6	8,401.4	15,153.0
Projected Benefits	8,009.0	7,612.7	15,621.7	7,490.8	8,494.8	15,985.6
Plan Assets at Fair Value	11,037.6	7,263.6	18,301.2	10,029.0	7,080.2	17,109.2
Projected Benefits less than/(in excess of) Plan Assets[a]	$ 3,028.6	$ (349.1)	$ 2,679.5	$ 2,538.2	$(1,414.6)	$ 1,123.6
Unamortized (Net Asset)/Net Transition Obligation[a]	(1,296.9)	847.5	(449.4)	(1,052.3)	777.9	(274.4)
Unamortized Prior Service Cost[b]	124.3	636.2	760.5	384.2	1,591.7	1,975.9
Unamortized Net (Gains)[c]	(1,258.7)	(705.7)	(1,964.4)	(1,049.5)	(755.4)	(1,804.9)
Adjustment Required to Recognize Minimum Liability[d]	—	(716.4)	(716.4)	—	(1,442.6)	(1,442.6)
Prepaid Pension Cost/(Liability) Recognized in the Balance Sheet	$ 597.3	$ (287.5)	$ 309.8	$ 820.6	$(1,243.0)	$ (422.4)
Significant Assumptions						
Discount Rate	8.3%				9.0%	
Rate of Increase in Compensation	6.0%				6.0%	
Long-Term Rate of Return on Assets	8.0%				9.0%	

[a]The balance of the initial difference between assets and obligation deferred for recognition over a 15-year period.
[b]The prior service effect of plan amendments deferred for recognition over remaining service.
[c]The deferred gain or loss resulting from investments, other experience and changes in assumptions.
[d]An adjustment to reflect the unfunded accumulated benefit obligation in the balance sheet for plans whose benefits exceed the assets—other assets include a corresponding intangible asset.

positive amount. Do these amounts equal the minimum liability reported on the balance sheet each year? If not, why not?

e. Assess the changes in the financial condition of Ford's pension plans during Year 4.

4.12 *Interpreting Income Tax Disclosures.* The income tax note of Westinghouse Electric Corporation for Year 3 and Year 4 reveals the following (amounts in millions):

Income Tax Expense	Year 4	Year 3
Current	$100.0	$ 70.3
Deferred	(95.9)	24.3
Total	$ 4.1	$ 94.6

Income Taxes Deferred	Year 4	Year 3
Depreciation	$ 46.3	$ 28.6
Product Warranty	25.4	(4.6)
Pensions	(49.7)	32.5
Leases	22.7	23.3
Other	(140.6)	(55.5)
Total	$ (95.9)	$ 24.3

Effective Tax Rate Reconciliation		
Federal Statutory Tax Rate	34.0%	34.0%
Foreign Rate Differences	(11.5)	.8
Research Tax Credits	(10.7)	(10.4)
Other	2.3	(1.7)
Effective Tax Rate	14.1%	22.7%

a. What is the likely relation between income before taxes (excluding permanent differences) and taxable income for Year 3? for Year 4?

b. Compute the amount of income before taxes for Year 3 and for Year 4. Note that GAAP defines the effective tax rate as income tax expense divided by income before income taxes.

c. What is the likely explanation for the behavior of the deferred tax provision over the two-year period for each of the following:

(1) Depreciation.

(2) Product warranty (recognized as an expense in the year Westinghouse sells its products for financial reporting but when it makes warranty expenditures for tax reporting).

(3) Pensions.

(4) Leases (Westinghouse is the lessor).

4.13 *Interpreting Income Tax Disclosures.* Income before income taxes of Cypres Corporation for Year 5 appears below:

Revenues	
Sales	$5,000
Rent	300
Interest on Municipal Bond	400
Total Revenues	$5,700

Expenses

Cost of Goods Sold (excluding depreciation)	$4,000
Selling and Administrative (excluding depreciation)	500
Depreciation	250
Goodwill Amortization	100
Total Expenses	$4,850
Income before Income Taxes	$ 850

For income tax purposes, interest on municipal bonds is not taxable and goodwill amortization is not deductible. Rent revenue is $400 and depreciation expense is $500, causing timing differences between financial reporting and taxable income. The income tax rate is 30 percent for Year 5. Cypres Corporation expects that rate to remain the same in future years.

    a. Compute the amount of income tax expense for Year 5. Indicate the portion that is currently payable and the portion that is deferred.

    b. Determine the components of deferred tax expense for Year 5 (that is, the individual items that sum to deferred tax expense).

    c. Prepare a reconciliation between income taxes at the statutory tax rate on income before taxes and income tax expense.

4.14 *Interpreting Income Tax Disclosures*. The income tax note to the financial statements of Weil Corporation reveals the following:

	Year 8	Year 7	Year 6
Income before Income Taxes	$(60)	$50	$120
Components of Income Tax Expense			
Current	$ 11.6	$ —	$ 25.8
Deferred	(34.0)	17.0	10.2
Total Expense	$(22.4)	$17.0	$ 36.0
Components of Deferred Tax Expense			
Depreciation	$(38.0)	$16.0	$ 12.2
Warranties	4.0	1.0	(2.0)
Total Deferred Expense	$(34.0)	$17.0	$ 10.2
Income Tax Reconciliation			
Taxes at 34% Statutory Rate	$(20.4)	$17.0	$ 40.8
Research and Energy Credits	(2.0)	—	(4.8)
Income Tax Expense	$(22.4)	$17.0	$ 36.0
Effective Tax Rate	(37.3%)	34.0%	30.0%

    a. What is the relation between income (loss) before taxes for financial reporting and taxable income (loss) for each of the three years?

    b. Why are there no taxes payable for Year 7 despite a positive income before income taxes for financial reporting?

    c. Why are there taxes payable for Year 8 despite a net loss before taxes for financial reporting?

    d. What explains the behavior of the components of deferred tax expense over the three years?

4.15 *Interpreting Income Tax Disclosures*. The income tax note to the financial statements of Egan Corporation for Year 5, Year 6, and Year 7 is shown below

	Year 5	Year 6	Year 7
Components of Income Tax Expense			
Current	$ —	$ 117	$ 772
Deferred	(787)	471	289
	$ (787)	$ 588	$ 1,061
Components of Deferred Taxes			
Depreciation	$ (450)	$ 210	$ 348
Warranties	40	(25)	(40)
Installment Sales	50	40	36
Rental Fees	(140)	(41)	(55)
Net Operating Loss	(287)	287	—
	$ (787)	$ 471	$ 289
Tax Reconciliation			
Pretax Book Income	$ (1,800)	$ 1,200	$ 3,000
Taxes at Statutory Rates, .46, .46, .34	$ (828)	$ 552	$ 1,020
Goodwill Amortization	41	46	41
Investment Credit	—	(10)	
Income Tax Expense	$ (787)	$ 588	$ 1,061
Effective Tax Rate	(43.7%)	49.0%	35.4%

a. What is the likely explanation for the behavior of deferred taxes relating to depreciation timing differences between Year 5 and Year 6?

b. What is the likely explanation for the behavior of deferred taxes relating to warranty timing differences between Year 5 and Year 6?

c. Explain the rationale for the item Net Operating Loss in the deferred tax components disclosure. Be sure to indicate consideration of the direction of the adjustment (decreases deferred tax expense in Year 5 and increases it in Year 6).

4.16 *Interpreting Income Tax Disclosures.* The notes to the financial statements of Alcoa reveal the following (amounts in millions):

Income Taxes

The components of income before U.S. and foreign taxes on income were:

	Year 5	Year 6
U.S.	$ 626.1	$ (177.2)
Foreign	1,539.7	1,224.4
Total	$2,165.8	$1,047.2

Income tax expense consists of the following:

		Year 5	Year 6
U.S. Taxes:	Current	$ 212.4	$ 98.7
	Deferred	97.2	(122.2)
Foreign Taxes:	Current	446.0	406.3
	Deferred	42.8	11.0
Total		$ 798.4	$ 393.8

The components of deferred income tax expense appear below:

	Year 5	Year 6
Depreciation	$ 72.5	$ 42.6
Employee Benefits	15.0	(10.7)
Loss Provisions Not Currently Deductible	.3	(121.0)
Deferred Income	53.7	(18.5)
Other	(1.5)	(3.6)
Total	$140.0	$(111.2)

The provisions for income taxes represent effective tax rates of 36.9 percent in Year 5 and 37.6 percent in Year 6. The difference between these rates and the U.S. statutory rate of 34 percent results from:

	Year 5	Year 6
Investment Credits	(.4)	(.6)
Taxes on Foreign Income	3.3	4.6
Other	─	(.4)
Total Difference from U.S. Statutory Tax Rate	2.9%	3.6%

a. Was income before taxes for financial reporting greater or less than taxable income for Year 5? for Year 6?

b. Alcoa generated a pretax loss for financial reporting in the United States during Year 6 yet paid the U.S. government $98.7 million in income taxes. Explain this apparent paradox.

c. What is the likely explanation for the behavior of deferred taxes relating to employee benefit timing differences between Year 5 and Year 6?

d. What is the likely explanation for the behavior of deferred taxes relative to deferred income timing differences between Year 5 and Year 6?

4.17 *Interpreting Income Tax Disclosures.* The income tax note for Bethlehem Steel Corporation reveals the following for Year 8, Year 9, and Year 10 (amounts in millions):

The provision for income taxes consisted of:

	Year 10	Year 9	Year 8
Federal—Current	$ 2.0	$ 5.0	$ 5.0
State and Foreign—Current	4.0	3.0	2.0
Total Current	6.0	8.0	7.0
Federal—Deferred	─	4.0	2.0
Total Provision	$ 6.0	$12.0	$ 9.0

The provision for income tax expense differs from the amount computed by applying the Federal statutory rate to pretax income (loss). The computed amounts and the items comprising the total differences are as follows (amounts in millions):

	Year 10	Year 9	Year 8
Pretax Income (loss)			
U.S.	$(474.2)	$240.2	$381.1
Foreign	16.7	17.5	9.5
Total	$(457.5)	$257.7	$390.6
Computed Amounts	$(155.6)	$ 87.6	$132.8
Loss in Excess of Allowable Carrybacks	155.6	—	—
Benefit from Financial Net Operating Loss Carryforward	—	(72.9)	(103.1)
Percentage Depletion	—	(7.6)	(9.2)
Dividend Received Deduction	—	(7.0)	(6.9)
Benefit from Interest Payment on Prior Years' Federal Income Tax Deficiencies	—	—	(14.4)
Alternative Minimum Tax	2.0	9.0	7.0
State and Foreign Taxes	4.0	3.0	2.0
Other differences — Net	—	(.1)	.8
Total Provision	$ 6.0	$ 12.0	$ 9.0

a. Bethlehem Steel Corporation generated positive amounts of income before taxes in Year 8 and Year 9 but paid only minor amounts of income taxes to governmental bodies in those years. What is the apparent explanation?

b. Bethlehem Steel Corporation generated a negative amount of income before taxes during Year 9. Why doesn't the income statement report a tax savings from this loss equal to the tax rate times the loss?

Generally Accepted Accounting Principles: Intercorporate Entities

5

This chapter continues the discussion of generally accepted accounting principles underlying corporate annual reports. As was the case in Chapters 3 and 4, the objective is to develop a sufficient understanding of the effects of alternative accounting methods so that the analyst can analyze and meaningfully interpret the financial statements. The focus, as before, is on GAAP in the United States, with significant differences from other countries noted. This chapter considers:

1. Corporate acquisitions.

2. Investments in securities.

3. Foreign currency translation.

4. Segment reporting.

Corporate Acquisitions

Corporate acquisitions occur when one corporation acquires all, or substantially all, of another corporation's common stock in a single transaction. GAAP permits two methods of accounting for corporate acquisitions, depending on the structure of the acquisition: the purchase method and the pooling of interests method.[1]

Exhibit 5.1 shows financial statement information for Company P and Company S, which we will use to illustrate these two accounting methods. Company P acquires 100 percent of the outstanding common stock of Company S. Management estimates that the combination will save $50,000 a year in operating expenses before income taxes. Columns (1) and (2) of Exhibit 5.1 show abbreviated

---

[1] Accounting Principles Board, *Accounting Principles Board Opinion No. 16*, "Business Combinations," (1970).

single-company financial statements for each company prior to the combination. Column (3) shows the market values of the assets, liabilities, and shareholders' equity of Company S. Company S has 22,000 shares of common stock outstanding that sell for $84 per share in the market. The market value of Company S's shareholders' equity is therefore $1,848,000 (= 22,000 × $84). The market value ($1,848,000) exceeds the book value ($450,000) of shareholders' equity by $1,398,000. There are three reasons for this difference:

1. Long-term depreciable assets have a market value of $850,000 but a book value of only $450,000. The lower book value of depreciable assets results from accounting's use of historical cost valuations for assets. Company S initially recorded its depreciable assets at acquisition cost. Over time, Company S recognized a portion of this acquisition cost as depreciation expense. GAAP does not permit the firm to recognize increases in the market values of these assets. The market value of Company S, as measured by the market value of its common stock, reflects the economic values, not book values, of assets.

2. Deferred income taxes of $136,000 arise because the firm cannot deduct the $400,000 excess of the market value over the book value of depreciable assets as depreciation expense for income tax purposes in future years ($400,000 × .34 = $136,000). This $136,000 amount represents the extra income taxes that the firm will pay in future years because taxable income will exceed book income before income taxes. Stated another way, the $136,000 represents the loss in future tax benefits because the company cannot base depreciation on the $850,000 market value of depreciable assets. We might show the $136,000 as a reduction in the market value of depreciable assets ($850,000 − $136,000 = $714,000) on the premise that the market value of these assets *to P* is only $714,000, not $850,000. As discussed later, GAAP includes the $136,000 in the Deferred Income Tax Liability account.

3. Goodwill of $1,134,000 exists. The amount of goodwill equals the difference between the acquisition cost ($1,848,000) and the market value of identifiable assets and liabilities ($450,000 + $850,000 − $450,000 − $136,000 = $714,000), or $1,134,000. Goodwill includes intangible attributes that a firm cannot separately identify (for example, well-trained labor force, reputation for high-quality products, superior managerial skills), as well as any merger premium that the acquiror had to pay to consummate the corporate acquisition. Because goodwill amortization is never deductible for income tax purposes, no deferred income taxes on goodwill arise.

Company P, the acquiring company, has 100,000 shares of common stock outstanding, which sell for $42 each in the market.

Purchase Method

Under the purchase method, the acquiror records the assets and liabilities of the acquired company at the amount of cash or market value of other consideration given in the exchange. The purchase method therefore follows the principles of ac-

Exhibit 5.1
Consolidated Statements Comparing Purchase and Pooling of Interests Methods

| | Historical Cost | | S Shown at Current Market Values (3) | Companies P and S Consolidated at Date of Acquisition | |
	P (1)	S (2)		Purchase (4)	Pooling of Interests (5)
Balance Sheets					
Assets					
Current Assets	$1,500,000	$ 450,000	$ 450,000	$1,950,000	$1,950,000
Depreciable Assets less Accum. Depreciation	1,700,000	450,000	850,000	2,550,000	2,150,000
Goodwill	—		1,134,000	1,134,000	
Total Assets	$3,200,000	$ 900,000	$2,434,000	$5,634,000	$4,100,000
Equities					
Liabilities	$1,300,000	$ 450,000	$ 450,000	$1,750,000	$1,750,000
Deferred Income Taxes	—		136,000	136,000	—
Shareholders' Equity	1,900,000	450,000	1,848,000	3,748,000	2,350,000
Total Equities	$3,200,000	$ 900,000	$2,434,000	$5,634,000	$4,100,000
Income Statements					
Precombination Income before Income Taxes From Combination	$ 300,000	$ 160,000		$ 460,000	$ 460,000
Cost Savings				50,000	50,000
Extra Depreciation Expense				(80,000)	
Base for Income Tax Expense	$ 300,000	$ 160,000		$ 430,000	$ 510,000
Income Tax Expense	(102,000)	(54,400)		(146,200)	(173,400)
Goodwill Amortization				(28,350)	—
Net Income	$ 198,000	$ 105,600		$ 255,450	$ 336,600
Number of Common Shares Outstanding	100,000	22,000		144,000	144,000
Earnings per Common Share	$ 1.98	$ 4.80		$ 1.77	$ 2.34

quisition cost accounting (that is, the acquiring company records assets and liabilities at the price it pays for them). To illustrate, assume that P issues (sells) 44,000 additional common shares on the market for $42 each, or $1,848,000 in total, and uses the proceeds to purchase 100 percent of the outstanding common shares of S. When cash is the only consideration used in a corporate acquisition, GAAP requires firms to use the purchase method (discussed more fully below). Column (4) of Exhibit 5.1 shows the combined, or consolidated, balance sheet of P and S on the date of the combination under the purchase method. The accountant combines the book values of P's assets and equities with the market values of S's assets and equities in applying the purchase method.

The lower panel of Exhibit 5.1 shows the effect of using the purchase method for the acquisition on income statements of subsequent years. The consolidated income statement starts with the combined pretax incomes of P and S assuming no acquisition had occurred. We add the $50,000 of cost savings resulting from more efficient operations after the combination. We subtract the additional depreciation arising from the asset revaluation. The additional depreciation expense of $80,000 reflects a five-year life and use of the straight-line depreciation method [$80,000 = .20($850,000 − $450,000)]. The $430,000 of book income before taxes and before amortization of goodwill is the basis for income tax *expense* of $146,200. Taxable income of $510,000 (= $460,000 + $50,000) is the basis for income tax *payable* of $173,400. The combined companies report the difference between income tax expense of $146,200 and income tax payable of $173,400, or $27,200, as a reduction in Deferred Income Taxes established at the date of acquisition. This $27,200 amount equals the income tax rate of 34 percent times the extra depreciation expense of $80,000. Goodwill amortization of $28,350 assumes straight-line amortization over 40 years ($28,350 = $1,134,000/40).

Pooling of Interests Method

The pooling of interests method accounts for a corporate acquisition as the uniting of ownership interests of two companies by an exchange of common stock. The pooling of interests method views the exchange of common shares as a change in *form*, not in *substance*; that is, the shareholders of the predecessor companies become shareholders in the new combined enterprise. Each of the predecessor companies continues its operations as before. Because no change occurs in either the ownership interests or the nature of the activities of the enterprises involved, no new basis of accountability arises. The accountant simply adds the book values of the assets and liabilities of both companies when accounting for a "corporate acquisition" as a pooling of interests. Unlike the purchase method, the consolidated balance sheet does not reflect the market values of the acquired company's assets and liabilities on the date of acquisition.

To illustrate the pooling of interests method, assume that P issues the 44,000 shares of its common stock directly to the owners of S in return for their shares. Previous shareholders of P and S now own the outstanding shares of P and S combined. The consolidated balance sheet in column (5) of Exhibit 5.1 is the sum of the separate company amounts in columns (1) and (2). The pooling of interests method requires no revaluations of assets, nor does it permit the recognition of goodwill.

The consolidated income statement is likewise the sum of the amounts for the separate companies (except for recognizing the projected cost savings). Because the balance sheet does not reflect asset revaluations and goodwill under the pooling of interests method, the accountant records no additional depreciation or amortization. For this reason, income under the pooling of interests method is higher than under the purchase method. Furthermore, assets and shareholders' equities are less under the pooling of interests method than under the purchase method. Rates of return on assets and on shareholders' equity (discussed in Chapters 7 and 8) will likely exceed those under the purchase method.

Criteria for Pooling of Interests

The concept of a pooling of interests envisions two independent companies agreeing to combine their shareholder groups and their operations and continuing to operate in a new combined form. It does not view the transaction as one company buying out the other.

To qualify for the pooling of interests method, the transaction must meet twelve criteria, set out in Exhibit 5.2. Unless the transaction satisfies all twelve criteria, the combining firms cannot use the pooling method. On the other hand, if the transaction satisfies all criteria, the combining firms must use the pooling method.

The first two criteria attempt to operationalize the notion that the combining companies acted independently in their decision to combine. The next seven criteria attempt to ensure that the shareholders of the predecessor companies become common equity holders in the new combined enterprise. GAAP includes several of these criteria to circumvent abuses of the pooling method. The aim of the last three criteria is to ensure continuity of the shareholder groups and of operations after the combination.

Managing Future Earnings

Critics of the pooling of interests method argue that it not only keeps reported expenses from increasing after the merger but may also allow the management of the pooled companies to manage the reported earnings in an arbitrary way. Suppose, as has happened, that Company P merges with an old, established firm, Company F, which has produced commercial films. Company F has amortized these films, made in the 1940s and 1950s, so that by the 1990s their book value is close to zero. But the market value of the films is much larger than zero, because television stations and cable networks find that old movies please their audiences. If Company P acquires Company F and uses the purchase method, the old films appear on the consolidated balance sheet at their current market values. If Company P merges with Company F and uses the pooling of interests method, the films appear on the consolidated balance sheet at their near-zero book values. Then, when Company P wants to boost reported earnings for the year, it can sell some old

Exhibit 5.2
Criteria for Pooling of Interests Method

Prior to the Combination

1. Each of the combining companies is autonomous and has not been a subsidiary or division of another corporation within two years before initiation of the plan to combine.

2. Each of the combining companies is independent of the other combining companies.

At the Time of the Combination

3. The combination occurs in a single transaction or in accordance with a specific plan that the combining entities complete within one year.

4. A corporation issues only common stock with rights identical to the majority of its outstanding voting stock in exchange for substantially all (at least 90 percent) of the voting stock of another company.

5. None of the combining companies change the equity interest of the voting common stock in contemplation of the combination either within two years before initiating the plan of combination or between the initiation and consummation dates; changes in contemplation of the combination may include distributions to shareholders and additional issuances, exchanges, and retirements of securities.

6. Each of the combining companies acquires shares of voting common stock only for purposes other than business combinations, and no company reacquires more than a normal number of shares between the initiation and consummation dates.

7. The ratio of the interest of an individual common shareholder to that of other common shareholders in a combining company remains the same as a result of the exchange of stock in the combination.

8. Shareholders can exercise the voting rights to which the common stock in the combined corporation entitle them; the combined company can neither deprive nor restrict the shareholders from exercising those rights.

9. The combining entities resolve all issues at the consummation date of the plan; no provisions of the plan relating to the issue of securities or other consideration are pending.

Subsequent to the Combination

10. The combined corporation does not agree directly or indirectly to retire or reacquire all or part of the common stock issued in the combination.

11. The combined corporation does not make special financial arrangements for the benefit of the former shareholders of a combining company, such as guaranteeing loans secured by stock issued in the combination, which in effect negate the exchange of equity securities.

12. The combined corporation does not intend or plan to dispose of a significant part of the assets of the combining companies within two years after the combination other than disposals in the ordinary course of business of the formerly separate companies and to eliminate duplicate facilities or excess capacity.

Source: Accounting Principles Board, *Accounting Principles Board Opinion No. 16*, "Business Combinations" (1970), para. 45–49.

movies to a television or cable network and report a large gain. Actually, of course, the owners of Company F enjoyed this gain when they "sold" to Company P for current asset values, not the obsolete book values.

Those who defend pooling of interests accounting argue that the management of the pooled enterprise has no more opportunity to manage earnings than did the management of Company F before the pooling. Management of Company F can sell old movies any time it chooses and report handsome gains. The use of the historical cost basis of accounting creates the opportunities for managing earnings. Defenders of pooling argue that there is no reason to penalize the management of a merged company relative to the management of an established company with many undervalued assets on its books. Opponents of pooling reply that it was the management of Company F that earned the holding gains, whereas it is the management of Company P that can report them as realized gains under pooling.

Proponents of the pooling of interests method point out that the purchase method also provides opportunities for managing future earnings. Under the purchase method, the combining companies allocate the aggregate purchase price to identifiable assets and liabilities based on their market values. The market values of many assets—particularly depreciable assets, patents, copyrights, and similar items—are difficult to measure objectively because of the absence of well-organized, used asset markets. Thus, the combining companies can allocate relatively low amounts to assets that the firm will write off quickly as expenses (such as machinery) and relatively large amounts to assets that it will write off over longer periods (such as buildings) or not at all (such as land). The combining companies must use appraisals or other independent evidence of market values to validate the purchase price allocation, but there is considerable latitude in selecting appraisers!

One common practice in applying the purchase method is the establishment of *acquisition reserves*. At the time one company acquires another company, it may not know fully the potential losses inherent in the acquired assets or the potential liabilities of the acquired company. The acquiring company will allocate a portion of the purchase price to various types of acquisition reserves (for example, estimated losses on long-term contracts, estimated liabilities for unsettled lawsuits). An acquiring company has up to one year after the date of acquisition to revalue these acquisition reserves as new information becomes available. After that, the acquisition reserve amounts remain in the accounts and absorb losses as they occur. That is, the firm charges actual losses against the acquisition reserves instead of against income for the period of the loss.

To illustrate, assume that at the date of acquisition there is unsettled litigation involving an acquired company. The acquiring company, based on the information it has available, estimates that a loss of $3 million will ultimately result. It allocates $3 million to an acquisition reserve. (It would presumably pay less for this company because of this potential liability.) Assume that settlement of the lawsuit occurs three years after the date of the acquisition for $2 million. The accountant charges the $2 million loss against the $3 million reserve instead of against net income for the year. Furthermore, the accountant eliminates the $1 million remaining in the acquisition reserve, increasing net income by that amount in the year of the settlement.

When used properly, acquisition reserves are an accounting mechanism to help ensure that the assets and liabilities of an acquired company reflect market values. However, given the estimates required in establishing such reserves, management has some latitude in managing earnings under the purchase method.

Corporate Acquisitions and Income Taxes

Most corporate acquisitions involve a transaction between the acquiring corporation and the *shareholders* of the acquired corporation. Although the board of directors and management of the acquired company may closely monitor the discussions and negotiations, the acquisition usually takes place with the acquiring corporation giving some type of consideration to the shareholders of the acquired corporation in exchange for their stock. From a legal standpoint, the acquired corporation remains a legally separate entity that has simply had a change in the makeup of its shareholder group.

The income tax treatment of corporate acquisitions follows these legal-entity notions. In most acquisitions, the acquired company does not restate its assets and liabilities to reflect the amount that the acquired corporation paid for the shares of common stock. Instead, the tax basis of assets and liabilities of the acquired company before the acquisition carries over after the acquisition.[2] In this sense, the tax treatment of a corporate acquisition is analogous in concept to a pooling of interests. Thus, even if the combining entities use the purchase method for financial reporting, they treat the transaction like a pooling of interests for tax purposes (actually called a nontaxable reorganization).

Interpreting Corporate Disclosures on Acquisitions

For the following discussion refer to Pepsi's Note 2 on acquisitions and investments in affiliates in Appendix B. Pepsi made acquisitions totaling $736 million in Year 8, $3.4 billion in Year 7, and $1.8 billion in Year 6. It used a combination of cash, notes payable, and Pepsi common stock as consideration. Because Pepsi common stock represents a minor proportion of the total consideration, Pepsi used the purchase method of accounting for these acquisitions. These acquisitions involved franchised bottling operations and consumer foods companies. Pepsi allocated a large portion of the purchase prices to intangible assets (franchise rights and goodwill). Note that goodwill and other intangibles comprise 34 percent (= $5,845.2/$17,143.4) of total assets at the end of Year 8, largely resulting from these

---

[2] An acquiring company can elect to liquidate the acquired company under Section 338 of the Internal Revenue Code and thereby record assets and liabilities at their market values for tax purposes. However, the acquired company must pay taxes immediately on differences between these market values and the tax basis of assets and liabilities.

acquisitions. Coke, in contrast, made virtually no acquisitions during this period. Its goodwill and other intangibles comprise three percent (= $275,126/$9,278,187) of total assets. A large portion of the difference in the total assets of Pepsi and Coke represents a difference in the amount of recorded intangibles. These companies must amortize the intangibles, thereby reducing net income. The firms cannot deduct the portion representing amortization of goodwill for tax purposes. Thus, Pepsi shows an increase in its effective tax rate each year (see Pepsi's Note 10 on income tax) for "nondeductible amortization of goodwill and other intangibles."

The analyst should examine carefully the financial statements of firms engaging in a merger accounted for as a pooling of interests. The market values for assets and liabilities often far exceed their recorded values. For example, May Department Stores (May) merged with Associated Dry Goods (Associated) in a transaction treated as a pooling of interests. The book values for Associated at the time of the merger were as follows (in millions):

Assets	$2,489
Liabilities	$1,589
Shareholders' Equity..	900
	$2,489

May used the above amounts to record the merger. The financial statements indicate that May exchanged 69.7 million shares of its common stock for all of the outstanding common stock of Associated. Based on a market price per share for May of approximately $38 on the date of the merger, the market value of Associated's shareholders' equity was $2,648.6 million (= 69.7 × $38). The book value of shareholders' equity was $900 million. The excess of market value over book value of shareholders' equity of $1,748.6 million (= $2,648.6 – $900.0) probably represents undervalued or nonrecorded assets. If the analyst assumes that all of the differential is goodwill and amortizes it over 40 years, then goodwill amortization of the merged enterprise increases $43.7 million ($1,748.6/40) using the purchase method instead of the pooling of interest method. Reported earnings of the combined enterprise for the year of the merger were $381 million. If the entities had used the purchase method, net income would be no greater than $337.3 million (= $381.0 – $43.7), an 11.5 percent decrease. If a portion of the excess purchase price were allocated to assets with lives shorter than the 40-year amortization period for goodwill, net income would be even less than $337.3 million.

The analyst should also exert care when comparing U.S. firms and non-U.S. firms engaged in corporate acquisitions. The pooling of interests method is either disallowed or allowed only under unusual circumstances (such as an inability to identify the purchaser) in most other countries. Furthermore, considerable diversity exists in accounting for goodwill. Firms in the United Kingdom can charge off goodwill directly against shareholders' equity accounts, bypassing the income statement. Firms in Japan amortize goodwill over five years, whereas firms in Germany use a period between five and fifteen years. These differences in accounting methods for corporate acquisitions will likely increase in importance as international acquisition activity accelerates in the 1990s.

Investments in Securities

Firms invest in the securities (debt, preferred stock, common stock) of other entities (corporations, government units) for a variety of reasons:

1. Short-term investments of temporarily excess cash.

2. Long-term investments to:
   a. Lock in high yields on debt securities.
   b. Exert significant influence on an important raw materials supplier, customer, technological innovator, or other valued entity.
   c. Gain voting control of another entity whose operations mesh well strategically with the investing firm.

Firms report investments of the first type in the Current Assets section of the balance sheet under the title Marketable Securities. These investments tend to be in government securities. Firms report investments of the second type under Investments in the noncurrent asset section of the balance sheet. These longer-term investments tend to be in equity, rather than debt, securities.

Types of Investments

The accounting for investments depends on the purpose of the investment and on the percentage of voting stock that one firm owns of another. Figure 5.1 identifies three types of investments:

1. *Minority, passive investments*: Firms view debt securities or shares of capital stock of another corporation as a good investment and acquire them for their anticipated interest or dividends and capital gains (increases in the market prices of the securities). The percentage owned of another corporation's voting shares is not so large that the acquiring company can control or exert significant influence over the other company. GAAP views investments in debt securities, preferred stock, or common stock where the firm holds less than 20 percent of the voting stock as a minority, passive investment.

2. *Minority, active investments*: Firms acquire shares of another corporation so that the acquiring corporation can exert significant influence over the other company's activities. This significant influence is usually at a broad policy-making level through representation on the other corporation's board of directors. Because of the wide dispersion of ownership of most publicly held corporations, many of whose shareholders do not vote their shares, firms can exert significant influence over another corporation with ownership of less than a majority of the voting stock. GAAP views investments of between 20 and 50 percent of the voting stock of another company as a minority, active investment unless evidence indicates that the acquiring firm cannot exert significant influence.

3. *Majority, active investments*: Firms acquire shares of another corporation so that the acquiring corporation can control the other company. This control is typ-

Figure 5.1

Types of Intercorporate Investments in Capital Stock

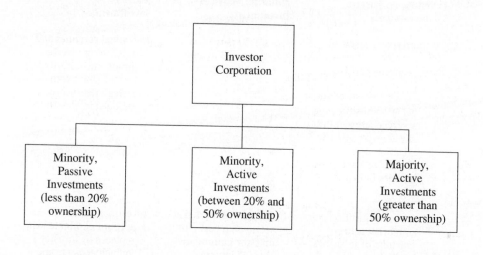

ically at both the broad policy-making level and at the day-to-day operational level. Ownership of more than 50 percent of the voting stock of another company implies an ability to control, unless available evidence indicates to the contrary.

The accounting for these three types of investments attempts to reflect the different purpose of each. Exhibit 5.3 summarizes the reporting for each type of investment in the financial statements.

Minority, Passive Investments

If a firm does not own a sufficient percentage of the voting stock of another corporation to control or significantly influence it, the management of the investment involves two activities: awaiting the receipt of interest or dividends and deciding when to sell the investment for a capital gain or loss. GAAP requires firms to account for minority, passive investments using the lower of cost or market method.[3] A summary of the accounting follows:

1. Firms initially record investments at acquisition cost.

2. Revenues each period equal interest and dividends received or receivable.

3. At the end of each period, firms compare the market value of the portfolio of securities with the acquisition cost of the portfolio. They make this comparison for

---

[3] Financial Accounting Standards Board, *Statement of Financial Accounting Standards No. 12,* "Accounting for Certain Marketable Securities," (1975).

Exhibit 5.3
Reporting Investments in Securities in the Financial Statements

Financial Statement	Minority, Passive Investments	Minority, Active Investments	Majority, Active Investments
Income Statement	Interest and dividend revenue. Unrealized decreases in the market value of Marketable Securities below acquisition cost and recoveries of unrealized losses up to acquisition cost. Realized gains and losses on sales of investments.	Investor's share of investee's net income.	Individual revenues and expenses of investee minus the minority interest's share of investee's net income included in consolidated net income.
Balance Sheet	Lower of acquisition cost or market value of portfolio of securities applied separately to Marketable Securities (current asset) and Investments in Securities (noncurrent asset). Unrealized decreases in the market value of Investments in Securities below acquisition cost included in Shareholders' Equity section of the balance sheet.	Investments reported at acquisition cost plus investor's cumulative share of investee's net income minus dividends received from investee since acquisition.	Investment in Securities account eliminated and replaced by investee's individual assets and liabilities in preparing consolidated balance sheet. Minority interest's claim on investee's net assets shown on equities side of consolidated balance sheet.
Statement of Cash Flows	Cash received from interest and dividends.	Cash received from interest and dividends.	Individual cash flows from operating, investing, and financing activities of investee included in consolidated statement of cash flows.

short-term investments in Marketable Securities (current asset) separately from long-term Investments in Securities (noncurrent asset). These firms report the investments at the lower of acquisition cost or current market value on the balance sheet. They report unrealized decreases in the market value of the portfolios during the period (as well as unrealized increases up to original acquisition cost) as follows:

   (a) Marketable Securities (current asset)—as part of net income for the period.

(b) Investments in Securities (noncurrent asset)—as a negative element in the shareholders' equity section of the balance sheet.

The rationale for treating the unrealized loss differently for these two types of investments is that GAAP considers short-term fluctuations in market prices as more relevant in evaluating investment performance in short-term investments of temporarily excess cash than in long-term investments in securities.

4. When a firm sells a particular investment, it recognizes the difference between the selling price and the acquisition cost of the investment as a gain or loss in the income statement.

Interpreting Financial Statement Disclosures for Investments in Securities

Coke and Pepsi both show investments in marketable securities in the current assets section of their balance sheets. They report these securities "at cost, which approximates market." Although this reporting appears to violate the required use of the lower of cost or market method, GAAP permits departures where the results are not materially different.

Because firms invest in marketable securities with temporarily excess cash, the analyst can generally presume that firms could sell these securities for an amount at least equal to the amount shown on the balance sheet. This is a reasonable presumption for firms located in countries that require the lower of cost or market method, such as the United States, France, and Great Britain. Certain countries, such as Canada, Japan, and Germany, require the valuation of marketable securities at acquisition cost unless the firms consider the price decline to be permanent. Firms in the latter countries seldom disclose the market value of their marketable securities. If interest rates have increased or stock prices have declined materially in one of these countries during the last several months of the accounting period, the analyst should interpret the reported amounts for these securities cautiously. The valuation of long-term minority, passive investments (acquisition cost or lower of cost or market) in other countries generally parallels the accounting for marketable securities shown as current assets.

Minority, Active Investments

When a firm owns less than a majority of the voting stock of another corporation, the accountant must exercise judgment in ascertaining whether the firm can exert significant influence. For the sake of uniformity, GAAP presumes that one company can significantly influence another company when it owns 20 percent or more of the voting stock of the other company. Ownership of less than 20 percent may permit a firm to exert significant influence, but in these cases management must demonstrate to the independent accountants that it is possible.

GAAP requires firms to account for minority, active investments, generally those where ownership is between 20 and 50 percent, using the *equity method*.[4] Under the equity method, the firm owning shares in another firm recognizes as revenue (expense) each period its share of the net income (loss) of the other firm. See, for example, the income statement of Coke. The line Equity Income includes Coke's share of the earnings from 20 percent to 50 percent owned affiliates. The investor treats dividends received from the investee as a return of investment and not as income. In the discussion that follows, we designate the firm owning shares as P and the firm whose shares P owns as S.

The rationale for using the equity method when significant influence is present is best understood by considering the financial statement effects of using the lower of cost or market method in these circumstances. Under the lower of cost or market method, P recognizes income or loss on the income statement only when it receives a dividend or sells all or part of the investment. Suppose, as often happens, that S follows a policy of financing its own growing operations through retention of earnings and consistently declares dividends significantly less than its net income. The market price of S's shares will probably increase to reflect the retention of assets generated by earnings. Under the lower of cost or market method, P will continue to show the investment at acquisition cost and P's only reported income from the investment will be the modest dividends received. P, because of its ownership percentage, can influence the dividend policy of S and thereby the amount of income recognized under the lower of cost or market method. Under these conditions, the lower of cost or market method may not reasonably reflect the earnings of S generated under P's influence. The equity method provides a better measure of a firm's earnings and of its investment when, because of its ownership interest, it can significantly influence the operations and dividend policy of another firm.

Under the equity method, firms report investments on the balance sheet at acquisition cost plus (minus) the investor's share of the investee's net income (loss) each period minus the dividends received from the investee each period. Thus, investments on the balance sheet accounted for using the equity method change each period in direct proportion to changes in retained earnings of the investee.

The statement of cash flows reports cash flows and not equity method earnings. Thus, in deriving cash flow from operations, the statement of cash flows subtracts the investor's share of the investee's earnings from net income and adds the cash dividends received. Most firms report this adjustment as a subtraction for the investor's share of the *undistributed* earnings (net income minus dividends) of the investee.

Interpreting Financial Statement Disclosures for Equity Method Investments

Refer to the financial statements for Coke in Appendix A for this discussion. Its balance sheet shows investments in Coca-Cola Enterprises, Coca-Cola Amatil, and Other, principally bottling operations. Note 3 sets out additional information

---

[4]Accounting Principles Board, *Accounting Principles Board Opinion No. 18,* "The Equity Method of Accounting for Investments in Common Stock," (1971).

about these investments. Coca-Cola Enterprises is a 49 percent owned bottler. Coca-Cola Amatil is a more than 50 percent owned bottler but Coke intends to reduce its ownership below 50 percent. Thus, Coke's investments represent minority, active investments for which it uses the equity method. The note indicates that these investees generated earnings of $282,584 (= $77,148 + $205,436) in Year 8. Coke's share of this income is $110,139 (= $34,429 + $75,710), which agrees with the amount that Coke shows as equity income on its income statement for Year 8. Coke's statement of cash flows shows a subtraction from net income of $93,816 for "equity income, net of dividends" in deriving cash flow from operations. Coke therefore received cash dividends of $16,323 (= $110,139 − $93,816) from these investments during Year 8.

We might wonder why Coke chooses to own only 49 percent or less of these bottlers, a critical component of its operating activities. A possible explanation is that this arrangement permits Coke to keep debt off its balance sheet. Note 3 indicates that these bottlers carry liabilities of $7,609,815 (= $3,394,117 + $4,215,698) on assets of $11,110,747 (= $5,020,596 + $6,090,151). Thus, the ratio of liabilities to total assets for the bottlers is 68.5 percent (= $7,609,815/$11,110,747). The corresponding percentage for Coke with these investments reported using the equity method is 58.5 percent. If Coke owned a majority interest, GAAP would require Coke to consolidate its financial statements with those of the bottlers (see discussion in the next section of this chapter) and Coke's debt/equity ratio would increase. Note that the total assets of these investees exceed those of Coke ($11,110,747 versus $9,278,187).

Refer now to the financial statements of Pepsi in Appendix B. Pepsi shows "Investments in Affiliates" on its balance sheet. Note 1 on accounting policies indicates that Pepsi accounts for these investments using the equity method. It nets equity income from these investments against selling, administrative, and other expenses, perhaps because the amounts are not sufficiently material to warrant a separate line in the income statement. Pepsi owns most of its bottling operations.

The analyst should address two questions in particular when examining the financial statements of firms with significant equity method intercorporate investments:

1. What is the relation between equity method income and cash flows received from the investees?

2. Are assets and liabilities essential to a firm's operations submerged in the intercorporate investment account?

The analyst answers the first question by comparing equity method income on the income statement with the adjustment to net income for undistributed earnings of investees in the statement of cash flows. Coke, for instance, derived more than 5 percent of its pretax earnings during Year 8 from equity method investees but received only a minor amount of cash from these investments.

The analyst answers the second question by studying the notes on intercorporate investments. Firms must disclose partial balance sheet and income statement information on significant intercorporate investments. As an earlier section discussed, Coke maintains 49 percent ownership in major bottling operations. The assets and liabilities of these bottlers do not appear on Coke's balance sheet. A later section demonstrates the procedure an analyst might follow to incorporate amounts for such investments on the balance sheet.

The analyst should also exert caution when examining the financial statements of firms in other countries. Firms commonly use the equity method for minority, active investments in Canada, France, and Great Britain and in certain filings with the Ministry of Finance in Japan. Countries that follow a strict legal definition of the entity, such as Germany, tend to report these intercorporate investments at acquisition cost, even when significant influence is present.

Majority, Active Investments

When one firm, P, owns more than 50 percent of the voting stock of another company, S, P can control the activities of S. This control may occur at both a broad policy-making level and a day-to-day operational level. The majority investor in this case is the *parent* and the majority-owned company is the *subsidiary*. GAAP requires the combining or *consolidating* of the financial statements of majority-owned companies with those of the parent.[5]

Reasons for Legally Separate Corporations. There are many reasons why a business firm prefers to operate as a group of legally separate corporations rather than as a single legal entity. From the viewpoint of the parent company, the more important reasons for maintaining legally separate subsidiary companies include the following:

1. To reduce financial risk. Separate corporations may mine raw materials, transport them to a manufacturing plant, produce the product, and sell the finished product to the public. If any one part of the total process proves to be unprofitable or inefficient, losses from insolvency fall only on the owners and creditors of the one subsidiary corporation.

2. To meet more effectively the requirements of state corporation laws and tax legislation. If an organization does business in many states, it must often contend with overlapping and inconsistent taxation, regulations, and requirements. Organizing separate corporations to conduct the operations in the various states may reduce administrative costs.

3. To expand or diversify with a minimum of capital investment. A firm may absorb another company by acquiring a controlling interest in its voting stock. It may accomplish this result with a substantially smaller capital investment, as well as with less difficulty, inconvenience, and risk, than if it had constructed a new plant or geared up for a new line of business.

---

[5] Financial Accounting Standards Board, *Statement of Financial Accounting Standards No. 94*, "Consolidation of Majority-Owned Subsidiaries," (1987).

Purpose of Consolidated Statements. For a variety of reasons, then, a parent and several legally separate subsidiaries may exist as a single economic entity. (The General Electric Company, for example, consists of about 150 legally separate companies.) A consolidation of the financial statements of the parent and each of its subsidiaries presents the results of operations, financial position, and changes in cash flows of an affiliated group of companies under the control of a parent, essentially as if the group of companies were a single entity. The parent and each subsidiary are legally separate entities, but they operate as one centrally controlled *economic entity*. Consolidated financial statements generally provide more useful information to the shareholders of the parent corporation than would separate financial statements of the parent and each subsidiary.

Consolidated financial statements also generally provide more useful information than does the equity method. The parent, because of its voting interest, can effectively control the use of the subsidiary's individual assets. Consolidation of the individual assets, liabilities, revenues, and expenses of both the parent and the subsidiary provides a more realistic picture of the operations and financial position of the single economic entity.

In a legal sense, consolidated statements merely supplement, and do not replace, the separate statements of the individual corporations, although it is common practice to present only the consolidated statements in published annual reports.

Consolidation Policy. GAAP requires that firms prepare consolidated financial statements when they meet the following two criteria:

1. The parent owns more than 50 percent of the voting stock of the subsidiary.

2. There are no important restrictions on the ability of the parent to exercise control of the subsidiary.

Ownership of more than 50 percent of the subsidiary's voting stock implies an ability to exert control over the activities of the subsidiary. As an example, the parent can control the subsidiary's corporate policies and dividend declarations. There may be situations where the parent cannot control the subsidiary's activities, despite the ownership of a majority of the voting stock. For example, the subsidiary may reside in a foreign country that severely restricts the withdrawal of funds from that country. Or, the subsidiary may be in bankruptcy and under the control of a court-appointed group of trustees. In these cases, the parent will probably not consolidate its financial statements with those of the subsidiary. When the parent owns more than 50 percent of the shares but cannot exercise control, it uses the lower of cost or market method.

Disclosure of Consolidation Policy. The note to the financial statements describing significant accounting policies includes a statement about the consolidation policy of the parent. If a parent does not consolidate a significant majority-owned subsidiary, the notes will disclose that fact. The notes to the financial statements of Coke and Pepsi indicate that they consolidate all majority-owned subsidiaries. The one exception is Coke's investment in Coca-Cola Amatil Limited. Coke states that its controlling interest is temporary because Coke intends to reduce its interest below 50 percent. Thus, it accounts for this investment using the equity method.

Understanding Consolidated Statements. This section discusses three concepts essential for understanding consolidated financial statements:

1. The need for intercompany eliminations.

2. The meaning of consolidated net income.

3. The nature of the external minority interest.

Need for Intercompany Eliminations. State corporation laws typically require each legally separate corporation to maintain its own set of books. Thus, during the accounting period, the accounting records of each corporation record transactions of that entity with all other entities (both affiliated and nonaffiliated). At the end of the period, each corporation prepares its own set of financial statements. The consolidation of these financial statements involves summing the amounts for various financial statement items across the separate company statements. The amounts resulting from the summation require adjustments, however, to eliminate double counting resulting from *intercompany transactions*. Consolidated financial statements reflect the results of an affiliated group of companies operating as a single company. Thus, consolidated financial statements include only the transactions between the consolidated entity and others outside the group.

The eliminations to remove intercompany transactions typically appear on a *consolidation worksheet* and not on the books of any of the legal entities comprising the consolidated group. The accountant prepares the consolidated financial statements directly from the worksheet. The consolidated entity generally maintains no separate set of books.

To illustrate the need for, and the nature of, *elimination entries*, refer to the data for Company P and Company S in Exhibit 5.4. Column (1) shows the balance sheet and income statement data for Company P taken from its separate company books. Column (2) shows similar data for Company S. Column (3) sums the amounts from columns (1) and (2). The amounts in column (3) include the effects of several intercompany items and, therefore, do not represent the correct amounts for *consolidated* assets, equities, revenues, or expenses.

Eliminating Double Counting of Intercompany Payables. Separate company records indicate that $12,000 of Company S's accounts receivable represent amounts payable by Company P. The amounts in column (3) count the current assets underlying this transaction twice: once as part of Accounts Receivable on Company S's books and a second time as Cash (or Other Assets) on Company P's books. Also, Accounts Payable in column (3) includes the liability shown on Com-

Exhibit 5.4

Illustrative Data for Preparation of Consolidated Financial Statements

	Single-Company Statements		
	Company P (1)	Company S (2)	Combined (3) = (1) + (2)
CONDENSED BALANCE SHEETS ON DECEMBER 31			
Assets			
Accounts Receivable	$ 200,000	$ 25,000	$ 225,000
Investment in Stock of Company S (at equity)	705,000	—	705,000
Other Assets	2,150,000	975,000	3,125,000
Total Assets	$3,055,000	$1,000,000	$4,055,000
Equities			
Accounts Payable	$ 75,000	$ 15,000	$ 90,000
Other Liabilities	70,000	280,000	350,000
Common Stock	2,500,000	500,000	3,000,000
Retained Earnings	410,000	205,000	615,000
Total Equities	$3,055,000	$1,000,000	$4,055,000
CONDENSED INCOME STATEMENTS FOR CURRENT YEAR			
Revenues			
Sales	$ 900,000	$ 250,000	$1,150,000
Equity in Earnings of Company S	48,000	—	48,000
Total Revenues	$ 948,000	$ 250,000	$1,198,000
Expenses			
Cost of Goods Sold (excluding depreciation)	$ 440,000	$ 80,000	$ 520,000
Depreciation Expense	120,000	50,000	170,000
Administrative Expenses	80,000	40,000	120,000
Income Tax Expense	104,000	32,000	136,000
Total Expenses	$ 744,000	$ 202,000	$ 946,000
Net Income	$ 204,000	$ 48,000	$ 252,000
Dividend Declarations	50,000	13,000	63,000
Increase in Retained Earnings for the Year	$ 154,000	$ 35,000	$ 189,000

pany P's books, even though the amount is not payable to an entity external to the consolidated group. To eliminate double counting on the asset side and to report Accounts Payable at the amount payable to external entities, the elimination entry reduces the amounts for Accounts Receivable and Accounts Payable in column (3) by $12,000.

Eliminating Double Counting of Investment. To consider a more complex example, Company P's balance sheet shows an asset, Investment in Stock of Company S. The subsidiary's balance sheet shows its individual assets. The combined balance sheet in column (3) includes both Company P's investment in Company S's net assets and the assets and liabilities themselves. We must eliminate Company P's account, Investment in Stock of Company S, from the sum of the balance sheets. Because the consolidated balance sheet must maintain the accounting equation, we must make corresponding eliminations on the right-hand, or equities, side as well.

To understand the eliminations from the right-hand side of the balance sheet, recall that the right-hand side shows the sources of the firm's financing. Creditors (liabilities) and owners (shareholders' equity) finance Company S. Company P owns 100 percent of Company S's voting shares. Thus, the creditors of both companies and Company P's shareholders finance the assets on the consolidated balance sheet of the single economic entity. In other words, the equities of the consolidated entity are the liabilities of both companies but the shareholders' equity of Company P alone. If we added the shareholders' equity accounts of Company S to those of Company P, we would count the financing from Company P's shareholders twice (once on the parent's books and once on the subsidiary's books). Hence, when we eliminate Company P's investment account from the sum of the two companies' assets, we maintain the accounting equation by eliminating the shareholders' equity accounts of Company S.

Eliminating Double Counting of Income. Similarly, we must eliminate certain intercompany items from the sum of income statement accounts to present meaningfully the operating performance of the consolidated entity. Company P's accounts show Equity in Earnings of Company S of $48,000. Company S's records show individual revenues and expenses that net to $48,000. If we merely summed the revenues and expenses of the two companies, as column (3) of Exhibit 5.4 illustrates, we would double count the earnings of Company S. We must eliminate the account, Equity in Earnings of Company S, in preparing consolidated statements.

Eliminating Intercompany Sales. Another example of an intercompany item involves intercompany sales of inventory. Separate company records indicate that Company S sold merchandise to Company P for $40,000 during the year. None of this inventory remains in Company P's inventory on December 31. The sale of the merchandise inventory increases Sales Revenue on both Company S's books (sale to Company P for $40,000) and on Company P's books (sale to an external entity for probably a higher price). Thus, the combined amount for Sales Revenue overstates sales from the standpoint of the consolidated entity by $40,000. Likewise, Cost of Goods Sold of both companies includes the separate-company costs of the goods sold. To eliminate double counting, we must eliminate $40,000 from consolidated Cost of Goods Sold.

Consolidated Income. The amount of consolidated net income for a period exactly equals the amount that the parent shows on its separate company books from applying the equity method; that is, consolidated net income equals

Parent Company's Net Income from Its Own Activities	+	Parent Company's Share of Subsidiary's Net Income	−	Profit (or + Loss) on Intercompany Transactions

A consolidated income statement differs from an equity method income statement in the *components* presented. When using the equity method for an unconsolidated subsidiary, the parent's share of the subsidiary's net income minus gain (or plus loss) on intercompany transactions appears on a single line, Equity in Earnings of Unconsolidated Subsidiary. In a consolidated income statement, we combine the individual revenues and expenses of the subsidiary (less intercompany adjustments) with those of the parent, and eliminate the account, Equity in Earnings of Unconsolidated Subsidiary, shown on the parent's books. Some accountants refer to the equity method as a *one-line consolidation* because it nets the individual revenues and expenses of the subsidiary into the one account, Equity in Earnings of Unconsolidated Subsidiary.

External Minority Interest in Consolidated Subsidiary. The parent does not always own 100 percent of the voting stock of a consolidated subsidiary. Accountants refer to the owners of the remaining shares of voting stock as the *minority interest*. These shareholders have a proportionate interest in the net assets (= Total Assets − Total Liabilities) of the subsidiary as shown on the subsidiary's separate corporate records. They also have a proportionate interest in the earnings of the subsidiary.

One issue that the accountant must confront in preparing consolidated statements is whether the statements should show only the parent's share of the assets and liabilities of the subsidiary or whether they should show all of the subsidiary's assets and liabilities along with the minority interest's claim on them. GAAP shows all of the assets and liabilities of the subsidiary because the parent, with its controlling voting interest, effectively directs the use of all of the assets and liabilities, not merely an amount equal to the parent's percentage of ownership. The consolidated balance sheet and income statement in these instances, however, must disclose the interest of the minority shareholders in the consolidated subsidiary.

The amount of the minority interest appearing on the balance sheet results from multiplying the common shareholders' equity of the subsidiary by the minority's percentage of ownership. For example, if the common shareholders' equity (or assets minus liabilities) of a consolidated subsidiary totals $500,000 and the minority owns 20 percent of the common stock, the minority interest appears on the consolidated balance sheet at $100,000 (= .20 × $500,000). The consolidated balance sheet typically shows the minority interest between the liabilities and shareholders' equity. The financial statements of Coke and Pepsi give no indication that a minority interest exists in any of its consolidated subsidiaries.

The amount of the minority interest in the subsidiary's income results from multiplying the subsidiary's net income by the minority's percentage of ownership. The consolidated income statement shows the proportion of consolidated income applicable to the parent company and the proportion of the subsidiary's income applicable to the minority interest. Typically, the minority interest in the subsidiary's income appears as a deduction in calculating consolidated net income.

Limitations of Consolidated Statements. The consolidated statements do not replace those of individual corporations; rather, they supplement those statements and aid in their interpretation. Creditors must rely on the resources of one corporation and may be misled if forced to rely entirely on a consolidated statement that combines the data of a company in good financial condition with one verging on insolvency. Firms can legally declare dividends only from their own retained earnings. Where the parent company does not own all of the shares of the subsidiary, the outside or minority stockholders can judge the dividend constraints, both legal and financial, only by inspecting the subsidiary's statements.

Consolidation of Unconsolidated Subsidiaries and Affiliates. The analyst may wish to assess the financial position of a firm with all important majority-owned subsidiaries and minority-owned affiliates consolidated. Coke, for instance, has significant investments in bottlers that are integral to its operations. Consolidation of the financial statements of these affiliates with those of Coke presents a more realistic picture of the assets and liabilities of Coke as an operating enterprise. Consolidation also places Coke on a more comparable basis with Pepsi, which owns most of its bottling operations.

Exhibit 5.5 presents a consolidation worksheet for Coke and its bottlers. Coke's balance sheet provides the amounts in column (1). Note 3 to Coke's financial statements provides the amounts for columns (2) and (3). The amounts in column (4) eliminate amounts in the intercorporate investment accounts on Coke's books against the shareholders' equity accounts of the affiliates. The column also shows the reclassification of a portion of the shareholders' equity accounts of the affiliates to recognize the minority interests' claim. The amount that Exhibit 5.5 shows for the minority interest equals the total shareholders' equity of the affiliates times the minority interests' ownership percentage. This percentage is 51 percent for Coca-Cola Enterprises. Coke does not disclose its ownership percentage in Other Equity Investments. We can approximate this percentage by comparing Coke's equity income from these investments ($75,710 in Note 3) to the total net income of the investees ($205,436 in Note 3). Coke appears to own 36.853 percent (= $75,710/$205,436) and the minority interest owns 63.147 percent. This procedure probably includes some measurement error. The amounts that Coke shows for its intercorporate investments ($666,847 + $1,310,209) do not equal Coke's share (49 percent and 36.853 percent) of the shareholders' equity of the investees. The difference represents goodwill (= –$130,128 + $619,417). Exhibit 5.5 includes this goodwill in noncurrent assets. The consolidated amounts in column (5) provide a better sense of the assets and obligations under Coke's influence and inte-

Exhibit 5.5
Consolidation Worksheet for Coke and Equity Method Affiliates

	Coke (1)	Coca-Cola Enterprises (2)	Other Equity Investments (3)	Eliminations (4)	Consolidated (5)
Current Assets	$4,142,778	$ 495,341	$1,658,341		$ 6,296,460
Investments in Securities	2,024,622	—	—	− 666,847[a]	
				− 1,310,209[a]	47,566
Noncurrent Assets	3,110,787	4,525,255	4,431,810	− 130,128[c]	12,557,141
				+ 619,417[e]	
Total Assets	$9,278,187	$5,020,596	$6,090,151		$18,901,167
Current Liabilities	$4,296,491	$1,054,791	$1,696,796		$7,048,078
Noncurrent Liabilities	1,132,532	2,339,326	2,518,902		5,990,760
Minority Interest				+ 829,504[b]	
				+ 1,183,661[d]	2,013,165
Shareholders' Equity	3,849,164	1,626,479	1,874,453	− 1,626,479[a]	3,849,164
				− 1,874,453[a]	
	$9,278,187	$5,020,596	$6,090,151		$18,901,167

[a]Given.
[b]$829,504 = .51 \times \$1,626,479$.
[c]$-\$130,128 = [\$666,847 - (.49 \times \$1,626,479)]$.
[d]$1,183,661 = (1 - .36853)(\$1,874,453)$.
[e]$619,417 = [\$1,310,209 - (.36853 \times \$1,874,453)]$.

gral to its operations. Net income for Coke remains the same regardless of whether Coke accounts for these investments using the equity method or by consolidating them. The components of net income (that is, sales, cost of goods sold) do change but not net income. As Chapter 7 discusses more fully, consolidation of these equity method affiliates reduces Coke's rate of return on assets (same net income but larger assets).

The consolidation of majority-owned subsidiaries is a relatively recent phenomenon in some countries (for instance, Germany and Japan). These countries tended to follow strict legal definitions of the reporting entity. GAAP in these countries now generally requires the preparation of consolidated financial statements, although the requirement in Japan applies only to filings with the Ministry of Finance.

Joint Venture Investments

Firms frequently join together in joint ventures to carry out their business activities. For instance, two chemical firms may join together to construct a chemical processing plant. Each firm agrees to purchase 50 percent of the output of the plant and to pay 50 percent of the operating and debt service costs. When they sell the plant, each firm receives half of the net cash proceeds. By joining together, they can perhaps construct a larger, more efficient plant than if each firm built its own smaller plant. Note 3 to Pepsi's financial statements indicates that Pepsi and

Mitsubishi Corporation jointly own the Kentucky Fried Chicken operation in Japan. The note does not provide much additional information on the assets, liabilities, or income of this joint venture.

Joint ventures are unique in that joint control is present. Neither firm has a majority voting position. Both firms must generally agree to make significant policy changes. These investments therefore fall between minority, active investments and majority, active investments.

Firms account for joint ventures using the equity method. They include the investment in the joint venture in the noncurrent asset section, Investments, on the balance sheet. The assets and liabilities of the joint venture do not appear on the balance sheet of either owner. Long-term debt typically finances most joint ventures. By accounting for the joint venture using the equity method, firms keep this debt off the balance sheet. As Chapter 4 discussed, firms commonly attempt to keep debt off the balance sheet in an effort to present a less risky position to potential lenders. Joint ventures have increased in popularity in recent years.

The Financial Accounting Standards Board is currently studying the accounting for joint ventures. At issue is whether firms should use the equity method or whether proportionate consolidation is more appropriate. Under proportionate consolidation, the investor's share of the assets and liabilities of the joint venture appear in separate sections on the assets and liabilities sides of the balance sheet, with the investment account eliminated. Some accountants argue that proportionate consolidation better captures the economics of these transactions where joint control is present.

Income Tax Consequences of Investments in Securities

For income tax purposes, investments fall into two categories:

1. Investments in debt securities, in preferred stock, or in less than 80 percent of the common stock of another entity. Firms recognize interest or dividends received or receivable each period as taxable income (subject to a partial dividend exclusion), as well as gains or losses when they sell the securities.

2. Investments in 80 percent or more of the common stock of another entity. Firms can prepare consolidated tax returns for these investments.

As is evident, the methods of accounting for investments for financial and tax reporting do not overlap precisely. Thus, timing differences will likely arise for which firms must recognize deferred taxes.

Foreign Currency Translation

U.S. parent companies must translate the financial statements of foreign branches and subsidiaries into U.S. dollars before preparing consolidated financial statements for shareholders and creditors. This section describes and illustrates the translation methodology and discusses the implications of the methodology both for managing international operations and for interpreting financial statement disclosures regarding such operations.

Two general issues arise in translating the financial statements of a foreign branch or subsidiary:

1. Should the firm translate individual financial statement items at the exchange rate at the time of the transaction (referred to as the historical exchange rate) or at the exchange rate during or at the end of the current period (referred to as the current exchange rate)? Financial statement items that firms translate using the historical exchange rates appear in the financial statements at the same U.S. dollar equivalent amount each period regardless of changes in the exchange rate. For example, land acquired in France for 10,000 French francs when the exchange rate was $.40 per French franc appears on the balance sheet at $4,000 each period. Financial statement items that firms translate using the current exchange rate appear in the financial statements at a different U.S. dollar amount each period when exchange rates change. Thus, a change in the exchange rate to $.60 per French franc results in reporting the land at $6,000 on the balance sheet. Financial statement items for which firms use the current exchange rate give rise to a *foreign exchange adjustment* each period.

2. Should the firm recognize the foreign exchange adjustment as a gain or loss in measuring net income each period as it arises or should the firm defer its recognition until a future period? The foreign exchange adjustment represents an unrealized gain or loss, much the same as changes in the market value of marketable securities, inventories, or other assets. Should GAAP require realization of the gain or loss through sale of the foreign operation before recognizing it or should the unrealized gain or loss flow directly to the income statement as the exchange rate changes?

The foreign currency translation methods differ across countries primarily with regard to the answers to these two questions. The section below describes GAAP in the United States. A later section considers GAAP in other countries.

Functional Currency Concept

Central to the translation of foreign currency items is the *functional currency concept.*[6] Foreign entities (whether branches or subsidiaries) are of two general types:

1. A foreign entity operates as a relatively self-contained and integrated unit within a particular foreign country. The functional currency for these operations is the currency of that foreign country.

---

[6] Financial Accounting Standards Board, *Statement of Financial Accounting Standards No. 52,* "Foreign Currency Translation," (1981).

2. The operations of a foreign entity are a direct and integral component or extension of the parent company's operations. The functional currency for these operations is the U.S. dollar.

FASB *Statement No. 52* sets out characteristics for determining whether the currency of the foreign unit or the U.S. dollar is the functional currency. Exhibit 5.6 summarizes these characteristics. The operating characteristics of a particular foreign operation may provide mixed signals regarding which currency is the functional currency. Management must exercise judgment in determining which functional currency best captures the economic effects of a foreign entity's operations and financial position. As a later section discusses, management may wish to structure certain financings or other transactions to swing the balance to favor selecting either the foreign currency or the U.S. dollar as the functional currency. Once a firm determines the functional currency of a foreign entity, it must use it consistently over time unless changes in economic circumstances clearly indicate a change in the functional currency.

FASB *Statement No. 52* provides for one exception to the guidelines in Exhibit 5.6 for determining the functional currency. If the foreign entity operates in a highly inflationary country, GAAP considers its currency to be too unstable to serve as the functional currency, and the firm must use the U.S. dollar instead. A highly inflationary country is one that has experienced cumulative inflation of at least 100 percent over a three-year period. Most South American countries and many developing nations fall within this exception and pose particular problems for the U.S. parent company, as a later section discusses.

Translation Methodology—Foreign Currency Is Functional Currency

When the functional currency is the currency of the foreign unit, GAAP requires firms to use the all-current translation method. The left-hand column of Exhibit 5.7 summarizes the translation procedure under the all-current method. Firms translate revenues and expenses at the average exchange rate during the period and balance sheet items at the end-of-the-period exchange rate. Net income includes only *transaction* exchange gains and losses of the foreign unit. That is, a foreign unit that has receivables and payables denominated in a currency other than its own must make a currency conversion upon settlement of the account. The gain or loss from changes in the exchange rate between the time the account originated and the time of settlement is a transaction gain or loss. Firms recognize this gain or loss during the periods while the account is outstanding, even though it is not yet realized, or settled.

When a foreign unit operates more or less independently of the U.S. parent, GAAP assumes that only the parent's equity investment in the foreign unit is subject to exchange rate risk. The firm measures the effect of exchange rate changes on this investment each period, but includes the resulting "translation adjust-

Exhibit 5.6
Factors for Determining Functional Currency of Foreign Unit

	Foreign Currency Is Functional Currency	U.S. Dollar Is Functional Curency
Cash Flows of Foreign Entity	Receivables and payables denominated in foreign currency and not usually remitted to parent currently.	Receivables and payables denominated in U.S. dollars and readily available for remittance to parent.
Sales Prices	Influenced primarily by local competitive conditions and not responsive on a short-term basis to exchange rate changes.	Influenced by worldwide competitive conditions and responsive on a short-term basis to exchange rate changes.
Cost Factors	Foreign unit obtains labor, materials, and other inputs primarily from its own country.	Foreign unit obtains labor, materials, and other inputs primarily from the United States.
Financing	Financing denominated in currency of foreign unit or generated internally by the foreign unit.	Financing denominated in U.S. dollars or ongoing fund transfers by the parent.
Relations between Parent and Foreign Unit	Low volume of intercompany transactions and few operational interrelations between parent and foreign unit.	High volume of intercompany transactions and extensive operational interrelations between parent and foreign unit.

Source: Financial Accounting Standards Board, *Statement of Financial Accounting Standards No. 52*, "Foreign Currency Translation," 1981.

ment" in a separate account in the shareholders' equity section of the balance sheet rather than in net income. GAAP's rationale for this treatment is that the firm's investment in the foreign unit is for the long term; short-term changes in exchange rates should not, therefore, affect periodic net income. Firms recognize the cumulative amount in the translation adjustment account when measuring any gain or loss from disposing of the foreign unit.

Illustration.   Exhibit 5.8 illustrates the all-current method for a foreign unit during its first year of operations. The exchange rate was $1:1FC on January 1, $2:1 FC on December 31, and $1.5:1 FC on average during the year. The firm translates all assets and liabilities on the balance sheet at the exchange rate on December 31. It translates common stock at the exchange rate on the date of issuance; the translation adjustment account includes the effects of changes in exchange rates on this investment. The translated amount of retained earnings results from translating the income statement and dividends. Note that the firm translates all revenues and expenses of the foreign unit at the average exchange rate. The foreign unit realized a transaction gain during the year and recorded it on its books. In addition, the translated amounts for the foreign unit include an

Exhibit 5.7
Summary of Translation Methodology

	Foreign Currency Is the Functional Currency (All-Current Method)	**U.S. Dollar Is the Functional Currency (Monetary/Non-Monetary Method)**
Income Statement	Firms translate revenues and expenses as measured in foreign currency into U.S. dollars using the average exchange rate during the period. Income includes (1) realized and unrealized transaction gains and losses and (2) realized translation gains and losses when the firm sells the foreign unit.	Firms translate revenues and expenses using the exchange rate in effect when the firm made the original measurements underlying the valuations. Firms translate revenues and most operating expenses using the average exchange rate during the period. However, they translate cost of goods sold and depreciation using the historical exchange rate appropriate to the related asset (inventory, fixed assets). Net income includes (1) realized and unrealized transaction gains and losses, and (2) unrealized translation gains and losses on the net monetary position of the foreign unit each period.
Balance Sheet	Firms translate assets and liabilities as measured in foreign currency into U.S. dollars using the end-of-the-period exchange rate. Use of the end-of-the-period exchange rate gives rise to unrealized transaction gains and losses on receivables and payables requiring currency conversions in the future. Firms include an unrealized translation adjustment on the net asset position of the foreign unit in a separate shareholders' equity account and not in net income until the firm sells the foreign unit.	Firms translate monetary assets and liabilities using the end-of-the-period exchange rate. They translate non-monetary assets and equities using the historical exchange rate.

unrealized transaction gain arising from exposed accounts that are not yet settled. Note *a* to Exhibit 5.8 shows the computation of translated retained earnings. The foreign unit paid the dividend on December 31. Note *b* shows the calculation of the translation adjustment. By investing $30 in the foreign unit on January 1 and allowing the $24.5 of earnings to remain in the foreign unit throughout the year while the foreign currency was increasing in value relative to the U.S. dollar, the parent has a potential exchange "gain" of $35.5. It reports this amount in the separate shareholders' equity account on the balance sheet.

Exhibit 5.8

Illustration of Translation Methodology When the Foreign Currency Is the Functional Currency

	Foreign Currency		U.S. Dollars	
Balance Sheet				
Assets				
Cash	FC	10	$2.0:1FC	$ 20.0
Receivables		20	$2.0:1FC	40.0
Inventories		30	$2.0:1FC	60.0
Fixed Assets (net)		40	$2.0:1FC	80.0
Total	FC	100		$200.0
Liabilities and Shareholders' Equity				
Accounts Payable	FC	40	$2.0:1FC	$ 80.0
Bonds Payable		20	$2.0:1FC	40.0
Total	FC	60		$120.0
Common Stock	FC	30	$1.0:1FC	$ 30.0
Retained Earnings		10		14.5[a]
Unrealized Translation Adjustment		—		35.5[b]
Total	FC	40		$ 80.0
Total	FC	100		$200.0
Income Statement				
Sales Revenue	FC	200	$1.5:1FC	$300.0
Realized Transaction Gain		2[c]	$1.5:1FC	3.0[c]
Unrealized Transaction Gain		—[d]	—	2.0[d]
Cost of Goods Sold		(120)	$1.5:1FC	(180.0)
Selling and Administrative Expense		(40)	$1.5:1FC	(60.0)
Depreciation Expense		(10)	$1.5:1FC	(15.0)
Interest Expense		(2)	$1.5:1FC	(3.0)
Income Tax Expense		(15)	$1.5:1FC	(22.5)
Net Income	FC	15		$ 24.5

	Foreign Currency		U.S. Dollars	
[a]Retained Earnings, Jan. 1	FC	0.0		$ 0.0
Plus Net Income		15.0		24.5
Less Dividends		(5.0)	$2.0:1FC	$(10.0)
Retained Earnings, Dec. 31	FC	10.0		$ 14.5
[b]Net Asset Position, Jan. 1	FC	30.0	$1.0:1FC	$ 30.0
Plus Net Income		15.0		24.5
Less Dividends		(5.0)	$2.0:1FC	$(10.0)
Net Asset Position, Dec. 31	FC	40.0		$ 44.5
Net Asset Position, Dec. 31		⟶	$2.0:1FC	80.0
Unrealized Translation "Gain"				$ 35.5

[c]The foreign unit had receivables and payables denominated in a currency other than its own. When it settled these accounts during the period, the foreign unit made a currency conversion and realized a transaction gain of FC2.

[d]The foreign unit has receivables and payables outstanding that will require a currency conversion in a future period when the foreign unit settles the accounts. Because the exchange rate changed while the receivables/payables were outstanding, the foreign unit reports an unrealized transaction gain for financial reporting.

Exhibit 5.9
Illustration of Translation Methodology When the U.S. Dollar Is the Functional Currency

Balance Sheet	Foreign Currency		U.S. Dollars	
Assets				
Cash	FC$	10	$2.0:1FC	$20.0
Receivables		20	$2.0:1FC	40.0
Inventories		30	$1.5:1FC	45.0
Fixed Assets (Net)		40	$1.0:1FC	40.0
Total	FC$	100		$145.0
Liabilities and Shareholders' Equity				
Accounts Payable	FC$	40	$2.0:1FC	$ 80.0
Bonds Payable		20	$2.0:1FC	40.0
Total	FC$	60		$120.0
Common Stock	FC$	30	$1.0:1FC	$ 30.0
Retained Earnings		10		(5.0)[a]
Total	FC$	40		$ 25.0
Total	FC$	100		$145.0
Income Statement				
Sales Revenue	FC$	200	$1.5:1FC	$300.0
Realized Transaction Gain		2	$1.5:1FC	3.0
Unrealized Transaction Gain		—	—	2.0
Unrealized Translation Loss		—		(24.5)[b]
Cost of Goods Sold		(120)	$1.5:1FC	(180.0)
Selling and Administrative Expense		(40)	$1.5:1FC	(60.0)
Depreciation Expense		(10)	$1.0:1FC	(10.0)
Interest Expense		(2)	$1.5:1FC	(3.0)
Income Tax Expense		(15)	$1.5:1FC	(22.5)
Net Income	FC$	15		$ 5.0
[a]Retained Earnings, Jan. 1	FC$	0	—	$0.0
Plus Net Income		15	See above	5.0
Less Dividends		(5)	$2.0:1FC	(10.0)
Retained Earnings, Dec. 31	FC$	10		$ (5.0)

[b]Income for financial reporting includes any unrealized translation gain or loss for the period. The net monetary position of a foreign unit during the period serves as the basis for computing the translation gain or loss. The foreign unit was in a net monetary liability position during a period when the U.S. dollar decreased in value relative to the foreign currency. The translation loss arises because the U.S. dollars required to settle the net monetary liability position at the end of the year exceed the U.S. dollars required to settle the obligation at the time the firm initially recorded the transactions giving rise to change in net monetary liabilities during the period. The calculations appear on the next page:

Translation Methodology—U.S. Dollar Is Functional Currency

When the functional currency is the U.S. dollar, GAAP requires firms to use the *monetary/non-monetary translation method*. The right-hand column of Exhibit 5.7 summarizes the translation procedure under the monetary/non-monetary

Exhibit 5.9 (*Continued*)

	Foreign Currency	U.S. Dollars	
Net Monetary Position, Jan. 1	FC$ 0.0	—	$ 0.0
Plus			
Issue of Common Stock	30.0	$1.0:1FC	$ 30.0
Sales for Cash and on Account	200.0	$1.5:1FC	300.0
Settlement of Exposed Receivable/Payable at a Gain	2.0	$1.5:1FC	3.0
Unrealized Gain on Exposed Receivable/Payable	—		2.0
Less			
Acquisition of Fixed Assets	(50.0)	$1.0:1FC	(50.0)
Acquisition of Inventory	(150.0)	$1.5:1FC	(225.0)
Selling and Admin. Costs Incurred	(40.0)	$1.5:1FC	(60.0)
Interest Cost Incurred	(2.0)	$1.5:1FC	(3.0)
Income Taxes Paid	(15.0)	$1.5:1FC	(22.5)
Dividend Paid	(5.0)	$2.0:1FC	(10.0)
Net Monetary Liability Position, Dec. 31	(30.0)		$ (35.5)
Unrealized Translation Loss		$2.0:1FC	(60.0)
			$ 24.5

method. The underlying premise of the monetary/non-monetary method is that the translated amounts reflect amounts that the firm would have reported if it had originally made all measurements in U.S. dollars. To implement this underlying premise, GAAP makes a distinction between monetary items and non-monetary items.

A monetary item is an account whose maturity amount does not change as the exchange rate changes. From a U.S. dollar perspective, these accounts give rise to exchange gains and losses because the number of U.S. dollars required to settle the fixed foreign currency amounts fluctuates over time with exchange rate changes. Monetary items include cash, receivables, accounts payable and other accrued liabilities, and long-term debt. Firms translate these items using the end-of-the-period exchange rate and recognize translation gains and losses. These translation gains and losses increase or decrease net income each period, whether or not the foreign unit must make an actual currency conversion to settle the monetary item.

A non-monetary item is any account that is not monetary and includes inventories, fixed assets, common stock, revenues, and expenses. Firms translate these accounts using the historical exchange rate in effect when the foreign unit initially made the measurements underlying these accounts. Inventories and cost of goods sold translate at the exchange rate when the foreign unit acquired the inventory items. Fixed assets and depreciation expense translate at the exchange rate when the foreign unit acquired the fixed assets. Most revenues and operating expenses other than cost of goods sold and depreciation translate at the average exchange rate during the period. The objective is to state these accounts at their U.S. dollar equivalent historical-cost amounts. In this way the translated amounts will reflect the U.S. dollar perspective that is appropriate when the U.S. dollar is the functional currency.

Illustration.   Exhibit 5.9 shows the application of the monetary/non-monetary method to the data considered earlier in Exhibit 5.8. Net income again includes both realized and unrealized transaction gains and losses. Net income under the monetary/non-monetary translation method also includes a $24.5 translation loss. As Exhibit 5.9 (note **b**) shows, the firm was in a net monetary liability position during a period when the U.S. dollar decreased in value relative to the foreign currency. The translation loss arises because the U.S. dollars required to settle these foreign-denominated net liabilities at the end of the year exceed the U.S. dollar amount required to settle the net liability position before the exchange rate changed.

Implications of Functional Currency Determination

As these illustrations demonstrate, the functional currency and related translation method can significantly affect translated financial statement amounts for a foreign unit. Some summary comparisons appear below:

	Functional Currency Is:	
	Foreign Currency	**U.S. Dollar**
Net Income	$ 24.5	$ 5.0
Total Assets	200.0	145.0
Shareholders' Equity	80.0	25.0
Return on Assets	12.3%	3.4%
Return on Equity	30.6%	20.0%

These differences arise for two principal reasons:

1.   The all-current translation method (foreign currency is the functional currency) uses current exchange rates, while the monetary/non-monetary translation method (U.S. dollar is the functional currency) uses a mixture of current and historical rates. Not only are net income and total asset amounts different, but the relative proportions of receivables, inventories, and fixed assets to total assets, debt/equity ratios, and gross and net profit margins differ. When firms use the all-current translation method, the translated amounts reflect the same financial statement relationships (for example, debt/equity ratios) as when measured in the foreign currency. When the U.S. dollar is the functional currency, financial statement relationships get measured (in U.S. dollar equivalent amounts) and financial ratios differ from their foreign currency amounts.

2.   The monetary/non-monetary method includes unrealized translation gains and losses in net income rather than in shareholders' equity. Much of the debate with respect to the predecessor to FASB *Statement No. 52*, which was *Statement No. 8*, involved the inclusion of this unrealized translation gain or loss in net income. Many companies argued that the gain or loss was a bookkeeping adjustment only and lacked economic significance, particularly when the transaction required no currency conversion to settle a monetary item. Also, its inclusion in net income often caused wide, unexpected swings in earnings, particularly in quarterly reports.

As discussed earlier, the organizational structure and operating policies of a particular foreign unit determine its functional currency. When these operating characteristics provide mixed signals, management must exercise judgment in identifying the functional currency. For reasons discussed above, most firms prefer to use the foreign currency as the functional currency because the all-current method generally results in fewer earnings surprises. Some actions that management might consider to swing the balance of factors toward use of the foreign currency as the functional currency include:

1. Decentralize decision making into foreign unit: The greater the degree of autonomy of the foreign unit, the more likely its currency will be the functional currency. The U.S. parent company can design effective control systems to monitor the activities of the foreign unit while at the same time permitting the foreign unit to operate with considerable freedom.

2. Minimize remittances/dividends: The greater the degree of earnings retention by the foreign unit, the more likely its currency will be the functional currency. The parent may obtain cash from a foreign unit indirectly rather than directly through remittances or dividends. For example, a foreign unit with mixed signals about its functional currency might, through loans or transfer prices for goods or services, send cash to another foreign unit whose functional currency is clearly its own currency. This second foreign unit can then remit it to the parent. Other possibilities for interunit transactions are possible to ensure that *some* foreign currency rather than the U.S. dollar is the functional currency.

Interpreting Financial Statement Disclosures

For the following discussion refer to the financial statements for Coke in Appendix A. Coke's Note 1 on accounting policies does not indicate the foreign currency translation method it uses for foreign operations. Note 20 discloses that Coke has substantial foreign involvements (61.2 percent of sales and 51.1 percent of assets in Year 8). Coke conducts a portion of these operations in Latin America and Africa, where high inflation rates often dictate use of the monetary/non-monetary translation method.

The "management discussion and analysis of operations" included elsewhere in Coke's annual report indicates that "other income (deductions)" on the income statement includes an exchange loss of $.5 million for Year 8 on foreign currency transactions and translations of balance sheet accounts for operations in countries for which the U.S. dollar serves as the functional currency. This loss is sufficiently immaterial that Coke does not provide additional disclosures in its notes to the financial statements. The small size of this loss suggests either that Coke maintains a net monetary position close to zero in these countries or that Coke hedges the foreign exchange exposure on its net monetary position.

Coke's balance sheet shows an account, "Foreign Currency Translation Adjustment," in the shareholders' equity section, suggesting that Coke uses the all-current translation method for a portion of its foreign operations. These operations resulted in a negative translation adjustment of $7.206 million at the end of Year 7 and a positive adjustment of $4.031 million at the end of Year 8, an increase of $11.237 million during Year 8. The all-current translation method assumes that Coke's net asset position (that is, assets minus liabilities, or shareholders' equity) is at risk to exchange-rate changes. The reporting of a positive increase in the translation adjustment account suggests that the foreign currency increased in value relative to the U.S. dollar during Year 8.

Refer now to Pepsi's financial statements in Appendix B. Note 14 indicates that Pepsi also has major foreign operations, although not as significant as those of Coke. Pepsi discloses no information about the foreign currency translation method it uses for foreign operations. Its balance sheet shows a "currency translation adjustment" account in the shareholders' equity section. This adjustment account reflects a positive increase during Year 8, the same as for Coke, suggesting that Pepsi also operated in countries whose currency increased in value relative to the U.S. dollar.

Both Coke and Pepsi have significant foreign operations. Changes in exchange rates can significantly affect interpretations of their profitability, independent of the translation method used. Consider the following examples:

	Foreign Subsidiary		U.S. Parent		
Scenario 1	**Foreign Currency**		**U.S. Dollars**	**U.S. Dollars**	**Consolidated**
Sales	FC100	$10:1FC	$1,000	$1,500	$2,500
Expenses	80	$10:1FC	800	1,000	1,800
Net Income	FC 20	$10:1FC	$ 200	$ 500	$ 700
Profit Margin			20%	33%	28%
Scenario 2					
Sales	FC100	$15:1FC	$1,500	$1,500	$3,000
Expenses	80	$15:1FC	1,200	1,000	2,200
Net Income	FC 20	$15:1FC	$ 300	$ 500	$ 800
Profit Margin			20%	33%	26.7%

Under the first scenario, the average exchange rate was $10:1FC during the period. Foreign sales represent 40 percent of consolidated sales (= $1,000/$2,500) and the consolidated profit margin is 28 percent. Under the second scenario, foreign operations as measured in the local currency are identical to those in the first scenario. In this case, however, the average exchange rate was $15:1FC. After translation, foreign sales represent 50 percent of consolidated sales ($1,500/$3,000) and the profit margin is now 26.7 percent. Although the operations of this foreign unit are largely self-contained within the foreign country and, on an operational level at least, not affected by exchange-rate changes, the extent to which the exchange rate changed did have an effect on consolidated financial statements in U.S. dollars. We analyze the impact of foreign operations on the profitability of Coke and Pepsi in later chapters.

Coke's and Pepsi's disclosures regarding foreign operations, though sparse, are not unusual. Most firms aggregate information for all foreign operations so that the analyst encounters difficulties trying to interpret the impact of international activities on profitability and risk. The interpretive difficulties increase when comparing U.S. companies with non-U.S. companies. Reporting practices vary widely. In addition to the all-current and monetary/non-monetary translation methods, some countries permit the current/non-current method (current assets and liabilities translate at the current exchange rate; non-current assets and liabilities translate at the historical exchange rate). In addition to recognizing translation adjustments in income immediately or in a separate shareholders' equity account, some countries require firms to amortize this adjustment into income over a future period of time. As capital markets become more integrated internationally, we would hope that greater uniformity in translation methods will evolve.

Foreign Currency Translation and Income Taxes

Income tax laws make a distinction between a foreign branch of a U.S. parent and a foreign subsidiary of a U.S. parent. A subsidiary is a legally separate entity from the parent, while a branch is not. The translation procedure of foreign branches is essentially the same as for financial reporting (except that taxable income does not include translation gains and losses until realized). That is, a firm selects a functional currency for each foreign branch and uses the all-current or monetary/non-monetary translation method as appropriate.

For foreign subsidiaries, taxable income includes only dividends received each period (translated at the exchange rate on the date of remittance). Because parent companies typically consolidate foreign subsidiaries for financial reporting but cannot consolidate them for tax reporting, temporary differences likely arise that require the provision of deferred taxes.

Segment Reporting

Each of the three topics discussed thus far in this chapter (corporate acquisitions, investments in securities, and foreign currency translation) involves the aggregation of information about various entities or units into a single set of financial statements. When these entities or units operate in an integrated or coordinated manner, it is useful to examine the results of operations and financial position for the combined entities as a whole.

The process of combining or aggregating information for various entities, however, can hinder the analyst in making judgments about the returns and risks of the subunits. For instance, General Electric Company (GE) manufactures and distributes a wide line of industrial and consumer products. Its wholly owned, consolidated subsidiary, General Electric Financial Services (GEFS), operates in leasing, venture capital, investment banking, and other financial services. The consolidated financial statements merge these different activities. Yet the assets of GE are primarily inventories and fixed assets while those of GEFS are largely receivables. The capital structure of GEFS includes considerably more debt than that of GE. To provide useful information about their subunits, GAAP requires firms to disclose certain segment data.[7] This section describes these disclosures, which later chapters use in analyzing the profitability of Coke and Pepsi.

Definition of Segments

GAAP requires firms to report segment data in three ways: (1) product/industry, (2) geographical location (foreign versus domestic), and (3) major customers (for example, U.S. government). However, firms provide segment data only for those segments that make up 10 percent or more of total sales, income, or assets. *Statement No. 14* does not prescribe a list of acceptable segment classes. Instead, firms are free to determine the segment groupings that best characterize their operations. Both Coke (Note 19) and Pepsi (Note 14) indicate that they operate in soft drinks and consumer foods, while Pepsi also operates in restaurants. Both firms have significant foreign operations but break out their segment data differently. Coke, for example, includes Canadian operations with Pacific operations while Pepsi includes Canadian operations with Mexican operations.

Transfer Pricing and Treatment of Central Corporate Expenses

Most firms operate with some degree of integration. As a consequence, most segments sell a portion of their output to other segments within the firm. Two questions arise with respect to intersegment sales:

1. Should segment sales include intersegment sales or should firms eliminate intersegment sales from the segment data?

2. At what transfer price should segments report intersegment sales (cost, market price)?

Statement No. 14 requires firms to disclose material intercompany sales in their segment reports. They must also disclose the transfer price used. Coke indicates in Note 19 that intersegment transfers are not material. Pepsi makes no such disclosure, implying that its intersegment transfers are also immaterial.

A second reporting issue is the treatment of central corporate costs (president's salary, corporate office expenses). Should firms allocate these costs to segments in measuring segment operating profit or should they remain unallocated? FASB *Statement No. 14* does not prescribe one treatment or the other but requires firms to disclose the nature and amount of corporate assets and expenses and indicate clearly how they treat such costs in the segment report.

Coke includes a column in its segment disclosures for "corporate." This column includes amounts that Coke chooses not to allocate to the segments. It does not disclose the items included in the $301.4 million on the operating income line for Year

---

[7]Financial Accounting Standards Board, *Statement of Financial Accounting Standard No. 14,* "Financial Reporting for Segments of a Business Enterprise," (1976).

8. An examination of Coke's income statement suggests that it primarily includes interest expense. Note that the consolidated operating income reported in the segment disclosures is pretax income. Pepsi's segment note indicates that it did not allocate interest and other corporate costs to segments, but provides no further detail.

Segment Items Disclosed

For each identifiable product or industry segment, firms must disclose five items of information:

1. Sales.
2. Operating profit.
3. Identifiable assets.
4. Capital expenditures.
5. Depreciation expense.

For geographic segments, firms must report only segment sales, operating income, and identifiable assets. For segment disclosures by major customers, firms need only report sales.

The segment disclosures required in Canada closely parallel those in the United States. European countries tend to require the reporting of sales by major industry grouping and by geographic location. Firms in these countries seldom disclose information about segment operating income or assets. Japanese companies provide segment sales data beginning in 1993.

Later chapters describe and illustrate the uses made of these disclosures. The following discussion provides an overview of these uses.

1. Profitability analysis: Later chapters discuss the rate of return on assets and its disaggregation into profit margin and asset turnover components. The segment disclosures permit similar calculations at a segment level:

$$\text{Rate of Return on Assets} = \text{Profit Margin} \times \text{Asset Turnover}$$

$$\frac{\text{Operating Profit}}{\text{Identifiable Assets}} = \frac{\text{Operating Profit}}{\text{Sales}} \times \frac{\text{Sales}}{\text{Identifiable Assets}}$$

2. Cash-generating ability of operations: Chapter 2, as will later chapters, discussed the analysis of a firm's cash-generating ability. We focus on cash flow from operations. A measure of a firm's ability to finance itself internally is cash flow from operations divided by capital expenditures. Operating profit plus depreciation expense is roughly equivalent to working capital provided by operations. Although this is not the same as cash flow from operations, it does provide some information about the liquidity characteristics of the segments. When we divide this amount by capital expenditures, the result is a rough measure of the segment's ability to finance itself from operations.

Summary

Unlike reporting topics such as inventories, leases, and deferred taxes (covered in Chapters 3 and 4), which affect only one or a few lines in the financial statements, this chapter's topics tend to affect many line items in the financial statements. The accounting for corporate acquisitions, intercorporate investments, foreign currency translation, and segment reporting is therefore more pervasive with respect to their effects on the financial statements. This situation both increases the potential significance of these topics to the financial analyst and provides a source for concern. Full disclosure of the effects of using the purchase method instead of the pooling of interests method or of translating the financial statements of a foreign unit using the all-current method instead of the monetary/non-monetary method is cumbersome and possibly confusing. The analyst must often contend with less than sufficient disclosures when interpreting financial statements affected by the topics considered in this chapter.

Problems

5.1 *Impact of Purchase versus Pooling of Interests Methods on the Balance Sheet and Income Statement.* Padre Company acquired all of the outstanding common stock of Sardis Company on January 1, Year 2, in exchange for 40,000 shares of Padre Company common stock that was selling for $20 per share. Exhibit 5.10 presents balance sheets of Padre Company and Sardis Company just prior to the acquisition. The firms will treat the acquisition as a nontaxable exchange for income tax purposes. The income tax rate is 34 percent.

    a.   Prepare a consolidated balance sheet for Padre Company and Sardis Company on January 1, Year 2, assuming that these firms account for the acquisition using the purchase method. Be sure to recognize the tax effect of temporary differences between the book and tax basis of assets.

    b.   Repeat part (*a*) using the pooling of interests method.

    c.   Partial income statements for Padre Company and Sardis Company for Year 2 from their separate company activities appear below:

	Padre Company	Sardis Company
Sales	$2,500,000	$1,200,000
Cost of Goods Sold	(1,850,000)	(820,000)
Selling and Administrative Expenses	(410,000)	(270,000)
Interest Expense	(17,000)	(8,000)
Income Tax Expense	(75,820)	(34,680)
Net Income	$ 147,180	$ 67,320

Make the following assumptions.

    (1) The income tax rate for the consolidated firm is 34 percent.

    (2) Both firms use a first-in, first-out cost-flow assumption for inventories.

Exhibit 5.10

Padre Company and Sardis Company Balance Sheets, December 31, Year 1

| | Padre Co. Book Value | Sardis Company | |
		Book Value	Market Value
Assets			
Cash	$ 100,000	$ 30,000	$ 30,000
Accounts Receivable	150,000	100,000	100,000
Inventory	300,000	120,000	180,000
Long-Term Investments	250,000	80,000	240,000
Plant and Equipment (Net)	430,000	160,000	310,000
Other Assets	80,000	40,000	45,000
Total Assets	$1,310,000	$530,000	$905,000
Liabilities and Shareholders' Equity			
Current Liabilities	$ 160,000	$ 50,000	$ 50,000
Bonds Payable	200,000	100,000	100,000
Common Stock, $5 Par Value	500,000	—	—
Common Stock, $2 Par Value	—	200,000	
Additional Paid-in Capital	50,000	80,000	
Retained Earnings	400,000	100,000	
	$1,310,000	$530,000	

(3) The long-term investments represent minority, passive investments (ownership of less than 20 percent) accounted for using
the lower of cost or market method.

(4) The combined company amortizes the difference between the
market value and book value of Sardis Company's plant and
equipment and other assets over 10 years using the straight-line
method, while it amortizes goodwill over 40 years for financial
reporting. The firms cannot deduct goodwill amortization for tax
purposes.

Prepare consolidated income statements for Year 2 assuming the firms
account for the acquisition using (i) the purchase method, and (ii) the
pooling of interests method.

5.2 *Impact of Purchase versus Pooling of Interests Methods on the Balance Sheet
and Income Statement.* Marmee Company and Small Enterprises agree to merge
when the balance sheets of the two companies are as follows:

	Marmee Company	Small Enterprises
Assets	$700,000	$312,000
Liabilities	$150,000	$100,000
Common Stock ($1 Par)	160,000	64,000
Additional Paid-in Capital	120,000	34,000
Retained Earnings	270,000	114,000
Total Equities	$700,000	$312,000

Marmee issues 50,000 shares of common stock with a market value of $800,000 in return for the 64,000 shares of Small Enterprises. An appraisal indicates that the market value of the fixed assets of Small exceeds their book value by $448,000.

a. Prepare consolidated balance sheets for Marmee and Small on the merger date assuming the firms account for the merger using (i) the purchase method, and (ii) the pooling of interests method. Be sure to consider income tax effects.

b. Partial income statements for Marmee and Small for the first year after the merger from their separate-company activities appear below:

	Marmee Company	Small Enterprises
Sales	$2,000,000	$1,500,000
Other Revenues	50,000	10,000
Total Revenues	$2,050,000	$1,510,000
Expenses except Income Taxes	1,700,000	1,300,000
Pretax Income	$ 350,000	$ 210,000

Make the following assumptions:

(1) The income tax rate for the consolidated firm is 34 percent.

(2) Fixed assets have a remaining life of five years on the date of the merger. Both firms use the straight-line depreciation method. The firm amortizes goodwill straight line over 40 years.

(3) The firms cannot deduct amortization of asset costs and goodwill arising from the purchase in computing taxable income for tax returns.

(4) Small Enterprises declared no dividends.

Prepare consolidated income statements and consolidated earnings per share for the first year following the merger. Assume that the firms accounted for the merger using (i) the purchase method, and (ii) the pooling of interests method.

5.3 *Effect of Purchase and Pooling of Interests Methods on Balance Sheet and Income Statement.* Bristol-Myers Corporation and Squibb, both pharmaceutical firms, agreed to merge as of October 1, Year 9. Bristol-Myers exchanged 234 million shares of its common stock for the outstanding shares of Squibb. The shares of Bristol-Myers sold for $55 per share on the merger date, resulting in a transaction with a market value of $12.87 billion. The firms accounted for the merger as a pooling of interests.

a. The most recent balance sheets of Bristol-Myers and Squibb prior to the merger reveal the following (amounts in millions):

	Bristol-Myers	Squibb
Assets	$5,190	$3,083
Liabilities	$1,643	$1,682
Shareholders' Equity	3,547	1,401
	$5,190	$3,083

Prepare summary consolidated balance sheets such as those above for Bristol-Myers and Squibb assuming that the firms accounted for the merger using (i) the pooling of interests method, and (ii) the purchase method. Assume that any excess of market value over book value relates to goodwill.

b. Net income of Bristol-Myers and Squibb prior to and subsequent to the merger appears below (amounts in millions). The amounts for Year 9 exclude a special charge for merger-related expenses.

	Pre-Merger			Post-Merger	
	Year 7	Year 8	First Nine Months of Year 9	Last Three Months of Year 9	Year 10
Bristol-Myers	$710	$829	$716	—	—
Squibb	$358	$425	$384	—	—
Combined	—	—	—	$340	$1,748

Compute the amount of net income that Bristol-Myers Squibb would report for Year 9 using the pooling of interests method.

c. Compute the amount of net income that Bristol-Myers Squibb would report for Year 9 using the purchase method. Assume that the firm amortizes goodwill over 40 years. Note that net income under the purchase method excludes earnings of Squibb prior to the merger.

d. Compute the amount of net income that Bristol-Myers Squibb would report for Year 10 using the purchase method.

e. Complete the following schedule of net income:

	Bristol-Myers Company		Bristol-Myers Squibb Company	
	Year 7	Year 8	Year 9	Year 10
Pooling of Interests Method				
Purchase Method				

f. Refer to the analysis in part (e). Compare the levels and growth rates in net income for the purchase and pooling of interests methods.

5.4 *Effect of Financing on Accounting for Corporate Acquisition at Date of Acquisition and Subsequent Year.* Certain data regarding Frye Corporation and Webster Corporation on January 1, Year 3 appear below:

	Historical Cost		Market Value
	Frye	Webster	Webster
Assets			
Current Assets	$ 800	$ 300	$ 400
Depreciable Assets (Net)	1,200	700	900
	$2,000	$1,000	
Equities			
Liabilities	$ 800	$ 200	200
Common Stock	300	300	} 1,300
Retained Earnings	900	500	
	$2,000	$1,000	

The shares of Webster are selling in the market for $1,300. Frye wishes to acquire 100 percent of Webster's common stock as of January 1, Year 3, and is considering three alternative ways of structuring the transaction.

Alternative A—Issue at par 14 percent, 20-year bonds for $1,300. Use the proceeds to acquire the stock of Webster. Alternative A accounts for the transaction using the purchase method.

Alternative B—Issue to the shareholders of Webster 100 shares of a new Frye convertible preferred stock that have a total par and market value of $1,200 and pay dividends totaling $55 each year. Alternative B accounts for the transaction using the purchase method.

Alternative C—Issue to the shareholders of Webster 500 shares of Frye common stock having a market value of $1,100. Alternative C accounts for the transaction using the pooling of interests method.

The undervalued current assets represent inventories accounted for using a FIFO cost-flow assumption. The undervalued depreciable assets have an average remaining life of 10 years. The firms use the straight-line method. They amortize goodwill over 20 years. The income tax rate is 34 percent. The transaction is a nontaxable exchange for tax purposes in all three cases.

    a.   Prepare a consolidated balance sheet for Frye and Webster as of the date of acquisition on January 1, Year 3, under each of these three alternatives.

    b.   Estimated net incomes for Year 3 if the acquisition had not taken place are as follows: Frye: $1,000; Webster: $500. Compute the amount of consolidated net income to common stock for Frye and Webster for Year 3 under each alternative.

5.5 *Preparing a Consolidated Balance Sheet at Date of Acquisition Using the Purchase Method.* P Company acquired all of the outstanding common stock of S Company on January 1, Year 5. P Co. gave a combination of cash and shares of its own common stock in the exchange. The total market value of the consideration given by P Co. was $140,000. S Co. will remain a legally separate subsidiary but P Co. will consolidate its financial statements with those of S Co. each year. P Co. accounts for the transaction using the purchase method for financial reporting and as a nontaxable exchange for tax purposes. Exhibit 5.11 presents the balance sheets of P Co. and S Co. on January 1, Year 5 (amounts in thousands). The following information applies to S Co.

1. S Co. uses a LIFO cost-flow assumption. The market value of S Co.'s inventory was $60,000 and of its fixed assets was $150,000 on the date of acquisition.

2. S Co. expects to settle a lawsuit pending against it for $5,000 pretax in Year 5. S Co. carries no insurance for such lawsuits. P Co. wishes to establish an acquisition reserve for this lawsuit.

3. S Co. has an unfunded pension obligation of $20,000 as of the date of acquisition. It expects to fund and expense this obligation evenly over the years Year 5 through Year 8.

4. Both companies are subject to an income tax rate of 34 percent.
   a. Prepare an analysis that compares the acquisition cost to the book value of the net assets of S Co. and show the allocation of any excess cost assuming that P Co. uses the purchase method to account for the acquisition.
   b. Prepare a consolidated balance sheet for P Co. and S Co. as of the date of acquisition on January 1, Year 5.

Exhibit 5.11
Consolidation Worksheet as of January 1, Year 5 (Date of Acquisition)

	P Co.	S Co.	Consolidated	Supporting Calculations
Cash	$ 15	$ 10		
Accounts Receivable	30	20		
Inventories	50	40		
Other Current Assets	5	—		
Investment in S Co.	140	—		
Fixed Assets—Net	100	110		
Other Noncurrent Assets	20	—		
Total Assets	$360	$180		
Accounts Payable	$ 50	$ 30		
Other Current Liabilities	30	20		
Long-Term Debt	40	50		
Other Noncurrent Liabilities	10	—		
Common Stock	50	10		
Additional Paid-in Capital	140	30		
Retained Earnings	40	40		
Total Equities	$360	$180		

5.6 *Preparing a Consolidated Balance Sheet and Income Statement One Year after a Purchase Method Acquisition.* Refer to the data for P Co. and S Co. in Problem 5.5. Exhibit 5.12 presents income statements and balance sheets taken from the separate-company books of each company at the end of Year 5 (end of first year after the acquisition). The following information pertains to P Co. and S Co.:

1. P Co. uses the equity method to account for its investment in S Co.

2. Neither company dipped into its LIFO inventory layers during Year 5.

3. S Co.'s fixed assets had an average remaining life of ten years as of the date of acquisition. P Co. and S Co. use the straight-line depreciation method. All depreciation relates to manufacturing operations.

4. S Co. settled the lawsuit during Year 5 for $5,000 pretax and included the loss in selling and administrative expenses of S Co.

Exhibit 5.12
Consolidation Worksheet for Year 5 (First Year after Acquisition)

	P Co.	S Co.	Consolidated	Supporting Calculations
Income Statement				
Sales	$300	$200		
Equity in Earnings of S Co.	15	—		
Total Revenues	$315	$200		
Cost of Goods Sold	$180	$140		
Selling and Administrative Expenses	65	30		
Interest Expense	5	5		
Income Tax Expense	20	10		
Total Expenses	$270	$185		
Net Income	$ 45	$ 15		
Balance Sheet				
Cash	$ 20	$ 15		
Accounts Receivable	40	30		
Inventories	60	50		
Other Current Assets	10	—		
Investment in S Co.	155	—		
Fixed Assets—Net	145	120		
Other Noncurrent Assets	—	—		
Total Assets	$430	$215		
Accounts Payable	$ 60	$ 40		
Other Current Liabilities	40	30		
Long-Term Debt	50	50		
Other Noncurrent Liabilities	5	—		
Common Stock	50	10		
Additional Paid-in Capital	140	30		
Retained Earnings	85	55		
Total Equities	$430	$215		

5. S Co. funded the unfunded pension liability, which relates entirely to factory workers, as anticipated during Year 5.

6. P Co. and S Co. amortize goodwill straight-line over ten years.

Prepare a consolidated income statement for Year 5 and a consolidated balance sheet at the end of Year 5 for P Co. and S Co.

5.7 *Consolidating a Less than Wholly Owned Subsidiary*. Exhibit 5.13 presents amounts taken from the separate company books of Company A and Company B (partial), as well as consolidated amounts for Company A and Company B.

    a. Complete this worksheet by determining the amounts shown on the *separate-company books of Company B*. Enter the appropriate amounts in the "Co. B" column of the worksheet. You may wish to proceed by entering the elimination entries made to prepare the consolidated amounts in the "eliminations" section of the worksheet. Neither company paid dividends during the year.

    b. Based only on the data available after completing part (*a*), what is the apparent operating relationship between Company A and Company B?

Exhibit 5.13
Consolidation Worksheet for Company A and Company B

	Co. A	Co. B	Adjustments and Eliminations	Consolidated
Cash	$ 30			$ 40
Accounts Receivable	50	$ 20		45
Inventories	80			110
Investment in Co. B (80%)	40	—		—
Fixed Assets (Net)	150			200
Goodwill	—	—		16
	$350			$411
Accounts Payable	$ 70	$ 20		$ 65
Other Current Liabilities	40			70
Long-Term Debt	100			130
Minority Interest in Co. B	—			6
Common Stock	70	10		70
Retained Earnings	70			70
	$350			$411
Sales	$400	$220		$440
Equity in Earnings of Co. B	8	—		—
Cost of Goods Sold	(270)	(150)		(240)
Selling and Administrative Expense.	(106)			(156)
Income Taxes	(16)			(26)
Minority Interest in Co. B	—			(2)
Net Income	$ 16			$ 16

5.8 *Consolidating a Less than Wholly Owned Subsidiary.* Parent acquired a controlling interest (but less than 100 percent) in the common stock of Sub on January 1, Year 6. Any excess purchase price relates goodwill, amortized over ten years. Although Parent is a manufacturer and Sub is a consumer finance company, they prepare consolidated financial statements for the two entities together [see column (5) of Exhibit 5.14]. The notes to the financial statements present information for Sub by itself [see column (2) of Exhibit 5.14]. The notes also indicate that Sub owes Parent $20 on December 31, Year 6, for a short-term cash advance made by Parent.

a. Determine the amounts appearing on the separate-company books of Parent and enter the amounts in column (1) of Exhibit 5.14. You may wish to enter the consolidation elimination entries made, placing the amounts in columns (3) and (4), and then working backwards toward the amounts in column (1).

b. Compute the amount paid by Parent on January 1, Year 6, for its investment in Sub.

Exhibit 5.14
Consolidation Worksheet for Parent and Sub
December 31, Year 6

	Parent (1)	Sub (2)	Eliminations Debit (3)	Eliminations Credit (4)	Consolidated (5)
Balance Sheet					
Cash		$ 40			$ 60
Accounts and Notes Receivable		430			460
Inventories		—			90
Investment in Sub's Stock (Equity Method)		—			—
Fixed Assets (Net)		30			161
Goodwill		—			9
		$500			$780
Accounts Payable		$ 20			$ 60
Other Current Liabilities		320			370
Long-Term Debt		80			180
Minority Interest in S		—			20
Common Stock		20			50
Retained Earnings		60			100
		$500			$780
Income Statement for Year 6					
Revenues		$ 97			$807
Equity in Earnings of Sub.		—			—
Cost of Goods Sold		—			(420)
Selling and Admin. Expense		(30)			(272)
Interest Expense		(45)			(55)
Income Tax Expense		(6)			(26)
Min. Int. in Sub's Net Income		—			(4)
		$ 16			$ 30
Dividends Declared		$ 10			$ 20

5.9 *Interpreting Financial Statement Disclosures Regarding Intercorporate Investments in Securities.* Exhibit 5.15 presents a consolidated balance sheet, Exhibit 5.16 presents a consolidated income statement, and Exhibit 5.17 presents a consolidated statement of cash flows for Kaplan Corporation. Excerpts from the notes to Kaplan Corporation's financial statements provide additional information.

Note 1: Summary of Accounting Policies

- *Basis of Consolidation.* Kaplan Corporation consolidates its financial statements with Heimann Corporation, an 80 percent-owned subsidiary acquired on January 2, Year 1.
- *Marketable Securities.* Marketable securities appear at the lower of acquisition cost or market.
- *Investments.* Investments of less than 20 percent of the outstanding common stock of other companies appear at the lower of cost or market. Kaplan Corporation accounts for investments of 20 to 50 percent of the outstanding common stock of unconsolidated affiliates using the equity method.
- *Goodwill.* Kaplan Corporation amortizes goodwill over a period of ten years.

Note 2: Marketable securities appear net of an allowance for market price declines below acquisition cost of $50,000 on December 31, Year 1, and $70,000 on December 31, Year 2.

Note 3: Burton Corporation had a net income of $400,000 and paid dividends of $75,000 in Year 2.

Burton Corporation
(amounts in thousands)

	December 31, Year 1	December 31, Year 2
BALANCE SHEET		
Cash and Marketable Securities	$ 760	$ 840
Accounts Receivable (Net)	6,590	7,400
Other Assets	1,050	1,260
Total Assets	$8,400	$9,500
Notes Payable due within 1 year	$3,900	$4,300
Long-Term Note Payable	2,000	2,000
Other Liabilities	500	875
Common Stock	100	100
Additional Paid-in Capital	1,500	1,500
Retained Earnings	400	725
Total Equities	$8,400	$9,500

	Year 2
STATEMENT OF INCOME AND RETAINED EARNINGS	
Revenues	$ 920
Expenses	(520)
Net Income	$ 400
Less Dividends	(75)
Retained Earnings, December 31, Year 1	400
Retained Earnings, December 31, Year 2	$ 725

Exhibit 5.15
Kaplan Corporation Consolidated Balance Sheets December 31, Year 1 and Year 2 (amounts in thousands)

	December 31, Year 1	December 31, Year 2
ASSETS		
Current Assets		
Cash	$ 1,470	$ 2,919
Marketable Securities (Note 2)	450	550
Accounts Receivable	2,300	2,850
Inventories	2,590	3,110
Prepayments	800	970
Total Current Assets	$ 7,610	$10,399
Investments (Note 3)		
Investment in Maher Corporation (10%)	$ 200	$ 185
Investment in Johnson Corporation (30%)	310	410
Investment in Burton Corporation (40%)	800	930
Total Investments	$ 1,310	$ 1,525
Property, Plant, and Equipment		
Land	$ 400	$ 500
Buildings	800	940
Equipment	3,300	3,800
Total Cost	$ 4,500	$ 5,240
Less Accumulated Depreciation	(1,200)	(930)
Net Property, Plant, and Equipment	$ 3,300	$ 4,310
Goodwill (Note 4)	90	80
Total Assets	$12,310	$16,314
LIABILITIES AND SHAREHOLDERS' EQUITY		
Current Liabilities		
Note Payable	$ —	$ 1,000
Accounts Payable	1,070	2,425
Salaries Payable	800	600
Interest Payable	300	400
Income Taxes Payable	250	375
Total Current Liabilities	$ 2,420	$ 4,800
Long-Term Liabilities		
Bonds Payable	$ 6,209	$ 6,209
Deferred Income Taxes	820	940
Total Long-Term Liabilities	$ 7,029	$ 7,149
Minority Interest in Net Assets	$ 180	$ 214

Exhibit 5.15 (*continued*)

	December 31, Year 1	December 31, Year 2
Shareholders' Equity		
Common Shares ($10 Par Value)	$ 500	$ 600
Additional Paid-in Capital	800	1,205
Unrealized Loss on Valuation of Investments	(25)	(40)
Retained Earnings	1,436	2,406
Total	$ 2,711	$ 4,171
Less Treasury Shares (at Cost)	(30)	(20)
Total Shareholders' Equity	$ 2,681	$ 4,151
Total Liabilities and Shareholders' Equity	$12,310	$16,314

Exhibit 5.16

Kaplan Corporation Consolidated Income Statement for Year 2 (amounts in thousands)

Revenues

Sales	$12,000
Equity in Earnings of Unconsolidated Affiliates	300
Dividend Revenue	20
Gain on Sale of Marketable Securities	30
Total Revenues	$12,350

Expenses

Cost of Goods Sold	$ 7,200
Selling and Administrative	2,689
Loss on Sale of Equipment	80
Unrealized Loss from Price Decline of Marketable Equity Securities	20
Interest	561
Total Expenses	$10,550
Net Income before Income Taxes and Minority Interest	$ 1,800
Income Tax Expense	540
Net Income before Minority Interest	$ 1,260
Minority Interest in Earnings	40
Net Income	$ 1,220

Exhibit 5.17
Kaplan Corporation Consolidated Statement of Cash Flows for Year 2 (amounts in thousands)

Operations

Net Income	$1,220	
Additions		
Depreciation	560	
Deferred Taxes	120	
Loss on Sale of Equipment	80	
Minority Interest in Undistributed Earnings of Consolidated Subsidiary	34	
Amortization of Discount on Bonds	28	
Amortization of Goodwill	10	
Unrealized Loss from Price Decline of Marketable Securities	20	
Increase in Accounts Payable	1,355	
Increase in Interest Payable	100	
Increase in Income Taxes Payable	125	
Subtractions		
Gain on Sale of Marketable Securities	(30)	
Equity in Earnings of Affiliates in Excess of Dividends Received	(180)	
Amortization of Premium on Bonds	(28)	
Increase in Accounts Receivable	(550)	
Increase in Inventories	(520)	
Increase in Prepayments	(170)	
Decrease in Salaries Payable	(200)	
Cash Flow from Operations		$ 1,974

Investing

Sale of Marketable Securities	$ 210	
Sale of Equipment	150	
Investment in Johnson Corporation	(50)	
Purchase of Marketable Securities	(300)	
Acquisition of Land	(100)	
Building	(300)	
Equipment	(1,400)	
Cash Flow from Investing		$ (1,790)

Financing

Increase in Notes Payable	$1,000	
Common Stock Issued	500	
Treasury Stock Sold	15	
Dividends	(250)	
Cash Flow from Financing		1,265
Net Change in Cash		$ 1,449

Note 4: On January 2, Year 1, Kaplan Corporation acquired 80 percent of the outstanding common shares of Heimann Corporation by issuing 20,000 shares of Kaplan Corporation common stock. The Kaplan Corporation shares were selling on January 2, Year 1, for $40 a share. Kaplan Corporation treats any difference between the acquisition price and the book value of the net assets acquired as goodwill and amortizes it straight line over a period of ten years from the date of acquisition.

a. Complete the following analysis of changes in Marketable Securities during Year 2.

Marketable Securities at Acquisition Cost

Balance, December 31, Year 1	$ 500
Plus Purchases	
Less Cost of Marketable Securities Sold	———
Balance, December 31, Year 2	═══

Allowance for Market Price Declines of Marketable Securities

Balance, December 31, Year 1	$ 50
Unrealized Loss during Year 2	
Balance, December 31, Year 2	———

b. Prepare an analysis that explains the changes in the three intercorporate investment accounts during Year 2.

c. The notes to the financial statements indicate that Kaplan owns 80 percent of the outstanding stock of Heimann Corporation. Why isn't this intercorporate investment included among "Investments" on the assets side of the balance sheet?

d. Describe the nature of the account "Minority Interest in Net Assets" that Kaplan Corporation reports on the balance sheet. How is its amount determined?

e. Describe the nature of the account "Minority Interest in Earnings" that appears on the income statement. How is its amount determined?

f. Refer to the statement of cash flows in Exhibit 5.17. Explain the rationale for inclusion of each of the following items in the derivation of cash flow from operations:

(1) Minority interest in undistributed earnings of consolidated subsidiary	$ 34
(2) Amortization of goodwill	$ 10
(3) Unrealized loss from price declines of marketable securities	$ 20
(4) Gain on sale of marketable securities	$ (30)
(5) Equity in earnings of affiliates in excess of dividends received	$(180)

5.10 *Translating the Financial Statements of a Foreign Subsidiary When the Foreign Currency Is the Functional Currency; Consolidation with Domestic Parent.* Powell Corporation, a U.S. parent company, organized Selling, Inc., a wholly owned Colombian subsidiary, to carry out its marketing activities in that country.

Powell contributed $100,000 to establish the subsidiary at a time when the exchange rate between the Colombian peso and the U.S. dollar was $.02. Exhibit 5.18 presents financial statement data for the subsidiary for Year 1. Exhibit 5.19 presents a partial consolidation worksheet for Powell and its Colombian subsidiary. The following additional information pertains to these companies for Year 1.

1. During Year 1, Powell Corporation sold merchandise on account to its Colombian subsidiary totaling $100,000. The subsidiary sold all of the merchandise by year end. Accounts receivable and payable of $25,000 arising from these intercompany sales remain outstanding at year end. The firms denominated the intercompany transaction in Colombian pesos. Powell Corporation has included a transaction loss on its accounts receivable from the subsidiary in Other Expenses.

2. The subsidiary declared and paid its dividend on December 31, Year 1.

Exhibit 5.18
Translation of Financial Statements of Colombian Subsidiary—Year 1

	Colombian Pesos	Exchange Rate	U.S. Dollars
Balance Sheet			
Assets			
Cash	P 500,000		
Accounts Receivable	4,000,000		
Inventories	3,500,000		
Fixed Assets (Net)	1,900,000		
	P9,900,000		
Liabilities and Equity			
Accounts Payable	P2,400,000		
Bonds Payable	2,000,000		
Common Stock	5,000,000		
Translation Adjustment	—		
Retained Earnings	500,000		
	P 9,900,000		
Income Statement			
Revenues	P15,000,000		
Cost of Goods Sold	(10,000,000)		
Depreciation Expense	(100,000)		
Other Expenses	(2,700,000)		
Net Income	P 2,200,000		
Retained Earnings Statement			
Balance, January 1, Year 1	P —		
Plus Net Income	2,200,000		
Less Dividends	(1,700,000)		
Balance, December 31, Year 1	P 500,000		

Exhibit 5.19

Consolidation Worksheet for Powell Corporation and Colombian Subsidiary

	Powell Corp.	Colombian Subsidiary	Adjustments and Eliminations	Consolidated
Balance Sheet				
Cash	$ 48,000			
Accounts Receivable	125,000			
Inventories	260,000			
Investment in Colombian Subsidiary	114,100			
Fixed Assets (Net)	120,000			
Total Assets	$ 667,100			
Accounts Payable	$ 280,000			
Bonds Payable	50,000			
Common Stock	100,000			
Translation Adjustment	—			
Retained Earnings	237,100			
Total Equities	$ 667,100			
Income Statement				
Sales Revenue	$ 500,000			
Equity in Earnings of Colombian Subs. .	39,600			
Cost of Goods Sold	(400,000)			
Depreciation Expense	(20,000)			
Other Expenses	(30,000)			
Net Income	$ 89,600			
Dividends	(20,000)			
Increase in Retained Earnings	$ 69,600			
Retained Earnings, Jan. 1	167,500			
Retained Earnings, Dec. 31	$ 237,100			

3. The exchange rates during Year 1 were:

When Subsidiary Was Organized	$.020:1P
Average for Year 1	$.018:1P
December 31, Year 1	$.015:1P

a. Complete Exhibit 5.18 showing the translation of the subsidiary's accounts into U.S. dollars assuming that the Colombian peso is the functional currency. Include a separate calculation of the translation adjustment.

b. Using the translated amounts from part (*a*), complete the consolidation worksheet in Exhibit 5.19.

5.11 *Translating the Financial Statements of a Foreign Subsidiary When the U.S. Dollar Is the Functional Currency; Consolidation with Domestic Parent.* Refer to the data in Problem 5.10 for Powell Corporation and its Colombian subsidiary. Assume now that the U.S. dollar is the functional currency. Additional information appears below.

Exhibit 5.20
Translation of Financial Statements of Colombian Subsidiary—Year 1

	Colombian Pesos	Exchange Rate	U.S. Dollars
Balance Sheet			
Assets			
Cash	P 500,000		
Accounts Receivable	4,000,000		
Inventories	3,500,000		
Fixed Assets (Net)	1,900,000		
	P 9,900,000		
Liabilities and Equity			
Accounts Payable	P 2,400,000		
Bonds Payable	2,000,000		
Common Stock	5,000,000		
Retained Earnings	500,000		
	P 9,900,000		
Income Statement			
Revenues	P 15,000,000		
Cost of Goods Sold	(10,000,000)		
Depreciation Expense	(100,000)		
Other Expenses	(2,700,000)		
Translation Exchange Loss	—		
Net Income	P 2,200,000		
Retained Earnings Statement			
Balance, January 1, Year 1	P —		
Plus Net Income	2,200,000		
Less Dividends	(1,700,000)		
Balance, December 31, Year 1	P 500,000		

1. The subsidiary issued the bonds and acquired the fixed assets when the exchange rate was $.02.

2. The subsidiary acquired merchandise evenly over the year.

    a. Complete Exhibit 5.20 showing the translation of the subsidiary's accounts into U.S. dollars. Show supporting computations for the translation exchange loss.

    b. Using data from Exhibit 5.20, complete the consolidation worksheet in Exhibit 5.21.

5.12 *Translating the Financial Statements of a Foreign Subsidiary; Comparison of Translation Methods.* Stebbins Corporation established a wholly owned Canadian subsidiary on January 1, Year 6, by contributing US$500,000 for all of

Exhibit 5.21

Consolidation Worksheet for Powell Corporation and Colombian Subsidiary

	Powell Corp.	Colombian Subsidiary	Adjustments and Eliminations	Consolidated
Balance Sheet				
Cash	$ 48,000			
Accounts Receivable	125,000			
Inventories	260,000			
Investment in Colombian Subsidiary	102,500			
Fixed Assets (Net)	120,000			
Total Assets	$ 655,500			
Accounts Payable	$ 280,000			
Bonds Payable	50,000			
Common Stock	100,000			
Retained Earnings	225,500			
Total Equities	$ 655,500			
Income Statement				
Sales Revenue	$ 500,000			
Equity in Earnings of Colombian Subs ..	28,000			
Cost of Goods Sold	(400,000)			
Depreciation Expense	(20,000)			
Translation Exchange Gain (Loss)	—			
Other Expenses	(30,000)			
Net Income	$ 78,000			
Dividends	(20,000)			
Increase in Retained Earnings	$ 58,000			
Retained Earnings, Jan. 1	167,500			
Retained Earnings, Dec. 31	$ 225,500			

the subsidiary's common stock. The exchange rate on that date was C$1:US$.90 (that is, 1 Canadian dollar equaled 90 U.S. cents). The Canadian subsidiary invested C$500,000 in a building with an expected life of 20 years and rented it to various tenants for the year. The average exchange rate during Year 6 was C$1:US$.85 and the exchange rate on December 31, Year 6, was C$1:US$.80. Exhibit 5.22 shows the amounts taken from the books of the Canadian subsidiary at the end of Year 6 measured in Canadian dollars.

a. Prepare a balance sheet, income statement, and retained earnings statement for the Canadian subsidiary for Year 6 in U.S. dollars assuming that the Canadian dollar is the functional currency. Include a separate schedule showing the computation of the translation adjustment account.

b. Repeat part (a) but assume that the U.S. dollar is the functional currency. Include a separate schedule showing the computation of the translation gain or loss.

Exhibit 5.22
Financial Statements of Canadian Subsidiary for Year 6

Balance Sheet December 31, Year 6
Assets

Cash	C$ 77,555
Rent Receivable	25,000
Building (Net)	475,000
	C$ 577,555

Liabilities and Equity

Accounts Payable	6,000
Salaries Payable	4,000
Common Stock	555,555
Retained Earnings	12,000
	C$ 577,555

Income Statement for Year 6

Rent Revenue	C$ 125,000
Operating Expenses	(28,000)
Depreciation Expense	(25,000)
Translation Exchange Loss	—
Net Income	C$ 72,000

Retained Earnings Statement for Year 6

Balance, January 1, Year 6	C$ —
Net Income	72,000
Dividends	(60,000)
Balance, December 31, Year 6	C$ 12,000

c. Why is the sign of the translation adjustment for Year 6 under the all-current translation method and the sign of the translation gain or loss for Year 6 under the monetary/non-monetary translation method the same? Why do their amounts differ?

d. Assuming that the firm could justify either translation method, which method would the management of Stebbins Corporation likely prefer for Year 6?

5.13 *Translating the Financial Statements of a Foreign Subsidiary; Second Year of Operations.* Refer to Problem 5.13 for Stebbins Corporation for Year 6, its first year of operations. Exhibit 5.23 shows the amounts for the Canadian subsidiary for Year 7. The average exchange rate during Year 7 was C$1:US$.82 and the exchange rate on December 31, Year 7, was C$1:US$.84. The Canadian subsidiary declared and paid dividends on December 31, Year 7.

a. Prepare a balance sheet, income statement, and retained earnings statement for the Canadian subsidiary for Year 7 in U.S. dollars assuming that

Exhibit 5.23
Financial Statements of Canadian Subsidiary for Year 7

Balance Sheet
Assets

Cash	C$ 116,555
Rent Receivable	30,000
Building (Net)	450,000
	C$ 596,555

Liabilities and Equity

Accounts Payable	C$ 7,500
Salaries Payable	5,500
Common Stock	555,555
Retained Earnings	28,000
	C$ 596,555

Income Statement

Rent Revenue	C$ 150,000
Operating Expenses	(34,000)
Depreciation Expense	(25,000)
Translation Exchange Gain	—
Net Income	C$ 91,000

Retained Earnings Statement

Balance, January 1, Year 7	C$ 12,000
Net Income	91,000
Dividends	(75,000)
Balance, December 31, Year 7	C$ 28,000

the Canadian dollar is the functional currency. Include a separate schedule showing the computation of the translation adjustment for Year 7 and the change in the translation adjustment account.

b. Repeat part (*a*) but assume that the U.S. dollar is the functional currency. Include a separate schedule showing the computation of the translation gain or loss.

c. Why is the sign of the translation adjustment for Year 7 under the all-current translation method and the sign of the translation gain or loss under the monetary/non-monetary translation method the same? Why do their amounts differ?

d. Assuming that the firm could justify either translation method, which method would the management of Stebbins Corporation likely prefer for Year 7?

5.14 *Interpreting Translated Financial Statements When U.S. Dollar and Foreign Currency Are the Functional Currency.* Exhibit 5.24 presents the translated

Exhibit 5.24
Translated Financial Statements of Foreign Sub

Balance Sheet of Foreign Sub	U.S. Dollar Is Functional Currency (1)	Foreign Currency Is Functional Currency (2)
Cash	$ 6,000	$ 6,000
Accounts Receivable	24,000	24,000
Inventories (FIFO)	20,000	18,000
Property, Plant, and Equipment	50,000	40,000
Total	$100,000	$ 88,000
Accounts Payable	$ 30,000	$ 30,000
Long-term Debt	24,000	24,000
Common Stock	40,000	40,000
Translation Adjustment	—	(12,600)
Retained Earnings	6,000	6,600
Total	$100,000	$ 88,000

Income Statement of Foreign Sub	U.S. Dollar Is Functional Currency (1)	Foreign Currency Is Functional Currency (2)
Sales	$ 76,000	$ 76,000
Cost of Goods Sold	(40,000)	(36,000)
Selling & Administrative	(18,000)	(18,000)
Depreciation	(8,000)	(6,400)
Interest	(2,000)	(2,000)
Income Taxes	(6,000)	(6,000)
Realized Transaction Loss on Receivables	(1,000)	(1,000)
Unrealized Translation Gain	5,000	
Net Income	$ 6,000	$ 6,600

financial statements of Foreign Sub for its first year of operations. Column (1) shows the statements assuming that the U.S. dollar is the functional currency. Column (2) shows the statements assuming that the currency of Foreign Sub is the functional currency.

a.   Did the foreign currency increase or decrease in value relative to the U.S. dollar during the year? Explain.

b.   Describe the likely nature of the transaction that gave rise to the "realized transaction loss on receivables" of $1,000.

c.   Describe the cause of the "unrealized translation gain" of $5,000.

d.   Describe the cause of the "translation adjustment" of ($12,600) on the balance sheet.

e.   What is the profit margin (net income/sales) of Foreign Sub as originally measured in its foreign currency for the year? Explain.

5.15 *Calculating and Comparing the Translation Adjustment with the Translation Gain or Loss.* Foreign Sub is a wholly owned subsidiary of U.S. Domestic Corporation. U.S. Domestic Corporation acquired the subsidiary several years ago. The financial statements of Foreign Sub for Year 6 in its own currency appear below.

	December 31	
	Year 5	Year 6
ASSETS		
Cash	FC 150	FC 250
Accounts Receivable	250	400
Inventories (FIFO)	400	500
Land	600	800
	FC 1,400	FC 1,950
EQUITIES		
Accounts Payable	FC 250	FC 300
Long-Term Debt	200	300
Common Stock	600	600
Retained Earnings	350	750
	FC 1,400	FC 1,950

INCOME STATEMENT	For Year 6
Sales	FC 3,000
Cost of Goods Sold	(2,300)
Selling and Administrative Expenses	(200)
Net Income	FC 500
Less Dividends	(100)
Increase in Retained Earnings	FC 400

The exchange rates between the U.S. dollar and the foreign currency of the subsidiary were:

December 31, Year 5	$ 8:1FC
Average for Year 6	$10:1FC
December 31, Year 6	$12:1FC

On January 1, Year 6, Foreign Sub acquired additional land and financed it in part by assuming long-term debt. It declared and paid dividends on December 31, Year 6. Operating activities occur evenly over the year (that is, not seasonally).

a. Assuming that the currency of Foreign Sub is the functional currency, compute the amount of the change in the cumulative translation adjustment account for Year 6. Indicate whether the change increases or decreases shareholders' equity.

b. Assuming that the U.S. dollar is the functional currency, compute the amount of the translation gain or loss for Year 6. Indicate whether the amount is a gain or loss.

c. Why is the direction of the change in the cumulative translation adjustment account in part (*a*) different from the translation gain or loss in part (*b*)?

5.16 *Comparing the Translation Gain or Loss with the Cumulative Translation Adjustment Account.* International Sub is a wholly owned subsidiary of U.S. Domestic Corporation. The financial statements of International Sub for Year 4 in its own currency are as follows:

		December 31			
		Year 3		**Year 4**	
ASSETS					
Cash	FC	100	FC	150	
Accounts Receivable		300		350	
Inventories		250		300	
Fixed Assets (Net)		550		600	
	FC	1,200	FC	1,400	
LIABILITIES AND SHAREHOLDERS' EQUITY					
Accounts Payable	FC	400	FC	450	
Long-Term Debt		400		450	
Common Stock		100		150	
Retained Earnings		300		350	
	FC	1,200	FC	1,400	

		For Year 4
Sales	FC	1,500
Cost of Goods Sold		(1,000)
Selling and Administrative Expenses		(425)
Net Income	FC	75
Less Dividends		(25)
Increase in Retained Earnings	FC	50

The exchange rates between the U.S. dollar and the foreign currency of the subsidiary were:

December 31, Year 3	$3:1FC
December 31, Year 4	$5:1FC
Average for Year 4	$4:1FC

a. Assume that the functional currency of International Sub is the U.S. dollar. Indicate the sign (debit or credit) of any translation adjustment, explain the reason for the direction of the sign, and describe how the translation adjustment appears in the financial statements for Year 4.

b. Assume now that the currency of International Sub is the functional currency. Repeat the instructions from part (*a*) for this assumption.

5.17 *Identifying the Functional Currency.* Electronic Computer Systems (ECS) designs, manufactures, sells, and services networked computer systems, associated peripheral equipment, and related network, communications, and software products.

Exhibit 5.25 presents segment geographical data. ECS conducts sales and marketing operations outside the United States principally through sales subsidiaries in Canada, Europe, Central and South America, and East Asia, by direct sales from the parent corporation and through various representative and distributorship arrangements. The Company's international manufacturing operations include plants in Canada, East Asia and Europe. These manufacturing plants sell their output to the Company's sales subsidiaries, the parent corporation or other manufacturing plants for further processing.

ECS accounts for intercompany transfers between geographic areas at prices representative of unaffiliated party transactions.

Exhibit 5.25
**Geographical Segment Data for Electronic Computer Systems
(amounts in thousands)**

	Year 3	Year 4	Year 5
Revenues			
U.S. Customers	$ 4,472,195	$ 5,016,606	$ 5,810,598
Intercompany	1,354,339	1,921,043	2,017,928
Total	$ 5,826,534	$ 6,937,649	$ 7,828,526
Europe Customers	$ 2,259,743	$ 3,252,482	$ 4,221,631
Intercompany	82,649	114,582	137,669
Total	$ 2,342,392	$ 3,367,064	$ 4,359,300
Canada, East Asia, Americas customers	$ 858,419	$ 1,120,356	$ 1,443,217
Intercompany	577,934	659,204	912,786
Total	$ 1,436,353	$ 1,779,560	$ 2,356,003
Eliminations	(2,014,922)	(2,694,829)	(3,068,383)
Net revenue	$ 7,590,357	$ 9,389,444	$11,475,446
Income			
United States	$ 342,657	$ 758,795	$ 512,754
Europe	405,636	634,543	770,135
Canada, East Asia, Americas	207,187	278,359	390,787
Eliminations	(126,771)	(59,690)	(38,676)
Operating Income	$ 828,709	$ 1,612,007	$ 1,635,000
Interest Income	116,899	122,149	143,665
Interest Expense	(88,079)	(45,203)	(37,820)
Income before Income Taxes	$ 857,529	$ 1,688,953	$ 1,740,845
Assets			
United States	$ 3,911,491	$ 4,627,838	$ 5,245,439
Europe	1,817,584	2,246,333	3,093,818
Canada, East Asia, Americas	815,067	843,067	1,293,906
Corporate Assets (temporary cash investments)	2,035,557	1,979,470	2,057,528
Eliminations	(1,406,373)	(1,289,322)	(1,579,135)
Total Assets	$ 7,173,326	$ 8,407,386	$10,111,556

Sales to unaffiliated customers outside the United States, including U.S. export sales, were $5,729,879,000 for Year 5, $4,412,527,000 for Year 4, and $3,179,143,000 for Year 3, which represented 50 percent, 47 percent, and 42 percent, respectively, of total operating revenues. The international subsidiaries have reinvested substantially all of their earnings to support operations. These accumulated retained earnings, before elimination of intercompany transactions, aggregated $2,793,239,000 at the end of Year 5, $2,070,337,000 at the end of Year 4, and $1,473,081,000 at the end of Year 3.

The Company enters into forward exchange contracts to reduce the impact of foreign currency fluctuations on operations and the asset and liability positions of foreign subsidiaries. The gains and losses on these contracts increase or decrease net income in the same period as the related revenues and expenses, and for assets and liabilities, in the period in which the exchange rate changes.

Discuss whether ECS should use the U.S. dollar or the currencies of its foreign subsidiaries as its functional currency.

5.18 *Issues in Interpreting Segment Data.* Exhibit 5.26 presents segment data for Hennessey Corporation and Dingman Corporation. Both firms manufacture chemical and automotive products.

Exhibit 5.26
Segment Data for Hennessey Corporation and Dingman Corporation

	Hennessey Corporation		Dingman Corporation	
	Year 4	Year 5	Year 4	Year 5
Sales				
Chemical	$ 580	$ 660	$1,200	$1,400
Automotive	720	840	1,800	2,100
Less Intersegment Sales	(100)	(100)	—	—
Total Sales	$1,200	$1,400	$3,000	$3,500
Operating Income				
Chemical	$ 43	$ 62	$ 120	$ 168
Automotive	65	92	180	252
Total	$ 108	$ 154	$ 300	$ 420
Interest Expense	(4)	(5)	(10)	(12)
Corporate Expense	(4)	(9)	(40)	(58)
Income Tax Expense	(40)	(56)	(100)	(140)
Net Income	$ 60	$ 84	$ 150	$ 210
Assets				
Chemical	$ 960	$1,120	$2,400	$2,800
Automotive	1,080	1,260	2,700	3,150
Total Assets	$2,040	$2,380	$5,100	$5,950

a. Calculate the ratio of net income to total assets for each firm and each year. How do these firms compare on this measure of profitability?

b. Calculate the ratio of total segment operating income to total assets for each firm and each year. How do these firms compare on this measure of profitability?

c. Why do your conclusions on profitability in part (*a*) differ from those in part (*b*)?

d. Calculate the sales mix for each firm and each year assuming (1) the chemical segment makes all intersegment sales, and (2) the automotive segment makes all intersegment sales. Comment on the results.

5.19 *Definition of Segments for Segment Disclosures.* Diversified Chemicals Corporation (DCC) manufactures a variety of chemical products for industrial and consumer markets. Exhibit 5.27 presents sales, operating income, and asset data for its nine principal product groupings.

DCC wishes to establish segment groupings to use in presenting segment financial information in its annual report. You are asked to calculate the ratio: operating income/assets for the following groupings of segments:

a. Each of the segments listed in Exhibit 5.27.

b. Four product groupings: drugs, chemicals, paints, and plastics.

c. Two customer segments: consumer products (drugs, household chemicals, paints, and consumer plastics) and industrial products (industrial and specialty chemicals, and industrial plastics).

d. All segments combined.

e. If you were a financial analyst, which segment grouping would you find most informative?

f. If you were the chief financial officer of DCC, which segment grouping from those identified in parts (*a*), (*b*), and (*c*) would you prefer to report?

Exhibit 5.27
Segment Data for Diversified Chemicals Corporation
(amounts in millions)

Segment	Sales	Operating Income	Assets
Ethical Drugs	$ 300	$ 48	$ 400
Nonprescription Drugs	325	28	350
Generic Drugs	125	19	75
Industrial Chemicals	75	12	225
Specialty Chemicals	130	30	300
Household Chemicals	225	50	450
Paints	110	(30)	225
Industrial Plastics	290	28	555
Consumer Plastics	110	22	200
Total	$1,690	$ 207	$2,780

Case 5.1:
Fisher Corporation*

Effective January 1, 1993, Weston Corporation (Weston) and Fisher Corporation (Fisher) will merge their respective companies. Under the terms of the merger agreement, Weston will acquire all of the outstanding common shares of Fisher. Fisher will remain a legally separate entity. However, Weston will consolidate its financial statements with those of Fisher at the end of each accounting period. According to the merger agreement, Weston can structure the transaction under any of the following three alternatives:

Alternative A   Weston would acquire all of the outstanding common shares of Fisher for $58,500,000 in cash. To obtain the necessary cash, Weston would issue $59,000,000 of 10 percent, 20-year bonds on the open market. For financial reporting purposes, Weston would account for the merger using the purchase method. For tax purposes, the merger transaction is a taxable event to Fisher's shareholders. The tax basis of Fisher's net assets remains the same after the acquisition as before the acquisition; the tax law does not allow a revaluation of these net assets to market value.

Alternative B   Weston would acquire all of the outstanding common shares of Fisher in exchange for the issuance of 1,800,000 shares of a new Weston preferred stock. The preferred stock would carry an annual dividend of $2.00 per share and would be convertible into .75 shares of Weston common stock at any time. The exchange ratio would be one share of the new preferred stock for each common share of Fisher which is outstanding. These preferred shares would not be considered common stock equivalents for purposes of calculating earnings per share. An independent investment banking firm has valued the preferred shares at $50,000,000. For financial reporting purposes, Weston would account for the merger using the purchase method. For tax purposes, the merger transaction is a nontaxable event to Fisher's shareholders. The tax basis of Fisher's net assets carries over after the acquisition.

Alternative C   Weston would acquire all of the outstanding common shares of Fisher in exchange for 1,517,787 shares of Weston's $.30 par value common stock. Based on the market price at the merger date, these shares would have a market value of $48,000,000. For financial reporting purposes, Weston would account for the merger using the pooling of interests method. For tax purposes, the merger transaction is a nontaxable event to Fisher's shareholders. The tax basis of Fisher's net assets carries over after the acquisition.

Summarizing the alternatives:

*The author gratefully acknowledges the assistance of Gary M. Cypres in the preparation of this case.

	Alternative A	Alternative B	Alternative C
Type of Consideration Given	Cash	Convertible Preferred Stock	Common Stock
Value of Consideration Given	$58,500,000	$50,000,000	$48,000,000
Financial Reporting Method	Purchase	Purchase	Pooling of Interests
Tax Reporting Method—Shareholders	Taxable	Nontaxable	Nontaxable
Tax Reporting Method—Fisher	Nontaxable	Nontaxable	Nontaxable

COMPANY BACKGROUND— WESTON (AS OF JANUARY 1, 1993)

Weston was formed on November 4, 1964, in a merger of four companies and has grown continually since that date. Weston is a worldwide Fortune 500 company with 1992 revenues of $482,000,000. The Company designs and manufactures environmental, energy, and engineered products and makes chemicals and specialty products.

The Company's long involvement with environmental protection systems began in 1935 with the development of the Weston machine for cleaning rust and scale from structural steel and other materials. Each Weston machine included air pollution controls to prevent the debris of the cleaning process from spreading. The Weston requires less time and less than one-tenth the energy of sandblasting. Further savings resulted from recycling the abrasive shot used in the cleaning process. As the Weston business grew, the Company expanded its manufacturing capability. In addition to making Westons, spare parts, and associated pollution control equipment, the Company began to produce consumables, such as the abrasives used by the Westons and the replacement filter bags that collected the fine particulate matter resulting from the cleaning process. Soon after the development of the Weston, growing customer interest in separately purchasing the pollution control devices utilized in the Weston machines resulted in the Company's entry into the air pollution control business. By the early 1950s, it was offering a full range of fabric filter systems for a variety of industrial and utility uses. In the mid-1960s, the Company became the North American licensee for certain European air pollution technologies, including "Lurgi" electrostatic precipitators.

To enable Weston to offer more comprehensive systems to solve environmental problems and to broaden its activities into related energy areas, the Company sought an engineering and technological capability to complement its established manufacturing capacity. In 1985 it acquired Metallurgical Engineering Company. The Company also increased its manufacturing capacity by constructing new facilities for its existing product lines and by acquiring additional facilities for the production of industrial fans and blowers and the means to design, erect, and service industrial chimneys. It further augmented its manufacturing capabilities by purchasing, in 1989, BPM Corporation, a manufacturer of precision and industrial ball and roller bearings, motion transmission devices, and related products.

The Company is the exclusive licensee in the United States of certain European technology for the production of steam through the combustion of refuse. The same process permits the recovery of metal and other commercially valuable resources. The steam is used for a variety of purposes, including heating and the generation of electricity. In 1988, the Company completed the construction of its first refuse-to-energy plant using such technology, at Saugus, Massachusetts. The Company is active in designing facilities and seeking to develop processes that allow the efficient and economical use of high-sulfur coal in an environmentally acceptable way on a commercial scale. The Company also participates in developing other clean energy technologies such as the burning of biomass (primarily wood refuse).

The Company's other broad product category is its Chemicals and Specialty Products. The Company is a manufacturer of chemicals, including urethane-based products, pigments, resins, varnishes, dispersions, and color flushes. The Company offers various specialty products used in numerous printing processes including letterpress, offset, silk screen, flexographic, and gravure processes. The Company also produces one-time carbon paper for business forms, data processing, and carbonless reproduction paper.

For the five years ended 1992 (see Exhibit 1), the Company's revenues, net income and earnings per share had each grown at an average compounded annual rate of 23 percent. Growth in 1992 exceeded the average in all categories. These five-year growth rates include the recession year of 1990 when the Company's net income increased by 14 percent despite a sales decline of 5 percent. Weston accomplished this growth rate both from operations and from aggressive corporate acquisitions. The company intends to continue making acquisitions in the future.

Although the Company has exhibited strong financial growth, it has consistently maintained a conservative balance sheet (see Exhibit 2). The Company's debt has steadily declined from 31 percent of long-term capital in 1988 to 24 percent in 1992 (See Exhibit 3). Dividends per share have ranged between 27 percent and 32 percent of earnings per share in each of the last five years.

The Company currently projects 25 percent growth in net income and earnings per share in 1993, with revenues increasing by 16 percent.

COMPANY BACKGROUND—FISHER (AS OF JANUARY 1, 1993)

Fisher Corporation is a leading designer and manufacturer of material handling and processing equipment for heavy industry in the United States and abroad. Its sales have more than doubled and its earnings increased more than sixfold in the past five years. In material handling, Fisher is a major producer of electric overhead and gantry cranes, ranging from 5 tons in capacity to 600-ton giants, the latter used primarily in nuclear and conventional power generating plants. It also builds underhung cranes and monorail systems for general industrial use carrying loads up to 40 tons, railcar movers, railroad and mass transit shop maintenance equipment, plus a broad line of advanced package conveyors. Fisher is a world leader in evaporation and crystallization systems and also furnishes dryers, heat exchangers, and filters to complete its line of chemical processing equipment sold internationally to the chemical, fertilizer, food, drug, and paper industries. For the metallurgical industry, it designs and manufactures electric arc and induction furnaces, cupolas, ladles, and hot metal distribution equipment.

Exhibit 4 presents comparative income statements and Exhibit 5 presents comparative balance sheets for Fisher.

Fisher's management estimates that revenues will remain approximately flat between 1992 and 1993, but that Fisher's net income for 1993 will decline to $2,500,000, compared with $6,600,000 in 1992. This decrease in net income results from a $1,000,000 increase in labor costs in 1993, a $3,000,000 loss in the construction of a crystallization system, a $1,000,000 expenditure to meet expected OSHA requirements, and a $1,000,000 expenditure to relocate one of its product lines to a new plant facility. Fisher has 1,800,000 shares outstanding on January 1, 1993. It currently pays a dividend of $1.22 per share.

Allocation of Purchase Price   Exhibit 6 shows the calculation of the purchase price and the allocation of any excess cost under each of the three alternatives for structuring the acquisition of Fisher. Exhibits 7 to 13 present pro forma consolidated financial statements for Weston and Fisher under each of the three alternatives.

REQUIRED

a. As a shareholder of Fisher, which alternative would you choose and why? Would your answer differ if you were an individual investor versus a pension fund?

b. As the chief financial officer of Weston, which alternative would you choose and why?

Exhibit 1
Weston Corporation Income Statements for the Years Ended December 31
(amounts in thousands)

	1988	1989	1990	1991	1992	Estimated 1993*
Sales	$233,000	$321,300	$306,500	$361,500	$482,100	$560,000
Cost and Expenses						
Cost of Sales	(180,700)	(251,100)	(232,800)	(273,900)	(360,600)	(415,700)
Selling and Admin.	(36,500)	(51,600)	(51,900)	(58,300)	(86,921)	(105,632)
Operating Income	$ 15,800	$ 18,600	$ 21,800	$ 29,300	$ 34,579	$ 38,668
Equity in Net Income of Nonconsolidated						
Entities	2,300	3,800	3,600	2,600	3,200	4,000
	(1,300)	(2,100)	(900)	(400)	(1,600)	(1,000)
Other Income (Expense)	$ 16,800	$ 20,300	$ 24,500	$ 31,500	$ 36,179	$ 41,668
Income before Taxes	(6,800)	(7,500)	(9,900)	(14,000)	(14,179)	(14,168)
Provision for Income Taxes	$ 10,000	$ 12,800	$ 14,600	$ 17,500	$ 22,000	$ 27,500
Net Income	$ 1.25	$ 1.60	$ 1.83	$ 2.22	$ 2.82	$ 3.53
Earnings per Share	$ .40	$ .40	$ .45	$ .63	$ .88	$ 1.20
Dividends per Share of Common Stock						
Ave. Number of Shares of Common Stock						
Outstanding	8,000	8,000	8,000	7,900	7,800	7,800

*Before consideration of the merger with Fisher.

Exhibit 2

**Weston Corporation Consolidated Balance Sheets December 31
(amounts in thousands)**

	1991	1992	Estimated 1993*
ASSETS			
Cash	$ 28,000	$ 28,000	$ 32,000
Accounts Receivable	84,000	90,000	100,000
Inventory	58,000	71,000	82,000
Other	4,000	13,000	13,000
Total Current Assets	$174,000	$202,000	$227,000
Property, Plant, and Equipment	$ 96,000	$116,000	$131,000
Less Accumulated Depreciation	(29,000)	(38,000)	(48,000)
Net	$ 67,000	$ 78,000	$ 83,000
Investment in Nonconsolidated Entities	42,000	45,000	47,000
Goodwill	8,400	8,000	7,800
Other Assets	6,000	7,000	7,200
Total Assets	$297,400	$340,000	$372,000
Liabilities			
Current Portion Long-Term Debt	$ 400	$ 2,000	$ —
Accounts Payable	23,000	30,000	40,000
Accrued Liabilities and Advances	67,000	78,000	91,000
Income Taxes	12,000	21,000	14,000
Total Current Liabilities	$102,400	$131,000	$145,000
Long-Term Debt	48,000	48,000	48,000
Deferred Taxes	9,000	10,000	10,000
Total Liabilities	$159,400	$189,000	$203,000
Shareholders' Equity			
Common Stock	$ 11,000	$ 11,000	$ 11,000
Capital Surplus	55,000	55,000	55,000
Retained Earnings	72,000	85,000	103,000
Total Shareholders' Equity	$138,000	$151,000	$169,000
Total Liabilities and Shareholders' Equity	$297,400	$340,000	$372,000

*Before consideration of the merger with Fisher.

Exhibit 3
Weston Corporation Key Financial Highlights 1989–1993 Estimated

	1989	1990	1991	1992	1993 (E)*
Earnings per Share	$ 1.60	$ 1.83	$ 2.22	$ 2.82	$ 3.53
Dividends per Share	$ .40	$ .45	$ .63	$ .88	$ 1.20
Current Ratio	1.8	2.0	1.7	1.5	1.6
Long-Term Debt as a Percentage of Long-Term Capital	28.9%	26.5%	25.8%	24.1%	22.1%
Return on Average Common Shareholders' Equity	12.4%	12.9%	13.6%	15.2%	17.2%
Book Value per Share	$ 13.50	$ 14.88	$ 17.69	$ 19.36	$ 21.68
Tangible Net Worth ($000)	$99,300	$111,600	$129,600	$143,000	$161,200
Times Interest Earned	5.7	7.8	9.8	10.9	10.0

*Before consideration of the merger with Fisher.

Exhibit 4
**Fisher Corporation Income Statement
(amounts in thousands)**

	1988	1989	1990	1991	1992	Estimated 1993
Sales	$41,428	$53,541	$76,328	$109,373	$102,699	$100,000
Other Revenue and Gains	0	41	0	0	211	200
Cost of Goods Sold	(33,269)	(43,142)	(60,000)	(85,364)	(80,260)	(85,600)
Sell. and Admin. Expense	(6,175)	(7,215)	(9,325)	(13,416)	(12,090)	(10,820)
Other Expenses and Losses	(2)	0	(11)	(31)	(1)	—
Earnings before Interest and Taxes	$ 1,982	$ 3,225	$ 6,992	$ 10,562	$ 10,559	$ 3,780
Interest Expense	(43)	(21)	(284)	(276)	(13)	—
Income Tax Expense	(894)	(1,471)	(2,992)	(3,703)	(3,944)	(1,280)
Income from Contin. Ops.	$ 1,045	$ 1,733	$ 3,716	$ 6,583	$ 6,602	$ 2,500

Exhibit 5

**Fisher Corporation Balance Sheet
(amounts in thousands)**

	1987	1988	1989	1990	1991	1992
Cash	$ 955	$ 961	$ 865	$ 1,247	$ 1,540	$ 3,100
Marketable Securities	0	0	0	0	0	2,900
Accts./Notes Receivable	6,545	7,295	9,718	13,307	18,759	15,000
Inventories	7,298	8,686	12,797	20,426	18,559	18,000
Current Assets	$14,798	$16,942	$23,380	$34,980	$38,858	$39,000
Property, Plant, and Equipment	12,216	12,445	13,126	13,792	14,903	15,000
Less Accum. Depreciation	(7,846)	(8,236)	(8,558)	(8,988)	(9,258)	(9,000)
Other Assets	470	420	400	299	343	1,000
Total Assets	$19,638	$21,571	$28,348	$40,083	$44,846	$46,000
Accts. Payable—Trade	$ 2,894	$ 4,122	$ 6,496	$ 7,889	$ 6,779	$ 7,000
Notes Payable—Nontrade	0	0	700	3,500	0	0
Current Part LT Debt	170	170	170	170	0	0
Other Current Liab.	550	1,022	3,888	8,624	12,879	8,000
Current Liabilities	$ 3,614	$ 5,314	$11,254	$20,183	$19,828	$15,000
Long-Term Debt	680	510	340	170	0	0
Deferred Taxes	0	0	5	228	357	1,000
Total Liabilities	$ 4,294	$ 5,824	$11,599	$20,581	$20,185	$16,000
Preferred Stock	$ 0	$ 0	$ 0	$ 0	$ 0	$ 0
Common Stock	2,927	2,927	2,927	5,855	7,303	9,000
Additional Paid-in Cap.	5,075	5,075	5,075	5,075	5,061	5,000
Retained Earnings	7,342	7,772	8,774	8,599	12,297	16,000
Treasury Stock	0	−27	−27	−27	0	0
Shareholders' Equity	$15,344	$15,747	$16,749	$19,502	$24,661	$30,000
Total Equities	$19,638	$21,571	$28,348	$40,083	$44,846	$46,000

Exhibit 6
Calculation of Purchase Price and Allocation of Excess Cost (amounts in thousands)

	Alternative A	Alternative B	Alternative C*
Purchase Price			
Base Price	$ 58,500	$ 50,000	$ 14,000
Acquisition Costs (Note 1)	500	500	500
Total	$ 59,000	$ 50,500	$ 14,500
Book Value of Contributed Capital of Fisher	(30,000)	(30,000)	(14,000)
Excess of Cost over Book Value to be Allocated to Assets and Liabilities	$ 29,000	$ 20,500	$ 500
Allocation of Excess Cost			
Recognition of "Reserve" for Losses on Long-Term Contracts (Note 2)	3,000 Cr.	3,000 Cr.	—
Write-up of Building and Equipment (Note 3)	17,000 Dr.	17,000 Dr.	—
Recognition of Unfunded Pension Liability (Note 4)	5,000 Cr.	5,000 Cr.	—
Recognition of Estimated Liability to Meet OSHA Requirements (Note 5)	1,000 Cr.	1,000 Cr.	—
Recognition of Estimated Costs to Relocate Facilities in Connection with Product Move (Note 6)	1,000 Cr.	1,000 Cr.	—
Total Allocated to Identifiable Assets and Liabilities	7,000 Dr.	7,000 Dr.	—
Deferred Tax Effect (Note 7)	2,380 Cr.	2,380 Cr.	—
Residual to Goodwill (Note 8)	24,380 Dr.	15,880 Dr.	—
Total Allocated	$29,000 Dr.	$20,500 Dr.	—

*The pooling of interests method ignores the market value of Weston's common shares of $48,000,000. The shares exchanged receive a value equal to the book value of Fisher's contributed capital, $14,000,000. Weston must expense the acquisition costs in the year incurred.

Note 1: Acquisition costs consist of printing, legal, auditing, and finders' fees and increase the cost of the shares of Fisher acquired under Alternatives A and B.

Note 2: The book value of certain long-term contracts of Fisher (relating to a crystallization system) exceeds their market value by $3,000,000. Fisher expects to complete these contracts during 1993. Weston establishes a "reserve" for this loss as of the date of acquisition and includes it among current liabilities. When Fisher completes the contracts in 1993, the consolidated entity will charge the actual loss against the "reserve" for financial reporting. It will then claim a deduction for the loss in calculating taxable income.

Note 3: The market value of Fisher's property, plant, and equipment on January 1, 1993, is $23,000. Their book value and tax basis is $6,000. Thus, Weston allocates $17,000 (= $23,000 – $6,000) of the excess cost to property, plant, and equipment. The consolidated entity will depreciate the excess using the straight-line method over ten years for financial reporting. It cannot depreciate the excess for tax purposes.

Note 4: Fisher has an unfunded pension obligation of $5,000 on January 1, 1993. Fisher had planned to amortize this obligation straight-line over 20 years from January 1, 1993. Weston allocates a portion of the purchase price to this obligation on the date of the acquisition.

Note 5: Fisher expects to incur $1,000 of costs during 1993 on its facilities to comply with various health and safety provisions of OSHA. Weston allocates a portion of the purchase price to recognize this expected cost.

Note 6: Weston intends to relocate the manufacture of certain product lines of Fisher to a new plant facility during 1993. The estimated costs of relocation are $1,000. Weston allocates a portion of the purchase price to recognize this expected cost.

Note 7: FASB *Statement No. 96* requires firms to provide deferred taxes for differences between the book basis and tax basis of assets and liabilities. Weston allocates the $7,000 amount of excess cost shown in Exhibit 6 to individual assets and liabilities for financial reporting. For tax reporting, the basis of these assets and liabilities remains the same as the amounts shown on Fisher's books before the acquisition. Thus, Weston provides deferred taxes of $2,380 (=.34 × $7,000), of which $1,700 [=.34 × ($3,000 Cr. + $1,000 Cr. + $1,000 Cr.)] is a current asset and $4,080 [=.34 × ($17,000 Dr. – $5,000 Cr.)] is a noncurrent liability. The consolidated entity eliminates these deferred taxes as it amortizes the related asset or liability.

Note 8: Weston allocates the remaining excess cost to goodwill. The consolidated entity amortizes goodwill over 40 years.

Exhibit 7

Weston Corporation and Fisher Corporation
Pro Forma Consolidated Balance Sheet as of January 1, 1993, Assuming Cash Exchange
(amounts in thousands)

	Weston (before Acquisition) (1)	To Record Acquisition of Fisher's Shares (2)	(3)	Weston (after Acquisition) (4)	Fisher (after Acquisition) (5)	Consolidation Worksheet Entries (6)	(7)	Pro Forma Consolidated (8)
Assets								
Cash	$ 28,000	(A) 59,000	(B) 59,000	$ 28,000	$ 6,000			$ 34,000
Accounts Receivable	90,000			90,000	15,000			105,000
Inventory	71,000			71,000	18,000			89,000
Other	13,000			13,000		(C) 1,700		14,700
Total Current Assets	$202,000			$202,000	$39,000			$242,700
Property, Plant, and Equipment	$116,000			$116,000	$15,000	(C) 8,000		$139,000
Less: Accumulated Depr.	(38,000)			(38,000)	(9,000)	(C) 9,000		(38,000)
Net Property, Plant, and Equip.	$ 78,000			$ 78,000	$ 6,000			$101,000
Investment in Nonconsolidated Entities	45,000			45,000	—			45,000
Investment in Fisher	—	(B) 59,000		59,000	—	(C) 59,000		
Goodwill	8,000			8,000	—	(C) 24,380		32,380
Other Assets	7,000			7,000	1,000			8,000
Total Assets	$340,000			$399,000	$46,000			$429,080
Liabilities								
Current Portion Long-Term Debt	$ 2,000			$ 2,000	$ —			$ 2,000
Accounts Payable	30,000			30,000	7,000			37,000
Accrued Liabilities and Advances	78,000			78,000	7,000			90,000
Income Taxes	21,000			21,000	1,000		(C) 3,000	22,000
Total Current Liabilities	$131,000			$131,000	$15,000		(C) 1,000	$151,000
Long-Term Debt	48,000		(A) 59,000	107,000			(C) 1,000	107,000
Other Liabilities	—			—	1,000			6,000
Deferred Taxes	10,000			10,000			(C) 5,000	14,080
Total Liabilities	$189,000			$248,000	$16,000		(C) 4,080	$278,080
Shareholders' Equity								
Preferred Stock	$ —			$ —	$ —			$ —
Common Stock	11,000			11,000	9,000	(C) 9,000		11,000
Additional Paid-in Capital	55,000			55,000	5,000	(C) 5,000		55,000
Retained Earnings	85,000			85,000	16,000	(C) 16,000		85,000
Total Shareholders' Equity	$151,000			$151,000	$30,000			$151,000
Total Liabilities and Shareholders' Equity	$340,000			$399,000	$46,000			$429,080

(A) Issue of bonds for cash.

(B) Purchase of Fisher's outstanding common stock and payment of acquisition costs.

(C) Elimination of investment in Fisher and Fisher's shareholders' equity accounts and allocation of excess purchase price (see Exhibit 6 for amounts).

Exhibit 8

Weston Corporation and Fisher Corporation
Pro Forma Consolidated Income Statement for the Year Ending December 31, 1993,
Assuming Cash Exchange
(amounts in thousands)

	Weston	Fisher	Consolidation Worksheet Entries Dr.	Consolidation Worksheet Entries Cr.	Pro Forma Consolidated
Sales	$560,000	$100,000			$660,000
Cost of Sales					
Cost of Sales	(415,700)	(85,600)	(B) 1,700	(E) 5,000	(498,000)
Selling and Administrative	(105,632)	(10,820)	(C) 610	(D) 250	(116,812)
Operating Income	38,668	3,580			$ 45,188
Equity in Net Income of Nonconsolidated Entities	4,000	—			4,000
Other Income (Expense)	(1,000)	200	(A) 5,900		(6,700)
Income before Taxes	41,668	3,780			$ 42,488
Provision for Income Taxes	14,168	1,280	(D) 85	(A) 2,006	14,649
			(E) 1,700	(B) 578	
Net Income	$ 27,500	$ 2,500			$ 27,839
Earnings per Share—Primary	$ 3.53	$ 1.39			$ 3.57
Average Number Shares of Common Stock Outstanding	7,800	1,800			7,800

(A) Interest on debt: .10 × $59,000 = $5,900, tax effect = $2,006
(B) Depreciation expense: $17,000/10 = $1,700; deferred tax effects = .34 × $1,700 = $578
(C) Goodwill amortization: $24,380/40 = $610; tax effect = 0
(D) Elimination of pension expense: $5,000/20 = $250; deferred tax effect = .34 × $250 = $85
(E) Elimination of contract loss, OSHA cost, and relocation costs = $5,000; deferred tax effect: .34 × $5,000 = $1,700

Exhibit 9

Weston Corporation and Fisher Corporation
Pro Forma Consolidated Balance Sheet as of January 1, 1993, Assuming Preferred Stock Exchange
(amounts in thousands)

	Weston (before Acquisition) (1)	To Record Acquisition of Fisher's Shares (2)		Weston (after Acquisition) (4)	Fisher (after Acquisition) (5)	Consolidation Worksheet Entries (6)	Consolidation Worksheet Entries (7)	Pro Forma Consolidated (8)
Assets								
Cash	$ 28,000		(A) 500	$ 27,500	$ 6,000			$ 34,000
Accounts Receivable	90,000			90,000	15,000			105,000
Inventory	71,000			71,000	18,000			89,000
Other	13,000			13,000		(B) 1,700		14,700
Total Current Assets	$202,000			$201,500	$39,000			$242,700
Property, Plant, and Equipment	$116,000			$116,000	$15,000	(B) 8,000		$139,000
Less: Accumulated Depr.	(38,000)			(38,000)	(9,000)	(B) 9,000		(38,000)
Net Property, Plant, and Equip.	$ 78,000			$ 78,000	$ 6,000			$101,000
Investment in Nonconsolidated Entities	45,000			45,000	—			45,000
Investment in Fisher	—	(A) 50,500		50,500	—		50,500 (B)	—
Goodwill	8,000			8,000	—	(B) 15,880		23,880
Other Assets	7,000			7,000	1,000			8,000
Total Assets	$340,000			$390,000	$46,000			$420,580
Liabilities								
Current Portion Long-Term Debt	$ 2,000			$ 2,000	$ —			$2,000
Accounts Payable	30,000			30,000	7,000		3,000 (B)	37,000
Accrued Liabilities and Advances	78,000			78,000	7,000		1,000 (B)	90,000
Income Taxes	21,000			21,000	1,000		1,000 (B)	22,000
Total Current Liabilities	$131,000			$131,000	$15,000			$151,000
Long-Term Debt	48,000			48,000				48,000
Other Liabilities	—			—	1,000			6,000
Deferred Taxes	10,000			10,000			5,000 (B)	6,000
Total Liabilities	$189,000			$189,000	$16,000		4,080 (B)	14,080
								$219,080
Shareholders' Equity								
Preferred Stock	$ —	(A) 50,000		$ 50,000	$ —			$ 50,000
Common Stock	11,000			11,000	9,000	(B) 9,000		11,000
Additional Paid-in Capital	55,000			55,000	5,000	(B) 5,000		55,000
Retained Earnings	85,000			85,000	16,000	(B) 16,000		85,000
Total Shareholders' Equity	$151,000			$201,000	$30,000			$201,000
Total Liabilities and Shareholders' Equity	$340,000			$390,000	$46,000			$420,080

(A) Issue of preferred stock for the outstanding common shares of Fisher and payment of acquisition costs.

(B) Elimination of investment in Fisher and Fisher's shareholders' equity accounts and allocation of excess purchase price (see Exhibit 6 for amounts).

Exhibit 10
Weston Corporation and Fisher Corporation
Pro Forma Consolidated Income Statement for the Year Ending December 31, 1993,
Assuming Preferred Stock Exchange
(amounts in thousands)

	Weston	Fisher	Consolidation Worksheet Entries Dr.	Cr.	Pro Forma Consolidated
Sales	$560,000	$100,000			$660,000
Cost of Sales					
Cost of Sales	(415,700)	(85,600)	(A) 1,700	(D) 5,000	(498,000)
Selling and Administrative	(105,632)	(10,820)	(B) 397	(C) 250	(116,599)
Operating Income	38,668	3,580			$ 45,401
Equity in Net Income of Nonconsolidated Entities	4,000	—			4,000
Other Income (Expense)	(1,000)	200			(800)
Income before Taxes	$ 41,668	$ 3,780			$ 48,601
Provision for Income Taxes	(14,168)	(1,280)	(C) 85	(A) 578	(16,655)
			(D) 1,700		
Net Income	$ 27,500	$ 2,500			$ 31,946
Earnings per Share—Primary	$ 3.53	$ 1.39			*
Average Number Shares of Common Stock Outstanding	7,800	1,800			7,800

(A) Depreciation expense = $17,000/10 = $1,700; deferred tax effect = .34 × 1,700 = $578.
(B) Goodwill amortization = $15,880/40 = $397; tax effect = 0.
(C) Pension expense: $5,000/20 = $250; deferred tax effect = .34 × $250 = $85.
(D) Loss on contract, OSHA and relocation costs = $5,000; deferred tax effect = .34 × $5,000 = $1,700.
*Primary EPS: ($31,946 – $3,600)/7,800   =   3.63
Fully Diluted EPS: $31,946/(7,800 + 1,350)   =   3.49

Exhibit 11

Weston Corporation and Fisher Corporation
Pro Forma Consolidated Balance Sheet as of January 1, 1993, Assuming Common Stock Exchange
(amounts in thousands)

	Weston (before Acquisition) (1)	To Record Acquisition of Fisher's Shares (2)	(3)	Weston (after Acquisition) (4)	Fisher (after Acquisition) (5)	Consolidation Worksheet Entries (6)	(7)	Pro Forma Consolidated (8)
Assets								
Cash	$ 28,000		(B) 500	$ 27,500	$ 6,000			$ 33,500
Accounts Receivable	90,000			90,000	15,000			105,000
Inventory	71,000			71,000	18,000			89,000
Other	13,000			13,000	—			13,000
Total Current Assets	$202,000			$201,500	$39,000			$240,500
Property, Plant, and Equipment	$116,000			$116,000	$15,000			$131,000
Less: Accumulated Depr.	(38,000)			(38,000)	(9,000)			(47,000)
Net Property, Plant, and Equip.	$ 78,000			$ 78,000	$ 6,000			$ 84,000
Investment in Nonconsolidated Entities	45,000			45,000	—			45,000
Investment in Fisher		(A) 14,000		14,000	—		14,000 (C)	—
Goodwill	8,000			8,000	—			8,000
Other Assets	7,000			7,000	1,000			8,000
Total Assets	$340,000			$353,500	$46,000			$385,500
Liabilities								
Current Portion Long-Term Debt	$ 2,000			$2,000	$ —			$2,000
Accounts Payable	30,000			30,000	7,000			37,000
Accrued Liabilities and Advances	78,000			78,000	7,000			85,000
Income Taxes	21,000			21,000	1,000			22,000
Total Current Liabilities	$131,000			$131,000	$15,000			$146,000
Long-Term Debt	48,000			48,000	—			48,000
Other Liabilities	—			—	1,000			1,000
Deferred Taxes	10,000			10,000	—			10,000
Total Liabilities	$189,000			$189,000	$16,000			$205,000
Shareholders' Equity								
Preferred Stock	$ —			$ —	$ —			$ 0
Common Stock	11,000		(A) 455	11,455	9,000	(C) 9,000		11,455
Additional Paid-In Capital	55,000		(A)13,545	68,545	5,000	(C) 5,000		68,545
Retained Earnings	85,000	(B) 500		84,500	16,000			100,500
Total Shareholders' Equity	$151,000			$164,500	$30,000			$180,500
Total Liabilities and Shareholders' Equity	$340,000			$353,500	$46,000			$385,500

(A) Issue of common stock for the outstanding common shares of Fisher.
(B) Immediate expensing of the acquisition costs of $500. See Exhibit 6 for the explanation. The same amount affects net income for 1993; see Exhibit 12.
(C) Elimination of investment in Fisher and Fisher's shareholders' equity accounts.

Exhibit 12

Weston Corporation and Fisher Corporation
Pro Forma Consolidated Income Statement for the Year Ending December 31, 1993,
Assuming Common Stock Exchange
(amounts in thousands)

	Weston	Fisher	Consolidation Worksheet Entries Dr.	Consolidation Worksheet Entries Cr.	Pro Forma Consolidated
Sales	$560,000	$100,000			$660,000
Cost of Sales					
Cost of Sales	(415,700)	(85,600)			(501,300)
Selling and Administrative	(105,632)	(10,820)			(116,452)
Operating Income	$ 38,668	$ 3,580			$ 42,248
Equity in Net Income of Nonconsolidated					
Entities	4,000	—			4,000
Other Income (Expense)	(1,000)	200	(A) 500		(1,300)
Income before Taxes	$ 41,668	$ 3,780			$ 44,948
Provision for Income Taxes	(14,168)	(1,280)		(A) 170	(15,278)
Net Income	$ 27,500	$ 2,500			$ 29,670
Earnings per Share—Primary	$ 3.53	$ 1.39			$ 3.18
Average Number Shares of Common					
Stock Outstanding	7,800	1,800			9,318

(A)   Expensing the cost of acquisition = $500. Income tax effect = .34 × $500 = $170.

EXHIBIT 13
Weston Corporation and Fisher Corporation
Key Financial Highlights

	Actual for Weston Corporation				Weston Corporation and Fisher Corporation—Pro Forma for 1993		
	1989	1990	1991	1992	Alter. A	Alter. B	Alter. C
Earnings per							
Common Share (Primary)	$ 1.60	$ 1.83	$ 2.22	$ 2.82	$ 3.57	$ 3.63	$ 3.18
(Fully Diluted)	—	—	—	—	—	$ 3.49	—
Dividends per							
Common Share*	$ .40	$ .45	$ .63	$.88	$ 1.20	$ 1.20	$ 1.20
Current Ratio*	1.8	2.0	1.7	1.5	1.6	1.6	1.6
Long-Term Debt as Percentage							
of Long-Term Capital*	28.9%	26.5%	25.8%	24.1%	41.5%	19.3%	21.0%
Return on Average Common							
Shareholders' Equity	12.4%	12.9%	13.6%	15.2%	17.4%	17.7%	15.6%
Book Value per Common Share	$ 13.50	$ 14.88	$ 17.69	$ 19.36	$ 19.36	$ 19.36	$ 19.37
Tangible Net Worth ($000)*	$99,300	$111,600	$129,600	$143,000	$118,620	$127,620	$172,500
Times Interest Earned	5.7	7.8	9.8	10.9	5.0	11.5	10.7
(with Preferred Dividend)	—	—	—	—	—	6.5	—

*Pro forma amounts for these ratios are at date of acquisition of Fisher.

Calculation of Key Financial Ratios—Alternative A

Primary earnings per share: $27,839/7,800 = $3.57

Current ratio: $242,700/$151,000 = 1.6

Long-term debt to long-term capital: $107,000/($107,000 + $151,000) = 41.5%

Return on common equity: $27,839/.5[$151,000 + ($151,000 + $27,839 − $9,360)] = 17.4%

   Common dividend = 7,800 × $1.20 = $9,360

Book value per share: $151,000/7,800 = $19.36

Tangible net worth: $429,080 − $32,380 − $278,080 = $118,620

Times interest earned: ($27,839 + $14,649 + $4,630 + $5,900)/($4,630 + $5,900) = 5.0

   Interest expense with no merger: ($27,500 + $14,168 + X)/X = 10.0; X = $4,630

Calculation of Key Financial Ratios—Alternative B

Primary earnings per share: ($31,946 − $3,600)/7,800 = $3.63

   Preferred dividend = 1,800 × $2.00 = $3,600

Fully diluted earnings per share: $31,946/(7,800 + 1,350) = 3.49

Common shares issued upon conversion of preferred: 1.800 × .75 = 1,350

Current ratio: $242,700/$151,000 = 1.6

Long-term debt to long-term capital: $48,000/($48,000 + $201,000) = 19.3%

Return on common equity: ($31,946 − $3,600)/.5[$151,000 + ($151,000 + $31,946 − $3,600 − $9,360)] = 17.7%

Book value per common share: $151,000/7,800 = $19.36

Tangible net worth: $420,580 − $23,880 − $219,080 − $50,000 = $127,620

Times interest earned: ($31,946 + $16,655 + $4,630)/$4,630 = 11.5 With preferred dividend: ($31,946 + $16,655 + $4,630)/($4,630 + $3,600) = 6.5

Calculation of Key Financial Ratios—Alternative C

Primary earnings per share: $29,670/(7,800 + 1,518) = $3.18

Current ratio: $240,500/$146,000 = 1.6

Long-term debt to long-term capital: $48,000/($48,000 + $180,500) = 21.0%

Return on common equity: $29,670/5[$180,500 + ($180,500 + $29,670 − $11,182)] = 15.6%

Common dividend: (7,800 + 1,518) × $1.20 = $11,182

Book value per common share: $180,500/(7,800 + 1,518) = $19.37

Tangible net worth: $385,500 − $8,000 − $205,000 = $172,500

Times interest earned: ($29,670 + $15,278 + $4,630)/4,630 = 10.7

Data Issues in Analyzing Financial Statements

The analytical tools discussed in the remainder of this book use data from the financial statements as inputs. The financial statement data should reflect comparable measurement and reporting procedures both across time and across firms so that the analyst can identify economic differences. This chapter discusses several financial statement data issues that the analyst should consider before applying the analytical tools, including:

1. Restated financial statements.
2. Account classification differences.
3. Accounting principles differences.
4. Reporting period differences.

The chapter also considers issues that arise when using average industry ratios as a basis of comparison when interpreting a particular firm's financial statement ratios.

Restated Financial Statement Data

There are several situations in which GAAP requires firms to restate retroactively the financial statements of prior years when the current year's annual report includes prior years' financial statements for comparative purposes:

1. If a firm decides during the current year to discontinue its involvement in a particular line of business, the revenues and expenses of that business for the current year plus any loss the firm expects to incur at the time of disposal (firms do

not recognize anticipated gains prior to realization) appear in the income statement under "discontinued operations." Likewise, the balance sheet segregates the net assets of discontinued businesses into a single line. The revenues and expenses of such businesses for prior years, which the firm had previously classified under continuing operations, now appear as part of discontinued operations in comparative income statements for those years.

2. If a firm merges with another firm in a transaction accounted for as a pooling of interests, it must restate prior years' financial statements to reflect the results for the two entities combined.

3. Certain changes in accounting principles (for instance, change from a LIFO cost-flow assumption for inventories to any other cost-flow assumption, change in the method of income recognition on long-term contracts) require the restatement of prior years' financial statements to reflect the new method.

The analyst must decide whether to use the financial statement data as originally reported for each year or as restated to reflect the new conditions. Because the objective of most financial statement analysis is to evaluate the past as a guide for projecting the future, the logical response is to use the restated data.

The analyst encounters difficulties, however, in using restated data. Most companies include balance sheets for two years and income statements and statements of cash flows for three years in their annual reports. Analysts can calculate ratios based on balance sheet data only (for example, current assets/current liabilities, long-term debt/shareholders' equity) for two years at most on a consistent basis. Analysts can calculate ratios based on data from the income statement (for example, cost of goods sold/sales) or from the statement of cash flows for three years at most on a consistent basis. However, many important ratios rely on data from both the balance sheet and either the income statement or the statement of cash flows. For instance, the rate of return on common shareholders' equity equals net income to common stock divided by average common shareholders' equity. The denominator of this ratio requires two years of balance sheet data. Thus, it is possible to calculate ratios based on average data from the balance sheet and one of the other two financial statements for only one year under the new conditions. The analyst could obtain balance sheet amounts for prior years from earlier annual reports, but this results in comparing restated income statement or statement of cash flow data for those earlier years with nonrestated balance sheet data.

To illustrate this issue, refer to the financial statements of General Mills (Mills) in Exhibits 6.1 (income statement) and 6.2 (balance sheet). The notes to Mills' financial statements indicate that Mills decided in Year 5 to dispose of its toy and fashion segments and the nonapparel retailing businesses within its specialty retailing segment. It reported a loss of $188.3 million from these discontinued operations in its income statement for Year 5 (see first column of Exhibit 6.1). In its comparative income statements for Year 4 and Year 3 (second and third columns), the income from these discontinued operations appears on the line Discontinued Operations after Tax. Exhibit 6.1 also shows the amounts as originally reported for Year 4 and Year 3 (columns four and five) in which Mills included the revenues and expenses from these operations in continuing operations. Exhibit 6.2 shows the

Exhibit 6.1

Consolidated Statement of Earnings for General Mills, Inc., and Subsidiaries
(amounts in millions, except per share data)

	Fiscal Year Ended			As Originally Reported	
	May 26, Year 5 (52 weeks)	May 27, Year 4 (52 Weeks)	May 29, Year 3 (52 Weeks)	May 27, Year 4 (52 Weeks)	May 29, Year 3 (52 Weeks)
Continuing Operations					
Sales	$ 4,285.2	$ 4,118.4	$ 4,082.3	$ 5,600.8	$ 5,550.8
Costs and Expenses					
Cost of Sales, Exclusive of Items Below	2,474.8	2,432.8	2,394.8	3,165.9	3,123.3
Selling, General and Administrative Expenses	1,368.1	1,251.5	1,288.3	1,849.4	1,831.6
Depreciation and Amortization Expenses	110.4	99.0	94.2	133.1	127.5
Interest Expense	60.2	31.5	39.5	61.4	58.7
Total Costs and Expenses	4,013.5	3,814.8	3,816.8	5,209.8	5,141.1
Earnings from Continuing Operations—Pretax	271.7	303.6	265.5	391.0	409.7
Gain (Loss) from Redeployments	(75.8)	53.0	2.7	7.7	—
Earnings from Continuing Operations after Redeployments—Pretax	195.9	356.6	268.2	398.7	409.7
Income Taxes	80.5	153.9	106.1	165.3	164.6
Earnings from Continuing Operations after Redeployments	115.4	202.7	162.1	233.4	245.1
Earnings per Share—Continuing Operations after Redeployments	$ 2.58	$ 4.32	$ 3.24	$ 4.98	$ 4.89
Discontinued Operations after Tax	(188.3)	30.7	83.0	—	—
Net Earnings (Loss)	$ (72.9)	$ 233.4	$ 245.1	$ 233.4	$ 245.1
Net Earnings (Loss) per Share	$ (1.63)	$ 4.98	$ 4.89	$ 4.98	$ 4.89
Average Number of Common Shares	44.7	46.9	50.1	46.9	50.1

Exhibit 6.2
Consolidated Balance Sheets for General Mills, Inc., and Subsidiaries
(amounts in millions)

	Fiscal Year Ended	
	May 26, Year 5	May 27, Year 4
ASSETS		
Current Assets		
Cash and Short-Term Investments	$ 66.8	$ 66.0
Receivables, Less Allowance for Doubtful Accounts of $4.0 in Yr. 5 and $18.8 in Yr. 4	284.5	550.6
Inventories	377.7	661.7
Investments in Tax Leases	—	49.6
Prepaid Expenses	40.1	43.6
Net Assets of Discontinued Operations and Redeployments	517.5	18.4
Total Current Assets	1,286.6	1,389.9
Land, Buildings, and Equipment, at Cost		
Land	$ 93.3	$ 125.9
Buildings	524.4	668.6
Equipment	788.1	904.7
Construction in Progress	80.2	130.0
Total Land, Buildings, and Equipment	1,486.0	1,829.2
Less Accumulated Depreciation	(530.0)	(599.8)
Net Land, Buildings, and Equipment	956.0	1,229.4
Other Assets		
Net Noncurrent Assets of Businesses to Be Spun Off	$ 206.5	$ —
Intangible Assets, Principally Goodwill	50.8	146.0
Investments and Miscellaneous Assets	162.7	92.8
Total Other Assets	420.0	238.8
Total Assets	**$2,662.6**	**$2,858.1**
LIABILITIES AND STOCKHOLDERS' EQUITY		
Current Liabilities		
Accounts Payable	$ 360.8	$ 477.8
Current Portion of Long-Term Debt	59.4	60.3
Notes Payable	379.8	251.0
Accrued Taxes	1.4	74.3
Accrued Payroll	91.8	119.1
Other Current Liabilities	164.0	162.9
Total Current Liabilities	1,057.2	1,145.4
Long-Term Debt	449.5	362.6
Deferred Income Taxes	29.8	76.5
Deferred Income Taxes—Tax Leases	60.8	—
Other Liabilities and Deferred Credits	42.0	49.0
Total Liabilities	1,639.3	1,633.5
Stockholders' Equity		
Common Stock	$ 213.7	$ 215.4
Retained Earnings	1,201.7	1,375.0
Less Common Stock in Treasury, at Cost	(333.9)	(291.8)
Cumulative Foreign Currency Adjustment	(58.2)	(74.0)
Total Stockholders' Equity	1,023.3	1,224.6
Total Liabilities and Stockholders' Equity	**$2,662.6**	**$2,858.1**

comparative balance sheets for Year 5 and Year 4. Note that the net assets of these discontinued businesses appear on a separate line in the Year 5 balance sheet. However, individual asset and liability accounts include the amounts for these discontinued activities in the Year 4 balance sheet. Thus, Mills provides three years of income statements with the operations of these discontinued businesses set out separately, but only one balance sheet. The analyst cannot even calculate ratios using income statement and average balance sheet data for one year on a consistent basis in this case.

In cases where the firm provides sufficient information to restate prior years' financial statements without injecting an intolerable number of assumptions, the analyst should use retroactively restated financial statement data. In cases where the firm does not provide sufficient information to do the restatements, the analyst should use the amounts as originally reported for each year. When making *interpretations* of the resulting ratios, the analyst attempts to assess how much of the change in the ratios results from the new reporting condition and how much relates to other factors.

Account Classification Differences

Firms frequently classify items in their financial statements in different ways. For example, one firm might report depreciation and amortization expense as a separate item in its income statement, whereas another firm might include it in cost of goods sold and selling and administrative expenses. The analyst cannot compare directly financial statement ratios involving these accounts across the two firms. The analyst must either allocate the amounts for depreciation and amortization expense for the first firm to cost of goods sold and selling and administrative expenses or extract the amounts for depreciation and amortization expense for the second firm from cost of goods sold and selling and administrative expenses and report them separately.

The goal when comparing two or more companies is to obtain comparable data sets. A scan of the financial statements should permit the analyst to identify significant differences that might affect the analysis and interpretations. When the analyst can easily and unambiguously reclassify accounts, the reclassified data should serve as the basis for analysis. If the reclassifications require numerous assumptions, then it is probably better not to reclassify the data. The analyst should make note of the differences in account classification for further reference when interpreting the financial statement analysis.

Accounting Principles Differences

A potentially important source of difference in the data sets between firms is the use of different accounting principles, or methods. Within constraints imposed by generally accepted accounting principles, firms can select the accounting methods they will follow in preparing their financial statements. Exhibit 6.3 lists some of the

Exhibit 6.3
Summary of Generally Accepted Accounting Principles for Major Industrialized Countries

	United States	Canada	France	Japan	Great Britain	Germany
Marketable Securities (Current Asset)	Lower of cost or market	Lower of cost or market	Lower of cost or market	Cost (unless price declines considered permanent)	Lower of cost or market	Lower of cost or market
Bad Debts	Allowance method	Allowance method	Allowance method for identifiable uncollectible accounts	Allowance method	Allowance method	Allowance method for identifiable uncollectible accounts
Inventories —Valuation	Lower of cost or market	Lower of cost or market	Lower of cost or market	Lower of cost or market	Lower of cost or market	Lower of cost or market
—Cost Flow Assumption	FIFO, LIFO, average	FIFO, average	FIFO, average	FIFO, LIFO average	FIFO, average	Average (unless physical flow is FIFO or LIFO)
Fixed Assets—Valuation	Acquisition cost less depreciation	Acquisition cost less depreciation	Acquisition cost less depreciation[a]	Acquisition cost less depreciation	Acquisition cost less depreciation[b]	Acquisition cost less depreciation
—Depreciation	Straight-line, declining balance, sum-of-the-years'-digits	Straight-line, accelerated	Straight-line, accelerated	Straight-line, declining balance, sum-of-the-years'-digits	Straight-line, declining balance, sum-of-the-years'-digits	Straight-line, accelerated
Research and Development	Expensed when incurred	Expensed when incurred	Generally expensed when incurred, but may be capitalized and amortized	Expensed when incurred or capitalized and amortized	Expensed when incurred	Expensed when incurred
Leases	Operating and capital lease methods	Operating and capital lease methods	Operating lease method	Operating lease method	Operating and capital lease methods	Operating and capital lease methods
Deferred Taxes	Deferred tax accounting required	Deferred tax accounting required	Book/tax conformity generally required so deferred tax accounting not an issue	Book/tax conformity generally required so deferred tax accounting not an issue	Deferred tax accounting required based on probability that liability or asset will crystallize	Book/tax conformity generally required so deferred tax accounting not an issue

Investments in Securities

0%–20%	Lower of cost or market	Cost (unless price declines considered permanent)	Lower of cost or market^a	Cost (unless price declines considered permanent)	Lower of cost or market	Cost (unless price declines considered permanent)
20%–50%	Equity method	Equity method	Equity method	Cost (unless price declines considered permanent)	Equity method	Cost (unless price declines considered permanent)
Greater Than 50%	Consolidation required	Consolidation generally required	Consolidation required	Consolidation not required (except in certain filings with the Ministry of Finance)	Both parent company and group (consolidated) financial statements presented	Consolidation required
Corporate Acquisitions Accounting Method	Purchase and pooling of interests methods	Purchase method (pooling permitted only when acquirer cannot be identified)	Purchase method	Purchase method	Purchase and pooling of interests methods	Purchase method
Amortization of Goodwill	Amortized over maximum of 40 years	Amortized over maximum of 40 years	Amortization required	Amortized over maximum of 5 years	Goodwill either written off immediately against a retained earnings reserve or capitalized and amortized over its expected useful life.	Amortized over period of 5 to 15 years

^{a}Generally accepted accounting principles in France permit periodic revaluations of tangible fixed assets and investments to current market values. However, the book/tax conformity requirement in France results in immediate taxation of unrealized gains. As a consequence, revaluations are unusual.

^{b}Generally accepted accounting principles in Great Britain permit periodic revaluations of land, buildings, and certain intangibles to current market values. The firm credits a revaluation reserve account, a component of shareholders' equity.

Exhibit 6.4
Accounting Principles Followed by Coke and Pepsi

	Coke	Pepsi
Inventory Valuation	Lower of cost or market	Lower of cost or market
Inventory Cost-Flow Assumption	FIFO, LIFO, and average	FIFO, LIFO, and average
Depreciation Method	Straight-line	Straight-line
Consolidation	All majority-owned subsidiaries (unless control is temporary)	All majority-owned subsidiaries
Foreign Currency Translation	All-current and monetary/non-monetary	All-current (perhaps monetary/non-monetary as well)
Leases	Operating	Operating and capital

more important areas where differences may exist across firms, both within the United States and between the United States and other countries. Chapters 3, 4, and 5 discussed most of these accounting principles. A reading of the financial statements will reveal important differences that the analyst should consider. The first note to the financial statements usually lists the accounting principles followed.

Exhibit 6.4 compares the accounting principles followed by Coke and Pepsi. The only difference of potential concern is Coke's practice of holding 49 percent interests in its bottlers, thereby avoiding consolidation (see the discussion in Chapter 5). We consider the effect of Coke's practice of avoiding consolidation on profitability and risk analysis in later chapters.

A question similar to that raised earlier for restated data applies here as well. Should the analyst restate the financial statement data of the companies so that they are comparable? Or, should the analyst use the reported amounts in performing the ratio analysis and consider the impact of different accounting methods at the interpretation stage? The response to this question again depends on whether the financial statements and notes provide sufficient information to make reasonably reliable restatements. Chapters 3, 4, and 5 showed the adjustments that the analyst can make for inventory cost-flow assumptions, depreciation methods, leases, deferred taxes, corporate acquisition method, and consolidation policy.[1]

---

[1] A study of the effect of restating financial statements for inventory cost-flow assumptions, depreciation methods, consolidation policy, pension accounting, and deferred tax accounting revealed rank order correlations of the reported and the restated data generally above 95 percent on 16 different profitability and risk ratios. These results should at least lead the analyst to think carefully about the need to make adjustments for differences in accounting principles unless it appears that the differences materially affect the financial statements. See James P. Dawson, Peter M. Neupert, and Clyde P. Stickney, "Restating Financial Statements for Alternative GAAPs: Is It Worth the Effort?" *Financial Analysts Journal* (November–December 1980), pp. 3–11.

Reporting Period Differences

Although the majority of publicly held corporations in the United States use a December year end, there are several industries in which the principal competitors use different year ends. Consider the following example of the consumer foods industry:

Company	Year End
Campbell Soup	August
General Mills	May
Heinz	April
Kellogg	December
Quaker Oats	June

The question arises as to whether the analyst should place firms on a comparable reporting period before performing financial statement analysis.

The response depends on (1) the length of the time period by which the year ends differ, and (2) the occurrence of events during that time period that precludes reasonable comparisons between companies. If the year ends differ by three months or less, then the analyst generally need not make adjustments. If the year ends differ by more than three months and the industry is either cyclical or subject to major strikes, raw materials shortages, or similar problems in the intervening period, then the analyst should examine the impact of different year ends. Note that the analyst need not make adjustments when sales are seasonal (as opposed to cyclical), because the fiscal year for each firm will include a full set of seasonal and nonseasonal quarters.

The analyst obtains the data needed to make adjustments for different year ends from quarterly reports. Publicly held firms provide certain income statement and balance sheet data quarterly, although they do not need to present a full set of financial statements.

The annual report usually includes summary information from these quarterly reports. Exhibit 6.5 presents quarterly information from a recent annual report for Campbell Soup Company. Campbell shows various income statement items for each of the quarters of the last two fiscal years. With this information, the analyst can compute sales or earnings for various periods as follows (amounts in millions):

Year Ended May, Year 8

Sales ($998.8 + $1,179.1 + $1,336.1 + $1,207.4)	=	$4,721.4
Net Earnings ($70.1 + $94.9 + $84.6 + $22.4)	=	$ 272.0

Year Ended February, Year 8

Sales ($1,128.3 + $998.8 + $1,179.1 + $1,336.1)	=	$4,642.3
Net Earnings ($48.1 + $70.1 + $94.9 + $84.6)	=	$ 297.7

Year Ended November, Year 7

Sales ($1,248.6 + $1,128.3 + $998.8 + $1,179.1)	=	$4,554.8
Net Earnings ($70.4 + $48.1 + $70.1 + $94.9)	=	$ 283.5

Because each of these time periods represents the end of a quarter in Campbell's fiscal year, the quarterly report will include the balance sheet for that period end.

Exhibit 6.5
Quarterly Data for Campbell Soup Company
(amounts in millions)

	Year 7			
	First	**Second**	**Third**	**Fourth**
Net Sales...	$1,114.6	$1,248.6	$1,128.3	$998.8
Cost of Products Sold.............................	798.7	872.8	812.0	697.0
Net Earnings	58.7	70.4	48.1	70.1
Per Share				
Net Earnings	.45	.54	.37	.54
Dividends...	.165	.18	.18	.18
Market Price				
High..	33.25	31.88	35.38	34.88
Low..	26.38	28.00	29.44	30.13

	Year 8			
	First	**Second**	**Third**	**Fourth**
Net Sales	$1,179.1	$1,336.1	$1,207.4	$1,146.3
Cost of Products Sold	830.7	920.3	857.8	784.0
Earnings before Cumulative				
Effect of Accounting Change..............	62.4	84.6	22.4	72.2
Cumulative Effect of Change				
in Accounting for Income Taxes	32.5			
Net Earnings...	94.9	84.6	22.4	72.2
Per Share				
Earnings before Cumulative				
Effect of Accounting Change.........	.48	.65	.17	.56
Cumulative Effect of Change				
in Accounting for Income Taxes ...	.25			
Net Earnings.....................................	.73	.65	.17	.56
Dividends	.18	.21	.21	.21
Market Price				
High	34.19	30.00	31.25	26.88
Low...	22.75	24.38	25.75	23.88

Thus, the analyst would use the May data when comparing Campbell and General
Mills. The analyst would use the November year-end data when comparing Campbell with Kellogg because the year ends are sufficiently close. Coke and Pepsi use a
December year end so no adjustment is necessary.

Interpreting Financial Statement Ratios

The analyst can compare financial ratios for a particular firm with similar ratios
for the same firm for earlier periods (time-series analysis) or with those of other
firms for the same period (cross-section analysis). This section discusses some of
the issues involved in making such comparisons.

Comparisons with Corresponding Ratios of Earlier Periods

A time-series analysis of a particular firm's financial statement ratios permits a historical tracking of the trends and variability in the ratios over time. The analyst can study the impact of economic conditions (recession, inflation), industry conditions (shift in regulatory status, new technology), and firm-specific conditions (shift in corporate strategy, new management) on the time pattern of these ratios.

Some of the questions that the analyst should raise before using ratios of past financial statement data as a basis for interpreting ratios for the current period include:

1. Has the firm made a significant change in its product, geographical, or customer mix that affects the comparability of financial statement ratios over time?

2. Has the firm made a major acquisition or divestiture?

3. Has the firm changed its methods of accounting over time? For example, does the firm now consolidate a previously unconsolidated entity?

One major concern with using past performance as a basis for comparison is that the earlier performance might have been at an unsatisfactory level. Any improvement during the current year still leaves the firm at an undesirable level. An improved profitability ratio may mean little if a firm ranks last in its industry in terms of profitability in both years.

Another concern is with interpreting the rate of change in a ratio over time. The analyst's interpretation of a 10 percent increase in profit margin differs depending on whether other firms in the industry experienced a 15 percent versus a 5 percent increase. Comparing a particular firm's ratios with those of similar firms lessens the concerns discussed above.

Comparisons with Corresponding Ratios of Other Firms

The major task confronting the analyst in performing a cross-section analysis is identifying the other firms to use for comparison. The objective is to select firms with similar products and strategies and similar size and age. Few firms may meet these criteria. However, one common approach is to use average industry ratios, such as those published by Dun & Bradstreet and Robert Morris Associates or as derived from computerized data bases. Exhibit 6.6 summarizes the information provided in these published surveys. These published ratios provide an overview of the performance of an industry.

The analyst should consider the following issues when using industry ratios:

1. Definition of an industry: Publishers of average industry ratios generally classify diversified firms into the industry of their major product. General Mills, for example, appears as a "consumer foods" company, even though it generates almost one-fourth of its sales from restaurants. Similarly, General Mills has one of the largest restaurant chains in the United States (Red Lobster and Olive Garden), but the "restaurant" category in these publications does not include amounts for General Mills' restaurants. The "industry" also excludes privately held and foreign

Exhibit 6.6
Description of Published Industry Ratios

Robert Morris Associates, *Annual Statement Studies*

1. Presents common size balance sheets and income statements and 16 financial statement ratios by four-digit standard industrial classification (SIC) code.

2. Provides data for all firms within each four-digit industry code for each of the last five years.

3. Provides data for the most recent year only by size of firm, using assets as the size variable. Data include only firms with assets less than $100 million.

4. Common size statements represent the average for each industry category (not clear whether this is a simple or a weighted average).

5. The summaries present the median and upper and lower quartiles for each ratio.

Dun and Bradstreet, *Industry Norms and Key Financial Ratios*

1. Presents common size balance sheets and income statements and 14 financial statement ratios by four-digit SIC code.

2. Presents data for the most recent year only.

3. Gives no breakdown by size of company.

4. Common size statements constructed for the industry using total assets (balance sheet) and sales (income statement) as the base. The common size percentages times the median level of assets and sales for the industry result in a balance sheet and income statement for the median-size firm.

5. The summaries present the median and upper and lower quartiles for each ratio.

firms. If these types of firms are significant for a particular industry, the analyst should recognize the possible impact of their absence from the published data.

2. Calculation of industry average: Is the published ratio a simple (unweighted) average of the ratios of the included firms or is it weighted by size of firm? Is the weighting based on sales, assets, market value, or some other factor? Is the median of the distribution used instead of the mean?

3. Distribution of ratios around the mean: To interpret a deviation of a particular firm's ratio from the industry average requires information on the distribution around the mean. The analyst interprets a ratio that is 10 percent larger than the industry mean differently depending on whether the standard deviation is 5 percent versus 15 percent greater or less than the mean. The published sources of industry ratios give either the quartiles or the range of the distribution.

4. Definition of financial statement ratios: The analyst should examine the definition of each published ratio to ensure that it is consistent with that calculated by the analyst. For instance, is the rate of return on common shareholders' equity based on average or beginning-of-the-period common shareholders' equity? Does the debt/equity ratio include all liabilities or just long-term debt?

Average industry ratios serve as a useful basis of comparison as long as the analyst recognizes their possible limitations.

Summary

The first six chapters of this book have discussed issues that the analyst should consider *before* calculating financial statement ratios and employing other analytical tools. A checklist is as follows:

1. What is the purpose of the analysis (equity investment, bank loan)?

2. What are the economic characteristics and current conditions in the industry of the firm to be analyzed?

3. What particular strategy has the firm selected to compete within its industry?

4. Are unusual or nonrecurring events reflected in the financial statements that affect the comparability of reported amounts over time (restructuring changes, discontinued operations, extraordinary items, changes in accounting principles)?

5. Are there significant differences in the reported amounts of firms to be compared (accounting principles followed, account classifications, reporting periods)?

A careful and patient reading of the financial statements, notes, and other information presented in the annual report will better focus the analyst's efforts and likely result in more meaningful interpretations.

The next three chapters describe and illustrate analytical tools for assessing the profitability and risk of a firm. Chapter 7 considers the rate of return on assets and its components, and Chapter 8 considers the rate of return on common shareholders' equity and its components. These are the primary tools for assessing a firm's profitability. Chapter 9 discusses the analysis of risk.

Problems

6.1 *Using Originally Reported versus Restated Data.* Grant Corporation manufactures chemical and automotive products. During Year 8, it disposed of its automotive segment and recognized a gain on the sale of $100 million net of taxes. Exhibit 6.7 presents income statements for Grant Corporation for Years 6, 7, and 8. The first three columns show the amounts as originally reported for each year.

Exhibit 6.7
Income Statements for Grant Corporation
(amounts in millions)

	As Originally Reported			As Retroactively Restated in Year 8 Annual Report		
	Year 6	Year 7	Year 8	Year 6	Year 7	Year 8
Sales	$ 3,870	$ 4,060	$ 4,220	$ 3,490	$ 3,836	$ 4,220
Cost of Goods Sold................................	(2,518)	(2,621)	(2,666)	(2,233)	(2,442)	(2,666)
Selling and Administrative....................	(902)	(1,033)	(1,013)	(838)	(920)	(1,013)
Interest...	(67)	(73)	(84)	(70)	(77)	(84)
Income Taxes...	(153)	(133)	(183)	(140)	(159)	(183)
Income from Continuing Operations ...	$ 230	$ 200	$ 274	$ 209	$ 238	$ 274
Discontinued Operations.......................	—	—	56	21	(38)	56
Net Income	$ 230	$ 200	$ 330	$ 230	$ 200	$ 330

The last three columns show the amounts as reported for Year 8 along with restated amounts for Years 6 and 7 to reflect the discontinuance of the automotive business.

a. Compute the profit margin (that is, net income divided by sales) for each of the three years based on the amounts as originally reported.

b. Recompute the profit margin for each of the three years based on the originally reported amounts but use income from continuing operations in the numerator.

c. Recompute the profit margin for each of the three years based on the restated amounts and using income from continuing operations in the numerator.

d. Which set of profit margins from parts (a) to (c) provides the most useful information about the past profitability performance of Grant Corporation? Explain.

e. Which set of profit margins from parts (a) to (c) provides the most useful information for predicting the future profitability of Grant Corporation? Explain.

6.2 *Using Originally Reported versus Restated Data.* In an effort to defend itself against an unfriendly corporate takeover, Union Carbide Corporation sold off a significant portion of its business during Year 6. Exhibit 6.8 presents income statement data and Exhibit 6.9 presents balance sheet data for Union Carbide for Year 5 and Year 6. The first column of each exhibit shows the amounts as originally reported in the Year 5 annual report; the second column shows the amounts for Year 5 as retroactively restated in the Year 6 annual report; the third column shows the amounts reported for Year 6. The income tax rate was 46 percent in both years.

a. If the analyst wished to compare the change in operating performance between Year 5 and Year 6, which columns and amounts in Exhibit 6.8 would the analyst use? Explain.

Exhibit 6.8

**Income Statements for Union Carbide
(amounts in millions)**

	Year 5 as Originally Reported	Year 5 as Restated in Year 6 Annual Report	Year 6 as Reported
Sales	$ 9,003	$ 6,390	$ 6,343
Cost of Goods Sold..............................	(6,252)	(4,597)	(4,343)
Selling and Administrative......................	(2,160)	(1,386)	(1,341)
Interest..	(292)	(279)	(543)
Income Taxes.....................................	441	398	(64)
All Other Items[a]..................................	(1,339)	(1,029)	78
Income—Continuing Operations..............	$ (599)	$ (503)	$ 130
Discontinued Operations[b].......................	—	(96)	569
Extraordinary Items[c]............................	18	18	(473)
Cumulative Effect of Change in Accounting Principle[d]......................			270
Net Income.......................................	$ (581)	$ (581)	$ 496

[a]Includes losses of $858 million ($475 million after taxes) from restructuring ongoing operations during Year 5.
[b]Sale of several major lines of business.
[c]Gains and losses on early extinguishments of debt.
[d]Gain from reversion of excess pension funds back to Company.

Exhibit 6.9

**Balance Sheets for Union Carbide
(amounts in millions)**

	Year 5 as Originally Reported	Year 5 as Restated in Year 6 Annual Report	Year 6 as Reported
Cash and Marketable Securities	$ 459	$ 430	$ 299
Receivables.......................................	1,644	1,114	1,085
Inventories..	1,422	831	746
Prepayments......................................	353	218	247
Net Assets of Discontinued Businesses.....................................	—	1,833	37
Total Current Assets	$ 3,878	$4,426	$2,414
Property, Plant, and Equipment (Net)	5,780	4,527	4,379
Other Assets	923	717	778
Total Assets	$10,581	$9,670	$7,571
Current Liabilities................................	$ 3,055	$2,382	$1,881
Long-Term Debt	1,750	1,713	3,057
Other Noncurrent Liabilities....................	1,757	1,556	1,628
Total Liabilities	$ 6,562	$5,651	$6,566
Contributed Capital	$ 751	$ 751	$1,349
Retained Earnings...............................	3,434	3,434	1,878
Treasury Stock...................................	(166)	(166)	(2,222)
Total Shareholders' Equity.....................	$ 4,019	$4,019	$1,005
Total Liabilities and Shareholders' Equity	$10,581	$9,670	$7,571

b. If the analyst wished to analyze changes in the structure of assets and equities between Year 5 and Year 6, which columns and amounts in Exhibit 6.9 would the analyst use? Explain.

c. If the analyst wished to compute the ratio of income from continuing operations divided by average total assets from continuing operations for Year 6, which amounts from Exhibit 6.9 would the analyst use for Year 5 total assets? Explain.

d. Part of Union Carbide's defensive strategy against an unfriendly takeover was to sell poorly performing assets for cash. By comparing the Year 5 and Year 6 balance sheets, what other actions did Union Carbide apparently take to defend itself during Year 6?

6.3 *Using Originally Reported versus Restated Data.* INTERCO is a manufacturer and retailer of a broad line of consumer products, including London Fog, Florsheim Shoes, Converse, Ethan Allen Furniture, and Lane Furniture. During Year 9, INTERCO became the target of an unfriendly takeover attempt. In an effort to defend itself against the takeover, INTERCO declared a special dividend of $1.4 billion. It financed the dividend by issuing long-term debt and preferred stock. INTERCO planned to dispose of certain businesses to repay a portion of this debt. Exhibits 6.10, 6.11, and 6.12 present balance sheets, income statements, and statements of cash flows, respectively, for INTERCO. The first column of each exhibit

Exhibit 6.10
Balance Sheets for INTERCO
(amounts in thousands)

	Year 8 as Originally Reported	Year 8 as Restated in Year 9 Annual Report	Year 9 as Reported
Cash and Marketable Securities	$ 31,882	$ 23,299	$ 77,625
Receivables	486,657	310,053	329,299
Inventories	805,095	514,193	490,967
Prepayments	35,665	24,984	41,625
Net Assets of Discontinued Businesses	—	521,644	346,372
Total Current Assets	$1,359,299	$1,394,173	$ 1,285,888
Property, Plant, and Equipment (Net)	479,499	317,238	327,070
Other Assets	146,788	118,989	162,344
Total Assets	$1,985,586	$1,830,400	$ 1,775,302
Current Liabilities	$ 373,343	$ 269,315	$ 736,268
Long-Term Debt	299,140	266,191	1,986,837
Other Noncurrent Liabilities	61,766	43,557	57,947
Total Liabilities	$ 734,249	$ 579,063	$ 2,781,052
Contributed Capital	$ 256,740	$ 256,740	$ 339,656
Retained Earnings	1,179,964	1,179,964	(1,208,250)
Treasury Stock	(185,367)	(185,367)	(137,156)
Total Shareholders' Equity	$1,251,337	$1,251,337	$(1,005,750)
Total Liabilities and Shareholders' Equity	$1,985,586	$1,830,400	$ 1,775,302

Exhibit 6.11
Income Statements for INTERCO
(amounts in thousands)

	Year 8 as Originally Reported	Year 8 as Restated in Year 9 Annual Report	Year 9 as Reported
Sales..	$3,341,423	$1,995,974	$2,011,962
Other Income	29,237	13,714	18,943
Total Revenues...............................	$3,370,660	$2,009,688	$2,030,905
Cost of Goods Sold	$2,284,640	$1,288,748	$1,335,678
Selling and Administrative	799,025	493,015	537,797
Interest	33,535	29,188	141,735
Income Taxes......................................	108,457	85,303	19,977
Total Expenses...............................	$3,225,657	$1,896,254	$2,035,187
Income from Continuing Operations..............	$ 145,003	$ 113,434	$ (4,282)
Income from Discontinued Operations...........	—	31,569	74,432
Net Income..	$ 145,003	$ 145,003	$ 70,150

Exhibit 6.12
Statements of Cash Flows for INTERCO
(amounts in thousands)

	Year 8 as Originally Reported	Year 8 as Restated in Year 9 Annual Report	Year 9 as Reported
Operations			
Income (Loss) from Continuing Operations....	$ 145,003	$ 113,434	$ (4,282)
Depreciation	62,772	40,570	40,037
Other Addbacks (Subtractions).........................	13,957	8,750	(24,230)
Change in Operating Working Capital Accounts	(103,958)	(96,271)	29,015
Cash Flow from Continuing Operations	$ 117,774	$ 66,483	$ 40,540
Cash Flow from Discontinued Operations.......	—	27,964	249,704
Cash Flow from Operations	$ 117,774	$ 94,447	$ 290,244
Investing			
Sale of Fixed Assets	$ 8,102	$ 1,145	$ 4,134
Acquisition of Fixed Assets................................	(65,880)	(45,925)	(50,966)
Cash Flow from Investing............................	$ (57,778)	$ (44,780)	$ (46,832)
Financing			
Increase in Short-Term Borrowing.................	$ 1,677	$ 1,677	$ —
Increase in Long-Term Borrowing.................	205,673	205,533	1,967,500
Increase in Capital Stock	4,606	4,606	19,994
Decrease in Long-Term Borrowing................	(95,841)	(85,570)	(617,401)
Decrease in Capital Stock	(160,442)	(160,442)	(102,341)
Dividends..	(64,219)	(64,219)	(1,456,162)
Other..	54	252	(676)
Cash Flow from Financing	$(108,492)	$ (98,163)	$ (189,086)
Net Change in Cash..	$ (48,496)	$ (48,496)	$ 54,326

shows the amounts as originally reported for Year 8. The second column shows the restated amounts for Year 8 to reflect the decision to dispose of certain businesses that the Company had previously included in continuing operations. The third column shows the amounts reported for Year 9.

a. Refer to the balance sheets of INTERCO in Exhibit 6.10. Why is the restated amount for total assets for Year 8 of $1,830,400 different from the originally reported amount for total assets of $1,985,586?

b. Refer to the income statements of INTERCO in Exhibit 6.11. Why are the originally reported and restated net income amounts the same ($145,003) when each of the Company's individual revenues and expenses decreased upon restatement?

c. Refer to the statements of cash flows for INTERCO in Exhibit 6.12. Why is the restated amount of cash flow from operations for Year 8 of $94,447 less than the originally reported amount of $117,774?

d. If the analyst wished to analyze changes in the structure of assets and equities between Year 8 and Year 9, which columns and which amounts in Exhibit 6.10 would the analyst use? Explain.

e. If the analyst wishes to compare the change in operating performance between Year 8 and Year 9, which columns and amounts in Exhibit 6.11 would the analyst use? Explain.

f. Describe briefly how INTERCO's actions during Year 9 might have thwarted an unfriendly takeover attempt.

6.4 *Effect of Different Reporting Periods.* American Airlines, Delta Airlines, and United Airlines dominate the U.S. airline industry. The companies frequently compare themselves on size, route structure, airplane fleet, and other dimensions. Financial analysts frequently compare the operating performance of these airlines. The use of different year ends makes the latter task more difficult. American and United use a calendar-year reporting period whereas Delta uses a fiscal year ending in June. Recessions, tensions in the Middle East, increases in interest rates, and other factors affect the comparability of the financial data for these companies. Quarterly data for each company appear below (amounts in millions):

American Airlines

Calendar Year Ended December 31, Year 9

Operating Revenues....... $2,451.0	$2,715.7	$2,727.4	$2,585.5
Operating Income.......... $ 156.7	$ 286.5	$ 230.8	$ 70.0

Calendar Year Ended December 31, Year 10

Operating Revenues....... $2,688.2	$2,974.4	$3,054.7	$3,007.3
Operating Income.......... $ (8.2)	$ 233.7	$ 143.6	$ (245.1)

Delta Airlines

Fiscal Year Ended June 30, Year 9

Operating Revenues....... $1,881.6	$1,858.1	$2,038.1	$2,311.7
Operating Income.......... $ 148.3	$ 119.9	$ 125.9	$ 284.2

Fiscal Year Ended June 30, Year 10

Operating Revenues....... $2,173.4	$2,048.6	$2,120.4	$2,239.9
Operating Income.......... $ 190.6	$ 70.6	$ 48.1	$ 110.3

Fiscal Year Ended June 30, Year 11		
Operating Revenues....... $2,217.5	$2,129.7	
Operating Income.......... $ (73.6)	$ (312.0)	

United Airlines

	Calendar Year Ended December 31, Year 9		
Operating Revenues....... $2,328.0	$2,516.0	$2,582.0	$2,368.0
Operating Income.......... $ 143.0	$ 222.0	$ 132.0	$ (32.0)

	Calendar Year Ended December 31, Year 10		
Operating Revenues....... $2,156.0	$2,744.0	$2,973.0	$2,804.0
Operating Income.......... $ (47.0)	$ 179.0	$ 129.0	$ (297.0)

a. Calculate the profit margin (operating income divided by operating revenues) for each firm based on their reported amounts for Year 9 and Year 10 (December year end for American and United and June year end for Delta).

b. Recompute the profit margin for Delta for Year 9 and Year 10 using a calendar-year reporting period.

c. What observations would you make, based on the above analysis, about the need to place firms on comparable reporting periods?

6.5 *Effect of Different Reporting Periods.* Digital Equipment and Apollo Computer both manufacture computers and related products. Digital uses a fiscal year ending in June of each year as its accounting period, while Apollo uses the calendar year as its accounting period. Quarterly data for each company appear below:

Digital (amounts in millions)

	Fiscal Year Ended June 30, Year 4		
Sales... $1,074.3	$1,423.8	$1,430.8	$1,655.5
Net Income .... $ 15.9	$ 80.5	$ 101.8	$ 130.6

	Fiscal Year Ended June 30, Year 5		
Sales... $1,515.3	$1,628.0	$1,691.1	$1,851.9
Net Income .... $ 144.2	$ 110.3	$ 91.7	$ 100.5

Apollo (amounts in thousands)

	Calendar Year Ended December 31, Year 3		
Sales... $14,121	$17,607	$21,158	$27,773
Net Income .... $ 2,508	$ 3,867	$ 3,080	$ 3,672

	Calendar Year Ended December 31, Year 4		
Sales... $36,678	$46,007	$57,380	$75,685
Net Income .... $ 4,074	$ 5,142	$ 6,340	$ 8,352

	Calendar Year Ended December 31, Year 5		
Sales... $82,120	$87,548	$ 55,232	$70,675
Net Income (Loss) .... $ 8,846	$ 7,365	$(18,459)	$ 729

a. Calculate the profit margin (net income divided by sales) for Digital Equipment for its Year 4 and Year 5 accounting periods (year ending June of each year).

b. Calculate the profit margin of Apollo Computer for its Year 4 and Year 5 accounting periods (year ending December of each year).

    c. Calculate the profit margin of Apollo Computer for a fiscal year ending in June of Year 4 and Year 5 to place its results on a comparable basis with those of Digital Equipment.

    d. What observations would you make, based on the above analysis, about the need to place firms on comparable reporting periods?

6.6 *Effect of Different Reporting Periods.* Hospital management companies have experienced declining profitability in recent years. More restrictive Medicare reimbursement policies have curtailed hospital admissions and average lengths of stay. The reduction in utilization of their capital-intensive facilities has caused hospitals to report sharply lower earnings and even losses.

    Two leading hospital management companies are Hospital Corporation of America (HCA) and Humana. HCA uses a year ending in December as its accounting period, while Humana uses a year ending in August. Quarterly data for HCA and Humana appear below (amounts in millions):

HCA

Calendar Year Ended December 31, Year 4

Sales	$1,093.9	$1,038.4	$1,001.7	$1,043.9
Net Income	$ 86.5	$ 73.9	$ 69.1	$ 67.2

Calendar Year Ended December 31, Year 5

Sales	$1,184.8	$1,201.1	$1,257.0	$1,355.1
Net Income	$ 104.2	$ 92.6	$ 78.5	$ 63.3

Calendar Year Ended December 31, Year 6

Sales	$1,250.4	$1,250.9	$1,235.1	$1,194.2
Net Income	$ 94.1	$ 68.9	$ 53.8	$ (42.0)

Humana

Fiscal Year Ended August 31, Year 4

Sales	$468.4	$482.4	$507.1	$503.3
Net Income	$ 48.7	$ 47.2	$ 52.0	$ 45.4

Fiscal Year Ended August 31, Year 5

Sales	$515.1	$532.2	$566.5	$574.6
Net Income	$ 54.6	$ 51.2	$ 58.1	$ 52.3

Fiscal Year Ended August 31, Year 6

Sales	$607.1	$651.6	$682.4	$ 659.5
Net Income	$ 56.1	$ 53.7	$ 52.7	$(108.0)

    a. Calculate the profit margins (net income divided by sales) for HCA and Humana for their Year 5 and Year 6 reporting periods.

    b. Calculate the profit margin for HCA for Year 5 and Year 6 on as near a comparable reporting period with Humana as possible.

    c. Calculate the percentage change in sales between Year 5 and Year 6 for HCA and Humana based on their selected reporting periods.

    d. Calculate the percentage change in sales between Year 5 and Year 6 for HCA on as near a comparable reporting period with Humana as possible.

e. What observations would you make, based on the above analysis, about the need to place firms on comparable reporting periods?

6.7 *Calculating Average Industry Ratios.* Selected financial data for seven consumer foods companies for a recent year appear below (amounts in millions):

Company	Rate of Return on Common Equity	Sales	Assets
Campbell Soup	15.0%	$4,378.7	$2,437.5
General Foods...................	17.2%	9,022.4	4,553.7
General Mills	-6.5%	4,285.2	2,662.6
Heinz	22.6%	4,047.9	2,473.8
Kellogg............................	34.2%	2,930.1	1,726.1
Pillsbury	17.4%	4,670.6	2,778.5
Quaker Oats.....................	20.3%	3,520.1	1,841.9
Total..............................		$32,855.0	$18,474.1

a. Determine the median rate of return on common equity for the consumer foods industry.
b. Calculate the average rate of return on common equity for the consumer foods industry, with the mean defined as: (1) simple (unweighted) mean, (2) weighted mean using sales, and (3) weighted mean using assets.
c. How well did General Foods perform relative to its industry?
d. Which of the industry measures from parts (*a*) and (*b*) do you think best captures the profitability of the industry?

6.8 *Calculating Average Industry Ratios.* Shown below are selected financial data for seven New York commercial banks for a recent year (amounts in millions):

Company	Rate of Return on Common Stock Equity	Revenues	Assets
Bankers Trust....................	16.30%	$3,849.7	$43,180
Bank of New York.............	16.23%	1,833.2	18,268
Chase Manhattan..............	13.07%	11,365.7	106,841
Chemical Bank	13.53%	4,399.6	45,947
Citicorp...........................	13.27%	26,214.4	206,486
Manufacturers Hanover ...	12.08%	8,127.1	76,394
J.P. Morgan......................	18.98%	5,316.2	56,465
Total..............................		$61,105.9	$553,581

a. Determine the median rate of return on common equity for these New York banks.
b. Calculate the mean rate of return on common equity for these New York banks, with the mean defined as (1) simple (unweighted) mean, (2) weighted mean using revenues, and (3) weighted mean using assets.
c. Why do these measures of central tendency differ for this set of New York banks?
d. The standard deviation of the set of rates of return on common stock equity is 2.27 around the simple mean of 14.78 percent. A particular analyst views a firm that has a rate of return greater than one standard deviation

away from the mean as "significantly" underperforming or overperforming the industry. Indicate the firms in the commercial banking industry above that the analyst would classify as underperformers or overperformers.

6.9 *Calculating Common Size Income Statement for Computer Industry.* Exhibit 6.13 presents income statement data for a recent year for five manufacturers of mainframe computers. A common size income statement for each company also appears.

    a. Prepare a common size income statement for this segment of the computer industry using as the measure of central tendency the (1) median, (2) simple average, and (3) weighted average based on sales.

    b. The median for each income statement item (for example, cost of goods sold, interest expense) will not net to the median profit margin. Why does this occur?

    c. Why does the common size income statement based on simple averaging differ so much from the corresponding statement based on a weighted average?

    d. The standard deviation of profit margin around the simple mean is 3.4. A particular financial analyst views a firm that has a profit margin more than one standard deviation away from the mean to be significantly underperforming or overperforming the industry. Identify the underperformers or overperformers by this definition.

Exhibit 6.13
Income Statement Data for Mainframe Computer Industry
(amounts in millions)

	Amdahl		Control Data		Honeywell		IBM		UNISYS	
	Amount	%	Amount	%	Amount	%	Amount	%	Amount	%
Sales.........................	$1,505	100.0%	$3,366	100.0%	$6,679	100.0%	$54,217	100.0%	$9,714	100.0%
Cost of Goods Sold ...	(826)	(54.9)	(2,347)	(69.7)	(4,780)	(71.6)	(24,610)	(45.4)	(5,639)	(58.1)
Selling and Adminis- trative Expenses ...	(248)	(16.5)	(601)	(17.9)	(1,092)	(16.3)	(16,431)	(30.3)	(2,350)	(24.2)
Research and Devel- opment Expense...	(179)	(11.9)	(389)	(11.6)	(290)	(4.3)	(5,434)	(10.0)	(597)	(6.1)
Interest Expense.......	(18)	(1.2)	(64)	(1.9)	(125)	(1.9)	(485)	(.9)	(256)	(2.6)
Income Tax Expense.	(125)	(8.3)	(32)	(.9)	(158)	(2.4)	(3,351)	(6.2)	(370)	(3.8)
All Other Items.........	33	2.2	92	2.7	20	.3	1,352	2.5	76	.8
Net Income..............	$ 142	9.4%	$ 25	.7%	$ 254	3.8%	$ 5,258	9.7%	$ 578	6.0%

CASE 6.1:
Tanaguchi Corporation—Part A*

Dave Ando and Yoshi Yashima, recent business school graduates, work as research security analysts for a mutual fund specializing in international equity investments. Based on several strategy meetings, senior managers of the fund decided to invest in the machine tool industry. One international company under consideration is Tanaguchi Corporation, a Japanese manufacturer of machine tools. As staff analysts assigned to perform fundamental analysis on all new investment options, Ando and Yashima obtain a copy of Tanaguchi Corporation's unconsolidated financial statements (Appendix A of this case) and set out to calculate their usual spreadsheet of financial statement ratios. Exhibit 1 presents the results of their efforts. As a basis for comparison, Exhibit 1 also presents the median ratios for U.S. machine tool companies for a comparable year. The following conversation ensues.

Dave:　　Tanaguchi Corporation does not appear to be as profitable as comparable U.S. firms. Its operating margin and rate of return on assets are significantly less than the median ratios for U.S. machine tool operators. Its rate of return on common equity is only slightly less than its U.S. counterparts, but this is at the expense of assuming much more financial leverage and therefore risk. Most of this leverage is in the form of short-term borrowing. You can see this in its higher total liabilities to total assets ratio combined with its lower long-term debt ratio. This short-term borrowing and higher risk are also evidenced by the lower current and quick ratios. Finally, the market price of Tanaguchi Corporation's shares are selling at a higher multiple of net income and stockholders' equity than those of U.S. machine tool companies. I can't see how we can justify paying more for a company that is less profitable and more risky than comparable U.S. companies. It doesn't seem to me that it is worth exploring this investment possibility any further.

Yoshi:　　You may be right, Dave. However, I wonder if we are not comparing apples and oranges. As a Japanese company, Tanaguchi Corporation operates in an entirely different institutional and cultural environment than U.S. machine tool companies. Furthermore, it prepares its financial statements in accordance with Japanese generally accepted accounting principles (GAAP), which differ from those in the United States.

Dave:　　Well, I think we need to explore this further. I recall seeing a report on an associate's desk comparing U.S. and Japanese accounting principles. I will get a copy for us (Appendix B of this case).

---

*Paul R. Brown of New York University coauthored this case. It appeared in *Issues in Accounting Education* (Spring 1992), pp. 57–79 and is reproduced with permission of the American Accounting Association.

Exhibit 1

Comparative Financial Ratio Analysis for Tanaguchi Corporation and U.S. Machine Tool Companies

	Tanaguchi Corporation	Median Ratio for U.S. Tool Companies[a]
Profitability Ratios		
Operating Margin after Taxes (before interest expense and related tax effects)	2.8%	3.3%
× Total Assets Turnover	1.5	1.8
= Return on Assets	4.2%	5.9%
× Common's Share of Operating Earnings[b]	.83	.91
× Capital Structure Leverage[c]	3.8	2.6
= Return on Common Equity	13.3%[d]	13.9%[d]
Operating Margin Analysis		
Sales	100.0%	100.0%
Other Revenues/Sales	.4	—
Cost of Goods Sold/Sales	(73.2)	(69.3)
Selling and Administrative/Sales	(21.0)	(25.8)
Income Taxes/Sales	(3.4)	(1.6)
Operating Margin (excluding interest and related tax effects)	2.8%	3.3%
Assets Turnover Analysis		
Receivable Turnover	5.1	6.9
Inventory Turnover	6.3	5.2
Fixed Asset Turnover	7.5	7.0
Risk Analysis		
Current Ratio	1.1	1.6
Quick Ratio	.7	.9
Total Liabilities/Total Assets	73.8%	61.1%
Long-Term Debt/Total Assets	4.7%	16.1%
Long-Term Debt/Stockholders' Equity	17.9%	43.2%
Times Interest Covered	5.8	3.1
Market Price Ratios (per common share)		
Market Price/Net Income	45.0	9.0
Market Price/Stockholders' Equity	5.7	1.2

[a]Source: Robert Morris Associates, *Annual Statement Studies* (except price earnings ratio).

[b]Common's Share of Operating Earnings = Net Income to Common/Operating Income after Taxes (before interest expense and related tax effects). Chapter 8 describes this ratio as the common earnings leverage ratio.

[c]Capital Structure Leverage = Average Total Assets/Average Common Stockholders' Equity.

[d]The amounts for return on common equity may not be precisely equal to the product of return on assets, common's share of operating earnings, and capital structure leverage due to rounding.

REQUIRED

Using the report comparing U.S. and Japanese accounting principles (Appendix B) and Tanaguchi Corporation's financial statements and notes (Appendix A), identify the most important differences between U.S. and Japanese GAAP. Consider both the differences in acceptable methods and in the methods commonly used. For each major difference, indicate the likely effect (increase, decrease, or no effect) of converting Tanaguchi's financial statements to U.S. GAAP (1) on net income, (2) on total assets, and (3) on the ratio of liabilities divided by stockholders' equity.

Appendix A
Unconsolidated Financial Statements for Tanaguchi Corporation

Tanaguchi Corporation Balance Sheet (amounts in billions of yen)

	March 31	
	Year 4	Year 5
ASSETS		
Current Assets		
Cash	¥ 30	¥ 27
Marketable Securities (Note 1)	20	25
Notes and Accounts Receivable (Note 2)		
Trade Notes and Accounts	200	210
Affiliated Company	30	45
Less Allowance for Doubtful Accounts	(5)	(7)
Inventories (Note 3)	130	150
Other Current Assets	25	30
Total Current Assets	¥ 430	¥ 480
Investments		
Investments in and Loans to Affiliated Companies (Note 4)	¥ 110	¥ 140
Investments in Other Companies (Note 5)	60	60
Total Investments	¥ 170	¥ 200
Property, Plant, and Equipment (Note 6)		
Land	¥ 25	¥ 25
Buildings	110	130
Machinery and Equipment	155	180
Less Depreciation to Date	(140)	(165)
Total Property, Plant, and Equipment	¥ 150	¥ 170
Total Assets	¥ 750	¥ 850
LIABILITIES AND STOCKHOLDERS' EQUITY		
Current Liabilities		
Short-Term Bank Loans	¥ 185	¥ 200
Notes and Accounts Payable		
Trade Notes and Accounts	140	164
Affiliated Company	25	20
Other Current Liabilities	40	50
Total Current Liabilities	¥ 390	¥ 434
Long-Term Liabilities		
Bonds Payable (Note 7)	¥ 20	¥ 20
Convertible Debt	20	20
Retirement and Severance Allowance (Note 8)	122	153
Total Long-Term Liabilities	¥ 162	¥ 193
Stockholders' Equity		
Common Stock, 10 par value	¥ 15	¥ 15
Capital Surplus	40	40
Legal Reserve (Note 9)	16	17
Retained Earnings (Note 9)	127	151
Total Stockholders' Equity	¥ 198	¥ 223
Total Liabilities and Stockholders' Equity	¥ 750	¥ 850

Tanaguchi Corporation Statement of Income and Retained Earnings for Fiscal Year 5 (amounts in billions of yen)

Revenues

Sales (Note 10).....................................	¥ 1,200
Interest and Dividends (Note 11)..........	5
Total Revenues...................................	¥ 1,205

Expenses

Cost of Goods Sold..............................	¥ 878
Selling and Administrative....................	252
Interest..	13
Total Expenses....................................	¥ 1,143
Income before Income Taxes	¥ 62
Income Taxes (Note 12)........................	(34)
Net Income	¥ 28

Retained Earnings

Balance, Beginning of Fiscal Year 5......	¥ 127
Net Income	28
Deductions	
Cash Dividends	(3)
Transfer to Legal Reserve (Note 9) ...	(1)
Balance, End of Fiscal Year 5................	¥ 151

TANAGUCHI CORPORATION NOTES TO FINANCIAL STATEMENTS

NOTE 1: Marketable Securities Marketable securities appear on the balance sheet at acquisition cost.

NOTE 2: Accounts Receivable Accounts and notes receivable are noninterest bearing. Within 15 days of sales on open account, customers typically sign noninterest-bearing, single-payment notes. Customers usually pay these notes within 60 to 180 days after signing. When Tanaguchi Corporation needs cash, it discounts these notes with Menji Bank. Tanaguchi Corporation remains contingently liable in the event customers do not pay these notes at maturity. Receivables from (and payables to) affiliated company are with Takahashi Corporation (see Note 4) and are noninterest bearing.

NOTE 3: Inventories Inventories appear on the balance sheet at lower of cost or market. The measurement of acquisition cost uses a weighted average cost-flow assumption.

NOTE 4: Investments and Loans to Affiliated Companies Intercorporate investments appear on the balance sheet at acquisition cost. The balances in this account at the end of Year 4 and Year 5 comprise the following:

	Year 4	Year 5
Investment in Tanaka Corporation (25%)	¥ 15	¥ 15
Investment in Takahashi Corporation (80%)	70	70
Loans to Takahashi Corporation	25	55
	¥ 110	¥ 140

NOTE 5: Investments in Other Companies   Other investments represent ownership shares of less than 20 percent and appear at acquisition cost.

NOTE 6: Property, Plant, and Equipment   Fixed assets appear on the balance sheet at acquisition cost. The firm capitalizes expenditures that increase the service lives of fixed assets, whereas it expenses immediately expenditures that maintain the originally expected useful lives. It computes depreciation using the declining balance method. Depreciable lives for buildings are 30 to 40 years and for machinery and equipment are 6 to 10 years.

NOTE 7: Bonds Payable   Bonds payable comprises two bond issues as follows:

	Year 4	Year 5
12% semiannual, ¥10 billion face value bonds, with interest payable on March 31 and September 30 and the principal payable at maturity on March 31, Year 20; the bonds were initially priced on the market to yield 10%, compounded semiannually	¥ 11.50	¥ 11.45
8% semiannual, ¥10 billion face value bonds, with interest payable on March 31 and September 30 and the principal payable at maturity on March 31, Year 22; the bonds were initially priced on the market to yield 10%, compounded semiannually	¥ 8.50	¥ 8.55
	¥ 20.00	¥ 20.00

NOTE 8: Retirement and Severance Allowance   The firm provides amounts as a charge against income each year for estimated retirement and severance benefits but does not fund these amounts until it makes actual payments to former employees.

NOTE 9: Legal Reserve and Retained Earnings   The firm reduces retained earnings and increases the Legal Reserve account for a specified percentage of dividends paid during the year. The following plan for appropriation of retained earnings was approved by shareholders at the annual meeting held on June 29, Year 5:

Transfer to Legal Reserve	¥ (1)
Cash Dividend	(3)
Directors' and Statutory Auditors' Bonuses	(1)
Elimination of Special Tax Reserve Relating to Sale of Equipment	1

NOTE 10: Sales Revenue   The firm recognizes revenues from sales of machine tools at the time of delivery. Reported sales for Year 5 are net of a provision for doubtful accounts of ¥50 billion.

NOTE 11: Interest and Dividend Revenue   Interest and Dividend Revenue includes ¥1.5 billion from loans to Takahashi Corporation, an unconsolidated subsidiary.

NOTE 12: Income Tax Expense   The firm computes income taxes based on a statutory tax rate of 55 percent for Year 5. Deferred tax accounting is not a common practice in Japan.

Appendix B
Comparison of U.S. and Japanese GAAP

1. Standard Setting Process

U.S.   The U.S. Congress has the legal authority to prescribe acceptable accounting principles, but it has delegated that authority to the Securities and Exchange Commission (SEC). The SEC has stated that it will recognize pronouncements of the Financial Accounting Standards Board (FASB), a private-sector entity, as the primary vehicle for specifying generally accepted accounting standards.

Japan   The Japanese Diet has the legal authority to prescribe acceptable accounting principles. All Japanese corporations (both publicly and privately held) must periodically issue financial statements to their stockholders following provisions of the Japanese Commercial Code. This Code is promulgated by the Diet. The financial statements follow strict legal-entity concepts.

Publicly listed corporations in Japan must also file financial statements with the Securities Division of the Ministry of Finance following accounting principles promulgated by the Diet in the Securities and Exchange Law. The Diet, through the Ministry of Finance, obtains advice on accounting principles from the Business Advisory Deliberations Council (BADC), a body composed of representatives from business, the accounting profession, and the Ministry of Finance. The BADC has no authority on its own to set acceptable accounting principles. The financial statements filed with the Securities Division of the Ministry of Finance tend to follow economic entity concepts, with intercorporate investments either accounted for using the equity method or consolidated.

All Japanese corporations file income tax returns with the Taxation Division of the Ministry of Finance. The accounting principles followed in preparing tax returns mirror closely those used in preparing financial statements for stockholders under the Japanese Commercial Code. The Ministry of Finance will sometimes need to reconcile conflicting preferences of the Securities Division (desiring financial information better reflecting economic reality) and the Taxation Division (desiring to raise adequate tax revenues to run the government).

2. Principal Financial Statements

U.S.   Balance sheet, income statement, statement of cash flows.

Japan   Balance sheet, income statement, proposal for appropriation of profit or disposition of loss. The financial statements filed with the Ministry of Finance contain some supplemental information on cash flows.

3. Income Statement

U.S.   Accrual basis.

Japan   Accrual basis.

4. Revenue Recognition

U.S.   Generally at time of sale; percentage-of-completion method usually required on long-term contracts; installment and cost-recovery-first methods permitted when there is high uncertainty regarding cash collectibility.

Japan   Generally at time of sale; percentage-of-completion method permitted on long-term contracts; installment method common when collection period exceeds two years regardless of degree of uncertainty of cash collectibility.

5. Uncollectible Accounts

U.S.   Allowance method.

Japan   Allowance method.

6. Inventories and Cost of Goods Sold

U.S.   Inventories valued at lower of cost or market. Cost determined by FIFO, LIFO, weighted average, or standard cost. Most firms use FIFO, LIFO, or a combination of the two.

Japan   Inventories valued at lower of cost or market. Cost determined by specific identification, FIFO, LIFO, weighted average, or standard cost. Most firms use weighted average or specific identification.

7. Fixed Assets and Depreciation Expense

U.S.   Fixed assets valued at acquisition cost. Depreciation computed using straight-line, declining balance, and sum-of-the-years'-digits methods. Permanent declines in value are recognized. Most firms use the straight-line method for financial reporting and an accelerated method for tax reporting.

Japan   Fixed assets valued at acquisition cost. Depreciation computed using straight-line, declining balance, and sum-of-the-years'-digits methods. Permanent declines in value are recognized. Most firms use a declining balance method for financial and tax reporting.

8. Intangible Assets and Amortization Expense

U.S.   Internally developed intangibles expensed when expenditures are made. Externally purchased intangibles capitalized as assets and amortized over expected useful life (not to exceed 40 years). Goodwill cannot be amortized for tax purposes.

Japan   The cost of intangibles (both internally developed and externally purchased) can be expensed when incurred or capitalized and amortized over the period allowed for tax purposes (generally 5 to 20 years). Goodwill is amortized over 5 years. Some intangibles (e.g., property rights) are not amortized.

9. Liabilities Related to Estimated Expenses (Warranties, Vacation Pay, Employee Bonuses)

U.S.   Estimated amount recognized as an expense and as a liability. Actual expenditures are charged against the liability.

Japan   Estimated amount recognized as an expense and as a liability. Actual expenditures are charged against the liability. Annual bonuses paid to members of the Board of Directors and to the Commercial Code auditors are not considered expenses, but a distribution of profits. Consequently, such bonuses are charged against retained earnings.

10. Liabilities Related to Employee Retirement and Severance Benefits

U.S.   Liability recognized for unfunded accumulated benefits.

Japan   Severance benefits more common than pension benefits. An estimated amount is recognized each period as an expense and as a liability for financial reporting. The maximum liability recognized equals 40 percent of the amount payable if all eligible employees were terminated currently. There is wide variability in the amount recognized. Benefits are deducted for tax purposes only when actual payments are made to terminated employees. Such benefits are seldom funded beforehand.

11. Liabilities Related to Income Tax

U.S.   Income tax expense based on book income amounts. Deferred tax expense and deferred tax liability recognized for temporary (timing) differences between book and taxable income.

Japan   Income tax expense based on taxable income amounts. Deferred tax accounting not practiced. In consolidated statements submitted to the Ministry of Finance by listed companies (see No. 18), deferred tax accounting is permitted.

12. Noninterest-Bearing Notes

U.S.   Notes stated at present value of future cash flows and interest recognized over term of the note.

Japan   Notes stated at face amount and no interest recognized over term of the note. Commonly used as a substitute for Accounts Payable.

13. Bond Discount or Premium

U.S.   Subtracted from or added to the face value of the bond and reported among liabilities on the balance sheet. Amortized over the life of the bond as an adjustment to interest expense.

Japan   Bond discount usually included among intangible assets and amortized over the life of the bonds. Bond discount and premium may also be subtracted from or added to the face value of bonds on the balance sheet and amortized as an adjustment of interest expense over the life of the bonds.

14. Leases

U.S.   Distinction made between operating leases (not capitalized) and capital leases (capitalized).

Japan   All leases treated as operating leases.

15. Legal Reserve (Part of Shareholders' Equity)

U.S.   Not applicable.

Japan   When dividends are declared and paid, unappropriated retained earnings and cash are reduced by the amount of the dividend. In addition, unappropriated retained earnings are reduced and the legal reserve account is increased by a percentage of this dividend, usually 10 percent, until such time as the legal reserve equals 25 percent of stated capital. The effect of the latter entry is to capitalize a portion of retained earnings to make it part of permanent capital.

16. Appropriations of Retained Earnings

U.S.   Not a common practice in the U.S. Appropriations have no legal status when they do appear.

Japan   Stockholders must approve each year the "proposal for appropriation of profit or disposition of loss." Four items commonly appear: dividend declarations, annual bonuses for directors and Commercial Code auditors, transfers to legal reserves, and changes in reserves.

    The income tax law permits certain costs to be deducted earlier for tax than for financial reporting and permits certain gains to be recognized later for tax than for financial reporting. To obtain these tax benefits, the tax law requires that these items "be reflected on the company's books." The *pretax effects* of these timing differences *do not appear* on the income statement. Instead, an entry is made decreasing unappropriated retained earnings and increasing special retained earnings reserves (a form of appropriated retained earnings). When the timing difference reverses, the above entry is reversed. The *tax effects* of these timing differences *do appear* on the income statement, however. In the year that the timing difference originates, income tax expense and income tax payable are reduced by the tax effect of the timing difference. When the timing difference reverses, income tax expense and income tax payable are increased by a corresponding amount.

17. Treasury Stock

U.S.   Shown at acquisition cost as a subtraction from total shareholders' equity. No income recognized from treasury stock transactions.

Japan   Reacquired shares are either canceled immediately or shown as a current asset on the balance sheet. Dividends "received" on treasury shares are included in income.

18. Investments in Securities

A. Marketable Securities (Current Asset)

U.S.   Lower of cost or market method.

Japan   Reported at acquisition cost, unless price declines are considered permanent, in which case lower of cost or market.

B. Investments (Noncurrent Asset)

U.S.   Accounting depends on ownership: Less than 20%, lower of cost or market; 20% to 50%, equity method; greater than 50%, consolidated.

Japan   The principal financial statements are those of the parent company only (that is, unconsolidated statements). Intercorporate investments are carried at acquisition cost. Listed companies must provide consolidated financial statements as supplements to the principal statements in filings to the Ministry of Finance. The accounting for investments in securities in these supplementary statements is essentially the same as in the U.S.

19. Corporate Acquisitions

U.S.   Purchase method or pooling of interests method.

Japan   Purchase method.

20. Foreign Currency Translation

U.S.   The translation method depends on whether the foreign unit operates as a self-contained entity (all-current method) or as an extension of the U.S. parent (monetary/non-monetary method). Any translation adjustment that arises from using the all-current method appears in a separate shareholders' equity account. Any translation adjustment that arises from using the monetary/non-monetary method affects net income for the period.

Japan   For branches, the monetary/non-monetary translation method is used, with any translation adjustment flowing through income. For subsidiaries, current monetary items are translated using the current rate, other balance sheet items use the historical rate, and the translation adjustment is part of shareholders' equity.

21. Segment Reporting

U.S.   Segment information (sales, operating income, assets) disclosed by industry segment, geographical location, and type of customer.

Japan   Since 1990, sales data by segment (industry, geographical location) have been required. No disclosure by type of customer.

Sources: The Japanese Institute of Certified Public Accountants, *Corporate Disclosure in Japan* (July 1987); KPMG Peat Marwick, *Comparison of Japanese and U.S. Reporting and Financial Practices* (1989).

Profitability Analysis: Rate of Return on Assets

7

How profitable were a firm's operations during the past period? This chapter and Chapter 8 describe and illustrate the analytical tools used to answer this question. This chapter considers the rate of return on assets (ROA), a measure that relates operating profits to assets in use independent of the financing of those assets. Chapter 8 considers the rate of return on common shareholders' equity, a measure that extends ROA to include the financing (debt versus equity) of assets.

Calculating the Rate of Return on Assets

The rate of return on assets measures the success of a firm in using assets to generate earnings independent of the financing of those assets. Refer to Figure 7.1. ROA takes the particular set of environmental factors and strategic choices that a firm makes as given and focuses on the profitability of its operations relative to the investments (assets) in place. ROA ignores, however, the means of financing these investments. This measure therefore separates financing activities from operating and investing activities. ROA is particularly useful in assessing the performance of business segments of a firm when, as is typical, financing for those segments comes from a central corporate pool of resources. As this and the next chapter show, ROA calculated at a firmwide level also provides useful insights about operating performance.

The analyst calculates ROA as follows:

$$\text{ROA} = \frac{\text{Net Income} + (1 - \text{Tax Rate})(\text{Interest Expense}) + \text{Minority Interest in Earnings}}{\text{Average Total Assets}}$$

Figure 7.1
Summary of Business Activities (Shaded Area Shows the Focus of ROA)

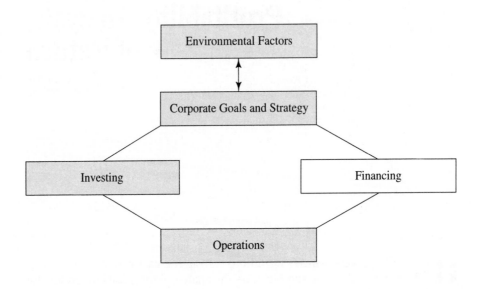

The numerator measures operating profits after income taxes, excluding any financing costs. Calculating the numerator is usually easiest if the analyst starts with net income[1] and then adjusts that number for financing costs. Because accountants subtract interest expense in computing net income, the analyst must add it back. However, the firm can deduct interest expense in measuring taxable income. The *incremental* effect of interest expense on net income therefore equals one minus the marginal (not average)[2] tax rate times interest expense. That is, the analyst adds back the full amount of interest expense to net income and then subtracts the tax savings from that interest expense. Because accountants do not sub-

---

[1]The analyst should use income from continuing operations instead of net income if the objective is to assess a firm's profitability as a going concern.

[2] The marginal tax rate is the statutory tax rate appropriate to a particular type of income or expense. In previous years, the statutory tax rate for capital gains and losses differed from the statutory tax rates applicable to ordinary income and expenses. Under current income tax law in the United States, the statutory tax rates for corporations are the same for both capital and ordinary income and expenses. The income tax note will disclose the statutory, or marginal, tax rate each year. The income tax note will also show a reconciliation between the statutory tax rate and the effective, or average, tax rate. The latter rate is equal to income tax expense divided by book income before taxes (see the discussion in Chapter 4). Revenues and expenses that are included in the calculation of book income but do not impact income tax expense (for example, interest on state and municipal securities, goodwill amortization) affect the effective tax rate.

tract dividends on preferred and common stocks in measuring net income, the analyst need not make an adjustment for dividends in calculating ROA.[3]

The rationale for adding back the minority interest in earnings is as follows: The denominator of ROA includes all assets of the consolidated entity, not just the parent's share. Net income in the numerator, however, represents the parent's earnings plus the parent's share of the earnings of consolidated subsidiaries. The accountant subtracts the minority interest's claim on the earnings of a consolidated subsidiary in measuring net income. Consistency with the inclusion of all of the assets of the consolidated entity in the denominator of ROA requires that the numerator include all of the earnings of the consolidated entity. The analyst accomplishes that objective by adding back the minority interest in earnings. Most publicly held corporations do not disclose the minority interest in earnings because its amount is usually immaterial. Thus, the analyst makes this adjustment only for significant minority interests.

Because operating income in the numerator of ROA reports the results *for a period of time*, the denominator uses a measure of average assets in use during that same period. For a nonseasonal business, an average of assets at the beginning and end of the year is usually satisfactory. For a seasonal business, the analyst should use an average of assets at the end of each quarter.

Refer to the financial statements for Coke and Pepsi in Appendix A and Appendix B repectively for the following illustration. The calculation of ROA for Year 8 is as follows:

$$\text{Coke} \quad \frac{\$1,381.9 + (1 - .34)(\$231.0)}{.5(\$8,282.5 + \$9,278.2)} = \frac{\$1,534.4}{\$8,780.4} = 17.5\%$$

$$\text{Pepsi} \quad \frac{\$1,076.9 + (1 - .34)(\$688.5)}{.5(\$15,126.7 + \$17,143.4)} = \frac{\$1,531.3}{\$16,135.1} = 9.5\%$$

Two nonrecurring items affect the ROA of Pepsi for Year 8: (1) a gain of $118.2 million ($53.0 million after tax; see Pepsi's Note 3) resulting from an initial stock offering of Pepsi's joint venture of Kentucky Fried Chicken in Japan, and (2) a $13.7 million discontinued operation charge relating to lawsuits and claims of a business that Pepsi sold in a prior year (see Pepsi's Note 4). These nonrecurring items should not influence the analyst's evaluation of Pepsi's ongoing profitability. The recomputed ROA for Year 8 excluding these items is therefore:

$$\text{ROA} = \frac{(\$1,076.9 - \$53.0 + \$13.7 + (1 - .34)(\$688.5)}{.5(\$15,126.7 + \$17,143.4)} = \frac{\$1,492.0}{\$16,135.1} = 9.2\%$$

[3] One could argue that the analyst should exclude returns from short-term investments of excess cash (that is, interest revenue) from the numerator of ROA under the view that such investments are really negative financings. We make no such adjustment in this book.

Coke's ROA substantially exceeds that of Pepsi for Year 8. Their operating income amounts are similar, but Pepsi has almost twice as many assets as Coke. Chapter 5 discussed Coke's operating strategy of holding a 49 percent interest in its bottlers. This level of ownership permits Coke to account for its investment in these bottlers using the equity method. Coke's assets include only its investment in the shareholders' equity of these entities, which is substantially less than their total assets. Exhibit 5.5 in Chapter 5 shows that Coke's total assets at the end of Year 8 are $18,901.2 if Coke consolidates these bottlers. Similarly, total assets on a consolidated basis are $16,858.7 at the end of Year 7.

Operating income in the numerator of ROA does not change as a result of consolidation. Recall from Chapter 5 that net income using the equity method equals consolidated net income; only the individual revenues and expenses differ. To exclude the effect of financing from the numerator of ROA, we must add back the interest expense (net of taxes) recognized by Coke's bottlers. Coke's Note 3 does not provide the amount of interest expense for those entities. We might approximate this amount by assuming that the noncurrent liabilities represent interest-bearing debt. Using an assumed interest rate of 8 percent yields interest expense of $354.5 [.08 × .5($2,055.7 + $2,339.3 + $1,947.9 + $2,518.9)] for Year 8. We inject some error into the calculation of ROA to the extent that some of the current liabilities of these entities bear interest, that some of the noncurrent liabilities do not bear interest, and that 8 percent is not a reasonable interest rate.

The final adjustment to the numerator of ROA to consolidate these bottlers is to add the minority interest in earnings. This adjustment permits the numerator to include 100 percent of the operating income of Coke and its bottlers and the denominator to include 100 percent of the assets of these entities. Coke's Note 3 shows the total income of these bottlers for Year 8 ($77,148 + $205,436 = $282,584), as well as Coke's equity share ($34,429 + $75,710 = $110,139). The share of the external minority interest is therefore $172,445 (= $282,584 − $110,139). Consolidating Coke's bottlers results in the following recomputed ROA for Year 8:

$$\text{ROA} = \frac{(\$1,381.9 + (1 - .34)(\$231.0 + \$354.5) + \$172.4}{.5(\$16,858.7 + \$18,901.2)} = \frac{\$1,940.7}{\$17,880.0} = 10.9\%$$

Thus, Coke's ROA for Year 8 still exceeds that of Pepsi, but consolidation of the bottlers eliminates most of the differences we observed when using Coke's reported amounts.

The analyst could adjust Coke's financial statements to consolidate these bottlers for all years and use only the restated amounts in making interpretations. Two difficulties arise, however, in such a procedure. First, the adjustment to the numerator of ROA for interest expense rests, perhaps, on inappropriate assumptions. Second, the financial statement data in Note 3 for these bottlers will not permit more than a few aggregate-level adjustments (for example, current assets, total assets, total revenues). A lack of information about individual assets, liabilities, revenues, and expenses precludes the analyst from gaining much depth of understanding as to why the ROAs of Coke and Pepsi differ or why they change over time. The approach we follow in this chapter is to use the reported financial statement data for Coke, with the investment in the bottlers accounted for using the equity method. We incorporate Coke's consolidation policy regarding these entities into our interpretations where appropriate.

A comparison of the ROAs of Coke and Pepsi over the last three years after eliminating nonrecurring items from Coke's amounts for Year 7, is as follows:

	Coke	Pepsi
Year 6	15.2%	9.8%
Year 7	17.2%	9.9%
Year 8	17.5%	9.2%

Thus, Coke's ROA increased over the last three years, while Pepsi's ROA decreased in Year 8. Coke's ROA in each year exceeded that of Pepsi.

Disaggregating ROA

The analyst obtains further insight into the behavior of ROA by disaggregating it into profit margin and total assets turnover (hereafter referred to as assets turnover) components as follows:

$$\text{ROA} = \text{Profit Margin} \times \text{Assets Turnover}$$

$$\frac{\substack{\text{Net Income + Interest} \\ \text{Expense (net of taxes)} \\ \text{+ Minority Interest} \\ \text{in Earnings}}}{\text{Average Total Assets}} = \frac{\substack{\text{Net Income + Interest} \\ \text{Expense (net of taxes)} \\ \text{+ Minority Interest} \\ \text{in Earnings}}}{\text{Sales}} \times \frac{\text{Sales}}{\text{Average Total Assets}}$$

The profit margin indicates the ability of a firm to generate operating profit from a particular level of sales.[4] The assets turnover indicates the ability to manage the level of investment in assets for a particular level of revenues or, to put it another way, the ability to generate revenues from a particular investment in assets.

The disaggregation of ROA for Coke and Pepsi for Year 8 is as follows:

	ROA	=	Profit Margin	×	Assets Turnover
Coke	$\dfrac{\$\ 1{,}534.4}{\$\ 8{,}780.4}$	=	$\dfrac{\$\ 1{,}534.4}{\$10{,}236.4}$	×	$\dfrac{\$10{,}236.4}{\$\ 8{,}780.4}$
	17.5%	=	15.0%	×	1.2
Pepsi	$\dfrac{\$\ 1{,}492.0}{\$16{,}135.1}$	=	$\dfrac{\$\ 1{,}492.0}{\$17{,}802.7}$	×	$\dfrac{\$17{,}802.7}{\$16{,}135.1}$
	9.2%	=	8.4%	×	1.1

---

[4] One might argue that the analyst should use total revenues, not just sales, in the denominator because assets generate returns in forms other than sales (for example, interest, equity in earnings of affiliates). However, interpretations of various expense ratios (discussed later in this chapter) are usually easier when we use sales in the denominator.

Exhibit 7.1
**ROAs, Profit Margins and Assets Turnovers
for Coke and Pepsi—Year 6 to Year 8**

	Year 6	Year 7	Year 8
Coke			
ROA	15.2%	17.2%	17.5%
Profit Margin	14.4%	15.1%	15.0%
Assets Turnover	1.1	1.1	1.2
Pepsi			
ROA	9.8%	9.9%	9.2%
Profit Margin	7.6%	8.6%	8.4%
Assets Turnover	1.3	1.2	1.1

Exhibit 7.1 summarizes ROA, profit margin, and assets turnover for the two companies for Year 6, Year 7, and Year 8. Coke has experienced a higher ROA than Pepsi in each of the last three years. Its higher ROA derives from a higher profit margin; these firms realized similar assets turnovers. A later section of this chapter examines these differences in profitability in greater depth.

Figure 7.2 depicts graphically the average ROAs, profit margins, and assets turnovers of 21 industries for the 1980 to 1989 time period. The two isoquants reflect ROAs of 4 percent and 8 percent. The isoquants show the various combinations of profit margin and assets turnover that yield an ROA of 4 percent or 8 percent. For instance, an ROA of 8 percent results from any of the following profit margin/assets turnover combinations: 8%/1.0, 4%/2.0, 2%/4.0, 1%/8.0.

The data for ROA, profit margin, and assets turnover underlying the plots in Figure 7.2 reflect aggregated amounts across firms and across years. The focus of financial statement analysis is on the ROAs of specific firms, or even segments of specific firms, for particular years (or even quarters). We can obtain some useful insights about the behavior of ROA at the segment or firm level, however, by examining the industry-level data. In particular,

1.   What factors seem to explain the consistently superior or consistently weak ROAs of some industries relative to the average of all industries (that is, reasons for differences in the distribution of industries in the bottom left versus top right in Figure 7.2)?

2.   What factors seem to explain the fact that certain industries tend to have high profit margins but low assets turnovers, while other industries experience low profit margins and high assets turnovers (that is, reasons for differences in the distribution of industries in the upper left versus lower right in Figure 7.2)?

The microeconomics and business strategy literatures provide useful background for interpreting the behavior of ROA, profit margin and assets turnover.

Figure 7.2

Average ROAs, Profit Margins and Assets Turnovers for 21 Industries for the Period 1980–89

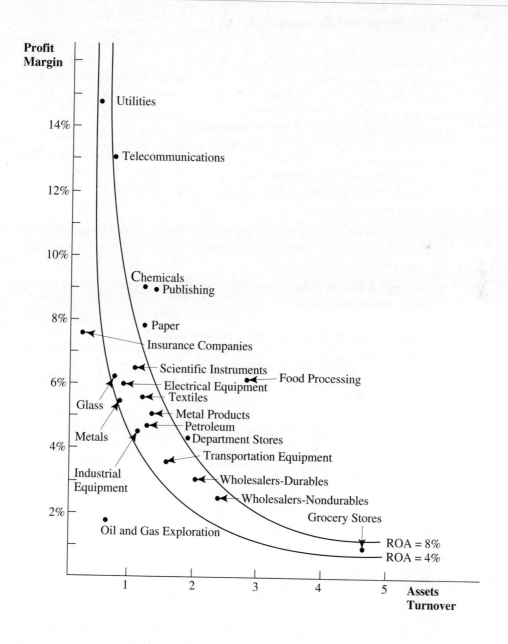

Interpreting the Rate of Return on Assets[5]

Differences or Changes in ROA

Economic theory posits that higher levels of perceived risk in any activity should lead to higher levels of expected return if that activity is to attract capital. The extra return compensates for the extra risk assumed. Realized rates of return (ROAs) derived from financial statement data for any particular period will not necessarily correlate as predicted with the level of risk involved in an activity as economic theory suggests for the following reasons:

1. Realized ROAs may differ from expected ROAs (a) because of the use of faulty assumptions in deriving expected ROAs, or (b) because changes in the environment after forming expectations cause realized ROAs to deviate from those anticipated.

2. Realized ROAs use data for discrete periods shorter than the projected life of an activity, whereas rates of return based on economic theory represent average rates over multiple periods.

3. Realized ROAs use data on actual results of a past period whereas expected ROAs look to the future.[6]

Despite these weaknesses, ROAs based on reported financial statement data do provide useful information for tracking the past, periodic performance of a firm and its segments and for developing expectations about future earnings potential. Differences or changes in ROAs relate to operating-leverage and product life-cycle phenomena.

Operating Leverage.   Firms operate with different mixtures of fixed and variable costs in their cost structures. Steel, glass, and oil exploration are capital-intensive industries. Depreciation and many operating costs are more or less fixed for any given period. Most retailers and wholesalers, on the other hand, have high proportions of variable costs in their cost structures. Firms with high proportions of fixed costs will experience significant increases in operating income as sales increase. The increased income occurs because the firm spreads fixed costs over a larger number of units sold, resulting in a decrease in average unit cost. Likewise, when sales decrease, these firms experience sharp decreases in operating income. Economists refer to this process of operating with high proportions of fixed costs

---

[5]The material in this section draws heavily from Thomas I. Selling and Clyde P. Stickney, "The Effects of Business Environments and Strategy on a Firm's Rate of Return on Assets," *Financial Analysts Journal* (January/February 1989), pp. 43–52.

[6]If the income statement and balance sheet included changes in the market value of assets and liabilities, then ROAs based on financial statement data would more closely coincide with those posited by economic theory.

Figure 7.3
Cost Structure and Operating Leverage

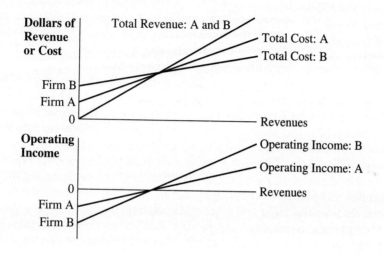

as operating leverage. Firms with high levels of operating leverage experience greater variability in their ROAs than firms with low levels of operating leverage.

Measuring the degree of operating leverage of a firm or its segments requires information about the fixed and variable cost structure. In Figure 7.3, the top panel shows the total revenue and total cost functions of two firms, A and B. The graphs assume that the two firms are the same size, have the same total revenue functions, and the same breakeven points. These assumptions simplify the discussion of operating leverage but are not necessary when comparing actual companies.

Firm B has a higher level of fixed costs than Firm A, as measured by the intersection of the vertical axis at zero sales in the top panel of Figure 7.3. Firm A has a higher level of variable costs than Firm B, as measured by the slope of its total cost functions as revenues increase above zero. The lower panel nets the total revenue and total cost functions to derive the operating income function. Operating income is negative in an amount equal to fixed costs when revenues are zero and operating income is zero at breakeven revenues. We use the slope of the operating income line as a measure of the extent of operating leverage. Firm B, with its higher fixed cost and lower variable cost mix, has more operating leverage. As revenues increase, its operating income increases more than that for Firm A. On the downside, however, income decreases more sharply as revenues decrease.

Another useful concept when studying operating leverage is contribution margin. Contribution margin equals revenues minus variable costs. The contribution margin percentage equals contribution margin divided by revenues. For every one dollar increase in sales, contribution margin increases by the contribution margin percentage. Because fixed costs do not change as revenues increase, operating income also increases by the contribution margin percentage as sales increase. *Thus, the slopes of the contribution margin function and the operating income function are the same.* This relationship is important when the analyst attempts to measure operating leverage for actual firms.

Unfortunately, firms do not publicly disclose information about their fixed and variable cost structures. To examine the influence of operating leverage on the behavior of ROA for a particular firm or its segments, the analyst must estimate the fixed/variable cost structure. One approach to such estimation is to study the various cost items of a firm and attempt to identify those items that are likely to behave as fixed costs. Firms incur some costs in particular amounts, referred to as *committed fixed costs*, regardless of the actual level of activity during the period. Examples include depreciation, amortization, and rent, all net of their tax effects. Firms can alter the amount of other costs, referred to as *discretionary fixed costs*, in the short run in response to operating conditions but, in general, these costs do not vary directly with the level of activity. Examples include research and development, maintenance, advertising, and central corporate staff expenses. Whether the analyst should classify these latter costs as fixed costs or as variable costs in measuring operating leverage depends on their behavior in each firm.

Assuming that depreciation, amortization, and rent are the only fixed costs for Coke and Pepsi, Exhibit 7.2 illustrates the calculation of operating leverage. We net these costs of their tax savings at the statutory tax rate. We then add the net fixed operating costs to operating income to derive the contribution margin (thus, the calculations move from bottom to top in Exhibit 7.2). The contribution margin percentage equals contribution margin divided by revenues. The contribution margin percentage represents the slope of the operating income line in the lower panel of Figure 7.3 and indicates the degree of operating leverage. There is some imprecision in this approach to measuring operating leverage, so the analyst should interpret the resulting measurements cautiously.

These calculations indicate that Coke carries the greater amount of operating leverage. At first glance this result may seem surprising. Pepsi has a major involvement in restaurants, a more capital-intensive activity than soft drinks or consumer foods. Pepsi also has a higher percentage of its assets invested in fixed assets. The explanation probably relates to Coke's investments in its bottlers. Adding the fixed costs of these bottlers increases total fixed costs, does not change operating income, and therefore decreases the contribution margin. Consolidating these bottlers also increases revenues. The net effect of consolidation is a smaller contribution margin percentage for Coke (lower contribution margin divided by higher revenues). Note that both Coke and Pepsi carry relatively low levels of operating leverage compared to many other industries.

Exhibit 7.2
Estimation of Fixed and Variable Cost Structure of Coke and Pepsi

Classification of Cost Items

	Coke			Pepsi		
	Year 6	Year 7	Year 8	Year 6	Year 7	Year 8
Depreciation and Amortization.........	$ 169.8	$ 183.8	$ 243.9	$ 629.3	$ 772.0	$ 884.0
Rent...	—	—	—	219.7	236.9	272.7
	$ 169.8	$ 183.8	$ 243.9	$ 849.0	$ 1,008.9	$ 1,156.7
Tax Effect	(57.7)	(62.5)	(82.9)	(288.7)	(343.0)	(393.3)
Fixed Costs–Net.................................	$ 112.1	$ 121.3	$ 161.0	$ 560.3	$665.9	$ 763.4
Revenues..	$8,357.2	$8,902.3	$10,516.4	$12,655.4	$15,419.6	$17,984.8
Variable Costs	(7,047.6)	(7,425.0)	(8,821.0)	(11,105.4)	(13,450.1)	(15,729.4)
Contribution Margin	$1,309.6	$1,477.3	$ 1,695.4	$ 1,550.0	$ 1,969.5	$ 2,255.4
Fixed Cost	(112.1)	(121.3)	(161.0)	(560.3)	(665.9)	(763.4)
Operating Income..............................	$1,197.5	$1,356.0	$ 1,534.4	$ 989.7	$ 1,303.6	$ 1,492.0
Contribution Margin Percentage......	15.7%	16.6%	16.1%	12.2%	12.8%	12.5%

Product Life Cycle.   A second explanation for differences in ROA uses the product life-cycle theory. Products move through four identifiable phases: introduction, growth, maturity, and decline. During the introduction and growth phases, a firm focuses on product development (product R&D spending), market development (advertising and other promotion spending) and capacity enlargement (capital spending). The objective is to gain market acceptance and market share. During the maturity phase, competition becomes more intense, and the emphasis shifts to reducing costs through improved capacity utilization (economies of scale) and more efficient production (process R&D spending). During the decline phase, firms exit the industry as sales decline and profit opportunities diminish.

Figure 7.4 depicts the behavior of revenues, operating income, investment, and ROA that corresponds to these four product life cycles. During the introduction and early growth phases, expenditures on product development and marketing, coupled with relatively low sales levels, lead to operating losses and negative ROAs. As sales accelerate during the high growth phase, operating income and ROAs turn positive. Extensive product development, marketing, and depreciation expenses during this phase moderate operating income, while heavy capital expenditures to build capacity for expected higher future sales increase the denominator of ROA. Thus ROA does not grow as rapidly as sales. ROA increases significantly during the maturity phase due to benefits of economies of scale and learning curve phenomena and to curtailments of capital expenditures. ROA deteriorates during the decline phase as operating income decreases, but may remain positive or even increase for some time into this phase. Thus, as products move through their life cycles, their ROAs should move to the upper right area in Figure 7.2, peak during the maturity stage, and then move to the lower left area as the decline phase sets in.

Figure 7.4
Relation between Sales, Operating Income, Investment and ROA during Product Life Cycle

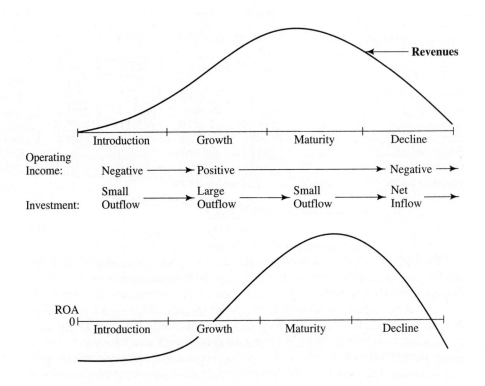

Note that the product life cycle theory focuses on individual products. We can extend the theory to an industry level by examining the average stage in the product life cycle of all products within that industry. For instance, the products in the computer industry range from the introduction to the decline phases, but the overall industry is probably in the latter part of the high growth phase. The soft drink and food processing industries, the primary involvements of Coke and Pepsi, are mature, although these firms and their competitors continually introduce new products. We might view the steel industry, at least in the United States, as in the early decline phase, although some companies have modernized production sufficiently to stave off the decline. Thus, differences among industries in their ROAs and changes over time in the ROAs of particular firms and industries relate to economies and diseconomies of scale arising from operating leverage and to movements through product life cycles.

Differences in the Profit Margin/Assets Turnover Mix

The second relationship examined is the relative mix of profit margin and assets turnover at which a firm or industry operates. Explanations come from both the microeconomics and business strategy literatures.

Microeconomic Theory.   Figure 7.5 sets out some important economic factors that constrain certain firms and industries to operate in particular segments of the profit margin/assets turnover array. Firms and industries characterized by heavy fixed capacity costs and lengthy periods required to add new capacity operate under a capacity constraint. There is an upper limit on the size of assets turnover achievable. In order to attract sufficient capital, these firms must generate a relatively high profit margin. Such firms will therefore operate in the area of Figure 7.5 marked Ⓐ. The firms usually achieve the high profit margin through some form of entry barrier. The entry barrier may take the form of large required capital outlays, high risks, or regulation. Such factors help explain the profit margin/assets turnover mix of telecommunications and utilities in Figure 7.2. The lack of such barriers coupled with high fixed capacity costs help explain the low ROAs in recent years of firms in the metals, industrial equipment, and glass industries.

Firms whose products are commodity-like in nature, where there are few entry barriers, and where competition is intense operate under a competitive constraint. There is an upper limit on the level of profit margin achievable. In order to attract sufficient capital, these firms must strive for high assets turnovers. Such firms will therefore operate in the area of Figure 7.5 marked Ⓒ. Firms achieve the high assets turnover by keeping costs as low as possible (for example, minimizing fixed overhead costs, purchasing in sufficient quantities to realize discounts, integrating vertically or horizontally to obtain cost savings, and similar moves). These firms match such actions to control costs with aggressively low prices to gain market share and drive out marginal firms. Most retailers and wholesalers operate in the Ⓒ area of Figure 7.5.

Firms that operate in the area of Figure 7.5 marked Ⓑ are not as subject to either capacity or competitive constraints as those that operate in the tails of the ROA curves. They thus have more flexibility to take actions that will increase profit margin, assets turnover, or both to achieve a higher ROA.

The notion of flexibility in trading off profit margin for assets turnover (or vice versa) is important when a firm considers strategic alternatives. The underlying economic concept is the marginal rate of substitution. Consider first a firm with a profit margin/assets turnover combination that puts it in the Ⓐ area of Figure 7.5. Such a firm will have to give up a significant amount of profit margin to obtain a meaningful increase in assets turnover. To increase ROA, such a firm should therefore emphasize actions that increase profit margin. Likewise, a firm in area Ⓒ of Figure 7.5 will have to give up considerable assets turnover to achieve a higher profit margin. To increase ROA, such a firm should emphasize actions that increase assets turnover. For firms operating in the tails of the ROA curves, the poor marginal rates of substitution do not favor trading off one variable for the other. Such firms must generally emphasize only one of these factors.

Figure 7.5
Economic Factors Affecting the Profit Margin/Assets Turnover Mix

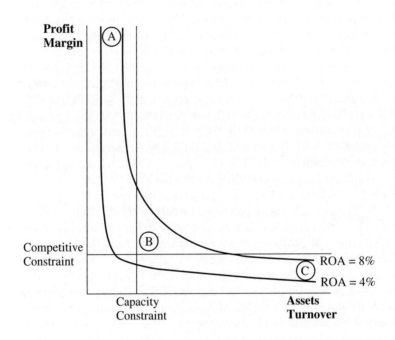

For firms operating in the area marked Ⓑ in Figure 7.5, the marginal rate of substitution of profit margin for assets turnover is more equal. Such firms therefore have more flexibility to design strategies that promote profit margin, assets turnover, or some combination when striving to increase ROA.

In summary, the economic concepts underlying the profit margin/assets turnover mix are the following:

Area of Firm in Figure 7.5	Capital Intensity	Competition	Likely Strategic Focus
Ⓐ	High	Monopoly	Profit Margin
Ⓑ	Medium	Oligopolistic or Monopolistic Competition	Profit Margin, Assets Turnover, or Some Combination
Ⓒ	Low	Pure Competition	Assets Turnover

Business Strategy.   Both Hall[7] and Porter[8] suggest that firms have two generic, alternative strategies for any particular product: product differentiation and low cost leadership. The thrust of the product-differentiation strategy is to differentiate a product in such a way as to obtain market power over revenues and therefore profit margins. The differentiation could relate to product capabilities, product quality, service, channels of distribution or some other factor. The thrust of the low-cost leadership strategy is to become the lowest cost producer, thereby enabling the firm to charge the lowest prices and achieve the highest volume. Such firms can achieve the low-cost position through economies of scale, production efficiencies, outsourcing, or similar factors or by asset parsimony (maintaining strict controls on investments in receivables, inventories, and capital expenditures).

In terms of Figure 7.5, movements in the direction of area Ⓐ *from any point along the ROA curves* focus on product differentiation. Likewise, movements in the direction of area Ⓒ *from any point along the ROA curves* focus on low-cost leadership. To illustrate, let us look at the average profit margins and assets turnovers for three types of retailers during the period 1980 to 1989:

	Profit Margin	Assets Turnover
Specialty Retailers	5.67%	1.8
Department Stores	4.20%	2.2
Grocery Stores	1.94%	4.5

Within the retailing industry, specialty retailers have differentiated themselves by following a niche strategy and achieved a higher profit margin than the other two segments. Competition severely constrains the profit margin of grocery stores and they must pursue more low-cost leadership strategies. Thus, a firm does not have to be in the tails of the ROA curves to be described as a product differentiator or low-cost leader. The appropriate basis of comparison is not other industries but other firms in the same industry. Remember, however, that the relative location along the ROA curve affects a firm's flexibility to trade off profit margin (product differentiation) for asset turnover (low-cost leadership).

Figure 7.6 shows the ROA, profit margin, and assets turnover for Coke and Pepsi for Year 8. These two firms dominate the soft drink industry. An average of their ratios essentially represents the soft drink industry's averages. Figure 7.6 also shows the average ROA, profit margin, and assets turnover for the consumer foods industry, which includes soft drinks as well as other food products. Note the following:

1. The ROA of Pepsi is slightly higher than the consumer foods industry average for Year 8, while Coke's is significantly higher.

2. Both Coke and Pepsi experienced higher profit margins than the consumer foods industry average. This performance reflects brand recognition and brand loyalty as well as the lack of major competitors.

---

[7] W. K. Hall, "Survival Strategies in a Hostile Environment," *Harvard Business Review* (September–October 1980), pp. 78–85.

[8] M. E. Porter, *Competitive Strategy,* (New York: Free Press, 1980). Porter suggests that firms might also pursue a niche strategy. Because a niche strategy essentially represents differentiation within a market segment, we include it here under product differentiation strategy.

Figure 7.6
**ROA, Profit Margin and Assets Turnover
for Consumer Foods, Coke and Pepsi for Year 8**

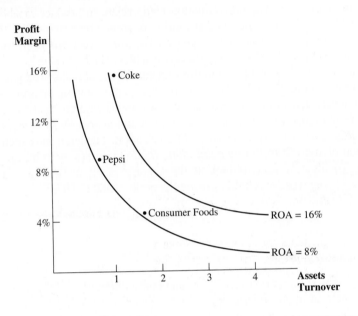

3.   Both Coke and Pepsi had slower assets turnovers than the consumer foods in-
     dustry average. Possible explanations include greater capital intensity of bot-
     tling operations and more extensive foreign involvements.

Generalizations such as those above provide a useful first pass but require more
in-depth analysis before drawing conclusions. We will examine the performance of
these two companies more fully in the next section.

     Thus, differences in the profit margin/assets turnover mix relate to factors ex-
ternal to a firm, such as degree of competition, extent of regulation, entry barriers
and similar factors, and to internal strategic choices, such as product differentiation and low-cost leadership. The external and internal factors are, of course,
interdependent and in a continual state of change.

Further Analysis of ROA

Thus far, we have demonstrated the calculation of ROA, profit margin, and assets
turnover and discussed some of the reasons why ROA and the profit margin/assets
turnover mix might differ between firms and industries. When attempting to understand reasons for differences in the operating performance of particular firms,

it is usually necessary to explore these relationships in greater depth. This section presents such an analysis for Coke and Pepsi.

We will perform the analysis at four levels, each one at a greater degree of disaggregation. The objective is to analyze the data in sufficient depth so that the analyst can identify reasons for differences in profitability. The four levels are as follows:

Level 1:   ROA for the firm as a whole.

Level 2:   Disaggregation of ROA into profit margin and assets turnover for the firm as a whole.

Level 3a: Disaggregation of profit margin into expense ratios for various cost items.

3b: Disaggregation of assets turnover into turnovers for individual assets.

Level 4:   Calculation of ROA, profit margin, and assets turnover for each of the operating segments of the firm, both by product line and geographically.

Exhibit 7.3 presents the analyses for Coke and Pepsi at the first three levels. Exhibits 7.4 and 7.5 present the analyses at the fourth level for the segments of each firm. Exhibit 7.6 defines the various ratios used in these analyses. A brief review of Coke's and Pepsi's common size and percentage change balance sheets and income statements in Exhibits 1.2 to 1.5 may provide useful background to the discussion that follows.

When interpreting this analysis, we will consider changes over time for each firm (time-series analysis) and differences between firms for the same period of time (cross-section analysis). By examining the data from both angles, we obtain a more complete picture of operating performance.

Time Series Analysis—Coke

Coke experienced an increased ROA over the three-year period, with most of the increase occurring between Year 6 and Year 7. The profit margin increased between Year 6 and Year 7, while the assets turnover increased slightly between Year 7 and Year 8.

The analyst gains further understanding of changes in the profit margin by examining a common size income statement. This statement shows the relation between operating expenses and sales. Exhibit 7.3 indicates that Coke's improved profit margin between Year 6 and Year 7 relates to an increase in the "other (net)" line. Coke discloses elsewhere in its annual report that a switch from exchange losses to exchange gains explains this improvement. Note that Coke's decreased cost of goods sold percentage between Year 6 and Year 7 offsets an increased selling and administrative expense percentage. This same pattern continued between Year 7 and Year 8. The decreased cost of goods sold percentage probably relates to a sales mix shift away from lower profit margin consumer foods and toward higher

Exhibit 7.3
Profitability Analysis for Coke and Pepsi, Levels 1, 2, and 3

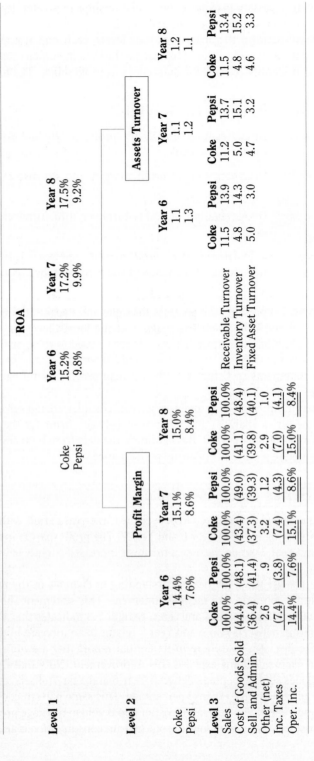

Level 1

ROA

	Year 6	Year 7	Year 8
Coke	15.2%	17.2%	17.5%
Pepsi	9.8%	9.9%	9.2%

Level 2

Profit Margin

	Year 6	Year 7	Year 8
Coke	14.4%	15.1%	15.0%
Pepsi	7.6%	8.6%	8.4%

Assets Turnover

	Year 6	Year 7	Year 8
Coke	1.1	1.1	1.2
Pepsi	1.3	1.2	1.1

Level 3

	Year 6		Year 7		Year 8	
	Coke	Pepsi	Coke	Pepsi	Coke	Pepsi
Sales	100.0%	100.0%	100.0%	100.0%	100.0%	100.0%
Cost of Goods Sold	(44.4)	(48.1)	(43.4)	(49.0)	(41.1)	(48.4)
Sell. and Admin.	(36.4)	(41.4)	(37.3)	(39.3)	(39.8)	(40.1)
Other (net)	2.6	.9	3.2	1.2	2.9	1.0
Inc. Taxes	(7.4)	(3.8)	(7.4)	(4.3)	(7.0)	(4.1)
Oper. Inc.	14.4%	7.6%	15.1%	8.6%	15.0%	8.4%

	Year 6		Year 7		Year 8	
	Coke	Pepsi	Coke	Pepsi	Coke	Pepsi
Receivable Turnover	11.5	13.9	11.2	13.7	11.5	13.4
Inventory Turnover	4.8	14.3	5.0	15.1	4.8	15.2
Fixed Asset Turnover	5.0	3.0	4.7	3.2	4.6	3.3

Exhibit 7.4
Profitability Analysis for Coke and Pepsi, Level 4

ROA

	Year 6		Year 7		Year 8	
	Coke	Pepsi	Coke	Pepsi	Coke	Pepsi
Soft Drinks	44.4%	11.4%	41.3%	10.9%	40.3%	11.9%
Consumer Foods	12.9%	39.3%	12.6%	24.3%	12.3%	24.0%
Restaurants	—	11.1%	—	13.5%	—	15.1%

Profit Margin

	Year 6		Year 7		Year 8	
	Coke	Pepsi	Coke	Pepsi	Coke	Pepsi
Soft Drinks	25.9%	9.8%	27.3%	11.7%	25.1%	11.8%
Consumer Foods	5.9%	18.0%	5.5%	19.1%	5.8%	18.5%
Restaurants	—	7.8%	—	7.9%	—	8.4%

Assets Turnover

	Year 6		Year 7		Year 8	
	Coke	Pepsi	Coke	Pepsi	Coke	Pepsi
Soft Drinks	1.7	1.2	1.5	.9	1.6	1.0
Consumer Foods	2.2	2.2	2.3	1.3	2.1	1.3
Restaurants	—	1.4	—	1.7	—	1.8

Exhibit 7.5
Profitability Analysis for Coke and Pepsi, Level 4

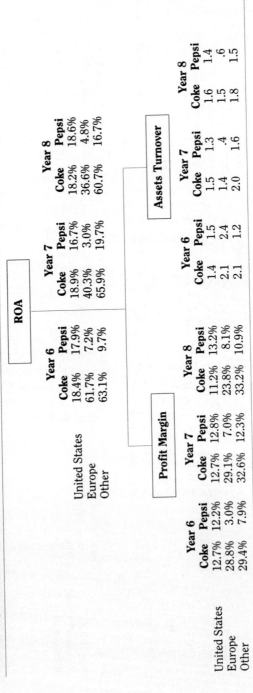

ROA

	Year 6 Coke	Year 6 Pepsi	Year 7 Coke	Year 7 Pepsi	Year 8 Coke	Year 8 Pepsi
United States	18.4%	17.9%	18.9%	16.7%	18.2%	18.6%
Europe	61.7%	7.2%	40.3%	3.0%	36.6%	4.8%
Other	63.1%	9.7%	65.9%	19.7%	60.7%	16.7%

Profit Margin

	Year 6 Coke	Year 6 Pepsi	Year 7 Coke	Year 7 Pepsi	Year 8 Coke	Year 8 Pepsi
United States	12.7%	12.2%	12.7%	12.8%	11.2%	13.2%
Europe	28.8%	3.0%	29.1%	7.0%	23.8%	8.1%
Other	29.4%	7.9%	32.6%	12.3%	33.2%	10.9%

Assets Turnover

	Year 6 Coke	Year 6 Pepsi	Year 7 Coke	Year 7 Pepsi	Year 8 Coke	Year 8 Pepsi
United States	1.4	1.5	1.5	1.3	1.6	1.4
Europe	2.1	2.4	1.4	.4	1.5	.6
Other	2.1	1.2	2.0	1.6	1.8	1.5

profit margin soft drinks. Coke states that it increased marketing expenditures over the three years to expand business. The company provides little additional insight regarding the shift in these expense ratios. Note, however, that the shift has virtually no net effect on Coke's profit margin. Although the shift in expense percentages may suggest a change in strategy, product mix, or other factors, the shift did not affect overall profitability.

The analyst gains further understanding of changes in assets turnover by examining the individual asset turnovers for accounts receivable, inventories, and fixed assets. Coke's total assets turnover, as well as its individual asset turnovers, were relatively flat over the three-year period. The slight deterioration of the fixed asset turnover results because capital expenditures increased more rapidly than sales during Year 7 and Year 8.

The analyst obtains further insight into changes in a firm's profitability by studying ROA, profit margin, and assets turnover data for the product and geographical segments. Exhibits 7.4 and 7.5 show the relevant ratios. Coke experienced slightly decreased ROA over the three-year period in both its soft drink and consumer foods segments. The declines result from slight declines in both profit margin and assets turnover, although the pattern of changes varies somewhat over the three years. The geographical segment data in Exhibit 7.5 indicate that the declining ROA occurred primarily in Europe. Coke's investments in assets in Europe more than doubled over the last two years, while sales increased 73 percent, decreasing the total assets turnover of European operations. The latter result probably explains Coke's declining fixed asset turnover noted above. With growth rates such as those Coke experienced in Europe, the declining fixed asset turnover is of little concern.

Coke's declining segment profitability appears inconsistent with the increased profitability for Coke overall. Changes in other income and unallocated central corporate expenses account for the conflicting trends. However, neither directional movement is particularly dramatic. Overall, Coke maintains relatively stable but high rates of return on assets, driven by a high profit margin (see Figure 7.6). We will compare Coke with Pepsi in a later section.

Time Series Analysis—Pepsi

Pepsi's ROA was flat between Year 6 and Year 7 and then declined in Year 8. The flat ROA between Year 6 and Year 7 results from an increased profit margin offset by a decreased assets turnover. The declining ROA in Year 8 results from both decreased profit margin and assets turnover. Pepsi's recent acquisitions explain most of these changes. Recall from previous chapters that Pepsi made major acquisitions during the last three years, with total assets almost doubling over that period. A large portion of the increased assets represents goodwill and other intangibles (see Pepsi's percentage change balance sheet in Exhibit 1.3). The amortization of these intangibles increases administrative expenses. The existence of these intangible assets also decreases total assets turnover. Note that Pepsi's total assets turnover declined, despite a relatively flat accounts receivable turnover and an increased inventory and fixed asset turnover.

The product-line profitability data for Pepsi's segments in Exhibit 7.4 indicate that the ROA of soft drinks was relatively flat, with increased profit margin offset by decreased assets turnover. The ROA of consumer foods decreased sharply between Year 6 and Year 7, largely as a result of decreased assets turnover. Major acquisitions during Year 7 in the United Kingdom explain this result (see Pepsi's Note 2). The ROA, profit margin and assets turnover of restaurants showed steady improvement over the three years as a result of operating efficiencies, improved quality controls, and more aggressive marketing.

The geographical segment data in Exhibit 7.5 indicate decreased profitability in Europe offset by increased profitability elsewhere. The decreased profitability in Europe relates to the major consumer foods acquisition in Year 7. The improved profitability elsewhere reflects expansion of restaurants worldwide.

Pepsi, like Coke, does not exhibit dramatic changes in its ROA over the period studied. Pepsi's acquisition actively dominates the changes observed at the segment level and the minor changes observed at the companywide level.

Cross Section Analysis—Coke versus Pepsi

Figure 7.6 shows that Coke outperformed Pepsi in terms of ROA, profit margin, and assets turnover for Year 8. Exhibit 7.3 indicates that Coke's ROA consistently dominates that of Pepsi, largely as a result of a higher profit margin. Their assets turnovers are essentially equivalent.

An examination of the common size income statement data shows that Coke's advantage derives from lower cost of goods sold and lower selling and administrative expense percentages. Chapter 3 demonstrated that the use of different cost-flow assumptions does not explain the differences in the cost of goods sold percentages. The product-line segment data in Exhibit 7.4 show that Coke's soft drink business is significantly more profitable than Pepsi's, while Pepsi's consumer foods business is significantly more profitable than Coke's. Soft drinks comprise 84 percent of Coke's sales mix, while consumer foods comprise only 28 percent of Pepsi's sales mix. The net effect is a higher profit margin for Coke. Exhibit 7.5 indicates that the two companies experience similar profitability in the United States. Coke, however, dominates Pepsi abroad. Note from the segment data that Coke's soft drink sales abroad are four times as large as Pepsi's, suggesting that Coke enjoys a competitive (perhaps monopoly) position in other countries.

Although the two companies experience similar total assets turnovers, their individual asset turnovers differ. Pepsi's accounts receivable and inventory turnovers are larger than Coke's, primarily as a result of their restaurant businesses. Pepsi's fixed assets turnovers are smaller than Coke's, again because of the capital intensity of restaurants.

Summary

This chapter has described and illustrated the analytical tools used to assess the operating profitability of a firm. The rate of return on assets, a measure that relates operating income to assets in use independent of the financing of those assets, is

Exhibit 7.6
Summary of Financial Statement Ratios

	Numerator	Denominator
Profitability Ratios		
Rate of Return on Assets	Net Income + Interest Expense (net of tax effects)[a]	Average Total Assets during the Period
Profit Margin Ratio (before interest effects)	Net Income + Interest Expense (net of tax effects)[a]	Sales
Various Expense Ratios	Various Expenses	Sales
Assets Turnover Ratio	Sales	Average Total Assets during the Period
Accounts Receivable Turnover Ratio	Net Sales on Account	Average Accounts Receivable during the Period
Inventory Turnover Ratio	Cost of Goods Sold	Average Inventory during the Period
Fixed Asset Turnover Ratio	Sales	Average Fixed Assets during the Period

[a]If a parent company does not own 100 percent of the common stock of a consolidated subsidiary, we add back to net income the minority interest share of earnings.

the starting point for this analysis. We disaggregated ROA into its components, profit margin and assets turnover, and then in turn disaggregated these components still further until we reached sufficient analytical depth to identify reasons for time-series and cross-sectional differences in ROA. Developing explanations for such differences requires that the analyst understand the underlying strategy of the business and the economics and current conditions existing in its industries.

Problems

7.1 *Relating Profit Margin and Assets Turnover to Type of Business.* Selected data for three retail firms are as follows:

	Firm A	Firm B	Firm C
Sales	$14,111.8	$15,471.0	$15,959.3
Operating Income (before Interest and Related Tax Effects)	$ 1,039.1	$ 789.5	$ 510.7
Average Total Assets	$ 5,930.0	$ 9,360.8	$ 4,590.5

One of these firms is a discount store chain, with its stores located primarily in suburban and rural locations. Another firm is a department store chain that carries a broad line of products and locates its stores in urban areas and suburban shopping centers. A third firm is a specialty retail clothing chain for teenagers, with store space rented in suburban shopping centers.

    a. Calculate the rate of return on assets for each firm. Disaggregate ROA into profit margin and assets turnover components.

    b. Indicate which firm is the discount store chain, which is the department store chain, and which is the specialty retailer. Discuss the reasoning for your selection.

7.2 *Relating ROA, Profit Margin, and Assets Turnover to Type of Business.* The ROA, profit margin (PM), and assets turnover (T/O) of three capital-intensive firms for three recent years are as follows:

	Year 5	Year 6	Year 7
	ROA = PM × T/O	ROA = PM × T/O	ROA = PM × T/O
Firm A	7.9% = 5.7% × 1.39	10.0% = 7.6% × 1.32	7.5% = 6.0% × 1.25
Firm B	7.7% = 11.8% × .65	7.4% = 12.3% × .60	7.8% = 14.2% × .55
Firm C	7.6% = 7.4% × 1.03	2.9% = 3.3% × .88	5.6% = 6.9% × .81

One of these firms is Consolidated Edison (electric utility), one is Delta Airlines, and one is Exxon. Match these three firms with the appropriate data sets above. Explain your reasoning.

7.3 *Effect of Operating Leverage on Gross Margin.* Computer Electronics Corporation reported the following in its income statement for its three most recent years:

	Year 2	Year 3	Year 4
Sales	$3,550	$4,080	$4,690
Cost of Goods Sold..............	2,730	3,048	3,414
Gross Margin........................	$ 820	$1,032	$1,276
Gross Margin Percentage....	23.1%	25.3%	27.2%

a. Assuming that the cost structure of Computer Electronics has not changed over the three-year period, determine the total fixed cost and the variable cost as a percentage of sales for these years. (Hint: Begin by computing the change in cost of goods sold relative to the change in sales; is this amount the variable cost or fixed cost portion of total costs?)

b. What factors seem to explain the changes in the gross margin percentage over this three-year period?

c. Analysts expect computer sales to decrease industrywide in Year 5. Computer Electronics expects its sales to decrease 20 percent. Assuming that the cost structure computed in part (a) continues to apply, estimate the gross margin percentage anticipated for Year 5.

7.4 *Measuring Operating Leverage Using Segment Data.* Lev Corporation operates in two business segments. The operating policies and strategies of these two segments have remained largely the same over the last two years. Data for these segments for Year 4 and Year 5 are as follows:

	Segment A	Segment B
Sales		
Year 4...	$400	$1,300
Year 5...	$440	$1,500
Operating Income (before Income Taxes)		
Year 4...	$ 48	$ 104
Year 5...	$ 60	$ 135

Average Assets

Year 4	$260	$ 845
Year 5	$285	$ 975

Capital Expenditures

Year 4	$ 80	$ 132
Year 5	$ 94	$ 154

Depreciation

Year 4	$ 40	$ 54
Year 5	$ 43	$ 58

a. Assuming that depreciation expense is the only fixed cost, determine the pretax variable and fixed cost structure of each of these two segments for each year.

b. Which segment carries more operating leverage? Explain.

c. Which segment appears to be more profitable? Analyze the data to the maximum depth possible in responding to this question.

7.5 *Reconciling Income Tax Expense Percentages with Effective Tax Rates.* Selected data taken from the financial statements of Merck, a pharmaceutical company, appear below (amounts in millions). The statutory tax rate is 34 percent in each year.

	Year 3	Year 4	Year 5
Sales	$ 3,547.5	$ 4,128.9	$ 5,061.3
Other Expenses	(2,622.5)	(3,011.0)	(3,599.7)
Income Tax Expense	(348.4)	(418.1)	(521.4)
Net Operating Income	$ 576.6	$ 699.8	$ 940.2

a. Compute the income tax expense percentage for each year (that is, income tax expense/sales).

b. Compute the effective tax rate on operating income before taxes (that is, income tax expense/operating income before taxes).

c. Why do these two measures of income taxes seemingly give conflicting information about Merck's tax burden?

7.6 *Analyzing Accounts Receivable for Two Companies.* Union Camp and Westvaco both manufacture pulp and paper products. Information about the two companies for Year 2, Year 3, and Year 4 are (amounts in millions):

Union Camp	Year 2	Year 3	Year 4
Sales	$1,865.9	$2,045.2	$2,307.6
Average Accounts Receivable (Net)	213.4	227.4	250.1

Westvaco			
Sales	$1,796.3	$1,818.2	$1,811.9
Average Accounts Receivable (Net)	143.9	158.1	165.6

a. Calculate the accounts receivable turnover for each company for each year.

b. The allowance for uncollectible accounts averages 4 percent of gross receivables for Union Camp and 4.4 percent of gross receivables for Westvaco. Recalculate the accounts receivable turnover for Union Camp for Year 4 assuming that its allowance for uncollectible accounts had averaged 4.4 percent instead of 4 percent. Is it likely that different levels of estimated uncollectible accounts explain the differences in accounts receivable turnover computed in part (*a*)?

c. Both companies offer credit terms of a 2 percent discount if customers pay within 10 days of purchase; otherwise the full amount is due in 30 days. What do the levels of the accounts receivable turnover suggest about the taking of discounts by customers of these two companies?

d. What factors might explain the trend in the accounts receivable turnover for each company?

e. What factors might explain the difference in the accounts receivable turnovers of the two companies?

7.7 *Analyzing Inventory Turnovers of Two Companies.* Eli Lilly and Warner Lambert are both pharmaceutical companies. Eli Lilly derives virtually all of its revenues from sales of ethical, or prescription, drugs. Warner Lambert derives approximately 50 percent of its revenues from ethical drugs and 50 percent from nonprescription drugs and personal health-care products. Eli Lilly uses a LIFO cost-flow assumption and Warner Lambert uses a FIFO cost-flow assumption. Data for the two companies for three recent years are as follows (amounts in millions):

	Eli Lilly	**Warner Lambert**
Cost of Goods Sold		
Year 7	$1,175.4	$1,169.9
Year 8	$1,346.2	$1,052.8
Year 9	$1,302.8	$1,169.7
Ending Inventories		
Year 6	$ 630.2[a]	$ 425.4
Year 7	$ 694.2[a]	$ 389.6
Year 8	$ 694.6[a]	$ 317.2
Year 9	$ 615.5[a]	$ 379.0

[a]The LIFO reserve was as follows: Year 6, $67.9; Year 7, $54.4; Year 8, $53.9; Year 9, $41.2.

a. Compute the inventory turnovers of each company for each of the three years using their reported inventory cost-flow assumptions.

b. Recompute the inventory turnovers for Eli Lilly using a FIFO cost-flow assumption. Refer to Exhibit 3.3 in Chapter 3 to review the conversion from LIFO to FIFO if necessary.

c. Some have suggested that the analyst obtains the same insights about inventory turnover by dividing sales, instead of cost of goods sold, by average inventory. Do you agree? Why or why not?

d. What factors might explain the trend of the inventory turnover ratio for each company?

e. What factors might explain the difference in inventory turnover ratios of the two companies?

7.8 *Analyzing Changes in the Fixed Asset Turnover*. Certain data for Inland Steel Industries appear below (amounts in millions):

	Sales	Capital Expenditures
Year 5	$2,999.4	$ 174.8
Year 6	$3,173.2	$ 124.8
Year 7	$3,453.2	$ 128.0

	Gross Fixed Assets	Net Fixed Assets
End of Year 4	$3,795.0	$1,730.8
End of Year 5	$3,923.3	$1,745.2
End of Year 6	$3,704.3	$1,552.4
End of Year 7	$3,703.5	$1,488.1

a. Calculate the fixed asset turnover for Year 5, Year 6, and Year 7, using average net fixed assets in the denominator.

b. Calculate the fixed asset turnover for Year 5, Year 6, and Year 7, using average gross fixed assets in the denominator.

c. The trends in the fixed asset turnovers computed in parts (*a*) and (*b*) are the same, but the rate of increase for the fixed asset turnover using net fixed assets is more rapid than that for the fixed asset turnover using gross fixed assets. What is the explanation for these differing rates of increase?

d. What factors seem to explain the changes in Inland Steel's fixed asset turnover?

7.9 *Interpreting Data on ROA and Its Components*. Exhibit 7.7 presents a set of financial ratios based on data from the financial statements of Sweet Corporation for Year 1, Year 2, and Year 3.

a. What is the likely explanation for the increasing profit margin for ROA over the three years? Consider the variable and fixed cost structure to the extent possible with the data provided. (Hint: Compute the change in various costs relative to the change in sales. Is this amount the variable cost or fixed cost portion of total costs?)

b. How has the income tax burden of Sweet Corporation changed over the three years?

Exhibit 7.7
Profitability Ratios for Sweet Corporation

	Year 1	Year 2	Year 3
Rate of Return on Assets...	8.0%	8.2%	8.1%
Profit Margin for ROA...	5.1%	5.4%	5.7%
Assets Turnover..	1.6	1.5	1.4
Cost of Goods Sold/Sales	59.8%	59.3%	58.9%
Selling and Administrative Expense/Sales.................	31.7%	31.7%	31.6%
Income Tax Expense[a]/Sales	3.4%	3.6%	3.8%
Accounts Receivable Turnover	8.2	8.1	8.2
Inventory Turnover...	4.9	5.0	4.9
Fixed Asset Turnover	2.8	2.6	2.4
Trend (Year 1 = 100)			
Sales	100	120	144
Net Income..	100	133	182
Capital Expenditures...	100	122	152

[a]Excluding tax effects of interest expense.

    c.   What is the apparent reason for the decreasing total assets turnover?

7.10 *Interpreting Data for ROA and Its Components at Firm and Segment Levels.*
Exhibits 7.8 to 7.11 present partial financial statements for Fin Stat Corporation
for Year 7 to Year 9. Analyze the data for Fin Stat Corporation to the maximum extent possible and respond to the following questions:
    a.   What is the likely reason for the decreasing rate of return on assets?
    b.   Assuming that the cost structure for cost of goods sold did not change
         over the three-year period, compute the fixed cost and variable cost per
         dollar of sales for cost of goods sold. (Hint: Compute the change in cost of
         goods sold relative to the change in sales. Is this amount the variable cost
         or the fixed cost portion of total costs?)
    c.   What is the likely explanation for the decreasing cost of goods sold per-
         centage coupled with the increasing inventory turnover?

Exhibit 7.8
Income Statements for Fin Stat Corporation

	For the Year		
	Year 7	Year 8	Year 9
Sales	$1,000	$1,200	$1,500
Cost of Goods Sold...................................	(660)	(756)	(900)
Selling and Administrative	(230)	(300)	(435)
Interest...	(10)	(24)	(45)
Income Taxes	(46)	(55)	(48)
Net Income..	$ 54	$ 65	$ 72

d. What is the likely explanation for the decrease in the income tax expense percentage between Year 8 and Year 9?

e. What is the apparent strategy being followed by Segment A?

Exhibit 7.9
Balance Sheets for Fin Stat Corporation

	December 31			
	Year 6	Year 7	Year 8	Year 9
Assets				
Cash..	$ 15	$ 33	$ 99	$ 29
Accounts Receivable	110	130	152	192
Inventories	155	185	193	247
Fixed Assets (Net).................................	250	310	490	660
Total Assets	$530	$658	$934	$1,128
Liabilities and Shareholders' Equity				
Bank Loans..	$ 24	$ 54	$231	$ 328
Accounts Payable	89	107	117	173
Long-Term Debt	106	132	187	226
Common Stock	200	200	200	200
Retained Earnings.................................	111	165	199	201
Total Equities.......................................	$530	$658	$934	$1,128

Exhibit 7.10
Segment Data for Fin Stat Corporation

	Year 7		Year 8		Year 9	
Sales						
Segment A...........................	$ 200	20%	$ 240	20%	$ 300	20%
Segment B...........................	500	50	540	45	600	40
Segment C...........................	300	30	420	35	600	40
	$1,000	100%	$1,200	100%	$1,500	100%
Operating Income						
Segment A...........................	$ 22	20%	$ 23	16%	$ 16	10%
Segment B...........................	59	54	80	56	91	55
Segment C...........................	29	26	41	28	58	35
	$ 110	100%	$ 144	100%	$ 165	100%
Operating Assets						
Segment A...........................	$ 132	20%	$ 140	15%	$ 95	8%
Segment B...........................	394	60	458	49	461	41
Segment C...........................	132	20	336	36	572	51
	$ 658	100%	$ 934	100%	$1,128	100%

Exhibit 7.11
Financial Ratio Analysis for Fin Stat Corporation

	Year 7	Year 8	Year 9
Return on Assets	10.0%	9.8%	9.6%
Profit Margin for ROA	5.9%	6.5%	6.6%
Assets Turnover	1.68	1.51	1.45
Cost of Goods Sold/Sales	66.0%	63.0%	60.0%
Selling and Admin. Expense/Sales	23.0%	25.0%	29.0%
Income Tax Expense/Sales[a]	5.15%	5.55%	4.45%
Accounts Receivable Turnover	8.3	8.5	8.7
Inventory Turnover	3.9	4.0	4.1
Fixed Asset Turnover	3.6	3.0	2.6

[a]Excluding tax effects of interest expense.

7.11 *Interpreting Data on ROA and Its Components.* Exhibit 7.12 presents a set of ratios based on financial statement data of Stebbins Corporation for Year 3, Year 4, and Year 5. Stebbins Corporation made no major changes in its product line over this period. Analyze the preceding data to the maximum depth possible and respond to the following questions:

    a.   What is the most likely explanation for the decreasing profit margin?

    b.   What is the likely explanation for the increasing assets turnover?

Exhibit 7.12
Profitability Ratios for Stebbins Corporation

	Year 3	Year 4	Year 5
Rate of Return on Assets	10.0%	11.0%	12.0%
Profit Margin (before Interest and Related Taxes)	18.0%	16.0%	14.0%
Assets Turnover	.56	.69	.86
Cost of Goods Sold/Sales	62.0%	63.0%	65.0%
Selling and Administrative Expenses/Sales	10.0%	10.0%	10.0%
Income Tax Expense[a]/Sales	10.0%	11.0%	11.0%
Accounts Receivable Turnover	2.6	2.5	2.4
Inventory Turnover	3.2	2.8	2.5
Fixed Asset Turnover	.9	1.4	2.6
Sales as a Percentage of Year 3 Sales	100	102	99
Net Income as a Percentage of Year 3 Net Income	100	102	99
Capital Expenditures as a Percentage of Year 3 Capital Expenditures	100	90	85
Assets as a Percentage of Year 3 Assets	100	82	64

[a]Excluding the tax effects of interest expense.

7.12 *Calculating and Interpreting Profitability Ratios.* Mercer Corporation manufactures electrical equipment that is used by a variety of other industries. Prior to Year 8, its only plant was in New Jersey. Desirous of establishing a West Coast presence, it acquired a new plant in Oregon early in Year 8. The new plant is more capital-intensive than the New Jersey facility and Mercer Corporation expects the plant to reduce labor costs. The Company instituted new "just-in-time" inventory control systems in the new plant in the hope of reducing raw materials storage costs. Mercer Corporation hired and trained a new sales staff for the West Coast operation. Production commenced in the new facility in February, Year 8.

Selected financial statement data for Mercer Corporation are as follows:

Balance Sheet	Dec. 31, Year 6	Dec. 31, Year 7	Dec. 31, Year 8
Cash...	$ 20	$ 30	$ 3
Accounts Receivable	18	20	55
Inventories	25	30	50
Fixed Assets (Net)..	75	80	185
Total Assets	$138	$160	$293

Income Statement	For Year 7	For Year 8
Sales	$160	$250
Cost of Goods Sold[a].....................................	(78)	(120)
Selling and Administrative[a]..........................	(30)	(48)
Depreciation..	(12)	(28)
Interest..	(2)	(4)
Income Taxes	(16)	(18)
Net Income..	$ 22	$ 32

[a]Excludes depreciation expense.

a.   Calculate the following ratios for Mercer Corporation for Year 7 and Year 8 (the statutory income tax rate was 40 percent in Year 7 and 34 percent in Year 8):

  (1) Rate of return on assets.
  (2) Profit margin percentage for ROA.
  (3) Assets turnover.
  (4) Cost of goods sold percentage.
  (5) Selling and administrative expense percentage.
  (6) Depreciation expense percentage.
  (7) Income tax expense (excluding tax effects of interest expense) percentage.
  (8) Accounts receivable turnover.
  (9) Inventory turnover.
  (10) Fixed asset turnover.

b.   Prepare a memorandum addressed to the president of Mercer Corporation explaining how and why its operating profitability changed between Year 7 and Year 8.

7.13 *Calculating and Interpreting Profitability Ratios.* General Mills (Mills) is a leading marketer of consumer foods and one of the largest operators of full-service restaurants in the United States. Exhibit 7.13 indicates that Mills generates just over 70 percent of its sales and approximately 80 percent of its operating profit from the consumer foods segment. However, the restaurant segment comprised a growing percentage of Mills' sales mix and asset mix in recent years.

Exhibit 7.14 presents comparative balance sheets of Mills for Years 5 through 8. Exhibit 7.15 presents comparative income statements and Exhibit 7.16 presents comparative statements of cash flows for Year 6, Year 7, and Year 8. Exhibit 7.17 presents profitability ratios for Year 6 and Year 7.

a. Compute the values for each of the ratios shown in Exhibit 7.17 for Year 8. The income tax rate during Year 6 and Year 7 was 46 percent and during Year 8 was 35 percent.

b. Evaluate the changes in profitability of Mills to the maximum extent permitted by the data.

Exhibit 7.13
Segment Data for General Mills
(amounts in millions)

Sales	Consumer Foods		Restaurants	
Year 6	$3,061.3	74%	$1,051.0	26%
Year 7	$3,449.9	73%	$1,249.1	27%
Year 8	$3,752.6	72%	$1,426.2	28%
Operating Profit				
Year 6	$ 284.2	77%	$ 84.8	23%
Year 7	$ 369.5	80%	$ 92.5	20%
Year 8	$ 411.3	82%	$ 88.9	18%
Operating Assets				
Year 6	$1,091.8	70%	$ 467.8	30%
Year 7	$1,211.7	67%	$ 594.0	33%
Year 8	$1,441.7	65%	$ 772.0	35%
Capital Expenditures				
Year 6	$ 153.6	67%	$ 74.0	33%
Year 7	$ 151.5	51%	$ 145.3	49%
Year 8	$ 191.2	54%	$ 163.8	46%
Depreciation Expense				
Year 6	$ 69.2	68%	$ 32.7	32%
Year 7	$ 78.9	67%	$ 39.4	33%
Year 8	$ 88.0	65%	$ 47.9	35%

Exhibit 7.14

Comparative Balance Sheets for General Mills (amounts in millions)

	End of Year 5	End of Year 6	End of Year 7	End of Year 8
Assets				
Cash...	$ 67	$ 190	$ 180	$ 14
Accounts Receivable	284	220	237	230
Inventories	378	351	388	424
Prepayments......................................	558[a]	43	136	142
Total Current Assets	$1,287	$ 804	$ 941	$ 810
Property, Plants, and Equipment (Net)............................	956	1,085	1,249	1,376
Other Assets	419[b]	197	165	486
Total Assets	$2,662	$2,086	$2,355	$2,672
Liabilities and Shareholders' Equity				
Accounts Payable —Trade..	$ 361	$ 382	$ 434	$ 461
Notes Payable —Nontrade.....................................	380	5	2	370
Current Portion of Long-Term Debt	59	11	94	1
Other Current Liabilities....................	257	365	393	359
Total Current Liabilities.................	$1,057	$ 763	$ 923	$1,191
Long-Term Debt	450	458	285	362
Deferred Taxes...................................	90	128	357	407
Other Noncurrent Liabilities..............	42	55	60	63
Total Liabilities	$1,639	$1,404	$1,625	$2,023
Common Stock	$ 38	$ 38	$ 38	$ 38
Additional Paid-in Capital..................	176	177	182	185
Retained Earnings..............................	1,201	813	924	1,068
Cumulative Translation Adjustment...................................	(58)	(32)	(35)	(34)
Treasury Stock	(334)	(314)	(379)	(608)
Total Shareholders' Equity......................................	$1,023	$ 682	$ 730	$ 649
Total Liabilities and Shareholders' Equity	$2,662	$2,086	$2,355	$2,672

[a]Includes assets totaling $253 million that Mills expects to sell and $265 million that Mills expects to spin off to shareholders during Year 6.

[b]Includes assets totaling $206 million that Mills expects to spin off to shareholders during Year 6.

Exhibit 7.15
Comparative Income Statements for General Mills (amounts in millions)

Revenues	Year 6	Year 7	Year 8
Sales	$4,112	$4,699	$5,179
Other Revenues	21	14	13
Total Revenues	$4,133	$4,713	$5,192

Expenses			
Cost of Goods Sold	$2,289	$2,577	$2,848
Selling and Administrative	1,377	1,564	1,711
Depreciation	104	123	140
Interest	53	43	51
Income Taxes	135	198	177
Total Expenses	$3,958	$4,505	$4,927
Net Income	$ 175	$ 208	$ 265

Exhibit 7.16
Comparative Statements of Cash Flows for General Mills (amounts in millions)

Operations	Year 6	Year 7	Year 8
Net Income	$ 175	$ 208	$ 265
Depreciation	104	123	140
Other Addbacks	31	32	28
Other Subtractions	—	—	(27)
Working Capital from Operations	$ 310	$ 363	$ 406
(Increase) Decrease in Receivables	81	(15)	(14)
(Increase) Decrease in Inventories	29	(52)	(101)
(Increase) Decrease in Prepayments	20	(3)	(10)
Increase (Decrease) in Accounts Payable	30	52	27
Increase (Decrease) in Other Current Liabilities	(40)	85	22
Cash Flow from Operations	$ 430	$ 430	$ 330

Investing			
Fixed Assets Sold	$ 19	$ 18	$ 13
Fixed Assets Acquired	(245)	(329)	(411)
Other Investing Transactions	296	79	(11)
Cash Flow from Investing	$ 70	$(232)	$(409)

Financing			
Increase in Short-Term Borrowing	—	—	$ 367
Increase in Long-Term Borrowing	$ 99	$ 51	87
Issue of Common Stock	22	20	20
Decrease in Short-Term Borrowing	(376)	(4)	—
Decrease in Long-Term Borrowing	(145)	(177)	(108)
Reacquisition of Common Stock	—	(81)	(247)
Dividends	(101)	(111)	(139)
Other Financing Transactions	125	93	(66)
Cash Flow from Financing	$(376)	$(209)	$ (86)
Net Change in Cash	$ 124	$ (11)	$(165)

Exhibit 7.17
Profitability Analysis for General Mills

	Year 6	Year 7	Year 8
Rate of Return on Assets	8.6%	10.4%	
Profit Margin for ROA	5.0%	4.9%	
Total Assets Turnover	1.7	2.1	
Cost of Goods and Services Sold Percentage	55.6%	54.9%	
Selling and Administrative			
Expense Percentage	33.5%	33.3%	
Depreciation Expense Percentage	2.5%	2.6%	
Income Tax Expense Percentage (Excluding			
Tax Effects of Interest Expense)	3.9%	4.6%	
Accounts Receivable Turnover	16.3	20.6	
Inventory Turnover	6.3	7.0	
Fixed Asset Turnover	4.0	4.0	
Consumer Foods Segment			
Rate of Return on Assets	26.0%	30.5%	
Profit Margin	9.3%	10.7%	
Assets Turnover	2.8	2.8	
Restaurant Segment			
Rate of Return on Assets	18.1%	15.6%	
Profit Margin	8.1%	7.4%	
Assets Turnover	2.2	2.1	

7.14 *Analyzing and Interpreting the Rate of Return on Assets and Its Components.* Digital Equipment Corporation (DEC) manufactures and markets a broad line of computer hardware and software, primarily for business and scientific applications. During Year 9, it derived 50 percent of its sales and 71 percent of its income from outside of the United States. Product sales account for approximately two-thirds of its revenues and service revenues account for the remainder. Exhibits 7.18, 7.19, and 7.20 present income statements, balance sheets, and statements of cash flow respectively for DEC. Assume that labor costs make up most of the cost of service revenues in Exhibit 7.18. Exhibit 7.21 presents a partial financial ratio analysis for DEC for Year 7, Year 8, and Year 9. The income tax rate for Year 9 is 34 percent.

   a. Compute the missing financial ratio amounts in Exhibit 7.21 for DEC for Year 9.

   b. What is the likely explanation for the decrease in the rate of return on assets between fiscal Year 7 (14.9%) and fiscal Year 8 (14.4%)? Analyze the data to the maximum feasible depth.

   c. What is the likely explanation for the increase in the cost of goods and services sold/sales percentage between fiscal Year 8 (47.6%) and fiscal Year 9 (49.0%)?

   d. What is the likely explanation for the decrease in the income tax expense to sales percentage between fiscal Year 8 (3.8%) and fiscal Year 9 (2.7%)?

Exhibit 7.18

Digital Equipment Corporation Income Statements (amounts in millions)

	Year Ended		
	June 27, Year 7	July 2, Year 8	July 1, Year 9
Revenues			
Product Sales..	$6,254	$ 7,542	$ 8,190
Service Revenues.......................................	3,135	3,934	4,552
Total Operating Revenues....................	$9,389	$11,476	$12,742
Costs and Expenses			
Cost of Product Sales	$2,532	$ 3,042	$ 3,468
Cost of Service Revenues	1,982	2,426	2,774
Research and Development Expenses	1,010	1,307	1,525
Selling and Administrative Expenses	2,253	3,066	3,639
Total Operating Expenses	$7,777	$ 9,841	$11,406
Operating Income	$1,612	$ 1,635	$ 1,336
Interest Income...	122	144	124
Interest Expense.......................................	(45)	(38)	(39)
Income before Income Taxes..................	$1,689	$ 1,741	$ 1,421
Income Tax Expense	(552)	(435)	(348)
Net Income...	$1,137	$ 1,306	$ 1,073

Exhibit 7.19

Digital Equipment Corporation Balance Sheets (amounts in millions)

	July 2, Year 8	July 1, Year 9
Assets		
Cash and Temporary Investments.....................................	$ 2,164	$ 1,655
Accounts Receivable..	2,592	2,965
Inventories...	1,575	1,638
Prepayments..	599	636
Total Current Assets..	$ 6,930	$ 6,894
Property, Plant, and Equipment (Cost)............................	$ 5,210	$ 6,249
Less Accumulated Depreciation	(2,115)	(2,603)
Net Property, Plant, and Equipment............................	$ 3,095	$ 3,646
Other Assets..	87	128
Total Assets...	$10,112	$10,668
Liabilities and Shareholders' Equity		
Bank Loans and Current Portion of Long-Term Debt....	$ 155	$ 30
Accounts Payable..	523	554
Other Current Liabilities	1,736	1,810
Total Current Liabilities	$ 2,414	$ 2,394
Long-Term Debt..	124	136
Deferred Income Taxes	63	102
Total Liabilities...	$ 2,601	$ 2,632
Common Stock...	$ 130	$ 130
Additional Paid-in Capital..	2,428	2,470
Retained Earnings...	5,460	6,366
Treasury Stock	(507)	(930)
Total Shareholders' Equity...	$ 7,511	$ 8,036
Total Liabilities and Shareholders' Equity.................	$10,112	$10,668

Exhibit 7.20

Digital Equipment Corporation Statement of Cash Flows (amounts in millions)

	Year Ended		
	June 27, Year 7	July 2, Year 8	July 1, Year 9
Operations			
Net Income	$ 1,137	$ 1,306	$ 1,073
Depreciation	436	527	687
Other Adjustments	74	66	50
(Increase) Decrease in Accounts Receivable	(409)	(280)	(373)
(Increase) Decrease in Inventories	(253)	(122)	(63)
(Increase) Decrease in Prepayments	(34)	(155)	19
Increase (Decrease) in Accounts Payable	171	93	30
Increase (Decrease) in Other Current Liabilities	588	264	56
Cash Flow from Operations	$ 1,710	$ 1,699	$ 1,479
Investing			
Acquisition of Property, Plant, and Equipment	(748)	(1,518)	(1,223)
Increase in Other Assets	(81)	(19)	(68)
Cash Flow from Investing	$ (829)	$ (1,537)	$ (1,291)
Financing			
Issue of Long-Term Debt	—	$ 7	$ 40
Retirement of Long-Term Debt	$ (81)	(3)	(153)
Purchase of Treasury Stock	(782)	(363)	(815)
Proceeds from Issue of Treasury Stock	189	243	231
Cash Flow from Financing	$ (674)	$ (116)	$ (697)
Change in Cash	$ 207	$ 46	$ (509)
Cash at Beginning of Year	1,911	2,118	2,164
Cash at End of Year	$ 2,118	$ 2,164	$ 1,655

7.15 *Interpreting Data on Return on Assets and Its Components.* Boyd Corporation is an integrated forest products company. Its sales mix and income mix for the last three years are as follows:

	Sales Mix			Income Mix		
	Year 3	Year 4	Year 5	Year 3	Year 4	Year 5
Pulp and Paper	54%	59%	55%	69%	81%	69%
Office Products	19	20	22	10	10	12
Building Products	26	20	22	20	8	18
Other	1	1	1	1	1	1
	100%	100%	100%	100%	100%	100%

The pulp and paper segment takes timber from company-owned forests and grinds it up into pulp. Boyd Corporation then either sells the pulp on the open market to other paper processors or converts it into paperboard or lineboard for boxes or into

Exhibit 7.21
Financial Statement Ratios for Digital Equipment Computation

	Year 7	Year 8	Year 9
Profit Margin for ROA	12.4%	11.6%	
Assets Turnover	1.2	1.2	
Return on Assets	14.9%	14.4%	
Cost of Goods Sold/Sales	48.1%	47.6%	
Sell. and Admin. Exp./Sales	24.0%	26.7%	
R&D Exp./Sales	10.8%	11.4%	
Interest Exp./Sales	.5%	.3%	
Income Tax Exp./Sales	5.9%	3.8%	
Accounts Receivable Turnover	4.5	4.7	
Inventory Turnover	1.9	2.0	
Fixed Asset Turnover	4.7	4.4	
SEGMENT DATA			
Sales Mix			
U.S.	57%	54%	50%
Europe	28	30	33
Other	15	16	17
	100%	100%	100%
Income Mix			
U.S.	45%	31%	29%
Europe	38	46	50
Other	17	23	21
	100%	100%	100%
Asset Mix			
U.S.	60%	55%	54%
Europe	29	32	33
Other	11	13	13
	100%	100%	100%
ROA			
U.S.	16.4%	9.8%	9.3%
Europe	28.2%	24.9%	23.8%
Other	33.0%	30.2%	31.7%
Profit Margin			
U.S.	10.9%	6.6%	6.4%
Europe	18.8%	17.7%	15.6%
Other	15.6%	16.6%	14.5%
Assets Turnover			
U.S.	1.5	1.5	1.4
Europe	1.5	1.4	1.5
Other	2.1	1.8	2.2
Product Sales Mix			
Product Sales	67%	66%	64%
Service	33	34	36
	100%	100%	100%
Gross Margin			
Product Sales	59.5%	59.7%	57.7%
Service	36.8%	38.3%	39.1%
Interperiod Percentage Changes			
Sales	23.7%	22.2%	11.0%
Cost of Goods Sold	5.4%	21.1%	14.2%
Sell. and Admin. Exp.	35.6%	39.6%	18.7%
Total Assets	17.2%	20.3%	5.5%
Capital Expenditures	33.7%	202.8%	-19.4%

Exhibit 7.22
Ratio Analysis for Boyd Corporation

	Year 3	Year 4	Year 5
Return on Assets			
Profit Margin for ROA	6.4%	8.7%	7.6%
Assets Turnover	1.1	1.2	1.1
Return on Assets	7.1%	10.2%	8.5%
Return on Common Equity			
Return on Assets	7.1%	10.2%	8.5%
Common Earnings Leverage	71.5%	80.6%	77.6%
Capital Structure Leverage	2.3	2.2	2.4
Return on Common Equity	11.7%	18.2%	15.9%
Common Size Income Statement			
Sales	100.0%	100.0%	100.0%
Cost of Goods Sold	(80.3)	(77.2)	(78.8)
Selling and Administration	(8.9)	(8.9)	(9.4)
Other	.2	.2	.4
Income Taxes—Operations	(4.6)	(5.4)	(4.6)
Profit Margin for ROA	6.4%	8.7%	7.6%
Interest Expense	(2.7)	(2.4)	(2.1)
Inc. Tax Savings on Interest	1.1	.8	.7
Net Income	4.8%	7.1%	6.2%
Asset Turnovers			
Receivables	10.9	11.0	10.6
Inventories	8.0	8.2	8.3
Fixed Assets	1.6	1.7	1.6
Liquidity			
Current Ratio	1.47	1.27	1.37
Quick Ratio	.68	.61	.66
Days Receivables Held	33	33	34
Days Inventory Held	46	45	44
Days Payables Held	33	35	40
Operating Cash Flow/Current Liabilities	71.1%	91.8%	72.8%
Solvency			
Total Liabilities/Total Assets	53.8%	53.5%	62.0%
L.T. Debt/Total Assets	27.8%	25.6%	36.2%
L.T. Debt/Owners' Equity	60.1%	55.2%	95.1%
Operating Cash Flow/Total Liabilities	20.9%	30.5%	22.0%
Interest Coverage Ratio	4.03	5.78	5.55
Operating Cash Flow/Capital Expenditures	1.66	1.33	.71
Segment Return on Assets			
Pulp and Paper	16.0%	22.9%	15.3%
Office Products	15.6%	18.4%	17.1%
Building Products	22.4%	16.3%	28.3%
Segment Profit Margins			
Pulp and Paper	15.9%	20.7%	16.3%
Office Products	6.5%	7.1%	6.6%
Building Products	8.7%	6.5%	10.8%
Segment Assets Turnovers			
Pulp and Paper	1.0	1.1	.9
Office Products	2.4	2.6	2.6
Building Products	2.6	2.5	2.6

newsprint. The office products segment converts pulp into uncoated and coated paper for use in stationery and computer output. The building products segment converts timber into lumber, plywood, and other home-building products.

Exhibit 7.22 presents selected financial statement ratios for Boyd Corporation for Year 3 to Year 5. The questions below rely on the ratios studied in this chapter. Questions using rate of return on common shareholders' equity, liquidity, and solvency ratios appear in Chapters 8 and 9.

    a. What is the likely explanation for the increased rate of return on assets between Year 3 and Year 4? Respond to this question to the maximum extent permitted by the financial ratios in Exhibit 7.22.

    b. What is the likely explanation for the decreased rate of return on assets between Year 4 and Year 5? Respond to this question to the maximum extent permitted by the financial ratios in Exhibit 7.22.

Profitability Analysis: Rate of Return on Common Shareholders' Equity

8

Chapter 7 considered the rate of return on assets, a useful measure for assessing the profitability of operations independent of the type and mix of financing. The principal interest of investors in a firm's common stock is the portion of a firm's ROA that is allocable to them as residual claimants on the firm's assets. The measure of profitability of interest to common shareholders is the rate of return on common shareholders' equity (ROCE). This chapter demonstrates the calculation of ROCE, illustrates its usefulness in analyzing the profitability of Coke and Pepsi, and discusses some of the determinants of its behavior. This chapter also discusses earnings per share (EPS), another commonly used financial ratio for assessing the return to shareholders.

Calculating ROCE

The analyst calculates ROCE as follows:

$$\text{ROCE} = \frac{\text{Net Income} - \text{Preferred Stock Dividends}}{\text{Average Common Shareholders' Equity}}$$

The numerator measures the amount of income for the period allocable to the common shareholders after subtracting all amounts allocable to senior claimants. The accountant subtracts interest expense on debt in measuring net income, so the analyst makes no adjustment for creditors' claims on earnings. The analyst must subtract dividends paid or payable on preferred stock from net income to obtain income attributable to the common shareholders. The denominator of ROCE measures the average amount of common equity in use during the period. Common equity equals total shareholders' equity minus the par value of preferred stock. Firms seldom issue preferred stock significantly above par value, so the analyst can assume that the amount in the Additional Paid-in Capital account relates to common stock. Because net income to common shareholders in the numerator reflects a subtraction for the minority interest in earnings of consolidated subsidiaries, the denominator should exclude the minority interest in net assets (if any).

The ROCEs of Coke and Pepsi for Year 8 appear below. As was the case with ROA in Chapter 7, we base our calculations on income from continuing operations and exclude unusual, nonrecurring items. Pepsi reported a discontinued operations charge of $13.7 million and a gain from an initial stock offering of a joint venture of $53.0 million in Year 8. The calculation below eliminates the effect of these two items (both amounts are after-tax amounts). Only Coke had preferred stock outstanding during the year.

$$\text{Coke} \quad \frac{\$1,381.9 - \$18.2}{.5[(\$3,485.5 - \$300.0) + (\$3,849.2 - \$75.0)]} = 39.2\%$$

$$\text{Pepsi} \quad \frac{\$1,076.9 + \$13.7 - \$53.0}{.5(\$3,891.1 + \$4,904.2)} = 23.6\%$$

The ROCEs of Coke were 33.1 percent in Year 6 and 36.3 percent in Year 7, reflecting an increase over the three-year period. The ROCEs of Pepsi were 26.9 percent in Year 6 and 25.6 percent in Year 7, reflecting a decrease over the three years.

Relating ROA and ROCE

ROA measures operating performance independent of financing while ROCE explicitly considers the amount and cost of debt and preferred stock financing. The relation between ROA and ROCE is as follows:

Return on Assets	=	**Return to Creditors**	+	**Return to Preferred Shareholders**	+	**Return to Common Shareholders**
$\dfrac{\text{Net Income + Interest Expense Net of Taxes}}{\text{Average Total Assets}}$	=	$\dfrac{\text{Interest Expense Net of Taxes}}{\text{Average Total Liabilities}}$	+	$\dfrac{\text{Preferred Dividends}}{\text{Average Preferred Shareholders' Equity}}$	+	$\dfrac{\text{Net Income to Common}}{\text{Average Common Shareholders' Equity}}$

The accountant allocates each dollar of return generated from using assets to the various providers of capital. Creditors receive their return in the form of interest. The cost of this capital is its amount net of the income tax benefit derived from deducting interest in calculating taxable income. Many liabilities, such as accounts payable and salaries payable, carry no explicit cost. The preferred stock carries a cost equal to the preferred dividend rate. Firms cannot deduct preferred dividends in calculating taxable income. The income from operations (that is, the numerator of ROA) that is not allocable to creditors or preferred shareholders belongs to the common shareholders as the residual claimants. Likewise, the portion of a firm's assets not financed with capital provided by creditors or preferred shareholders represents the capital provided by the common shareholders.

Consider now the relation between ROA and ROCE. Under what circumstances will ROCE exceed ROA? Under what circumstances will ROCE be less than ROA?

ROCE will exceed ROA whenever ROA exceeds the cost of capital provided by creditors and preferred shareholders. If a firm can generate a greater return on capital provided by creditors and preferred shareholders than the cost of that capital, the excess return belongs to the common shareholders. Refer to Case 1 in Exhibit 8.1. Assets during the period generated a return of 10 percent. The after-tax cost of creditors' capital is 6 percent. The excess return on creditors' capital of 4 percent belongs to the common shareholders. The 2 percent excess return on preferred shareholders' capital likewise belongs to the common shareholders. The common shareholders of course also have a full claim on the 10 percent return generated on each dollar of capital that they provided. Thus, the return to the common shareholders comprises the following:

Excess Return on Capital Provided by Creditors: $.04 \times \$40 =$	$1.6
Excess Return on Capital Provided by Preferred Shareholders: $.02 \times \$20 =$	.4
Return on Capital Provided by Common Shareholders: $.10 \times \$40 =$	4.0
Total Return to Common Shareholders	$6.0
ROCE: $6/$40	15%

Exhibit 8.1
Illustrations of Financial Leverage

	Return on Assets →Return to Creditors +		Return to Preferred + Shareholders	Return to Common Shareholders
Case 1	$10	$2.4	$1.6	$6
	$100	$40	$20	$40
Rates of Return	10%	6%	8%	15%
Case 2	$10	$3.0	$1.6	$5.4
	$100	$50	$20	$30
Rates of Return	10%	6%	8%	18%
Case 3	$10	$4	$1.6	$4.4
	$100	$50	$20	$30
Rates of Return	10%	8%	8%	14.7%
Case 4	$14	$2.4	$1.6	$10
	$100	$40	$20	$40
Rates of Return	14%	6%	8%	25%
Case 5	$3	$2.4	$1.6	($1.0)
	$100	$40	$20	$40
Rates of Return	3%	6%	8%	(2.5%)

Common business terminology refers to the phenomenon of using lower-cost creditor and preferred stock capital to increase the return to the common shareholders as *financial leverage*. Financial leverage works to the benefit of the common shareholders in Case 1.

Common shareholders realize even greater advantage of financial leverage when the firm increases the percentage of debt and preferred stock in the capital structure. Case 2 in Exhibit 8.1 increases the percentage of debt in the capital structure from 40 percent to 50 percent and decreases the percentage of common equity capital from 40 percent to 30 percent. The ROCE increases to 18 percent, comprising the following:

Excess Return on Capital Provided by Creditors: $.04 \times \$50 =$	$2.0
Excess Return on Capital Provided by Preferred Shareholders: $.02 \times \$20 =$	.4
Return on Capital Provided by Common Shareholders: $.10 \times \$30 =$	3.0
Total Return to Common Shareholders	$5.4
ROCE: $5.4/$30	18%

A firm cannot, of course, increase financial leverage without limit. As the firm increases the proportion of debt or preferred stock in the capital structure, its overall risk increases. This increased riskiness occurs because of the increased commitment to pay interest and principal on debt and dividends on preferred stock. The firm will reach a point where the after-tax cost of debt or preferred stock capital will exceed the return generated on the assets obtained from that capital. Referring to Case 3 in Exhibit 8.1, suppose that, by increasing the proportion of debt in the capital structure in Case 2, the average after-tax cost of debt increases to 8 percent from 6 percent. Compared to Case 1, Case 3 shows that the ROCE decreases from 15 percent to 14.7 percent. Although financial leverage still benefits the common shareholders [that is, ROA of 10 percent exceeds the cost of debt (8 percent) and preferred shareholders' (8 percent) capital], its benefit may not be optimal. Determining the appropriate mix of debt and equity capital in the capital structure, involving a trade-off of returns and risk, is a major concern in the field of finance.

Financial leverage represents a two-edged sword. It can enhance the returns to common shareholders in "good" earnings years (see Case 4), but can hurt their returns in "bad" earnings years (see Case 5). Thus, increasing the degree of financial leverage increases the variability of returns to common shareholders.

Disaggregating ROCE

We can disaggregate ROCE into several components to aid in its interpretation, much as we did in Chapter 7 with ROA. The disaggregated components of ROCE are ROA and adjusted leverage. Adjusted leverage further disaggregates into common earnings leverage and capital structure leverage.

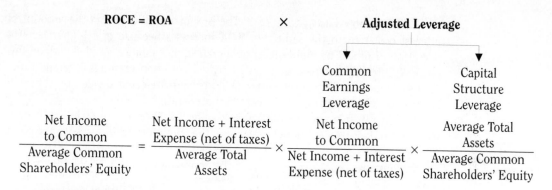

ROA indicates the return from operations independent of financing. Adjusted leverage indicates the multiplier effect of using debt and preferred stock financing to increase the return to common shareholders. Adjusted leverage is the product of two components: common earnings leverage and capital structure leverage. The common earnings leverage (CEL) ratio indicates the proportion of operating income (that is, net income before financing costs and related tax effects) allocable to the common shareholders. The capital structure leverage (CSL) ratio measures the degree to which a firm uses common shareholders' funds to finance assets.

This disaggregation of ROCE is illustrated here for the five cases in Exhibit 8.1:

Case	ROCE	=	ROA	×	Adjusted Leverage	Common Earnings Leverage	Capital Structure Leverage
1	15.0%	=	10%	×	1.50	.60	2.5
2	18.0%	=	10%	×	1.80	.54	3.3
3	14.7%	=	10%	×	1.47	.44	3.3
4	25.0%	=	14%	×	1.79	.71	2.5
5	(2.5%)	=	3%	×	(.83)	(.33)	2.5

Comparing Case 2 to Case 1, we see that the proportion of debt in the capital structure increased, with a consequent increase in the capital structure leverage ratio. However, the interest cost on this increased debt level reduces the portion of operating income allocable to the common shareholders. Thus, the common earnings leverage ratio decreased. The net effect of these two components was an increase in the adjusted leverage ratio and an increase in ROCE.

Comparing Case 3 to Case 1, we find the proportion of debt again increased while the common earnings leverage ratio decreased. In the third case, however, the common earnings leverage ratio decreased both because there is more debt in the capital structure and because the average interest cost of debt increased. The net effect of an increased capital structure leverage ratio and a decreased common earnings leverage ratio in this case is a decrease in the adjusted leverage ratio and a decrease in ROCE.

In general, increases in the capital structure leverage ratio result in decreases in the common earnings leverage ratio. Only by examining the net effect of these offsetting factors can the analyst assess the success of additional leveraging efforts.

Compare now Case 4 to Case 1. The proportion of debt and the amount of interest cost remain the same, but ROA increases because of a higher level of operating income. The higher level of operating profitability coupled with an unchanged interest cost results in an increased common earnings leverage ratio. That is, once the firm covers interest costs and preferred dividends, common shareholders have a claim on all increases in operating income.

In general, increases in ROA increase the common earnings leverage ratio (Case 4) and decreases in ROA decrease the common earnings leverage ratio (Case 5).

In summary the relations between the components of ROCE look like this:

Variables	Relationship
Capital Structure Leverage and Common Earnings Leverage	Negative Relation
Rate of Return on Assets and Common Earnings Leverage	Positive Relation

The disaggregation of ROCE for Coke and Pepsi for Year 8 appears as follows:

	ROCE	=	ROA	×	Common Earnings Leverage	×	Capital Structure Leverage
Coke	$\dfrac{\$1,381.9 - \$18.2}{.5[(\$3,485.5 - \$300.0) + (\$3,849.2 - \$75.0)]}$	=	$\dfrac{\$1,381.9 + (1 - .34)(\$231.0)}{.5(\$8,282.5 + \$9,278.2)}$	×	$\dfrac{\$1,381.9 - \$18.2}{\$1,381.9 + (1 - .34)(\$231.0)}$	×	$\dfrac{.5(\$8,282.5 + \$9,278.2)}{.5[(\$3,485.5 - \$300.0) + (\$3,849.2 - \$75.0)]}$
	39.2%	=	17.5%	×	.89	×	2.5
Pepsi	$\dfrac{\$1,037.6 - \$0}{.5(\$3,891.4 + \$4,904.2)}$	=	$\dfrac{\$1,037.6 + (1 - .34)(\$688.5)}{.5(\$15,126.7 + \$17,143.4)}$	×	$\dfrac{\$1,037.6 - \$0}{\$1,037.6 + (1 - .34)(\$688.5)}$	×	$\dfrac{.5(\$15,126.7 + \$17,143.4)}{.5(\$3,891.4 + \$4,904.2)}$
	23.6%	=	9.2%	×	.70	×	3.7

The higher ROCE of Coke results from a higher ROA. Pepsi carries more debt in its capital structure, resulting in a higher capital structure leverage ratio. Pepsi's common earnings leverage ratio is lower than Coke's, both because of lower ROA and a higher capital structure leverage ratio.

Exhibit 8.2 presents the disaggregation of ROCE of Coke and Pepsi for Year 6 to Year 8. The increasing ROCE of Coke results almost entirely from an increasing ROA. Except for some minor changes resulting from rounding, little change occurred in adjusted leverage. The decreased ROCE of Pepsi between Year 6 and Year 7 results from a decrease in adjusted leverage, in as much as ROA increased slightly. The capital structure leverage ratio increased to reflect a higher level of debt. However, the increased interest cost on this debt, and perhaps on existing variable rate debt as well, caused the common earnings leverage ratio to decrease. The changes in capital structure between Year 6 and Year 7 decreased rather than increased the return to Pepsi's shareholders. The decreased ROCE of Pepsi between Year 7 and Year 8 results from a decreased ROA. The adjusted leverage and capital structure leverage ratios remained approximately the same.

Exhibit 8.2
Disaggregation of ROCE of Coke and Pepsi Year 6 to Year 8

	ROCE	=	ROA	×	Adjusted Leverage	Common Earnings Leverage	×	Capital Structure Leverage
Coke								
Year 6	33.1%	=	15.2%	×	2.2	.87	×	2.5
Year 7	36.3%	=	17.2%	×	2.1	.83	×	2.5
Year 8	39.2%	=	17.5%	×	2.2	.89	×	2.5
Pepsi								
Year 6	26.9%	=	9.8%	×	2.7	.77	×	3.6
Year 7	25.6%	=	9.9%	×	2.6	.69	×	3.7
Year 8	23.6%	=	9.2%	×	2.6	.70	×	3.7

Determinants of the Behavior of ROCE

The discussion in the previous sections of this chapter suggests that ROCE relates to (1) an ability to generate a return from using assets in operations (that is, ROA) and (2) an ability to successfully leverage this return to benefit shareholders. This section explores more fully the association of ROA and financial leverage to ROCE, with the aim of enhancing understanding of the behavior of this important measure of profitability.

Exhibit 8.3 classifies 22 industries into a three-by-three matrix based on the level of their average ROA and capital structure leverage ratio for the years 1980 to 1989. The cells represent the lower, middle, and upper thirds in the rank orderings on each of these ratios. The average ROCE for each industry over the same time period appears in parentheses.

Observe the high degree of association between the level of ROA and the level of ROCE. The Spearman rank order correlation coefficient is .57. If we remove insurance and depository institutions, which have very low ROAs and very high capital structure leverage ratios, the Spearman rank order correlation is .73. Although we would expect firms with high ROAs to have high ROCEs, and vice versa, the important insight from Exhibit 8.3 is that the extent of financial leverage does not seem to make much difference in the rank ordering of ROA and ROCE (that is, the industries do not line up on a diagonal suggestive of a positive relation between ROA and capital structure leverage). The lack of association between ROCE and the capital structure leverage ratio lends further support to the observation that enhancing ROCE does not appear to drive firms' capital structure decisions.

A research study of firms in 22 industries for the years 1977 to 1986 found that the major portion of the annual changes in ROCE results from changes in

Exhibit 8.3
**Relation of ROCE to ROA and Capital Structure Leverage Ratio 1980 to 1989
(ROCE in Parentheses)**

	Capital Structure Leverage Ratio			
	Lower Third	**Middle Third**	**Upper Third**	
ROA				**Mean ROCE**
Upper Third	Chemicals (15.8%) Paper (13.9%) Publishing (15.8%)	Department Stores (13.9%) Food Processing (15.1%)	Telecommunications (13.6%) Grocery Stores (18.8%)	15.3%
Middle Third	Elec. Equip. (10.4%) Glass Prod. (9.0%) Metal Prod. (9.0%) Scient. Instr. (12.0%)	Textiles (7.6%) Trans. Equipment (10.9%) Wholesalers—Durables (9.2%)	Utilities (12.4%)	10.1%
Lower Third		Indus. Equipment (8.4%) Oil & Gas Expl. (1.3%) Primary Metals (3.1%)	Depository Inst. (14.6%) Insurance (12.2%) Petroleum (11.1%) Wholesalers—Nondur. (11.7%)	8.9%
Mean ROCE	12.3%	8.7%	13.5%	

ROA and not from financial leveraging activities.[1] Firms did not appear to make significant changes in their capital structure, at least during the annual reporting periods studied, to compensate for changes in ROA. This result makes intuitive sense since major changes in capital structure take time and are costly to execute. The results are also consistent with the philosophy of identifying and maintaining an optimal or desired capital structure over time, independent of short-term changes in operating profitability.

If assuming greater leverage does not result in changing the rank ordering of firms on ROA and ROCE, then why do firms differ in their degrees of financial leverage? The following factors, not all independent and in some cases offsetting, help to explain differences in the capital structure leverage ratio:

1. Level of capital intensity: Firms with high levels of fixed assets need large amounts of capital to finance their acquisition. They also have substantial assets that can serve as collateral for borrowing. Observe that among the industries with the highest capital structure leverage ratios are telecommunications, utilities, and petroleum, all highly capital intensive. (Note: The high capital structure leverage ratios for grocery stores result from supplier financing of inventories and those for

---

[1]Thomas I. Selling and Clyde P. Stickney, "Disaggregating the Rate of Return on Common Shareholders' Equity: A New Approach," *Accounting Horizons* (December 1990), pp. 9–17.

financial institutions—insurance, depository institutions—result from their historically stable customer bases.)

2. Cash-generating ability of operations: Firms unable to generate sufficient cash flow from operations to sustain ongoing or growing operations, pay dividends, and acquire needed capital equipment will assume debt financing. On the other hand, firms with high cash-generating ability relative to capital needed for dividends and capital expenditures will tend not to assume much debt financing. Such firms are better able to finance themselves internally. This explanation probably accounts for the low debt levels of the chemicals, paper, and publishing industries in Exhibit 8.3.

3. Variability in operating performance: Firms with high levels of variability in operating performance increase their overall risks by assuming financial leverage as well. Firms in the computer industry, for example, face high variability in their ROAs because of short product life cycles (high technological risks) and cyclical capital spending patterns by their customers and tend to maintain low levels of debt. This explanation probably accounts for the low levels of debt of the electronic equipment and scientific instruments industries in Exhibit 8.3. Firms in the telecommunications and utilities industries experience little variation in their ROAs because of regulation and assume high levels of debt to finance their capital-intensive operations.

In the late 1980s, a fourth explanation for differences in leverage emerged. Firms with high and stable cash-generating ability (for instance, department stores, consumer foods companies) increased their levels of debt from the low levels historically experienced as a defensive mechanism against an unfriendly takeover or as part of a leveraged buyout. In the early 1990s, these same firms found that they were often unable to service the high levels of debt and began reducing it. These phenomena have increased the difficulty of developing a model that systematically explains differences in capital structure leverage ratios across firms.

Relating ROCE to Market Values of Common Stock

Previous sections discussed ROCE as an accounting measure of return to the common shareholders. The common shareholder is likely to ask, How does ROCE relate to market returns to common stock (that is, dividends plus stock price changes divided by the market price at the beginning of the period) and to changes in those returns over time? This section describes the relation between ROCE and market returns and summarizes empirical research addressing this question.

To illustrate the relation between ROCE and stock prices, assume that common shareholders invest $100 in a newly formed firm on January 1. The shareholders expect the firm to earn 15 percent each year on the capital invested and consider 15 percent an appropriate discount rate for this expected level of return, given the level of risk involved. The market value of shareholders' equity equals the book value of shareholders' equity on January 1 (that is, the market to book ratio equals one). The projected earnings of 15 percent per year on the $100 of invested capital when discounted to January 1 at 15 percent have a present value of $100. If we define January 1 as time t, then:

$$\text{Market Price}_t = \text{Book Value}_t \times (\text{ROCE/Discount Rate})$$

Since ROCE and the discount rate for all future periods are the same,

$$\text{Market Price}_t = \text{Book Value}_t$$

Now assume that the realized ROCE during period $t + 1$ equals the 15 percent expected and that the discount rate of 15 percent does not change. The book value of shareholders' equity increases by 15 percent to $115. If the firm distributes this $15 of earnings to shareholders, the market price should remain at $100. That is, the realized return equals the expected return and future ROCEs and discount rates do not change, so market price will not change. The market rate of return of 15 percent (= $15 dividend/$100 beginning of period market price) equals ROCE (= $15 earnings/$100 beginning of period common shareholders' equity).[2] If the firm retains the $15 of earnings, the market price should increase by $15 to reflect the present value of expected future earnings on the $15 retained. The market rate of return of 15 percent (= $15 price increase/$100 beginning of period market price) again equals ROCE ($15 earnings/$100 beginning of period common shareholders' equity). Thus, if realized ROCEs coincide with expectations and the discount rate does not change, then the market rate of return equals ROCE.

Penman correlated market rates of return with ROCE for all firms on the New York and American Stock Exchanges for each of the years 1969 to 1985.[3] He found positive correlations for all years except two. The R-square values ranged from .02 to .19, with a mean of .09. Thus, ROCEs did not explain much of the cross-sectional variation in market rates of return.

At least two explanations for this low correlation are possible. First, the low correlations may result because firms experience temporary deviations from their long-run ROCEs. Several studies have demonstrated that ROCEs are mean reverting.[4] That is, firms with ROCEs higher (lower) than those of other firms with comparable risk subsequently experience lower (higher) ROCEs. Deviations from the long-run level result in considerable variation of realized ROCEs around long-run ROCE and lower the correlations between market rates of return and ROCEs.

---

[2] We calculate market rates of return and ROCE using the beginning-of-the-period amounts instead of average amounts for the year for ease of exposition.

[3] Stephen H. Penman, "An Evaluation of Accounting Rate of Return," *Journal of Accounting, Auditing and Finance* (Spring 1991), pp. 233–255.

[4] William H. Beaver, "The Time Series Behavior of Earnings," *Journal of Accounting Research Supplement 1970*, (1970) pp. 62–89; Robert N. Freeman, James A. Ohlson, and Stephen H. Pennman, "Book Rate of Return and Prediction of Future Earnings: An Empirical Investigation," *Journal of Accounting Research* (Autumn 1982), pp. 639–653.

Second, the deviations of realized ROCEs from their expected level are subject to two different interpretations. First, a substantially higher or lower ROCE than normal may represent a transitory event that should not persist. If so, the market should not respond to the higher or lower ROCE by altering the market price. On the other hand, the higher or lower ROCE may signal a permanent change in profitability that should increase or decrease market price. Changes in ROCE that the market expects will be temporary should have low correlation with market rates of return, whereas changes in ROCE that the market judges to be permanent should show high correlation. The low overall correlations between market rates of return and ROCEs perhaps reflects this ambiguity.

The challenge to the analyst is to disentangle temporary and permanent changes in ROCE. Such information is helpful to the analyst in deciding whether to purchase or sell a particular firm's common stock at the current market price. Board and Walker regressed unexpected ROCEs and unexpected market rates of return for 193 firms over the period 1963 to 1982.[5] Expected ROCEs equaled the realized ROCE of the preceding year. Expected market rates of return resulted from a regression of each firm's market rate of return on an index of returns for all firms for the 72 months preceding the particular year studied. The R-square of the regression of unexpected ROCE and unexpected market rates of return was .26, with systematic variation across firms and across time. Inflation accounted for part of the variation across time. Penman found the ratio of the market value to the book value of shareholders' equity to discriminate between transitory and permanent changes in ROCEs.[6] Firms experiencing higher ROCEs than other firms of comparable risk that the market expected would be permanent had higher market to book ratios than firms experiencing the higher ROCEs but which the market expected would be temporary. Similarly, firms experiencing lower ROCEs than other firms of comparable risk that the market expected would be temporary experienced higher market to book ratios than firms experiencing the lower ROCEs that the market expected would be permanent.

The following illustration may clarify these relations. Recall the earlier example where a newly created firm had shareholders' equity measured using both market and book values of $100 and an expected ROCE and discount rate of 15 percent. Suppose that during the first year the firm generated an ROCE of 18 percent. If the market viewed the increased ROCE as a permanent change in profitability, the market price should increase to reflect the present value of the expected permanent increase in earnings (assuming the discount rate remains at 15 percent). If the firm pays out the $18 of earnings as a dividend, the book value of shareholders' equity remains the same. Thus, the higher market to book ratio signals a permanent increase in ROCE. If the firm does not pay out the full $18 as a dividend, the market price should increase even more to reflect the return on the retained earnings. Even though shareholders' equity increases for the excess of earnings

[5] J. L. G. Board and M. Walker, "Intertemporal and Cross-Sectional Variation in the Association Between Unexpected Accounting Rates of Return and Abnormal Returns," *Journal of Accounting Research* (Spring 1990), pp. 182–192.

[6] Penman, "Evaluation of Accounting Rate of Return," pp. 237–243.

over dividends, the market to book ratio still increases to signal the permanent increase in ROCE.

Assume now that the market views the excess ROCE returns of three percent (= .18 − .15) as transitory. The market price should not change. If the firm pays out the full $18 as a dividend, shareholders' equity will likewise not change. Thus, the market to book ratio remains at one. If the firm does not pay out the full $18 as a dividend, the market price and shareholders' equity both increase to reflect the retention of earnings but the market to book ratio remains at one. A similar situation occurs when the realized ROCE is less than 15 percent and the market expects the deviation to be temporary. The market price again should not change. As long as the firm reduces its dividend to the lower earnings level, shareholders' equity should not change and the market to book ratio remains at one. Altering the dividend payout rate should change both market price and shareholders' equity and leave the market to book ratio at one.

Finally, consider the case where the market interprets the lower ROCE as a signal of permanently reduced profitability. The market price should decrease to reflect the reduced expected earnings stream (assuming no change in the discount rate). The book value of shareholders' equity remains the same, assuming the firm pays out all earnings as dividends. Thus, the market to book ratio decreases below one. Altering the dividend payout rate again changes market price and shareholders' equity but results in a decline in the market to book ratio.

These examples use a market to book ratio of one as the initial condition merely for ease of exposition. The examples could use other centering values (for example, 1.2 or .9), with the comments about high and low market to book ratios scaled against these alternative values.

An element of circularity exists in relating the market to book value ratio to changes in ROCE. The analyst desires to interpret realized changes in ROCE as either temporary or permanent in order to decide whether to buy or sell a common stock security at its current price. However, the analyst must use the current stock price to measure the market to book ratio that serves as the signal as to whether the change in ROCE is temporary or permanent.

We can study the applicability of this research to data for Coke and Pepsi. Exhibit 8.4 shows the ROCE, market rate of return (dividends + change in market price divided by market price at the beginning of the year), and market value to book value at year end for Coke and Pepsi for Year 6, Year 7, Year 8, and an average of the three years.

Consider first the three-year average amounts. Coke experienced a higher average ROCE than Pepsi and likewise a higher average market rate of return. Coke also has a higher average market value to book value ratio, suggesting that the market expects Coke to maintain this return advantage relative to Pepsi.

The year-to-year relations do not hold as well as the three-year averages. Coke experienced a higher ROCE in Year 6 and Year 8 but Pepsi experienced a higher market rate of return in those years. Coke's ROCE increased between Year 6 and Year 7. The increase in its market to book ratio suggests that the market viewed this increased profitability as sustainable. Coke did maintain (and even increased) its ROCE in Year 8. The drop in Coke's market to book ratio in Year 8 suggests that

Exhibit 8.4
Return Data for Coke and Pepsi

	Year 6		Year 7		Year 8		Three-Year Average	
	Coke	Pepsi	Coke	Pepsi	Coke	Pepsi	Coke	Pepsi
Rate of Return on Common Shareholders' Equity (ROCE)	33.1%	26.9%	36.7%	25.6%	39.2%	23.6%	36.3%	25.4%
Market Rate of Return	19.9%	20.8%	76.7%	54.0%	22.5%	32.2%	39.7%	35.7%
Market Value/Book Value	5.32	3.27	8.40	4.34	8.24	4.14	7.32	3.92

the market does not view the increased profitability as sustainable. Pepsi's ROCE declined between Year 6 and Year 7 but its market to book ratio increased. The market apparently viewed the decreased profitability as temporary. Pepsi's decline in ROCE in Year 8 perhaps convinced the market that the reduced profitability was not transitory because its market to book ratio declined.

The above interpretations reflect a rather crude effort to relate the results of empirical research to individual firm data for particular years. The difficulty in applying the results of this research illustrates the conflicts often encountered when academic researchers attempt to study relations between accounting data and stock prices and analysts attempt to use the results of these studies in their day-to-day activities. The academics provide theoretical models and empirical studies of large databases over extended periods of time in an effort to identify systematic relations. The security analyst must make buy and sell recommendations for particular firms' shares over a shorter period of time. Academic research perhaps points the analyst in the right direction but cannot provide a perfectly reliable decision model or criterion.

Earnings per Common Share

A second financial statement ratio that common equity investors frequently use to assess profitability is earnings per common share (EPS). This section describes briefly the calculation of EPS and discusses some of its uses and limitations.

Calculating EPS

Firms that do not have (1) convertible bonds or convertible preferred stock outstanding that holders can exchange for shares of common stock or (2) options or warrants outstanding that holders can use to acquire common stock have *simple capital structures*. For such firms, the accountant calculates EPS as follows:

$$\text{EPS (simple capital structure)} = \frac{\text{Net Income} - \text{Preferred Stock Dividends}}{\text{Weighted Average Number of Common Shares Outstanding}}$$

The numerator of EPS for a simple capital structure is identical to the numerator of ROCE. The denominator is a daily average of common shares outstanding, reflecting new stock issues, treasury stock acquisitions, and similar transactions.

Example 1. Brown Corporation had the following capital structure during its most recent year:

	January 1	December 31
Preferred Stock, $20 par Value, 500 Shares Issued and Outstanding..	$ 10,000	$ 10,000
Common Stock, $10 par Value, 4,000 Shares Issued......	40,000	40,000
Additional Paid in Capital	50,000	50,000
Retained Earnings...	80,000	85,600
Treasury Shares—Common (1,000 Shares)....................	—	(30,000)
Total Shareholders' Equity	$180,000	$155,600

Retained earnings changed during the year as follows:

Retained Earnings, January 1	$80,000
Plus Net Income.......................................	7,500
Less Dividends	
Preferred Stock.......................................	(500)
Common Stock..	(1,400)
Retained Earnings, December 31	$85,600

The preferred stock is not convertible into common stock. The firm acquired the treasury stock on July 1. There are no stock options or warrants outstanding. The calculation of earnings per share for Brown Corporation is:

$$\frac{\$7,500 - \$500}{(.5 \times 4,000) + (.5 \times 3,000)} = \frac{\$7,000}{3,500} = \$2.00 \text{ per share}$$

Firms that have either convertible securities or option or warrants outstanding have *complex capital structures*. Such firms must present two EPS amounts: primary EPS and fully diluted EPS. Both EPS amounts reflect in differing degrees the dilution potential of convertible securities, options, and warrants. The calculation of primary and fully diluted EPS is complex. This section describes these two EPS amounts in general terms.

First, we need two definitions:

1. Common stock equivalent: A security that derives most or all of its value from the right of its holder to exchange the security for common stock is a *common stock equivalent*. The market value of the security tends to track changes in the market value of the common stock. Stock options and warrants are always common stock equivalents because they have no cash yields on their own. Convertible bonds and convertible preferred stock may or may not represent a common stock equivalent. The accountant performs a test to ascertain whether the market prices

the convertible security more for its periodic cash yield (not a common stock equivalent) or more for its conversion feature (a common stock equivalent).

2. Other potentially dilutive security: All convertible securities that the accountant does not classify as common stock equivalents are *other potentially dilutive securities.*

Accountants calculate primary EPS as follows:

$$\text{Primary EPS} \atop \text{(complex capital structure)} = \frac{\text{Net Income} - \text{Preferred Stock Dividends} + \text{Adjustments for Common Stock Equivalents}}{\text{Weighted Average No. of Common Shares Outstanding} + \text{Weighted Average Number of Shares Issuable as Common Stock Equivalents}}$$

For purposes of calculating primary EPS only, the accountant assumes that a convertible security that is classified as a common stock equivalent is converted into common stock. The accountant adds back any interest expense (net of taxes) or dividends on that convertible security that the firm subtracted in calculating net income to common to calculate the numerator of primary EPS. The accountant adds (1) the weighted average number of shares of common stock actually outstanding, (2) the number of shares of common stock that the firm would issue upon conversion of these securities, and (3) the number of shares issuable for outstanding stock options and warrants, to calculate the denominator of primary EPS.

Example 2. Continuing with the data for Brown Corporation in Example 1, assume now that there were stock options outstanding throughout the year which, if exercised, would result in the issuance of an additional 300 shares of common stock.[7] Also assume that the preferred stock is convertible into 1,000 shares of common stock. The preferred stock, however, is not a common stock equivalent. The calculation of primary earnings per share is:

$$\frac{\$7,500 - \$500}{(.5 \times 4,000) + (.5 \times 3,000) + (1.0 \times 300)} = \frac{\$7,000}{3,800} = \$1.84 \text{ per share}$$

The stock options do not affect the measurement of net income, so the accountant makes no adjustment in the numerator of primary EPS. The accountant adds the 300 shares issuable upon exercise of the stock options to the denominator.

The calculation of fully diluted EPS assumes the conversion of convertible securities and exercise of outstanding options and warrants. Fully diluted EPS reflects

---

[7]The computation of the additional shares to be issued upon the exercise of stock options assumes that the firm would use any cash proceeds from such exercise to repurchase common shares on the open market. Only the net incremental shares issued (shares issued under option less shares repurchased) enter the computation of earnings per share.

the maximum potential dilution at the date of the balance sheet. The difference between primary and fully diluted EPS relates primarily to convertible securities that are not common stock equivalents (that is, they are other potentially dilutive securities). The calculation of fully diluted EPS, then, is:

$$
\begin{array}{l}
\text{Fully Diluted EPS} \\
\text{(complex capital} \\
\text{structure)}
\end{array}
=
\frac{
\begin{array}{l}
\text{Net Income – Preferred} \\
\text{Stock Dividends}
\end{array}
+
\begin{array}{l}
\text{Adjustments for} \\
\text{Common Stock} \\
\text{Equivalents}
\end{array}
+
\begin{array}{l}
\text{Adjustments for Other} \\
\text{Potentially Dilutive} \\
\text{Securities}
\end{array}
}{
\begin{array}{l}
\text{Weighted Average} \\
\text{Number of Common} \\
\text{Shares Outstanding}
\end{array}
+
\begin{array}{l}
\text{Weighted Average} \\
\text{Number of Shares} \\
\text{Issuable as Common} \\
\text{Stock Equivalents}
\end{array}
+
\begin{array}{l}
\text{Weighted Average} \\
\text{Number of Shares Issuable} \\
\text{as Other Potentially} \\
\text{Dilutive Securities}
\end{array}
}
$$

The adjustments for other potentially dilutive securities mirror those for common stock equivalents.

Example 3.   The calculation of fully diluted EPS for Brown Corporation appears below:

$$
\frac{\$7{,}500 - \$500 + \$500}{(.5 \times 4{,}000) + (.5 \times 3{,}000) + (1.0 \times 300) + (1.0 \times 1{,}000)} = \frac{\$7{,}500}{4{,}800} = \$1.56 \text{ per share}
$$

The calculation assumes the conversion of the convertible preferred stock into common stock as of January 1. If conversion had taken place, the firm would not have paid preferred dividends during the year. Thus, the analyst adds back the $500 preferred dividends, which the accountant subtracted in computing net income available to common stock, to calculate the numerator of fully diluted earnings per share. The weighted average number of shares in the denominator increases for the 1,000 common shares that the firm would issue upon conversion of the preferred stock.

The accountant makes these adjustments to EPS for complex capital structures only if their effect is dilutive (that is, the adjustments reduce EPS relative to the amounts calculated for a simple capital structure) and only if primary or fully dilutive EPS differ by at least 3 percent from EPS for a simple capital structure. These EPS amounts appear on the income statement.

In the income statements and notes on accounting policies of Coke and Pepsi, both companies show only a single EPS (although both companies separate continuing and discontinued operations). Both companies have stock options outstanding but neither company has convertible debt or preferred stock outstanding. Coke reports in Note 1 that its EPS uses the weighted average number of common shares outstanding in the denominator, implying that the dilutive effect of options is immaterial. Pepsi reports in Note 1 that its EPS uses the weighted average number of shares and share equivalents outstanding in the denominator, implying that outstanding options affected the calculation. Neither company reports a fully diluted EPS because of the absence of convertible securities.

Using EPS to Value Firms

Firms must present EPS information in the income statement under GAAP.[8] Security analysts also frequently use EPS as a measure of profitability because of the ease of relating EPS to the market price of a firm's stock using a price-earnings (P-E) ratio.

To understand the nature of the P-E ratio, consider the pricing of a firm's common shares. An investor in such shares will project the future cash flows anticipated from owning the stock (that is, periodic dividends plus the residual value from sale of the shares, both net of their tax effects). The investor discounts these cash flows to a present value using a risk-adjusted discount rate appropriate to such cash flows. The resulting present value is the highest price that the investor should pay for the shares.

To project future cash flows from owning the shares, the investor projects the future cash flows of the firm. The firm's cash flows are the source for the payment of dividends. The firm will reinvest cash flows not paid out as dividends to generate additional cash flows, which in turn should affect the residual value of the shares.

The next step is to link a firm's cash flows with its net income. Over sufficiently long time periods, net income equals cash receipts minus cash disbursements. That is, revenues result in the receipt of cash either at the time of sale or sometime after the time of sale when the firm collects the receivable. Expenses relate to a cash disbursement that either precedes the recognition of expenses (such as, purchase of depreciable assets), coincides with the recognition of expenses (such as, most employees' salaries and wages), or follows the recognition of expenses (such as, payment of accounts payable and other current liabilities for goods or services received). The accrual basis of accounting matches revenues with expenses independent of when the cash flows occur. However, net income measured over a period of several years should approximate the net amount of cash generated by a firm. Thus, projected net income serves as a surrogate for a firm's projected cash flows.

The final step in the logic underlying P-E ratios is to link earnings of the current period with future, or projected, earnings. Unless there is evidence that the firm will be unable to sustain the earnings of the current period into the future (for example, because of the inclusion of discontinued operations, extraordinary items, or other nonrecurring gains or losses in net income or because of changes in a firm's competitive position, economic conditions, or other factors affecting the future), then the analyst uses the current period's earnings to project future earnings. The chain of logic looks like this:

---

[8] Accounting Principles Board, *Accounting Principles Board Opinion No. 15,* "Earnings per Share," 1969.

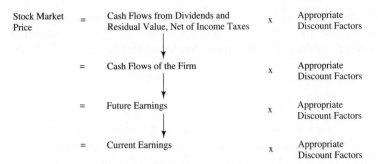

The discount factor in the four equations above ties into the P-E ratio. The P-E ratio is the reciprocal of the discount rate that the market deems appropriate for the particular earnings stream of the firm. To illustrate:

Appropriate Discount Rate	Calculation of P-E Ratio	P-E Ratio
8%	1.0/.08	12.5
10%	1.0/.10	10.0
12%	1.0/.12	8.3

When we multiply the EPS for the current period by the appropriate P-E ratio, the resulting market price reflects a particular yield based on the current period's earnings.

The first column of Exhibit 8.5 shows the mean P-E ratios for 22 U.S. industries for the period 1980 to 1989. The P-E ratios range from a low of 8.49 for de-

Exhibit 8.5
Price-Earnings Ratios and Related Data for 22 Industries, 1980–1989

	Price-Earnings Ratio	ROCE	Market Beta	CSL
Chemicals	13.75	15.82%	1.10	2.04
Department Stores	17.79	13.88%	1.20	2.60
Depository Institutions	8.49	14.63%	.95	4.99
Electrical/Electronic Equipment	16.99	10.35%	1.08	2.05
Food Processors	13.31	15.04%	.96	2.59
Grocery Stores	14.44	18.82%	.91	2.71
Industrial Equipment	16.22	8.42%	1.04	2.23
Insurance	9.98	12.20%	.80	4.45
Metal Products	14.94	8.99%	.95	2.19
Oil and Gas Extraction	17.27	1.30%	1.88	2.29
Paper Products	13.05	13.85%	1.16	2.10
Petroleum	13.63	11.14%	.78	2.68
Primary Metals	13.06	3.11%	1.14	2.52
Scientific Instruments	16.72	12.01%	.98	1.99
Stone/Glass Products	11.61	8.96%	.97	2.08
Telecommunications	12.77	13.58%	.84	2.64
Textiles	11.77	7.56%	1.14	2.59
Transportation Equipment	11.75	10.94%	1.08	2.38
Utilities	9.37	12.42%	.55	3.29
Wholesalers—Durable Goods	17.13	9.17%	1.00	2.36
Wholesalers—Nondurable Goods	12.56	11.65%	.94	2.99

pository institutions to 17.79 for department stores. Empirical research examining P-E ratios has identified three possible reasons for differences in P-E ratios across industries: (1) growth, (2) risk, and (3) accounting methods.

Growth. Researchers have hypothesized a positive relation between growth and the P-E ratio. The current year's earnings for rapidly growing firms is less than the long-run expected permanent earnings of such firms. Because the market values firms based on their permanent earnings, the P-E ratio applied to the current period's earnings will be greater than the appropriate multiple applied to permanent earnings. Likewise, firms experiencing slow or no growth are probably in declining industries. Their current period's earnings likely exceed long-run permanent earnings. The P-E ratio applied to the current period's earnings will be less than the appropriate multiple applied to permanent earnings. A related argument is that earnings over sufficiently long periods are mean reverting. Firms currently experiencing lower earnings than appropriate, given their level of capital and risk, will experience increasing profitability in the future. Firms currently experiencing higher earnings than appropriate will subsequently experience decreasing profitability. The mean-reverting level is permanent earnings.

Beaver and Morse correlated growth rates and differences in P-E ratios for a sample of firms between 1956 and 1974.[9] They defined growth as the percentage change in EPS from the preceding year. These researchers formed portfolios of securities based on the level of their P-E ratios. They found that the growth rate explained virtually none of the difference in P-E ratios. In addition, the initial P-E ratio differences across the portfolios tended to persist for up to 14 years, suggesting that any mean-reversion process was slow at best.

Zarowin[10] replicated the Beaver and Morse study but used analysts' five-year *forecasts* of growth for each firm rather than the one-year realized growth rate used by Beaver and Morse. Zarowin's results indicate that approximately 70 percent of the differences in P-E ratios relate to long-term forecasted growth rates. Initial differences in P-E ratios were also found to persist.

Another approach to examining the relation between P-E ratios and growth is to relate P-E ratios to ROCE. If earnings and ROCEs follow a mean reversion process, firms with low ROCEs should have high P-E ratios and vice versa. The second column of Exhibit 8.5 shows the average ROCEs of 22 industries for the period 1980 to 1989. Testing for an inverse relation between average industry P-E ratios and average ROCEs, the Spearman rank order correlation is 8.5 percent. Thus, realized ROCEs appear to explain very little of the interindustry differences in P-E ratios.

Risk. A previous section developed the rationale for treating the reciprocal of the P-E ratio as a discount rate to derive the present value of a firm's future earnings stream. This discount rate should reflect investors' desired rate of return, given the level of risk. Thus, the P-E ratio should be inversely related to risk. We

---

[9]William Beaver and Dale Morse,"What Determines Price-Earnings Ratios?" *Financial Analysts Journal* (July–August 1978), pp. 65–76.

[10] Paul Zarowin, "What Determines Price-Earnings Ratios—Revisited," *Journal of Accounting, Auditing and Finance* (Summer 1990), pp. 439–457.

will study the concept and measurement of risk in Chapter 9. At this point, we must consider two aspects of risk, however, in order to understand its possible relation to P-E ratios. Economic theory distinguishes systematic and nonsystematic risk. Systematic risk refers to the degree to which a particular firm's stock price varies with the stock prices of all firms. The beta coefficient that results from regressing a particular firm's stock price changes on a marketwide index of stock price changes measures this systematic risk. Firms whose share prices increase or decrease at a faster rate than the market average will have a beta greater than 1.0. Firms whose share prices increase or decrease at a slower rate than the market average will have a beta less than 1.0. Economists view this greater or lesser sensitivity to marketwide price changes as a measure of systematic risk. Nonsystematic risk refers to all elements of risk peculiar to a firm that market beta does not capture. (We will develop the relation between systematic and nonsystematic risk more fully in Chapter 9.)

Beaver and Morse studied the correlation between P-E ratios and market beta. They found that beta explained very little of the difference in P-E ratios.[11] Zarowin conducted similar tests and found similar results.[12] The third column of Exhibit 8.5 shows the average market beta for 22 industries for the period 1980 to 1989. Testing for an inverse relation between P-E ratio and beta, the Spearman rank order correlation is 46.9 percent. This latter result suggests that market beta may exhibit greater explanatory power for differences in P-E ratios over longer periods of time. Note that the data in Exhibit 8.5 represent averages for a ten-year period.

The fourth column of Exhibit 8.5 shows the average capital structure leverage ratio for each industry. This ratio is firm-specific (although Chapter 9 demonstrates a link between the CSL ratio and market beta) and captures an element of nonsystematic risk. The Spearman rank order correlation between P-E ratios and CSL (inverse relation) is 49.7 percent, again suggesting a link between P-E ratios and risk over this aggregated ten-year period.

Accounting Principles. A third possible reason for interindustry differences in P-E ratios is the use of different accounting principles in measuring earnings. Exhibit 8.5 shows the average P-E ratio of food processors as 13.31 and the average P-E ratio of paper products firms as 13.05. If food processors used a LIFO cost-flow assumption and accelerated depreciation and paper producers used a FIFO cost-flow assumption and straight-line depreciation, then adjusting earnings and P-E ratio to reflect the same accounting principles might eliminate differences in P-E ratios.

This explanation for differences in P-E ratios is suspect, at least for firms in the United States. Virtually all U.S. firms use the straight-line depreciation method for financial reporting. Firms roughly divide evenly on their use of a FIFO, LIFO, and average cost-flow assumption. Most firms using FIFO are in decreasing cost industries (computers, semiconductors, consumer electronics). Their use of FIFO

---

[11] Beaver and Morse, "Price-Earnings Ratios," pp. 70–72.

[12] Zarowin, "Price-Earnings Ratios—Revisited," pp. 449–453.

Exhibit 8.6
Price-Earnings Ratios and Related Data for Coke and Pepsi

	Price-Earnings Ratio	Five-Year Growth Rate in EPS	Market Beta	Capital Structure Leverage Ratio	Rate of Return on Common Shareholders' Equity
Coke					
Year 6	15.1	19.0%	.71	2.5	33.1%
Year 7	22.9	19.6%	.85	2.5	36.7%
Year 8	22.8	23.1%	.90	2.5	39.2%
Pepsi					
Year 6	13.5	24.1%	.90	3.6	26.9%
Year 7	18.9	17.3%	1.05	3.7	25.6%
Year 8	18.8	18.3%	1.04	3.7	23.6%

provides the same tax-saving opportunities as LIFO provides for firms experiencing increasing costs. Thus, the use of different cost-flow assumptions for inventories does not necessarily lead to noncomparable earnings amounts. There are other areas where accounting principle differences exist (for example, income recognition, leases), but they are unlikely to affect a sufficient number of firms to account for the differences in P-E ratios.

Zarowin adjusted the earnings numbers used in his study for consolidation of subsidiaries, depreciation, and investment credits.[13] The initial differences in P-E ratios across the portfolios studied using these adjusted earnings persisted in the same manner as the initial differences in P-E ratios persisted in the Beaver-Morse study using reported earnings. Zarowin interpreted these similarities as suggesting that differences in accounting principles do not explain differences in P-E ratios.

Brown et. al. adjusted the P-E ratios of U.S. firms for differences in inventory cost-flow assumptions and depreciation methods for 13 industries for each of the years 1985 to 1988.[14] They found no significant difference between the reported and restated data either by year across industries or by industry across years. Thus, differences in accounting principles do not appear to explain interindustry differences in P-E ratios.

Projected growth and risk seem to provide partial explanations for differences in P-E ratios. A well-integrated, well-tested theory explaining P-E ratios has not yet evolved.

We can study the applicability of these research findings to data for Coke and Pepsi. In the data in Exhibit 8.6, Coke's P-E ratio consistently exceeds Pepsi's. Coke's faster five-year growth rates in Year 7 and Year 8 and lower risk measures

---

[13]*Ibid.,* pp. 446.

[14]Paul R. Brown, Virginia E. Soybel, and Clyde P. Stickney, "Achieving Comparability of U.S. and Japanese Financial Statement Data," *Japan and the World Economy,* (Spring, 1993), pp. 51–72.

(market beta and CSL) are consistent with a positive relation between P-E ratios and growth and a negative relation between P-E ratios and risk.

Criticisms of EPS

Critics of EPS as a measure of profitability point out that it does not consider the amount of assets or capital required to generate a particular level of earnings. Two firms with the same earnings and EPS are not equally profitable if one firm requires twice the amount of assets or capital to generate those earnings as does the other firm. The number of shares of common stock outstanding serves as a poor measure of the amount of capital in use. The number of shares outstanding usually relates to a firm's attempts to achieve a desirable trading range for its common stock. For example, suppose a firm has an aggregate market value for its common shares of $10 million. If the firm has 500,000 shares outstanding, the shares will sell for $20 per share. If the firm has 1,000,000 shares outstanding, the shares will sell for $10 per share. The amount of capital in place is the same in both instances but the number of shares outstanding, and therefore EPS, are different.

For similar reasons, analysts cannot compare EPS amounts across firms. Two firms can have identical earnings, common shareholders' equity, and ROCE, but their EPSs will differ if they have different numbers of shares outstanding.

EPS is also an ambiguous measure of profitability because it reflects (1) operating performance in the numerator, and (2) capital structure decisions in the denominator. For example, a firm can experience reduced earnings during the year but report a higher EPS than the previous year if it has repurchased sufficient shares during the period. When assessing earnings performance, the analyst must separate the impact of these two factors on EPS.

The analyst should interpret the size of the P-E ratio as indicated by a firm's current market price and current EPS with caution. Firms experiencing rapid growth in EPS may trade at 25 (or more) times current earnings. This does not mean that the market expects a yield of only 4 percent (=1.0/.25). The market likely applies a multiple to expected future, or permanent, earnings which exceeds current EPS. If the analyst divides the current market price by expected EPS, then a more normal P-E ratio results.

Summary

This chapter has considered the assessment of profitability from the viewpoint of an investor in a firm's common stock. The chapter emphasized the rate of return on common shareholders' equity as the tool for making this assessment. Empirical data suggest a high degree of association between changes or differences in ROA and ROCE. Thus, the analytical tools that Chapter 7 discussed for gaining insight into the behavior of ROA are equally relevant to interpreting ROCE.

Differences in the levels of ROA and ROCE for a particular firm relate to financial leverage. The extent of a firm's financial leverage appears related to the degree of capital intensity, cash-generating ability of operations, and variability of earnings. Firms in the United States that significantly increased their financial leverage in the late 1980s are now engaging in debt reduction. High levels of debt service costs coupled with weak economic conditions necessitate these decreases in financial leverage.

Problems

8.1 *Relating Profitability to Financial Leverage.* Data for six independent cases is as follows:

Case	Average Total Assets	Interest-Bearing Debt	Average Common Share-holders' Equity	Rate of Return on Assets	After-Tax Cost of Interest-Bearing Debt
1	$200	$100	$100	6%	6%
2	200	100	100	8	6
3	200	120	80	8	6
4	200	100	100	4	6
5	200	50	100	6	6
6	200	50	100	5	6

a. Compute the rate of return on common shareholders' equity for each of the six cases. Disaggregate ROCE into ROA, common earnings leverage, and capital structure leverage components.

b. In which cases is financial leverage working to the advantage of common shareholders? Explain.

8.2 *Calculating and Interpreting ROCE and Its Components.* Ashford Electronics Corporation is a wholesale distributor of electronic equipment and supplies. It maintains eight regional warehouse distribution centers throughout the United States. Exhibit 8.7 presents a partial balance sheet and Exhibit 8.8 presents a partial income statement for Ashford Electronics Corporation for Year 8 and Year 9.

a. Compute the rate of return on common shareholders' equity for Year 8 and Year 9. Disaggregate ROCE into ROA, common earnings leverage, and capital structure leverage components.

b. What is the likely explanation for the change in ROCE between Year 8 and Year 9?

Exhibit 8.7
Partial Balance Sheet for Ashford Electronics Corporation

	December 31, Year 7	December 31, Year 8	December 31, Year 9
Assets	$37,650	$40,660	$43,900
Accounts Payable......	$ 7,530	$ 8,130	$ 8,780
Bank Loans	5,650	6,100	6,580
Long-Term Debt.......	9,400	10,160	10,970
Common Stock.........	5,000	5,000	5,000
Retained Earnings....	10,070	11,270	12,570
Total Equities	$37,650	$40,660	$43,900

Exhibit 8.8
Partial Income Statements for Ashford Electronics Corporation

	Year 8	Year 9
Sales..	$78,310	$84,560
Cost of Goods Sold	(58,730)	(63,420)
Selling and Administrative Expenses	(11,750)	(12,684)
Interest Expense..	(1,250)	(2,030)
Income Tax Expense (34 percent)	(2,237)	(2,185)
Net Income..	$ 4,343	$4,241

8.3 *Calculating and Interpreting ROCE and Its Components.* Neslin Corporation manufactures pulp and paper products. The firm locates its processing plants in the northwestern part of the United States. These plants currently operate at 90 percent of capacity. Neslin Corporation has several additional processing plants under construction. Typical construction time of a new plant is three years. Exhibit 8.9 presents a partial balance sheet and Exhibit 8.10 presents a partial income statement for Neslin Corporation for Year 4, Year 5, and Year 6. Dividends declared and paid are:

	Year 4	Year 5	Year 6
Preferred Stock	$114.3	$116.1	$116.7
Common Stock	518.6	574.2	598.6

a. Compute the rate of return on common shareholders' equity for Year 4, Year 5, and Year 6. Disaggregate ROCE into its ROA, common earnings leverage, and capital structure leverage components.

b. What explanations seem to account for the change in ROCE over the three years?

Exhibit 8.9
Partial Balance Sheet for Neslin Corporation

	December 31, Year 3	December 31, Year 4	December 31, Year 5	December 31, Year 6
Property, Plant, and Equipment.................	$12,070.2	$13,328.7	$14,696.2	$15,823.4
All Other Assets..............	1,563.4	1,384.2	1,588.8	1,581.8
Total Assets	$13,633.6	$14,712.9	$16,285.0	$17,405.2
Current Liabilities	$ 1,239.1	$ 1,556.5	$ 2,081.6	$ 2,289.5
Long-Term Debt.............	5,876.0	5,984.4	6,161.6	6,276.7
Other Liabilities..............	714.4	907.2	1,003.3	1,266.5
Preferred Stock..............	1,198.3	1,205.5	1,203.7	1,165.5
Common Stock..............	3,581.7	3,792.6	4,302.7	4,540.6
Retained Earnings	1,024.1	1,266.7	1,532.1	1,866.4
Total Equities.............	$13,633.6	$14,712.9	$16,285.0	$17,405.2

Exhibit 8.10
Income Statements for Neslin Corporation

	Year 4	Year 5	Year 6
Revenues...	$ 4,929.7	$ 4,964.2	$ 5,478.5
Operating Expenses.....................................	(2,997.1)	(2,860.4)	(3,191.1)
Interest Expense	(606.1)	(655.8)	(697.1)
Income Tax Expense (34 percent).................	(451.0)	(492.3)	(540.7)
Net Income	$ 875.5	$ 955.7	$ 1,049.6

8.4 *Interpreting ROCE and Its Components.* Refer to the data for Sweet Corporation in Problem 7.9. Consider the following additional information:

	Year 1	Year 2	Year 3
Rate of Return on Common Shareholders' Equity.........	13.2%	14.4%	15.5%
Adjusted Leverage Ratio...	1.7	1.8	1.9
Common Earnings Leverage Ratio..................................	.66	.68	.70
Capital Structure Leverage Ratio	2.5	2.6	2.7
Total Liabilities/Total Assets (12/31)	60.9%	62.3%	63.5%
Interest-Bearing Debt/Total Assets (12/31).....................	37.6%	32.9%	29.2%

What is the likely explanation for the increasing rate of return on common shareholders' equity? Respond to this question to the maximum extent permitted by the data.

8.5 *Interpreting ROCE and Its Components.* Refer to the data for Fin Stat Corporation in Problem 7.10. Consider the following additional information:

	Year 7	Year 8	Year 9
Rate of Return on Common Shareholders' Equity.........	16.0%	17.0%	18.0%
Adjusted Leverage Ratio...	1.6	1.7	1.9
Common Earnings Leverage Ratio..................................	.91	.83	.73
Capital Structure Leverage Ratio	1.8	2.1	2.6

What is the likely explanation for the increasing rate of return on common shareholders' equity? Respond to this question to the maximum extent permitted by the data. You do not need to explain the reasons for the change in ROA.

8.6 *Interpreting ROCE and Its Components.* Refer to the data for Stebbins Corporation in Problem 7.11. Consider the following additional information:

	Year 3	Year 4	Year 5
Rate of Return on Common Shareholders' Equity.........	18.0%	16.0%	14.0%
Adjusted Leverage Ratio...	1.8	1.5	1.2
Common Earnings Leverage Ratio..................................	.56	.63	.73
Capital Structure Leverage Ratio	3.2	2.3	1.6

What is the likely explanation for the decreasing rate of return on common shareholders' equity? Respond to this question to the maximum extent permitted by the data.

8.7 *Calculating and Interpreting ROCE and Its Components.* Refer to the data for Mercer Corporation in Problem 7.12. Consider the following additional information:

Capital Structure	December 31, Year 6	December 31, Year 7	December 31, Year 8
Accounts Payable	$ 53	$ 67	$ 90
Long-Term Debt	20	20	98
Common Stock	25	25	25
Retained Earnings	40	48	80
Total Equities	$138	$160	$293

  a. Calculate the rate of return on common shareholders' equity for Year 7 and Year 8. Disaggregate ROCE into its three components (ROA, common earnings leverage, and capital structure leverage).
  b. Explain the reasons for the change in ROCE over the two years.

8.8 *Calculating and Interpreting ROCE and Its Components.* Refer to the data for General Mills in Problem 7.13.
  a. Calculate the rate of return on common shareholders' equity for Year 6, Year 7, and Year 8. Disaggregate ROCE into its three components (ROA, common earnings leverage, and capital structure leverage).
  b. Calculate the percentage change in ROCE and in each of its three components between Year 6 and Year 7 and between Year 7 and Year 8.
  c. Evaluate the change in ROCE over the three years to the maximum extent permitted by the data. You do not need to explain the reasons for the change in ROA.

8.9 *Calculating and Interpreting ROCE and Its Components.* Refer to the data for Digital Equipment Corporation in Problem 7.14. Consider the following additional information:

	Year 7	Year 8	Year 9
Rate of Return on Assets	14.95%	14.4%	
Common Earnings Leverage	.977	.981	
Capital Structure Leverage	1.3	1.3	
Rate of Return on Common Shareholders' Equity	18.9%	18.9%	

  a. Calculate the rate of return on common shareholders' equity and its components for Year 9.
  b. Evaluate the changes in ROCE over the three years to the maximum extent permitted by the data. You do not need to explain reasons for the changes in ROA.

8.10 *Interpreting ROCE and Its Components.* Refer to the data for Boyd Corporation in Problem 7.15. Evaluate the changes in ROCE over the three-year period to the maximum extent permitted by the data. You do not need to explain reasons for the changes in ROA.

8.11 *Impact of Takeover Defenses on ROCE and Its Components.* Butkus Corporation projects the following amounts for the coming year:

Balance Sheet

Average Total Assets...	$ 16,950
Average Common Shareholders' Equity............	10,357

Income Statement

Revenues	$ 33,900
Operating Expenses	(28,815)
Interest Expense	(660)
Income Tax Expense (40 percent)......................	(1,770)
Net Income...	$ 2,655

a. Calculate the rate of return on common shareholders' equity anticipated for the coming year. Disaggregate ROCE into ROA, common earnings leverage, and capital structure leverage components.

b. Rumors appearing in the financial press suggest that Butkus Corporation is a takeover candidate. The firm is considering several defensive actions and desires to know their impact on ROCE and its components for the coming year. In each case, assume that Butkus Corporation will take the actions at a level rate during the year.

   (1) The firm will issue long-term debt totaling $8,000 (average of $4,000) and use the proceeds to repurchase shares of common stock. The debt will carry a 14 percent interest cost.

   (2) The firm will issue long-term debt totaling $8,000 (average of $4,000) and use the proceeds to pay a special dividend to shareholders. The debt will carry a 14 percent interest cost.

   (3) The firm will spin off assets with a market value and book value of $8,000 (average of $4,000) to shareholders as a special dividend. If Butkus Corporation had continued to hold these assets during the coming year, the firm would have generated an ROA of 15 percent.

c. Which of the three alternatives appears to provide the most effective defense against an unfriendly takeover?

8.12 *Interpreting Earnings per Share.* Company A and Company B both start Year 1 with $1 million of common shareholders' equity and 100,000 shares of common stock outstanding. Company A follows a policy of paying a dividend each year equal to 60 percent of net income, whereas Company B retains all of its earnings and declares no dividends.

Net income and dividends of the two companies for Year 1, Year 2, and Year 3 appear below:

	Company A		Company B	
	Net Income	**Dividends**	**Net Income**	**Dividends**
Year 1............................	$100,000	$60,000	$100,000	$-0-
Year 2............................	103,958	62,375	110,000	-0-
Year 3............................	108,014	64,808	104,822	-0-

On January 2, Year 3, Company B repurchased 10,000 shares of its outstanding common stock for $20 per share and held them as treasury stock throughout the remainder of Year 3.

a. Compute the amount of earnings per common share for each company for Year 1, Year 2, and Year 3.

b. Compute the rate of return on common shareholders' equity for each company for Year 1, Year 2, and Year 3.

c. Using the analyses prepared in parts (*a*) and (*b*) as illustrations, discuss the difficulties encountered in interpreting changes in earnings per share over time and differences in earnings per share between firms.

8.13 *Calculating and Interpreting ROCE and EPS for Complex Capital Structures.* Partial balance sheets and income statements of Bower Corporation for Year 3 and Year 4 appear in Exhibits 8.11 and 8.12 respectively.

Dividends declared and paid were as follows (amounts in thousands):

	Year 3	Year 4
Preferred Stock..................	$200	$150
Common Stock..................	322	338

Exhibit 8.11
Bower Corporation Partial Balance Sheets
(amounts in thousands)

	December 31, Year 2	December 31, Year 3	December 31, Year 4
Assets...	$20,600	$22,660	$25,000
Accounts Payable	$ 5,500	$ 6,460	$ 7,885
Long-Term Debt	4,860	5,100	7,100
Convertible Preferred Stock	2,000	2,000	1,000
Common Stock ($10 par value)..........	1,000	1,000	1,180
Additional Paid-in Capital...................	4,000	4,000	4,820
Retained Earnings...............................	3,240	4,100	5,015
Treasury Stock	—	—	(2,000)
	$20,600	$22,660	$25,000

Exhibit 8.12
Bower Corporation Partial Income Statements
(amounts in thousands)

	Year 3	Year 4
Sales..	$ 43,260	$ 47,660
Operating Expenses...........................	(40,377)	(44,602)
Interest Expense................................	(580)	(720)
Income Tax Expense (40 percent)	(921)	(935)
Net Income..	$ 1,382	$ 1,403

On July 1, Year 4, Bower Corporation issued $2 million of long-term bonds at face value on the open market and used the proceeds to repurchase 32,000 shares of common stock at $62.50 per share. Also on this date, holders of preferred stock with a par value of $1 million converted their shares into 18,000 shares of common stock. The remaining shares of preferred stock are also convertible into 18,000 shares of common stock.

 a. Compute the rate of return on common shareholders' equity for Year 3 and Year 4. Disaggregate ROCE into ROA, common earnings leverage, and capital structure leverage components.

 b. Compute primary and fully diluted earnings per share for Year 3 and Year 4. The convertible preferred stock is not a "common stock equivalent" but it is an "other potentially dilutive security."

 c. Calculate the percentage change in ROCE, primary and fully diluted earnings per share between Year 3 and Year 4.

 d. Using the analysis in parts (*a*), (*b*), and (*c*), discuss how the profitability of Bower Corporation changed between Year 3 and Year 4.

8.14 *Interpreting ROCE and Its Components.* Exhibit 8.13 presents ROCE and its disaggregated components for five firms. Discuss briefly the changes in profitability of each of these firms over the two-year period.

Exhibit 8.13
ROCE and Its Components for Five Firms

	ROCE = ROA ×	Common Earnings Leverage	×	Capital Structure Leverage
Delta Airlines				
Year 7	16.3% = 5.6% ×	.71	×	4.1
Year 8	14.8% = 6.1% ×	.57	×	4.3
Georgia Pacific				
Year 7	17.8% = 9.7% ×	.86	×	2.1
Year 8	17.6% = 9.2% ×	.78	×	2.4
National Medical Enterprises				
Year 7	14.5% = 5.8% ×	.60	×	4.2
Year 8	18.0% = 7.2% ×	.56	×	4.5
Digital Equipment Corporation				
Year 7	18.9% = 14.5% ×	.93	×	1.4
Year 8	18.9% = 13.7% ×	.95	×	1.5
Wal-Mart				
Year 7	31.8% = 13.6% ×	.84	×	2.8
Year 8	31.8% = 14.5% ×	.84	×	2.6

Exhibit 8.14
Selected Data for Three Breakfast Cereal Companies

	ROCE	ROA	Common Earnings Leverage	Capital Structure Leverage	Growth in Earnings per Share	Market Rate of Return	Price Earnings Ratio	Market to Book Value Ratio	Market Beta
General Mills									
Year 8	38.5%	11.9%	.89	3.6	19.8%	(12.3%)	15.0	5.9	.80
Year 9	45.7%	12.7%	.90	4.0	18.8%	51.7%	17.5	7.4	.80
Year 10	48.5%	13.4%	.90	4.0	18.2%	18.6%	17.1	7.9	.82
Three-Year Ave.	44.2%	12.7%	.90	3.9	22.3%	19.3%	16.5	7.1	.81
Kellogg									
Year 8	35.7%	16.9%	.95	2.2	21.9%	25.6%	16.5	5.3	.79
Year 9	27.1%	13.6%	.93	2.2	(1.3%)	7.7%	17.5	5.0	.81
Year 10	28.4%	15.3%	.92	2.0	8.1%	15.3%	18.2	4.8	.76
Three-Year Ave.	30.4%	15.3%	.93	2.1	9.6%	16.2%	17.4	5.0	.79
Quaker Oats									
Year 8	16.8%	7.8%	.84	2.6	25.0%	(12.5%)	18.1	2.8	.82
Year 9	12.5%	6.5%	.77	2.5	(23.6%)	42.6%	33.1	4.3	.72
Year 10	20.8%	9.3%	.75	3.0	55.9%	(21.0%)	16.3	3.5	.77
Three-Year Ave.	17.0%	7.9%	.79	2.7	19.1%	3.0%	22.5	3.5	.77

8.15 *Relating Accounting and Market Return Data.* Exhibit 8.14 presents selected data for the three dominant companies in the breakfast cereal food market. Each company also offers other consumer foods, while General Mills has a restaurant segment. General Mills spun off its toy business to shareholders as a special dividend in Year 6 and made significant purchases of treasury stock during Year 7 to Year 9 to defend against a possible unfriendly takeover attempt. Quaker Oats was the target of an unfriendly (unsuccessful) takeover attempt in Year 9.

a. Compare the three-year average ROCE and three-year average market rate of return for each company. Are these relations consistent with the chapter's discussion? Explain.

b. Compare the three-year average price-earnings ratios of the three companies. Is the ordering of these average price-earnings ratios consistent with the discussion in the chapter? Explain.

c. The capital structure leverage ratios of General Mills significantly exceed those of Kellogg, yet the common earnings leverage ratios of General Mills are only slightly lower than those of Kellogg. Explain.

Risk Analysis

When examining investment alternatives, the investor assesses the level of return expected from each alternative relative to the risk involved. Chapters 7 and 8 discussed the tools for analyzing past profitability and generating expectations about future returns. This chapter considers the analytical tools for studying risk.

The finance literature makes a distinction between (1) systematic risk and (2) nonsystematic, or firm-specific, risk. Systematic risk refers to the covariability of changes in a particular firm's stock prices with changes in the market prices of all firms in the market. We use the market beta of a firm's stock to measure systematic risk. Most of this chapter discusses the assessment of firm-specific risk, but we attempt to integrate these two dimensions of risk at the end of the chapter.

Overview of Risk Analysis

The sources and types of risk that a firm faces are numerous and often interrelated. They include:

Source	Type or Nature
International	Host government regulations or attitudes
	Political unrest
	Exchange rate changes
Domestic	Recession
	Inflation or deflation
	Interest rate changes
	Demographic changes
	Political changes
Industry	Technology
	Competition
	Regulation
	Availability of raw materials
	Unionization
Firm-Specific	Management competence
	Strategic direction
	Lawsuits

Exhibit 9.1
Structure for Financial Statement Analysis of Risk

Activity	Ability to Generate Cash	Need to Use Cash	Financial Statement Analysis Performed
Operations	Profitability of products	Working capital requirements	Short-term liquidity risk
Investing	Sales of existing plant assets or investments	Plant capacity requirements	Long-term liquidity (solvency) risk
Financing	Borrowing capacity	Debt service requirements	

Although a firm should continually monitor each of these types of risk, we focus our attention on the financial consequences of these elements of risk using data from the financial statements. Each of these types of risk ultimately affects net income and cash flows. A firm usually enters bankruptcy because it is unable either to generate sufficient cash internally or to obtain needed cash from external sources to sustain operating, investing, and financing activities. The statement of cash flows, which reports the net amount of cash generated or used by (1) operating, (2) investing, and (3) financing activities, is an important source of information for studying risk.

Publicly held corporations in the United States present a statement of cash flows for the most recent three years in their published financial statements. Small, privately held firms, however, usually prepare only a balance sheet and an income statement. Also, many non-U.S. firms do not prepare a cash-flow statement. Chapter 2 discussed the statement of cash flows and described a procedure for preparing this financial statement using information from the balance sheet and income statement.

Framework for Risk Analysis

Exhibit 9.1 relates the factors affecting a firm's ability to generate cash with its need to use cash. Most risk analysis focuses on a comparison of the supply of and demand for cash. Risk analysis using financial statement data typically examines (1) the near-term ability to generate cash to service working capital needs and debt service costs, and (2) the longer-term ability to generate cash internally or from external sources to satisfy plant capacity and debt repayment needs. We therefore structure our discussion of the analytical tools for assessing risk around short-term liquidity risk and long-term solvency risk.

Short-Term Liquidity Risk

The analysis of short-term liquidity risk requires an understanding of the *operating cycle* of a firm. Consider a typical manufacturing firm. It acquires raw materials on account, promising to pay suppliers within 30 or 60 days. The firm then combines the raw material, labor services, and other factor inputs to produce a product. It pays for some of these costs at the time of incurrence and delays payment of other costs. At some point, the firm sells the product either for cash or on account. It then collects the account and pays suppliers and others for purchases on account.

If a firm (1) can delay all cash outflows to suppliers, employees, and others until it receives cash from customers, and (2) receives more cash than it must disburse, then the firm will not likely encounter short-term liquidity problems. Most firms, however, cannot time their cash inflows and outflows precisely. Employees may require weekly or semimonthly payments, whereas customers may delay payment for 30 days or more. Firms may experience rapid growth and need to produce more units of product during a period than it sells. Even if perfectly timed, the cash outflows to support the higher level of production can exceed cash inflows from customers from the lower level of sales. Firms that operate at a net loss for a period often find that the completion of the operating cycle results in a net cash outflow instead of a net cash inflow.

Short-term liquidity problems also arise from longer-term solvency difficulties. For example, a firm may assume a high percentage of debt in its capital structure, as many firms did in the leveraged buyout movement of the late 1980s. This level of debt usually requires periodic interest payments and may require repayments of principal as well. For some firms, interest expense is their largest single cost. The operating cycle must not only generate sufficient cash to supply operating working capital needs, it must generally throw off sufficient cash to service debt as well.

Financially healthy firms frequently close any cash-flow gap in their operating cycles with short-term borrowing. Such firms may issue commercial paper on the market or obtain three- to six-month bank loans. Most such firms maintain a line of credit with their banks so they can obtain cash for working capital needs quickly. The notes to the financial statements usually disclose the amount of the line of credit and the level of borrowing utilized on that line during the year.

We will discuss seven financial statement ratios for assessing short-term liquidity risk in this section. Three ratios relate the level of resources available to meet short-term commitments with the level of those commitments: (1) current ratio, (2) quick ratio, and (3) operating cash flow to current liabilities ratio. Three ratios relate the amount of working capital required for the level of sales generated: (4) accounts receivable turnover, (5) inventory turnover, and (6) accounts payable turnover. And one ratio considers the demands of debt service costs on operating cash flows: (7) operating cash flows to cash interest costs.

Current Ratio

The current ratio equals current assets divided by current liabilities. It indicates the amount of cash available at the balance sheet date plus the amount of current assets that the firm expects to turn into cash within one year of the balance sheet date (from collection of receivables and sale of inventory) relative to obligations coming due within that period. The current ratios for Coke and Pepsi for Year 8 are:

$$\text{Current Ratio} = \frac{\text{Current Assets}}{\text{Current Liabilities}}$$

Coke   \$4,142.8/\$4,296.5   = .96:1

Pepsi   \$4,081.4/\$4,770.5   = .86:1

The current ratio for Coke was 1.13 in Year 6 and .99 in Year 7 and for Pepsi was .84 in Year 6 and .96 in Year 7. Thus, Coke experienced a decrease in its current ratio during the last three years, while Pepsi's current ratio increased in Year 7 and decreased to approximately its Year 6 level in Year 8.

Historically, analysts considered a current ratio of 2.0 or 1.5 adequate or satisfactory. As interest rates increased in the early 1980s, firms attempted to stretch their accounts payable and permit suppliers to finance a greater portion of their working capital needs (that is, receivables, inventories). As a consequence, current ratios began moving in the direction of 1.0. Current ratios hovering around this level are now not uncommon. Although this directional movement suggests an increase in short-term liquidity risk, the level of risk is not necessarily intolerable. Recall that accountants report inventories, a major component of current assets, at acquisition cost. Firms will likely sell these inventories for an amount greater than acquisition cost. Thus, the cash that the firm expects to generate from inventories is larger than the amount used in calculating the current ratio.

The current ratios of Coke and Pepsi are less than 1.0. Although this level of current ratio is low from an historical perspective, note that 35 percent of current assets for Coke and 44 percent of current assets for Pepsi represent cash and readily marketable securities. Recall also from the discussion in Chapter 7 that these companies realize gross margins (that is, sales minus cost of goods sold) of 50 percent to 60 percent. Thus, inventories have selling prices of 2 to 2.5 times the amount appearing on the balance sheet. Also, Coke reports in Note 5 that it has a \$600 million unused line of credit at the end of Year 8, while Pepsi reports in Note 8 that it has a \$3.5 billion unused line of credit at the end of Year 8. Thus, a current ratio less than 1.0 is not a major concern for these companies.

A second explanation for the decreasing current ratios of many firms in recent years is the shift from a first-in, first-out (FIFO) to a last-in, first-out (LIFO) cost-flow assumption for inventories. Under LIFO, inventories appear at the historical cost of the year of each LIFO layer. As time passes and inflation continues, the amount that the balance sheet reports for LIFO inventories increasingly deviates from current market value. This phenomenon results in a decreasing current ratio over time. Coke and Pepsi have used a combination of FIFO, LIFO, and average cost-flow assumptions for inventories for many years. The differences between the current cost and book value of inventories accounted for using LIFO are insignificant (see Coke's Note 1 and Pepsi's Note 5) and have virtually no effect on their current ratios.

Several additional interpretive problems arise with the current ratio:

1. An increase of equal amount in both current assets and current liabilities (for example, purchasing inventory on account) results in a decrease in the current ratio when the ratio is greater than 1.0 before the transaction but an increase in the current ratio if it is less than 1.0 before the transaction. Similar interpretive difficulties arise when current assets and current liabilities decrease by an equal amount. With current ratios for many firms now in the neighborhood of 1.0, this concern with the current ratio gains greater significance.

2. A very high current ratio may accompany unsatisfactory business conditions, whereas a falling ratio may accompany profitable operations. In a recessionary period, business contracts, firms pay current liabilities, and, even though current assets reach a low point, the current ratio can increase to very high levels. In a boom period, just the reverse can occur.

3. The current ratio is susceptible to "window dressing"; that is, management can take deliberate steps at the balance sheet date to produce a better current ratio than is the normal or average ratio for the period. For instance, towards the end of the period a firm may accelerate normal purchases on account (current ratio is less than 1.0) or delay such purchases (current ratio is greater than 1.0) in an effort to improve the current ratio. Alternatively, a firm may collect loans to officers, classified as noncurrent assets, and use the proceeds to reduce current liabilities.

Given these interpretive problems with the current ratio, the analyst may find its widespread use as a measure of short-term liquidity risk surprising. The explanation lies partially in its ease of calculation. In addition, empirical studies of bond default, bankruptcy, and similar financial distress have found the current ratio to have strong predictive power. A later section of this chapter discusses these studies more fully.

Quick Ratio

A variation of the current ratio is the quick ratio or acid test ratio. The analyst computes the quick ratio by including in the numerator only those current assets that the firm could quickly convert into cash. Analysts customarily include cash, marketable securities, and receivables. However, the analyst should study the facts in each case before deciding whether or not to include receivables and to exclude inventories. Some businesses can convert their inventory of merchandise into cash more quickly than other businesses can collect their receivables.

Assuming that we include accounts receivable but exclude inventories, the quick ratios of Coke and Pepsi for Year 8 are:

$$\text{Quick Ratio} = \frac{\text{Cash} + \text{Marketable Securities} + \text{Receivables}}{\text{Current Liabilities}}$$

Coke
$$\frac{\$1{,}429.6 + \$62.6 + \$913.5 + \$38.2}{\$4{,}296.5} = .57$$

Pepsi
$$\frac{\$170.8 + \$1{,}644.9 + \$1{,}414.7}{\$4{,}770.5} = .68$$

The quick ratio of Coke was .70 in Year 6 and .55 in Year 7, while Pepsi's was .67 in Year 6 and .75 in Year 7. In general, the trends in the quick ratio and the current ratio highly correlate. That is, the analyst obtains the same information about improving or deteriorating short-term liquidity by examining either ratio. Note that the current and quick ratios for each firm follow similar trends. With current ratios recently trending toward 1.0, quick ratios have trended toward .5.

Operating Cash Flow to Current Liabilities Ratio

The analyst can overcome the deficiencies discussed above in using current assets as an indicator of a firm's ability to generate cash in the near term by using cash flow from operations instead. Cash flow from operations, reported on the statement of cash flows, indicates the excess amount of cash that the firm derived from operations during the past period after funding working capital needs and making required payments on current liabilities. Because the numerator of this ratio uses amounts for a period of time, the denominator uses an average of current liabilities for the period. This ratio for Coke and Pepsi for Year 8 is:

$$\text{Operating Cash Flow to Current Liabilities Ratio} = \frac{\text{Cash Flow from (Continuing) Operations}}{\text{Average Current Liabilities}}$$

$$\text{Coke} \qquad \frac{\$1,283.9}{.5(\$3,657.9 + \$4,296.5)} = .32$$

$$\text{Pepsi} \qquad \frac{\$2,110.0}{.5(\$3,691.8 + \$4,770.5)} = .50$$

The ratio for Coke was .33 in Year 6 and .34 in Year 7 and for Pepsi was .57 in Year 6 and .50 in Year 7. An empirical study utilizing the operating cash flow to current liabilities ratio found that a ratio of .40 or more was common for a healthy manufacturing or retailing firm.[1] Coke has a higher current ratio than Pepsi but a lower quick ratio and cash flow from operations to current liabilities ratio. The latter ratio for Coke is less than the .40 benchmark. Although Coke appears to have more short-term liquidity risk than Pepsi using two of the three measures discussed thus far, neither company is subject to substantial risk in this regard for the reasons discussed above.

Working Capital Activity Ratios

The analyst uses three measures of the rate of activity in working capital accounts to study the cash-generating ability of operations and the short-term liquidity risk of a firm:

---

[1]Cornelius Casey and Norman Bartzcak, "Cash Flow—It's Not the Bottom Line," *Harvard Business Review* (July-August 1984), pp. 61–66.

$$\text{Accounts Receivable Turnover} = \frac{\text{Sales}}{\text{Average Accounts Receivable}}$$

$$\text{Inventory Turnover} = \frac{\text{Cost of Goods Sold}}{\text{Average Inventories}}$$

$$\text{Accounts Payable Turnover} = \frac{\text{Purchases}}{\text{Average Accounts Payable}}$$

Chapter 7 discussed the accounts receivable and inventory turnovers, components of the total assets turnover. We use these ratios here as measures of the speed with which firms turn accounts receivable into cash or sell inventories. The accounts payable turnover indicates the speed by which a firm pays for purchases on account. Purchases is not an amount that the financial statements typically disclose. The analyst can approximate purchases as follows:

Purchases = Cost of Goods Sold + Ending Inventory − Beginning Inventory.

The analyst often expresses these three ratios in terms of the number of days each balance sheet item (that is, receivables, inventories, accounts payable) is outstanding. To do so, divide 365 days by the three turnover amounts.

Exhibit 9.2 presents the calculation of these three turnover ratios for Coke and Pepsi for Year 8. Pepsi's accounts receivable turn over more rapidly than

Exhibit 9.2
Working Capital Activity Ratios for Coke and Pepsi for Year 8

	Accounts Receivable Turnover	**Days Receivables Outstanding**
Coke	$\dfrac{\$10,236.4}{.5(\$768.4 + \$52.1 + \$913.5 + \$38.2)} = 11.5$ times per year	$\dfrac{365}{11.5} = 32$ days
Pepsi	$\dfrac{\$17,802.7}{.5(\$1,239.7 + \$1,414.7)} = 13.4$ times per year	$\dfrac{365}{13.4} = 27$ days

	Inventory Turnover	**Days Inventory Held**
Coke	$\dfrac{\$4,208.9}{.5(\$789.1 + \$982.3)} = 4.8$ times per year	$\dfrac{365}{4.8} = 77$ days
Pepsi	$\dfrac{\$8,609.9}{.5(\$546.1 + \$585.8)} = 15.2$ times per year	$\dfrac{365}{15.2} = 24$ days

	Accounts Payable Turnover	**Days Accounts Payable Outstanding**
Coke	$\dfrac{(\$4,208.9 + \$982.3 - \$789.1)}{.5(\$1,386.5 + \$1,576.4)} = 3.0$ times per year	$\dfrac{365}{3.0} = 123$ days
Pepsi	$\dfrac{\$8,609.9 + \$585.8 - \$546.1}{.5(\$1,054.5 + \$1,116.3)} = 8.0$ times per year	$\dfrac{365}{8.0} = 46$ days

Coke's. The faster receivable turnover for Pepsi results from its involvement with restaurants. Refer to the segment data for Pepsi in Note 14. We can recompute Pepsi's accounts receivable turnover for Year 8 by eliminating sales of the restaurant segment. The computation is as follows:

$$\frac{\text{Restated Accounts Receivable}}{\text{Turnover for Pepsi for Year 8}} = \frac{\$17,802.7 - \$6,225.7}{.5(\$1,239.7 + \$1,414.7)} = 8.7$$

$$\text{Restated Days Receivable for Pepsi for Year 8} = \frac{365}{8.7} = 42 \text{ days}$$

These computations probably include some error because an unknown portion of the receivables relates to restaurant operations. Thus, removing all sales revenues of restaurants biases the accounts receivable turnover downward. Nonetheless, it appears that the difference in the accounts receivable turnover results from a different product mix between the two firms.

A similar explanation relates to the difference in inventory turnovers. Because restaurant food products turn over quickly, we would expect Pepsi's inventory turnover to exceed Coke's. We cannot restate Pepsi's inventory turnover to eliminate restaurant activities because the segment data do not disclose cost of goods sold for restaurants.

Pepsi's accounts payable turnover substantially exceeds Coke's. The principal explanation for this difference relates to differences in disclosure. Note from Coke's balance sheet in Appendix A that it combines accounts payable and accrued expenses, whereas Pepsi separates accounts payable from other current liabilities. Their accounts payable turnovers are therefore not comparable. The desirable procedure is to eliminate the liability for accrued expenses from Coke's calculations. Lacking the necessary information to make such an elimination, we instead add other current liabilities to accounts payable for Pepsi to assess the effect of the reporting differences on the accounts payable turnover. The restated amounts for Pepsi are:

$$\frac{\text{Restated Accounts Payable Turnover}}{\text{for Pepsi for Year 8}} = \frac{\$8,609.9 + \$585.8 - \$546.1}{.5(\$1,054.5 + \$1,457.3 + \$1,116.3 + \$1,584.0)} = 3.3$$

Pepsi's restated accounts payable turnover is similar to Coke's.
The relation between these three turnover ratios are as follows:[2]

Working Capital Investment: |—— Days Inventory Held ——|—— Days Receivables Outstanding ——|

Working Capital Financing: |—— Days Payables Outstanding ——|—— Required Financing Period ——|

The elapsed time between the acquisition of inventories (raw materials for a manufacturer and finished goods for a wholesaler or retailer) and the collection of cash

---

[2] The ideas in this section result from discussions with Professor George Sorter.

Exhibit 9.3

Calculation of Required Financing Period for Coke and Pepsi

	Days Receivable Outstanding	+	Days Inventory Outstanding	–	Days Payables Outstanding	=	Required Financing Period
Coke							
Year 6	32	+	77	–	47	=	62
Year 7	33	+	74	–	47	=	60
Year 8	32	+	77	–	46	=	63
Pepsi							
Year 6	26	+	26	–	47	=	5
Year 7	27	+	24	–	47	=	4
Year 8	27	+	24	–	46	=	5

from customers from sales on accounts equals the sum of the days inventories held and the days receivables outstanding. The firm must obtain financing for this working capital investment. Suppliers usually provide financing for a portion of this period, measured by the days payables outstanding. The firm must obtain other financing for the remaining period. One possibility is to use cash or marketable securities on hand, in which case the firm loses the opportunity to earn interest or other revenues on these assets. Alternatively, the firm can borrow in the commercial paper market or from a bank, in which case it incurs interest expense. Thus, the length of the required financing period indicates the time during which the firm incurs the risk of short-term changes in interest rates.

Coke's disclosure of accounts payable and accrued expenses on a single line means that we have measured the number of days accounts payable are outstanding improperly. We therefore cannot compute the required financing period for Coke using the reported data. We demonstrated above that Pepsi's accounts payable turnover restated to conform to Coke's disclosure is similar to Coke's. To illustrate the calculation and interpretation of the required financing period, we assume that *Coke's* corrected accounts payable turnover and days payables outstanding are identical to Pepsi's for each of the last three years. The calculation of the required financing period appears in Exhibit 9.3. This analysis shows clearly Coke's greater short-term liquidity risk, consistent with the interpretation of the quick ratio and operating cash flow to current liabilities ratio. Neither firm experienced much change in the three turnover ratios nor in their required financing periods during the last three years.

Operating Cash Flow to Cash Interest Costs Ratio

A firm burdened with heavy commitments to service debt can experience short-term liquidity problems just as much as a firm with working capital management problems. A ratio that assesses a firm's ability to service its debt from operating cash flows is the operating cash flow to cash interest costs ratio.

The numerator of this ratio is cash flow from operations before the payment of interest and income taxes. We calculate the numerator by adding the cash outflow for interest and income taxes to cash flow from operations in the statement of cash flows. The denominator is the cash outflow for interest. Coke discloses the cash outflow for interest in Note 7 ($233 million in Year 8) and for income taxes in Note 13 ($803 million in Year 8). Pepsi discloses the amounts for these items at the bottom of its statement of cash flows ($656.9 million and $375.0 million respectively for Year 8). The calculation of the operating cash flow to cash interest costs ratios for Year 8 is as follows:

$$\text{Operating Cash Flow to Cash Interest Costs Ratio} = \frac{\text{Cash Flow from Operations} + \text{Cash Outflow for Interest} + \text{Cash Outflow for Income Taxes}}{\text{Cash Outflow for Interest}}$$

Coke: = ($1,283.9 + $233.0 + $803.0)/$233.0   = 10.0

Pepsi: = ($2,110.0 + $656.9 + $375.0)/$656.9   = 4.8

Both companies generated more than sufficient cash flow from operations to meet both working capital needs and interest service requirements on debt. As the next section discusses more fully, Pepsi carries heavier long-term debt financing than Coke and therefore has a lower operating cash flow to cash interest costs ratio.

Analysts often approximate this ratio using amounts from the income statement instead of the statement of cash flows. Referred to as the interest coverage ratio, the computation is as follows:

$$\text{Interest Coverage Ratio} = \frac{\text{Income from Continuing Operations} + \text{Interest Expense} + \text{Income Tax Expense}}{\text{Interest Expense}}$$

Coke: = ($1,381.9 + $231.0 + $632.5)/$231.0   = 9.7

Pepsi: = ($1,090.6 + $688.5 + $576.8)/$688.5   = 3.4

Note that the interest coverage ratio provides the same insights about the ability of operations to service debt for Coke and Pepsi as does the operating cash flow to cash interest cost ratio. These two ratios tend to correlate highly. They differ under the following conditions:

1. The firm experiences rapid growth, with additional working capital investments causing income from continuing operations to exceed cash flow from operations.

2. The firm issues debt that does not require periodic cash interest payments (for example, zero-coupon debt or payment-in-kind debt).

3. The firm experiences significant timing differences between financial reporting and taxable income, so that income tax expense differs from income tax payments.

Note the similarity for Coke between income from continuing operations and cash flow from operations and of interest expense and cash payments for interest. The difference between income tax expense and income taxes paid causes the minor difference between the operating cash flow to cash interest costs ratio and the interest coverage ratio. On the other hand, Pepsi's cash flow from operations substantially exceeds its income from continuing operations and its cash payment for income taxes is less than income tax expense. Interest expense and cash payments of interest are similar. Thus, Pepsi's operating cash flow to cash interest costs ratio exceeds its interest coverage ratio.

In cases where the three listed conditions are not present, the interest coverage ratio usually serves as a useful surrogate for the operating cash flow to cash interest costs ratio. When the conditions are present and when the interest coverage ratio is less than approximately 2.0, then the analyst should use the cash-flow version of the ratio to assess short-term liquidity risk.

Summary of Short-Term Liquidity Risk Analysis

The short-term liquidity risk ratios suggest that Coke has more short-term liquidity risk than Pepsi. However, neither firm's ratios are at levels that should cause the analyst alarm. Both companies have established brand names and dominate the soft drink industry. Chapters 7 and 8 discussed their healthy profitability picture, suggesting that both firms could obtain short-term financing if needed. Their established lines of credit provide a cushion if short-term liquidity becomes a problem.

Long-Term Solvency Risk

Analysts use measures of long-term liquidity, or solvency, risk to examine a firm's ability to meet interest and principal payments on long-term debt and similar obligations as they come due. If the firm cannot make payments on time, it becomes insolvent and may require reorganization or liquidation.

Perhaps the best indicator for assessing long-term solvency risk is a firm's ability to generate profits over a period of years. Profitable firms either generate sufficient cash from operations or obtain needed cash from creditors or owners. The measures of profitability discussed in Chapters 7 and 8 therefore apply for this purpose as well. Four other measures used in examining long-term solvency risk are (1) debt ratios, (2) interest coverage ratio, (3) operating cash flow to total liabilities ratio, and (4) operating cash flow to capital expenditures ratio.

Debt Ratios

Analysts use debt ratios to measure the amount of long-term debt financing in a firm's capital structure. The higher this proportion, the greater the long-term solvency risk. Several variations in debt ratios exist. Three commonly encountered measures are:

$$\text{Long-Term Debt Ratio} = \frac{\text{Long-Term Debt}}{\text{Long-Term Debt} + \text{Shareholders' Equity}}$$

$$\text{Debt/Equity Ratio} = \frac{\text{Long-Term Debt}}{\text{Shareholders' Equity}}$$

$$\text{Long-Term Debt to Assets Ratio} = \frac{\text{Long-Term Debt}}{\text{Total Assets (Equities)}}$$

The debt ratios for Coke and Pepsi for Year 8 are as follows:

	Coke		**Pepsi**	
Long-Term Debt Ratio	$\dfrac{\$535.9}{\$535.9 + \$3,849.2}$	$= 12.2\%$	$\dfrac{\$5,600.1}{\$5,600.1 + \$4,904.2}$	$= 53.3\%$
Debt/Equity Ratio	$\dfrac{\$535.9}{\$3,849.2}$	$= 13.9\%$	$\dfrac{\$5,600.1}{\$4,904.2}$	$= 114.2\%$
Long-Term Debt to Assets Ratio	$\dfrac{\$535.9}{\$9,278.2}$	$= 5.8\%$	$\dfrac{\$5,600.1}{\$17,143.4}$	$= 32.7\%$

Exhibit 9.4 shows the debt ratios for Coke and Pepsi during the last three years. Pepsi has substantially higher debt ratios than Coke. The high debt ratios relate in part to Pepsi's greater involvement in capital-intensive restaurant operations. Pepsi also used debt to finance acquisitions, particularly in Year 7. Note the high correlation between changes in these three debt ratios over time. This result is not surprising since they use essentially the same financial statement data. The analyst can generally select one of these ratios and use it consistently over time. Because different debt ratios exist, the analyst should use caution when reading financial periodicals and discussing debt ratios with others to be sure of the particular version of the debt ratio being used. It is not unusual to find a debt/equity ratio greater than 1.0 (that is, more long-term debt than shareholders' equity), but a long-term debt ratio or long-term debt to assets ratio greater than 1.0 is highly unusual (requiring a negative shareholders' equity).

Chapter 4 discussed the increasingly common practice in recent years for firms to structure the financing of assets in such a way that they keep long-term

Exhibit 9.4
Debt Ratios for Coke and Pepsi Year 6 to Year 8

	Coke			**Pepsi**		
	Year 6	**Year 7**	**Year 8**	**Year 6**	**Year 7**	**Year 8**
Long-Term Debt Ratio	18.5%	13.6%	12.2%	45.7%	61.0%	53.3%
Debt/Equity Ratio	22.8%	15.7%	13.9%	84.0%	156.2%	114.2%
Long-Term Debt to Assets Ratio	10.2%	6.6%	5.8%	23.9%	40.2%	32.7%

debt off of the balance sheet. The supposed rationale for this practice is that analysts will view a firm as less risky and lend at a lower interest rate or invest with a lower expected return. This practice assumes a certain amount of naiveté on the part of financial statement users that lacks support from empirical research. Nonetheless, ample evidence exists that firms practice off-balance sheet financing.

It is desirable to search the financial statements and notes for obligations that the analyst should include in long-term debt. Chapter 4 discussed the accounting for each of the possible obligations considered below.

Obligation Not Classified as Long-Term Debt.   Firms have increasingly issued hybrid securities in recent years. These securities have both debt and equity characteristics. Long-term debt on the balance sheet typically already includes convertible bonds. However, preferred stock sometimes has debt characteristics. For example, some firms have issued preferred stock with mandatory redemption requirements in recent years. GAAP requires that the issuing firm classify such preferred stock on a separate line in the balance sheet between long-term debt and shareholders' equity.

In Note 9 for Coke in Appendix A, we see that Coke has preferred stock outstanding whose annual dividend varies with changes in short-term money market interest rates. The annual yield on this security resembles a debt instrument. However, Coke pays a dividend each year only if declared by the board of directors. Furthermore, the preferred stock has no mandatory time for redemption. Thus, the security has more equity than debt characteristics. The analysts should probably exclude it from long-term debt in computing debt ratios.

In Note 9 for Pepsi in Appendix B, we see that Pepsi shows a nonrecourse obligation on the financing side of its balance sheet but excludes it from long-term debt. The note indicates that Pepsi initially received $299 million relating to this borrowing. Pepsi probably then lent the funds to unaffiliated franchisees to finance restaurant facilities. The franchisees periodically pay royalties to Pepsi, which Pepsi in turn remits to the lending institution to repay the initial loan. Pepsi acts as an agent between the lending institution and the franchisees. Pepsi reports this obligation as a liability because it must make future cash payments when it receives royalties from franchisees. However, the nonrecourse nature of the obligation means that Pepsi will make no payment unless it receives such royalties. A failure to repay the loan does not appear to affect directly the solvency risk of Pepsi. However, such failure to repay affects the solvency of Pepsi's franchisees and thereby indirectly affects Pepsi's ability to generate funds to repay its own debt. A conservative approach to analyzing Pepsi's long-term solvency risk includes this obligation in long-term debt. A later section demonstrates the recalculation of Pepsi's debt ratios to include this nonrecourse obligation.

Off-Balance Sheet Commitments.   Recall from the discussion in Chapter 4 that firms recognize contingent obligations as liabilities only when:

1. Information available prior to the issuance of the financial statements indicates that it is probable that the firm has incurred a liability.

2. The firm can estimate the amount of the commitment with reasonable precision.[3]

Contingent obligations that a firm does not recognize as liabilities appear in notes to the financial statements.

In Coke's financial statements, Note 7 indicates that Coke is contingently liable for guarantees of debt owed by third parties of $139 million at the end of Year 8. The probability that Coke will incur a liability for this guarantee is sufficiently low that it excludes the contingent obligation from the balance sheet. The analyst can take a conservative position and include the potential obligation as a liability. A later section includes this commitment in the recalculation of the debt ratios for Coke.

Notes 4 and 8 to Coke's financial statements indicate that it has commitments on interest rate swaps and foreign currency forward exchange contracts. These commitments hedge Coke against changes in interest rates and foreign exchange rates. Coke's potential obligation is not the full amount reported for these two items ($60 million in Note 4 and $1.3 billion in Note 8). Coke's potential benefit or potential obligation is for the *change* in interest rates or exchange rates on the $1.36 billion amount. Because these contracts hedge existing receivables or payables, any benefit or cost of the hedging instrument presumably offsets any cost or benefit realized on the receivable or payable, and thus neutralizes Coke's risk. Coke's primary risk is that it does not collect its receivables or another party fails to deliver on the interest or exchange rate hedge. We make no adjustment to Coke's liabilities for these items.

In Pepsi's financial statements, Note 13 indicates that Pepsi is contingently liable on guarantees of $97 million. As with Coke, we include this contingent obligation in Pepsi's debt ratios in a later section. Note 8 indicates that Pepsi entered into interest rate swap agreements and forward foreign exchange contracts. We exclude these commitments from Pepsi's liabilities for the same reasons as discussed above for Coke.

Leases.   Chapter 4 discussed the accounting for leases, showing that a thin line often separates capital leases (recognized as liabilities) and operating leases (not recognized as liabilities). The conservative approach capitalizes all operating leases as if they were capital leases. Coke reports no operating leases in its notes. Pepsi discloses its commitments under operating leases in Note 7. Chapter 4 demonstrated the calculation of the $815.1 million present value of these operating lease commitments at the end of Year 8. We include this commitment in the recalculated amounts of Pepsi's debt ratios in a later section.

Pensions.   Chapter 4 also discussed the accounting for retirement plans, both for pensions and health-care benefits. Accountants distinguish between the accumulated benefit obligation of a pension plan (which uses current salaries and accumulated service to date) and the projected benefit obligation (which uses projected salaries and accumulated service to date). Firms must recognize a liability

---

[3]Financial Accounting Standards Board, *Statement of Financial Accounting Standards No. 5*, "Accounting for Contingencies," 1975, para. 8.

for an excess of the *accumulated* benefit obligation over assets in the pension fund. Firms disclose in the notes any excess of the *projected* benefit obligation over pension fund assets. The analyst obtains a more conservative measure of debt ratios by including the underfunded projected benefit obligation as a liability. Coke indicates in Note 12 that its underfunded projected benefit obligation totals $116.399 million (= $64.892 + $51.507) at the end of Year 8. We include this obligation in Coke's debt ratios in a later section. Pepsi indicates in Note 11 that pension fund assets exceed its projected benefit obligation.

Another potential liability is the obligation to provide health-care benefits to retired employees. GAAP requires firms to disclose the present value of this obligation in notes to the financial statements beginning in 1993. We therefore have no information on this obligation to include it in the recalculated debt ratios for Coke and Pepsi.

Debt of Nonconsolidated Entities. Chapter 5 discussed the GAAP requirement that firms prepare consolidated financial statements for majority-owned intercorporate investments. The debt of such entities appears among liabilities on the consolidated balance sheet. When a firm owns between 20 percent and 50 percent of another entity, it uses the equity method. The debt of such entities does not appear on the investor's balance sheet. The operating relationship between the investor and investee is often so closely intertwined that the debt effectively belongs to the investor. For example, the investor may guarantee the investee's debt, promise to purchase a certain amount of goods or services from the investee, or guarantee a certain level of income to the investee.

Chapter 5 discussed Coke's strategy of holding 49 percent ownership interests in its bottlers. As a consequence, Coke leaves a considerable amount of debt off of its balance sheet. Exhibit 5.5 shows that consolidating these bottlers adds $4,858.2 million to Coke's liabilities at the end of Year 8. The consolidation of these entities also adds $2,013.2 million to shareholders' equity for the remaining interests (that is, 51 percent) in those bottlers. Pepsi does not disclose financial statement information for unconsolidated entities, suggesting that they are not significant.

Recalculating the Debt Ratios. Exhibit 9.5 shows the revised long-term debt, shareholders' equity, and total assets for Coke and Pepsi incorporating the various obligations discussed in the preceding sections. The debt ratios using the reported and restated data are as follows:

	Coke		Pepsi	
	Reported	**Restated**	**Reported**	**Restated**
Long-Term Debt Ratio	12.2%	49.1%	53.3%	58.1%
Debt/Equity Ratio	13.9%	96.4%	114.2%	138.9%
Long-Term Debt to Assets Ratio	5.8%	29.5%	32.7%	37.7%

Coke's debt ratios increase considerably, primarily because of the debt of unconsolidated bottlers. The revised debt ratios of Coke and Pepsi are similar, although those for Pepsi are somewhat higher.

Exhibit 9.5
**Revised Financial Statement Amounts for
Coke and Pepsi to Reflect Off-Balance Sheet Debt**

	Coke	Pepsi
Reported Long-Term Debt	$ 535.9	$ 5,600.1
Nonrecourse Debt Obligation	—	299.0
Loan Guarantees	139.0	97.0
Operating Leases	—	815.1
Underfunded Projected Benefit Pension Obligation	116.4	—
Long-Term Debt of Unconsolidated Entities	4,858.2	—
Revised Long-Term Debt	$ 5,649.5	$ 6,811.2
Reported Shareholders' Equity	$ 3,849.2	$ 4,904.2
Remaining Equity Interests in Unconsolidated Entities	2,013.2	—
Revised Shareholders' Equity	$ 5,862.4	$ 4,904.2
Reported Total Assets	$ 9,278.2	$17,143.4
Additional Assets from		
Nonrecourse Debt Obligation	—	97.0
Loan Guarantees	139.0	815.1
Operating Leases	—	—
Pension Obligation	116.4	—
Consolidation of Bottlers	9,623.0[a]	—
	$19,156.6	$18,055.1

[a]$18,901.2 – $9,278.2 = $9,623.0 (see Exhibit 5.5).

Interest Coverage Ratio

The interest coverage ratio indicates the number of times that net income before interest expense and income taxes exceeds interest expense. The rationale is that the firm uses cash derived from operating income before income taxes to pay interest.

The interest coverage ratios for Coke and Pepsi for Year 8 are:

$$\text{Interest Coverage Ratio}^4 = \frac{\text{Net Income + Interest Expense + Income Tax Expense}}{\text{Interest Expense}}$$

Coke

$$\frac{\$1,381.9 + \$231.0 + \$632.5}{\$231.0} = 9.7$$

Pepsi

$$\frac{\$1,090.6 + \$688.5 + \$576.8}{\$688.5} = 3.4$$

---

[4] Increased precision suggests that the denominator include total interest cost for the year, not just the amount recognized as interest expense. If a firm self-constructs fixed assets, it must capitalize a portion of its interest cost each year and add it to the cost of the self-constructed assets. The analyst should probably only apply this refinement of the interest coverage ratio to electric utilities, which engage in heavy borrowing to construct their capital intensive plants.

The interest coverage ratios for Coke were 7.9 in Year 6 and 6.7 in Year 7 and for Pepsi were 4.3 in Year 6 and 3.2 in Year 7. Excluding interest on the debt of Coke's bottlers overstates its interest coverage ratio. We can approximate its effect by assuming an interest rate for the long-term borrowing by Coke's bottlers. Interest expense divided by average interest-bearing debt for Coke during Year 8 was 10.2 percent. Applying this interest rate to the average long-term debt of Coke's bottlers yields interest expense of $452.0 million [= (.102)(.5)($2,055.7 + $2,339.3 + $1,947.9 + $2,518.9)]. The revised interest coverage ratio for Coke for Year 8 is 4.5. (The numerator requires addbacks for interest expense and income taxes for both Coke and its bottlers, as well as the external interest in earnings of these bottlers.) Analysts typically view coverage ratios of less than approximately 2.0 as risky situations. Thus, neither Coke nor Pepsi appear to have much long-term solvency risk by this measure.

If a firm has other required periodic payments (for example, pensions, leases), then the analyst could include these amounts in the calculations as well. If so, the analyst refers to the ratio as the fixed charges coverage ratio.

One criticism of the interest or fixed charges coverage ratios as measures of long-term solvency risk is that they use earnings rather than cash flows in the numerator. (The justification is that income over sufficiently long time periods equals cash inflows minus cash outflows from operating and investing activities. A long-term perspective is appropriate when assessing long-term solvency risk.) Firms pay interest and other fixed charges with cash, however, and not with earnings. When the value of the ratio is relatively low, the analyst should use the cash-flow version of this ratio discussed under short-term liquidity risk.

Operating Cash Flow to Total Liabilities Ratio

The debt and interest coverage ratios give no recognition to the ability of a firm to generate cash flow from operations to service debt. The ratio of cash flow from operations to total liabilities overcomes this deficiency. This cash flow ratio is similar to the one used in assessing short-term liquidity, but here the denominator includes all liabilities (current and noncurrent).

The operating cash flow to total liabilities ratios for Year 8 for Coke and Pepsi using their reported amounts are as follows:

$$\text{Operating Cash Flow to Total Liabilities Ratio} = \frac{\text{Cash Flow from Continuing Operations}}{\text{Average Total Liabilities}}$$

Coke

$$\frac{\$1,283.9}{.5(\$4,797.1 + \$5,429.0)} = .25$$

Pepsi

$$\frac{\$2,110.0}{.5(\$11,235.6 + \$12,239.2)} = .18$$

The ratio for Coke was .25 in Year 6 and .25 in Year 7 and for Pepsi was .26 in Year 6 and .20 in Year 7. A ratio of 20 percent or more is common for a financially healthy company. Thus, both companies appear to have low long-term solvency risk by this measure, although Pepsi's declining ratio warrants close scrutiny.

Recalculating the operating cash flow to total liabilities ratio to include off-balance sheet debt is desirable. The major adjustment required is for the debt of Coke's bottlers. We can add the debt of these bottlers to Coke's total liabilities. Unfortunately, we cannot make a similar adjustment to cash flow from operations in the numerator because Note 3 to Coke's financial statements provides no cash flow information for these bottlers.

Operating Cash Flow to Capital Expenditures Ratio

A final ratio for assessing long-term solvency risk provides information about the ability of a firm to generate cash flow from operations in excess of capital expenditures needed to maintain and build plant capacity. The firm can use any excess cash flow to service debt. The analyst calculates this ratio as follows:

$$\text{Operating Cash Flow to Capital Expenditures Ratio} = \frac{\text{Cash Flow from Continuing Operations}}{\text{Capital Expenditures}}$$

$$\text{Coke} \qquad \frac{\$1,283.9}{\$\ 593.0} = 2.17$$

$$\text{Pepsi} \qquad \frac{\$2,110.0}{\$1,180.1} = 1.79$$

The corresponding ratios for Year 6 and Year 7 were 3.02 and 2.40 for Coke and 2.61 and 2.00 for Pepsi. Thus, both of these firms are throwing off more than enough cash from operations to finance capital expenditures and have amounts remaining to service debt. Recall that consumer foods products are in the maturity stage of their product life cycles and thus the analyst should expect a ratio greater than 1.0.

We can explore this ratio in more depth by examining segment data. The required segment disclosures indicate the operating income, depreciation expense, and capital expenditures for each product segment. With this information we can approximate the cash thrown off by each segment:

$$\frac{\text{Segment Cash Flow to}}{\text{Capital Expenditures Ratio}} = \frac{\text{Segment Operating Income} + \text{Segment Depreciation}}{\text{Segment Capital Expenditures}}$$

The numerator of this ratio is actually working capital from operations before interest, central corporate expenses, and income taxes. We cannot make an adjustment for additional working capital investments required within the segment, as is done in calculating cash flow from operations for the firm as a whole, because the segment disclosures do not provide the necessary information.

Exhibit 9.6
Segment Operating Cash Flow to
Capital Expenditures Ratios for Coke and Pepsi

	Coke			Pepsi		
	Year 6	Year 7	Year 8	Year 6	Year 7	Year 8
Soft Drinks..................	7.5	5.8	5.1	3.3	3.7	3.3
Consumer Foods.........	1.5	1.9	1.8	4.6	3.9	3.1
Restaurants	—	—	—	1.8	1.6	1.8

Using the segment data for Coke in Notes 19 and 20 and for Pepsi in Note 14, Exhibit 9.6 shows the segment operating cash flow to capital expenditures ratios. Because these ratios use segment operating income before taxes in computing the numerator, a ratio greater than approximately 1.7 suggests that the segment finances itself internally. Coke's soft drink segment throws off significantly more cash than needed to finance capital expenditures, whereas its consumer foods segment just about breaks even in terms of financing its capital expenditures. Pepsi's soft drink and consumer foods segments throw off excess cash to help finance its growing restaurant segment.

The operating cash flow to capital expenditures ratio indicates the *ability* to service debt but does not explicitly consider the future level of debt that a firm must pay. Also, management's discretionary latitude to alter the level of capital expenditures each year affects the ratio. A firm experiencing a poor year in terms of profitability may cut back its capital expenditures sufficiently to induce an increase in the ratio. Thus, the analyst should interpret trends in the ratio cautiously.

Summary of Long-Term Solvency Risk Analysis

The debt, interest coverage, and cash flow ratios indicate that Coke and Pepsi do not have substantial long-term solvency risk. Both firms are profitable and generate the needed cash flow to service their debt.

Bankruptcy Prediction Analysis

We might view the financial health of a firm along a continuum such as the following:

| Financially | Financially | Bankrupt | Liquidated |
| Healthy | Troubled | | |

The objective in performing a risk analysis of a firm is to obtain early warning signals that a firm is moving toward financially troubled or bankruptcy status. If management can predict such events several years before they occur, then it can take corrective action. Also, shareholders and creditors can take appropriate actions with the capital they have committed to the firm.

A stream of research over the last decade has attempted to discriminate the financial characteristics of healthy firms from those experiencing difficulty.[5] The objective is to build a discriminant or logit model using financial statement ratios which indicates the probability that a firm will go bankrupt several years before the event occurs. The typical approach involves selecting a sample of bankrupt or financially distressed firms and a matching set of healthy firms. The matching typically occurs on industry and size variables. The researcher calculates various profitability and risk ratios such as those discussed in Chapters 7, 8, and 9. Processing these ratios through a computerized discriminant or logit model yields a subset of the financial statement ratios that best discriminates between the financially distressed and healthy firms. Each financial ratio has a coefficient. Multiplying the coefficient times the value of each ratio for a particular firm yields a composite score. The discriminant or logit model indicates the score levels that suggest high or low probabilities of financial distress.

Perhaps the best known bankruptcy prediction model is Altman's Z-score.[6] Altman used manufacturing firms in developing the model. The calculation of the Z-score is:

$$Z - score \ = \ 1.2 \left[\frac{\text{Net Working Capital}}{\text{Total Assets}} \right] + 1.4 \left[\frac{\text{Retained Earnings}}{\text{Total Assets}} \right]$$

$$+ \ 3.3 \left[\frac{\text{Earnings before Interest and Taxes}}{\text{Total Assets}} \right]$$

$$+ \ .6 \left[\frac{\text{Market Value of Equity}}{\text{Book Value of Liabilities}} \right] + 1.0 \left[\frac{\text{Sales}}{\text{Total Assets}} \right]$$

Each of the ratios captures a different dimension of profitability or risk:

1. Net working capital/total assets: The proportion of total assets comprising relatively liquid net current assets (current assets minus current liabilities). This ratio captures short-term liquidity risk.

2. Retained earnings/total assets: Accumulated profitability and relative age of a firm.

3. Earnings before interest and taxes/total assets: A version of ROA. This ratio captures current profitability.

4. Market value of equity/book value of debt: This is a form of the debt/equity ratio, but it incorporates the market's assessment of the value of the firm's

[5]For an excellent summary of this research, see George Foster, *Financial Statement Analysis*, 2d edition (Englewood Cliffs, New Jersey: Prentice-Hall, 1986).

[6]Edward Altman, "Financial Ratios, Discriminant Analysis, and the Prediction of Corporate Bankruptcy," *Journal of Finance* (September 1968), pp. 589–609.

shareholders' equity. This ratio therefore captures long-term solvency risk and the market's overall view about the profitability and risk of the firm.

5. Sales/total assets: This ratio is similar to the total assets turnover and indicates the ability of a firm to use assets to generate sales.

The coefficients on each of the ratios do not necessarily indicate relative importance. They represent in part scaling devices for each ratio. For example, the 3.3 coefficient for earnings before interest and taxes divided by total assets reflects the fact that this ratio usually falls in the range of .04 to .10. The 1.0 coefficient for sales divided by total assets reflects the fact that this ratio usually falls in the range of .8 to 2.5 or more. In applying this model, Altman found that Z-scores of less than 1.81 indicated a high probability of bankruptcy, while Z-scores higher than 3.00 indicated a low probability of bankruptcy. Scores between 1.81 and 3.00 were in the gray area.

The Z-scores for Coke and Pepsi for Year 8 appear in Exhibit 9.7. The Z-scores for Coke and Pepsi differ for two reasons: (1) Coke's stronger profitability (see the discussion in Chapters 7 and 8) increases its values for the second and third ratios, and (2) Coke's nonconsolidation of its bottlers leaves significant debt out of the fourth ratio. Because Altman's original discriminant model used reported liabilities on the balance sheet, it is inappropriate to apply this model incorporating off-balance sheet liabilities. If Altman had included off-balance sheet liabilities, the coefficients would likely have differed from those above.

Altman and others subsequently extended this line of research to include other variables (cash-flow ratios, noncapitalized leases), specialized industries (railroads, savings and loans, and so on), and international settings. The models vary considerably, but tend to predict accurately 70 percent to 90 percent of bankruptcies in their samples up to two years prior to bankruptcy.

Critics of this line of research offer the following observations:

1. No accepted theory underlies the decline and ultimate bankruptcy of a firm. Thus, it is unclear which variables the researcher should include in the discriminant or logit models.

2. The researcher develops the discriminant and logit models by matching a bankrupt firm with a similar (as to product line, size) healthy firm. Most large firms operate in several industries. The researcher often encounters difficulties identifying a matched pair. Also, matching firms in the sample based on industry and size effectively precludes inclusion of these variables as discriminating factors. Yet, several studies have found these variables to have discriminatory power.

3. Bankruptcy studies have used samples of firms that are known to have gone bankrupt as of a particular date and examined the financial characteristics of these firms one, two, or more years prior to bankruptcy. This is a backward-looking exercise. Researchers need to conduct research that predicts the *timing* of bankruptcy for firms experiencing financial difficulty (a forward-looking exercise).

Despite these criticisms, analysts regularly use Z-score and similar discriminant and logit models. Their appeal is the use of a small number of financial statement ratios and the aggregation of these ratios into an easy-to-apply multivariate

Exhibit 9.7
Z-Score Analysis for Coke and Pepsi

$$Z\text{-score} = 1.2\left[\frac{\text{Net Working Capital}}{\text{Total Assets}}\right] + 1.4\left[\frac{\text{Retained Earnings}}{\text{Total Assets}}\right] + 3.3\left[\frac{\text{Earnings before Interest and Taxes}}{\text{Total Assets}}\right] + .6\left[\frac{\text{Market Value of Equity}}{\text{Book Value of Liabilities}}\right] + 1.0\left[\frac{\text{Sales}}{\text{Total Assets}}\right]$$

Coke

$$= 1.2\left[\frac{(\$153.7)}{\$9,278.2}\right] + 1.4\left[\frac{\$6,447.6}{\$9,278.2}\right] + 3.3\left[\frac{\$2,245.4}{\$9,278.2}\right] + .6\left[\frac{\$31,148.1}{\$5,429.0}\right] + 1.0\left[\frac{\$10,236.4}{\$9,278.2}\right]$$

$$6.29 = (.02) + .97 + .80 + 3.44 + 1.10$$

Pepsi

$$= 1.2\left[\frac{(\$689.1)}{\$17,143.4}\right] + 1.4\left[\frac{\$4,753.0}{\$17,143.4}\right] + 3.3\left[\frac{\$2,355.9}{\$17,143.4}\right] + .6\left[\frac{\$20,301.1}{\$12,239.2}\right] + 1.0\left[\frac{\$17,802.7}{\$17,143.4}\right]$$

$$2.83 = (.05) + .39 + .45 + 1.00 + 1.04$$

model. The Z-scores, like the financial statement ratios that serve as inputs, are merely signals or indicators of potential concern that the analyst needs to explore further. Viewed in this way, analysts are less likely to misuse or overemphasize them.

From Firm-Specific to Systematic Risk

The traditional theory of portfolio investments suggests that investors can largely eliminate firm-specific differences in risk (management skill, technological change, asset/equity mixes, and so on) by investing in a diversified portfolio of securities. The dimension of risk that investors cannot eliminate by diversification is systematic risk. Systematic risk refers to the covariability of changes in the market prices of a particular firm's stock with changes in market prices of all firms in the market. A firm whose stock prices change proportionally with the average for the market will have a beta of 1.0. A firm whose stock tends to increase or decrease 20 percent more than the average will have a beta of 1.2. A firm whose prices increase or decrease 20 percent less than the average will have a beta of .8. The investor must select the level of systematic risk desired and accept the level of return commensurate with that risk level. Of course, the higher the beta, the higher the expected return.

The factors that cause a particular firm's stock to vary in a certain way with the market depend on a complex set of economy-wide, industry, and firm-specific factors. Researchers in recent years have attempted to tie firm-specific risk analysis, as discussed previously in this chapter, with market beta. The objective is to identify changes in firm-specific elements of risk that might signal a change in market beta.

Gahlon and Gentry modeled the relation between nonsystematic and systematic risk using the concepts of operating leverage and financial leverage, discussed in Chapters 7 and 8, and variability of sales.[7] A firm with high operating leverage will have a high proportion of fixed costs in its cost structure (depreciation, rent, and so on). A firm with high financial leverage will likewise have a high proportion of fixed costs for interest expense. Such firms will find that their profits and cash flows increase by a higher percentage of each dollar increase in sales than is the case for firms with lower degrees of leverage. Likewise, their profits and cash flows will decrease by a higher percentage of each dollar decrease in sales than is the case for less leveraged firms. In other words, operating and financial leverage provide greater upside potential for profits and cash flows but greater variability as well. The greater the variability, the greater the risk.

Chapter 7 tied operating leverage to the level and variability of ROA. Chapter 8 tied operating and financial leverage to the level and variability of ROCE. We can now examine the relation between the level and variability of ROCE and beta. Exhibit 9.8 places each of the 22 industries examined in Chapters 7 and 8 into a three-by-three matrix based on the level and variability of ROCE. Exhibit 9.8 also shows the average market beta for each row and column of the matrix.

---

[7]James M. Gahlon and James A. Gentry, "On the Relationship Between Systematic Risk and the Degrees of Operating and Financial Leverage," *Financial Management* (Summer 1982), pp. 15–23.

Exhibit 9.8
Relation Between Level and Variability of ROCE and Market Beta
(market beta shown in parentheses)

	Standard Deviation of ROCE			
ROCE	**Low**	**Medium**	**High**	**Average Beta**
High	Chemicals (1.10) Paper Products (1.16)	Food Processors (.96) Publishing (1.13) Department Stores (1.20)	Grocery Stores (.91) Depository Institutions (.95)	1.06
Medium	Insurance (.80) Telecommunications (.84) Utilities (.55)	Petroleum (.78) Scientific Instruments (.98) Wholesalers—Nondurables (.94)	Electrical Equipment (1.08) Transportation Equipment (1.08)	.88
Low	Glass Products (.97) Metal Products (.95)	Industrial Machinery (1.04) Wholesalers—Durables (1.00)	Oil & Gas Extraction (1.18) Primary Metals (1.14) Textiles (1.14)	1.06
Average Beta	.91	1.00	1.07	

Perhaps the most surprising result in Exhibit 9.8 is the lack of an association between the level and variability of ROCE. Economic theory suggests that greater variability (risk) requires greater return. Thus, we expect the firms to align along a diagonal reflecting a positive association between the level and variability of ROCE, instead of a pattern with almost the same number of firms in each cell.

The data do indicate that firms with the lowest variability in their profitability have the smallest market beta (and vice versa). This relation makes intuitive sense. Changes in economic conditions do not significantly impact firms with low variability in their ROCEs. A regression of the average market beta of each firm in these 22 industries on the standard deviation of ROCE over the period 1980 to 1989 reveals a statistically significant relation at a .001 level of significance and an R-square of .08. Thus, the standard deviation of ROCE appears to explain only a small portion of the variability of market beta across firms. Research linking non-systematic and systematic risk continues to evolve.

Summary

The analysis of risk involves a comparison of (1) a firm's *ability* to generate or obtain cash with (2) the *need* for cash to pay obligations as they come due. This matching must occur with respect to both the amount and timing of cash flows. With the exception of the debt ratios, each of the risk ratios discussed in this chapter relates ability to needs as follows:

Short-Term Liquidity Risk	Ability	Needs
Current Ratio	Current Assets	Current Liabilities
Quick Ratio	Quick Assets	Current Liabilities
Operating Cash Flow to Current Liabilities Ratio	Cash Flow from Operations	Current Liabilities
Working Capital Activity Ratios	Receivable and Inventory Turnovers	Accounts Payable Turnover
Operating Cash Flow to Cash Interest Cost	Cash Flow from Operations before Cash Outflow for Interest and Income Taxes	Cash Outflow for Interest

Long-Term Solvency Risk		
Interest Coverage Ratio	Income before Interest and Taxes	Interest Expense
Operating Cash Flow to Total Liabilities Ratio	Cash Flow from Operations	Total Liabilities
Operating Cash Flow to Capital Expenditures Ratio	Cash Flow from Operations	Capital Expenditures

Because the ability to generate cash and the need for cash can differ depending on the time horizon, the analyst assesses both short-term liquidity risk and long-term solvency risk.

Problems

9.1 *Analyzing Short-Term Liquidity Risk.* Unlimited Creations, Inc. retails women's apparel in stores located in shopping centers throughout the United States. Customers charge their purchases using one of several bank credit cards or use an Unlimited Creations card that the firm first offered to customers in Year 5. The firm also instituted a new computer-based control system for inventories in Year 5 to provide more useful information for merchandise purchasing, timing of special sales, and similar inventory decisions. Exhibit 9.9 presents partial comparative balance sheets and Exhibit 9.10 presents comparative income statements for Unlimited Creations for its most recent three years.

    a. Compute the amount of cash flow provided by operations for Year 5, Year 6, and Year 7. Refer to Exhibit 2.7 for a worksheet format for computing the amount of operating cash flow.

    b. Compute the amount of the following financial statement ratios for Year 5, Year 6, and Year 7:

        (1)   Current ratio.

        (2)   Quick ratio.

        (3)   Accounts receivable turnover ratio.

        (4)   Inventory turnover ratio.

        (5)   Accounts payable turnover ratio.

        (6)   Operating cash flow to current liabilities ratio.

    c. How has the short-term liquidity risk of Unlimited Creations changed over the three years?

Exhibit 9.9
Comparative Partial Balance Sheets for Unlimited Creations

	December 31, Year 4	December 31, Year 5	December 31, Year 6	December 31, Year 7
Current Assets				
Cash..	$ 1,650	$ 1,430	$ 975	$ 925
Receivables.............................	6,270	7,650	9,485	11,950
Inventories..............................	11,545	13,245	15,485	17,795
Prepayments	850	1,020	1,225	1,470
Total Current Assets...........	$20,315	$23,345	$27,170	$32,140
Current Liabilities				
Accounts Payable....................	$13,901	$16,655	$20,739	$24,677
Bank Loans	400	400	500	900
Other Current Liabilities.......	3,940	4,730	5,670	6,800
Total Current Liabilities....	$18,241	$21,785	$26,909	$32,377

Exhibit 9.10
Comparative Income Statements for Unlimited Creations

	Year 5	Year 6	Year 7
Sales..	$65,000	$78,000	$93,600
Cost of Goods Sold	(53,300)	(63,200)	(74,880)
Selling and Administrative	(6,500)	(8,000)	(9,150)
Depreciation......................................	(1,500)	(1,800)	(2,200)
Interest..	(250)	(300)	(370)
Income Taxes.....................................	(1,380)	(1,880)	(2,800)
Net Income..	$ 2,070	$ 2,820	$ 4,200

9.2 *Analyzing Short-Term Liquidity Risk* (adapted from a problem by Leonard Morrissey). R. V. Supplies, Incorporated, founded in January Year 1, manufactures "Kaps." A "Kap" is a relatively low-cost camping unit attached to a pickup truck. Most units consist of an extruded aluminum frame and a fiberglass skin.

After a loss in its initial year, the company was barely profitable in Year 2 and Year 3. The firm realized more substantial profits in Years 4 and 5 as the financial statements in Exhibits 9.11 and 9.12 show.

However, in Year 6, ended just last month, the company suffered a loss of $13,400. Sales dropped from $424,000 in Year 5 to $247,400 in Year 6. The outlook for Year 7 is not encouraging. Potential buyers continue to shun pickup trucks in preference to more energy-efficient small foreign and domestic automobiles.

Exhibit 9.11
R.V. Suppliers, Incorporated, Balance Sheets (amounts in thousands)

	Dec. 31, Year 4	Dec. 31, Year 5	Dec. 31, Year 6
ASSETS			
Current Assets			
Cash	$ 14.0	$ 12.0	$ 5.2
Accounts Receivable	28.8	55.6	24.2
Inventories	54.0	85.6	81.0
Tax Refund Receivable	0	0	5.0
Prepayments	4.8	7.4	5.6
Total Current Assets	$101.6	$160.6	$121.0
Property, Plant, and Equipment—Net(Note 1)	30.2	73.4	72.2
Total Assets	$131.8	$234.0	$193.2
LIABILITIES AND SHAREHOLDERS' EQUITY			
Current Liabilities			
Bank Notes Payable	$ 10.0	$ 52.0	$ 70.0
Accounts Payable	31.6	53.4	17.4
Income Taxes Payable	5.8	7.0	0
Other Current Liabilities	4.2	6.8	4.4
Total Current Liabilities	$ 51.6	$119.2	$ 91.8
SHAREHOLDERS' EQUITY			
Capital Stock	$ 44.6	$ 44.6	$ 44.6
Retained Earnings	35.6	70.2	56.8
Total Shareholders' Equity	$ 80.2	$114.8	$101.4
Total Liabilities and Shareholders' Equity	$131.8	$234.0	$193.2

Note 1	**Year 4**	**Year 5**	**Year 6**
Acquisitions	$13.4	$48.4	$11.8
Depreciation Expense	(1.7)	(4.8)	(7.6)
Book Value and Sales Proceeds from Retirements	(.4)	(.4)	(5.4)
Net Change in Property, Plant, and Equipment	$11.3	$43.2	$(1.2)

Exhibit 9.12
R. V. Suppliers, Incorporated, Income Statements (amounts in thousands)

	Year 4	Year 5	Year 6
Net Sales	$266.4	$424.0	$247.4
Cost of Goods Sold	(191.4)	(314.6)	(210.6)
Gross Margin	$ 75.0	$109.4	$ 36.8
Operating Expenses[a]	(35.5)	(58.4)	(55.2)
Income (Loss) before Income Taxes	$ 39.5	$ 51.0	$(18.4)
Income Taxes	(12.3)	(16.4)	5.0
Net Income (Loss)	$ 27.2	$ 34.6	$(13.4)

[a]Includes depreciation expense of $1.7 in Year 4, $4.8 in Year 5, and $7.6 in Year 6.

   a. Complete worksheets for the preparation of a statement of cash flows for Year 5 and Year 6. Refer to Exhibit 2.7 for the format for these worksheets.
   b. Calculate the amount of the following short-term liquidity risk ratios for Year 5 and Year 6:

   (1) Current ratio (year end).
   (2) Quick ratio (year end).
   (3) Accounts receivable turnover.
   (4) Inventory turnover.
   (5) Accounts payable turnover.
   (6) Operating cash flow to current liabilities.

   c. How has the short-term liquidity risk of R.V. Suppliers changed over these two years?

9.3 *Analyzing Short-Term Liquidity Risk.* Collins Machine Tools, Inc., manufactures machine tool parts used in a variety of industries. Sales of machine tool parts are cyclical, derived from the demand for products sold by customers of Collins Machine Tools. Exhibit 9.13 presents partial comparative balance sheets

Exhibit 9.13
Partial Comparative Balance Sheets for Collins Machine Tools

	December 31, Year 6	December 31, Year 7	December 31, Year 8	December 31, Year 9
Current Assets				
Cash	$ 750	$ 540	$ 480	$ 320
Accounts Receivable	2,250	2,383	2,666	1,201
Inventories	2,175	2,571	2,957	1,432
Prepayments	120	140	160	110
Total Current Assets	$5,295	$5,634	$6,263	$3,063
Current Liabilities				
Accounts Payable	$2,300	$2,764	$3,070	$1,590
Other Current Liabilities	890	1,010	1,170	730
Total Current Liabilities	$3,190	$3,774	$4,240	$2,320

Exhibit 9.14
Comparative Income Statements for Collins Machine Tools

	Year 7	Year 8	Year 9
Sales	$13,900	$15,400	$11,600
Cost of Goods Sold	(9,730)	(10,780)	(8,120)
Selling and Administrative	(1,100)	(1,230)	(930)
Depreciation	(1,500)	(1,550)	(1,600)
Interest	(400)	(450)	(500)
Income Taxes	(470)	(555)	(180)
Net Income	$ 700	$ 835	$ 270

and Exhibit 9.14 presents comparative income statements of Collins Machine Tools for the most recent three years.

   a. Calculate the amount of cash flow from operations for Year 7, Year 8, and Year 9. Refer to Exhibit 2.7 for a format for this calculation.

   b. Compute the amount of each of the following ratios for Year 7, Year 8, and Year 9:

     (1) Current ratio.
     (2) Quick ratio.
     (3) Accounts receivable turnover.
     (4) Inventory turnover.
     (5) Accounts payable turnover.
     (6) Operating cash flow to current liabilities ratio.

   c. How has the short-term liquidity risk of Collins Machine Tools changed over the three years?

9.4 *Analyzing Long-Term Solvency Risk.* Northwest Airlines is a major U.S. airline, with operations centered in the Midwest, East Asia, and Northern Europe. During Year 6, it acquired Republic Airlines. Selected data taken or derived from its financial statements appear in Exhibit 9.15.

Exhibit 9.15
Selected Financial Data for Northwest Airlines
(amounts in millions)

Balance Sheet	December 31, Year 5	December 31, Year 6	December 31, Year 7
Long-Term Debt	$ 88	$ 809	$ 387
Capitalized Lease Obligations	406	578	562
Noncapitalized Operating Lease Obligations	387	1,277	1,876
Shareholders' Equity	947	1,106	1,523
Total Assets	2,320	4,219	4,323

Income Statement	Year 6	Year 7
Sales	$ 3,589	$ 5,142
Operating Expenses	(3,422)	(4,946)
Operating Income	$ 167	$ 196
Other Income (Net)	12	88
Interest Expense	(77)	(105)
Income Tax Expense	(25)	(76)
Net Income	$ 77	$ 103

Statement of Cash Flows	Year 6	Year 7
Cash Flow from Operations	$ 290	$ 496
Proceeds from Sale of Fixed Assets	410	566
Capital Expenditures[a]	669	693

[a]Excludes acquisition of Republic Airlines.

a. Compute the amounts of the following financial statement ratios for Year 6 and Year 7:

(1) Long-term debt ratio based on reported amounts (year end).
(2) Long-term debt ratio with operating leases capitalized (year end).
(3) Long-term debt to assets ratio based on reported amounts (year end).
(4) Long-term debt to assets ratio with operating leases capitalized (year end).
(5) Interest coverage ratio.
(6) Operating cash flow to total liabilities ratio based on reported amounts.
(7) Operating cash flow to total liabilities ratio with operating leases capitalized.
(8) Operating cash flow to capital expenditures ratio.
(9) Operating cash flow to capital expenditures (net of proceeds from sales of fixed assets) ratio.

b. How has the long-term solvency risk of Northwest Airlines changed over the period studied?

9.5 *Analyzing Long-Term Solvency Risk.* The Gillette Company manufactures a wide range of products for personal care. It was recently a target for an unfriendly takeover and took actions to defend itself. Selected data taken from its financial statements appear in Exhibit 9.16.

a. Compute the amount of the following long-term solvency ratios for Year 5 and Year 6:

(1) Long-term debt ratio (year end).
(2) Long-term debt to assets ratio (year end).
(3) Interest coverage ratio (based on reported data).
(4) Interest coverage ratio (excluding restructuring charge).
(5) Operating cash flow to total liabilities ratio.
(6) Operating cash flow to capital expenditures ratio.

b. How has the long-term solvency risk of the Gillette Company changed over the two years?

9.6 *Predicting Bankruptcy* (based on a problem by Norman Bartczak). Henderson Corporation manufactures processing equipment for the electronics, automotive, and appliance industries. Selected data from its financial statements for Year 3 to Year 7 appear in Exhibit 9.17.

a. Prepare a Z-score analysis for Henderson Corporation for each of the five years.

b. Identify the major contributing factors for changes in the Z-scores for Henderson Corporation over the five years.

c. Based only on the information presented and the analysis in parts (*a*) and (*b*), do you think Henderson Corporation can avoid bankruptcy?

Exhibit 9.16
Selected Financial Data for the Gillette Company (amounts in millions)

Balance Sheet	December 31, Year 4	December 31, Year 5	December 31, Year 6
Bank Loans...	$ 216.0	$ 414.9	$ 199.7
Current Operating Liabilities	430.3	486.1	701.2
Long-Term Debt.......................................	443.1	435.9	915.2
Other Noncurrent Liabilities..................	144.2	189.4	262.8
Total Liabilities.................................	$1,233.6	$1,526.3	$2,078.7
Contributed Capital...............................	$ 87.7	$ 90.5	$ 245.9
Retained Earnings..................................	934.8	1,014.4	944.3
Cumulative Translation Adjustment.......	(231.5)	(206.4)	(161.6)
Treasury Stock	(.2)	(.2)	(567.8)
Total Shareholders' Equity	$ 790.8	$ 898.3	$ 460.8
Total Equities	$2,024.4	$2,424.6	$2,539.5

Income Statement	Year 5	Year 6
Sales...	$2,400.0	$2,818.3
Cost of Goods Sold	(992.1)	(1,183.8)
Selling and Administrative	(1,027.5)	(1,223.7)
Interest..	(88.5)	(85.2)
Other (Net)	(19.5)	(69.1)
Restructuring Charge (Pretax)	—	(205.0)
Income Taxes...	(112.5)	(35.7)
Net Income..	$ 159.9	$ 15.8

Statement of Cash Flows		
Cash Flow from Operations	$ 218.4	$ 282.7
Capital Expenditures..............................	156.6	198.6

Exhibit 9.17
Selected Data for Henderson Corporation

Balance Sheet at End of Year	Year 3	Year 4	Year 5	Year 6	Year 7
Current Assets	$ 6,965	$ 9,109	$13,296	$15,295	$10,256
Total Assets...	14,022	14,853	21,299	25,609	19,221
Current Liabilities.................................	4,229	3,497	5,331	3,635	7,400
Long-Term Debt....................................	788	2,223	4,705	9,383	4,168
Retained Earnings (Deficit)...................	(520)	(136)	2,070	2,880	(2,520)
Shareholders' Equity.............................	8,420	8,804	11,010	12,414	7,021
Common Shares Outstanding................	4,234	4,234	4,234	4,239	4,242
Income Statement for Year					
Sales..	$17,414	$24,590	$38,548	$45,666	$23,780
Earnings before Interest and Taxes (Loss)	(596)	1,408	3,560	3,378	(5,134)
Market Price Information					
Market Price per Common Share at Year End	$1.875	$3.50	$2.50	$.875	$.75

9.7 *Predicting Bankruptcy.* CCB Corporation produces steel used in the automotive, appliance, and construction industries. Selected data from its financial statements for the most recent four years appear in Exhibit 9.18.

    a. Prepare a Z-score analysis for CCB Corporation for each of the last four years.

    b. Identify the major contributing factors for changes in the Z-scores for CCB Corporation over the four years.

Exhibit 9.18
Selected Data for CCB Corporation
(amounts in millions except per share amounts)

	Year 2	Year 3	Year 4	Year 5
Current Assets	$2,030	$2,208	$1,796	$1,848
Total Assets	4,030	4,333	4,023	4,406
Current Liablities	1,227	1,210	977	1,310
Total Liabilities	3,211	3,047	2,907	3,264
Retained Earnings	318	662	484	283
Shareholders' Equity	819	1,285	1,116	1,142
Common Shares Outstanding	36	48	49	55
Sales	8,010	7,511	4,777	4,578
Earnings (Loss) before Interest and Taxes	302	623	(165)	(97)
Market Price per Common Share	19.375	16.375	11.375	18.375

9.8 *Preparing and Interpreting the Statement of Cash Flows and Risk Ratios.* Refer to the information for Fin Stat Corporation presented in Problems 7.10 and 8.5.

    a. Complete worksheets for the preparation of a statement of cash flows for Year 7, Year 8, and Year 9. Refer to Exhibit 2.7 for the format for these worksheets. Depreciation expense was $25 in Year 7, $31 in Year 8, and $49 in Year 9.

    b. Calculate the following financial statement ratios for Fin Stat Corporation for each year:

        (1) Current ratio.
        (2) Quick ratio.
        (3) Operating cash flow to current liabilities ratio.
        (4) Accounts payable turnover ratio.
        (5) Interest coverage ratio.
        (6) Operating cash flow to total liabilities ratio.
        (7) Operating cash flow to capital expenditures ratio.

    c. How has the short-term liquidity risk of Fin Stat Corporation changed over the three-year period?

    d. How has the long-term solvency risk of Fin Stat Corporation changed over the three-year period?

9.9 *Preparing and Interpreting the Statement of Cash Flows and Risk Ratios.*
Refer to the information for Mercer Corporation presented in Problems 7.12 and 8.7.

   a. Complete worksheets for the preparation of a statement of cash flows for Year 7 and Year 8. Refer to Exhibit 2.7 for the format for these worksheets.

   b. Calculate the following financial statement ratios for Mercer Corporation for Year 7 and Year 8:

     (1) Current ratio.
     (2) Quick ratio.
     (3) Operating cash flow to current liabilities ratio.
     (4) Accounts payable turnover ratio.
     (5) Interest coverage ratio.
     (6) Operating cash flow to total liabilities ratio.
     (7) Operating cash flow to capital expenditures ratio.

   c. Assess the short-term liquidity risk of Mercer Corporation.
   d. Assess the long-term solvency risk of Mercer Corporation.

9.10 *Calculating and Interpreting Risk Ratios.* Refer to the information for General Mills in Problems 7.13 and 8.8. Short-term liquidity and long-term solvency risk ratios for Year 6 and Year 7 appear in Exhibit 9.19.

   a. Calculate the amounts of these ratios for Year 8.
   b. Assess the short-term liquidity risk of General Mills.
   c. Assess the long-term solvency risk of General Mills.

9.11 *Calculating and Interpreting Risk Ratios.* Refer to the information for Digital Equipment Corporation (DEC) in Problems 7.14 and 8.9. Short-term liquidity and long-term solvency risk ratios for Year 7 and Year 8 appear in Exhibit 9.20.

Exhibit 9.19
Risk Ratios for General Mills

Short-Term Liquidity	**Year 6**	**Year 7**
Current Ratio (End of Year)	1.05	1.02
Quick Ratio (End of Year)	.54	.45
Operating Cash Flow to Current Liabilities Ratio	47.3%	51.0%
Accounts Payable Turnover Ratio	6.1	6.4
Long-Term Solvency		
Long-Term Debt Ratio (End of Year)	40.2%	28.1%
Debt/Equity Ratio (End of Year)	67.2%	39.0%
Long-Term Debt to Assets Ratio (End of Year)	22.0%	12.1%
Interest Coverage Ratio	6.8	10.4
Operating Cash Flow to Total Liabilities Ratio	28.3%	28.4%
Operating Cash Flow to Capital Expenditures Ratio	1.8	1.3
Segment Cash Flow to Capital Expenditures Ratio		
Consumer Foods	2.3	3.0
Restaurants	1.6	.9

Exhibit 9.20
Risk Ratios for Digital Equipment Corporation

Short-Term Liquidity	**Year 7**	**Year 8**
Current Ratio (End of Year)..	3.40	2.87
Quick Ratio (End of Year)..	2.43	1.97
Operating Cash Flow to Current Liabilities Ratio	113.9%	80.2%
Days Receivables...	82	78
Days Inventories..	191	182
Days Payables	45	55

Long-Term Solvency		
Long-Term Debt Ratio (End of Year)	1.69%	1.79%
Debt/Equity Ratio (End of Year)..	1.72%	1.7%
Long-Term Debt to Assets Ratio (End of Year)......................	3.2%	1.2%
Interest Coverage Ratio...	17.6	46.8
Operating Cash Flow to Total Liabilities Ratio......................	93.1%	77.1%
Operating Cash Flow to Capital Expenditures Ratio	2.2	1.1

a. Calculate the amounts of these ratios for Year 9.
b. Assess the short-term liquidity risk of DEC.
c. Assess the long-term solvency risk of DEC.

9.12 *Interpreting Risk Ratios.* Refer to the data for Boyd Corporation in Problems 7.15 and 8.10.
a. Evaluate the changes in Boyd Corporation's short-term liquidity risk over the three-year period.
b. Evaluate the changes in Boyd Corporation's long-term solvency risk over the three-year period.

9.13 *Relating Systematic Risk to Nonsystematic Risk.* Exhibit 9.21 presents the average market beta for six industries and the average of selected financial statement ratios for a recent ten-year period. The six industries are:

1. Food processing.

2. Oil exploration and drilling.

3. Publishing.

4. Regulated utilities.

5. Trucking.

6. Wholesalers of equipment.

a. Use whatever clues you can to match the industries in Exhibit 9.21 with the six industries above. State your reasoning.
b. What general relationships do you observe between the level of market beta and the financial statement ratios presented in Exhibit 9.21?

Exhibit 9.21
Selected Data for Six Industries

Industry	Market Beta	Fixed Assets/ Total Assets	Operating Cash Flow/Capital Expenditures	ROA	Capital Structure Leverage	ROCE	Standard Deviation ROCE
A	.58	.82	.85	7.0%	3.44	14.9%	5.6
B	.78	.38	1.54	8.5%	2.56	15.1%	11.2
C	1.04	.35	1.97	11.5%	2.05	18.4%	11.9
D	1.22	.58	.74	5.6%	3.28	9.7%	14.2
E	1.39	.70	.75	5.1%	3.10	4.3%	33.4
F	1.48	.18	2.11	6.3%	2.40	8.7%	15.0

9.14 *Interpreting Profitability and Risk Ratios.* Exhibit 9.22 presents financial statement ratios for Abbott Corporation for Year 1, Year 2, and Year 3.
   a. What is the likely explanation for the decreasing rate of return on assets?
   b. What is the likely explanation for the increasing rate of return on common shareholders' equity?
   c. What is the likely explanation for the behavior of the current and quick ratios?
   d. What is the likely explanation for the decreases in the two cash flows from operations to liabilities ratios?

Exhibit 9.22
Abbott Corporation Ratio Analysis

	Year 1	Year 2	Year 3
Rate of Return on Assets..	10.0%	9.6%	9.2%
Profit Margin (before Interest and Related Tax Effects)....	6.0%	6.1%	6.1%
Total Assets Turnover	1.7	1.6	1.5
Cost of Goods Sold/Sales	62.5%	62.3%	62.6%
Selling Expenses/Sales..	10.3%	10.2%	10.4%
Interest Expense/Sales...	1.5%	2.0%	2.5%
Accounts Receivable Turnover	4.3	4.3	4.2
Inventory Turnover..	3.2	3.4	3.6
Plant Asset Turnover	.8	.7	.6
Rate of Return on Common Shareholders' Equity............	14.0%	14.2%	14.5%
Common Earnings Leverage..	85.0%	80.3%	75.4%
Capital Structure Leverage..	1.6	1.8	2.1
Current Ratio	1.4	1.3	1.2
Quick Ratio	1.0	.9	1.0
Cash Flow from Operations to Current Liabilities	38.2%	37.3%	36.4%
Long-Term Debt Ratio...	27.2%	33.8%	43.3%
Debt/Equity Ratio	37.5%	44.4%	52.4%
Cash Flow from Operations to Total Liabilities.................	16.3%	13.4%	11.1%
Interest Coverage Ratio	6.7	5.1	4.1

Case 9.1:
Fly-By-Night International Group*

Douglas C. Mather, founder, chairman, and chief executive of Fly-By-Night International Group (FBN), lived the fast-paced, risk-seeking life that he tried to inject into his company. Flying the company's Learjets, he logged 28 world speed records. Once he throttled a company plane to the top of Mount Everest in 3 ½ minutes.

These activities seemed perfectly appropriate at the time. Mather was a Navy fighter pilot in Vietnam and then flew commercial airliners. In the mid-1970s, he started FBN as a pilot training school. With the defense buildup beginning in the early 1980s, Mather branched out into government contracting. He equipped the company's Learjets with radar jammers and other sophisticated electronic devices to mimic enemy aircraft. He then contracted his "rent-an-enemy" fleet to the Navy and Air Force for use in fighter-pilot training. The Pentagon liked the idea and FBN's revenues grew to $55 million in the fiscal year ending April 30, 1992. Its common stock, issued to the public in 1987 at $8.50 a share, reached a high of $16.50 in mid-1991. Mather and FBN received glowing writeups in *Business Week* and *Fortune*.

In mid-1992, however, FBN began a rapid descent. Although still growing rapidly, its cash flow was inadequate to service its debt. According to Mather, he was "just dumbfounded. There was never an inkling of a problem with cash."

In the fall of 1992, the Board of Directors withdrew the company's financial statements for the year ending April 30, 1992, stating that there appeared to be material misstatements that needed investigation. In December 1992, Mather was asked to step aside as manager and director of the company pending completion of an investigation of certain transactions between Mather and the company. On December 29, 1992, NASDAQ (over-the-counter stock market) discontinued quoting the company's common shares. In February 1993, the Board of Directors, following its investigation, terminated Mather's employment and membership on the Board.

Exhibits 1 to 3 present the financial statements and related notes of FBN for the five years ending April 1988 through April 1992. The financial statements for 1988 to 1990 use the amounts as originally reported for each year. The amounts reported on the statement of cash flows for 1988 (for example, the change in accounts receivable) do not precisely reconcile to the amounts on the balance sheet at the beginning and end of the year because certain items classified as relating to continuing operations on the balance sheet at the beginning of 1988 were reclassified as relating to discontinued operations on the balance sheet at the end of 1988. The financial statements for 1991 and 1992 represent the restated financial statements for those years after the Board of Directors completed its investigation of suspected material misstatements that caused it to withdraw the originally issued financial statements for fiscal 1992.

REQUIRED

Study these financial statements and notes and respond to the following questions:

---

*The author gratefully acknowledges the assistance of Lawrence C. Calcano in the preparation of this case.

a. What evidence can you observe from analyzing the financial statements that might signal the cash flow problems experienced in mid-1992?

b. Can FBN avoid bankruptcy during 1993? What changes in either the design or implementation of FBN's strategy would you recommend?

Exhibit 1

Fly-By-Night International Group Comparative Balance Sheet
(amounts in thousands)

	April 30					
	1987	**1988**	**1989**	**1990**	**1991**	**1992**
Current Assets						
Cash	$ 192	$ 753	$ 142	$ 313	$ 583	$ 159
Notes Receivable	—	—	1,000	—	—	—
Accounts Receivable	2,036	1,083	1,490	2,675	4,874	6,545
Inventories	686	642	602	1,552	2,514	5,106
Prepayments	387	303	57	469	829	665
Net Assets of Discontinued Businesses	—	1,926	—	—	—	—
Total Current Assets	$ 3,301	$ 4,707	$ 3,291	$ 5,009	$ 8,800	$ 12,475
Property, Plant, and Equipment	$17,471	$37,250	$17,809	$24,039	$76,975	$106,529
Less Accumulated Depreciation	(2,593)	(4,462)	(4,288)	(5,713)	(8,843)	(17,231)
Net	$14,878	$32,788	$13,521	$18,326	$68,132	$ 89,298
Other Assets	$ 1,278	$ 1,566	$1,112	$ 641	$ 665	$ 470
Total Assets	$19,457	$39,061	$17,924	$23,976	$77,597	$102,243
Current Liabilities						
Accounts Payable	$ 1,436	$ 2,285	$ 939	$ 993	$ 6,279	$ 12,428
Notes Payable	—	4,766	1,021	140	945	—
Current Portion of Long-Term Debt	1,239	2,774	1,104	1,789	7,018	60,590
Other Current Liabilities	435	1,845	1,310	2,423	12,124	12,903
Total Current Liabilities	$ 3,110	$11,670	$ 4,374	$ 5,345	$26,366	$85,921
Noncurrent Liabilities						
Long-Term Debt	9,060	20,041	6,738	9,804	41,021	—
Deferred Income Taxes	1,412	1,322	—	803	900	—
Other Noncurrent Liabilities	—	248	—	226	—	—
Total Liabilities	$13,582	$33,281	$11,112	$16,178	$68,287	$85,921
Shareholders' Equity						
Common Stock	$ 20	$ 20	$ 20	$ 21	$ 22	$ 34
Additional Paid-in Capital	3,611	3,611	4,323	4,569	5,685	16,516
Retained Earnings	2,244	2,149	2,469	3,208	3,802	(29)
Treasury Stock	—	—	—	—	(199)	(199)
Total Shareholders' Equity	$ 5,875	$ 5,780	$ 6,812	$ 7,798	$ 9,310	$ 16,322
Total Liabilities and Shareholders' Equity	$19,457	$39,061	$17,924	$23,976	$77,597	$102,243

Exhibit 2

**Fly-By-Night International Group Comparative Income Statement
for the Year Ended April 30 (amounts in thousands)**

Continuing Operations	1988	1989	1990	1991	1992
Sales	$31,992	$19,266	$20,758	$36,597	$54,988
Expenses					
Cost of Services	22,003	9,087	12,544	26,444	38,187
Selling and Administrative	4,236	2,989	3,467	3,020	5,880
Depreciation	3,003	2,798	1,703	3,150	9,810
Interest	2,600	2,743	1,101	3,058	5,841
Income Taxes	74	671	803	379	(900)
Total Expenses	$31,916	$18,288	$19,618	$36,051	$58,818
Income (Loss)— Continuing Operations	$ 76	$ 978	$ 1,140	$ 546	$ (3,830)
Income— Discontinued Operations	(171)	(659)	(400)	47	—
Net Income (Loss)	$ (95)	$ 319	$ 740	$ 593	$ (3,830)

NOTES TO FINANCIAL STATEMENTS

1.   Summary of Significant Accounting Policies

Consolidation.   The consolidated financial statements include the accounts of the Company and its wholly owned subsidiaries. The Company uses the equity method for subsidiaries not majority owned (50 percent or less) and eliminates significant intercompany transactions and balances.

Inventories.   Inventories, which consist of aircraft fuel, spare parts, and supplies, appear at lower of FIFO cost or market.

Property and Equipment.   Property and equipment appear at acquisition cost. The Company capitalizes major inspections, renewals, and improvements, while it expenses replacements, maintenance, and repairs which do not improve or extend the life of the respective assets. The Company computes depreciation of property and equipment using the straight-line method.

Contract Income Recognition.   Contractual specifications (that is, revenue rates, reimbursement terms, functional considerations) vary among contracts; accordingly, the Company recognizes guaranteed contract income (guaranteed revenue less related direct costs) either as it logs flight hours or on a straight-line monthly basis over the contract year, whichever method better reflects the economics of the contract. The Company recognizes income from discretionary hours flown in excess of the minimum guaranteed amount each month as it logs such discretionary hours.

Exhibit 3

Fly-By-Night International Group Comparative Statements of Cash Flows for the Year Ended April 30 (amounts in thousands)

Operations	1988	1989	1990	1991	1992
Income—Continuing Operations	$ 76	$ 978	$ 1,140	$ 546	$ (3,830)
Depreciation	3,003	2,798	1,703	3,150	9,810
Other Adjustments	74	671	1,119	1,817	1,074
Working Capital from Operations	$ 3,153	$ 4,447	$ 3,962	$ 5,513	$ 7,054
Changes in Working Capital					
(Inc.) Decr. in Receivables	403	(407)	(1,185)	(2,199)	(1,671)
(Inc.) Decr. in Inventories	19	40	(950)	(962)	(2,592)
(Inc.) Decr. in Prepayments	36	246	(412)	(360)	164
Inc. (Decr.) in Accounts Payable	359	(1,346)	54	5,286	6,149
Inc. (Decr.) in Other Current Liabilities	596	(535)	1,113	9,701	779
Cash Flow from Continuing Operations	$ 4,566	$ 2,445	$ 2,582	$ 16,979	$ 9,883
Cash Flow from Discontinued Operations	(335)	(752)	(472)	(77)	—
Net Cash Flow from Operations	$ 4,231	$ 1,693	$ 2,110	$ 16,902	$ 9,883
Investing					
Sale of Property, Plant, and Equipment	$ 12	$ 18,387	$ 119	$ 3	$ 259
Acquisition of Property, Plant, and Equipment	(20,953)	(2,424)	(6,573)	(52,960)	(33,035)
Other	30	(679)	1,017	78	(1,484)
Net Cash Flow from Investing	$(20,911)	$ 15,284	$ (5,437)	$(52,879)	$(34,260)
Financing					
Increase in Short-Term Borrowing	$ 4,766	$ —	$ —	$ 805	$ —
Increase in Long-Term Borrowing	14,739	5,869	5,397	42,152	43,279
Issue of Common Stock	—	—	428	191	12,266
Decrease in Short-Term Borrowing	—	(3,745)	(881)	—	(945)
Decrease in Long-Term Borrowing	(2,264)	(19,712)	(1,647)	(7,024)	(30,522)
Acquisition of Common Stock	—	—	—	(198)	—
Other	—	—	201	321	(125)
Net Cash Flow from Financing	$ 17,241	$(17,588)	$ 3,498	$ 36,247	$ 23,953
Change in Cash	$ 561	$ (611)	$ 171	$ 270	$ (424)

Income Taxes. The Company recognizes deferred income taxes for timing differences between financial and tax reporting amounts.

2. Transactions with Major Customers

The Company provides contract flight services to three major customers: the U.S. Air Force, U.S. Navy, and the Federal Reserve Bank System. These contracts have termination dates in 1994 or 1995. Revenues from all government contracts as a percentage of total revenues were as follows: 1988, 31 percent; 1989, 68 percent; 1990, 73 percent; 1991, 72 percent; 1992, 62 percent.

3. Segment Data

During 1988, the Company operated in five business segments as follows:

Flight Operations—Business. Provides combat readiness training to the military and nightly transfer of negotiable instruments for the Federal Reserve Bank System, both under multi-year contracts.

Flight Operations—Transport. Provides charter transport services to a variety of customers.

Fixed Base Operations. Provides ground support operations (fuel, maintenance) to commercial airlines at several major airports.

Education and Training. Provides training for nonmilitary pilots.

Aircraft Sales and Leasing. Acquires aircraft that the Company then either resells or leases to various firms.

The Company discontinued the Flight Operations—Transport and Education and Training segments in 1989. It sold most of the assets of the Aircraft Sales and Leasing segment in 1989.

Segment revenue, operating profit, and asset data for the various segments appear below (amounts in thousands):

	April 30				
	1988	**1989**	**1990**	**1991**	**1992**
Revenues					
Flight Operations—Business	$10,803	$11,236	$16,026	$31,297	$ 44,062
Flight Operations—Transport....	13,805	—	—	—	—
Fixed Base Operations	3,647	3,911	4,651	4,832	9,597
Education and Training..............	542	—	—	—	—
Aircraft Sales and Leasing	3,195	4,119	81	468	1,329
Total	$31,992	$19,266	$20,758	$36,597	$ 54,988
Operating Profit					
Flight Operations—Business	$ 849	$ 2,463	$ 3,455	$ 4,863	$ 5,707
Flight Operations—Transport....	(994)	—	—	—	—
Fixed Base Operations	332	174	1,038	1,362	(2,041)
Education and Training..............	12	—	—	—	—
Aircraft Sales and Leasing	2,726[a]	1,217[b]	(15)	378	1,175
Total	$ 2,925	$ 3,854	$ 4,478	$ 6,603	$ 4,841
Assets					
Flight Operations—Business	$13,684	$11,130	$17,738	$64,162	$ 85,263
Flight Operations—Transport....	1,771	—	—	—	—
Fixed Base Operations	4,784	5,011	5,754	13,209	16,544
Education and Training..............	1,789	—	—	—	—
Aircraft Sales and Leasing	18,524	1,262	438	226	436
Total	$40,552	$17,403	$23,930	$77,597	$102,243

[a]Includes a gain of $2.6 million on the sale of aircraft.

[b]Includes a gain of $1.2 million on the sale of aircraft.

4. Discontinued Operations

Income from discontinued operations consists of the following (amounts in thousands):

1988
Loss from Operations of Charter Tour Business,
net of income tax benefits of $164 .... $(171)

1989
Loss from Operations of Flight Operations—
Transport ($1,261) and Education and Training ($172)
segments, net of income tax benefits of $685...................... $(748)
Gain on Disposal of Education and Training Business,
net of income taxes of $85... 89
Total .... $(659)

1990
Loss from Write-off of Airline Operations Certificates
in Flight Operations—Transport Business........................... $(400)

1991
Income from Operations of Flight Operations—
Transport ($78), net of income taxes of $31 .... $ 47

5. Related Party Transactions

On April 30, 1989, the Company sold most of the net assets of the Aircraft Sales and Leasing segment to Interlease, Inc., a Georgia corporation wholly owned by the Company's majority stockholder, whose personal holdings represented at that time approximately 75 percent of the Company.

Under the terms of the sale, the sales price was $1,368,000, of which the buyer paid $368,000 in cash and gave a promissory note for the remaining $1,000,000. The Company treated the proceeds received in excess of the book value of the net assets sold of $712,367 as a capital contribution due to the related party nature of the transaction. FBN originally acquired the assets of the Aircraft Sales and Leasing segment during 1988.

On September 29, 1992, the Company's Board of Directors established a Transaction Committee to examine certain transactions between the Company and Douglas Mather, its Chairman, President and majority stockholder. These transactions appear below:

Eastwind Transaction. On April 27, 1992, the Company acquired four Eastwind aircraft from a German company. FBN subsequently sold these aircraft to Transreco, a corporation owned by Douglas Mather, for a profit of $1,600,000. In late September and early October, Transreco sold these four aircraft at a profit of $780,000 to unaffiliated third parties. The Transactions Committee determined that none of the officers or directors of the Company were aware of the Eastwind transaction until late September 1992.

ESOP Transaction. On February 28, 1992, the Company's Employee Stock Ownership Plan (ESOP) acquired 100,000 shares of the Company's common stock from Mr. Mather at $14.25 per share. FBN financed the purchase. The

ESOP gave the Company a $1,425,000 unsecured demand note. To complete the transaction, the Company cancelled a $1,000,000 promissory note from Mr. Mather and paid the remaining $425,000 in cash. The Transaction Committee determined that the Board of Directors did not authorize the $1,425,000 loan to the ESOP, the cancellation of Mather's $1,000,000 note, or the payment of $425,000 in cash.

Certain Loans to Mr. Mather. In early September 1991, the Board of Directors authorized a $1,000,000 loan to Mr. Mather at the Company's cost of borrowing plus 1/8 percent. On September 19, 1991, Mr. Mather tendered a $1,000,000 check to the Company in repayment of the loan. On September 22, 1991, at Mr. Mather's direction, the Company made an additional $1,000,000 loan to him, the proceeds of which Mather apparently used to cover his check in repayment of the first $1,000,000 loan. The Transaction Committee concluded that the Board of Directors did not authorize the September 22, 1991, loan to Mr. Mather nor was any director aware of the loan at the time other than Mr. Mather. The Company's 1991 Proxy Statement, dated September 27, 1991, incorrectly stated that "as of September 19, 1991, Mr. Mather had repaid the principal amount of his indebtedness to the Company." Mr. Mather's $1,000,000 loan remained outstanding until it was cancelled in connection with the ESOP Transaction discussed above.

On December 12, 1992, the Company announced that Mr. Mather had agreed to step aside as Chairman and a Director and take no part in the management of the Company pending resolution of the matters presented to the Board by the Transactions Committee. On February 13, 1993, the Company announced that it had entered into a settlement agreement with Mr. Mather and Transreco resolving certain of the issues addressed by the Transactions Committee. Pursuant to the agreement, the Company will receive $211,000, the bonus paid to Mr. Mather for fiscal 1992, and $780,000, the gain recognized by Transreco on the sale of the Eastwind aircraft. Also pursuant to the settlement, Mr. Mather will resign all positions with the Company and waive his rights under his employment agreement to any future compensation or benefits to which he might otherwise have a claim.

6. Long-Term Debt

Long-term debt consists of the following (amounts in thousands):

	April 30				
	1988	**1989**	**1990**	**1991**	**1992**
Notes Payable to Banks					
Variable Rate	$ 3,497	$ 2,504	$ 2,086	$30,495	$ 44,702
Fixed Rate	1,228	3,562	6,292	14,679	13,555
Notes Payable to Finance Companies					
Variable Rate	10,808	1,667	1,320	—	—
Fixed Rate	325	—	—	—	—
Capitalized Lease Obligations	5,297	70	1,295	2,865	2,333
Other	1,660	39	600	—	—
Total	$22,815	$ 7,842	$11,593	$48,039	$ 60,590
Less Current Portion	(2,774)	(1,104)	(1,789)	(7,018)	(60,590)
Net	$20,041	$ 6,738	$ 9,804	$41,021	$

Substantially all of the Company's property, plant, and equipment serves as collateral for this debt. The borrowings from bank and finance companies contain restrictive covenants, the most restrictive of which appear below:

	1988	1989	1990	1991	1992
Liabilities/Tangible Net Assets	≤ 6.7	≤ 5.5	≤ 4.2	≤ 3.0	≤ 2.5
Tangible Net Assets........................	≥ 5,100	≥ 5,300	≥ 5,400	≥ 5,800	≥ 20,000
Working Capital............................					≥ 5,000
Interest Coverage Ratio................					≥ 1.15

As of April 30, 1992, the Company is in default of its debt covenants. It is also in default with respect to covenants underlying its capitalized lease obligations. As a result, lenders have the right to accelerate repayment of their loans. Accordingly, the Company has classified all of its long-term debt as a current liability.

The Company has entered into operating leases for aircraft and other equipment. The estimated present value of the minimum lease payments under these operating leases as of April 30 of each year is

1988	$4,083
1989	3,971
1990	3,594
1991	3,142
1992	2,706

7.   Income Taxes

Income tax expense consists of the following:

	Year Ended April 30				
	1988	1989	1990	1991	1992
Current					
Federal....................................	$ —	$ —	$ —	$ —	$ —
State..	—	—	—	—	—
Deferred					
Federal....................................	$ (85)	$ 67	$ 685	$ 380	$(845)
State..	(5)	4	118	30	(55)
Total....................................	$ (90)	$ 71	$ 803	$ 410	$(900)

The cumulative tax loss and tax credit carryovers as of April 30 of each year are as follows:

	Tax Loss	Tax Credit
1988	$ 4,500	$750
1989	2,100	450
1990	1,400	300
1991	5,200	280
1992	10,300	250

The deferred tax provision results from timing differences in the recognition of revenues and expenses for income tax and financial reporting. The sources and amounts of these differences for each year are as follows:

	1988	1989	1990	1991	1992
Depreciation	$ 778	$(770)	$ 336	$ 503	$ —
Aircraft Modification Costs	703	982	382	1,218	—
Net Operating Losses	(1,729)	—	290	(1,384)	(900)
Other	158	(141)	(205)	93	—
	$ (90)	$ 71	$ 803	$ 430	$(900)

A reconciliation of the effective tax rate with the statutory tax rate is as follows:

	1988	1989	1990	1991	1992
Federal Taxes at Statutory Rate	(40.0%)	34.0%	34.0%	34.0%	(34.0%)
State Income Taxes	(3.0)	3.0	3.0	3.0	(2.5)
Effect of Net Operating Loss and Investment Credits	—	(29.9)	(7.2)	—	16.5
Other	(6.0)	11.1	22.2	3.9	1.0
	(49.0%)	18.2%	52.0%	40.9%	(19.0%)

8. Market Price Information

The Company's common stock trades on the NASDAQ National Market System under the symbol FBN. Trading in the Company common stock commenced on January 10, 1988. High and low bid prices during each fiscal year are as follows:

	High Bid	Low Bid
1988	$ 5.25	$3.25
1989	$ 4.63	$3.00
1990	$11.25	$3.25
1991	$14.63	$6.25
1992	$16.50	$9.50

On December 29, 1992, the Company announced that the NASDAQ decided to discontinue quoting the Company's common stock because of the Company's failure to comply with NASDAQ's filing requirements.

Ownership of the Company's stock at various dates appears below:

	April 30				
	1988	1989	1990	1991	1992
Douglas Mather	75%	75%	72%	68%	42%
Public	25	25	24	23	48
Company ESOP	—	—	4	9	10
	100%	100%	100%	100%	100%
Common Shares Outstanding (000's)	2,000.0	2,000.0	2,095.0	2,222.8	3,357.5

Case 9.2:
Kroger Company*

The Kroger Company (Kroger) operates one of the largest supermarket chains in the United States. During the fall of 1988, Kroger became the target of unfriendly takeover bids by the Haft family and Kohlberg, Kravis, Roberts and Company. Prior to these bids, Kroger's common shares traded for $34 per share. The bidding was started at a price of $55 per share and increased to $64 per share. To defend itself against a takeover, Kroger issued a package of senior and subordinated debt totaling $3.6 billion and used the proceeds to partially fund a special dividend of $3.9 billion. The special dividend included cash of $40 per share (total of $3.2 billion) and a senior subordinated, increasing rate debenture with a face value of $12.50 and a market value of $8.69 per share (total of $695 million).

This case analyzes the factors that made Kroger an attractive buyout candidate in 1988 and the subsequent effect of the special dividend on its profitability and risk. Exhibits 1, 2, and 3 present Kroger's financial statements for its fiscal years ending December 1986 to December 1990. Several unusual items affect these financial statements:

1. Disposal of drug store operations: Kroger sold its drug store operations in 1986 and included a loss in discontinued operations for that year.

2. Restructuring provisions: Kroger made two major provisions for restructuring its business. It made a pretax provision of $164 million in 1986 to downsize corporate headquarters staff and close 100 stores and related manufacturing operations. Kroger made a pretax provision of $195 million in 1988 to cover a portion of the cost of its financial restructuring and special dividend.

3. Change in accounting for income taxes: Kroger adopted the liability method of accounting for deferred income taxes in 1987. Because income tax rates declined as a result of the Tax Reform Act of 1986, Kroger's deferred tax liability overstated the amount of taxes it expected to pay when timing differences reversed. Kroger reduced its deferred tax liability and included a special credit in earnings of $63 million in 1987.

4. Write off of deferred restructuring costs: Kroger originally capitalized as assets certain debt issue costs incurred in connection with its corporate restructuring in 1988. Kroger later refinanced some of the debt in 1989 and wrote off deferred costs totaling $56 million in 1989 and $1 million in 1990.

5. Operating lease commitments: Kroger leases a substantial portion of its stores under operating lease arrangements. The present value of these operating lease commitments when discounted at 10 percent appear below (in millions):

1985	$1,785	1987	$1,823	1989	$1,692
1986	$1,693	1988	$1,732	1990	$2,936

*The author gratefully acknowledges the assistance of Yannis Vasatis in the preparation of this Case.

Exhibit 1

Kroger Company

Comparative Income Statements

(in millions)

	1986	1987	1988	1989	1990
Sales	$ 17,123	$ 17,660	$ 19,053	$ 19,104	$ 20,261
Other Revenues and Gains	13	11	10	16	6
Cost of Goods Sold	(13,163)	(13,696)	(14,824)	(14,846)	(15,670)
Sell. and Admin. Expense	(3,609)	(3,553)	(3,784)	(3,652)	(3,918)
Restructuring (Charges) Credits[a]	(164)	8	(195)	18	27
Interest Expense	(104)	(107)	(208)	(649)	(564)
Income Tax Expense[a]	(40)	(140)	(17)	(7)	(59)
Income from Contin. Ops.	$ 56	$ 183	$ 35	$ (16)	$ 83
Income from Discont. Ops.	(4)[b]	0	0	0	0
Extra. Gains (Losses)	0	0	0	(56)[d]	(1)[d]
Changes in Acct. Princ.	0	63[c]	0	0	0
Preferred Stock Dividend	(3)	(6)	(16)	(2)	0
Net Income to Common	$ 49	$ 240	$ 19	$ (74)	$ 82
Average Number of Shares Outstanding	86.9	80.4	79.3	81.6	86.6

[a]Includes restructuring changes and credits (and related tax effects) as follows:

1986:	Provision for downsizing corporate overhead staff and closing of 100 stores, $164 million charge; tax effect, $82 million.
1987:	Reversal of provision in 1986 when actual charges and costs were less than expected, $8 million credit; tax effect, $4 million.
1988:	Provision for corporate restructuring relating to issue of debt and distribution of special dividend, $195 million charge; tax effect, $67 million.
1989, 1990:	Reversal of provision for corporate restructuring when actual charges were less than anticipated, $18 million credit in 1989 (tax effect $6 million); $27 million credit in 1990 (tax effect, $9 million).

[b]Loss from operations of drug store operations sold during 1986.

[c]Change to the liability method of accounting for deferred income taxes.

[d]Write off of deferred costs incurred in corporate restructuring in 1988 (net of tax effects).

Exhibit 4 presents selected financial statement and market price data for Kroger and three leading competitors for fiscal years 1985, 1986, and 1987, the three years prior to Kroger's special dividend. These data use the originally reported amounts for each company (except for the elimination of Kroger restructuring charge for 1986). The rates of return ratios use end-of-the-period values for assets and common shareholders' equity instead of the average values for these items.

REQUIRED

a.   An analyst desires to study the changes in the profitability and risk of Kroger prior to and subsequent to the special dividend to assess why

Exhibit 2
Kroger Company
Comparative Balance Sheets
(in millions)

Assets	1985	1986	1987	1988	1989	1990
Cash	$ 106	$ 212	$ 113	$ 211	$ 115	$ 55
Accounts Receivable	215	262	253	258	280	277
Inventories	1,473	1,197	1,448	1,275	1,395	1,448
Other Current Assets[a]	208	277	341	726	258	170
Current Assets	$2,002	$1,948	$2,155	$ 2,470	$ 2,048	$1,950
Investments	0	0	0	0	0	0
Property, Plant, and Equip. (Net)	1,991	1,968	2,137	1,910	1,912	1,874
Other Assets	185	170	168	234	282	295
Total Assets	$4,178	$4,086	$4,460	$ 4,614	$ 4,242	$4,119

Liabilities and Shareholders' Equity	1985	1986	1987	1988	1989	1990
Accts. Payable—Trade	$ 986	$ 912	$1,005	$ 1,095	$ 1,132	$ 1,198
Notes Payable—Nontrade	122	10	315	6	13	0
Current Part L-T Debt	42	50	29	341	171	96
Other Current Liab.	577	738	614	723	753	768
Current Liabilities	$1,727	$1,710	$1,963	$ 2,165	$ 2,069	$ 2,062
Long-Term Debt	925	830	987	4,724	4,724	4,558
Deferred Tax	314	292	292	302	294	273
Other Noncurrent Liabilities	23	99	84	102	120	86
Total Liabilities	$2,989	$2,931	$3,326	$ 7,293	$ 7,207	$ 6,979
Preferred Stock	$ 0	$ 125	$ 125	$ 250	$ 0	$ 0
Common Stock	396	410	424	101	102	104
Retained Earnings	980	939	1,095	(2,517)	(2,609)	(2,541)
Treasury Stock	(187)	(319)	(510)	(513)	(458)	(423)
Shareholders' Equity	$1,189	$1,155	$1,134	$(2,679)	$(2,965)	$(2,860)
Total Equities	$4,178	$4,086	$4,460	$ 4,614	$ 4,242	$ 4,119

[a]Includes assets that Kroger expects to sell at a net realizable value of $88 million in 1985, $101 million in 1986, $115 million in 1987, $483 million in 1988, $37 million in 1989, and $23 million in 1990.

Kroger needed to pay the special dividend and how well it performed with its heavier debt load after the special dividend. Discuss the adjustments that the analyst should make to the financial statement data in Exhibits 1 to 3 before performing the profitability and risk analysis.

b. Prepare a profitability and risk analysis of Kroger for 1986 and 1987. Using this analysis and the data in Exhibit 4, indicate the apparent reasons that Kroger became a takeover target in the fall of 1988.

c. Prepare a profitability and risk analysis of Kroger for 1987 to 1990. Evaluate the changes in Kroger's profitability and risk since the special dividend.

Exhibit 3
Kroger Company
Comparative Statement of Cash Flows
(in millions)

Operations	1986	1987	1988	1989	1990
Income from Continuing Operations.........	$ 56	$ 183	$ 35	$ (16)	$ 83
Depreciation and Amort.	231	223	254	241	245
Other Addbacks......................................	52	0	8	104	113
Other Subtractions	0	(20)	0	0	0
WC Provided by Ops.............................	$ 339	$ 386	$ 297	$ 329	$ 441
(Inc.) Decr. in Receivables...........................	(45)	8	(6)	(1)	4
(Inc.) Decr. in Inventories	83	(261)	15	(84)	(53)
(Inc.) Decr. in Other CA........................	(50)	(39)	(24)	42	75
Inc. (Decr.) Acct. Pay-Trade........................	(74)	93	90	37	66
Inc. (Decr.) in Other CL............................	120	(7)	157	85	(35)
Cash from Cont. Ops..............................	$ 373	$ 180	$ 529	$ 408	$ 498
Cash from Discontinued Ops......................	(4)	0	0	0	0
Cash from Extr. Gain/Loss........................	0	0	0	0	0
Net Cash Flow from Operations	$ 369	$ 180	$ 529	$ 408	$ 498
Investing					
Fixed Assets Sold.....................................	$ 129	$ 62	$ 93	$ 13	$ 25
Investments Sold	406[a]	21	0	0	30
Fixed Assets Acquired	(475)	(416)	(324)	(131)	(219)
Investments Acquired................................	(26)	0	(86)	(15)	(14)
Other Invest. Transact.	(22)	(76)	7	299[b]	(13)
Net Cash Flow from Investing....................	$ 12	$(409)	$ (310)	$ 166	$(191)
Financing					
Incr. S-T Borrowing.................................	$ 0	$ 305	$ 0	$ 0	$ 0
Incr. L-T Borrowing.................................	164	141	4,191[c]	2,706[f]	306
Issue of Capital Stock	146	12	181	16	22
Decr. S-T Borrowing.................................	(112)	0	(309)	0	0
Decr. L-T Borrowing.................................	(241)	(48)	(861)[d]	(3,141)[f]	(697)
Acquisit. of Cap. Stock.............................	(140)	(191)	(3)	(251)	0
Dividends...	(93)	(91)	(3,347)[e]	(2)	0
Other Financing Trans.	2	2	26	2	1
Net Cash Flow from Financing	$ (274)	$ 130	$ (122)	$ (670)	$(368)
Net Change in Cash	$ 107	$ (99)	$ 97	$ (96)	$ (61)

[a]Represents proceeds from the sale of drug store operations.

[b]Includes $224 million from the sale of assets; see Note a to Exhibit 2.

[c]Includes $3.6 billion of financing for payment of special dividend.

[d]Includes $360 million of existing debt obligations refinanced as part of restructuring.

[e]Includes approximately $3.2 billion for the cash portion of the special dividend.

[f]Includes $625 million of senior debentures and $625 million of subordinated debentures, the proceeds of which refinanced $1,000 million of senior, increasing rate subordinated debentures issued in 1988 to finance the special dividend.

Exhibit 4

Comparative Data for Supermarket Competitors

	Total Assets	Return on Assets	Long-Term Debt/Long-Term Capital	Return on Common Equity	Current Ratio	Price-Earnings Ratio
Kroger						
1985	$4,178	4.7%	38.1%	15.7%	1.2	12
1986	$4,086	3.4%[a]	34.4%[a]	11.8%[a]	1.1	11[a]
1987	$4,460	4.4%	40.9%	18.0%	1.1	11
A&P						
1985	$1,664	3.7%	33.6%	8.9%	1.3	15
1986	$2,080	3.7%	35.3%	9.7%	1.1	14
1987	$2,243	4.8%	30.4%	12.9%	1.1	14
American Stores						
1985	$3,463	4.4%	50.5%	18.0%	1.2	15
1986	$3,590	4.1%	47.0%	14.9%	1.2	15
1987	$3,650	4.3%	46.6%	15.2%	1.2	15
Winn Dixie Stores						
1985	$ 705	9.0%	12.8%	17.7%	1.6	14
1986	$ 830	8.9%	12.3%	17.1%	1.7	16
1987	$ 851	8.1%	12.2%	15.6%	1.6	17

[a]The amounts for Kroger for 1986 exclude a $164 million ($82 million net of taxes) restructuring charge.

Source: Standard & Poor, *Stock Reports*.

Case 9.3:
Tanaguchi Corporation—Part B*

(NOTE: Refer to Case 6.1, Tanaguchi Corporation—Part A, for background for this case.)

Dave Ando and Yoshi Yashima spent the next several days converting the financial statements of Tanaguchi Corporation from Japanese to U.S. GAAP. Although their conversions required them to make several estimates, Dave and Yoshi felt comfortable that they had largely filtered out the effects of different accounting principles. Exhibit 2 of this case presents the profitability and risk ratios for Tanaguchi Corporation based on Japanese GAAP (column 1) and as restated to U.S. GAAP (column 2). Column 3 shows the median ratios for U.S. machine tool

*Paul R. Brown of New York University coauthored this case. It appeared in *Issues in Accounting Education* (Spring 1992), pp. 57–79 and is reproduced with permission of the American Accounting Association.

Exhibit 2
Comparative Financial Ratio Analysis for
Tanaguchi Corporation and U.S. Machine Tool Companies

	Tanaguchi Corp. (Japanese GAAP) (1)	Tanaguchi Corp. (U.S. GAAP) (2)	Median Ratio for U.S. Machine Tool Companies[a] (3)
Profitability Ratios			
Operating Margin after Taxes (before Interest Expense and Related Tax Effects)	2.8%	2.9%	3.3%
× Total Assets Turnover	1.5	1.5	1.8
= Return on Assets	4.2%	4.5%	5.9%
× Common's Share of Operating Earnings[b]	.83	.83	.91
× Capital Structure Leverage[c]	3.8	4.0	2.6
= Return on Common Equity	13.3%[d]	14.8%	13.9%[d]
Operating Margin Analysis			
Sales..	100.0%	100.0%	100.0%
Other Revenue/Sales	.4	.4	—
Cost of Goods Sold/Sales..	(73.2)	(73.4)	(69.3)
Selling and Administrative/Sales.............................	(21.0)	(20.6)	(25.8)
Income Taxes/Sales	(3.4)	(3.5)	(1.6)
Operating Margin (Excluding Interest and Related Tax Effects)..	2.8%	2.9%	3.3%
Asset Turnover Analysis			
Receivable Turnover...	5.1	5.0	6.9
Inventory Turnover...	6.3	6.5	5.2
Fixed Asset Turnover..	7.5	7.2	7.0
Risk Analysis			
Current Ratio	1.1	1.0	1.6
Quick Ratio...	.7	.7	.9
Total Liabilities/Total Assets	73.8%	74.5%	61.1%
Long-Term Debt/Total Assets	4.7%	5.1%	16.1%
Long-Term Debt/Stockholders' Equity	17.9%	18.3%	43.2%
Times Interest Covered	5.8	5.7	3.1
Market Price Ratios (per Common Share)			
Market Price/Net Income..	45.0	30.9	9.0
Market Price/Stockholders' Equity..........................	5.7	4.6	1.2

[a]Source: Robert Morris Associates, *Annual Statement Studies* (except price-earnings ratio).

[b]Common's Share of Operating Earnings = Net Income to Common/Operating Income after Taxes (before interest expense and related tax effects). Chapter 8 describes this ratio as the common earnings leverage ratio.

[c]Capital Structure Leverage = Average Total Assets/Average Common Stockholders' Equity.

[d]The amounts for return on common equity may not precisely equal to the product of return on assets, common's share of operating earnings and capital structure leverage due to rounding.

companies (the same as those reported in Exhibit 1). After studying the financial statement ratios in Exhibit 2, the following conversation ensues.

Dave: The operating profitability of Tanaguchi Corporation, as evidenced by the rate of return on assets, is still lower than comparable U.S. firms, even after adjusting for differences in accounting principles. Although Tanaguchi's rate of return on common equity is now higher than its U.S. counterparts, the higher return occurs at the expense of taking on substantially more debt and therefore more risk. A significant portion of the differences in price-earnings ratios between Tanaguchi Corporation and U.S. companies results from differences in accounting principles. However, large differences still remain. I'm still not convinced that investing in Tanaguchi Corporation makes sense. Yoshi, am I on track with my interpretations or am I missing something?

Yoshi: I'm not sure we are yet to the point where we can make a recommendation regarding an investment in the shares of Tanaguchi Corporation. We need to develop a better understanding of why the restated financial ratios for Tanaguchi Corporation still differ so much from those for U.S. machine tool companies.

One possible explanation might relate to the practice of many Japanese companies to operate in corporate groups, which the Japanese call *keiretsus*. Tanaguchi Corporation is a member of the Menji *keiretsu*. Each *keiretsu* typically comprises firms in eight or ten different industries (for example, one *keiretsu* might include firms in the steel, chemicals, forest products, retailing, insurance, and banking industries). The companies usually hold stock in each other; investments in the 25 percent to 30 percent range are common. These investments are not made for the purpose of controlling or even significantly influencing other members of the corporate group. Rather, they serve as a mechanism for providing operating links between the entities. It is common for one corporation in the *keiretsu* to source many of its raw materials from another group member and to sell a substantial portion of its products to entities within the group. Each *keiretsu* includes a bank that provides needed funds to group members. It is rare that the bank would allow a member of the group to experience significant operating problems or to go bankrupt due to lack of funds.

A second, but related, institutional difference between the U.S. and Japan concerns stock ownership patterns. Roughly one-third of Japanese companies' shares is held by members of its *keiretsu* and another one-third is held by financial institutions, typically banks and insurance companies not affiliated with the *keiretsu*. This leaves only one-third of the shares held by individuals. The large percentage of intercorporate stock holdings has historically lessened the concern about keeping investors happy by paying large dividends or reporting ever-increasing earnings per share, as seems to be the case in the U.S.

Instead, the emphasis of Japanese companies has been on serving new or growing markets, increasing market share, and strengthening the members of the *keiretsu*. The Japanese economy has grown more rapidly than the U.S. economy during the last several decades. In addition, Japanese companies have built their export markets and added operations abroad. The strategic emphasis has been on gaining market dominance in this growth environment and not on attaining particular levels of profit margin, rates of return, or earnings per share.

Finally, stock price changes in Japan appear related more to changes in real estate values than to the operating performance of individual companies. Real estate values and stock prices moved dramatically upward during the 1980s, although significant decreases have occurred recently. The increasing stock prices appeared to keep investors happy, leading them to deemphasize the kinds of profitability performance evaluation common in the U.S.

(NOTE: Your instructor may assign additional references in conjunction with this case that elaborate on strategic, institutional, and cultural differences between the United States and Japan.)

REQUIRED

After studying the financial statements and notes for Tanaguchi Corporation, develop explanations for the differences in the profitability and risk ratios for Tanaguchi Corporation reported in column 2 of Exhibit 2 as compared to those reported in column 3 for U.S. machine tool companies.

Pro Forma Financial Statements and Valuation

Chapter 1 indicated that financial statement analysis serves two principal purposes: (1) evaluating a firm's recent operating performance and current financial position (a backward-looking exercise), and (2) projecting its future operating performance and financial position (a forward-looking exercise). Previous chapters examined the tools analysts use to assess operating performance and financial position. This chapter describes and illustrates the techniques for preparing projected financial statements, referred to as **pro forma financial statements,** and demonstrates their use in valuation.

Uses of Pro Forma Financial Statements

Decision makers (managers, investors) examine the probable future consequences of alternatives under consideration when they make decisions (for example, adding a product line or acquiring shares of a particular company's common stock). The financial statements reflect the results of past decisions. The decision maker analyzes these financial statements to gain insights that will enhance predictions about the future. Pro forma financial statements set out the financial consequences of various alternatives under consideration. The following examples illustrate several uses of pro forma financial statements.

Example 1. The managers of Selling Corporation wish to expand geographically and must decide whether to locate new operations in Canada or in Europe. Both alternatives involve constructing capital-intensive plants and building a sales organization in the respective geographic areas. The decision maker studies the cash-flow effects of these two alternatives in making this decision. Deriving the cash-flow effects requires projecting sales, expenses, assets, and financing. Pro forma financial statements summarize these projections.

Example 2.   The managers of Fisher Corporation desire to acquire all of the firm's outstanding common stock and take Fisher Corporation private. To obtain the cash needed to acquire the common stock, the managers will use the assets of Fisher Corporation as collateral. Thus, the assets of Fisher Corporation will not change as a result of the buyout, but the proportion of debt on the balance sheet will increase substantially. The cash flows of Fisher Corporation will service the new debt. To assess the feasibility of this management-led leveraged buyout, these managers must project the future cash flows from operating, investing, and financing activities. Projected income statements and balance sheets reflecting the higher level of debt provide the necessary information to determine the projected cash flows. If cash flows from operations are not sufficient to service the debt, then management must consider either using a lower proportion of debt, selling assets, or pursuing other alternatives.

Example 3.   Soybel Corporation, a publicly held company, wishes to acquire Shank Corporation. The management of Soybel Corporation must decide the price it will pay for Shank Corporation. It also desires to know the effect of the acquisition on the consolidated financial statements. To establish a price, Soybel Corporation projects the amount of cash it expects Shank Corporation to generate from operations net of required capital expenditures and debt service payments. The present value of these amounts establishes the maximum price Soybel Corporation should pay. Soybel Corporation prepares pro forma financial statements for both Soybel and Shank to examine the expected effect of the acquisition on the published consolidated financial statements.

The preparation of pro forma financial statements requires numerous assumptions (growth rate in sales, cost behavior of various expenses, levels of investment in working capital and fixed assets, mix of financing). The decision maker should study the sensitivity of the pro forma financial statements to the assumptions made and to the impact of different assumptions. Spreadsheet computer programs assist in this sensitivity analysis. The decision maker can study alternative assumptions quickly and trace through their effects on the financial statements.

The analyst should keep the following two comments in mind when preparing pro forma financial statements:

1.   The preparation of pro forma financial statements can easily deteriorate into a mechanical exercise. Spreadsheet computer programs permit the analyst to input a handful of assumptions and the programs output financial statements for many years into the future. The old adage of "garbage in, garbage out" applies particularly forcefully to the preparation of pro forma financial statements. The analyst should (1) carefully study past financial statement relations to gain an understanding of the economic characteristics of the business, and (2) consider changes in economic conditions, business strategy, and other factors that affect the projections. Projecting more than four or five years into the future probably results in projections of questionable reliability.

2.   The analyst should ensure that the pro forma financial statements are internally consistent. Assumptions made about sales and various expenses should articulate with the levels of accounts receivable, inventories, and other assets. Amounts on the statement of cash flows should articulate with changes in balance sheet accounts and with related income statement amounts.

Preparing Pro Forma Financial Statements

The procedure for preparing pro forma financial statements involves the following steps:

1. Project sales revenue for the desired number of future periods.

2. Project operating expenses (cost of goods sold, selling and administrative, income taxes excluding interest) and derive projected operating income. Operating income is the numerator of ROA. It excludes all financing costs.

3. Project the assets, liabilities, and shareholders' equity needed to support the level of operations projected in steps 1 and 2.

4. Determine the cost of financing the capital structure derived in step 3. Subtract the after-tax cost of this financing from operating income to obtain projected net income.

5. Derive the statement of cash flows from the projected income statement and comparative balance sheets.

We will illustrate this five-step procedure for Pepsi for Year 9, Year 10, and Year 11. Appendix B presents the financial statements for Pepsi for Year 8. Appendix C presents printouts of FSAP for Pepsi. We will use selected data from these printouts in making the projections for Pepsi.

Projecting Sales

The key starting point is to project sales. The expected level of sales serves as a basis for deriving many of the other amounts in the pro forma financial statements. If sales have grown at a reasonably steady rate in prior periods, then the analyst can project this growth rate into the future. If a major acquisition or sale affects the historical growth rate, then the analyst should filter out the effect of this event on the historical growth rate. The most difficult sales projections occur for firms with cyclical sales patterns (for example, heavy machinery, computers). Their historical growth rates for sales might reflect wide variations in both direction and amount from year to year. The analyst should probably project a varying growth rate that maintains this cyclical sales pattern in these cases.

The historical growth rates in sales for Pepsi are as follows:

Year 5	23.6%
Year 6	13.3%
Year 7	17.2%
Year 8	16.8%
Four-year Compound Average	17.7%

Earlier chapters indicated that the consumer foods industry in the United States is in its mature phase. Industry sales have grown recently at the growth rate for the general population, approximately 2 percent per year. The primary vehicles for growth by consumer foods companies are acquisitions and international sales. Pepsi made acquisitions in each of the last four years. Presuming that Pepsi continues to grow through acquisitions and international expansion, we use a compound annual growth rate of 17 percent in projecting sales, just slightly less than the 17.7 percent compound annual growth rate over the last five years. Projected sales are (in millions):

	Amount	Percentage Change
Year 8 Actual Sales	$17,802.7	—
Year 9 Projected Sales	$20,829.2	17.0%
Year 10 Projected Sales	$24,370.1	17.0%
Year 11 Projected Sales	$28,513.0	17.0%

Projecting Operating Expenses

The procedure for projecting operating expenses depends on the behavior of various cost items. If all costs behave as variable costs and the analyst anticipates no changes in their behavior relative to sales, then the common size income statement relations serve as the basis for projecting future operating expenses. We multiply projected sales by the cost of goods sold percentage, selling and administrative expense percentage, and so on to derive the amounts for operating expenses. Alternatively, we can project each operating expense to grow at the same rate as sales (17.0 percent for Pepsi).

On the other hand, if the cost structure reflects a high proportion of fixed costs that will not change as sales increase, then using the common size income statement approach described above can result in poor projections. In this case, the analyst should attempt to estimate the variable and fixed cost structure of the firm. Alternatively, the analyst can use the historical growth rates for individual cost items. Capital-intensive manufacturing firms often have high proportions of fixed costs in their cost structures. One clue suggesting the presence of fixed costs is that the percentage change in cost of goods sold differs significantly each year from the percentage change in sales. Using the historical growth rates for individual cost items is one way of reflecting the effects of different mixes of variable and fixed costs.

Chapter 7 demonstrated that Pepsi has a relatively low level of fixed costs. Thus, we project Pepsi's operating expenses using the common size income statement approach. Exhibit 10.1 presents pro forma income statements for Pepsi for Year 9, Year 10, and Year 11. The percentages for cost of goods sold, selling and administrative expenses, and other revenues represent an average of the common size percentages for the last three years. Note 10 to Pepsi's financial statements shows that the effective income tax rate was approximately 33 percent during the last three years. We use that rate in projecting income taxes in Exhibit 10.1. Note that "other items" in Exhibit 10.1 includes Pepsi's gain of $53 million (after taxes)

Exhibit 10.1
Pro Forma Income Statements for Pepsi
(amounts in millions)

	Year 8 Actual	Year 9 Projected	Year 10 Projected	Year 11 Projected
Sales...................................	$17,802.7[a]	$20,829.2	$24,370.1	$28,513.0
Cost of Goods Sold........................	(8,609.9)[b]	(10,102.2)	(11,819.5)	(13,828.8)
Selling and Administrative............	(7,137.2)[c]	(8,331.7)	(9,748.0)	(11,405.2)
Other Revenues and Expenses	182.1[d]	208.3	243.7	285.1
Income Taxes.................................	(745.7)[e]	(859.2)	(1,005.3)	(1,176.2)
Operating Income.........................	$ 1,492.0	$ 1,744.4	$ 2,041.0	$ 2,387.9
Interest Expense (Net of Taxes)[f]....	(454.4)	(522.0)	(607.9)	(708.0)
Other Items..................................	39.3	—	—	—
Net Income	$ 1,076.9	$ 1,222.4	$ 1,433.1	$ 1,679.9

[a]Projected using 17 percent growth rate.

[b]Projected assuming 48.5 percent of sales.

[c]Projected assuming 40.0 percent of sales.

[d]Projected assuming 1 percent of sales.

[e]Projected assuming 33 percent of operating income before taxes.

[f]Projected assuming a 9.5 percent interest rate and a 34 percent tax savings at the statutory marginal tax rate.

on a joint venture stock offering and a $13.7 million discontinued operations charge. These items are nonrecurring and therefore we exclude them from the projected income statement.

We will consider the projection of interest expense after projecting the firm's financing.

Projecting the Balance Sheet

Next we prepare the projected balance sheet. The analyst most easily accomplishes this step by projecting the assets side of the balance sheet first, and then determining the appropriate mix of financing for the projected level of assets.

Two general approaches to projecting assets are:

1. Project total assets and then use the common size balance sheet percentages to allocate this total among individual asset items.

2. Project individual asset items and then sum individual asset amounts to obtain total assets.

Projecting Total Assets Approach.   We can project total assets using the historical growth rate in assets. Pepsi's assets grew at a 23.9 percent compound annual growth rate during the last five years. If this growth rate continues, total assets will increase as follows (in millions):

	Amount	Percentage Change
Year 8 Actual Assets......................	$17,143.4	—
Year 9 Projected Assets..................	$21,240.7	23.9%
Year 10 Projected Assets................	$26,317.2	23.9%
Year 11 Projected Assets................	$32,607.0	23.9%

Using historical growth rates to project total assets can result in erroneous projections if the analyst fails to consider the link between sales growth and assets growth. We assumed a sales growth rate for Pepsi of 17 percent in Exhibit 10.1. Pepsi would not likely increase assets by 23.9 percent each year if sales continue to grow by only 17 percent. Pepsi made major acquisitions in recent years that inflated the historical growth rate in its assets. Because sales usually lag increases in assets, the analyst should probably use a lower growth rate than the historical rate.

An alternative approach to projecting total assets uses the total assets turnover. Pepsi's total assets turnover was 1.1 in Year 8, having decreased from a level of 1.3 in Year 6. The decrease results from recent acquisitions. The growth rate for sales in Exhibit 10.1 assumes Pepsi will continue to make acquisitions. Thus, the total assets turnover could decrease still further. On the other hand, *Coke's* assets turnover varied between 1.1 and 1.2 during the last three years. We assume that Pepsi's total assets turnover will remain at 1.1 over the next three years. The calculation of projected total assets using the assets turnover is as follows (in millions):

	Sales	Total Assets Turnover	Average Total Assets	Total Assets Beginning of Year	Total Assets End of Year
Year 9 Projected	$20,829.2	1.1	$18,935.6	$17,143.4	$20,727.9
Year 10 Projected	24,370.1	1.1	22,154.6	20,727.9	23,581.4
Year 11 Projected	28,513.0	1.1	25,920.9	23,581.4	28,260.4

This approach ties the projection of total assets to the level of projected sales. One difficulty sometimes encountered with using total assets turnover to project total assets is that it can result in unusual patterns for projected total assets. The total assets turnover uses *average* total assets in the denominator. If total assets changed by an unusually large (small) percentage in the most recent year before making the projections, then the next year's assets must change by an unusually small (large) proportion to compensate. As an illustration, refer to Figure 10.1. Assume that a firm has historically experienced a total assets turnover of 2.0. An acquisition late in Year 3 caused its total assets to increase, but the firm expects the assets turnover to remain at 2.0 longer term (dotted line). Projecting Year 4 assets using an assets turnover of 2.0 means that projected assets must decrease to maintain the *average* total assets commensurate with an assets turnover of 2.0. This "sawtooth" pattern makes little intuitive sense, given the growth rate in sales.

We encounter this problem when projecting total assets for Pepsi using its total assets turnover. Note that Pepsi's total assets increased 13.3 percent during Year 8, which is less than its average rate of increase in recent years. Using an assets turnover of 1.1 to project total assets, we determined above that total assets would increase as shown in the first two columns of the following data (in millions):

Figure 10.1
**Illustration of Difficulty Sometimes Encountered
When Projecting Total Assets Using Assets Turnover**

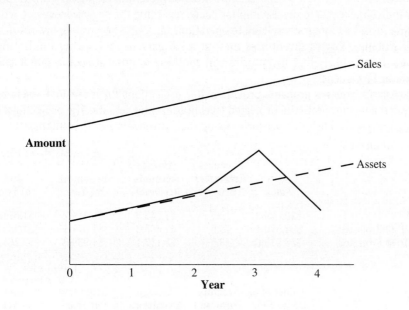

	Period End Assets	Percentage Increase	Period End Assets	Percentage Increase
Year 8..........................	$17,143.4	13.3%	$17,143.4	
Year 9..........................	20,727.9	20.9%	20,251.5	18.1%
Year 10........................	23,581.4	13.8%	23,923.1	18.1%
Year 11........................	28,260.4	19.8%	28,260.4	18.1%

Note that the growth rate in total assets fluctuates in a systematic pattern each year. The analyst can deal with that "sawtooth problem" by smoothing the rate of increase in assets. An increase in assets from $17,143.4 million to $28,260.4 million over three periods grows at a compound average annual rate of 18.1 percent. The last two columns above show the revised projected assets following this smoothed approach. Note that total assets equal $28,260.4 million at the end of Year 11 in both cases. The amounts in the last two columns smooth this growth in assets to obtain this asset level. We use these revised assets amounts in preparing the pro forma balance sheet for Pepsi.

Once the analyst projects total assets, common size balance sheet percentages provide the basis for allocating this total to individual assets. Exhibit 10.2 presents a pro forma balance sheet for Pepsi. We use the common size balance sheet percentages for Year 8 to allocate the total assets to cash, receivables, and so on.

Projecting Individual Asset Items Approach. The second general approach to projecting total assets focuses on each asset individually. We can again use either historical growth rates or asset turnovers. As with using historical growth rates to project total assets, the analyst must link historical growth rates for individual assets to the assumption made regarding the growth in sales, particularly for assets integrally related to operations (accounts receivable, inventories). For instance, Pepsi's inventories grew at a 9.0 percent rate during the last five years. It is unlikely that inventories will continue to grow at such a rate if sales grow at 17 percent.

Asset turnovers probably provide better projections for individual assets because they incorporate the projected level of operating activity. The projections of accounts receivable and inventories using their turnovers are (in millions):

	Sales	Accounts Receivable Turnover	Average Accounts Receivable	Accounts Receivable Beginning of Year	Accounts Receivable End of Year
Year 9 Projected	$20,829.2	13.5	$1,542.9	$1,414.7	$1,671.1
Year 10 Projected	$24,370.1	13.5	$1,805.2	$1,671.1	$1,939.3
Year 11 Projected	$28,513.0	13.5	$2,112.1	$1,939.3	$2,284.9

	Cost of Goods Sold	Inventory Turnover	Average Inventories	Inventories Beginning of Year	Inventories End of Year
Year 9 Projected	$10,102.2	15.2	$664.6	$585.8	$ 743.4
Year 10 Projected	$11,819.5	15.2	$777.6	$743.4	$ 811.8
Year 11 Projected	$13,828.8	15.2	$909.8	$811.8	$1,007.8

The following diagram summarizes the approaches for projecting assets:

	Project Total Assets	Project Individual Assets
Use Historical Growth Rates for Projections		
Use Assets Turnovers for Projections		

These four possible combinations yield similar projections when a firm has experienced relatively stable historical growth rates for total assets and individual asset items and relatively stable assets turnovers. If these changes have varied significantly from year to year, then using *average* historical growth rates provide more reasonable projections than those provided using assets turnovers. One desirable feature of using assets turnovers, however, is that projected assets amounts incorporate projections of the level of sales. Also, management's actions to improve profitability often focus on improving assets turnovers. The analyst can incorporate the effects of these actions into the projections more easily by using the assets turnovers approach than by adjusting the compound annual growth rates or common size balance sheet percentages.

Exhibit 10.2
Pro Forma Balance Sheets for Pepsi
(amounts in millions)

Assets	Year 8 Actual	Year 9 Projected	Year 10 Projected	Year 11 Projected
Cash...	$ 170.8	$ 201.8	$ 238.5	$ 281.8
Marketable Securities....................	1,644.9	1,944.9	2,297.3	2,713.8
Accounts Receivable	1,414.7	1,680.8	1,985.6	2,345.6
Inventories....................................	585.8	688.6	813.4	960.9
Prepayments	265.2	303.8	358.9	423.9
Total Current Assets..................	$ 4,081.4	$ 4,819.9	$ 5,693.7	$ 6,726.0
Investments	1,505.9	1,782.1	2,105.2	2,486.9
Property, Plant, and Equipment (Net)........................	5,710.9	6,743.7	7,966.4	9,410.7
Intangible Assets............................	5,845.2	6,905.8	8,157.8	9,636.8
Total Assets	$17,143.4	$20,251.5	$23,923.1	$28,260.4
Liabilities and Shareholders' Equity				
Accounts Payable	$ 1,116.3	$ 1,316.3	$ 1,555.0	$ 1,836.9
Notes Payable................................	1,626.5	1,923.9	2,272.7	2,684.7
Other Current Liabilities...............	2,027.7	2,389.7	2,822.9	3,334.7
Total Current Liabilities...........	$ 4,770.5	$ 5,629.9	$ 6,650.6	$ 7,856.3
Long-Term Debt............................	5,600.1	6,622.2	7,822.9	9,241.2
Deferred Income Taxes..................	942.8	1,113.8	1,315.8	1,554.3
Other Noncurrent Liabilities	925.8	1,093.7	1,291.8	1,526.1
Total Liabilities..........................	$12,239.2	$14,459.6	$17,081.1	$20,177.9
Common Stock..............................	$ 14.4	$ 14.4	$ 14.4	$ 14.4
Additional Paid-in Capital	365.0	441.4	535.8	635.7
Retained Earnings	4,753.0	5,609.7	6,626.7	7,828.1
Cumulative Translation Adjustment	383.2	455.5	526.3	621.7
Treasury Stock..............................	(611.4)	(729.1)	(861.2)	(1,017.4)
Total Shareholders' Equity	$ 4,904.2	$ 5,791.9	$ 6,842.0	$ 8,082.5
Total Liabilities and Shareholders' Equity.............	$17,143.4	$20,251.5	$23,923.1	$28,260.4

Projecting Liabilities and Shareholders' Equity. Once the analyst completes the assets side of the pro forma balance sheet, projections of liabilities and shareholders' equity come next. The analyst can assume some particular mix of debt and equity financing and apply this mix to the balance sheet at the end of each period. This approach provides reasonable projections for firms that target and maintain an optimal capital structure. Exhibit 10.2 projects the financing side of Pepsi's balance sheet using the common size balance sheet percentages at the end of Year 8. Total equities equal projected total assets.

In a corporate acquisition or leveraged buyout, the acquiror often changes the mix of debt and equity financing without necessarily changing total assets. For example, a leveraged buyout of Pepsi might result in the following changes in its capital structure:

	Current Capital Structure	Leveraged Buyout Capital Structure
Current Liabilities...	27.8%	30.0%
Long-Term Debt...	32.7	41.0
Other Current Liabilities	10.9	9.0
Total Liabilities...	71.4%	80.0%
Shareholders' Equity..	28.6	20.0
Total Liabilities and Shareholders' Equity..........	100.0%	100.0%

The analyst could apply the leveraged buyout financing mix percentages to the total assets amounts projected earlier to ascertain the capital structure amounts.

Projecting the Cost of Financing

With the capital structure now projected, we can estimate the cost of financing. This step requires assumptions about the mix of fixed- and adjustable-rate debt and the likely changes in interest rates in the future. If the analyst expects the risk characteristics of a firm to change in the future, which occurs as a result of a leveraged buyout, then the analyst must adjust interest rates to compensate for the change in risk.

The pro forma balance sheets in Exhibit 10.2 assume that Pepsi's capital structure in the future will remain the same as that at the end of Year 8. The after-tax cost of interest-bearing debt for Year 8 was 6.3 percent as the following analysis shows (in millions):

$$\frac{\text{Interest Expense Net of Tax Savings}}{\text{Average Interest-Bearing Debt}} = \frac{(1 - .34)(\$688.5)}{.5(\$866.3 + \$5,777.1 + \$299.4 + \$1,626.5 + \$5,600.1 + \$299.5)} = \frac{\$\ 454.4}{\$7,234.5} = 6.3\%$$

We apply this percentage to the average level of interest-bearing debt (short-term borrowing, long-term debt, and nonrecourse obligation) in the pro forma balance sheet in Exhibit 10.2 as follows (in millions):

	Interest-Bearing Debt				
	Beginning of Year	End of Year	Average Interest-Bearing Debt	Interest Cost	Interest Expense (Net of Taxes)
Year 9	$ 7,526.1	$ 9,046.7	$ 8,286.4	6.3%	$522.0
Year 10	$ 9,046.7	$10,250.8	$ 9,648.8	6.3%	$607.9
Year 11	$10,250.8	$12,255.4	$11,238.1	6.3%	$708.0

We subtract these after-tax interest cost amounts from operating income in Exhibit 10.1 to derive projected net income for each year.

Projecting the Statement of Cash Flows

The final step involves preparing a projected statement of cash flows. We prepare the statement of cash flows directly from the projected income statements and projected balance sheets. We follow the usual procedure for preparing this statement described in Chapter 2. Exhibit 10.3 presents the pro forma statements of cash flows for Pepsi. The derivation of each of the line items is as follows:

(1) Net Income: We use the amounts in the pro forma income statements (Exhibit 10.1).

(2) Depreciation and Amortization: We assume that these items will increase at the same rate as the respective assets (property, plant, and equipment and intangible assets). Exhibit 10.2 indicates that these assets grow at an 18.1 percent rate. We use these rates of increase for depreciation and amortization in Exhibit 10.3.

(3) Deferred Income Taxes: Change in deferred income taxes on the pro forma balance sheets.

(4), (5), (6), (7), (8) Changes in operating current asset and current liability accounts other than cash appearing on the pro forma balance sheets.

(9) Acquisition of Marketable Securities and Investments: The statement of cash flows classifies purchases and sales of marketable securities (current asset) and investments in securities (noncurrent asset) as "investing" transactions. We use the changes in these accounts on the pro forma balance sheets to derive the amounts for these items on the statement of cash flows. If part of the change relates to an income item (for example, equity in earnings of an affiliate), then the analyst should include the associated amount in the operations section instead of the investing section.

(10) Acquisition of Property, Plant, and Equipment: This line includes the net acquisition or disposition of fixed assets. Because the operations section already includes depreciation [line (2)], the derivation of the amount for acquisition of property, plant, and equipment appearing on line (10) must exclude the effect of depreciation on the change in property, plant, and equipment. For example, the comparative balance sheets indicate that property, plant, and equipment increase by $1,032.8 million (= $6,743.7 − $5,710.9) between Year 8 and Year 9. Projected depreciation for Year 9 is $810.2 million. Thus, net acquisitions of fixed assets must equal $1,843.0 million (= $1,032.8 + $810.2).

(11) Acquisition of Intangibles: Most of Pepsi's intangibles represent franchise rights and goodwill arising from corporate acquisitions. We enter the change in the balance sheet account plus amortization (appearing in the operations section) on line (11).

(12), (13), (17): Increases in borrowings (notes payable and long-term debt) and other noncurrent liabilities relate to financing activities unless the financial statements suggest otherwise. We included the change in deferred income taxes in the operations section because it represents an expense that does not use cash.

(14), (16) Changes in Common Stock: The amounts entered on lines (14) and (16) represent the changes in the Common Stock, Additional Paid-in Capital, and Treasury Stock accounts on the pro forma balance sheets.

Exhibit 10.3
Pro Forma Statements of Cash Flows for Pepsi
(amount in millions)

Operations	Year 8 Actual	Year 9 Projected	Year 10 Projected	Year 11 Projected
(1) Net Income	$ 1,090.6	$ 1,222.4	$ 1,433.1	$ 1,679.9
(2) Depreciation	686.0	810.2	956.8	1,130.0
(2) Amortization	198.0	233.8	276.2	326.1
(3) Deferred Income Taxes	120.3	171.0	202.0	238.5
Other	2.1	—	—	—
(4) (Increase) Decrease in Accounts Receivable	(124.8)	(266.1)	(304.8)	(360.0)
(5) (Increase) Decrease in Inventories	(20.9)	(102.8)	(124.8)	(147.5)
(6) (Increase) Decrease in Prepayments	(61.6)	(38.6)	(55.1)	(65.0)
(7) Increase (Decrease) in Accounts Payable	25.4	200.0	238.7	281.9
(8) Increase (Decrease) in Other Current Liabilities	209.1	362.0	433.2	511.8
Cash Flow from Operations	$ 2,110.0	$ 2,591.9	$ 3,055.3	$ 3,595.7
Investing				
(9) Acquisition of Marketable Securities	$ (181.8)	$ (300.0)	$ (352.4)	$ (416.5)
(9) Acquisition of Investments	(630.6)	(276.2)	(323.1)	(381.7)
(10) Acquisition of Property, Plant, and Equipment	(1,134.8)	(1,843.0)	(2,179.5)	(2,574.3)
(11) Acquisition of Intangibles	—	(1,294.4)	(1,528.2)	(1,805.1)
Other	9.9	—	—	—
Cash Flow from Investing	$ (1,937.3)	$ (3,713.6)	$ (4,383.2)	$ (5,177.6)
Financing				
(12) Increase in Notes Payable	$ (86.2)	$ 297.4	$ 348.8	$ 412.0
(13) Increase in Long-Term Debt	479.3	1,022.1	1,200.7	1,418.3
(14) Increase in Common Stock	—	76.4	94.4	99.9
(15) Dividends	(293.9)	(365.7)	(416.1)	(478.5)
(16) Acquisition of Common Stock	(147.7)	(117.7)	(132.1)	(156.2)
(17) Other	(28.6)	167.9	198.1	234.3
Cash Flow from Financing	$ (77.1)	$ 1,080.4	$ 1,293.8	$ 1,529.8
(18) Effect of Exchange Rate Changes	$ (1.0)	$ 72.3	$ 70.8	$ 95.4
(19) Change in Cash	$ 94.6	$ 31.0	$ 36.7	$ 43.3
Cash—Beginning of Year	76.2	170.8	201.8	238.5
Cash—End of Year	$ 170.8	$ 201.8	$ 238.5	$ 281.8

(15) Dividends: The amount shown for dividends equals the change in retained earnings on the pro forma balance sheets minus net income [$365.7 million for Year 9 = ($5,609.7 – $4,753.0) – $1,222.4)]. Alternatively, the analyst can assume a constant dividend payout ratio relative to net income or a constant growth rate in dividends. These alternative dividend assumptions require an adjustment of cash and retained earnings on the pro forma balance sheets.

(18) Effect of Exchange Rate Changes: The amount on this line reflects the change in the Cumulative Translation Adjustment account on the pro forma balance sheets. In published statements of cash flows, the amount on this line represents the effects of exchange rate changes on cash only. The effect of exchange rate changes on other accounts appears in one of the three main sections of the statement of cash flows. Because the amounts involved are immaterial, we do not employ this refinement in Exhibit 10.3.

(19) Change in Cash: The amounts on lines (1) to (18) net to the change in cash on the comparative balance sheets.

Analyzing Pro Forma Financial Statements

We can analyze the pro forma financial statements using the same ratios and other analytical tools discussed in previous chapters. Exhibit 10.4 presents a ratio analysis for Pepsi based on actual results for Year 8 and pro forma results for Year 9, Year 10, and Year 11.

Exhibit 10.4

Ratio Analysis for Pepsi Based on Pro Forma Financial Statements

Profitability	Year 8 Actual	Year 9 Projected	Year 10 Projected	Year 11 Projected
Profit Margin for ROA	8.6%	8.4%	8.4%	8.4%
Assets Turnover	1.1	1.1	1.1	1.1
Rate of Return on Assets	9.5%	9.3%	9.2%	9.2%
Common Earnings Leverage	.70	.70	.70	.70
Capital Structure Leverage	3.7	3.5	3.5	3.5
Rate of Return on Common Shareholders' Equity	24.5%	22.9%	22.7%	22.5%
Cost of Goods Sold/Sales	48.1%	48.5%	48.5%	48.5%
Selling and Administrative Expense/Sales	40.1%	40.0%	40.0%	40.0%
Interest Expense/Sales	3.9%	3.8%	3.8%	3.8%
Income Tax Expense/Sales	2.8%	2.8%	2.8%	2.8%
Accounts Receivable Turnover	13.4	13.5	13.3	13.2
Inventory Turnover	15.2	15.9	15.7	15.6
Fixed Asset Turnover	3.3	3.3	3.3	3.3
Short-Term Liquidity				
Current Ratio	.86	.86	.86	.86
Quick Ratio	.68	.68	.68	.68
Operating Cash Flow to Current Liabilities	49.9%	49.8%	49.8%	49.6%
Long-Term Solvency				
Long-Term Debt Ratio	53.3%	53.3%	53.3%	53.3%
Debt-Equity Ratio	114.2%	114.3%	114.3%	114.3%
Long-Term Debt to Assets Ratio	32.7%	32.7%	32.7%	32.7%
Times Interest Earned	3.42	3.29	3.31	3.32
Operating Cash Flow to Total Liabilities	18.0%	19.4%	19.4%	19.3%
Operating Cash Flow to Capital Expenditures	1.79	1.41	1.40	1.40

Note that the projected financial statement ratios for Pepsi remain essentially the same as the amounts for Year 8. This occurs because all income statement, balance sheet, and statement of cash flows amounts tie directly or indirectly to the increases in sales revenue. These pro forma financial statements might serve as the base case from which the analyst can assess the impact of various changes in assumptions for Pepsi.

For instance, assume that Pepsi anticipates an economic recession during Year 9. To maintain the same volume of units sold, Pepsi will need to lower prices by 3.5 percent. Assuming no changes in inventory holding policies, Pepsi's revised profitability ratios are:

	Originally Projected	Revised Projected
Profit Margin	8.4%	6.3%
Assets Turnover	1.1	1.1
Rate of Return on Assets	9.3%	6.8%
Common Earnings Leverage	.70	.59
Capital Structure Leverage	3.5	3.6
Rate of Return on Common Shareholders' Equity	22.9%	14.5%

Various other changes in assumptions are also possible. For example, the analyst might question Pepsi's ability to continue making major acquisitions each year. Slowing the rate of growth in sales and assets provides an alternative scenario for Pepsi's future.

Valuation

Valuing the shareholders' equity of a firm occupies much of the time and attention of security analysts. The analyst is likely to ask, Does the market price for a firm's common shares accurately reflect its operating performance and financial position and expected changes in profitability, risk, cash flows, and other factors? This section illustrates several approaches to valuation that use as inputs the analysis of a firm's financial statements. No single approach is consistently better or more accurate than the others. The analyst should use several approaches to valuation to determine if a consensus valuation or a range of values emerges. The three valuation approaches illustrated are (1) present value of future cash flows, (2) multiples of earnings, cash flows, or book value of shareholders' equity, and (3) current value of assets net of liabilities.

Valuation Using Present Value of Cash Flows

Rationale and Example.   Economic theory teaches that the value of any resource (asset) equals the present value of the future cash flows from that resource discounted at a risk-adjusted discount rate. The market value of a firm's common stock should therefore equal the present value of the expected dividends plus the present value of the amount received from the sale of the stock, both net of their income tax effects. Projecting future dividends and residual values requires assumptions about the future profitability of a firm. The analyst can use pro forma financial statements, such as those developed for Pepsi in the previous section, to aid in this valuation. This approach to valuation is particularly useful when the analyst expects major changes in the operating, investing, or financing activities of a firm.

To illustrate this valuation approach, refer to the pro forma statements of cash flows for Pepsi in Exhibit 10.3. Suppose the analyst concludes that the pro forma cash flows reliably reflect Pepsi's expected cash flows during Years 9 through 11. The net cash flows available to common shareholders are as follows (in millions):

	Year 9	Year 10	Year 11
Cash Flow from Operations	$ 2,591.9	$ 3,055.3	$ 3,595.7
Cash Flow from Investing	(3,713.6)	(4,383.2)	(5,177.6)
Cash Flow from Debt Financing	1,487.4	1,747.6	2,064.6
Effect of Exchange Rate Changes	72.3	70.8	95.4
Net Cash Flow Available for Common Shareholders	$ 438.0	$ 490.5	$ 578.1

The analyst must make some assumption about net cash flows anticipated after Year 11. One possibility is to assume that the growth rate in net cash flows available to common shareholders between Year 9 and Year 11 of 14.9 percent will continue into the future. Another approach is to assume a residual value at the end of the projection period (Year 11) equal to a multiple of earnings or cash flows. We assume a continuous 14.9 percent increase in net cash flows.

The analyst must discount these cash flows to their present value. The discount rate should reflect the investor's desired rate of return, incorporating the risk inherent in investing in Pepsi. For example, suppose that an investor desired a rate of return of 17 percent from an equity investment in Pepsi. To induce this investor to acquire Pepsi's common stock, the aggregate current market value of Pepsi should not exceed $18,281.6 million, as the following computations show:

Year	Cash Flow	Present Value Factor at 17 Percent	Present Value
9	$ 438.0	.85470	$ 374.4
10	$ 490.5	.73051	358.3
11	$ 578.1	.62437	360.9
After Year 11	$27,528.6[a]	.62437	17,188.0[a]
Total Present Value			$18,281.6

[a]578.1/(.17 − .149) = $27,528.6

The calculation of the present value of the cash flows after Year 11 assumes that the Year 11 net cash flow to common shareholders of $578.1 millon grows at 14.9 percent and gets discounted at 17 percent.[1] Based on the 788.4 million shares outstanding at the end of Year 8, the market price should be $23.19 (= $18,281.6/788.4) to

---

[1] This valuation model does not work well when the discount rate and growth rate are similar. The denominator approaches zero and the present value becomes extraordinarily large. Pepsi's growth rate of 14.9 percent is probably not sustainable in perpetuity, as this valuation model assumes.

yield a pretax return of 17 percent. Pepsi's actual market price at the end of Year 8 is $25.75 per share, implying a market rate of return less than 17 percent.

Example Using ROCE as Discount Rate.   An alternative approach to selecting a discount rate for the equity capital is to use the rate of return on common shareholders' equity. Chapter 8 discussed the theoretical relation between ROCE and the market rate of return on common equity (dividends plus market price changes). Exhibit 10.4 shows that Pepsi's ROCE was 24.5 percent for Year 8. The aggregate market value of Pepsi sufficient to yield 24.5 percent return to common equity holders is $4,088.3 million, computed as follows:

Year	Cash Flow	Present Value Factor at 24.5 Percent	Present Value
9	$ 438.0	.80321	$ 351.8
10	$ 490.5	.64515	316.4
11	$ 578.1	.51819	299.6
After Year 11	$6,021.9[a]	.51819	3,120.5
Total Present Value			$4,088.3

[a]$578.1/(.245 − .149)

Based on the 788.4 million shares outstanding at the end of Year 8, the market price per share should be $5.19 (= $4,088.3/788.4). If the investor uses ROCE as a surrogate for the market rate of return and anticipates that Pepsi's ROCE will remain at 24.5 percent, then Pepsi's current market price of $25.75 per share significantly overstates its economic value.

Exhibit 10.4, however, projects a declining ROCE for Pepsi during the next three years. Assume that we anticipate that Pepsi's ROCE will stabilize at 16.8 percent. Also assume that Pepsi's long-term growth rate in net cash flows remains at 14.9 percent. The aggregate market value of Pepsi should be $20,192.2 million, computed as follows:

Year	Cash Flow	Present Value Factor at 16.8 Percent	Present Value
9	$ 438.0	.85016	$ 375.0
10	$ 490.5	.73302	359.5
11	$ 578.1	.62758	362.8
After Year 11	$30,426.3[a]	.62758	19,094.9[a]
Total Present Value			$20,192.2

[a]$578.1/(.168 − .149) = $30,426.3

This aggregate market value suggests a market price of $25.61 per share (= $20,192.2/788.4), an amount close to Pepsi's actual market price at the end of Year 8.

Example in Financing Mix Decision.   Another appropriate setting for applying the present value approach to valuation involves changes in the mix of debt and equity financing. For instance, assume a firm wishes to issue additional debt and use the proceeds to repurchase shares of its common stock. The increased debt may provide additional financial leverage benefits to common shareholders as well as tax shields on the interest, and thereby increase the price of the firm's common stock. The analyst can revalue the common equity using the new capital structure to ascertain the maximum price the firm should pay, given the firm's desired rate of return.

To illustrate the analysis, assume that Pepsi issues $100 million of 20-year, 10 percent coupon bonds and uses the proceeds to repurchase 3.9 million shares of its common stock. Also assume that the increased debt level does not increase the risk to equity holders sufficiently to induce a change in the required rate of return of approximately 16.8 percent (see previous example). The aggregate market value of Pepsi should increase for two reasons:

1. The present value of the future cash flows required to service the debt at the 16.8 percent discount rate is $61.3 million, an amount which is less than the $100 million debt issue proceeds. This value increase reflects the benefits of additional financial leverage. By assuming greater financial leverage, the firm signals the market that its future prospects look sufficiently bright that common shareholders will benefit from the additional leverage without any increase in risk.

2. The present value of the future tax savings from interest expense on the debt. The new debt produces tax savings of $3.4 million (= .34 × .10 × $100) per year for 20 years. The present value of the tax savings at a discount rate of 16.8 percent is $19.3 million.[2]

Thus, the market value of Pepsi should increase as follows:

Current Market Value: $25.75 × 788.4 shares	$20,301.3
Issue Price of New Debt	100.0
Present Value of Cash Flow to Service the New Debt	(61.3)
Present Value of Tax Savings from Interest	19.3
Revised Aggregate Market Value	$20,359.3

This aggregate market value of $20,359.3 spread over the 784.5 million shares (= 788.4 – 3.9) implies a market price of $25.95 per share (= $20,359.3/784.5). If the market price increases to a level of $25.95, then engaging in the debt issue/stock repurchase yields the equity holders' desired rate of return of 16.8 percent.

The increased debt level may, however, increase the risk level sufficiently to induce the common shareholders to increase their required rate of return. Suppose that the increased debt level of $100 million causes Pepsi's shareholders to increase their desired rate of return from 16.8 percent to 16.9 percent. The market value of Pepsi should change as follows:

---

[2]Some theorists argue that a risk-free rate is the appropriate discount rate if the firm expects to have sufficient taxable income to benefit from the tax savings. A lower discount rate increases the present value of the tax savings.

Projected Cash Flows

Year 9:	$438.0 × .85543	$ 374.7
Year 10:	$490.5 × .73176	358.9
Year 11:	$578.1 × .62597	361.9
After Year 11:	$578.1/(.169 − .149) × .62597	18,093.7 $19,189.2
Issue Price of New Debt		100.0
Present Value of Cash Flows to Service Debt.........................		(61.0)
Present Value of Tax Savings from Interest...........................		19.2
Revised Present Value at 16.9 Percent		$19,247.4

In this case, the increase in debt reduces the market value of the common equity and the market price per share. The increased risk to the common shareholders does not justify the extra return.

Example in LBO Setting. Another setting for applying the present value approach to valuation involves the leveraged buyout (LBO). In a leveraged buyout, the acquiring entity alters the capital structure of the target company by adding substantially more debt. The acquiring entity uses the proceeds of the debt offering to purchase a controlling interest in the target firm from existing shareholders. The principal differences between the stock repurchase using additional debt (discussed above) and a leveraged buyout are (1) the LBO generally results in substantially more debt (although companies using a stock repurchase as a defensive mechanism against an unfriendly takeover often increase debt levels similar to an LBO), and (2) the target company transacts the stock repurchase, whereas another entity usually engages in the LBO (although a target company's management can form the other entity to conduct the LBO, labeled a management buyout or MBO).

Suppose we wish to conduct an LBO of Pepsi and must determine the price we should pay for Pepsi's common stock. We begin our analysis by ascertaining if the increased debt for Pepsi arising from the LBO violates its debt covenants. If so, the entity conducting the LBO must obtain sufficient funds both to repay existing debt and to acquire the common stock. Pepsi already has substantial debt in its capital structure. Interest-bearing debt comprises 43.9 percent of total assets [= ($1,626.5 + $5,600.1 + $299.5)/$17,143.4] and total liabilities comprise 71.4 percent of total assets. The LBO will likely require the repayment of the $7,526.1 million of existing debt.

The next step requires the computation of the present value of Pepsi's future cash flows. Exhibit 10.3 shows Pepsi's projected cash flows assuming continuation of its existing debt levels. Because we must repay this debt as part of the LBO, we should add back cash flows for interest expense on the debt (net of any tax savings) to projected cash flow from operations. The analysis is as follows (in millions):

	Year 9	Year 10	Year 11
Projected Cash Flow from Operations............................	$2,591.9	$3,055.3	$3,595.7
Cash Outflow for Interest Expense (Net of Taxes); see Exhibit 10.1	522.0	607.9	708.0
Revised Projected Cash Flow from Operations	$3,113.9	$3,663.2	$4,303.7

Pepsi's projected cash flows for investing activities result in a negative cash flow to cover financing for the LBO:

Revised Projected Cash Flow from Operations	$3,113.9	$3,663.2	$4,303.7
Projected Cash Flow for Investing..................................	(3,713.6)	(4,383.2)	(5,177.6)
Net Cash Flow Available to Cover Financing	$ (599.7)	$ (720.0)	$ (873.9)

Pepsi's rapid growth requires substantial cash outflows for fixed assets and acquisitions. Thus, Pepsi represents a poor candidate for an LBO. The acquiring entity must not only repay $7,526.1 million of debt but must also pay at least the current market value of the common equity (approximately $20 billion) to acquire Pepsi's outstanding shares. Cash flow from operations net of investing activities is negative, so the acquiring entity will encounter difficulties attempting to finance an LBO of Pepsi.

To illustrate the valuation of an LBO candidate using the present value approach, assume we project the following cash flows before debt service payment for a hypothetical target company (amounts in millions):

	Year 9	Year 10	Year 11	Year 12	Year 13
Cash Flow from Operations.....................................	$20.0	$22.0	$25.0	$28.0	$32.0
Cash Outflow for Interest (Net of Taxes) on $50 million of Existing Debt........................	3.3	3.3	3.3	3.3	3.3
Cash Flow for Investing...	(5.3)	(6.3)	(7.3)	(8.3)	(9.3)
Net Cash Flow before LBO Financing...................	$18.0	$19.0	$21.0	$23.0	$26.0

We add back to cash flow from operations the cash outflow required to service the debt to obtain operating cash flow excluding financing costs. We must discount these projected net cash flows plus cash flows anticipated after Year 13 to a present value to ascertain the value of the target company. We assume for illustration purposes that the target company continues to generate $26 million per year in cash flows after Year 13. This assumption is probably unrealistic, given that cash flows increased at a 9.6 percent rate between Year 9 and Year 13. One justification for such an assumption is that cash flows more than five years into the future are difficult to predict accurately so that a conservative assumption about future growth is appropriate. We can assess the sensitivity of the valuation to the no-growth assumption by providing for various positive growth rates.

The remaining item of information needed to compute present values is the discount rate. Assume the following capital structure for the target company after the LBO:

Senior Debt, 12% interest, 7-year term.......................................	50%
Subordinated Debt, 16% interest, 10-year term........................	30
Common Shareholders' Equity...	20
	100%

Also assume that the common equity investors desire a 40 percent pretax return. The weighted average cost of capital of the target company after the LBO is 15.13 percent computed as follows (assuming a 34 percent income tax rate):

	Pretax Cost	After-Tax Cost	Weight	Weighted Average
Senior Debt..	.12	.0792	.5	.0396
Subordinate Debt...................................	.16	.1056	.3	.0317
Common Shareholders' Equity.............		.4000	.2	.0800
			1.0	.1513

The present value of the projected cash flows at the weighted average cost of capital is as follows (in millions):

Year	Cash Flow	Present Value at 15.13%
9	18.0	$ 15.6
10	19.0	14.3
11	21.0	13.8
12	23.0	13.1
13	26.0	12.9
After 13	26.0	84.9[a]
Total Present Value...		$154.6

[a]($26.0/.1513) × .49438 = $84.9.

This analysis indicates a value of $154.6 million for the target company ($50 million for existing debt and $104.6 million for the common equity) using the present value of future cash flows.

Before discussing other valuation methods, note in this case that the target company will not generate sufficient cash flows from operating and investing activities to service the required debt. The firm needs $154.6 million of capital for the LBO. The debt service costs (net of tax savings) on the portion of this $154.6 million represented by debt exceeds the available projected cash flow. The acquiror must either (1) attempt to pay a lower price, (2) structure the debt service requirements so as to delay cash payments (balloon payments of principal, zero-coupon debt), or (3) arrange to sell a portion of the target company's assets to reduce debt.

Valuation Using Market Multiples

A second valuation approach relies on market multiples for comparable firms. The multiples might use earnings, cash flows, or shareholders' equity as the base, or some combination of the three. Exhibit 8.5 shows the average price-earnings ratios of firms in 22 industries for the period 1980 to 1989. Although the analyst would use a current price-earnings ratio in valuing a firm, this exhibit does show that P-E ratios differ across industries. They also differ within industries. The analyst should identify several competitors of similar size, operating strategies, financial structure, and other characteristics. The various market multiples provide clues about valuation.

To illustrate this approach, refer to the data in Exhibit 10.5 for five leading pharmaceutical firms in the United States for their most recent year. Pharmco Holdings, a privately held pharmaceutical company in the United Kingdom,

Exhibit 10.5
Selected Data for U.S. Pharmaceutical Firms (amounts in millions)

	Sales	ROCE	Five-Year Annual Growth Rate in EPS	Price-Earnings Ratio	Price-Cash Flow Ratio	Market Value to Book Value
Abbott Laboratories...............	$ 6,158.7	34.7%	18.0%	20.3	16.1	6.8
Bristol-Myers Squibb.............	$10,300.0	32.3%	19.8%	20.1	20.1	6.5
Eli Lilly....................................	$ 5,191.6	31.2%	16.2%	18.8	15.3	8.6
Merck	$ 7,671.5	48.4%	29.3%	19.7	16.9	9.1
Upjohn	$ 3,020.9	26.1%	17.6%	15.3	15.0	3.8

intends to make its initial public offering of stock in the United States. The following information pertains to the firm for its most recent year (in millions):

Sales	$5,708
Rate of Return on Common Shareholders' Equity....................	31.6%
Five-Year Growth Rate in EPS	15.1%
Earnings per Share..	1.06
Cash Flow per Share..	1.22
Book Value of Shareholders' Equity per Share.........................	3.20

A comparison of the data for Pharmco Holdings with similar data for U.S. pharmaceutical companies provides a basis for pricing the initial public offering. The sales and ROCE of Pharmco Holdings are similar to those of Eli Lilly. Pharmco Holdings' EPS grew more slowly than that of any of the U.S. pharmaceutical companies during the last five years. The analyst should ascertain whether the slower growth results from operating in slower growth markets (United Kingdom versus United States) or from less aggressive development and/or marketing of products. The initial public offering in the United States may signal an intention to move into the U.S. pharmaceutical market, with the possibility of higher growth in the future. Market multiples slightly less than those of Eli Lilly appear reasonable. Application of the various market multiples suggests the following initial offering prices for Pharmco Holdings:

	Financial Ratio	Market Multiple	Market Price
Earnings Per Share...	$1.06	18	$19.08
Cash Flow Per Share	$1.22	15	$18.90
Book Value of Shareholders' Equity per share....................	$3.20	8	$25.60

The implied market price using the market to book value multiple appears out of line with those based on earnings and cash flow. Eli Lilly's market to book value ratio also appears out of line relative to the other U.S. pharmaceutical companies. The analyst should ascertain the reason for Eli Lilly's higher multiple before using it to price Pharmco Holdings. Perhaps Eli Lilly recently repurchased a significant portion of its common stock, decreasing common shareholders' equity and driving up its stock price. If Pharmco Holdings has not engaged in a similar transaction, then Eli Lilly's market multiple may not apply to Pharmco Holdings. The average market to book value ratio for the five U.S. pharmaceutical companies is 6.96. Using a market multiple of 6.5 yields a market price of $20.80 (= $3.20 × 6.5) for Pharmco Holdings, a price closer to those indicated by the price-earnings and price-cash flow ratios.

Valuation Using Current Values of Net Assets

A third valuation approach uses valuations of individual assets and liabilities. This approach is particularly difficult for the analyst to apply because of the lack of sufficient publicly available information to make the valuation. One issue that the analyst faces is whether to make valuations assuming the firm is a going concern or to make valuations assuming the firm has to sell assets. The value-in-use of an asset likely differs from its value-in-exchange.

Accounts receivable generally have a current value close to their book value, unless evidence indicates that the firm has inadequately provided for uncollectible accounts. Whether the book value for inventories accurately reflects current values depends in part on whether the firm uses a FIFO or a LIFO cost-flow assumption. Inventories stated using a FIFO cost-flow assumption should approximate current values. Inventories stated using a LIFO cost-flow assumption probably understate current values. The notes to the financial statements disclose the difference between the current cost and LIFO valuation of inventories. The analyst can ascertain the current value of intercorporate investments in securities if the firm indicates the names of its investees and the shares of such investees trade publicly. For example, Coca Cola Enterprises, a majority unconsolidated investment of Coke, trades publicly. The analyst can estimate the value of Coke's 49 percent investment using the value of the remaining 51 percent held by the public. If the firm does not disclose the names of its investees or if the investees' shares do not trade publicly, then the analyst will experience difficulty determining the current value of investments.

The property, plant, and equipment account of most firms includes various kinds of assets located throughout the world. The analyst might estimate the current value of such assets using price indices prepared by governmental bodies (for example, indices for real estate, commercial buildings, equipment). Chapter 3 indicated a procedure for approximating the age of depreciable assets using information on depreciation expense and accumulated depreciation. As an example, Note 6 to Pepsi's financial statements indicates that accumulated depreciation totals $3,266.8 million at the end of Year 8 and depreciation expense for Year 8 was $686.0 million. Because Pepsi uses the straight-line depreciation method, Pepsi's depreciable assets are approximately 4.8 years old ($3,266.8/$686.0) at the end of Year 8 (this relatively young age reflects Pepsi's recent acquisitions). If government indices indicate that the prices of property, plant, and equipment increased at a compound average rate of 8 percent per year during the last five years, then the current value of Pepsi's depreciable assets exceeds their book value by 46.9 percent (= $(1.08)^5 - 1$). Thus, the current value is approximately $8,389.3 million (= 1.469 × $5,710.9).

The valuation of goodwill and other intangibles is even more difficult than other assets because the balance sheet often excludes such items. One approach is to compare a particular firm's ROA and ROCE to those of its competitors. An excess return suggests the presence of brand names, customer loyalty, or other favorable characteristics. To illustrate, assume that a firm consistently generates an ROA of 4 percentage points greater than its competitors. If assets as of the valuation date total $100 million, then the firm generates excess operating earnings of $4 million each year. We can use a market multiple, such as a price-earnings ratio, to ascertain the current value of this excess earnings capacity and use it as the value for intangibles. Alternatively, we can assume that the $4 million represents a cash flow and discount it to a present value at some appropriate discount rate.

Most liabilities have current values close to their book values. The analyst, however, must search the notes to the financial statements for off-balance sheet obligations and commitments that affect the current value of a firm's net assets, or shareholders' equity. Chapters 4 and 9 discussed several examples of off-balance sheet obligations.

Summary

Previous chapters discussed the interpretation and analysis of published financial statements. Although this interpretation and analysis require the analyst to make numerous judgments about the financial statement information, the material in this chapter moves the analyst to still higher levels of subjectivity. Preparing pro forma financial statements requires numerous assumptions. The quality of the inputs affects the quality of the outputs. The process of valuing firms relies on these assumptions still further. An analytical task that appears at the outset to embody the objectivity of a science turns out to resemble more closely the subjectivity of an art!

Case 10.1:
Holmes Corporation

Holmes Corporation is a leading designer and manufacturer of material handling and process equipment for heavy industry in the United States and abroad. Its sales have more than doubled and its earnings increased more than sixfold in the past five years. In material handling, Holmes is a major producer of electric overhead and gantry cranes, ranging from 5 tons in capacity to 600-ton giants, the latter used primarily in nuclear and conventional power generating plants. It also builds underhung cranes and monorail systems for general industrial use carrying loads up to 40 tons, railcar movers, railroad and mass transit shop maintenance equipment, plus a broad line of advanced package conveyors. Holmes is a world leader in evaporation and crystallization systems and also furnishes dryers, heat exchangers, and filters to complete its line of chemical processing equipment sold internationally to the chemical, fertilizer, food, drug, and paper industries. For the metallurgical industry, it designs and manufactures electric arc and induction furnaces, cupolas, ladles, and hot metal distribution equipment.

The information on the following pages appears in the 1992 annual report of Holmes Corporation.

HIGHLIGHTS

	1992	1991
Net Sales	$102,698,836	$109,372,718
Net Earnings	6,601,908	6,583,360
Net Earnings per Share	3.62*	3.61*
Cash Dividends Paid	2,241,892	1,426,502
Cash Dividends per Share	1.22*	.78*
Shareholders' Equity	29,333,803	24,659,214
Shareholders' Equity per Share	16.07*	13.51*
Working Capital	23,100,863	19,029,626
Orders Received	95,436,103	80,707,576
Unfilled Orders at End of Period	77,455,900	84,718,633
Average Number of Common Shares Outstanding during Period	1,824,853*	1,824,754*

*Adjusted for June 1992 and June 1991 5-for-4 stock distributions.

Net Sales, Net Earnings, and Net Earnings per Share by Quarter (adjusted for 5-for-4 stock distribution in June 1992 and June 1991)

	1992			1991		
	Net Sales	**Net Earnings**	**Per Share**	**Net Sales**	**Net Earnings**	**Per Share**
First Quarter	$ 25,931,457	$1,602,837	$ .88	$ 21,768,077	$1,126,470	$ .62
Second Quarter	24,390,079	1,727,112	.95	28,514,298	1,716,910	.94
Third Quarter	25,327,226	1,505,118	.82	28,798,564	1,510,958	.82
Fourth Quarter	27,050,074	1,766,841	.97	30,291,779	2,229,022	1.23
	$102,698,836	$6,601,908	$3.62	$109,372,718	$6,583,360	$3.61

Common Stock Prices and Cash Dividends Paid per Common Share by Quarter (adjusted for 5-for-4 stock distribution in June 1992 and June 1991)

	1992			1991		
	Stock Prices		Cash Dividends per Share	Stock Prices		Cash Dividends per Share
	High	Low		High	Low	
First Quarter	22 ½	18 ½	$ .26	11 ¼	9 ½	$.16
Second Quarter...........	25 ¼	19 ½	.26	12 ⅜	8 ⅞	.16
Third Quarter..............	26 ¼	19 ¾	.325	15 ⅞	11 ⅝	.20
Fourth Quarter	28 ⅛	23 ¼	.375	20 ⅞	15 ⅞	.26
			$1.22			$.78

MANAGEMENT'S REPORT TO SHAREHOLDERS

1992 was a pleasant surprise for all of us at Holmes Corporation. When the year started, it looked as though 1992 would be a good year but not up to the record performance of 1991. However, due to the excellent performance of our employees and the benefit of a favorable acquisition, 1992 produced both record earnings and the largest cash dividend outlay in the company's 93-year history.

There is no doubt that some of the attractive orders received in late 1989 and early 1990 contributed to 1992 profit. But of major significance was our organization's favorable response to several new management policies instituted to emphasize higher corporate profitability. 1992 showed a net profit on net sales of 6.4 percent, which not only exceeded the 6.0 percent of last year but represents the highest net margin in several decades.

Net sales for the year were $102,698,836, down 6 percent from the $109,372,718 of a year ago but still the second largest volume in our history. Net earnings, however, set a new record at $6,601,908, or $3.62 per common share, which slightly exceeded the $6,583,360, or $3.61 per common share earned last year.

Cash dividends paid in 1992 of $2,241,892 were 57 percent above the $1,426,502 paid a year ago. The record total resulted from your Board's approval of two increases during the year. When we implemented the 5-for-4 stock distribution in June 1992, we maintained the quarterly dividend rate of $.325 on the increased number of shares for the January payment. Then in December 1992, we increased the quarterly rate to $.375 per share.

1992 certainly was not the most exuberant year in the capital equipment markets. Fortunately, our heavy involvement in ecology improvement, power generation, and international markets continued to serve us well, with the result that new orders of $95,436,103 were 18 percent over the $80,707,576 of 1991.

Economists have predicted a substantial capital spending upturn for well over a year but so far our customers have displayed stubborn reluctance to place new orders amid the uncertainty concerning the economy. Confidence is the answer. As soon as potential buyers can see clearly the future direction of the economy, we expect the unleashing of a large latent demand for capital goods, producing a much-expanded market for Holmes' products.

Fortunately, the accelerating pace of international markets continues to yield new business. 1992 was an excellent year on the international front as our foreign customers continue to recognize our technological leadership in several product lines. Net sales of Holmes products shipped overseas and fees from foreign licensees amounted to $30,495,041, which represents a 31 percent increase over the $23,351,980 of a year ago.

Management fully recognizes and intends to take maximum advantage of our technological leadership in foreign lands. The latest manifestation of this policy was the acquisition of a controlling interest in Societé Francaise Holmes Fermont, our Swenson process equipment licensee located in Paris. Holmes and a partner started this firm 14 years ago as a sales and engineering organization to function in the Common Market. The company currently operates in the same mode. It owns no physical manufacturing assets, subcontracting all production. Its markets have expanded to include Spain and the Eastern bloc countries.

Holmes Fermont is experiencing strong demand in Europe. For example, in early May a $5.5 million order for a large potash crystallization system was received from a French engineering company representing a Russian client. Management estimates that Holmes Fermont will contribute approximately $6 to $8 million of net sales in 1993.

Holmes' other wholly owned subsidiaries—Holmes Equipment Limited in Canada, Ermanco Incorporated in Michigan, and Holmes International, Inc., our FSC (Foreign Sales Corporation)—again contributed substantially to the success of 1992. Holmes Equipment Limited registered its second best year. However, capital equipment markets in Canada have virtually come to a standstill in the past two quarters. Ermanco achieved the best year in its history, while Holmes International, Inc., had a truly exceptional year because of the very high level of activity in our international markets.

The financial condition of the company showed further improvement and is now unusually strong as a result of very stringent financial controls. Working capital increased to $23,100,863 from $19,029,626, a 21 percent improvement. Inventories decreased 6 percent from $18,559,231 to $17,491,741. The company currently has no long-term or short-term debt and has considerable cash in short-term instruments. Much of our cash position, however, results from customers' advance payments which we will absorb as we make shipments on the contracts. Shareholders' equity increased 19 percent to $29,393,803 from $24,690,214 a year ago.

Plant equipment expenditures for the year were $1,172,057, down 18 percent from $1,426,347 in 1991. Several appropriations approved during the year did not require expenditures because of delayed deliveries beyond 1992. The major emphasis again was on our continuing program of improving capacity and efficiency through the purchase of numerically controlled machine tools. We expanded the Ermanco plant by 50 percent, but since this is a leasehold arrangement, we made only minor direct investment. We also improved the Canadian operation by adding more manufacturing space and installing energy-saving insulation.

Labor relations were excellent throughout the year. The Harvey plant continues nonunion. We negotiated a new labor contract at the Canadian plant which extends to March 1, 1994. The Pioneer Division in Alabama has a labor contract that does not expire until April 1993. While the union contract at Ermanco expired June 1, 1992, work continues while negotiation proceeds on a new contract. We anticipate no difficulty in reaching a new agreement.

We exerted considerable effort during the year to improve Holmes' image in the investment community. Management held several informative meetings with security analyst groups to enhance the awareness of our activities and corporate performance.

The outlook for 1993, while generally favorable, depends in part on the course of capital spending over the next several months. If the spending rate accelerates, the quickening pace of new orders, coupled with present backlogs, will provide the conditions for another fine year. On the other hand, if general industry continues the reluctant spending pattern of the last two years, 1993 could be a year of maintaining market positions while awaiting better market conditions. Management takes an optimistic view and thus looks for a successful 1993.

The achievement of record earnings and the highest profit margin in decades demonstrates the capability and the dedication of our employees. Management is most grateful for their efforts throughout the excellent year.

T. R. Varnum
President

T. L. Fuller
Chairman

March 15, 1993

REVIEW OF OPERATIONS

1992 was a very active year although the pace was not at the hectic tempo of 1991. It was a year that showed continued strong demand in some product areas but a dampened rate in others. The product areas that had some special economic circumstances enhancing demand fared well. For example, the continuing effort toward ecological improvement fostered excellent activity in Swenson process equipment. Likewise, the energy concern and the need for more electrical power generation capacity boded well for large overhead cranes. On the other hand, Holmes' products that relate to general industry and depend on the overall capital spending rate for new equipment experienced lesser demand, resulting in lower new orders and reduced backlogs. The affected products were small cranes, underhung cranes, railcar movers, and metallurgical equipment.

1992 was the first full year of operations under some major policy changes instituted to improve Holmes' profitability. The two primary revisions were the restructuring of our marketing effort along product division lines and the conversion of the product division incentive plans to a profit-based formula. The corporate organization adapted extremely well to the new policies. The improved profit margin in 1992, in substantial part, was a result of the changes.

International activity increased markedly during the year. Surging foreign business and the expressed objective to capitalize on Holmes' technological leadership overseas resulted in the elevation of Mr. R. E. Foster to officer status as Vice President—International. The year involved heavy commitments of the product division staffs, engineering groups, and manufacturing organization to such important contracts as the $14 million Swenson order for Poland, the $8 million Swenson project for Mexico, $2 million crane order for Venezuela, and several millions of dollars of railcar movers for all areas of the world.

The acquisition of control and commencement of operating responsibility of Societé Francaise Holmes Fermont, the Swenson licensee in Paris, was a major milestone in our international strategy. This organization has the potential of becoming a very substantial contributor in the years immediately ahead. Its long-range market opportunities in Europe and Asia are excellent.

Material Handling Products   Material handling equipment activities portrayed conflicting trends. During the year when total backlog decreased, the crane division backlog increased. This was a result of several multimillion dollar contracts for power plant cranes. The small crane market, on the other hand, experienced depressed conditions during most of the year as general industry withheld appropriations for new plant and equipment. The underhung crane market experienced similar conditions. However, as Congressional attitudes and policies on investment unfold, we expect capital spending to show a substantial upturn.

The Transportation Equipment Division secured the second order for orbital service bridges, a new product for the containment vessels of nuclear power plants. This design is unique and allows considerable cost savings in erecting and maintaining containment shells.

The Ermanco Conveyor Division completed its best year with the growing acceptance of the unique XenoROL® design. We expanded the Grand Haven plant by 50 percent to effect further cost reductions and new concepts of marketing.

The railcar moving line continued to produce more business from international markets. We installed the new 11TM unit in six domestic locations, a product showing signs of exceptional performance. We shipped the first foreign 11TM machine to Sweden.

Process Equipment Products Process equipment again accounted for slightly more than half of the year's business.

Swenson activity reached an all-time high level with much of the division's effort going into international projects. The large foreign orders required considerable additional work to cover the necessary documentation, metrification when required, and general liaison.

We engaged in considerably more subcontracting during the year to accommodate one-piece shipment of the huge vessels pioneered by Swenson to effect greater equipment economies. The division continued to expand the use of computerization for design work and contract administration. We developed more capability during the year to handle the many additional tasks associated with turnkey projects. Swenson research and development efforts accelerated in search of better technology and new products. We conducted pilot plant test work at our facilities and in the field to convert several sales prospects into new contracts.

The metallurgical business proceeded at a slower pace in 1992. However, with construction activity showing early signs of improvement and automotive and farm machinery manufacturers increasing their operating rates, we see intensified interest in metallurgical equipment.

FINANCIAL STATEMENTS

The financial statements of Holmes Corporation and related notes appear on the following page.

NOTES TO CONSOLIDATED FINANCIAL STATEMENTS, 1992 AND 1991

Note A—Summary of Significant Accounting Policies Significant accounting policies consistently applied appear below to assist the reader in reviewing the Company's consolidated financial statements contained in this report.

Consolidation. The consolidated financial statements include the accounts of the Company and its subsidiaries after eliminating all intercompany transactions and balances.

Inventories. Inventories generally appear at the lower of cost or market, with cost determined principally on a first-in, first-out method.

Property, Plant, and Equipment. Property, plant, and equipment appear at acquisition cost less accumulated depreciation. When the Company retires or

Exhibit 1
Holmes Corporation
Balance Sheets
(amounts in thousands)

	1987	1988	1989	1990	1991	1992
Cash	$ 955	$ 962	$ 865	$ 1,247	$ 1,540	$ 3,857
Marketable Securities	0	0	0	0	0	2,990
Accts./Notes Receivable	6,545	7,295	9,718	13,307	18,759	14,303
Inventories	7,298	8,685	12,797	20,426	18,559	17,492
Current Assets	$ 14,798	$ 16,942	$ 23,380	$ 34,980	$ 38,858	$ 38,642
Investments	0	0	0	0	0	422
Property, Plant, and Equipment	12,216	12,445	13,126	13,792	14,903	15,876
Less: Accum. Depreciation	7,846	8,236	8,558	8,988	9,258	9,703
Other Assets	470	420	400	299	343	276
Total Assets	$ 19,638	$ 21,571	$ 28,348	$ 40,083	$ 44,846	$ 45,513
Accts. Payable—Trade	$ 2,894	$ 4,122	$ 6,496	$ 7,889	$ 6,779	$ 4,400
Notes Payable—Nontrade	0	0	700	3,500	0	0
Current Part L-T Debt	170	170	170	170	170	0
Other Current Liab.	550	1,022	3,888	8,624	12,879	11,142
Current Liabilities	$ 3,614	$ 5,314	$ 11,254	$ 20,183	$ 19,828	$ 15,542
Long-Term Debt	680	510	340	170	0	0
Deferred Tax (NCL)	0	0	0	216	328	577
Other Noncurrent Liab.	0	0	0	0	0	0
Total Liabilities	$ 4,294	$ 5,824	$ 11,594	$ 20,569	$ 20,156	$ 16,119
Common Stock	$ 2,927	$ 2,927	$ 2,927	$ 5,855	$ 7,303	$ 9,214
Additional Paid-in Cap.	5,075	5,075	5,075	5,075	5,061	5,286
Retained Earnings	7,342	7,772	8,774	8,599	12,297	14,834
Cum. Translation Adj.	0	0	5	12	29	60
Treasury Stock	0	−27	−27	−27	0	0
Shareholders' Equity	$ 15,344	$ 15,747	$ 16,754	$ 19,514	$ 24,690	$ 29,394
Total Equities	$ 19,638	$ 21,571	$ 28,348	$ 40,083	$ 44,846	$ 45,513

Exhibit 2
Holmes Corporation
Income Statements
(amounts in thousands)

	1988	1989	1990	1991	1992
Sales	$ 41,428	$ 53,541	$ 76,328	$ 109,373	$ 102,699
Other Revenues and Gains	0	41	0	0	211
Cost of Goods Sold	−33,269	−43,142	−60,000	−85,364	−80,260
Sell. and Admin. Expense	−6,175	−7,215	−9,325	−13,416	−12,090
Other Expenses and Losses	−2	0	−11	−31	−1
EBIT	$ 1,982	$ 3,225	$ 6,992	$ 10,562	$ 10,559
Interest Expense	−43	−21	−284	−276	−13
Income Tax Expense	−894	−1,471	−2,992	−3,703	−3,944
Net Income	$ 1,045	$ 1,733	$ 3,716	$ 6,583	$ 6,602

Exhibit 3
Holmes Corporation
Statement of Cash Flows
(amounts in thousands)

	1988	1989	1990	1991	1992
Operations					
Net Income.........................	$ 1,045	$ 1,733	$ 3,716	$ 6,583	$ 6,602
Depreciation and Amortization...........................	491	490	513	586	643
Other Addbacks.....................	20	25	243	151	299
Other Subtractions.....................	0	0	0	0	–97
WC Provided by Operations...........................	$ 1,556	$ 2,248	$ 4,472	$ 7,320	$ 7,447
(Inc.) Decr. in Receivables.................................	–750	–2,424	–3,589	–5,452	4,456
(Inc.) Decr. in Inventories.................................	–1,387	–4,111	–7,629	1,867	1,068
Inc. (Decr.) in Accts. Pay—Trade........................	1,228	2,374	1,393	1,496	–2,608
Inc. (Decr.) in Other Current Liabilities..............	473	2,865	4,737	1,649	–1,508
Cash from Operations.....................................	$ 1,120	$ 952	$ –616	$ 6,880	$ 8,855
Investing					
Fixed Assets Acquired (Net).................................	$ –347	$ –849	$ –749	$ –1,426	$ –1,172
Investments Acquired......................	0	0	0	0	–3,306
Other Invest. Transact.	45	0	81	–64	39
Cash Flow from Investing................................	$ –302	$ –849	$ –668	$ –1,490	$ –4,439
Financing					
Inc. in Short-Term Borrowing............................	$ 0	$ 700	$ 2,800	$ 0	$ 0
Inc. in Long-Term Borrowing.............................	0	0	0	0	0
Issue of Capital Stock........................	0	0	0	0	315
Decr. in Short-Term Borrowing........................	0	0	0	–3500	0
Decr. in Long-Term Borrowing.........................	–170	–170	–170	–170	–170
Acquisit. of Capital Stock.................................	–27	0	0	0	0
Dividends........................	–614	–730	–964	–1,427	–2,243
Other Financing Transactions............................	0	0	0	0	0
Cash Flow from Financing..............................	$ –811	$ –200	$ 1,666	$ –5,097	$ –2,098
Net Change in Cash..	$ 7	$ –97	$ 382	$ 293	$ 2,318

disposes of properties, it removes the related costs and accumulated depreciation from the respective accounts and credits or charges any gain or loss to earnings. The Company expenses maintenance and repairs as incurred. It capitalizes major betterments and renewals. Depreciation results from applying the straight-line method over the estimated useful lives of the assets as follows:

Buildings	30 to 45 years
Machinery and equipment	4 to 20 years
Furniture and fixtures	10 years

Intangible Assets.   The Company amortizes the unallocated excess of cost of a subsidiary over net assets acquired over a 17-year period.

Research and Development Costs. The Company charges research and development costs to operations as incurred ($479,410 in 1992 and $467,733 in 1991).

Pension Plans. The Company and its subsidiaries have noncontributory pension plans covering substantially all of their employees. The Company's policy is to fund accrued pension costs as determined by independent actuaries. Pension costs amounted to $471,826 in 1992 and $366,802 in 1991.

Revenue Recognition. The Company generally recognizes income on a per-centage-of-completion basis. It records advance payments as received and reports them as a deduction from billings when earned. The Company recognizes royalties, included in net sales, as income when received. Royalties total $656,043 in 1992 and $723,930 in 1991.

Income Taxes. The Company provides no income taxes on unremitted earnings of foreign subsidiaries since it anticipates no significant tax liabilities should foreign units remit such earnings. The Company makes provision for deferred income taxes applicable to timing differences between financial statement and income tax accounting, principally on the earnings of a foreign sales subsidiary which existing statutes defer in part from current taxation.

Note B—Foreign Operations The consolidated financial statements include net assets of $2,120,648 ($1,847,534 in 1991), undistributed earnings of $2,061,441 ($1,808,752 in 1991), sales of $7,287,566 ($8,603,225 in 1991), and net income of $454,999 ($641,454 in 1991) applicable to the Canadian subsidiary.

The Company translates balance sheet accounts of the Canadian subsidiary into U.S. dollars at the exchange rates at the end of the year, and operating results at the average of exchange rates for the year.

Note C—Inventories Inventories used in determining cost of sales appear below:

	1992	1991	1990
Raw Materials and Supplies...................	$ 8,889,147	$ 9,720,581	$ 8,900,911
Work in Process.....................................	8,602,594	8,838,650	11,524,805
	$17,491,741	$18,559,231	$20,425,716

Note D—Short-Term Borrowing The Company has short-term credit agreements which principally provide for loans of 90-day periods at varying interest rates. There were no borrowings in 1992. In 1991, the maximum borrowing at the end of any calendar month was $4,500,000 and the approximate average loan balance and weighted average interest rate, computed by using the days outstanding method, were $3,435,000 and 7.6 percent respectively. There were no restrictions upon the Company during the period of the loans and no compensating bank balance arrangements required by the lending institutions.

Note E—Income Taxes   Provision for income taxes consists of:

	1992	1991
Current		
Federal..................................	$2,931,152	$2,633,663
State	466,113	483,240
Canadian...............................	260,306	472,450
	3,657,571	3,589,353
Deferred		
Federal..................................	263,797	91,524
Canadian...............................	22,937	21,706
	286,734	113,230
	$3,944,305	$3,702,583

Reconciliation of the total provision for income taxes to the current federal statutory rate of 34 percent is as follows:

	1992		1991	
	Amount	%	Amount	%
Tax at Statutory Rate	$3,585,640	34.0%	$3,497,240	34.0%
State Taxes, Net of U.S. Tax Credit.............	251,701	2.4	260,950	2.5
All Other Items...	106,964	1.0	(55,607)	(.5)
	$3,944,305	37.4%	$3,702,583	36.0%

Note F—Pensions   The components of pension expense appear below:

	1992	1991
Service Cost	$ 476,490	$ 429,700
Interest Cost	567,159	446,605
Actual Return on Pension Investments...............	(614,210)	(592,900)
Amount Deferred..	55,837	98,817
Amortization of Actuarial Gains and Losses.........	(13,450)	(15,420)
Pension Expense..	$ 471,826	$ 366,802

The funded status of the pension plan appears below:

	December 31	
	1992	1991
Accumulated Benefit Obligation..........................	$5,763,450	$5,325,291
Effect of Salary Increases	1,031,970	976,480
Projected Benefit Obligation...............................	6,795,420	6,301,771
Pension Fund Assets...	6,247,940	5,583,730
Excess Pension Obligation	$ 547,480	$ 718,041

Assumptions used in accounting for pensions appear below:

	1992	1991
Expected Return on Pension Assets	10%	10%
Discount Rate for Projected Benefit Obligation..............	9%	8%
Salary Increases..	5%	5%

Note G—Common Stock   As of March 20, 1992, the Company increased the authorized number of shares of common stock from 1,800,000 shares to 5,000,000 shares.

On December 29, 1992, the Company increased its equity interest (from 45 percent to 85 percent) in Societé Francaise Holmes Fermont, a French affiliate, in exchange for 18,040 of its common shares in a transaction accounted for as a purchase. The Company credited the excess of the fair value ($224,373) of the Company's shares issued over their par value ($90,200) to additional contributed capital. The excess of the purchase cost over the underlying value of the assets acquired was insignificant.

The Company made a 25 percent common stock distribution on June 15, 1991, and on June 19, 1992, resulting in increases of 291,915 shares in 1991 and 364,433 shares in 1992, respectively. We capitalized the par value of these additional shares by a transfer of $1,457,575 in 1991 and $1,822,165 in 1992 from retained earnings to the common stock account. In 1991 and 1992, we paid cash of $2,611 and $15,340, respectively, in lieu of fractional share interests.

In addition, the Company retired 2,570 shares of treasury stock in June 1991. The earnings and dividends per share for 1991 and 1992 in the accompanying consolidated financial statements reflect the 25 percent stock distributions.

Note H—Contingent Liabilities   The Company has certain contingent liabilities with respect to litigation and claims arising in the ordinary course of business. The Company cannot determine the ultimate disposition of these contingent liabilities but, in the opinion of management, they will not result in any material effect upon the Company's consolidated financial position or results of operations.

Note I—Quarterly Data (unaudited)   Quarterly sales, gross profit, net earnings, and earnings per share for 1992 appear below:

	Net Sales	Gross Profit	Net Earnings	Earnings per Share
First	$ 25,931,457	$ 5,606,013	$1,602,837	$ .88
Second	24,390,079	6,148,725	1,727,112	.95
Third	25,327,226	5,706,407	1,505,118	.82
Fourth..............	27,050,074	4,977,774	1,766,841	.97
Year..............	$102,698,836	$22,438,919	$6,601,908	$3.62

The first quarterly results are restated for the 25 percent stock distribution on June 19, 1992.

AUDITORS' REPORT

Board of Directors and Stockholders
Holmes Corporation

We have examined the consolidated balance sheets of Holmes Corporation and Subsidiaries as of December 31, 1992 and 1991, and the related consolidated statements of earnings and cash flows for the years then ended. Our examination was made in accordance with generally accepted auditing standards, and accordingly included such tests of the accounting records and such other auditing procedures as we considered necessary in the circumstances.

In our opinion, the financial statements referred to above present fairly the consolidated financial position of Holmes Corporation and Subsidiaries at December 31, 1992 and 1991, and the consolidated results of their operations and changes in cash flows for the years then ended, in conformity with generally accepted accounting principles applied on a consistent basis.

Chicago, Illinois
March 15, 1993

FIVE-YEAR SUMMARY OF OPERATIONS

	1992	1991	1990	1989	1988
Orders Received	$ 95,436,103	$ 80,707,576	$121,445,731	$89,466,793	$55,454,188
Net Sales	102,698,836	109,372,718	76,327,664	53,540,699	41,427,702
Backlog of Unfilled Orders	77,455,900	84,718,633	113,383,775	68,265,708	32,339,614
Earnings before Taxes on Income	10,546,213	10,285,943	6,708,072	3,203,835	1,939,414
Taxes on Income	3,944,305	3,702,583	2,991,947	1,470,489	894,257
Net Earnings	6,601,908	6,583,360	3,716,125	1,733,346	1,045,157
Net Property, Plant, and Equipment	6,173,416	5,644,590	4,803,978	4,568,372	4,209,396
Net Additions to Property	1,172,057	1,426,347	748,791	848,685	346,549
Depreciation and Amortization	643,231	585,735	513,402	490,133	491,217
Cash Dividends Paid	2,242,892	1,426,502	963,935	730,254	614,378
Working Capital	23,100,863	19,029,626	14,796,931	12,126,491	11,627,875
Shareholders' Equity	29,392,803	24,690,214	19,514,358	15,747,166	15,344,116
Earnings per Share of Common (1)	3.62	3.61	2.03	.96	.57
Dividends per Share of Common (1)	1.22	.78	.53	.40	.34
Book Value per Share of Common (1)	16.07	13.51	10.68	9.18	8.62
Number of Shareholders December 31	2,157	2,024	1,834	1,792	1,787
Number of Employees December 31	1,549	1,550	1,551	1,425	1,303
Shares of Common Outstanding December 31 (1)	1,824,853	1,824,754	1,824,754	1,824,941	1,827,515
Percent Net Sales by Product Line					
Material Handling Equipment	46.1%	43.6%	51.3%	54.4%	63.0%
Processing Equipment	53.9%	56.4%	48.7%	45.6%	37.0%

Note: (1) Based on number of shares outstanding on December 31 adjusted for the 5-for-4 stock distributions in June 1990, 1991, and 1992.

REQUIRED

a. Describe briefly the factors that make Holmes an attractive leveraged buyout candidate and the factors that make it an unattractive leveraged buyout candidate.

b. Prepare pro forma financial statements for Holmes Corporation for 1993 to 1997 excluding all financing (that is, project the amount of operating income after taxes, assets, and cash flows from operating and investing activities). State the underlying assumptions made.

c. What price would you be willing to pay for Holmes Corporation's outstanding common stock? Provide supporting calculations.

d. Using the price from part (c) and the following financing package for the purchase, complete the pro forma financial statements from part (b).

Type	Proportion	Interest Rate	Term
Revolving Bank Loan	15%	10%	Continuous
Term Debt	45	10	7-Year Amortization
Subordinated Debt	25	14	10-Year Amortization
Shareholders' Equity	15		
	100%		

e. Would you attempt to acquire Holmes Corporation after completing the analyses in parts (a) to (d)? If not, how would you change the analyses to make this an attractive leveraged buyout?

Case 10.2:
Rodriguez Home Center, Inc.*

Rodriguez Home Center, Inc. ("RHC" or "the Company"), operates a specialty retail store in Los Angeles, California, offering (fiscal 1992 sales mix in parentheses) furniture (27%), appliances (15%), audio and video electronics products (47%), selected jewelry (4%), and related products and services (7%). The Company is known for low and competitive prices, a liberal return-of-merchandise policy, and a willingness to offer first-time credit to its customers. The Company's bilingual sales staff and liberal credit terms have supported the development of a substantial customer base that is mostly Hispanic. RHC operates out of one department store and uses one warehouse, both of which it leases.

The Company is wholly owned by Jose Rodriguez, who is 62 years old. His father founded RHC in 1955. The Company's competitive advantage is the goodwill generated among the Hispanic community over the years. Although its product offerings are not unique, its competitively low prices for brandname merchandise and credit extension policies have garnered an active customer list of 60,000 individuals. Two of its top three corporate officers are Hispanic as well as 14 of its 15

*The author acknowledges the assistance of Gary M. Cypres in the preparation of this case.

line managers. U.S. Census data indicate that the Hispanic community now comprises 25 percent of the State of California's total population.

Jose Rodriguez is interested in selling his ownership in RHC and has approached his bank to assist in finding a buyer. The bank approached you as a partner in Southern California Investment Partners to see if your investment group might have an interest. The bank provided you with the attached financial statements (Exhibits 3, 4, and 5) and notes for the most recent five fiscal years. The bank indicated its willingness to maintain the working capital loan facility with the Company on essentially the same terms as currently.

REQUIRED

You are asked to ascertain a reasonable purchase price for the equity ownership of Jose Rodriguez as of January 31, 1992. You should derive this valuation following three separate approaches:

1. Market values of comparable companies

2. Market values of individual assets and liabilities (including goodwill)

3. Present value of future cash flows of RHC.

The most comparable publicly traded companies in terms of product line are Second Family Group, Inc. (over-the-counter market), and Best Choice Co., Inc. (New York Stock Exchange). However, neither of these two companies offers in-store credit like Rodriguez. Dayton Hudson and J.C. Penney offer in-store credit but a much broader product line than Rodriguez. Exhibit 1 presents selected data for these four companies. Exhibit 2 presents financial statement ratios for appliance, electronic, and furniture retailers.

Jose Rodriguez indicates that he recently received an appraisal report of the store fixtures and equipment conducted by Price Waterhouse. The Company asked for this appraisal to assist in assessing the adequacy of its insurance coverage. The appraisal as of January 31, 1992, appears below (amounts in thousands):

Store Fixtures and Equipment	Fair Market Value
Automobiles and Trucks	$ 344.0
Furniture and Equipment	1,621.0
Leasehold Improvements	1,461.6
Total	$3,426.6

The report indicates that the valuation of automobiles and trucks uses information from *Truck Blue Book, Truck Gazette,* and *Kelley Blue Book.* The valuation of furniture, equipment and leasehold improvements uses various government price indices for the specific items to ascertain their reproduction cost in new condition. Price Waterhouse then adjusted this reproduction cost downward to reflect the current condition of these items.

Exhibit 1
**Selected Data for Certain Retailers
for 1992 Fiscal Year**

	Second Family Group	Best Choice Company	Dayton-Hudson	J.C. Penney
Sales (000's)	$78,222	$512,850	$14,739,000	$16,736,000
Assets (000's)	$32,779	$156,787	$ 8,524,000	$12,325,000
Net Income (000's)	$ 1,252	$ 5,683	$ 410,000	$ 577,000
Profit Margin for ROA	2.1%	1.6%	4.2%	4.6%
Assets Turnover	2.5	3.5	1.9	1.3
Rate of Return on Assets	5.1%	5.5%	8.2%	6.2%
Common Earnings Leverage..................	68.4%	70.1%	65.7%	74.4%
Capital Structure Leverage	2.5	2.3	5.0	3.4
Rate of Return on Common				
Shareholders' Equity......................	8.7%	9.0%	26.7%	15.7%
Cost of Goods Sold/Sales.......................	72.5%	76.5%	72.3%	65.5%
Selling and Admin. Expense/Sales........	24.7%	20.9%	18.6%	31.7%
Accounts Receivable Turnover..............	107.2	74.3	11.6	4.9
Inventory Turnover	4.3	4.0	5.5	4.2
Accounts Payable Turnover....................	4.8	6.2	8.9	6.4
Current Ratio..	1.2:1	1.6:1	1.5:1	2.6:1
Total Liabilities/Total Assets	58.6%	57.8%	75.7%	64.4%
Long-Term Debt/Total Assets.................	22.9%	22.4%	43.2%	25.4%
Interest Coverage Ratio..........................	2.6	3.6	3.0	3.8
Five-Year Growth Rate				
Sales..	10.4%	24.9%	12.3%	2.3%
Net Income	8.7%	15.7%	7.3%	4.8%
Market Value/Earnings...........................	14.2	16.8	11.8	10.3
Market Value/Earnings before				
Interest, Depr. and Taxes...................	6.1	7.3	3.6	4.1
Market Value/Book Value				
of Common Equity	1.31	1.44	2.86	1.61

Exhibit 2
**Financial Ratios for Selected Retailers
for 1992 Fiscal Year**

	Appliance Stores	Electronic Stores	Furniture Stores
Profit Margin for Return on Assets.......................	2.7%	3.6%	3.3%
Assets Turnover	2.3	2.0	1.6
Return on Assets..	6.3%	7.3%	5.4%
Return on Common Shareholders' Equity...........	13.3%	17.0%	10.2%
Cost of Goods Sold/Sales.......................................	69.6%	65.5%	63.0%
Accounts Receivable Turnover..............................	24.3	33.2	12.8
Inventory Turnover	3.8	3.9	3.0
Current Ratio..	2.0:1	2.1:1	2.9:1
Total Liabilities/Total Assets	51.8%	50.0%	45.0%

Exhibit 3
Rodriguez Home Center, Inc.
Comparative Income Statements (amounts in thousands)

	For the Year Ended January 31				
	1988	**1989**	**1990**	**1991**	**1992**
Sales.........................	$ 56,058	$ 69,670	$ 86,382	$ 98,534	$110,500
Cost of Goods Sold	(37,404)	(46,214)	(56,892)	(68,054)	(75,774)
Gross Margin	$ 18,654	$ 23,456	$ 29,490	$ 30,480	$ 34,726
Selling and Administrative Expenses	(20,832)	(23,678)	(30,064)	(33,284)	(38,032)
Finance Income..	6,294	6,454	9,498	11,396	13,508
Credit Insurance Income	1,060	1,312	1,698	2,022	3,388
Interest Expense...	(1,456)	(1,604)	(2,690)	(4,594)	(4,436)
Income before Income Taxes.........................	$ 3,720	$ 5,940	$ 7,932	$ 6,020	$ 9,154
Income Tax Expense	(1,914)	(2,822)	(3,184)	(2,796)	(4,119)
Net Income...	$ 1,806	$ 3,118	$ 4,748	$ 3,224	$ 5,035

Exhibit 4
Rodriguez Home Center, Inc.
Comparative Balance Sheets (amounts in thousands)

	For the Year Ended January 31					
Assets	**1987**	**1988**	**1989**	**1990**	**1991**	**1992**
Cash...	$ 243	$ 436	$ 786	$ 500	$ 802	$ 1,152
Accounts Receivable						
Gross	30,216	34,976	46,330	59,512	71,360	83,896
Deferred Interest	(2,288)	(2,648)	(4,904)	(5,520)	(7,174)	(9,224)
Allowance for Uncollectible Accounts...	(578)	(670)	(1,116)	(1,600)	(2,000)	(2,400)
Net...	$ 27,350	$ 31,658	$ 40,310	$ 52,392	$ 62,186	$ 72,272
Merchandise Inventories.............................	7,562	10,250	11,294	16,612	16,392	15,646
Prepayments	36	56	106	2,362	3,618	3,004
Total Current Assets..............................	$ 35,191	$ 42,400	$ 52,496	$ 71,866	$ 82,998	$ 92,074
Fixtures and Equipment (net)....................	3,038	2,906	2,454	2,338	3,116	2,870
Deposits..	38	68	192	192	176	178
Total Assets	$ 38,267	$ 45,374	$ 55,142	$ 74,396	$ 86,290	$ 95,122
Liabilities and Shareholders' Equity						
Notes Payable to Bank..............................	$ 16,410	$ 18,995	$ 24,186	$ 31,435	$ 37,312	$ 43,363
Current Portion of Long-Term Debt	—	—	—	—	218	268
Accounts and Notes Payable–Trade	9,869	11,646	11,154	13,514	16,764	14,305
Other Current Liabilities............................	2,486	3,425	5,376	10,273	8,794	9,165
Total Current Liabilities.......................	$ 28,765	$ 34,066	$ 40,716	$ 55,222	$ 63,088	$ 67,101
Long-Term Debt	—	—	—	—	804	588
Total Liabilities.....................................	$ 28,765	$ 34,066	$ 40,716	$ 55,222	$ 63,892	$ 67,689
Common Stock..	$ 36	$ 36	$ 36	$ 36	$ 36	$ 36
Retained Earnings	9,466	11,272	14,390	19,138	22,362	27,397
Total Stockholders' Equity....................	$ 9,502	$ 11,308	$ 14,426	$ 19,174	$ 22,398	$ 27,433
Total Liabilities and Stockholders' Equity	$ 38,267	$ 45,374	$ 55,142	$ 74,396	$ 86,290	$ 95,122

Exhibit 5
Rodriguez Home Center, Inc.
Comparative Statement of Cash Flows (amounts in thousands)

	For the Year Ended January 31				
	1988	**1989**	**1990**	**1991**	**1992**
Operations					
Net Income	$ 1,806	$ 3,118	$ 4,748	$ 3,224	$ 5,035
Depreciation	512	558	608	730	714
(Increase) Decrease in Receivables	(4,308)	(8,652)	(12,082)	(9,794)	(10,086)
(Increase) Decrease in Inventories	(2,688)	(1,044)	(5,318)	220	746
(Increase) Decrease in Prepayments	(20)	(50)	(2,256)	(1,256)	614
Increase (Decrease) in Accounts Payable	1,777	(492)	2,360	3,250	(2,459)
Increase (Decrease) in Other Current Liabilities	939	1,951	4,897	(1,479)	371
Cash Flow from Operations	$(1,982)	$(4,611)	$ (7,043)	$(5,105)	$ (5,065)
Investing					
Acquisition of Fixtures and Equipment	(380)	(106)	(492)	(1,508)	(468)
Other Investing Transactions	(30)	(124)	—	16	(2)
Cash Flow from Investing	$ (410)	$ (230)	$ (492)	$(1,492)	$ (470)
Financing					
Increase (Decrease) in Short-Term Debt	$ 2,585	$ 5,191	$ 7,249	$ 5,877	$ 6,051
Increase (Decrease) in Long-Term Debt	—	—	—	1,022	(166)
Cash Flow from Financing	$ 2,585	$ 5,191	$ 7,249	$ 6,899	$ 5,885
Net Change in Cash...	$ 193	$ 350	$ (286)	$ 302	$ 350

NOTES TO FINANCIAL STATEMENTS

1. Summary of Significant Accounting Policies

Revenue Recognition.   The Company recognizes revenue from the sale of merchandise at the time of sale. It typically provides customers with financing for their purchases. The Company adds interest at rates varying between 11 percent and 21 percent to the face (gross) amount of the receivable at the time of sale and recognizes this amount as revenue over the term of the installment contract using the interest method. The installment contracts provide for monthly payments and mature from 1 to 24 months from the time of the sale. The Company's balance sheet uses 24 months as the operating cycle in accordance with the terms of the installment contracts.

Merchandise Inventories.   The Company states its inventories at lower of cost (first-in, first-out) or market.

Store Fixtures and Equipment.   Store fixtures and equipment appear at acquisition cost. The Company computes depreciation and amortization using the straight-line method over the estimated lives of assets as follows:

Automobiles and Trucks	3–5 years
Furniture and Equipment	5–7 years
Leasehold Improvements	Life of lease

Income Taxes. The Company provides deferred taxes for timing differences between book and taxable income.

2. Accounts Receivable An aging of the accounts receivable on January 31, 1992, reveals the following (dollar amounts in thousands):

Days Past Due	Number of Accounts	Gross Amount Outstanding
31–60 Days	2,996	$2,061
61–90 Days	1,594	1,025
91–120 Days	840	549
121–150 Days	414	304
More than 150 Days	638	393
	6,482	$4,332

The allowance for uncollectible accounts changed as follows (amounts in thousands):

	Fiscal Year Ending January 31				
	1988	**1989**	**1990**	**1991**	**1992**
Balance, Beginning of Fiscal Year ...	$ 578	$ 670	$ 1,116	$ 1,600	$ 2,000
Plus Bad Debt Expense.....................	1,682	2,160	2,764	3,416	3,868
Minus Accounts Written Off	(1,590)	(1,714)	(2,280)	(3,016)	(3,468)
Balance, End of Fiscal Year..............	$ 670	$ 1,116	$ 1,600	$ 2,000	$ 2,400

3. Inventories The book value of inventories exceeded their market value by $800,000 on January 31, 1992, and the Company recorded a writedown to reflect a lower of cost or market valuation. The Company took its first complete physical inventory on January 31, 1991, and discovered that the book inventory exceeded the physical inventory by $2,600,000. The Company wrote down the book inventory to reflect this overstatement but did not restate inventory and cost of goods sold amounts for prior fiscal years.

4. Store Fixtures and Equipment Store fixtures and equipment consist of the following (amounts in thousands):

	January 31				
	1988	**1989**	**1990**	**1991**	**1992**
Automobiles and Trucks	$ 486	$ 544	$ 609	$ 683	$ 765
Furniture and Equipment................	2,809	2,320	2,457	3,021	2,622
Leasehold Improvements.................	1,210	1,546	1,604	2,099	1,886
Software Development Costs	210	˙ 360	440	507	698
Gross...	$ 4,715	$ 4,770	$ 5,110	$ 6,310	$ 5,971
Less Accumulated Depreciation	(1,809)	(2,316)	(2,772)	(3,194)	(3,101)
Net	$ 2,906	$ 2,454	$ 2,338	$ 3,116	$ 2,870

Software development costs are capitalized and amortized in accordance with a reporting standard of the Financial Accounting Standards Board.

5. Notes Payable to Bank The Company has a revolving line of credit agreement with a bank that provides for borrowings not to exceed the lower of $60,000,000 or 65 percent of eligible receivables. The amounts outstanding on this line bear interest at .5 percent over the bank's prime rate. Accounts receivable and inventories not otherwise secured by the Company's trade notes (Note 6) collateralize this line of credit. The bank may withdraw the line-of-credit facility at any time, with any unpaid notes then repayable over a maximum period of 12 months. The line-of-credit agreement contains restrictive covenants with regard to the maintenance of financial ratios.

At January 31, 1992, the Company's borrowings under the line-of-credit facility total $43,363,000. These borrowings bear interest at rates ranging from 9.46 percent to 10.01 percent and have maturities from February 13, 1992 to July 22, 1992. The amount of unused credit under this line was $2,446,000 on January 31, 1992.

6. Trade Notes Payable Trade notes payable result from inventory purchases made through a flooring arrangement with a finance company. The repayment terms typically require payment within 30 days. The flooring company possesses a first priority security interest in certain inventories. The supplier of the merchandise pays all finance charges.

7. Long-Term Debt Long-term debt consists of the following (amounts in thousands):

	January 31	
	1991	**1992**
Various equipment notes at interest rates ranging from 10.75% to 11.25%, secured by assets, maturing from 1993 to 1996.......	$ 808	$687
Obligations under capital leases......................	214	168
Total...	$1,022	$855
Less Current Portion......................................	218	267
	$ 804	$588

Maturities of the equipment notes and obligations under capital leases at January 31, 1992, are as follows (amounts in thousands):

Fiscal Year	Equipment Notes	Capital Leases
1993...	$217	$67
1994...	162	67
1995...	176	66
1996...	132	—
	$687	$200
Less Amount Representing Interest...........	—	32
	$687	$168

8. Income Taxes The provision for income taxes consists of the following (amounts in thousands):

	For the Year Ended January 31				
Current Taxes	**1988**	**1989**	**1990**	**1991**	**1992**
Federal.................................	$ 599	$1,144	$ 1,222	$ 2,286	$ 1,581
State.....................................	186	372	595	798	590
Deferred Taxes					
Federal.................................	$ 868	$ 966	$ 1,010	$ (213)	$ 1,440
State.....................................	261	340	357	(75)	508
Total Provision............................	$ 1,914	$2,822	$ 3,184	$ 2,796	$ 4,119

Deferred taxes arise from timing differences related to revenue recognition and depreciation.

9. Commitments The Company leases its warehouse and certain computer equipment under five-year, noncancellable operating leases expiring in fiscal 1995. The warehouse lease provides for a minimum 4 percent rent escalation per year from fiscal 1992 onward and has two five-year options to extend. The Company also leases its retail showroom under a noncancellable lease expiring in fiscal 1998. The lease provides for cost-of-living rent escalation plus payment of certain executory costs, excluding property taxes, and has two five-year options to extend.

Aggregate minimum lease payments are as follows (amounts in thousands):

Fiscal Year	**Total**
1993	2,995
1994	3,037
1995	2,344
1996	1,526
1997	1,526
Thereafter................	1,272
	12,700

Rent expense for fiscal years 1991 and 1992 were $2,389,566 and $2,424,826 respectively.

Case 10.3:
Revco D.S., Inc.*

Investors in a firm's debt securities that were issued to finance a leveraged buy-out (LBO) have increasingly used the legal concept of fraudulent conveyance in efforts to obtain financial restitution for losses they incurred when the issuing

---

*The author acknowledges the assistance of Dusty Philip in the preparation of this case.

firm is unable to service its debt adequately after the LBO. The sponsoring equity participants in an LBO use the assets of a target firm as collateral for substantial debt borrowings. The proceeds of the debt issues plus a relatively small amount of funds contributed by the sponsoring equity participants finance the buyout of the shares of the pre-LBO shareholders. A presumption exists on the part of the new debtholders that the firm is solvent after the LBO. That is, the value of the firm's assets exceeds the claims of creditors. A subsequent finding that a firm is unable to service the LBO debt may suggest (1) that the value of liabilities exceeded the value of assets just after the LBO (either because lenders overstated the perceived value of the assets or because more corporate assets were used to buy out the pre-LBO shareholders than was appropriate), or (2) subsequent management decisions or operating conditions led to a deterioration of asset values or increase in liability values. Claimants use the fraudulent conveyance concept in the first setting above, arguing that the sponsoring equity participants overpaid to buy out existing shareholders, leaving insufficient assets in the firm to service the debt.

Revco D.S., Inc., the largest retail drugstore chain in the United States, engaged in an LBO transaction totaling $1.45 billion on December 29, 1986. Revco subsequently filed for bankruptcy on July 28, 1988, causing substantial losses for debt and equity participants in the LBO. This case examines whether the value of Revco's net assets at the time of the LBO justified the buyout price.

ECONOMIC CHARACTERISTICS AND EXISTING CONDITIONS IN THE DRUGSTORE INDUSTRY

Between 1970 and 1985, the drugstore industry experienced a 15 percent annual growth rate in sales. Most of this growth occurred because of the increasingly dominating presence of large retail drugstore chains (Revco, Rite Aid, Eckerds, Walgreens). By 1985, these chains commanded a 60 percent market share, with independent drugstores, pharmacies, hospitals, variety stores, and supermarkets comprising the remainder. Drugstores compete on the basis of price, convenience, quality, reliability, and delivery. The drugstore chains increased their market share at the expense of the smaller players for the following reasons:

1. Lower prices due to volume purchasing.

2. Greater convenience due to the larger number of locations.

3. Greater diversity of merchandise beyond pharmaceuticals.

4. Improving professional image.

By the mid-1980s, however, the drugstore industry began approaching maturity. The number of retail outlets nationwide reached a saturation point. In 1986, drugstores reported their smallest sales gains in a decade. Competition intensified among drugstores for a larger share of the now slower growing market. Among the more important industry trends were the following:

1. Frequent price wars: Firms began to trade off reduced profit margin for increased assets turnover.

2. Increased focus on cost-cutting: Firms trimmed costs to offset the required price reductions. Many drugstores installed computer systems to improve productivity and service.

3. Recentralization: Firms began to reverse the trend over the preceding decade towards autonomous profit centers in an effort to eliminate overhead costs and increase coordination among drugstores.

4. Consolidation: Firms attempted to maintain their historical growth rates and increase their market share by acquiring existing drugstore chains. In addition, supermarket chains attempted to diversify into drugstores by participating in these acquisitions. Some of the major acquisitions included:

Acquiror/Acquiree

Pantry Pride/Adams Drugs
Kroger Co./Hook Drugs
K-Mart/Payless Drug Stores
Imasco/People's Drug Stores

5. Diversification: Drugstore chains diversified into higher growth, higher profit margin businesses, including auto parts, food distribution, children's toys, and books.

6. Changed product mix: Drugstores expanded their product line to include video cassette rentals and film processing.

Several positive signs appeared on the horizon for the drugstore industry in the mid-1980s:

1. Aging of the population: Demographers expected the number of individuals over 65 years of age to increase 30 percent between 1986 and 1990 and those over 75 to increase by 74 percent. These age groups typically require substantially more prescription drugs than the general population.

2. Increased health consciousness: Individuals placed increasing emphasis on exercise, diet, and health monitoring beginning in the early 1980s, a trend expected to continue for the foreseeable future. Drugstores added products to satisfy consumer needs in these areas.

3. Rising hospital costs: Rising hospital costs were expected to lead to shorter hospital stays and increased emphasis on outpatient and at-home care, increasing the likelihood that patients would purchase drugs from drugstore chains rather than in-hospital pharmacies.

4. New tax legislation: Drugstores expected to benefit from the decrease in the statutory income tax rate from 46 percent to 34 percent.

Exhibit 1
Operating Data for Revco

| | Fiscal Year Ended May | | | | | Compound Annual Growth Rate |
	1982	1983	1984	1985	1986	
Sales (in millions).................................	$ 1,555	$ 1,793	$ 2,227	$ 2,396	$ 2,743	15.2%
Number of Drugstores...........................	1,593	1,661	1,778	1,898	2,031	6.3%
Drugstore Retail Square Footage (in thousands)....................................	12,227	12,849	13,909	15,148	16,694	8.1%
Drugstore Sales as Percentage of Total Sales......................................	94.5%	94.9%	95.3%	95.1%	95.4%	—
Drugstore Sales per Square Foot..........	$ 120	$ 132	$ 153	$ 150	$ 157	6.9%
Same-Drugstore Percentage Sales Growth.................................	8.4%	12.3%	12.3%	5.8%	8.5%	—
Prescription Revenue as Percentage of Drugstore Sales	28.0%	29.6%	29.4%	30.5%	31.1%	—

HISTORICAL BACKGROUND OF REVCO

Exhibit 1 presents certain operating data for Revco for the fiscal years ending May 1982 to 1986. At the end of fiscal 1986, Revco operated more than 2,000 drugstores in the following geographical mix:

Southeast..................	52.5%
Middle Atlantic	8.5
Midwest.....................	19.9
Southwest.................	19.1
Total......................	100.0%

Revco's sales grew at a 15.2 percent compound annual rate during the five years preceding the LBO. Revco increased the number of drugstores at a 6.3 percent annual rate, using both internal growth and acquisitions. Prescription revenues remained a steady 30 percent of drugstore sales and drugstore revenues remained a steady 95 percent of total revenues. Revco employed an "everyday low prices" strategy during this period rather than opting for periodic sales.

Exhibit 2 presents comparative income statements, Exhibit 3 presents comparative balance sheets, and Exhibit 4 presents comparative statements of cash flows for the 1982 to 1986 fiscal years. Additional information pertaining to these financial statements appears below:

1. Revco leases drugstore and warehouse facilities using operating leases. The present value of its lease commitments when discounted at 10 percent appears below:

Exhibit 2
Revco D.S., Inc., Income Statements (amounts in millions)

	1982	1983	1984	1985	1986
Sales Revenue	$ 1,555	$ 1,793	$ 2,227	$ 2,396	$ 2,743
Interest Revenue	2	2	3	2	3
Total Revenues	$ 1,557	$ 1,795	$ 2,230	$ 2,398	$ 2,746
Cost of Goods Sold	(1,135)	(1,307)	(1,602)	(1,795)	(2,022)
Selling and Administrative Expenses	(321)	(360)	(448)	(520)	(596)
Interest Expense	(11)	(6)	(6)	(15)	(29)
Unusual Items	—	—	—	—	3
Income before Taxes	$ 90	$ 122	$ 174	$ 68	$ 102
Income Taxes	(40)	(56)	(81)	(29)	(45)
Net Income	$ 50	$ 66	$ 93	$ 39	$ 57

Exhibit 3
Revco D.S., Inc., Balance Sheets (amounts in millions)

Assets	1981	1982	1983	1984	1985	1986
Cash	$ 18	$ 27	$ 51	$ 18	$ 8	$ 45
Accounts Receivable	31	31	41	54	75	69
Inventories	258	276	317	472	492	502
Prepayments	11	11	16	19	26	24
Total Current Assets	$ 318	$ 345	$ 425	$ 563	$ 601	$ 640
Property, Plant, and Equipment						
Gross	$ 164	$ 199	$ 218	$ 271	$ 345	$ 428
Accumulated Depreciation	(46)	(58)	(69)	(84)	(102)	(127)
Net	$ 118	$ 141	$ 149	$ 187	$ 243	$ 301
Other Assets	11	15	24	27	31	46
Total Assets	$ 447	$ 501	$ 598	$ 777	$ 875	$ 987

Liabilities and Shareholders' Equity						
Accounts Payable	$ 78	$ 90	$ 100	$ 142	$ 145	$ 155
Notes Payable	—	—	—	51	121	—
Current Portion of Long-Term Debt	3	3	4	4	4	5
Other Current Liabilities	47	49	66	72	75	94
Total Current Liabilities	$ 128	$ 142	$ 170	$ 269	$ 345	$ 254
Long-Term Debt	66	66	43	39	45	305
Deferred Income Taxes	4	8	13	22	28	36
Total Liabilities	$ 198	$ 216	$ 226	$ 330	$ 418	$ 595
Common Stock	$ 14	$ 20	$ 32	$ 36	$ 36	$ 36
Additional Paid-in Capital	20	15	41	39	39	42
Retained Earnings	215	250	299	372	382	412
Treasury Stock	—	—	—	—	—	(98)
Total Shareholders' Equity	$ 249	$ 285	$ 372	$ 447	$ 457	$ 392
Total Liabilities and Shareholders' Equity	$ 447	$ 501	$ 598	$ 777	$ 875	$ 987

Exhibit 4
**Revco D.S., Inc., Statement of Cash Flows
(amounts in millions)**

Operating	1982	1983	1984	1985	1986
Net Income	$ 50	$ 66	$ 93	$ 39	$ 57
Depreciation	17	19	23	28	34
Other Addbacks	4	6	10	6	2
Wk. Cap. from Operations	$ 71	$ 91	$ 126	$ 73	$ 93
(Inc.) Decr. in Accounts Receivable	1	(11)	(7)	(22)	9
(Inc.) Decr. in Inventories	(18)	(41)	(142)	(20)	(10)
(Inc.) Decr. in Prepayments	—	(4)	(2)	(7)	2
Inc. (Decr.) in Accounts Payable	13	11	33	7	11
Inc. (Decr.) in Other Current Liabilities	1	17	(2)	(1)	18
Cash Flow from Operations	$ 68	$ 63	$ 6	$ 30	$ 123
Investing					
Sale of Property, Plant, and Equipment	$ 2	$ 2	$ 1	$ 6	$ 2
Acquisition of Property, Plant, and Equipment	(42)	(29)	(58)	(90)	(82)
Other	—	—	—	—	(16)
Cash Flow from Investing	$ (40)	$ (27)	$ (57)	$ (84)	$ (96)
Financing					
Inc. in Short-Term Borrowing	—	—	$ 49	$ 70	—
Inc. in Long-Term Borrowing	$ 3	—	—	11	$ 261
Inc. in Common Stock	1	$ 38	1	1	2
Decr. in Short-Term Borrowing	—	—	—	—	(121)
Decr. in Long-Term Borrowing	(3)	(24)	(7)	(5)	(5)
Decr. in Common Stock	—	—	—	—	(99)
Dividends	(15)	(17)	(22)	(29)	(27)
Other	(5)	(9)	(3)	(4)	(1)
Cash Flow from Financing	$ (19)	$ (12)	$ 18	$ 44	$ 10
Net Change in Cash	$ 9	$ 24	$ (33)	$ (10)	$ 37

May 31	Present Value of Operating Leases (in millions)
1981	$212
1982	$249
1983	$283
1984	$343
1985	$409
1986	$456

2. Revco uses a last-in, first-out (LIFO) cost-flow assumption for inventories and cost of goods sold. The excess of current cost over LIFO inventories at each year end appears on the next page.

May 31	Excess of Current Cost over LIFO Inventories (in millions)
1982	$ 82
1983	$ 94
1984	$103
1985	$118
1986	$128

3. Selected per share data appear below:

	Fiscal Year				
	1982	**1983**	**1984**	**1985**	**1986**
Earnings per Share	$ 1.39	$ 1.91	$ 2.54	$ 1.06	$ 1.72
Book Value per Share..............	$ 8.12	$10.24	$12.22	$12.48	$12.11

4. On May 24, 1984, Revco acquired the outstanding common shares of Odd Lot Trading Co. by issuing 4.4 million Revco common shares valued at $113 million. Revco treated the acquisition as a pooling of interests, recording the shares issued at the book value of the Odd Lot Trading Co. common shareholders' equity of $925,000. Odd Lot Trading Co. purchases closed-out merchandise and manufacturers' overruns from various vendors for resale at discount prices through their 153 stores located in nine states. Sales and earnings of Odd Lot Trading Co. generally comprise less than 5 percent of Revco's total sales each year. Prior to the acquisition, Revco sold certain merchandise to Odd Lot Trading Co. At the time of the acquisition, Revco was considered a target for an unfriendly takeover. The shares exchanged placed 4.4 million shares (12.0 percent) in what Revco considered friendly hands. Soon after the acquisition, the former owners and managers of Odd Lot Trading Co. made numerous suggestions to improve the operations and profitability of Revco's drugstore operations, suggestions that Sidney Dworkin, long-time chairman and CEO of Revco, did not appreciate. Revco fired these individuals in February 1985. On July 9, 1985, Revco repurchased the 4.4 million shares held by these individuals for $98.2 million in cash. Revco financed the stock repurchase using the proceeds from $95 million of long-term borrowing.

5. For the year ending May 1985, Revco recognized a pretax loss of $35 million from writing down inventories of Odd Lot Trading Co. The latter company operated at a net loss of $9.5 million in fiscal 1985 and at a net loss of $8.6 million in fiscal 1986.

6. On July 1, 1985, Revco acquired the Carls Drug Store chain for $35 million in cash.

7. The income statement for the fiscal year ending May 1986 includes the following unusual items (amounts shown are pretax in millions):

Gain from Sale of Computer Subsidiary	$ 6.6
Gain on Sale of Alarm Service Division...................	2.3
Premium for Short-Term Insurance Coverage	
Following Bankruptcy of Former Carrier	(5.0)
Expenses of Board of Directors to Examine	
Proposed LBO..	(1.1)
Total Unusual Items..	$ 2.8

The after-tax effect of the unusual items was $1.5 million.

8. Revco's market price per share was $27.50 in early 1986 just prior to rumors of an LBO hitting the market.

9. An independent appraisal of Revco's net assets as of September 1986 revealed assets (excluding any goodwill) of $1.433 billion and liabilities of .611 billion.

LBO TRANSACTION

The sponsoring equity participants in the LBO included the following:

Transcontinental Services Group............................	51.0%
Current Management...	28.9
Salomon Brothers	13.1
Golenberg & Co...	1.4
Holders of Exchangeable Preferred Stock...............	5.6
Total...	100.0%

These individuals obtained financing totaling $1.45 billion and used the proceeds to purchase the outstanding shares of Revco for $38.50 per share and to retire $117.5 million of existing debt. The new Revco entity also assumed $175.0 million of existing Revco debt carrying interest of 11.5 percent. Exhibit 5 presents a cash flow analysis relating to the LBO. Revco planned to sell seven nondrugstore subsidiaries soon after the LBO for their independently appraised value of $225 million and use the proceeds to repay a portion of the term debt.

REQUIRED

Your task is to assess the reasonableness of the $38.50 buyout price for Revco's common shares. Your analysis should proceed as follows:

a. Prepare a set of pro forma financial statements for Revco for the fiscal years 1987 to 1991, ignoring the financing for the LBO. That is, project (1) operating income after taxes but before interest expense and related tax effects, (2) assets and current liabilities excluding term debt and the current portion of long-term debt, and (3) cash flow from operations (excluding interest and related taxes) net of cash flow from investing activities. Discount the net cash flow from operating and investing activities, including any residual value at the end of fiscal 1991, using a weighted average cost of capital from the LBO. Assume a 40 percent income tax rate for fiscal 1987 and a 34 percent tax rate thereafter. The prime interest rate at the time of the transaction was 10 percent. The debentures were issued for their face value.

Exhibit 5

Sources and Uses of Cash Relating to Revco LBO (amounts in thousands)

Sources

Term Bank Loan, priced at prime plus 1.75% or LIBOR + 2.75%, Repayable over five years	$ 455,000
Senior Subordinated Debentures, 13.125%, due in December 1993 and 1994	400,000
Subordinated Debentures, 13.30%, due in December 1995 and 1996	210,000
Junior Subordinated Debentures, 13.30%, due in December 1997 to 2001	93,750
Convertible Preferred Stock, 850,000 shares with $12 per share dividend, convertible into 2.56 common shares each	85,000
Exchangeable Preferred Stock, 7,880,000 shares with $3.8125 per share dividend on liquidation preference ($25), exchangeable for $25 notes yielding 15.25%	130,020
Junior Preferred Stock, 1,203,875 shares with $4.40 per share dividend	30,098
Common Stock	34,381
Revco Cash	9,155
Total Sources	$1,447,404

Uses

Acquisition of Revco Common Stock, 32,433 shares at $38.50	$1,248,674
Repayment of Existing Debt	117,484
Cancellation of Revco Employee Stock Options	3,246
Fees and Commissions	78,000
Total Uses	$1,447,404

b. A second approach to assessing the reasonableness of the buyout price is to examine the valuation of other drugstore chains. Exhibits 6 through 9 present historical ratio analyses (assuming the capitalization of all operating leases) for four drugstore chains as follows:

Fay's Drug Company: This firm operated 150 drugstores throughout the Northeast in 1986. The average store size was approximately 15,000 square feet. Drugstore sales comprised the vast majority of revenues. Fay's also operated several auto parts and paper supplies outlets.

Perry Drugstores: This firm operated 139 drugstores, primarily in Michigan, in 1986. Perry focused its strategy on drugstores, auto parts, and health care, with drugstores the dominant segment by far.

Rite Aid Corporation: Rite Aid operated 1,403 drugstores throughout 20 states in 1986 (third largest in the industry behind Revco and Eckerd). The firm's average drugstore totaled 6,500 square feet. Rite Aid also operated auto parts, toy store, and book chains.

Walgreen Company: Walgreen operated 1,273 drugstores in 1986. Although Walgreen ranked fourth in number of stores, it ranked first in sales. The firm also operated a chain of restaurants.

(continued on page 486)

Exhibit 6
Ratio Analysis for Fay's Drug Company

PROFITABILITY ANALYSIS	1982	1983	1984	1985	1986
Return on Assets					
Profit Margin	1.8%	2.4%	3.1%	2.7%	1.3%
× Assets Turnover	2.9	3.0	2.7	2.3	2.2
= Return on Assets	5.3%	7.3%	8.1%	6.2%	2.9%
Return on Common Equity					
Return on Assets	5.3%	7.3%	8.1%	6.2%	2.9%
× Common Earnings Leverage	72.5%	84.3%	85.0%	86.1%	47.0%
× Capital Structure Leverage	4.1	3.8	3.0	2.9	3.4
= Return on Com. Equity	15.5%	23.4%	20.7%	15.5%	4.6%
Operating Performance					
Gross Margin/Sales	25.1%	24.9%	25.6%	25.5%	23.7%
Oper. Profit before Tax/Rev.	3.2%	4.6%	5.6%	4.5%	1.9%
Net Income—Cont. Ops./Revenues	1.3%	2.0%	2.6%	2.4%	0.6%
Assets Turnover					
Sales/Average Accts. Rec.	61.8	63.1	76.1	68.3	58.0
COGS/Average Inventory	5.9	7.0	6.3	5.5	5.5
Sales/Average Fixed Assets	11.4	12.7	11.5	10.7	10.4
RISK ANALYSIS					
Liquidity					
Current Ratio	1.78	1.98	1.74	1.81	2.56
Quick Ratio	0.52	0.76	0.49	0.52	0.68
Days Payables Held	38	30	33	38	32
Days Receivable Held	6	6	5	5	6
Days Inventory Held	62	52	58	67	66
Operating Cash Flow to Current Liabilities	44.4%	40.5%	30.9%	16.6%	−20.5%
Solvency					
Total Liabilities/Total Assets	73.8%	73.8%	61.8%	67.9%	72.2%
L-T Debt/Total Assets	46.0%	46.8%	35.3%	41.5%	53.5%
L-T Debt/Owners' Equity	175.6%	178.5%	92.5%	129.2%	192.6%
Operating Cash Flow to Total Liabilities	17.2%	15.0%	12.2%	6.5%	−6.2%
Interest Coverage Ratio	3.51	6.52	6.62	6.32	1.47
Operating Cash Flow to Cap. Exp.	2.16	1.42	0.80	0.68	−0.40

Exhibit 7
Ratio Analysis for Perry Drugstores

PROFITABILITY ANALYSIS	1982	1983	1984	1985	1986
Return on Assets					
Profit Margin	1.8%	2.1%	2.4%	2.5%	1.7%
× Assets Turnover	2.2	2.0	1.8	1.8	1.7
= Return on Assets	4.0%	4.2%	4.4%	4.4%	2.9%
Return on Common Equity					
Return on Assets	4.0%	4.2%	4.4%	4.4%	2.9%
× Common Earnings Leverage	65.1%	75.0%	87.2%	73.9%	51.9%
× Capital Structure Leverage	4.5	3.6	3.3	4.1	4.9
= Return on Com. Equity	11.7%	11.5%	12.7%	13.3%	7.4%
Operating Performance					
Gross Margin/Sales	29.8%	29.9%	31.1%	30.4%	31.1%
Oper. Profit before Tax/Rev.	3.0%	3.7%	3.9%	3.9%	2.9%
Net Income—Cont.Ops./Revenues	1.2%	1.6%	2.1%	1.8%	0.9%
Assets Turnover					
Sales/Average Accts. Rec.	65.3	72.2	59.5	38.4	33.2
COGS/Average Inventory	3.9	3.8	3.5	3.3	3.2
Sales/Average Fixed Assets	11.8	12.2	11.3	9.6	8.4
RISK ANALYSIS					
Liquidity					
Current Ratio	1.93	2.24	1.46	1.99	2.24
Quick Ratio	0.18	0.40	0.19	0.32	0.33
Days Payables Held	54	48	51	55	54
Days Receivable Held	6	5	6	10	11
Days Inventory Held	93	96	104	109	113
Operating Cash Flow to Current Liabilities	−12.8%	4.0%	31.4%	−36.9%	−5.3%
Solvency					
Total Liabilities/Total Assets	77.8%	68.4%	71.2%	78.8%	80.6%
L-T Debt/Total Assets	51.1%	47.2%	38.7%	54.2%	58.7%
L-T Debt/Owners' Equity	229.7%	149.5%	134.2%	255.8%	302.4%
Operating Cash Flow to Total Liabilities	−4.6%	1.2%	11.7%	−12.6%	−1.4%
Interest Coverage Ratio	2.55	3.73	6.90	3.23	1.86
Operating Cash Flow to Cap. Exp.	−0.83	0.21	0.69	−0.54	−0.15

Exhibit 8
Ratio Analysis for Rite Aid Corporation

PROFITABILITY ANALYSIS	1982	1983	1984	1985	1986
Return on Assets					
Profit Margin	4.5%	4.7%	5.0%	5.2%	4.8%
× Assets Turnover	2.1	2.1	2.0	1.9	1.8
= Return on Assets	9.5%	9.6%	10.1%	9.9%	8.4%
Return on Common Equity					
Return on Assets	9.5%	9.6%	10.1%	9.9%	8.4%
× Common Earnings Leverage	100.5%	101.6%	102.4%	98.0%	90.9%
× Capital Structure Leverage	2.0	2.1	2.1	2.2	2.5
= Return on Com. Equity	19.6%	20.8%	21.3%	21.6%	19.1%
Operating Performance					
Gross Margin/Sales	26.2%	27.1%	28.2%	28.9%	28.7%
Oper. Profit before Tax/Rev.	8.8%	9.1%	9.7%	10.1%	9.2%
Net Income—Cont. Ops./Revenues	4.6%	5.2%	6.1%	5.1%	4.3%
Assets Turnover					
Sales/Average Accts. Rec.	31.4	34.8	38.9	35.5	25.2
COGS/Average Inventory	3.9	4.0	4.0	3.9	3.7
Sales/Average Fixed Assets	9.2	8.8	8.5	7.7	7.0
RISK ANALYSIS					
Liquidity					
Current Ratio	1.90	1.77	2.26	1.74	2.09
Quick Ratio	0.31	0.36	0.34	0.30	0.45
Days Payables Held	32	29	30	30	27
Days Receivable Held	12	10	9	10	14
Days Inventory Held	94	90	91	93	98
Operating Cash Flow to Current Liabilities	25.5%	40.6%	65.0%	32.6%	0.8%
Solvency					
Total Liabilities/Total Assets	51.7%	54.1%	49.2%	60.1%	59.9%
L-T Debt/Total Assets	26.5%	26.3%	26.8%	32.7%	34.9%
L-T Debt/Owners' Equity	54.8%	57.4%	52.7%	82.0%	87.0%
Operating Cash Flow to Total Liabilities	12.5%	19.6%	28.5%	12.8%	0.3%
Interest Coverage Ratio	11.58	13.61	18.95	12.08	7.23
Operating Cash Flow to Cap. Exp.	0.70	1.10	1.59	0.35	0.28

Exhibit 9

Ratio Analysis for Walgreen Company

PROFITABILITY ANALYSIS	1982	1983	1984	1985	1986
Return on Assets					
Profit Margin	2.5%	2.9%	3.1%	3.1%	3.0%
× Assets Turnover	2.4	2.3	2.3	2.2	2.1
= Return on Assets	6.1%	6.8%	7.0%	6.8%	6.3%
Return on Common Equity					
Return on Assets	6.1%	6.8%	7.0%	6.8%	6.3%
× Common Earnings Leverage	108.2%	99.7%	97.7%	96.7%	94.6%
× Capital Structure Leverage	3.1	3.1	3.1	3.2	3.3
= Return on Com. Equity	20.4%	21.1%	21.4%	21.0%	19.9%
Operating Performance					
Gross Margin/Sales	30.5%	30.6%	30.7%	30.7%	30.3%
Oper. Profit before Tax/Rev.	4.5%	5.3%	5.7%	5.7%	5.4%
Net Income—Cont. Ops./Revenues	2.7%	3.0%	3.1%	3.0%	2.8%
Assets Turnover					
Sales/Average Accts. Rec.	139.7	148.0	83.2	79.3	100.8
COGS/Average Inventory	5.3	5.3	5.2	5.1	5.0
Sales/Average Fixed Assets	9.3	9.3	9.5	9.4	8.7
RISK ANALYSIS					
Liquidity					
Current Ratio	1.52	1.55	1.66	1.76	1.85
Quick Ratio	0.25	0.30	0.33	0.33	0.36
Days Payables Held	27	29	28	27	27
Days Receivable Held	3	2	4	5	4
Days Inventory Held	69	69	70	72	72
Operating Cash Flow to Current Liabilities	37.4%	38.9%	28.9%	29.6%	29.8%
Solvency					
Total Liabilities/Total Assets	67.4%	68.5%	67.9%	69.2%	70.5%
L-T Debt/Total Assets	38.7%	40.6%	39.0%	43.0%	44.9%
L-T Debt/Owners' Equity	118.5%	129.1%	121.4%	139.7%	152.3%
Operating Cash Flow to Total Liabilities	13.7%	14.3%	10.5%	9.9%	9.0%
Interest Coverage Ratio	14.92	20.45	26.73	30.33	18.33
Operating Cash Flow to Cap. Exp.	1.11	1.39	1.26	1.00	0.69

Exhibit 10
Valuation Data on Five Drugstore Acquisitions

			Purchase Price of Common Stock as a Multiple of		
Date	**Company Acquired**		**Sales**	**EBIT**[a]	**EBIDT**[b]
Jan. 1985	Payless Drug Stores	One-Year Prior	.58	8.3	6.9
	(144 store chain)	Five-Year Average	.69	11.0	9.0
Feb. 1985	Hook Drug, Inc.	One-Year Prior	.46	9.5	7.7
	(300 store chain)	Five-Year Average	.56	10.6	8.7
Oct. 1985	Jack Eckerd Corp.	One-Year Prior	.47	9.0	6.9
	(drugstores, optical centers, clothing stores)	Five-Year Average	.53	8.2	6.8
May 1986	Thrifty Corp.	One-Year Prior	.57	10.9	8.7
	(555 drugstores plus book, auto parts, and sporting goods stores)	Five-Year Average	.62	13.8	10.9
Dec. 1986	Revco	One-Year Prior	.44	9.2	7.4
	(2,000 drugstores)	Five-Year Average	.57	9.8	8.2

[a]EBIT is earnings before interest and taxes.

[b]EBIDT is earnings before interest, depreciation, and taxes.

Source: Amounts adapted from: Karen H. Wruck, "What Really Went Wrong with Revco?" *Journal of Applied Corporate Finance* (Summer 1991), pp. 79–92.

The following market price information as of the end of fiscal 1986 for each firm may assist in your valuation:

	Fay's	**Perry**	**Rite Aid**	**Walgreen**
Price-Earnings Ratio	17	19	19	22
Price to Book Value per Share	2.44	3.81	4.52	4.60

c. A third approach to assessing the reasonableness of the buyout price is to examine acquisitions of other drugstore chains around the time of the Revco LBO. Exhibit 10 presents data relating to five such acquisitions. The transaction involving Jack Eckerd Corp. was a management-led LBO, whereas the Payless Drug, Hook Drug, and Thrifty Corp. transactions involved acquisitions by other operating corporations.

Cases

Athletic Footwear Industry Analysis*

With products carrying such names as The Pump, Air Attack Plan, Workout, Brat, and Stardust and advertising endorsements ranging from athletes such as Joe Montana and Michael Jordan to entertainers such as Priscilla Presley and Paula Abdul, the debate rages on as to whether this industry is a performance-driven athletic footwear industry or a fashion-driven sneaker industry. This case analyzes the financial success of the three leading companies in the industry, each of which follows a different strategy along the performance-fashion continuum: NIKE, Reebok, and L.A. Gear.

A HISTORICAL OVERVIEW

Twenty-five years ago, German-based Adidas and Puma dominated the athletic footwear industry. NIKE, a U.S. company, and Reebok, a U.K. company, were in their infancy and L.A. Gear had not yet been born. During the 1960s and 1970s, the industry grew slowly but steadily, marketing its products primarily to the serious runner.

During the 1980s, however, the health and fitness craze in the United States combined with a fashion consciousness to create a sales boom. The market grew at a compound annual rate of approximately 26 percent during this decade. Athletic shoes designed specifically for running, basketball, tennis, aerobics, and other sports emerged. NIKE became the market leader in the United States during the early 1980s, emphasizing high performance athletic footwear backed by what most observers considered the most technologically advanced product development group in the industry. Reebok entered the U.S. market in 1979 and experienced rapid growth in the early 1980s, emphasizing fashion more than performance. L.A. Gear entered the industry in 1985 with a similar fashion emphasis.

Exhibit 1 sets forth market share data for each of the years 1987 to 1991. NIKE rested somewhat on its laurels during the mid-1980s and lost its dominant market share position to Reebok. NIKE began to reassert itself in 1986 by reorganizing management and by increasing its investment in new product development, maintaining that performance would dominate fashion in the long run. NIKE regained its market share dominance in 1989.

Reebok began a period of decreasing market share in 1987, being squeezed on the performance end by NIKE and on the fashion end by L.A. Gear. To compensate, it created and introduced "The Pump" in 1989. This technology allows air to be pumped into an internal bladder in the shoe to provide for greater safety and comfort. This new product introduction also signalled a strategic shift to focus on both performance and fashion, a strategy that the company labeled "performance-panache."

*The author gratefully acknowledges the assistance of Regina O'Neill in the preparation of this case.

Exhibit 1
Market Share—Domestic Wholesale Athletic Shoes

	1987	1988	1989	1990	1991
NIKE	18.2%	22.7%	24.7%	26.2%	30.0%
Reebok	30.1	27.1	23.5	23.5	23.0
L.A. Gear	2.2	4.7	11.0	15.4	8.0
All Other	49.5	45.5	40.8	34.9	41.0
	100.0%	100.0%	100.0%	100.0%	100.0%

Source: Sporting Goods Management News, Inc.

L.A. Gear experienced rapid growth during the 1986 to 1990 period, similar to that experienced by Reebok during the early 1980s. L.A. Gear markets its products primarily to teenage females, emphasizing casual styles and bright colors. Company executives state that they are selling the Los Angeles lifestyle, capitalizing on the country's seemingly insatiable appetite for anything Californian.

The "big three" companies now dominate the athletic footwear market, with their dominance expected to increase even more in the 1990s. These companies have brand name recognition and the necessary resources to advertise and promote their products on a domestic as well as global basis. The market leaders of 30 years ago, Adidas and Puma, are no longer major players.

INDUSTRY ECONOMICS

Product Lines   Industry analysts continue to debate the importance of technology in the athletic footwear industry. Proponents point to NIKE's dominant market position that results from continual innovation in product development. Opponents point to the rapid growth experienced by Reebok during the early 1980s and L.A. Gear during the late 1980s following essentially a fashion emphasis. They also note that only 20 percent of athletic footwear consumers in the United States use the footwear for its intended purpose. Uncertainty also exists as to whether patents can successfully protect technological improvements from competitor imitation. All three companies now market shoes with an inner air system, for example.

The substantial increases in advertising expenditures in recent years provide further evidence of the increasingly commodity nature of athletic footwear. Since 1985, the "big three" have increased advertising and promotion at a 40 percent annual rate. Endorsements by athletes have evolved increasingly into endorsements by entertainers.

One view of the athletic footwear industry is that it comprises two segments: (1) footwear for the dedicated athlete, where performance is essential, and (2) footwear for the general populace, where comfort, brand name, and fashion play a more dominant role. The latter segment is the larger and faster growing of the two. The strategies for success in these two segments probably differ. The ability to market a similar line of footwear to both markets is unclear.

Growth Characteristics With the U.S. population growing at only 1.5 percent per year, the 26 percent growth rate in sales of athletic footwear during the 1980s is not sustainable. Concern exists with respect to both volume increases (how many pairs of athletic shoes will consumers tolerate in their closets) and price increases (will consumers continue to pay prices for newly innovated athletic footwear that is often twice as costly as other footwear).

Athletic footwear companies diversified their revenue sources in two directions in recent years. One direction involves increased emphasis on international sales. With dress codes becoming more casual in Europe and East Asia and interest in American sports such as basketball and football becoming more widespread, industry analysts view international markets as the growth markets of the 1990s.

The second direction for diversification is sports apparel and other leisure-time products. Each of the "big three" capitalized on its brand name recognition and distribution channels to create a line of sportswear that coordinates with its footwear. In addition, some companies added leisure-time products such as watches and boats to their product lines.

Production Nearly 99 percent of the athletic footwear sold in the United States comes from factories in East Asia, primarily in South Korea, China, Taiwan, Thailand, Indonesia, and Malaysia. The footwear companies do not own any of these manufacturing facilities. They typically place company personnel in these plants to oversee the manufacturing process, helping to ensure quality control and serving as a link between the design and the manufacture of footwear. The manufacturing process is labor intensive, with sewing machines used as the primary equipment. As a consequence of this production strategy, footwear companies have few fixed assets on their balance sheets. Footwear companies typically price their purchases of footwear from these factories in U.S. dollars.

Marketing Footwear and sportswear companies sell their products through various department, specialty, and discount stores. In the United States, each of the "big three" companies maintains a sales force. This sales force functions to educate retailers on new product innovations, store display design, and similar activities. Because of the rapid growth in sales experienced in recent years, particularly for new, innovative products, the sales force operates more as order takers than demand creators. Maintaining good customer relations in an environment where demand often exceeds available supply is a particularly challenging task. The dominant market share of the "big three" and limits on retailers' shelf space will make it increasingly difficult for the remaining athletic footwear companies to gain market share in the future.

The "big three" companies have typically used independent distributors to market their products abroad. With increasing brand name recognition and anticipated growth in international sales, these companies are beginning to acquire their distributors to capture more of the profits generated abroad and maintain better control of international marketing.

Finance   Compared to other apparel firms, the athletic footwear firms generate higher profit margins and rates of return. These firms use the cash flow generated from this superior profitability to finance the working capital investments (receivables and inventories) required to sustain the rapid growth experienced in recent years. As a consequence, some firms have experienced negative cash flows from operations. These companies have used supplier and short-term bank borrowing to make up the shortfall. Long-term debt tends to be minimal, reflecting in part the absence of significant investments in fixed assets.

COMPANY STRATEGIES

NIKE   NIKE targets the serious athlete with performance-driven footwear. NIKE claims that the resilient, shock-absorbing layer of air-filled plastic membranes in the soles of its shoes gives the wearer added protection and a competitive advantage. NIKE's image is top athletic performance and this remains the most critical part of its product design and marketing appeal. Phil Knight, chairman, CEO, and 36 percent shareholder, sums up the company's philosophy and driving force behind NIKE's success by saying: "We have the edge because we are not shoe makers; we're athletes who make shoes."

NIKE's ultimate goal is to achieve and maintain a status as the leader in athletic performance footwear in all sports where it has a product offering. The company competes in 39 product categories and is now market leader in 22. Although only 20 percent of athletic footwear industry-wide is sold for its intended purpose, NIKE boasts a 40 percent rate among its customers. The company is a major supplier to high school and college sports teams.

In order to remain technologically innovative, NIKE changes approximately 50 percent of its product line every six months, introducing evolutionary improvements to some products, dropping others, and introducing new products. Most of the ideas for NIKE's technological innovations come from NIKE's Sport Research Laboratory, which "conducts extensive studies on a wide variety of basic and applied research projects, from children's foot mophology to the problem of turf toe in football to apparel aerodynamics."

NIKE's most recent innovation is the cross-training shoe. This shoe combines the stability of a court shoe with the cushioning of a running shoe to permit the wearer to perform a variety of activities with just one fitness shoe.

NIKE has experienced limited success in appealing to women. Sales of NIKE's women's shoes represent only 15 percent to 20 percent of the footwear product mix, compared to the industry average of 45 percent. Women often find the support in NIKE's shoes bulky and unattractive.

In recent years, domestic footwear provided two-thirds of total sales, domestic apparel and accessories represented 12 percent, and international sales 21 percent. International sales grew to 29 percent of sales in 1991. NIKE targets its apparel and accessories collection to an assortment of sports (basketball, tennis, and so on). Product designs fit with the company's overall theme that performance is paramount and that form follows function. NIKE expanded beyond athletic footwear by acquiring Cole Haan in 1988, a leading designer and marketer of quality casual and dress shoes. It has recently offered a new line of products that combine Cole Haan's styling with NIKE's air cushioning technology. NIKE views international sales as a primary growth market. It recently acquired a large proportion of its independent distributors abroad and restructured its worldwide organization to compete more effectively as a global company.

NIKE sources almost all of its athletic footwear abroad and about 50 percent of its sports apparel. It has diversified its production sources to reduce costs and political risks. NIKE manufactures its most technical products in Korea (50 percent of production) and Taiwan (15 percent to 20 percent); it produces many of the mid-level products in factories in Thailand (15 percent to 20 percent); and products manufactured for sports teams come from China (6 percent to 7 percent) and Indonesia (5 percent). It recently added plants in Mexico and Argentina. Factories producing exclusively or primarily for NIKE supply the majority of NIKE's athletic footwear. NIKE employees maintain a continual presence in these independently owned factories.

NIKE's reputation for timely delivery of product to its customers results from its "Futures" program. Under this program, retailers book orders five to six months in advance. NIKE guarantees 90 percent delivery of the order within 15 days of the promised date at the agreed price at the time of ordering. Approximately 80 percent of total orders received by NIKE comes through their "Futures" program. This program allows the company to improve production scheduling, thereby reducing inventory risk. However, the program locks in prices and increases NIKE's risk of changes in raw materials and labor costs.

Exhibit 2 presents sales mix data for NIKE by product line. Exhibit 3 presents geographical segment data. The present values of commitments under operating leases when discounted at 10 percent are as follows:

May 31	Present Value Operating Leases (000's)
1986	$42,407
1987	$40,712
1988	$51,759
1989	$68,838
1990	$75,296
1991	$87,715

Reebok An understanding of Reebok's current strategic positioning requires a historical perspective. Reebok's corporate antecedents trace back to the early part of the twentieth century when Joseph Foster, a famous English runner, designed high performance running shoes for world-class runners (names such as Harold Abrahams and Eric Liddell). During the 1950s, the company was renamed after the reebok, which the dictionary defines as "a swift and agile gazelle." Prior to 1979, the company remained primarily a designer and manufacturer of high performance running shoes marketed in the United Kingdom.

Exhibit 2
Sales Data by Product Line for NIKE

Sales Mix	1987	1988	1989	1990	1991
Domestic Footwear					
Athletic	58.2%	62.9%	62.3%	61.2%	55.9%
Nonathletic..................	—	—	5.1	5.4	4.6
Domestic Apparel	14.9	11.9	12.2	11.9	10.8
Total Domestic	73.1%	74.8%	79.6%	78.5%	71.3%
Total Foreign...................	26.9	25.2	20.4	21.5	28.7
Total Sales	100.0%	100.0%	100.0%	100.0%	100.0%

Growth Rate					
Domestic Footwear					
Athletic		+48.2%	+40.8%	+29.3%	+22.5%
Nonathletic..................		—	—	+26.2%	+15.7%
Domestic Apparel		+9.3%	+45.7%	+27.8%	+22.4%
Total Domestic		+40.3%	+51.3%	+28.9%	+22.0%
Total Foreign...................		+28.5%	+15.1%	+37.6%	+79.7%
Total Sales		+37.2%	+42.2%	+30.7%	+34.4%

Reebok entered the U.S. market in 1979. It merged existing technologies from its running shoes with a flair for style and fashion and rode the sports and fitness wave in the United States. Offering the right products at the right time, its sales increased from $1.3 million in 1981 to $919.4 million in 1986, overtaking NIKE for the largest U.S. market share.

A failure by Reebok to redesign either the technology or style of its classic line of shoes and increased competition from NIKE on the performance end of the spectrum and L.A. Gear on the fashion end resulted in decreasing market share for Reebok beginning in 1987 (see Exhibit 1). By 1989, NIKE recaptured market share leadership from Reebok. To regain momentum, Reebok introduced The Pump late in 1989 into its basketball shoe. By pressing a device on the side of the shoe, the user pumps air into a bladder lodged between the body of the shoe and the sole. This technology purportedly provides for greater comfort and shock resistance. Reebok has since extended the pump technology to its other athletic shoes.

Reebok's emphasis in the early 1980s on style and fashion and its recent emphasis on technology has sent mixed signals to the market regarding its corporate strategy. Further clouding the picture is a series of acquisitions made in recent years:

October 1986:	Rockport (casual and dress shoes) for $118.5 million
April 1986:	Avia (athletic footwear) for $181.2 million
January 1988:	Ellesse (sportswear) for $24.7 million
October 1989:	Boston Whaler (recreational boats) for $29.4 million

Despite these seemingly mixed signals regarding corporate strategy, Reebok's product line is not too dissimilar to NIKE's.

Exhibit 3
Geographical Segment Analysis for NIKE

Sales Mix	1987	1988	1989	1990	1991
United States	73.1%	74.8%	79.6%	78.5%	71.3%
Europe	21.8	19.4	14.1	15.0	22.1
Other Foreign	5.1	5.8	6.3	6.5	6.6
	100.0%	100.0%	100.0%	100.0%	100.0%

Income Mix

United States	61.7%	69.5%	77.8%	76.3%	63.6%
Europe	34.8	22.6	12.0	13.3	26.2
Other Foreign	3.5	7.9	10.2	10.4	10.2
	100.0%	100.0%	100.0%	100.0%	100.0%

Asset Mix

United States	72.2%	77.3%	79.7%	76.9%	71.4%
Europe	21.5	14.7	13.6	15.9	22.8
Other Foreign	6.3	8.0	6.7	7.2	5.8
	100.0%	100.0%	100.0%	100.0%	100.0%

Return on Assets

United States	16.9%	22.8%	38.3%	40.1%	28.1%
Europe	32.1%	39.0%	34.4%	33.9%	36.2%
Other Foreign	10.9%	25.2%	59.4%	57.7%	54.9%

Profit Margin

United States	7.6%	12.7%	16.9%	17.9%	15.2%
Europe	14.9%	15.9%	14.7%	16.5%	20.2%
Other Foreign	5.5%	17.5%	27.0%	28.4%	26.2%

Asset Turnover

United States	2.2	1.8	2.3	2.2	1.9
Europe	2.2	2.5	2.3	2.1	1.8
Other Foreign	2.0	1.4	2.2	2.0	2.1

	Sales Mix	
	NIKE	**Reebok**
Athletic Shoes	55.9%	54.7%
Nonathletic Shoes	4.6	9.2
Apparel	10.8	4.2
Other	—	1.4
International	28.7	30.5
	100.0%	100.0%

Reebok recently reorganized its marketing effort for athletic shoes into Technology and Lifestyle units to become more responsive to each market.

One might contrast NIKE and Reebok's strategies by observing that a single unifying thread—performance—appears to link NIKE's various product offerings, whereas Reebok exhibits a strategy that has evolved incrementally as the company has grown from entrepreneurial upstart to a maturing, increasingly globally oriented firm.

Reebok's fastest growing segment in recent years is its international operations. It markets through wholly owned subsidiaries in the United Kingdom, Canada, Germany, Holland and Austria, as well as distributors in over 50 countries. It has the largest market share in Canada, Australia, New Zealand, Hong Kong, and Singapore and a strong second position in the United Kingdom. It is positioning itself for the rapid growth in international sales expected in the athletic footwear industry in the years ahead.

Reebok sources all of its products from independently owned factories abroad. The vast majority of its athletic footwear come from factories in South Korea, while factories in Taiwan, China, Thailand, Indonesia, and the Philippines manufacture its other shoes and apparel. Reebok boasts merchandise delivery-time accuracy in excess of 99 percent.

Exhibit 4 presents sales mix data for Reebok by product line and Exhibit 5 presents geographical segment data. The present values of commitments under operating leases when discounted at 10 percent are as follows:

December 31	Present Value of Operating Leases (000's)
1986	$ 5,986
1987	$16,128
1988	$33,472
1989	$30,995
1990	$41,262
1991	$51,015

L.A. Gear   L.A. Gear introduced its first athletic footwear in 1985 and since that time has become the third largest brand in the United States. The company's commitment is "to provide consumers with attractively styled, high quality athletic footwear at prices intended to make L.A. Gear products attractive to the broadest spectrum of the buying public and to maximize the growth potential of the brand." L.A. Gear views itself as falling in the fashion rather than the performance end of the spectrum. A company spokesman stated: "NIKE has spent millions for years on research and development. They have such a lead on athletic shoe design, nobody is going to catch them on technology."

In 1987, L.A. Gear introduced a line of sports apparel and accessories to complement its athletic footwear. The firm discontinued its apparel business in 1991.

L.A. Gear designs its advertising and promotion campaigns with in-house advertising staff, arguing that it thereby avoids the "translation" problem often en-

Exhibit 4
Sales Data by Product Line for Reebok

Sales Mix	1987	1988	1989	1990	1991
Reebok Footwear	69.6%	64.3%	63.1%	54.3%	48.8%
Avia	10.8	11.3	10.8	7.1	5.9
Ellesse	—	1.9	1.1	2.2	2.3
Apparel	3.3	2.5	2.3	2.0	1.9
Rockport	10.6	9.6	10.5	10.7	9.2
Boston Whaler	—	—	.4	1.7	1.4
International	5.7	10.4	11.8	22.0	30.5
Total Sales	100.0%	100.0%	100.0%	100.0%	100.0%

Growth Rate					
Reebok Footwear	+17.8%	+16.0%	–.4%	+1.7%	+14.0%
Avia	+118.2%	+31.3%	–2.6%	–21.4%	+4.5%
Ellesse	—	—	–38.3%	+223.8%	+34.0%
Apparel	+19.2%	–4.1%	–7.1%	—	+26.2%
Rockport	—	+13.3%	+11.7%	+20.8%	+8.2%
Boston Whaler	—	—	—	+616.7%	+2.7%
International	+419.4%	+129.9%	+14.3%	+224.1%	+75.4%
Total Sales	+51.1%	+28.6%	+2.0%	+18.5%	+26.7%

countered when using an external agency and permits the company to react quickly to new developments. Its advertising campaigns have made the L.A. Gear brand name synonymous with "the lifestyle of Southern California, a lifestyle of sun, fitness and fun which intrigues people the world over." L.A. Gear's list of "unstoppable" celebrity endorsers includes Michael Jackson, Joe Montana, Kareem Abdul-Jabbar, and Priscilla Presley.

L.A. Gear sources all of its footwear from independent producers overseas, primarily in South Korea. It maintains a staff of over 100 people abroad to oversee the production and quality control of its products. It distributes its products in the United States through a broad range of department stores, shoe stores, specialty stores and sporting goods stores. It relies more heavily on department and shoe stores than does NIKE and Reebok. Under the company's "open stock" inventory system, customers may order as few as four pairs of shoes in any size, color, or style. L.A. Gear fills its orders from its own inventory rather than re-ordering from its manufacturers. This policy permits the company to respond quickly to customer orders and encourages retailers to continue devoting shelf space to L.A. Gear products. The company uses distributors in approximately 100 countries to distribute its products abroad.

Exhibit 6 presents product line sales data for L.A. Gear. The present values of operating leases when discounted at 10 percent are as follows:

Exhibit 5
Geographical Segment Analysis for Reebok

Sales Mix	1987	1988	1989	1990	1991
United States	94.3%	88.8%	87.0%	76.7%	68.8%
Europe	3.5	6.0	6.4	17.8	24.7
Other................................	2.2	5.2	6.6	5.5	6.5
	100.0%	100.0%	100.0%	100.0%	100.0%

Income Mix					
United States	76.6%	60.8%	65.5%	51.8%	59.5%
Europe	21.7	33.5	29.6	47.2	33.1
Other................................	1.7	5.7	4.9	1.0	7.4
	100.0%	100.0%	100.0%	100.0%	100.0%

Asset Mix					
United States	84.3%	80.7%	84.1%	82.2%	71.2%
Europe	11.1	14.6	11.0	14.8	18.9
Other................................	4.6	4.7	4.9	3.0	9.9
	100.0%	100.0%	100.0%	100.0%	100.0%

ROA Analysis					
United States					
ROA.............................	17.3%	9.7%	11.7%	7.9%	13.7%
Profit Margin	9.7%	5.2%	7.2%	5.5%	7.4%
Asset Turnover	1.8	1.8	1.6	1.4	1.8
Europe					
ROA.............................	37.4%	29.6%	40.4%	40.2%	28.7%
Profit Margin	74.8%	43.3%	44.2%	21.6%	11.5%
Asset Turnover	.5	.7	.9	1.9	2.5
Other					
ROA.............................	6.9%	15.6%	14.8%	4.2%	12.2%
Profit Margin	8.9%	8.3%	7.0%	1.5%	9.8%
Asset Turnover	.8	1.9	2.1	2.9	1.2

November 30	Present Value of Operating Leases (000's)
1986	$ 697
1987	$ 2,145
1988	$ 6,885
1989	$15,079
1990	$35,990
1991	$26,305

Exhibit 6
Sales Data by Product Line for L.A. Gear

Sales Mix	1987	1988	1989	1990	1991
Domestic Footwear					
Women..........................	72%	60%	47%	32%	29%
Men................................	15	13	19	22	29
Children.........................	9	17	20	19	22
Domestic Apparel and					
Accessories....................	—	1	5	9	—
International	4	9	9	18	20
	100%	100%	100%	100%	100%

Growth Rates

Domestic Footwear					
Women..........................		+164.2%	+116.1%	+1.4%	–37.5%
Men................................		+174.5%	+303.1%	+65.8%	–10.5%
Children.........................		+493.8%	+224.7%	+35.3%	–22.9%
Domestic Apparel and					
Accessories....................		—	+1,304.6%	+161.0%	—
International		+621.4%	+174.8%	+148.8%	–20.1%
Total Sales		+216.9%	+175.9%	+46.2%	–24.5%

REQUIRED

The financial statements for these companies appear at the end of this case (amounts in thousands). Assess the relative profitability and risk of NIKE, Reebok, and L.A. Gear, giving consideration to the different strategies that each company pursues.

NIKE Balance Sheet

	1986	1987	1988	1989	1990	1991
Cash	$ 8,107	$ 126,867	$ 75,357	$ 85,749	$ 90,449	$ 119,804
Marketable Securities	10,031	0	0	0	0	0
Accts./Notes Receivable	185,633	184,459	258,393	296,350	400,877	521,588
Inventories	180,205	120,663	198,470	222,924	309,476	586,594
Other Current Assets	27,534	17,293	21,362	33,358	36,880	52,274
Current Assets	$ 411,510	$ 449,282	$ 553,582	$ 638,381	$ 837,682	$1,280,260
Investments	0	0	0	0	0	0
Property, Plant, and Equipment	89,517	96,988	112,022	154,314	238,461	397,601
Less Accum. Depreciation	39,834	48,508	54,319	64,332	78,797	105,138
Other Assets	15,645	14,081	97,810	97,047	97,206	135,707
Total Assets	$ 476,838	$ 511,843	$ 709,095	$ 825,410	$1,094,552	$1,708,430
Accts. Payable—Trade	$ 23,648	$ 28,036	$ 50,288	$ 71,105	$ 107,423	$ 165,912
Notes Payable—Nontrade	61,634	43,145	135,215	39,170	31,102	300,364
Current Part L-T Debt	3,417	4,800	1,573	1,884	8,792	580
Other Current Liab.	44,027	48,101	67,690	103,744	125,844	161,616
Current Liabilities	$ 132,726	$ 124,082	$ 254,766	$ 215,903	$ 273,161	$ 628,472
Long-Term Debt	15,300	35,202	30,306	34,051	25,941	29,992
Deferred Tax (NCL)	11,666	14,242	11,949	13,352	10,931	16,877
Other Noncurrent Liab.	300	300	300	300	300	300
Minority Int. in Subs.	0	0	0	0	0	0
Total Liabilities	$ 159,992	$ 173,826	$ 297,321	$ 263,606	$ 310,333	$ 675,641
Preferred Stock	$ 0	$ 0	$ 0	$ 0	$ 0	$ 0
Common Stock	2,877	2,879	2,869	2,871	2,874	2,876
Additional Paid-in Cap.	81,633	83,542	69,737	74,227	78,582	84,681
Retained Earnings	232,843	253,534	340,325	486,862	701,728	949,660
Cum. Translation Adj.	−507	−1,938	−1,157	−2,156	1,035	−4,428
Treasury Stock	0	0	0	0	0	0
Shareholders' Equity	$ 316,846	$ 338,017	$ 411,774	$ 561,804	$ 784,219	$1,032,789
Total Equities	$ 476,838	$ 511,843	$ 709,095	$ 825,410	$1,094,552	$1,708,430

NIKE Income Statement

	1987	1988	1989	1990	1991
Sales	$ 877,357	$1,203,440	$1,710,803	$2,235,244	$3,003,610
Other Revenues and Gains	6,201	20,722	3,449	7,264	43
Cost of Goods Sold	−596,662	−803,380	−1,074,831	−1,384,172	−1,850,530
Sell. and Admin. Expense	−204,742	−246,583	−354,825	−454,521	−664,061
EBIT	$ 82,154	$ 174,199	$ 284,596	$ 403,815	$ 489,062
Interest Expense	−8,475	−8,004	−13,949	−10,457	−27,316
Income Tax Expense	−37,800	−64,500	−103,600	−150,400	−174,700
Minority Int. in Earnings	0	0	0	0	0
Income from Contin. Ops.	$ 35,879	$ 101,695	$ 167,047	$ 242,958	$ 287,046
Income from Discont. Ops.	0	0	0	0	0
Extra. Gains (Losses)	0	0	0	0	0
Changes in Acct. Princ.	0	0	0	0	0
Preferred Stock Dividend	−30	−30	−30	−30	−30
NI Avail. to Com.	$ 35,849	$ 101,665	$ 167,017	$ 242,928	$ 287,016

NIKE Statement of Cash Flows

	1987	1988	1989	1990	1991
Operations					
Net Income, Cont. Ops.	$ 35,879	$ 101,695	$ 167,047	$ 242,958	$ 287,046
Depreciation and Amort.	12,078	14,020	14,775	17,130	34,473
Other Addbacks	10,980	432	3,752	5,591	5,626
Other Subtractions	0	−211	−8,532	−946	−2,668
WC Provided by Ops.	$ 58,937	$ 115,936	$ 177,042	$ 264,733	$ 324,477
(Inc.)Decr. in Receivables	1,174	−64,187	−37,957	−104,527	−119,958
(Inc.)Decr. in Inventories	59,542	−60,082	−24,454	−86,552	−274,966
(Inc.)Decr. in Other CA	4,331	−5,624	−2,061	−4,997	−6,261
Inc.(Decr.) Acct. Pay.—Trade	4,388	22,252	20,817	36,318	58,489
Inc.(Decr.) in Other CL	4,074	10,724	36,054	22,100	32,385
Cash from Cont. Ops.	$ 132,446	$ 19,019	$ 169,441	$ 127,075	$ 14,166
Cash from Discont. Ops.	0	0	0	0	0
Cash fr. Extr. Gain/Loss	0	0	0	0	0
Net Cash Flow from Ops.	$ 132,446	$ 19,019	$ 169,441	$ 127,075	$ 14,166
Investing					
Fixed Assets Sold	$ 1,728	$ 8,863	$ 2,565	$ 810	$ 1,730
Investments Sold	0	0	0	0	0
Fixed Assets Acquired	−11,874	−25,513	−42,022	−87,195	−164,843
Investments Acquired	0	−95,130	0	0	−37,563
Other Invest. Trans.	−930	−1,445	−1,014	−3,044	10,511
Net Cash Flow from Investing	$ −11,076	$−113,225	$ −40,471	$ −89,429	$−211,187
Financing					
Incr. S-T Borrowing	$ 0	$ 82,185	$ 0	$ 0	$ 269,262
Incr. L-T Borrowing	30,332	12	0	903	5,149
Issue of Cap. Stock	1,911	8,075	2,517	1,652	3,211
Decr. S-T Borrowing	−18,489	0	−96,045	−8,068	0
Decr. L-T Borrowing	−10,678	−11,693	−4,019	−2,105	−9,974
Acquisit. of Cap. Stock	0	−21,890	0	0	0
Dividends	−15,188	−14,904	−20,510	−28,092	−39,114
Other Financing Trans.	−529	911	−521	2,764	−2,158
Net Cash Flow from Financing	$ −12,641	$ 42,696	$−118,578	$ −32,946	$ 226,376
Net Change in Cash	$ 108,729	$ −51,510	$ 10,392	$ 4,700	$ 29,355

Reebok Balance Sheet

	1986	1987	1988	1989	1990	1991
Cash	$ 66,077	$ 60,167	$ 99,349	$ 171,424	$ 227,140	$ 84,717
Marketable Securities	0	0	0	0	0	0
Accts./Notes Receivable	120,075	204,676	276,204	289,363	391,288	425,663
Inventories	122,522	240,898	301,920	276,911	367,233	436,576
Other Current Assets	7,913	30,355	36,198	46,580	44,001	80,167
Current Assets	$ 316,587	$ 536,096	$ 713,671	$ 784,278	$1,029,662	$1,027,123
Investments	0	0	0	0	0	0
Property, Plant, and Equipment	21,198	73,477	92,546	136,776	160,132	205,436
Less Accum. Depreciation	1,980	8,968	18,419	30,542	49,017	59,107
Other Assets	104,575	267,761	275,651	275,855	262,448	257,369
Total Assets	$ 440,380	$ 868,366	$1,063,449	$1,166,367	$1,403,225	$1,430,821
Accts. Payable—Trade	$ 84,351	$ 175,072	$ 137,125	$ 148,360	$ 166,061	$ 308,353
Notes Payable—Nontrade	22,111	54,626	75,208	1,651	68,660	11,562
Current Part L-T Debt	24	399	404	598	1,411	28,828
Other Current Liab.	34,384	38,272	43,124	52,372	57,647	75,740
Current Liabilities	$ 140,870	$ 268,369	$ 255,861	$ 202,981	$ 293,779	$ 424,483
Long-Term Debt	664	12,612	112,662	110,302	105,752	170,398
Deferred Tax (NCL)	1,245	2,622	4,224	8,788	6,965	12,403
Other Noncurrent Liab.	0	0	0	0	0	0
Minority Int. in Subs.	0	0	0	0	0	0
Total Liabilities	$ 142,779	$ 283,603	$ 372,747	$ 322,071	$ 406,496	$ 607,284
Preferred Stock	$ 0	$ 0	$ 0	$ 0	$ 0	$ 0
Common Stock	528	1,125	1,129	1,139	1,144	1,272
Additional Paid-in Cap.	119,433	263,877	266,564	275,336	281,478	502,962
Retained Earnings	176,194	315,515	421,194	564,463	707,145	912,928
Cum. Translation Adj.	1,446	4,246	1,815	3,358	6,962	9,616
Treasury Stock	0	0	0	0	0	-603,241
Shareholders' Equity	$ 297,601	$ 584,763	$ 690,702	$ 844,296	$ 996,729	$ 823,537
Total Equities	$ 440,380	$ 868,366	$1,063,449	$1,166,367	$1,403,225	$1,430,821

Reebok Income Statement

	1987	1988	1989	1990	1991
Sales	$1,389,196	$1,785,935	$1,822,092	$2,159,243	$2,734,474
Other Revenues and Gains	10,240	5,282	24,330	14,744	11,971
Cost of Goods Sold	-808,991	-1,122,226	-1,071,751	-1,288,314	-1,644,635
Sell. and Admin. Expense	-279,540	-424,302	-468,338	-571,981	-682,629
EBIT	$ 310,905	$ 244,689	$ 306,333	$ 313,692	$ 419,181
Interest Expense	-4,771	-14,129	-15,554	-18,857	-29,295
Income Tax Expense	-140,934	-93,558	-115,781	-118,229	-155,175
Minority Int. in Earnings	0	0	0	0	0
Income from Contin. Ops.	$ 165,200	$ 137,002	$ 174,998	$ 176,606	$ 234,711
Income from Discont. Ops.	0	0	0	0	0
Extra. Gains (Losses)	0	0	0	0	0
Changes in Acct. Princ.	0	0	0	0	0
Preferred Stock Dividend	0	0	0	0	0
NI Avail. to Com.	$ 165,200	$ 137,002	$ 174,998	$ 176,606	$ 234,711

Reebok Statement of Cash Flows

	1987	1988	1989	1990	1991
Operations					
Net Income, Cont. Ops.	$ 165,200	$ 137,002	$ 174,998	$ 176,606	$ 234,711
Depreciation and Amort.	20,112	23,353	28,535	36,523	38,338
Other Addbacks	3,265	0	0	1,349	117
Other Subtractions	−5,603	−5,157	−7,630	0	−8,544
WC Provided by Ops.	$ 182,974	$ 155,198	$ 195,903	$ 214,478	$ 264,622
(Inc.)Decr. in Receivables	−84,601	−66,684	−6,477	−94,389	1,079
(Inc.)Decr. in Inventories	−118,376	−53,960	35,603	−79,747	−43,414
(Inc.)Decr. in Other CA	−22,442	−5,109	−5,027	−2,841	−19,960
Inc.(Decr.) Acct. Pay.—Trade	49,952	1,335	33,463	−4,475	117,845
Inc.(Decr.) in Other CL	3,888	−1,491	14,817	6,193	18,874
Cash from Cont. Ops.	$ 11,395	$ 29,289	$ 268,282	$ 39,219	$ 339,046
Cash from Discont. Ops.	0	0	0	0	0
Cash fr. Extr. Gain/Loss	0	0	0	0	0
Net Cash Flow from Ops.	$ 11,395	$ 29,289	$ 268,282	$ 39,219	$ 339,046
Investing					
Fixed Assets Sold	$ 0	$ 0	$ 0	$ 0	$ 0
Investments Sold	0	0	1,109	0	0
Fixed Assets Acquired	−45,715	−31,923	−18,400	−24,073	−37,730
Investments Acquired	−163,060	−14,768	−32,850	0	−5,657
Other Invest. Trans.	−14,794	0	0	0	0
Net Cash Flow from Investing	$−223,569	$ −46,691	$ −50,141	$ −24,073	$ −43,387
Financing					
Incr. S-T Borrowing	$ 73,659	$ 10,623	$ 0	$ 75,452	$ 9,444
Incr. L-T Borrowing	9,302	96,465	0	5,209	215,000
Issue of Cap. Stock	143,548	2,878	8,381	4,450	11,080
Decr. S-T Borrowing	0	−25,377	−105,558	0	−73,547
Decr. L-T Borrowing	−491	−120	−11,762	−3,671	−158,723
Acquisit. of Cap. Stock	−117	−58	0	0	−396,147
Dividends	−22,158	−25,396	−33,965	−34,219	−30,805
Other Financing Trans.	2,521	−2,431	−3,162	−6,651	−14,384
Net Cash Flow from Financing	$ 206,264	$ 56,584	$−146,066	$ 40,570	$−438,082
Net Change in Cash	$ −5,910	$ 39,182	$ 72,075	$ 55,716	$−142,423

L.A. Gear Balance Sheet

	1986	1987	1988	1989	1990	1991
Cash	$ 3,509	$ 3,245	$ 4,205	$ 353	$ 3,291	$ 1,422
Marketable Securities	7,611	12	0	0	0	0
Accts./Notes Receivable	2,738	15,148	49,526	100,749	156,391	111,470
Inventories	13,823	15,813	66,556	139,516	160,668	141,115
Other Current Assets	340	939	3,383	16,596	18,009	43,064
Current Assets	$ 28,021	$ 35,157	$ 123,670	$ 257,214	$ 338,359	$ 297,071
Investments	0	0	0	0	0	0
Property, Plant, and Equipment	300	1,174	3,720	9,888	28,599	36,345
Less Accum. Depreciation	31	164	610	1,809	4,975	9,476
Other Assets	451	627	2,053	1,265	1,972	1,631
Total Assets	$ 28,741	$ 36,794	$ 128,833	$ 266,558	$ 363,955	$ 325,571
Accts. Payable—Trade	$ 2,230	$ 3,886	$ 7,748	$ 25,619	$ 22,056	$ 7,320
Notes Payable—NonTrade	2,560	7,126	57,230	37,400	94,000	20,000
Current Part L-T Debt	0	0	0	0	0	0
Other Current Liab.	6,203	3,663	22,546	35,316	42,022	66,536
Current Liabilities	$ 10,993	$ 14,675	$ 87,524	$ 98,335	$ 158,078	$ 93,856
Long-Term Debt	0	0	0	0	0	0
Deferred Tax (NCL)	0	0	0	0	0	0
Other Noncurrent Liab.	0	0	0	0	0	0
Minority Int. in Subs.	0	0	0	0	0	0
Total Liabilities	$ 10,993	$ 14,675	$ 87,524	$ 98,335	$ 158,078	$ 93,856
Preferred Stock	$ 0	$ 0	$ 0	$ 0	$ 0	$ 100,000
Common Stock	15,848	15,848	13,008	84,863	91,179	92,331
Additional Paid-in Cap.	0	0	0	0	0	0
Retained Earnings	1,900	6,271	28,301	83,360	114,698	39,384
Cum. Translation Adj.	0	0	0	0	0	0
Treasury Stock	0	0	0	0	0	0
Shareholders' Equity	$ 17,748	$ 22,119	$ 41,309	$ 168,223	$ 205,877	$ 231,715
Total Equities	$ 28,741	$ 36,794	$ 128,833	$ 266,558	$ 363,955	$ 325,571

L.A. Gear Income Statement

	1987	1988	1989	1990	1991
Sales	$ 70,575	$ 223,713	$ 617,080	$ 902,225	$ 618,092
Other Revenues and Gains	604	856	0	0	0
Cost of Goods Sold	−41,569	−129,103	−358,482	−591,740	−448,682
Sell. and Admin. Expense	−20,559	−54,024	−154,449	−240,596	−224,197
EBIT	$ 9,051	$ 41,442	$ 104,149	$ 69,889	$ −54,787
Interest Expense	−1,110	−4,102	−12,304	−18,515	−12,936
Income Tax Expense	−3,570	−15,310	−36,786	−20,036	22,727
Minority Int. in Earnings	0	0	0	0	0
Income from Contin. Ops.	$ 4,371	$ 22,030	$ 55,059	$ 31,338	$ −44,996
Income from Discont. Ops.	0	0	0	0	−21,204
Extra. Gains (Losses)	0	0	0	0	0
Changes in Acct. Princ.	0	0	0	0	−1,625
Preferred Stock Dividend	0	0	0	0	0
NI Avail. to Com.	$ 4,371	$ 22,030	$ 55,059	$ 31,338	$ −67,825

L.A. Gear Statement of Cash Flows

	1987	1988	1989	1990	1991
Operations					
Net Income, Cont. Ops.	$ 4,371	$ 22,030	$ 55,059	$ 31,338	$ -44,986
Depreciation and Amort.	133	446	1,199	3,394	7,182
Other Addbacks	65	0	558	0	4,528
Other Subtractions	-232	-1,020	0	0	0
WC Provided by Ops.	$ 4,337	$ 21,456	$ 56,816	$ 34,732	$ -33,286
(Inc.)Decr. in Receivables	-12,410	-34,378	-50,764	-56,101	44,431
(Inc.)Decr. in Inventories	-1,990	-50,743	-72,960	-21,152	19,553
(Inc.)Decr. in Other CA	-599	-2,432	-12,638	-954	-24,565
Inc.(Decr.) Acct. Pay.—Trade	1,656	7,197	17,871	-3,563	-14,736
Inc.(Decr.) in Other CL	-567	12,213	12,770	6,706	6,514
Cash from Cont. Ops.	$ -9,573	$ -46,687	$ -48,905	$ -40,332	$ -2,089
Cash from Discont. Ops.	-35	0	0	0	-3,204
Cash fr. Extr. Gain/Loss	0	0	0	0	0
Net Cash Flow from Ops.	$ -9,608	$ -46,687	$ -48,905	$ -40,332	$ -5,293
Investing					
Fixed Assets Sold	$ 0	$ 0	$ 0	$ 0	$ 0
Investments Sold	0	0	0	0	0
Fixed Assets Acquired	-874	-2,546	-6,168	-18,939	-14,188
Investments Acquired	0	0	0	0	0
Other Invest. Trans.	-9	-406	-246	-707	-44
Net Cash Flow from Investing	$ -883	$ -2,952	$ -6,414	$ -19,646	$ -14,232
Financing					
Incr. S-T Borrowing	$ 4,626	$ 50,104	$ 0	$ 56,600	$ 0
Incr. L-T Borrowing	0	0	0	0	0
Issue of Cap. Stock	0	0	69,925	908	93,281
Decr. S-T Borrowing	-1,998	0	-19,830	0	-74,000
Decr. L-T Borrowing	0	0	0	0	0
Acquisit. of Cap. Stock	0	0	0	0	0
Dividends	0	0	0	0	-1,625
Other Financing Trans.	7,599	495	1,372	5,408	0
Net Cash Flow from Financing	$ 10,227	$ 50,599	$ 51,467	$ 62,916	$ 17,656
Net Change in Cash	$ -264	$ 960	$ -3,852	$ 2,938	$ -1,869

Consumer Goods Retailing Industry Analysis*

The consumer goods segment of the retailing industry is in the midst of a period of rapid change. Compound annual growth rates in retail sales of 7 percent during the 1980s led to the construction of an excess number of retail stores nationwide, a phenomenon known as overstoring. Economic conditions and demographic changes now lead industry analysts to predict growth in retail sales of only 1 to 2 percent annually during the 1990s. Increased competition for consumers' dollars forces all retailers to rethink their strategic positioning with respect to the key characteristics that differentiate retailers: breadth and depth of product line, price, product quality, level of service, and cost structure.

This case analyzes the strategies and financial performance of three retailers that dominated their retailing categories as they exited the 1980s: The Limited (specialty stores), May Department Stores (department stores), and Wal-Mart Stores (discount stores). Whether these retailers continue to justify their label from a recent *Business Week* article as the "super retailers" is a focus of this case.

A HISTORICAL PERSPECTIVE

The current environment facing the retailing industry has its antecedents in events of the last four decades. Department store chains dominated consumer goods retailing in the 1950s and early 1960s. The notions of "one-stop shopping" and "being all things to all people" provided the rationale for the growth of this type of retailer. Most of the department stores during this period were located in the inner cities. The descriptive phrase for these department stores was probably more appropriately stated as "being all things to certain people" because the various department store chains targeted specific income groups. W.T. Grant aimed at the lower-income group; Sears, Penney, and Montgomery Ward at the middle-income group; and Marshall Field, Macy, and other large city retailers at upper-income individuals. Although these department stores differed in quality of merchandise, price, service, and other dimensions, their unifying theme was one-stop shopping.

Three events beginning in the mid-1960s altered the profile of the retailing industry. The movement to the suburbs led to the rapid growth of shopping malls. One or more department stores typically anchored these malls, complemented by a variety of specialty retail outlets. The department stores served as the major draw of customers to the malls and often contributed substantially to coverage of construction and overhead costs. The growth of shopping malls permitted the department stores to maintain their market share as customers left the inner city. It also provided opportunities for economies of scale in purchasing, advertising, store design and layout, and similar factors.

A second factor affecting retailing in the mid-1960s was the emergence of credit cards. Retailers found that customers were much more willing to purchase

*The author gratefully acknowledges the assistance of Catherine Frye and Mark Golan in the preparation of this case.

merchandise on credit than for cash, and credit cards proliferated. Department stores exerted little effort to check credit worthiness; the aim was to get the card in the customers' hands to enhance sales. Retailers thus not only had to finance and manage the merchandising function; they also needed skills and resources to manage and finance the credit function as well.

A third development of the mid-1960s was the emergence of the discount chains (K-Mart, Wal-Mart). The discounters competed on the basis of lower prices, lower margins, and higher turnovers. These retailers tended to locate in the suburbs in the vicinity of shopping malls. They were thus able to generate the traffic without incurring the overhead cost of the mall locations. Discounters achieved the lower prices through many of the scale economies anticipated by the department stores in moving to the malls (purchasing, advertising). There were two major differences, however: less expensive stores and less service provided. The primary impact of the discounters was on department stores that catered to the lower-income groups (W.T. Grant went bankrupt in 1975). Even the middle-income-oriented stores (Sears, Penney) found that they had to upscale their products and service to distance themselves from the discounters.

The 1970s was a period of rapid growth of shopping malls. The malls were larger than those built in the late 1960s and offered additional attractions (movie theaters, ice skating rinks) to draw customers from nearby competing malls. The department stores discovered the need to locate in an increasing number of malls just to maintain their market share. The department stores also found that specialty retailers located in their malls were beginning to erode market share.

The 1980s was the decade of the specialty retailer. Specialty retailers offer depth and breadth of selection in a particular product category. They benefit from mall traffic attracted by the anchor department store and can thus save on advertising costs (consider, for example, Crate & Barrel, most shoe stores). Their standard merchandise lines and nonspecialized physical requirements for stores permit them to open and close stores quickly (low barriers to entry and exit). Specialty retailers tend to price their merchandise as high or higher than their department store neighbors (better selection, service, and often display), but their cost structures are lower.

Thus, the discounters squeezed the department stores on their commodity-like products and the specialty retailers squeezed the department stores on their fashion and houseware products. The growing shop-at-home phenomena (catalogs, cable TV shopping networks) also negatively impacted the department stores. Finally, department stores were a primary target of several leveraged buyout transactions during the late 1980s, leaving certain firms with heavy debt burdens to service in an increasingly competitive retailing environment.

ECONOMICS OF CONSUMER GOODS RETAILING

The following chart provides an overview of the economic characteristics of three segments of the retailing industry. These descriptions relate to differences between these segments rather than in comparison with other industries.

Factor	Specialty Retailers	Department Stores	Discounters
1. Seasonality	High	High	Average
2. Cyclicality	High	High	Average
3. Operating Leverage	Average	High	Average
4. Importance of Employees	High	Average	Low
5. Capital Requirements	Low	High	Average
6. Barriers to Entry	Low	High	Average
7. Growth Potential	Average	Low	Average

Seasonality.   The department and specialty stores generate most of their sales (approximately 55 percent) and earnings during the Christmas season. They also experience an upturn in sales of clothing items in late summer in preparation for the new school year. These stores must cover their minimum levels of fixed costs (occupancy, salaries) during the off season to remain viable. Although the discounters experience some seasonality as well, the commodity nature of their product lines leads to more stable sales levels throughout the year.

Cyclicality.   The department and specialty stores are highly susceptible to economic downturns. Consumers can delay purchases or scale down and purchase from the discounters. Thus, changes in employment, prices, interest rates, tax rates, and so on significantly affect sales of these retailers. Such cycles do not affect the discounters as much. If anything, economic downturns tend to help the discounters.

Operating Leverage.   The department stores, because of their large investments in store buildings, commitments under leases, and maintenance of a minimum work force carry substantial operating leverage. Given the current competitive conditions in the retailing industry, this high operating leverage is more of a downside risk than an upside potential. The discounters and specialty retailers also carry operating leverage relating to the same factors as for the department stores. However, their relative levels of investment (that is, cost per square foot) are less and they probably have more flexibility to scale up and down than the department stores.

Importance of Employees.   The quantity and expertise of employees is least for the discounters and greatest for the specialty retailers, with department stores falling in between. The expertise will vary somewhat by the type of specialty retailer (for example, electronics versus shoes).

Capital Requirements.   The occupancy cost (construction plus operations) for the discounters is probably the lowest of the three types of retailers. However, these firms must generally obtain their own financing (unless they locate in a shopping center). The occupancy cost for the department and specialty stores is higher. The department stores may own or lease their space, but the specialty retailers almost always lease theirs. Thus, the capital requirements are least for the specialty retailers, followed by the discounters and the department stores.

Barriers to Entry. The specialty retailers have the lowest barriers to entry. Not only do they have lower capital cost, but their mall locations reduce their need to advertise to attract customers. The discounters have average capital requirements and must generally develop name recognition to attract customers. They therefore rank in the middle with respect to entry barriers. The department stores' high fixed cost and broad product lines create the highest barriers to entry of the three.

Growth Potential. The specialty retailers experienced their high growth phase during the 1980s and are now entering the maturity phase, the discounters are mature and will grow at the rate of the general population, and the traditional department store may be approaching its "product decline" phase.

FINANCIAL STATEMENT CHARACTERISTICS

Balance Sheet. Exhibit 1 presents common size balance sheets of the three types of retailers examined in this case.

The department stores usually carry receivables from their credit card operations. The discounters and specialty retailers sell for cash or use bank credit card services and have few receivables. Inventories are a major asset for all three types of retailers. Most firms use a dollar-value LIFO inventory flow assumption, which means that the current market value of their inventories can substantially exceed the book value. Fixed assets are the other major asset of retailers. Included here are store buildings that the retailer either owns or leases under capital leases, as well as store fixtures. Buildings leased under operating leases will not appear on the balance sheet, but firms disclose information about such leases in the notes to the financial statements.

Exhibit 1
Common Size Balance Sheets

	Specialty Retailers	**Department Stores**	**Discounters**
Cash	5%	5%	5%
Receivables	5	20	5
Inventories	55	30	50
Fixed Assets	30	40	35
Other Assets	5	5	5
Total	100%	100%	100%
Current Liabilities	35%	30%	35%
Long-Term Debt	15	20	20
Other Liabilities	5	5	5
Shareholders' Equity	45	45	40
Total	100%	100%	100%

Exhibit 2
Common Size Income Statements

	Specialty Retailers	Dept. Stores	Discounters
Sales...	100%	100%	100%
Cost of Goods Sold	(70)	(72)	(76)
Gross Margin	30%	28%	24%
Selling and Administrative	(19)	(20)	(18)
Interest	(1)	(2)	(1)
Income Taxes.............................	(4)	(2)	(2)
Net Income.................................	6%	4%	3%

The financing of the various types of retailers is remarkably similar. The department stores have somewhat larger current liabilities to support their receivables than discounters and specialty retailers. None of the retailers carry significant amounts of financial leverage (except for those involved in leveraged buyouts). However, they do report material amounts of commitments under operating leases in the notes to their financial statements. Retail operations tend to be cash cows. Unless the retailer grows rapidly and adds new stores, it tends to need little external debt financing. Much of the debt reported on the balance sheet is for capitalized leases.

Income Statement. Exhibit 2 presents common size income statements for the three segments of the consumer goods retailing industry. As one would expect, the profit margins of the specialty retailers are highest, the discounters are the lowest, and department stores are in between. These differences largely reflect differences in the gross margins realized, plus the extra overhead costs of department stores. All three types of retailers have effective tax rates close to the statutory rates.

CURRENT CONDITIONS AND STRATEGY IMPLICATIONS

Current characteristics of the retailing industry appear below:

1. Overstoring of Retail Outlets. The rapid growth of retail stores during the 1980s led retailers to assume that sales would continue to grow 7 percent or more annually during the 1990s. With sales growth of 1 to 2 percent annually now anticipated, too many stores are chasing too few consumers' dollars. Retailing now becomes essentially a zero-sum game, with one retailer's increased sales coming at the expense of another retailer.

2. Weak Economic Conditions and Low Consumer Confidence. Consumers increased their debt levels during the 1980s (from 14 percent of disposable income in 1983 to 18 percent in 1987) to finance purchases of furniture, appliances, automobiles, and other non-real estate items. The increased debt levels reflected consumer confidence from increasing real estate values, the tax deductibility of interest expense on consumer debt, and the general leveraging up of U.S. corporations. Declining real estate values, job layoffs, and uncertainty about the worldwide competitiveness of U.S. firms led consumers to curtail retail purchases and repay debt during the early 1990s.

3. Demographic Changes. Three demographic shifts add to the downward pressure on retail sales during the 1990s: (a) a shift in the purchasing patterns of the baby boomers away from furniture, appliances, and clothing during the 1980s to college education and retirement savings during the 1990s; (b) an aging of the population, with proportionately larger spending on services (for example, health care) than on goods; and (c) a slowdown in the growth rate of new household formations caused by lower birth rates during the 1970s and early 1980s, decisions to delay marriage, and higher divorce rates.

4. Rapid Maturity of New Store Concepts. The intense competition for consumers' retail dollars leads retailers to create innovative retailing concepts that competitors quickly copy. Catalog shopping and shop-at-home television concepts experienced their rapid growth and maturity phases in a few short years during the 1980s. Warehouse clubs and factory outlet malls are now experiencing rapid growth, but such retailing concepts may also quickly reach saturation points.

5. Technological Improvements. Computer systems now play critical roles in customer checkout, purchasing, market research, inventory control, and the physical movement of goods. The rapidly escalating expenditures on computer hardware and software have provided certain firms with a temporary, but probably not sustainable, competitive advantage.

These environmental factors impact the strategic positioning of retailers on each of the key characteristics that differentiate retailers:

1. Price. The overstoring of retailing outlets coupled with reduced consumer spending place downward pressure on prices throughout the retail industry. Strategies that emphasize "everyday low prices" will likely dominate strategies that emphasize "periodic sales." The latter strategy requires heavier promotional spending and runs the risk that consumers will "cherry pick" the sale items.

2. Product Quality. The high levels of product reliability experienced in consumer electronics, appliances, and automobiles during the last decade have led consumers to expect similar quality levels in other product categories. Branded merchandise sometimes serves as a signal of product quality.

3. Value/Cost Relation. The increasingly sophisticated consumer will likely assess the value added from a purchase relative to its cost more closely than was the case during the high-growth, free-spending 1980s.

4. Services.   Providing service to the customer both at the time of sale and subsequently is one means of differentiating one retailer from another, but it also adds to costs.

5. Cost Structure.   The downward pressure on prices requires all retailers to consider avenues for controlling costs more effectively. Expenditures on technology may increase employee productivity and lower costs overall. Volume purchasing and just-in-time purchasing can lower inventory costs. Eliminating periodic sales can lower promotion expenditures.

Discount firms that sell branded merchandise have benefited in recent years from these retail industry trends. The rapid growth in the number of discount outlets and increasing competition from other retailers (warehouse clubs, factory outlets) in the saturated retail market raise questions about the ability of the discounters to maintain their historical growth rates and levels of profitability.

Specialty retailers found a profitability niche during the 1980s by offering depth in a particular product category and coupling it with high service levels and attractive store layouts. Whether consumers will continue to purchase from these "category killers" during the 1990s remains uncertain. Exhibit 2 indicates that specialty retailers have historically realized some of the highest margins in the retailing industry, a position that they may not be able to sustain in the decade ahead. The rapid growth of factory outlet malls is perhaps one signal of their vulnerability.

The strategic positioning of the department stores is perhaps the most questionable of the three retail categories studied in this case. The pressure from the specialty retailers on the high end and the discounters on the low end continues to squeeze market share and profitability from the department stores. Their decision during the 1980s to move toward the specialty retailers by redesigning their stores into mini-boutiques subjects the department stores to some of the same risks discussed above for the specialty retailers.

COMPANIES ANALYZED

The Limited.   The Limited operates a variety of both upscale and discount retailing chains. Its chains include:

> *Upscale:*   Limited, Express, Victoria's Secret, Lane Bryant, Henri
> Bendel, Abercrombie & Fitch.
> *Discount:* Lerner, Lerner Woman

The Limited operates each chain as independent, competing entities. By locating several of its chains in a single shopping center, The Limited has the market power of a department store in that center. Its decentralized organization structure permits each chain to respond to changing fashion and competitive conditions in ways that department stores cannot.

Data for the last five years appear below:

	Fiscal Year				
	1988	**1989**	**1990**	**1991**	**1992**
Limited					
No. of Stores	711	754	766	778	773
Sq. Ft. (thousands)	2,633	*	3,361	3,526	3,927
Express					
No. of Stores	348	418	469	549	611
Sq. Ft. (thousands)	936	*	1,735	2,151	2,926
Victoria's Secret					
No. of Stores	236	328	384	442	507
Sq. Ft. (thousands)	455	*	966	1,210	1,666
Lane Bryant					
No. of Stores	631	687	720	752	786
Sq. Ft. (thousands)	2,630	*	3,037	3,295	3,522
Henri Bendel					
No. of Stores	1	1	1	4	4
Sq. Ft. (thousands)	14	*	14	72	93
Abercrombie & Fitch					
No. of Stores	—	25	25	27	36
Sq. Ft. (thousands)	—	*	166	192	287
Lerner					
No. of Stores	770	784	802	858	910
Sq. Ft. (thousands)	4,700	*	5,095	5,721	6,515
Lerner Woman					
No. of Stores	398	384	—	—	—
Sq. Ft. (thousands)	1,430	*	—	—	—
Other					
No. of Stores	—	—	—	447	567
Sq. Ft. (thousands)	—	—	—	841	1,419
Total Square Footage	12,798	14,296	14,374	17,008	20,335
Present Value of Operating Leases at 10% (millions)	$1,346	$1,517	$1,676	$2,016	$2,716
Number of Employees	50,200	56,700	63,000	72,500	83,800

*Not disclosed.

May Department Stores. The May Department Stores maintains its major presence in the department store segment (Lord & Taylor, May Co., Hechts, Robinson's, and others). In May 1986, May merged with Associated Dry Goods Corporation in a stock swap accounted for using the pooling of interests method. May also maintains a specialty retail shoe chain (Volume Shoe). Prior to fiscal year 1990, May also owned two regional discount store chains (Caldor and Venture). Selected data for May Department Stores appear on the next page.

Fiscal Year	Department Stores			Specialty Shoe Stores		
	Sales (millions)	No. of Stores	Sq. Feet (millions)	Sales (millions)	No. of Stores	Sq. Feet (millions)
1988	$6,205	258	45.0	$1,399	2,516	9.2
1989	$7,537	297	52.6	$1,132	2,602	8.5
1990	$8,106	288	53.1	$1,228	2,746	8.9
1991	$8,669	324	55.0	$1,366	2,967	9.6
1992	$8,854	318	51.8	$1,548	3,295	10.2

Fiscal Year	Discount Stores			Present Value of Operating Leases at 10% (millions)	Number of Employees
	Sales (millions)	No. of Stores	Sq. Feet (millions)		
1988	$2,170	186	18.4	$878	143,000
1989	$2,856	192	18.7	$920	152,000
1990	—	—	—	$748	115,000
1991	—	—	—	$862	116,000
1992	—	—	—	$936	115,000

Wal-Mart. Wal-Mart has successfully pursued the discount store strategy throughout the South and Midwest and is currently moving into the Northeast. In 1991, it ranked as the largest retailer in the United States in terms of sales. Its phenomenal growth and profitability during the 1980s and early 1990s result from a combination of (1) everyday low prices for a broad line of branded merchandise, (2) high service levels, with a generous return policy, (3) new store buildings with accessible floor layouts, and (4) the most technologically advanced computerized information system in the industry. Wal-Mart has placed increasing emphasis on its Sam's Clubs in recent years. Data for the last five years appear below:

Fiscal Year	Sales (millions)	No. of Wal-Mart Stores	No. of Sam's Clubs	Total Square Feet (millions)	Present Value of Operating Leases at 10% (millions)	Number of Employees
1988	$15,959	1,114	84	77.8	$1,031	183,000
1989	20,649	1,259	105	91.6	1,207	223,000
1990	25,811	1,402	123	106.6	1,498	271,000
1991	32,602	1,573	148	127.5	1,696	328,000
1992	43,887	1,720	208	151.9	1,782	371,000

FINANCIAL STATEMENT ANALYSIS OF A RETAILER

The traditional tools of profitability analysis (rates of return on assets and shareholders' equity and their sub-components) and risk analysis are appropriate for retailers. Several ratios particularly important for retailers appear below:

1. Sales per Square Foot. Indicates the ability to utilize space productively in generating revenues. Average sales per square foot in 1991 were approximately $170 for department stores, $230 for discount stores, and $255 for specialty retailers.

2. Same Store Sales Growth. The increase in retail sales between two periods provides a biased measure of growth because of new store additions. Analysts typically examine the growth in retail sales of a particular firm including only those stores that were open for at least one year as of the measurement date.

3. Gross Margin Percentage. Sales minus cost of goods sold equals gross margin. The percentage of gross margin to sales is the most important measure of a firm's success relative to its competitors in its merchandising function.

4. Inventory Turnover. Inventories represent the largest asset of most retailers. The inventory turnover ratio (cost of goods sold divided by average inventory) provides a measure of the firm's ability to manage the level of investment in this important asset. Typical inventory turnovers are 2.5 for specialty retailers and department stores and 5.0 for discounters.

5. Selling and Administrative Expense Percentage. Retail chains seek to achieve economies of scale in their selling and administrative functions by spreading these costs over a large retail sales base. The ratio of selling and administrative expense to sales provides a measure of their success in achieving these economies.

6. Employees per Square Foot. This ratio provides an indication of the level of service provided by a retailer. Because retailers do not disclose separately the number of employees involved in sales versus administrative functions, the analyst must interpret this ratio carefully.

REQUIRED

The financial statements for these companies appear at the end of the case (amounts in millions). Analyze the profitability and risk of these three companies, identifying strategic and other reasons for changes over time and differences between the firms.

The Limited Balance Sheet

		1987		1988		1989		1990		1991		1992
Cash	$	3	$	48	$	15	$	22	$	13	$	34
Marketable Securities		0		0		0		0		0		0
Accts./Notes Receivable		539		560		532		596		670		736
Inventories		361		354		407		482		585		730
Other Current Assets		32		48		70		64		96		105
Current Assets	$	935	$	1,010	$	1,024	$	1,164	$	1,364	$	1,605
Investments		0		0		0		0		0		0
Property, Plant, and Equipment		1,001		1,237		1,516		1,691		2,048		2,456
Less Accum. Depreciation		266		348		449		519		653		799
Other Assets		68		77		55		82		112		157
Total Assets	$	1,738	$	1,976	$	2,146	$	2,418	$	2,871	$	3,419
Accts. Payable—Trade	$	169	$	150	$	189	$	175	$	200	$	200
Notes Payable—Nontrade		0		0		0		0		0		0
Current Part L-T Debt		0		0		0		0		0		0
Other Current Liab.		166		180		267		303		281		320
Current Liabilities	$	335	$	330	$	456	$	478	$	481	$	520
Long-Term Debt		417		681		518		446		540		714
Deferred Tax (NCL)		169		174		199		215		254		267
Other Noncurrent Liab.		35		62		27		39		36		41
Minority Int. in Subs.		0		0		0		0		0		0
Total Liabilities	$	956	$	1,247	$	1,200	$	1,178	$	1,311	$	1,542
Preferred Stock	$	0	$	0	$	0	$	0	$	0	$	0
Common Stock		94		95		95		95		190		190
Additional Paid-in Cap.		200		205		204		196		99		101
Retained Earnings		488		669		879		1,169		1,481		1,783
Cum. Translation Adj.		0		0		0		0		0		0
Treasury Stock		0		−240		−232		−220		−210		−197
Shareholders' Equity	$	782	$	729	$	946	$	1,240	$	1,560	$	1,877
Total Equities	$	1,738	$	1,976	$	2,146	$	2,418	$	2,871	$	3,419

The Limited Income Statement

		1988		1989		1990		1991		1992
Sales	$	3,528	$	4,071	$	4,648	$	5,253	$	6,149
Other Revenues and Gains		9		0		6		13		12
Cost of Goods Sold		−2,535		−2,856		−3,201		−3,623		−4,356
Sell. and Admin. Expense		−584		−747		−821		−933		−1,081
Other Expenses and Losses		0		8		0		0		0
EBIT	$	418	$	460	$	632	$	710	$	724
Interest Expense		−40		−64		−58		−57		−64
Income Tax Expense		−143		−151		−227		−255		−257
Minority Int. in Earnings		0		0		0		0		0
Income from Contin. Ops.	$	235	$	245	$	347	$	398	$	403
Income from Discont. Ops.		0		0		0		0		0
Extra. Gains (Losses)		0		0		0		0		0
Changes in Acct. Princ.		0		0		0		0		0
Preferred Stock Dividend		0		0		0		0		0
NI Avail. to Com.	$	235	$	245	$	347	$	398	$	403

The Limited Statement of Cash Flows

	1988	1989	1990	1991	1992
Operations					
Net Income, Cont. Ops.	$ 235	$ 245	$ 347	$ 398	$ 403
Depreciation and Amort.	109	142	165	184	223
Other Addbacks	0	0	0	0	0
Other Subtractions	0	0	0	0	0
WC Provided by Ops.	$ 344	$ 387	$ 512	$ 582	$ 626
(Inc.)Decr. in Receivables	14	−17	−66	−73	−65
(Inc.)Decr. in Inventories	8	−44	−102	−102	−145
(Inc.)Decr. in Other CA		0	0	0	0
Inc.(Decr.) Acct. Pay.—Trade	−19	36	−14	−38	0
Inc.(Decr.) in Other CL	23	131	74	56	60
Cash from Cont. Ops.	$ 370	$ 493	$ 404	$ 425	$ 476
Cash from Discont. Ops.	0	0	0	0	0
Cash from Extr. Gain/Loss	0	0	0	0	0
Net Cash Flow from Ops.	$ 370	$ 493	$ 404	$ 425	$ 476
Investing					
Fixed Assets Sold	$ 0	$ 0	$ 0	$ 0	$ 0
Investments Sold	0	0	34	0	0
Fixed Assets Acquired	−283	−289	−319	−429	−523
Investments Acquired	0	0	0	−11	−19
Other Invest. Trans.	−26	−37	12	−9	0
Net Cash Flow from Investing	$ −309	$ −326	$ −273	$ −449	$ −542
Financing					
Incr. S-T Borrowing	$ 0	$ 0	$ 0	$ 0	$ 0
Incr. L-T Borrowing	264	0	250	300	173
Issue of Cap. Stock	0	0	0	0	15
Decr. S-T Borrowing	0	0	0	0	0
Decr. L-T Borrowing	0	−163	−322	−205	0
Acquisit. of Cap. Stock	−240	0	0	0	0
Dividends	−45	−43	−58	−86	−101
Other Financing Trans.	5	7	5	7	0
Net Cash Flow from Financing	$ −16	$ −199	$ −125	$ 16	$ 87
Net Change in Cash	$ 45	$ −32	$ 6	$ −8	$ 21

May Department Stores Balance Sheet

	1987	1988	1989	1990	1991	1992
Cash	$ 469	$ 172	$ 124	$ 92	$ 80	$ 207
Marketable Securities	0	0	0	0	0	0
Accts./Notes Receivable	1,591	1,670	2,160	2,274	2,494	2,404
Inventories (EOP)	1,432	1,481	1,788	1,491	1,628	1,741
Other Current Assets	33	58	96	196	175	222
Current Assets	$ 3,525	$ 3,381	$ 4,168	$ 4,053	$ 4,377	$ 4,574
Investments	0	0	0	0	0	0
Property, Plant, and Equip.	3,677	3,870	4,421	3,736	4,180	4,540
Less Accum. Depreciation	1,175	1,238	1,315	1,070	1,195	1,389
Other Assets	182	168	870	1,083	933	1,003
Total Assets	$ 6,209	$ 6,181	$ 8,144	$ 7,802	$ 8,295	$ 8,728
Accts. Payable—Trade	$ 838	$ 906	$ 1,075	$ 706	$ 729	$ 662
Notes Payable—Nontrade	0	0	0	0	0	0
Current Part L-T Debt	145	42	160	449	333	79
Other Current Liab.	621	612	839	839	680	781
Current Liabilities	$ 1,604	$ 1,560	$ 2,074	$ 1,994	$ 1,742	$ 1,522
Long-Term Debt	1,136	1,192	2,483	3,003	3,565	3,918
Deferred Tax (NCL)	471	404	360	307	352	331
Other Noncurrent Liab.	300	299	177	175	160	163
Minority Int. in Subs.	0	0	0	0	0	0
Total Liabilities	$ 3,511	$ 3,455	$ 5,094	$ 5,479	$ 5,819	$ 5,934
Preferred Stock	$ 103	$ 3	$ 0	$ 4	$ 9	$ 13
Common Stock	153	149	149	124	123	123
Additional Paid-in Cap.	179	41	18	0	0	15
Retained Earnings	2,263	2,533	2,883	2,195	2,344	2,643
Cum. Translation Adj.	0	0	0	0	0	0
Treasury Stock	0	0	0	0	0	0
Shareholders' Equity	$ 2,698	$ 2,726	$ 3,050	$ 2,323	$ 2,476	$ 2,794
Total Equities	$ 6,209	$ 6,181	$ 8,144	$ 7,802	$ 8,295	$ 8,728

May Department Stores Income Statement

	1988	1989	1990	1991	1992
Sales	$ 10,581	$ 11,742	$ 9,602	$ 10,066	$ 10,615
Other Revenues and Gains	22	18	22	0	0
Cost of Goods Sold	−7,706	−8,453	−6,581	−6,978	−7,339
Sell. and Admin. Expense	−2,019	−2,279	−1,989	−2,046	−2,164
Other Expenses and Losses	0	0	0	0	0
EBIT	$ 878	$ 1,028	$ 1,054	$ 1,042	$ 1,112
Interest Expense	−135	−247	−255	−280	−316
Income Tax Expense	−299	−278	−284	−262	−281
Minority Int. in Earnings	0	0	0	0	0
Income from Contin. Ops.	$ 444	$ 503	$ 515	$ 500	$ 515
Income from Discont. Ops.	0	31	−17	0	0
Extra. Gains (Losses)	0	0	0	0	0
Changes in Acct. Princ.	0	0	0	0	0
Preferred Stock Dividend	−4	0	0	0	0
NI Avail. to Com.	$ 440	$ 534	$ 498	$ 500	$ 515

May Department Stores Statement of Cash Flows

	1988	1989	1990	1991	1992
Operations					
Net Income, Cont. Ops.	$ 444	$ 503	$ 498	$ 500	$ 515
Depreciation and Amort.	270	330	269	294	319
Other Addbacks	45	50	63	37	35
Other Subtractions	0	0	0	–31	–86
WC Provided by Ops.	$ 759	$ 883	$ 830	$ 800	$ –783
(Inc.)Decr. in Receivables	–106	–203	–136	–98	90
(Inc.)Decr. in Inventories	–77	–108	–173	–30	–113
(Inc.)Decr. in Other CA	67	–35	–39	–47	–47
Inc.(Decr.) Acct. Pay.—Trade	77	134	–67	–33	–8
Inc.(Decr.) in Other CL	–261	–123	–38	–227	101
Cash from Cont. Ops.	$ 459	$ 548	$ 377	$ 365	$ 806
Cash from Discont. Ops.	0	2	–89	–31	0
Cash from Extr. Gain/Loss	0	0	0	0	0
Net Cash Flow from Ops.	$ 459	$ 550	$ 288	$ 334	$ 806
Investing					
Fixed Assets Sold	$ 41	$ 33	$ 34	$ 69	$ 46
Investments Sold	0	0	455	6	0
Fixed Assets Acquired	–501	–423	–522	–548	–512
Investments Acquired	0	–88	–17	–317	0
Other Invest. Trans.	183	–837	81	166	–49
Net Cash Flow from Investing	$ –277	$ –1,315	$ 31	$ –624	$ –515
Financing					
Incr. S-T Borrowing	$ 0	$ 36	$ 322	$ 0	$ 0
Incr. L-T Borrowing	100	1,074	374	719	434
Issue of Cap. Stock	52	628	470	59	44
Decr. S-T Borrowing	0	0	0	–144	214
Decr. L-T Borrowing	–163	–186	–219	0	–121
Acquisit. of Cap. Stock	–294	–651	–1,090	–147	–32
Dividends	–174	–184	–209	–209	–216
Other Financing Trans.	0	0	0	0	0
Net Cash Flow from Financing	$ –479	$ 717	$ –352	$ 278	$ –105
Net Change in Cash	$ –297	$ –48	$ –33	$ –12	$ 186

Wal–Mart Balance Sheet

	1987	1988	1989	1990	1991	1992
Cash	$ 166	$ 11	$ 13	$ 13	$ 13	$ 31
Marketable Securities	0	0	0	0	0	0
Accts./Notes Receivable	90	96	127	156	305	419
Inventories	2,031	2,652	3,351	4,428	5,809	7,384
Other Current Assets	66	146	140	116	288	741
Current Assets	$ 2,353	$ 2,905	$ 3,631	$ 4,713	$ 6,415	$ 8,575
Investments	0	0	0	0	0	0
Property, Plant, and Equipment	2,070	2,685	3,391	4,402	5,996	8,141
Less Accum. Depreciation	394	540	729	972	1,285	1,707
Other Assets	20	82	67	56	262	434
Total Assets	$ 4,049	$ 5,132	$ 6,360	$ 8,199	$ 11,388	$ 15,443
Accts. Payable—Trade	$ 925	$ 1,100	$ 1,390	$ 1,827	$ 2,651	$ 3,454
Notes Payable—Nontrade	0	104	19	185	395	454
Current Part L-T Debt	14	19	21	24	30	40
Other Current Liab.	401	521	636	810	913	1,056
Current Liabilities	$ 1,340	$ 1,744	$ 2,066	$ 2,846	$ 3,989	$ 5,004
Long-Term Debt	943	1,053	1,194	1,273	1,899	3,278
Deferred Tax (NCL)	75	78	92	115	134	172
Other Noncurrent Liab.	0	0	0	0	0	0
Minority Int. in Subs.	0	0	0	0	0	0
Total Liabilities	$ 2,358	$ 2,875	$ 3,352	$ 4,234	$ 6,022	$ 8,454
Preferred Stock	$ 0	$ 0	$ 0	$ 0	$ 0	$ 0
Common Stock	28	57	57	57	114	115
Additional Paid-in Cap.	192	170	174	180	416	625
Retained Earnings	1,471	2,030	2,777	3,728	4,836	6,249
Cum. Translation Adj.	0	0	0	0	0	0
Treasury Stock	0	0	0	0	0	0
Shareholders' Equity	$ 1,691	$ 2,257	$ 3,008	$ 3,965	$ 5,366	$ 6,989
Total Equities	$ 4,049	$ 5,132	$ 6,360	$ 8,199	$ 11,388	$ 15,443

Wal–Mart Income Statement

	1988	1989	1990	1991	1992
Sales	$ 15,959	$ 20,649	$ 25,811	$ 32,602	$ 43,887
Other Revenues and Gains	105	137	175	262	402
Cost of Goods Sold	–12,282	–16,057	–20,070	–25,500	–34,786
Sell. and Admin. Expense	–2,599	–3,268	–4,070	–5,152	–6,684
Other Expenses and Losses	0	0	0	0	0
EBIT	$ 1,183	$ 1,461	$ 1,846	$ 2,212	$ 2,819
Interest Expense	–114	–136	–138	–169	–266
Income Tax Expense	–441	–488	–632	–752	–945
Minority Int. in Earnings	0	0	0	0	0
Income from Contin. Ops.	$ 628	$ 837	$ 1,076	$ 1,291	$ 1,608
Income from Discont. Ops.	0	0	0	0	0
Extra. Gains (Losses)	0	0	0	0	0
Changes in Acct. Princ.	0	0	0	0	0
Preferred Stock Dividend	0	0	0	0	0
NI Avail. to Com.	$ 628	$ 837	$ 1,076	$ 1,291	$ 1,608

Wal–Mart Statement of Cash Flows

	1988	1989	1990	1991	1992
Operations					
Net Income, Cont. Ops.	$ 628	$ 837	$ 1,076	$ 1,291	$ −1,608
Depreciation and Amort.	166	214	269	347	475
Other Addbacks	0	1	5	3	0
Other Subtractions	−1	0	0	0	−8
WC Provided by Ops.	$ 793	$ 1,052	$ 1,350	$ 1,641	$ 2,075
(Inc.)Decr. in Receivables	−6	−31	−29	−58	−114
(Inc.)Decr. in Inventories	−575	−700	−1,077	−1,088	−1,460
(Inc.)Decr. in Other CA	0	−6	−11	12	−10
Inc.(Decr.) Acct. Pay.–Trade	127	290	437	689	710
Inc.(Decr.) in Other CL	120	129	197	100	156
Cash from Cont. Ops.	$ 459	$ 734	$ 867	$ 1,296	$ 1,357
Cash from Discont. Ops.	0	0	0	0	0
Cash from Extr. Gain/Loss	0	0	0	0	0
Net Cash Flow from Ops.	$ 459	$ 734	$ 867	$ 1,296	$ 1,357
Investing					
Fixed Assets Sold	$ 0	$ 0	$ 0	$ 0	$ 0
Investments Sold	0	0	0	0	0
Fixed Assets Acquired	−757	−797	−1,086	−1,533	−2,142
Investments Acquired	0	0	0	0	0
Other Invest. Trans.	−51	9	7	7	−8
Net Cash Flow from Investing	$ −808	$ −788	$ −1,079	$ −1,526	$ −2,150
Financing					
Incr. S-T Borrowing	$ 104	$ 0	$ 166	$ 30	$ 58
Incr. L-T Borrowing	194	248	189	500	1,010
Issue of Cap. Stock	7	4	6	5	13
Decr. S-T Borrowing	0	−85	0	0	0
Decr. L-T Borrowing	−42	−21	−25	−134	−75
Acquisit. of Cap. Stock	0	0	0	−26	0
Dividends	−68	−91	−124	−159	−195
Other Financing Trans.	0	0	0	14	0
Net Cash Flow from Financing	$ 195	$ 55	$ 212	$ 230	$ 811
Net Change in Cash	$ −154	$ 1	$ 0	$ 0	$ 18

Marketing Services Industry Analysis*

The independent advertising agency that offers advertising services primarily to domestic clients is a relic of the past. The changed nature of this industry results from three factors:

1. An expansion of services beyond advertising to include direct response marketing, public relations, marketing research, lobbying, and similar efforts. The companies in this industry now portray themselves as marketing services, or communications, specialists rather than as advertising agencies.

2. An expansion in the offering of services on a worldwide basis, reflecting the increasing globalization of their clients and their clients' products and the growth opportunities in Western and Eastern Europe and East Asia. The use of the term *worldwide* in the names of several of the large, multinational firms evidences this geographical outreach.

3. A rapid growth in the merger and acquisition of existing agencies, in large part to accomplish the product extensions and geographical expansions discussed above. The merger actively has resulted in a small number of mega-marketing services firms worldwide.

This case analyzes three of the largest marketing services firms in the world, each of which headquarters in a different country: Dentsu (Japan), The Interpublic Group of Companies (United States), and WPP (United Kingdom).

ECONOMIC CHARACTERISTICS OF MARKETING SERVICES

Marketing services firms are classic service businesses. Their major asset, their employees, provide marketing services for clients for a commission or fee. Because the balance sheet does not report this important "asset," analyzing the profitability and risk of these firms is a uniquely challenging task. This section describes the economic characteristics of marketing services firms.

Revenues   Marketing services firms derive 60 to 80 percent of their revenues from advertising services. Their main task is to create an advertising campaign for clients and the related advertising copy to support the campaign. These firms then purchase advertising time or space from various media (television, magazines, newspapers) and sell the time or space to their clients. Historically, the advertising firms charged a standard fee for their services of 15 percent of the billing price of advertisements placed. The agencies now price less than one-third of advertising

---

*Charles G. Crane provided much appreciated assistance in the preparation of this case.

services on this basis. This change reflects a recognition that a standardized fee does not adequately capture the differing amounts of services provided for various clients (that is, larger clients desire a discount). It also results from increasing competition in the industry, caused by overcapacity among advertising agencies and curtailments in the rate of growth in advertising spending by clients. Negotiated fees are rapidly replacing the standardized fee. The amount reported as sales in the income statements of marketing services firms represents commissions and fees, not the total billings to clients.

Agencies may subcontract the production of advertising copy or do the work themselves. In the latter case, they generate a fee for the production services. Marketing services firms price most other services (that is, direct response marketing, marketing research) on a negotiated-fee basis.

Marketing services expenditures are discretionary fixed costs. Once made, they go directly to the client's bottom line. Their discretionary nature, however, means that clients can increase or decrease their levels of expenditures quickly in response to economic conditions.

Advertising and other promotion spending by clients aims to (1) maintain or enhance market share for mature products or (2) rapidly disseminate information about new products. Most mature products are cash cows and the objective is to defend established brand franchises. Many of the leading brands of 50 years ago are also the leading brands today, largely through continued defensive advertising and promotion.

High rates of technological change in certain industries have shortened product life cycles and serve as a source of increased advertising and promotion spending. Advertising is particularly effective in establishing and reinforcing product niches and communicating technological product modifications. New food introductions have grown at a 15 to 20 percent rate annually in recent years, reflecting increased health consciousness, the desire for easier-to-fix meals, and the growth of the microwave market. Test marketing a new product costs approximately $1 million and rolling out a new product nationally can run $20 million. The marketing services industry obviously benefits from these expenditures. On the other hand, the high rate of new product fatalities (80 percent) often causes firms to delay new product introductions during recessionary periods, exacerbating the cyclicality of the industry.

The U.S. market has dominated advertising spending for decades. It was not until 1985 that the growth rate in spending outside of the United States exceeded that in the United States. It was not until 1988 that the non-U.S. advertising volume exceeded that in the United States. Industry specialists predict that the growth markets of the future will be Western Europe, Eastern Europe, and East Asia. The impetus for growth in Western Europe comes from the anticipated removal of trade barriers in 1992 and the privatization of television broadcasting. The democratization of Eastern Europe should provide large, untested markets for a wide range of consumer products denied the populace for decades. The rapid industrial growth and increased standard of living throughout East Asia should fuel increased advertising spending in that area.

Costs   The major costs of marketing services firms include compensation, rent, travel and communication, all of which tend to behave as fixed costs. Although this cost structure provides some limited opportunities for economies of scale on the upside (that is, operating leverage), the stickiness of these costs on the downside can result in significant risk of diseconomies. With the overcapacity in the industry and recent recessions, firms have been more willing to terminate employees, risking the permanent loss of creative talent for the short-term survival of the company.

The largest cost by far is for compensation, representing approximately 60 percent of revenues. In addition to cash compensation, firms often offer various forms of deferred and incentive compensation to motivate and retain highly skilled, creative individuals. Other operating costs average 30 to 35 percent of revenues. Included here are rent for operating leases on buildings and depreciation on furniture, fixtures, and leasehold improvements. The remaining major cost is income taxes, averaging 30 to 50 percent of income before taxes and 4 to 6 percent of revenues. Being labor rather than capital intensive, marketing services firms realize few of the benefits of accelerated depreciation.

The globalization of marketing services firms subjects their revenues and costs to foreign currency risks. Firms can reduce this risk somewhat by attempting to match revenues and costs by currency (for example, billings in Spain matched against compensation, rent, and other costs incurred within Spain). Such matching becomes increasingly difficult as firms create advertisements and other promotions in one location for products that clients market worldwide. The management of foreign currency risk requires financial expertise in an industry where creative talent dominates the management ranks.

The increased globalization also presents challenges when comparing the operating performance and financial condition of multinational marketing services firms. The consolidated financial statements will differ depending on the translation method used (all current, current/noncurrent, monetary/nonmonetary) and the treatment of exchange gains and losses (flow through the income statement or bypass the income statement and go directly to a shareholders' equity account).

To summarize, marketing services firms exhibit some operating leverage characteristics. Operating margins can increase dramatically when revenues increase, but revenue decreases quickly squeeze these margins. The sensitivity of revenues to both economic conditions and exchange rate changes adds to the potential benefits and risks of operating leverage in this industry.

Cash Flows   Because marketing services firms are not capital intensive, cash flow from operations tends to track net income fairly closely (with a lag). Although dividend payouts average 40 to 60 percent of net income, these firms still generate large amounts of cash flows from operations. Lacking collateralizable assets and the need for cash, marketing services firms have historically not required external debt or equity financing. The recent growth of mergers in the industry has led some firms to tap the external capital markets to finance these transactions.

Balance Sheet   The major recorded asset on the balance sheet of marketing services firms is receivables, representing 60 to 70 percent of total assets. Such receivables appear on two lines on the balance sheet. "Accounts Receivable" represents amounts due from clients for advertising that the firm has placed with various media. The amount shown includes both the commission or fee of the firm as well as the amount payable by the client for the advertising time or space. The firm serves as an agent for the media in collecting the fee from the client. "Expenditures Billable to Clients" represents production costs incurred plus profit on the preparation of advertising copy for clients. Except in cases where customers have gone bankrupt, firms generally collect these receivables. Offsetting these receivables is "Accounts Payable" on the liabilities side of the balance sheet. This obligation represents amounts owed to various media for advertisements placed for clients. Managing the net receivable/payable position becomes an important task, particularly during periods of high interest rates.

As indicated earlier, marketing services firms rent most of their physical facilities under operating leases. Thus, neither the buildings nor the lease obligations appear on the balance sheet. The notes to the financial statements sometimes provide data on these operating leases. Recorded long-term debt is an insignificant source of capital for these firms, partly because operations generate most of the needed funds and partly because such firms prefer not to add risk from financial leverage to their already large risk from operating leverage.

CURRENT INDUSTRY CONDITIONS

The following discussion summarizes some of the more important issues currently facing the marketing services industry.

1. Shift from Advertising to Promotion Spending.   In 1980, business firms spent 43 percent of their marketing budgets on advertising and 57 percent on promotion (coupons, price discounts, prizes). In 1990, the proportion was 30 percent for advertising and 70 percent for promotion. This shift reflects the following:

a. A greater cost consciousness on the part of consumers, putting downward pressure on prices. Coupons and other forms of price discounts cater to this increased emphasis on price. This shift in consumer emphasis results not only from recessionary conditions but from a longer-term concern for the growth and health of particular economies.

b. Rapid improvements in information technology permit firms to obtain precise information about the buying habits of their customers. Direct marketing to these customers, often through mailings, has replaced spending on broad, national advertising.

c. Increased pressure on marketers to demonstrate the benefits of marketing expenditures. The effect of a particular coupon campaign on sales is often easier to measure than the effect of an equivalent amount spent on advertising in the national media.

The extension of services of marketing services firms beyond advertising to include direct marketing reflects this shift in spending patterns. Most of these firms, however, still obtain the vast majority of their revenues from advertising.

2. Movement to Multinational, Multiservice Firms.

The jury is still out as to whether the assumptions underlying the movement to multinational, multiservice firms will play out. Will the idea of a world or global brand, marketed the same way around the world, work across various cultures? Are advances in communications knitting different cultures so closely together that advertising agencies can ignore cultural differences? Do clients want "one-stop shopping" for their marketing services? Does knowledge of a client's business and products obtained from offering advertising services carry over to marketing research and public relations services? Will the ability to offer services on a worldwide basis attract and retain multinational clients or will they opt for spreading their risks across several firms? Will the marketing services firms realize the economies-of-scale benefits anticipated from their size and be in a position to price their services competitively relative to smaller, domestic firms?

3. Digestion of Recent Mergers and Acquisitions.

Digesting the multiservice and multinational firms acquired in recent years, particularly given the recessionary conditions in some countries, has presented particularly challenging tasks for the marketing services firms. One difficulty relates to centralization/decentralization. Should the parent entity permit each acquired company to operate as an independent unit or should the parent centralize decision making and fully integrate the acquired company into the corporate structure? Will the choice affect the willingness of creative talent in the acquired company to remain after the merger? Will the choice affect the willingness of clients of the acquired company to remain with that entity, particularly when the parent entity provides marketing services for the client's competitors? In an effort to maintain both employee and client loyalties, parent entities have permitted acquired companies to operate as much as possible as independent agencies, maintaining their name, employee benefit programs, and so on. It is not uncommon for several wholly owned subsidiaries of international marketing services firms to compete with each other in a given market and to maintain separate offices in the same city. Whether this organizational structure is sustainable longer term is subject to question.

Because the creative talent of employees represents the major asset of most marketing services firms, much of the purchase price in these acquisitions is attributable to goodwill. Acceptable accounting principles differ across countries in the treatment of goodwill. The United States and Japan both require the capitalization of goodwill as an asset. The United States permits a 40-year amortization period, while Japan requires a 5-year period. The United Kingdom permits firms to report the goodwill in a reserve that is a negative element of shareholders' equity on the date of acquisition, bypassing the income statement. Subsequent amortization of the goodwill reserve reduces particular shareholders' equity accounts.

4. Separation of the Creation and Placement of Advertisement Copy. Advertising agencies have historically monopolized these two functions and priced them as a bundle of services. Changes are occurring on two fronts, however. First, client firms are creating their own in-house advertising departments. The impetus for this change stems from clients' desires to respond more quickly to new developments in their customer markets, to concerns about confidentiality of new product developments when marketing service firms also service the clients' competitors, and to a desire to maintain a tighter control on costs. Second, media buying specialists have emerged. These specialists purchase media time or space in bulk and sell it at more competitive prices than many marketing services firms can match. These recent developments are causing the marketing services firms to unbundle these services and price them on a negotiated-fee basis.

5. Constraints Imposed by Post-LBO Movement. Many leveraged buyouts of the late 1980s involved consumer foods and retailing entities, traditionally heavy advertisers. The need to conserve cash to service the LBO debt has resulted in cutbacks in marketing services expenditures. The recessionary conditions in many economies have heightened this need to conserve cash for debt servicing. In addition, evidence suggests that the merged entities tend to spend less on advertising after the merger than if the entities had remained independent. This reduction reflects in part the need to conserve cash for debt service and in part the hope for economies-of-scale benefits.

FIRMS STUDIED

Exhibit 1 sets forth the worldwide revenues of the top 10 marketing services firms for 1991. A brief description of the three companies analyzed in this case follows.

Exhibit 1
**Worldwide Agency Rankings
(amounts in millions of U.S. dollars)**

Rank 1991	Rank 1990	Agency	Revenues	Billings
1	1	WPP	$ 2,661.8	$ 17,915.8
2	2	Interpublic Group	1,798.9	12,100.8
3	3	Saatchi & Saatchi	1,705.5	11,663.4
4	4	Omnicom Group	1,471.2	10,442.9
5	5	Dentsu	1,451.0	10,680.1
6	6	Young & Rubicam	1,057.1	7,840.1
7	7	Euro RSCG	1,016.3	6,955.7
8	8	Grey Advertising	659.3	4,437.4
9	9	Hakuhodo	655.6	4,686.7
10	10	Foote, Cone & Belding Communications	616.0	4,651.0

Source: *Advertising Age*, April 13, 1992.

Exhibit 2

Comparative for Dentsu, Interpublic Group, and WPP Group (amounts in U.S. dollars)

Dentsu	1987	1988	1989	1990	1991
Number of Employees....................................	5,820	5,844	5,867	5,896	5,893
Revenues per Employee	$ 143,211	$ 186,214	$ 201,410	$ 215,486	$ 241,398
Compensation per Employee..........................	$ 83,324	$ 101,113	$ 101,154	$ 104,127	$ 122,505
Net Income per Employee	$ 6,974	$ 10,720	$ 15,890	$ 17,446	$ 23,818
Commissions and Fees/Total Billings	14.1%	14.4%	14.3%	14.3%	14.6%
Average Exchange Rate (Dollars per Yen).......	$ .0069	$ .0078	$ .0072	$ .0069	$ .0075
Ending Exchange Rate (Dollars per Yen)........	$ .0081	$ .0079	$ .0070	$ .0075	$ .0071

Interpublic Group					
Number of Employees....................................	13,300	14,700	14,700	16,800	16,800
Revenues per Employee	$ 72,986	$ 81,082	$ 85,500	$ 79,136	$ 97,302
Compensation per Employee..........................	$ 40,661	$ 44,639	$ 47,030	$ 45,413	$ 52,394
Net Income per Employee	$ 3,707	$ 4,090	$ 4,803	$ 4,766	$ 5,628
Commission and Fees/Total Billings..............	10.7%	11.7%	10.7%	11.6%	13.5%

WPP Group					
Number of Employees....................................	5,366	10,443	17,568	22,590	20,514
Revenues per Employee	$ 68,541	$ 73,371	$ 78,298	$ 85,127	$ 87,584
Compensation per Employee..........................	$ 38,267	$ 40,473	$ 41,501	$ 47,785	$ 50,257
Net Income per Employee	$ 1,565	$ 2,022	$ 1,349	$ 1,557	$ −1,465
Commission and Fees/Total Billings..............	25.95%	24.35%	22.87%	23.25%	23.50%
Average Exchange Rate (Dollars per Pound)...	$ 1.6800	$ 1.7815	$ 1.6317	$ 1.7872	1.7684
Ending Exchange Rate (Dollars per Pound) ...	$ 1.8785	$ 1.8090	$ 1.6125	$ 1.9300	1.8710

Exhibit 2 presents certain comparative data for the three companies expressed in U.S. dollars. Income statement amounts are translated using the average exchange rate for the period. Financial statements for the three firms expressed in their local currencies appear at the end of the case.

Dentsu Dentsu is the leading marketing services firm in Japan, with approximately a 45 percent market share. The next largest firm, Hakuhodo, has a 20 percent share. With the exception of some small joint ventures with non-Japanese firms, the Japanese marketing services firms dominate their market. Dentsu has recently expanded its product offerings to include sales promotion, marketing research, public relations, and the planning and organizing of sports and cultural events, conventions and expositions. Its foray into international markets takes the form of a joint venture with Young and Rubicam and a 40 percent interest in Collett Dickenson Pearce Europe. Exhibit 3 presents segment sales mix data for Dentsu. Dentsu does not disclose geographical sales data, nor does it report segment operating profit or asset data on either a product or geographical basis.

The financial statement amounts for Dentsu appear in millions of Japanese yen. The only conversion made for U.S. generally accepted accounting principles is

Exhibit 3
Segment Data for Dentsu

Sales Mix	1987	1988	1989	1990	1991
Newspapers	21%	21%	20%	20%	19%
Magazines	4	4	4	4	4
Radio	3	3	3	2	3
Television	40	38	38	37	38
Sales Promotion	14	15	16	16	15
Other	18	19	19	21	21
Total	100%	100%	100%	100%	100%

to treat director's bonuses as an expense in measuring net income (see line for "Changes in Accounting Principles" in the income statement). Dentsu does not disclose its commitments under operating leases.

Interpublic Group The Interpublic Group of Companies derives almost all of its revenues from advertising services (as opposed to broad-based marketing services). The company is an amalgamation of four independent advertising agencies which operate worldwide: McCann-Erickson Worldwide, Lintas Worldwide, Daily and Associates, and the Lowe Group. These entities operate as independent companies, often competing with each other in certain markets. Exhibit 4 presents sales, operating income and asset data by geographical segments of Interpublic. The present value of operating lease commitments when discounted at 10 percent are as follows (amounts in millions of U.S. dollars):

December 31	Present Value
1986	$247
1987	$316
1988	$363
1989	$394
1990	$481
1991	$467

WPP Group Prior to 1987, WPP Group engaged in manufacturing activities in the United Kingdom. The year 1987 marked the beginning of its strategic shift toward marketing services. In July 1987, WPP Group acquired JWT Group, comprising J. Walter Thompson Advertising (advertising), Hill and Knowlton (public relations), and MRD Group (marketing research). JWT Group had operated these agencies as independent entities with a worldwide network of offices. In June 1989, WPP Group acquired Ogilvy Group. Ogilvy Group also offered advertising, public relations, marketing research, and similar services on a worldwide basis but, unlike JWT, Ogilvy Group developed these services from within the organiza-

Exhibit 4
Segment Data for Interpublic Group

	1987	1988	1989	1990	1991
Revenue Mix					
United States	39%	39%	37%	30%	31%
Europe	40	38	29	46	48
East Asia	13	13	14	13	12
Other	8	10	10	11	9
	100%	100%	100%	100%	100%
Income Mix					
United States	42%	40%	39%	26%	34%
Europe	38	36	37	48	46
East Asia	12	15	15	13	12
Other	8	9	9	13	8
	100%	100%	100%	100%	100%
Asset Mix					
United States	36%	36%	35%	30%	27%
Europe	42	39	41	50	52
East Asia	15	15	14	11	13
Other	7	10	10	9	8
	100%	100%	100%	100%	100%
Return on Assets					
United States	9.4%	9.4%	9.5%	5.8%	9.7%
Europe	7.3%	7.6%	7.7%	6.1%	7.0%
East Asia	6.6%	8.3%	9.3%	7.3%	7.6%
Other	8.8%	7.3%	8.1%	9.4%	7.5%
Profit Margin					
United States	12.4%	11.9%	12.9%	11.1%	14.3%
Europe	11.1%	10.9%	11.5%	13.1%	13.0%
East Asia	10.8%	12.8%	13.9%	12.0%	14.1%
Other	10.8%	11.1%	10.9%	14.6%	11.5%
Asset Turnover					
United States	.8	.8	.7	.5	.7
Europe	.7	.7	.7	.5	.5
East Asia	.6	.6	.7	.6	.5
Other	.8	.7	.7	.6	.7

tion (instead of by acquisition) and integrated the full range of marketing services within each office. Exhibit 5 presents sales and operating income mix data for WPP Group's major products and geographical markets. The present value of operating lease commitments when discounted at 10 percent appear on the next page (amounts in millions of pounds):

Exhibit 5
Segment Data for WPP Group

Sales Mix—Products	1987	1988	1989	1990	1991
Media Advertising	54%	49%	53%	50%	51%
Nonmedia Advertising	14	15	12	13	12
Public Relations	13	15	10	11	10
Marketing Research	7	6	10	11	12
Specialist Communications	11	13	14	14	14
Other	1	2	1	1	1
	100%	100%	100%	100%	100%

Income Mix—Products					
Media Advertising	55%	49%	54%	54%	65%
Nonmedia Advertising	18	16	13	8	1
Public Relations	(1)	11	9	9	1
Marketing Research	10	7	7	8	11
Specialist Communications	17	15	15	19	20
Other	1	2	2	2	2
	100%	100%	100%	100%	100%

Sales Mix—Geographical					
United Kingdom	20%	24%	19%	22%	22%
United States and Canada	58	52	51	47	45
Rest of World	22	24	30	31	33
	100%	100%	100%	100%	100%

Income Mix—Geographical					
United Kingdom	35%	32%	20%	21%	17%
United States and Canada	34	38	49	47	46
Rest of World	31	30	31	32	37
	100%	100%	100%	100%	100%

December 31	Present Value
1987	£19
1988	£20
1989	£43
1990	£51
1991	£63

The financial statement amounts for WPP Group appear in millions of pounds. The negative amounts shown for WPP Group's retained earnings result from the U.K. practice of showing goodwill arising from corporate acquisitions as a negative element of shareholders' equity. The balance sheet for WPP Group appearing with this case reverses the goodwill out of shareholders' equity (see the amounts on the line "Cumulative Translation Adjustment") and adds it to "Other Assets." Amortization of this goodwill over a 40-year period appears on the line "Changes in Accounting Principles" on the income statement. The statement of cash flows shows the net change in operating working capital accounts instead of the changes in individual working capital accounts. As discussed above, WPP Group made significant acquisitions in 1987 and 1989. The annual reports disclose the effect of these acquisitions on net current assets, so it is possible to separate the aggregate change working capital accounts into the portions relating to operating and investing activities. WPP Group does not disclose the effect of acquisitions on accounts receivable, inventories, accounts payable, and so on, so it is not possible to detail the aggregate change in working capital any further.

REQUIRED

Assess the relative profitability and risk of Dentsu, The Interpublic Group of Companies, and WPP Group, identifying strategic reasons that might explain the differences observed. The line for "Cost of Goods Sold" in the income statement represents compensation expense. Give careful consideration to the types of financial ratios appropriate for analyzing a service business.

Dentsu Balance Sheet

	1986	1987	1988	1989	1990	1991
Cash	¥ 45,075	¥ 50,336	¥ 43,129	¥ 50,760	¥ 53,660	¥ 57,324
Marketable Securities	12,796	19,344	23,137	15,645	13,031	10,838
Accts./Notes Receivable	221,747	241,059	282,837	330,634	393,795	401,192
Inventories	8,419	7,080	15,079	19,309	18,260	16,679
Other Current Assets	4,731	4,094	3,093	15,058	7,703	8,685
Current Assets	¥ 292,768	¥ 321,913	¥ 367,275	¥ 431,406	¥ 486,449	¥ 494,718
Investments	9,947	12,921	21,090	24,502	28,147	32,500
Property, Plant, and Equipment	48,651	49,407	51,500	56,415	63,323	66,410
Less Accum. Depreciation	14,286	16,036	17,910	19,467	21,078	23,178
Other Assets	9,585	9,585	13,359	16,546	21,934	26,513
Total Assets	¥ 346,665	¥ 377,790	¥ 435,314	¥ 509,402	¥ 578,775	¥ 596,963
Accts. Payable—Trade	¥ 177,077	¥ 193,405	¥ 232,559	¥ 272,219	¥ 315,637	¥ 313,955
Notes Payable—Nontrade	26,495	29,469	31,617	32,346	35,012	30,742
Current Part L-T Debt	0	0	0	0	0	0
Other Current Liab.	27,204	30,294	35,961	50,821	52,305	53,026
Current Liabilities	¥ 230,776	¥ 253,168	¥ 300,137	¥ 355,386	¥ 402,954	¥ 397,723
Long-Term Debt	3,120	4,710	5,009	7,431	8,996	10,854
Deferred Tax (NCL)	0	0	0	0	0	0
Other Noncurrent Liab.	40,001	41,604	44,264	48,054	53,745	56,114
Minority Int. in Subs.	442	504	582	722	876	1,035
Total Liabilities	¥ 274,339	¥ 299,986	¥ 349,992	¥ 411,593	¥ 466,571	¥ 465,726
Preferred Stock	¥ 0	¥ 0	¥ 0	¥ 0	¥ 0	¥ 0
Common Stock	2,304	2,304	2,304	2,304	2,304	2,304
Additional Paid-in Cap.	12	12	12	12	12	12
Retained Earnings	70,010	75,488	83,006	95,493	109,888	128,921
Cum. Translation Adj.	0	0	0	0	0	0
Treasury Stock	0	0	0	0	0	0
Shareholders' Equity	¥ 72,326	¥ 77,804	¥ 85,322	¥ 97,809	¥ 112,204	¥ 131,237
Total Equities	¥ 346,665	¥ 377,790	¥ 435,314	¥ 509,402	¥ 578,775	¥ 596,963

Dentsu Income Statement

	1987	1988	1989	1990	1991
Sales	¥ 120,795	¥ 139,294	¥ 163,071	¥ 184,223	¥ 199,158
Other Revenues and Gains	5,522	2,926	4,087	3,556	7,081
Cost of Goods Sold	−74,856	−80,345	−86,902	−95,512	−101,069
Sell. and Admin. Expense	−27,986	−32,902	−38,306	−46,690	−50,522
Other Expenses and Losses	0	0	0	0	0
EBIT	¥ 23,475	¥ 28,973	¥ 41,950	¥ 45,577	¥ 54,648
Interest Expense	−2,518	−2,343	−2,653	−3,708	−5,426
Income Tax Expense	−14,790	−18,293	−26,056	−26,502	−29,395
Minority Int. in Earnings	74	93	155	170	177
Income from Contin. Ops.	¥ 6,093	¥ 8,244	¥ 13,086	¥ 15,197	¥ 19,650
Income from Discont. Ops.	0	0	0	0	0
Extra. Gains (Losses)	0	0	0	0	0
Changes in Acct. Princ.	−208	−225	−221	−282	−280
Preferred Stock Dividend	0	0	0	0	0
NI Avail. to Com.	¥ 5,885	¥ 8,019	¥ 12,865	¥ 14,915	¥ 19,370

Dentsu Statement of Cash Flows

	1987	1988	1989	1990	1991
Operations					
Net Income, Cont. Ops.	¥ 5,885	¥ 8,019	¥ 12,865	¥ 14,915	¥ 19,370
Depreciation and Amort.	1,750	1,874	1,852	2,031	2,447
Other Addbacks	2,337	3,355	5,012	7,786	6,996
Other Subtractions	0	−134	−892	−1,986	−4,122
WC Provided by Other Ops.	¥ 9,972	¥ 13,114	¥ 18,837	¥ 22,746	¥ 24,691
(Inc.) Decr. in Receivables	−19,312	−41,778	−47,797	−63,161	−7,397
(Inc.) Decr. in Inventories	1,339	−7,999	−1,811	−422	602
(Inc.) Decr. in Other CA	637	1,001	−2,419	1,471	979
Inc. (Decr.) Acct. Pay.—Trade	16,328	39,154	39,660	43,418	−1,682
Inc. (Decr.) in Other CL	3,090	5,667	2,696	8,549	−768
Cash from Cont. Ops.	¥ 12,054	¥ 9,159	¥ 9,166	¥ 12,601	¥ 16,425
Cash from Discont. Ops.	0	0	0	0	0
Cash from Extr. Gain/Loss	0	0	0	0	0
Net Cash Flow from Ops.	¥ 12,054	¥ 9,159	¥ 9,166	¥ 12,601	¥ 16,425
Investing					
Fixed Assets Sold	¥ 0	¥ 0	¥ 0	¥ 0	¥ 0
Investments Sold	0	0	9,520	4,988	2,949
Fixed Assets Acquired	−756	−2,093	−5,520	−12,371	−5,358
Investments Acquired	−6,548	−3,793	−5,580	−5,893	−5,631
Other Invest. Trans.	−2,974	−11,943	−2,737	−195	−1,940
Net Cash Flow from Investing	¥ −10,278	¥ −17,829	¥ −4,317	¥ −13,471	¥ −9,980
Financing					
Incr. S-T Borrowing	¥ 2,974	¥ 2,148	¥ 729	¥ 2,666	¥ 0
Incr. L-T Borrowing	1,590	1,153	2,980	2,198	2,497
Issue of Cap. Stock	0	0	0	0	0
Decr. S-T Borrowing	0	0	0	0	−4,270
Decr. L-T Borrowing	0	−854	−558	−633	−639
Acquisit. of Cap. Stock	0	0	0	0	0
Dividends	−369	−369	−369	−461	−369
Other Financing Trans.	−710	−615	0	0	0
Net Cash Flow from Financing	¥ 3,485	¥ 1,463	¥ 2,782	¥ 3,770	¥ −2,781
Net Change in Cash	¥ 5,261	¥ −7,207	¥ 7,631	¥ 2,900	¥ 3,664

Interpublic Group Balance Sheet

	1986	1987	1988	1989	1990	1991
Cash	$ 122	$ 143	$ 140	$ 89	$ 179	$ 240
Marketable Securities	25	38	40	34	37	36
Accts./Notes Receivable	725	931	1,093	1,225	1,656	1,705
Inventories	0	0	0	0	0	0
Other Current Assets	15	18	24	25	42	50
Current Assets	$ 887	$ 1,130	$ 1,297	$ 1,373	$ 1,914	$ 2,031
Investments	18	28	45	68	34	30
Property, Plant, and Equipment	88	152	195	226	305	333
Less Accum. Depreciation	16	69	83	94	127	146
Other Assets	102	106	146	168	458	536
Total Assets	$ 1,079	$ 1,347	$ 1,600	$ 1,741	$ 2,584	$ 2,784
Accts. Payable—Trade	$ 555	$ 738	$ 889	$ 981	$ 1,421	$ 1,456
Notes Payable–NonTrade	41	31	47	54	115	157
Current Part L-T Debt	0	0	0	0	0	0
Other Current Liab.	144	178	181	175	233	240
Current Liabilities	$ 740	$ 947	$ 1,117	$ 1,210	$ 1,769	$ 1,853
Long-Term Debt	21	21	43	37	144	170
Deferred Tax (NCL)	0	0	0	0	0	0
Other Noncurrent Liab.	68	87	92	113	147	157
Minority Int. in Subs.	7	12	15	13	14	17
Total Liabilities	$ 836	$ 1,067	$ 1,267	$ 1,373	$ 2,074	$ 2,197
Preferred Stock	$ 0	$ 0	$ 0	$ 0	$ 0	$ 0
Common Stock	2	2	2	4	4	4
Additional Paid-in Cap.	68	79	94	113	217	258
Retained Earnings	186	221	267	316	371	438
Cum. Translation Adj.	−7	6	0	2	17	4
Treasury Stock	−6	−28	−30	−67	−99	−117
Shareholders' Equity	$ 243	$ 280	$ 333	$ 368	$ 510	$ 587
Total Equities	$ 1,079	$ 1,347	$ 1,600	$ 1,741	$ 2,584	$ 2,784

Interpublic Group Income Statement

	1987	1988	1989	1990	1991
Sales	$ 943	$ 1,153	$ 1,218	$ 1,329	$ 1,635
Other Revenues and Gains	30	43	44	45	45
Cost of Goods Sold	−541	−656	−691	−763	−880
Sell. and Admin. Expense	−320	−397	−413	−437	−578
Other Expenses and Losses	0	0	0	0	0
EBIT	$ 112	$ 143	$ 158	$ 174	$ 222
Interest Expense	−9	−10	−15	−19	−34
Income Tax Expense	−51	−68	−68	−72	−88
Minority Int. in Earnings	−3	−5	−5	−3	−5
Income from Contin. Ops.	$ 49	$ 60	$ 70	$ 80	$ 95
Income from Discont. Ops.	0	0	0	0	0
Extra. Gains (Losses)	0	0	0	0	0
Changes in Acct. Princ.	0	0	0	0	0
Preferred Stock Dividend	0	0	0	0	0
NI Avail. to Com.	$ 49	$ 60	$ 70	$ 80	$ 95

Interpublic Group Statement of Cash Flows

	1987	1988	1989	1990	1991
Operations					
Net Income, Cont. Ops.	$ 49	$ 60	$ 70	$ 80	$ 95
Depreciation and Amort.	21	25	30	38	54
Other Addbacks	14	24	21	20	21
Other Subtractions	−12	−13	−24	−27	−16
WC Provided by Ops.	$ 72	$ 96	$ 97	$ 111	$ 154
(Inc.) Decr. in Receivables	−129	−214	−190	−167	−69
(Inc.) Decr. in Inventories	0	0	0	0	0
(Inc.) Decr. in Other CA	−1	−7	−1	−12	−7
Inc. (Decr.) Acct. Pay.—Trade	142	151	92	440	7
Inc. (Decr.) in Other CL	22	65	78	−184	8
Cash from Cont. Ops.	$ 106	$ 91	$ 76	$ 188	$ 93
Cash from Discont. Ops.	0	0	0	0	0
Cash from Extr. Gain/Loss	0	0	0	0	0
Net Cash Flow from Ops.	$ 106	$ 91	$ 76	$ 188	$ 93
Investing					
Fixed Assets Sold	$ 3	$ 7	$ 5	$ 6	$ 5
Investments Sold	0	0	0	2	5
Fixed Assets Acquired	−21	−44	−46	−37	−47
Investments Acquired	−6	−7	−11	−2	0
Other Invest. Trans.	−7	−73	−23	−83	−27
Net Cash Flow from Investing	$ −31	$ −117	$ −75	$ −114	$ −64
Financing					
Incr. S-T Borrowing	$ 0	$ 17	$ 6	$ 0	$ 36
Incr. L-T Borrowing	2	27	1	78	166
Issue of Cap. Stock	3	3	5	5	7
Decr. S-T Borrowing	−15	0	0	−7	0
Decr. L-T Borrowing	−8	−5	−6	−4	−132
Acquisit. of Cap. Stock	−22	−2	−36	−32	−17
Dividends	−14	−17	−22	−24	−29
Other Financing Trans.	0	0	0	0	0
Net Cash Flow from Financing	$ −54	$ 23	$ −52	$ 16	$ 31
Net Change in Cash	$ 21	$ −3	$ −51	$ 90	$ 60

WPP Group Balance Sheet

		1986		1987		1988		1989		1990		1991
Cash	£	8	£	73	£	93	£	233	£	229	£	205
Marketable Securities		0		5		14		7		9		2
Accts./Notes Receivable		12		208		217		533		491		518
Inventories		2		38		34		91		62		63
Other Current Assets		1		137		35		97		100		97
Current Assets	£	23	£	461	£	393	£	961	£	891	£	885
Investments		0		3		5		20		13		15
Property, Plant, and Equipment		7		86		98		189		184		202
Less Accum. Depreciation		2		7		19		39		55		75
Other Assets		9		103		396		1,206		1,212		1,172
Total Assets	£	37	£	646	£	873	£	2,337	£	2,245	£	2,199
Accts. Payable—Trade	£	6	£	229	£	244	£	605	£	560	£	599
Notes Payable—Nontrade		2		99		33		117		68		36
Current Part L-T Debt		0		0		0		0		0		0
Other Current Liab.		14		127		160		428		358		335
Current Liabilities	£	22	£	455	£	437	£	1,150	£	986	£	970
Long-Term Debt		2		82		100		443		459		503
Deferred Tax (NCL)		0		54		12		42		35		35
Other Noncurrent Liab.		1		30		63		202		159		150
Minority Int. in Subs.		1		1		1		12		10		10
Total Liabilities	£	26	£	622	£	613	£	1,849	£	1,649	£	1,668
Preferred Stock	£	0	£	0	£	0	£	22	£	22		21
Common Stock		1		4		4		4		4		6
Additional Paid-in Cap.		0		0		0		193		194		194
Retained Earnings		1		−69		56		−561		−464		−489
Cum. Translation Adj.		9		89		200		830		840		799
Treasury Stock		0		0		0		0		0		0
Shareholders' Equity	£	11	£	24	£	260	£	488	£	596	£	531
Total Equities	£	37	£	646	£	873	£	2,337	£	2,245	£	2,199

WPP Group Income Statement

		1987		1988		1989		1990		1991
Sales	£	219	£	442	£	843	£	1,076	£	1,106
Other Revenues and Gains		4		8		16		14		9
Cost of Goods Sold		−125		−237		−447		−604		−583
Sell. and Admin. Expense		−73		−154		−293		−339		−331
Other Expenses and Losses		0		0		0		0		0
EBIT	£	25	£	59	£	119	£	147	£	111
Interest Expense		−11		−19		−44		−57		−55
Income Tax Expense		−7		−19		−35		−36		−24
Minority Int. in Earnings		0		0		−2		−3		−1
Income from Contin. Ops.	£	7	£	21	£	38	£	51	£	31
Income from Discont. Ops.		0		0		0		0		0
Extra. Gains (Losses)		0		0		0		0		0
Changes in Acct. Princ.		0		−2		−4		−9		−48
Preferred Stock Dividend		0		0		−8		−18		−18
NI Avail. to Com.	£	7	£	19	£	26	£	24	£	−35

WPP Group Statement of Cash Flow

	1987	1988	1989	1990	1991
Operations					
Net Income, Cont. Ops.	£ 7	£ 21	£ 38	£ 51	£ 31
Depreciation and Amort.	5	12	20	25	26
Other Addbacks	0	56	0	0	0
Other Subtractions	−5	0	−61	−47	−42
WC Provided by Ops.	£ 7	£ 89	£ −3	£ 29	£ 15
Change in Wk. Capital Accounts	67	−30	145	−6	−3
Cash from Cont. Ops.	£ 74	£ 59	£ 142	£ 23	£ 12
Cash from Discont. Ops.	0	0	0	0	0
Cash from Extr. Gain/Loss	0	0	0	0	0
Net Cash Flow from Ops.	£ 74	£ 59	£ 142	£ 23	£ 12
Investing					
Fixed Assets Sold	£ 2	£ 0	£ 5	£ 8	£ 4
Investments Sold	0	122	0	0	8
Fixed Assets Acquired	−9	−17	−13	−33	−21
Investments Acquired	0	−1	−15	−7	−2
Other Invest. Trans.	−390	−63	−617	−31	−15
Net Cash Flow from Investing	£ −397	£ 41	£ −640	£ −63	£ −26
Financing					
Incr. S-T Borrowing	£ 96	£ 0	£ 91	£ 0	£ 0
Incr. L-T Borrowing	65	10	343	75	44
Issue of Cap. Stock	207	0	214	0	0
Decr. S-T Borrowing	0	−8	0	−18	−31
Decr. L-T Borrowing	0	−69	−7	−21	−13
Acquisit. of Cap. Stock	0	0	0	0	0
Dividends	0	−2	−12	−28	0
Other Financing Trans.	19	−11	10	28	−10
Net Cash Flow from Financing	£ 387	£ −80	£ 639	£ 36	£ −10
Net Change in Cash	£ 64	£ 20	£ 141	£ −4	£ −24

Commercial Banking Industry Analysis

The commercial banking industry is in turmoil. Uncollectible loans to underdeveloped countries, real estate developers, and leveraged buyout participants are hurting profitability and threatening the very survival of many banks. Competition from securities firms and mutual funds offering money market accounts is eroding the commercial banks' traditional deposit funding base. Federal regulators are imposing strict new controls to ensure the strength and credibility of the banking system. Yet signs of optimism appear on the horizon. Unimpeded interstate banking is rapidly approaching a reality. Bank mergers are accelerating in the expectation of realizing economies of scale in data processing, branch networking, and other activities. Substantial provisions for uncollectible loans during the last few years result in most banks having reserves equal to the amount of nonperforming loans. Declining interest rates provide banks with an increasing spread between the rates paid to depositors and the interest rates specified in existing fixed-rate loans.

This case examines the profitability and risk of three commercial banks that pursue different strategies in response to these industry conditions: Bank of Boston (super regional bank), Bankers Trust (global merchant bank), and Citibank (diversified strategy, with solid positions in consumer, commercial, domestic and international sectors and a growing involvement in investment banking services).

ECONOMIC CHARACTERISTICS OF COMMERCIAL BANKING

Commercial banks derive their earnings from two principal activities: (1) lending and investing and (2) fee-based services.

Lending and Investing   Exhibit 1 presents a common size balance sheet for all commercial banks as of December 31, 1986 to 1990. Exhibit 2 presents a common size income statement for these same years. Customer deposits serve as a bank's principal source of funds. Most of these deposits are interest bearing. Checking and NOW accounts generally offer variable interest rates and certificates of deposit generally offer fixed rates. Commercial banks also borrow short-term from other banks and issue commercial paper. They obtain a minor amount of funds from long-term borrowing. Shareholders' equity comprises a much smaller proportion of total financing than is the case for most industrial companies. Thus, a commercial bank's funding sources tilt heavily toward the short term.

Loans to customers comprise approximately 60 percent of total assets. Commercial banks make the vast majority of their loans to other business enterprises, as opposed to individuals. Commercial and industrial loans may extend from a few weeks or months (typical working capital loans) to many years (financing for major equipment) and may be secured or unsecured. Banks usually price these loans at the bank's prime rate plus an add-on, and may include compensating balance requirements and/or commitment fees. Commercial banks have not priced these

Exhibit 1
Common Size Balance Sheet for Commercial Banks

	1986	**1987**	**1988**	**1989**	**1990**
Assets					
Loans					
Commercial and Industrial	20.3%	19.6%	18.1%	19.1%	18.9%
Financial Institutions	6.5	7.3	7.1	5.9	6.4
Real Estate...............................	11.3	15.8	16.5	19.9	20.8
Consumer..................................	6.2	7.3	6.8	6.5	6.5
Other	12.7	11.6	12.7	6.4	7.4
Total Loans.............................	57.0%	61.6%	61.2%	57.8%	60.0%
Investments					
Federal Government...............	4.1	4.9	5.1	5.2	7.7
Other	5.0	5.7	5.7	4.7	4.1
Other Assets	33.9	27.8	28.0	32.3	28.2
	100.0%	100.0%	100.0%	100.0%	100.0%
Equities					
Deposits....................................	55.3%	58.1%	58.3%	58.6%	57.1%
Borrowings...............................	24.2	20.5	21.3	23.4	19.3
Other Liabilities.......................	12.0	13.7	11.5	10.1	15.0
Shareholders' Equity	8.5	7.7	8.9	7.9	8.6
	100.0%	100.0%	100.0%	100.0%	100.0%

loans competitively in recent years and business firms have relied increasingly on issuing their own commercial paper or borrowing in the Eurodollar market.

Loans to companies in less developed countries (LDC), such as Mexico, Brazil, and Argentina, comprised 16.5 percent of commercial and industrial loans at the end of 1990. During the late 1970s and early 1980s, large sums of petro dollars flowed into the United States. Money-center banks used the funds to extend loans to businesses in developing countries with the hope that these businesses would grow as their economies grew and represent a new source of revenues for the banks, both from lending and fee-based services. Most of these economies did not flourish as expected and the banks incurred substantial loan losses during the late 1980s. Commercial banks provided substantial bad debt reserves for these loans, particularly in 1987 and 1989. At the end of 1990, reserves averaged 60 percent of the outstanding LDC loans at eight lending money-center banks. Two other bright spots now appear in the LDC picture. Many LDC borrowers renegotiated their loans in accordance with the Brady Plan. Under this plan, borrowers could (1) reduce the face amount of their loans by 35 percent but pay a market rate of interest or (2) maintain the existing face amount but pay a below-market interest rate of 6.25 percent. In return for these debt restructurings, the governments of the companies guarantee the debt. Mexico and Venezuela have engaged in these arrangements, with other LDC countries expected to follow. The second bright spot in the LDC picture is the improving economic conditions in many South and Central American countries as a result of the privatization of telecommunications, air-

Exhibit 2
Common Size Income Statement for Commercial Banks

	1986	1987	1988	1989	1990
Revenues					
Interest Income	85.7%	85.1%	85.8%	86.3%	85.3%
Service Charges	2.9	3.1	3.0	2.8	3.1
Other Revenues	11.4	11.8	11.2	10.9	11.6
Total Revenues	100.0%	100.0%	100.0%	100.0%	100.0%
Expenses					
Interest Expense	51.6%	50.5%	52.0%	55.7%	54.6%
Provision for Loan Losses	7.9	12.9	5.2	8.1	8.3
Personnel Expenses	15.5	15.7	14.8	13.4	13.9
Other Operating Expenses	16.9	18.0	16.8	15.8	16.9
Total Expenses	91.9%	97.1%	88.8%	93.0%	93.7%
Income before Taxes	8.1%	2.9%	11.2%	7.0%	6.3%
Income Tax Expense	1.9	1.9	3.2	2.7	2.1
Net Income	6.2%	1.0%	8.0%	4.3%	4.2%
Profit Margin for ROA	6.2%	1.0%	8.0%	4.3%	4.2%
Assets Turnover	.10	.11	.10	.12	.12
Return on Assets (ROA)	.62%	.11%	.82%	.51%	.50%

lines, and other industries. Despite improvements in the LDC loan situation, commercial banks now face similar problems with leveraged buyout and real estate loans, as discussed below.

Commercial banks were a principal lender of senior debt in many leveraged buyout transactions during the late 1980s. These loans typically extend for five to seven years and generate higher yields than the average commercial loan. Banks also receive commitment fees ranging from 1 to 4 percent of the principal amount of these loans. The economic downturn during the early 1990s caused many of the borrowers on the heavily leveraged transactions (HLT) to default, resulting in loan restructurings and bankruptcies. HLT loans comprised 5.3 percent of total assets of the five largest banks engaged in such transactions at the end of 1990 and approximately 28 percent of commercial and industrial loans. Nonperforming HLT loans represented 8 percent of all HLT loans.

Commercial real estate loans are typically long term, secured, and subject to various degrees of risk depending on the location of the property. Exhibit 1 indicates that real estate loans represented an increasing percentage of total assets during the five years 1986 to 1990. Contributing factors to increased real estate loans included (1) income tax incentives prior to 1986 that encouraged real estate development, (2) passage of the Garn-St. Germain Act in 1982 that permitted banks to lend on undeveloped real estate and to provide 100 percent financing for new construction, and (3) skyrocketing real estate values. The overbuilding of commercial space that resulted from this attractive real estate environment led to high vacancy rates in most major cities (from 14 percent in New York to 24 percent in Houston at the end of 1990). Competition for tenants led to lower rents and declining property values. With inadequate cash flows to service real estate loans and little or no equity invested, owners and developers simply walked away from many projects. Commercial banks found themselves as landlords of many commercial properties after repossession. Federal regulators define a real estate loan as nonperforming if the market value of the property is less than the outstanding loan, even if the borrower makes all required loan payments. At the end of 1990, nonperforming real estate loans comprised 16.1 percent of total real estate loans.

Commercial banks seldom lend all of their available funds. They invest a portion in various financial assets, particularly U.S. government securities, both as a source of immediate liquidity and as a pool of loanable funds. "Other assets" appearing on the common size balance sheet in Exhibit 1 includes cash balances held in financial institutions and bank buildings.

Fee-Based Services   Competition among banks and other financial services firms for customers' deposits has forced upward the interest rates commercial banks must pay for funds. Likewise, competition from the commercial paper, private placement, and the Eurodollar market has forced downward the interest rates commercial banks can charge on business loans. The declining spread between these interest rates coupled with the problem of uncollectible loans discussed above has led commercial banks to increase their fee-based sources of revenue. Service charges for various banking services (checking accounts, trust services) comprise approximately 3 percent of total revenues but have grown more rapidly in recent years than interest revenues (see the trend income statement in Exhibit 3). Other fee-based services have grown even more rapidly. Included here are fees from loan commitments, guarantees of various financial transactions, and merger and acquisition advisory work. The offering of these services not only diversifies the sources of revenues but provides commercial banks an opportunity to differentiate their product line relative to the more commodity nature of lending.

Operating Costs   The operating costs of commercial banks tend to behave as fixed costs in the short run, although banks can alter the amount of employee compensation through hirings and firings. Personnel expenses declined as a percentage of total revenues between 1986 and 1990. A portion of this declining percentage results from elimination of duplicate personnel following the many mergers that have occurred in recent years (discussed below). An additional portion results from increased employee productivity brought about by increasingly powerful and sophisticated computer information systems.

Summary of Economic Characteristics   Commercial banks must manage the spread between the interest rate paid for funds and the return generated from using those funds for loans and investments in securities. Volatile interest rates, increased competition on both the borrowing and lending sides of the balance sheets of commercial banks, and a mismatch between the term structure of assets and liabilities result in both lower returns and higher risks. Fee-based revenues

Exhibit 3
Trend Income Statement for Commercial Banks (1985 = 100)

	1986	1987	1988	1989	1990
Revenues					
Interest Income......................	95	98	108	126	127
Service Charges......................	108	118	127	138	155
Other Revenues......................	125	135	139	157	171
Total Revenues......................	98	104	113	131	135
Expenses					
Interest Expense	90	92	103	128	129
Provision for Loan Losses.......	123	209	91	165	173
Personnel Expenses	107	113	116	122	129
Other Operating Expenses......	111	122	127	136	149
Total Expenses	101	110	110	134	138
Income before Taxes	96	36	151	108	100
Income Tax Expense	94	96	182	173	137
Net Income.................................	96	17	141	88	88

represent a more stable source of revenues and provide opportunities for product differentiation and the building of customer loyalty. Increased spending on information technology and closer monitoring of employee productivity offer opportunities for better control of costs.

CURRENT CONDITIONS IN THE COMMERCIAL BANKING INDUSTRY

The previous section discussed several important factors affecting commercial banks, including losses on LDC, HLT, and real estate loans, movement to fee-based services, increased investment in information technology, and personnel reductions. This section discusses several additional factors affecting the industry.

Effect of Bank Failures on FDIC Fund   The number of failing commercial banks increased from approximately 50 annually in the early 1980s to approximately 200 annually in the late 1980s, with the number projected to increase still further in the early 1990s. The Federal Deposit Insurance Corporation (FDIC) insures deposits up to $100,000 per account. The FDIC collects premiums from commercial banks on their deposit accounts to fund this insurance program. Bank failures essentially depleted the assets in the insurance fund at the end of 1991, despite an increase in the insurance premium from $.12 per $100 to $.23 per $100 between August 1990 and July 1991. Whether the FDIC will resort to additional increases in premiums or lobby Congress to replenish the insurance fund by raising income taxes remains an issue. Critics of FDIC insurance argue that it unnecessarily props up weak banks at the expense of strong banks. They argue for either risk-adjusted premiums based on the financial condition of the bank or elimination of FDIC insurance altogether.

Establishment of Capital Guidelines   Assets of a commercial bank equal to the amount of shareholders' equity serve as a cushion of protection for depositors and lenders. These assets are not subject to withdrawal (as with deposits) or debt service payments (as with borrowings). Analysts have used the ratio of shareholders' equity to total assets as a measure of liquidity and solvency risk. Differences across countries in the definition of shareholders' equity and differences across banks and countries in the riskiness of the portfolio of assets inhibit cross-bank comparisons using this ratio. In July 1988, central banks from the United States, Canada, Japan, and seven Western European countries established uniform capital guidelines for international banks. By 1992, all banks should have "capital" equal to 8 percent of "adjusted assets."

Obtaining agreement on the definition of capital proved difficult. Central bankers agreed on a two-tier system:

Tier I: Common stock, additional paid-in capital, retained earnings minus goodwill.
Noncumulative perpetual preferred stock.

Tier II: Other preferred stock.
Certain subordinated debt (up to 50 percent of Tier I capital).
Loan loss reserves (up to 1.25 percent of total assets).
A portion (45 percent) of the unrealized gains on real estate and marketable securities.

At least 4 percent of the 8 percent desired capital ratio should come from Tier I capital.

"Adjusted assets" that serve as a base for the capital guidelines reflect the risk inherent in different assets. The risk weights for various assets are as follows:

0 percent: Cash, gold, reserves at central banks, investments in the securities of the United States or other governments within the Organization of Economic Cooperation and Development (OECD).

20 percent: Deposits with, and loans to, or guarantees by, U.S. and OECD banks, loans to, or general obligation securities, of states and municipalities, residential-backed securities, shares of mutual funds investing in the above securities.

50 percent: State and municipal revenue bonds, credit equivalent of currency and interest rate swaps, residential mortgage loans.

100 percent: All other private sector loans, loans to other foreign governments, property, plant, and equipment, assets sold with recourse.

Off-balance sheet items, such as loan commitments, commercial letters of credit, and performance guarantees, require conversion into credit equivalents according to prescribed formulas and then their assignment to one of the four asset categories above. Multiplying each asset category by the appropriate weight yields the amount of "adjusted assets." Tier I capital should equal 4 percent of adjusted assets and Tier I plus Tier II capital should equal 8 percent of adjusted assets by 1992. Each country has authority to adjust these guidelines if warranted by local conditions, although extensive adjustments will reduce the effectiveness of the agreement.

Commercial banks disclose the computation of their capital ratios in accordance with the established guidelines. The guidelines provide for a transition to the 8 percent standard prior to 1992. Commercial banks have taken several actions in recent years in an effort to meet the capital ratio guidelines, including issuing common and preferred stock, curtailing dividends, and altering the asset mix away from loans and towards investments of U.S. government securities.

Bank Mergers   The commercial banking industry has experienced increasing consolidation in recent years as a result of bank mergers. The aim of many of these mergers is to obtain economies of scale by spreading the substantial cost of computerized information systems over a larger customer base. Some of these mergers involve crosstown rivals, whereby a merger not only provides a larger customer base but permits the banks to eliminate duplicate facilities and personnel. Conventional wisdom in the banking industry suggests that intramarket mergers yield approximately twice the cost savings as out-of-market mergers.

A significant portion of the merger activity has involved banks operating in different markets. The Supreme Court ruled in 1985 that a group of states could enter into reciprocal banking arrangements with each other and exclude banks incorporated in another state. This ruling set in motion a series of regional banking mergers, legally creating interstate banking. These "super-regional banks" aim not only to realize economies of scale in information systems but to compete more effectively with the large, money-center banks. Most of the highly populated states now either allow interstate banking or have a trigger date set within the next few years when any bank can establish a presence within the state.

Opponents of this consolidation movement argue that it will lessen competition and increase the cost of banking to consumers. The antitrust division of the Department of Justice serves as one control mechanism on mergers, examining the impact of a particular merger on competition in a given market. Another control mechanism is the likely strength and viability of small, local banks. Such banks offer the basic commercial banking functions (deposit-taking, lending) in a personal, friendly atmosphere and with a sensitivity to local conditions. Customers not needing the more sophisticated services of the larger banks can remain with their local bank.

Diversification into Other Financial Services   The Glass-Steagall Act of 1933 prohibits commercial banks from engaging in investment banking activities. The Congress was concerned that commercial banks would experience a conflict of interests if they were involved both in underwriting securities and investing depositors' funds in securities. A similar restriction applies to investment banks engaging in deposit-taking activities. Cracks in the so-called "glass wall" between underwriting and investing depositors' funds have continually appeared in recent years. Investment banks have offered money market accounts that invest customers' funds in U.S. government securities. Commercial banks have sequentially received authority to underwrite municipal bonds, then corporate bonds, and now certain large, healthy banks have authority to underwrite equity securities. The Bush administration has proposed the abolishment of the Glass-Steagall Act to permit commercial and investment banks to offer deposit-taking, lending, underwriting, and insurance services. Such action should increase competition for each of these financial services and place U.S. commercial banks on a more level playing field with banks in other countries.

ANALYZING A COMMERCIAL BANK'S FINANCIAL STATEMENTS

The financial statements of a commercial bank differ from those of a manufacturing or retailing firm. Because banks act as a conduit between those with funds and those needing funds, several related accounts appear on the assets and liabilities sides of the balance sheet. Loans and investments in securities comprise the majority of a bank's assets. Investments might appear in the following accounts:

- Federal Funds Sold: Excess reserves that the bank lends to other banks on an overnight or very short-term basis.

- Securities Purchased under Agreements to Resell: Temporarily excess funds that the bank lends to corporations or government units, usually on an overnight basis. Government securities that appear on the books of the borrowing entity collateralize such loans. If the borrowing entity is unable to repay the loan when due from its general cash account, it agrees to sell the securities in order to repay the loan.

- Investments in Securities: Investments in U.S. government securities (as a source of liquidity) or state and local government securities (to reduce income taxes).

- Trading Account Securities: A bank's inventory of securities in which it functions as an underwriter or dealer. The bank generally holds these securities for their capital gain potential.

The principal liabilities of a bank are demand and time deposits. Commercial banks have increasingly used three sources of short-term funds.

- Federal Funds Purchased: Funds borrowed from the excess reserves of other banks, usually on an overnight or short-term basis. Such borrowing is not subject to FDIC premiums or reserve requirements.

- Securities Sold under Agreements to Repurchase: Funds temporarily borrowed from corporations and governmental entities. The bank puts up government securities appearing on the assets side of its balance sheet as collateral for these borrowings. If the bank is unable to repay the loan when due from the general cash account, it agrees to sell the government securities to obtain the necessary cash. Funds obtained from these "repurchase agreements" typically have a lower cost than federal funds borrowings because they are collateralized. They are also not subject to FDIC premiums or reserve requirements as long as U.S. government securities serve as the collateral.

- Commercial Paper: Larger, money-center banks have increasingly issued their own commercial paper as a source of funds.

Most of the assets and equities of commercial banks are interest rate sensitive. Banks adopt varying strategies in dealing with interest rate risk. Some adopt a position of balancing interest rate sensitive assets and liabilities, particularly when interest rates change rapidly, to reduce or eliminate interest rate risk and earnings volatility. Others maintain a positive position (interest rate sensitive assets exceed liabilities) so as to benefit from an increase in interest rates. More recently, banks have written floating rate loans to offset interest rate risk on the liabilities side of their balance sheets.

The income statements of commercial banks separate the income from deposit-taking/lending activities and the income from fee-based services. The typical income statement appears in the following format:

       Interest Revenue
    − Interest Expense
    = Net Interest Margin
    − Provision for Loan Losses
    + Noninterest Income
    − Noninterest Expense
    = Net Income before Taxes
    − Income Taxes
    = Net Income

Although banks provide a statement of cash flows, the analyst must interpret this statement differently than for a manufacturing or retailing firm. A bank's principal source of financing (deposits) integrally relates to operations and a bank's primary investing activities (lending and acquiring and selling securities) likewise integrally relate to operations. Thus, the distinctions between operating, investing, and financing activities are not as clearcut as for other industries. The objectives in analyzing a bank's financial statements are the same as in analyzing those of an industrial firm: to assess expected return and risk.

Expected Return   The past profitability of a bank serves as useful information in projecting future rates of return. Analysts use the following profitability ratios to analyze a bank:

1. Rate of Return on Assets = Net Income/Average Total Assets. Unlike the case for an industrial firm, the analyst does not add back interest expense in the numerator. Because interest expense is essentially "cost of goods sold" for a bank, the analyst appropriately deducts it in measuring operating profitability.

2. Rate of Return on Common Shareholders' Equity = Net Income Available to Common/Average Common Shareholders' Equity. Because of the high degree of financial leverage employed by banks, the return on shareholders' equity usually differs substantially from the return on assets.

3. Gross Yield on Earning Assets = Interest Revenue/Average Earning Assets. Earning assets include loans and investments.

4. Rate Paid on Funds = Interest Expense/Average Earning Assets. This ratio indicates the cost of funds required to carry earning assets.

5. Net Interest Margin = Gross Yield on Earning Assets − Rate Paid on Funds. This is the most frequently used ratio to assess the profitability of a bank from its traditional deposit/lending activities.

6. Noninterest Revenue Percentage = Noninterest Revenue/Total Revenue. This ratio has become increasingly important as banks have diversified their revenue sources.

7. Noninterest Expense Percentage = Noninterest Expenses/Total Revenue. Analysts commonly use this ratio as a measure of operating productivity.

8. Loan Loss Provision Percentage = Loan Loss Provision for the Year/Interest Revenues. This ratio has increased in importance in recent years because of increases in loan loss reserves.

Risk   The analysis of risk focuses on three dimensions: credit risk, interest rate risk, and liquidity risk.

Credit risk arises primarily in connection with loans. Real estate, HLT, and some foreign loans have been particularly troublesome in recent years. Analysts use the following ratios in assessing credit risk:

1. Net Charge-Offs Ratio = Net Charge-Offs/Average Loans Receivable during the Year. Net charge-offs equals loans charged off during the year minus recoveries during the year of loans charged off in a previous year.

2. Nonperforming Loans Percentage = Nonperforming Loans/Total Loans Receivable. Both numerator and denominator are measured at their year-end amounts.

3. Loan Loss Reserve to Nonperforming Loans Ratio = Loan Loss Reserve/Nonperforming Loans. Both are measured at their year-end amounts.

4. Loan Loss Reserve Ratio to Total Loans Ratio = Loan Loss Reserve/Loans Receivable. Both are measured at year-end amounts.

Interest rate risk relates to the sensitivity of a bank's assets and liabilities to changes in interest rates. To analyze interest rate risk, it would be desirable to obtain a maturity profile of the bank's interest rate sensitive assets and liabilities. Banks, however, do not fully disclose such information. Banks must present, however, an analysis of changes in interest revenue and interest expense between the current year and the preceding year, attributing the change to volume and interest rate factors. The analyst can use this analysis to assess interest rate risk.

Liquidity risk relates to the ability of a bank to obtain cash quickly if needed. Having ready access to the federal funds, repurchase agreements, and commercial paper markets reduces a bank's liquidity risk. The portfolio of government securities also serves as a source of short-term liquidity. The larger the amount of long-term capital in a bank's capital structure, the less will be the near-term demand on cash and therefore the bank's liquidity risk. Two ratios used for assessing this dimension of liquidity risk are:

1. Long-Term Financing Ratio = Long-Term Debt + Shareholders' Equity/Total Assets. Both are measured at their average amounts during the year.

2. Capital Ratio. A previous section described the calculation of this ratio, which banks must report annually.

COMPANIES STUDIED

Bank of Boston   Bank of Boston pursues a super-regional banking strategy in New England, competing directly with Fleet/Northstar. The Bank of Boston obtains depositors' funds from a branch network located throughout the region. Commercial and institutional loans dominate its portfolio, with international loans comprising 18 percent of the total. It also offers a wide range of management consulting services, including mergers and acquisitions, restructuring, and leasing, to its business customers.

Bankers Trust   Bankers Trust pursues a global merchant banking strategy. A merchant bank provides both commercial and investment banking services. Bankers Trust does not maintain a retail branch network. It obtains deposits from its commercial customers and makes loans to these same firms. The bank emphasizes the offering of a wide range of fee-based services. Bankers Trust manages more corporate investment funds than any other U.S. institution and is expanding this activity in Europe and East Asia. It plays a major role in corporate restructurings, leveraged leasing, and similar transactions.

Citibank   Citibank, the largest commercial bank in the United States, attempts to provide a full range of financial services to consumers and businesses on a worldwide basis. Citibank's Consumer Banking division obtains deposits from individuals through its vast, worldwide retail branch network, a strategy that differentiates it from other international banks. It makes consumer loans for automobiles, home improvements, and similar items and maintains a 13 percent share in the mammoth credit card business. Citibank's Global Finance division plays a major role in managing corporate funds and lending to corporate customers worldwide, as well as offering fee-based advisory services that compete directly with the major investment banks. Citibank has recently increased its role in selling annuities, marking its entry into the insurance business. The bank has met resistance to such a move in certain states, which maintain regulatory authority over insurance activities.

REQUIRED

Financial statements (amounts in millions) for these banks appear next, followed by printouts of a bank analysis program called Bank2. Analyze the profitability and risk of Bank of Boston, Bankers Trust, and Citibank, identifying strategic reasons for observed changes over time and differences between banks.

Bank Name: Bank of Boston

Year (Most Recent, Last Col.)	1987	1988	1989	1990	1991
Period End Assets					
Interest-Bearing Deposits	$ 2,081	$ 1,447	$ 3,940	$ 1,226	$ 1,179
Resale Agreements	131	195	2,150	1,139	768
Domestic Loans	20,538	22,456	21,676	18,091	16,697
Foreign Loans	3,486	3,539	3,115	3,174	3,810
Trading Account Securities	327	477	299	172	189
Investment Securities	3,391	3,221	2,784	3,526	4,754
Total Earning Assets	$ 29,954	$ 31,335	$ 33,964	$ 27,328	$ 27,397
Other Assets	4,163	4,726	5,214	5,201	5,303
Total Assets	$ 34,117	$ 36,061	$ 39,178	$ 32,529	$ 32,700
Period End Equities					
Non-Int.-Bearing Deposits					
Domestic	$ 4,463	$ 4,168	$ 3,785	$ 3,774	$ 3,610
Foreign	368	385	263	300	394
Interest-Bearing Deposits					
Domestic	11,910	13,672	17,108	17,628	16,551
Foreign	5,730	5,366	7,541	4,807	4,183
Short-Term Borrowing	7,272	7,363	5,419	2,103	4,329
Long-Term Borrowing	1,526	1,633	1,608	1,090	1,049
Other Non-Int.-Bear. Liab.	1,099	1,389	1,357	1,171	970
Total Liabilities	$ 32,368	$ 33,976	$ 37,081	$ 30,873	$ 31,086
Preferred Stock	$ 208	$ 208	$ 208	$ 208	$ 208
Common Stock	1,541	1,877	1,889	1,448	1,406
Total Shareholders' Equity	$ 1,749	$ 2,085	$ 2,097	$ 1,656	$ 1,614
Total Equities	$ 34,117	$ 36,061	$ 39,178	$ 32,529	$ 32,700

Bank Name: Bank of Boston

Year (Most Recent, Last Col.)	1987	1988	1989	1990	1991
Average Assets					
Interest-Bearing Deposits	$ 1,620	$ 1,810	$ 2,022	$ 3,066	$ 1,158
Resale Agreements	157	156	457	2,894	1,318
Domestic Loans	19,197	21,234	23,497	20,693	18,437
Foreign Loans	3,943	3,610	3,269	3,138	3,512
Trading Account Securities	425	322	398	369	261
Investment Securities	2,821	3,267	3,153	2,712	3,623
Total Earning Assets	$ 28,163	$ 30,399	$ 32,796	$ 32,872	$ 28,309
Other Assets	3,057	3,295	3,696	3,619	3,438
Total Assets	$ 31,220	$ 33,694	$ 36,492	$ 36,491	$ 31,747
Average Equities					
Non-Int.-Bearing Deposits					
Domestic	$ 4,067	$ 3,760	$ 3,651	$ 3,374	$ 3,207
Foreign	270	306	229	279	291
Interest-Bearing Deposits					
Domestic	11,690	12,823	14,829	18,482	17,706
Foreign	4,222	4,673	5,450	5,929	3,781
Short-Term Borrowing	6,623	7,580	7,175	3,954	3,198
Long-Term Borrowing	1,482	1,558	1,613	1,399	1,048
Other Non-Int.-Bear. Liab.	1,085	1,106	1,395	1,084	943
Total Liabilities	$ 29,439	$ 31,806	$ 34,342	$ 34,501	$ 30,174
Preferred Stock	$ 208	$ 208	$ 208	$ 208	$ 208
Common Stock	1,573	1,680	1,942	1,782	1,365
Total Shareholders' Equity	$ 1,781	$ 1,888	$ 2,150	$ 1,990	$ 1,573
Total Equities	$ 31,220	$ 33,694	$ 36,492	$ 36,491	$ 31,747

Bank Name: Bank of Boston

Year (Most Recent, Last Col.)	1987	1988	1989	1990	1991
Income Statement					
Interest Revenues					
Deposits in Banks	$ 303	$ 509	$ 861	$ 558	$ 488
Resale Agreements	43	86	397	405	114
Domestic Loans	1,946	2,230	2,677	2,141	1,706
Foreign Loans	949	1,159	1,320	1,332	1,222
Trading Acct. Sec.	39	33	49	34	17
Investment Sec.	431	583	646	485	323
Total Int. Revenues	$ 3,711	$ 4,600	$ 5,950	$ 4,955	$ 3,870
Interest Expense					
Domestic Deposits	$ 703	$ 849	$ 1,178	$ 1,362	$ 1,082
Foreign Deposits	922	1,326	1,790	1,478	1,342
Other Int. Expense	936	1,293	1,828	1,115	540
Total Int. Expense	$ 2,561	$ 3,468	$ 4,796	$ 3,955	$ 2,964
Net Interest Margin	$ 1,150	$ 1,132	$ 1,154	$ 1,000	906
Loan Loss Provision	–632	–144	–722	–620	–328
Net Interest Income	$ 518	$ 988	$ 432	$ 380	$ 578
Non-Interest Revenue					
Fin. Ser. Fees	$ 244	$ 314	$ 340	$ 310	$ 318
Trust Fees	136	140	154	152	146
Trad. Acct. Gain and Loss	4	10	16	–8	22
Invest. Gains and Losses	13	13	16	13	18
Other Non-Int. Revenue	160	219	368	237	173
Total Non-Int. Rev.	$ 557	$ 696	$ 894	$ 704	$ 677
Non-Interest Expense					
Compensation	$ 575	$ 589	$ 608	$ 656	$ 594
Occup. and Equip.	197	213	226	254	204
Other Non-Int. Expense	348	385	373	560	537
Total Non-Int. Exp.	$ 1,120	$ 1,187	$ 1,207	$ 1,470	$ 1,335
Income before Taxes	$ –45	$ 497	$ 119	$ –386	$ –80
Income Tax Expense	65	–175	–49	–52	46
Income before Ext. Items	$ 20	$ 322	$ 70	$ –438	$ –34
Ext. Gains and Losses	0	0	0	44	8
Net Income	$ 20	$ 322	$ 70	$ –394	$ –26
Preferred Dividends	–13	–14	–14	–14	–13
Net Income to Common	$ 7	$ 308	$ 56	$ –408	$ –39
Other Data					
Loan Loss Reserve (EOP)	$ 733	$ 690	$ 923	$ 924	$ 924
Net Charge-Offs	$ 354	$ 194	$ 489	$ 619	$ 328
Nonperforming Loans	$ 1,294	$ 1,028	$ 1,074	$ 1,154	$ 909

Bank Name: Bank of Boston

Year (Most Recent, Last Col.)	1987	1988	1989	1990	1991
Overall Profitability Analysis					
Profit Margin for ROA	0.47%	6.08%	1.02%	−6.96%	−.57%
× Asset Turnover	0.14	0.16	0.19	0.16	0.14
= Return on Assets	0.06%	0.96%	0.19%	−1.08%	−.08%
Profit Margin for ROCE	0.16%	5.82%	0.82%	−7.21%	−.86%
× Asset Turnover	0.14	0.16	0.19	0.16	.14
× Leverage Ratio	19.85	20.06	18.79	20.48	23.26
= Return On Common Equity	0.45%	18.33%	2.88%	−22.90%	−2.86%
Operating Performance Analysis					
Gross Yield on Earn. Asset	13.18%	15.13%	18.14%	15.07%	13.67%
Rate Paid on Funds	9.09%	11.41%	14.62%	12.03%	10.47%
Net Interest Margin	4.08%	3.72%	3.52%	3.04%	3.20%
Non-Int. Rev. Percentage	13.05%	13.14%	13.06%	12.44%	14.89%
Non-Int. Exp. Percentage	30.43%	25.50%	20.11%	27.10%	31.05%
Loan Loss Prov. Percentage	17.03%	3.13%	12.13%	12.51%	8.48%
Segment Profitability Analysis					
Return from Bank Deposits	18.70%	28.12%	42.58%	18.20%	42.14%
Return from Resale Agrmnts	27.39%	55.13%	86.87%	13.99%	8.65%
Return from Domestic Loans	10.14%	10.50%	11.39%	10.35%	9.25%
Return from Foreign Loans	24.07%	32.11%	40.38%	42.45%	34.79%
Return from Trad. Acct. Sec.	10.12%	13.35%	16.33%	7.05%	14.94%
Return from Invest. Sec.	15.74%	18.24%	21.00%	18.36%	9.41%
Cost of Domestic Deposits	6.01%	6.62%	7.94%	7.37%	6.11%
Cost of Foreign Deposits	21.84%	28.38%	32.84%	24.93%	35.49%
Cost of Other Borrowing	11.55%	14.15%	20.80%	20.83%	12.72%
Risk Analysis					
Net Charge-Off Ratio	1.53%	0.78%	1.83%	2.60%	1.49%
Nonperform. Loans Perc.	5.39%	3.95%	4.33%	5.43%	4.43%
Loan Loss Reserve to Nonperform. Loan Ratio	56.6%	67.1%	85.9%	80.1%	101.7%
Loan Loss Reserve to Total Loans Ratio	3.05%	2.65%	3.72%	4.35%	4.51%
Long-Term Financing Ratio	45.42%	45.21%	42.86%	41.28%	39.98%
Capital Ratio	N/A	N/A	9.67%	9.66%	9.53%

Bank Name: Bank of Boston

Year (Most Recent, Last Col.)	1987	1988	1989	1990	1991
Common Size Statement **Period End Assets**					
Interest-Bearing Deposits	6.10%	4.01%	10.06%	3.77%	3.61%
Resale Agreements	0.38	0.54	5.49	3.50	2.35
Domestic Loans	60.20	62.27	55.33	55.61	51.06
Foreign Loans	10.22	9.81	7.95	9.76	11.65
Trading Account Securities	0.96	1.32	0.76	0.53	.58
Investment Securities	9.94	8.93	7.11	10.84	14.54
Total Earning Assets	87.80%	86.89%	86.69%	84.01%	83.78%
Other Assets	12.20	13.11	13.31	15.99	16.22
Total Assets	100.00%	100.00%	100.00%	100.00%	100.00%
Common Size Statement **Period End Equities**					
Non-Int.-Bearing Deposits					
Domestic	13.08%	11.56%	9.66%	11.60%	11.04%
Foreign	1.08	1.07	0.67	0.92	1.20
Interest-Bearing Deposits					
Domestic	34.91	37.91	43.67	54.19	50.61
Foreign	16.80	14.88	19.5	14.78	12.79
Short-Term Borrowing	21.31	20.42	13.83	6.47	13.24
Long-Term Borrowing	4.47	4.53	4.10	3.35	3.21
Other Non-Int.-Bear. Liab.	3.22	3.85	3.46	3.60	2.97
Total Liabilities	94.87%	94.22%	94.65%	94.91%	95.06%
Preferred Stock	0.61%	0.58%	0.53%	0.64%	.64%
Common Stock	4.52	5.21	4.82	4.45	4.30
Total Shareholders' Equity	5.13%	5.78%	5.35%	5.09%	4.94%
Total Equities	100.00%	100.00%	100.00%	100.00%	100.00%

Bank Name: Bank of Boston

Year (Most Recent, Last Col.)	1987	1988	1989	1990	1991
Common Size Statement **Average Assets**					
Interest-Bearing Deposits	5.19%	5.37%	5.54%	8.40%	3.65%
Resale Agreements	0.50	0.46	1.25	7.93	4.15
Domestic Loans	61.49	63.02	64.39	56.71	58.07
Foreign Loans	12.63	10.71	8.96	8.60	11.06
Trading Account Securities	1.36	0.96	1.09	1.01	.82
Investment Securities	9.04	9.70	8.64	7.43	11.41
Total Earning Assets	90.21%	90.22%	89.87%	90.08%	89.17%
Other Assets	9.79	9.78	10.13	9.92	10.83
Total Assets	100.00%	100.00%	100.00%	100.00%	100.00%
Common Size Statement **Average Equities**					
Non-Int.-Bearing Deposits					
Domestic	13.03%	11.16%	10.00%	9.25%	10.10%
Foreign	0.86	0.91	0.63	0.76	0.92
Interest-Bearing Deposits					
Domestic	37.44	38.06	40.64	50.65	55.77
Foreign	13.52	13.87	14.93	16.25	11.91
Short-Term Borrowing	21.21	22.50	19.6	10.84	10.07
Long-Term Borrowing	4.75	4.62	4.42%	3.83	3.30
Other Non-Int.-Bear. Liab.	3.48	3.28	3.82	2.97	2.97
Total Liabilities	94.30%	94.40%	94.11%	94.55%	95.05%
Preferred Stock	0.67%	0.62%	0.57%	0.57%	.66%
Common Stock	5.04	4.99	5.32	4.88	4.30
Total Shareholders' Equity	5.70%	5.60%	5.89%	5.45%	4.95%
Total Equities	100.00%	100.00%	100.00%	100.00%	100.00%

Bank Name: Bank of Boston

Year (Most Recent, Last Col.)	1987	1988	1989	1990	1991
Common Size Statement **Income Statement**					
Interest Revenues					
Deposits in Banks	7.10%	9.61%	12.58%	9.86%	10.73%
Resale Agreements	1.01	1.62	5.80	7.16	2.51
Domestic Loans	45.60	42.11	39.11	37.83	37.52
Foreign Loans	22.24	21.88	19.29	23.54	26.87
Trading Acct. Sec.	0.91	0.62	0.72	0.60	.37
Investment Sec.	10.10	11.01	9.44	8.57	7.10
Total Int. Revenues	86.95%	86.86%	86.94%	87.56%	85.11%
Interest Expense					
Domestic Deposits	16.47%	16.03%	17.21%	24.07%	23.80%
Foreign Deposits	21.60	25.04	26.15	26.12	29.51
Other Int. Expense	21.93	24.41	26.71	19.70	11.88
Total Int. Expense	60.00%	65.48%	70.08%	69.89%	65.19%
Net Interest Margin	26.94%	21.37%	16.86%	17.67%	19.93%
Loan Loss Provision	−14.81	−2.72	−10.55	−10.96	−7.21
Net Interest Income	12.14%	18.66%	6.31%	6.71%	12.71%
Non-Interest Revenue					
Fin. Ser. Fees	5.72%	5.93%	4.97%	5.48%	6.99%
Trust Fees	3.19	2.64	2.25	2.69	3.21
Trad. Acct. Gain and Loss	0.09	0.1	0.23	−0.14	.48
Invest. Gains and Losses	0.30	0.25%	0.23	0.23	.40
Other Non-Int. Revenue	3.75	4.14	5.38	4.19	3.80
Total Non-Int. Rev.	13.05%	13.14%	13.06%	12.44%	14.89%
Non-Interest Expense					
Compensation	13.47%	11.12%	8.88%	11.59%	13.06%
Occup. and Equip.	4.62	4.02	3.30	4.49	4.49
Other Non-Int. Expense	8.15	7.27	5.45	9.90	11.81
Total Non-Int. Exp.	26.24%	22.41%	17.64%	25.98%	29.36%
Income before Taxes	−1.05%	9.38%	1.74%	−6.82%	−1.76%
Income Tax Expense	1.52	−3.30	−0.72	−0.92	1.01
Income before Ext. Items	0.47%	6.08%	1.02%	−7.74%	−.75%
Ext. Gains and Losses	0.00	0.00	0.00	0.78	.18
Net Income	0.47%	6.08%	1.02%	−6.96%	−.57%
Preferred Dividends	−0.30	−0.26	−0.20	−0.25	−.29
Net Income to Common	0.16%	5.82%	0.82%	−7.21%	−.86%

Bank Name: Bank of Boston

Year (Most Recent, Last Col.)	1987	1988	1989	1990	1991
Trend Income Statement					
Interest Revenues					
Deposits in Banks	100.0	168.0	284.2	184.2	161.1
Resale Agreements	100.0	200.0	923.3	941.9	265.1
Domestic Loans	100.0	114.6	137.6	110.0	87.7
Foreign Loans	100.0	122.1	139.1	140.4	128.8
Trading Acct. Sec.	100.0	84.6	125.6	87.2	43.6
Investment Sec.	100.0	135.3	149.9	112.5	74.9
Total Int. Revenues	100.0	124.0	160.3	133.5	104.3
Interest Expense					
Domestic Deposits	100.0	120.8	167.6	193.7	153.9
Foreign Deposits	100.0	143.8	194.1	160.3	145.6
Other Int. Expense	100.0	138.1	195.3	119.1	57.7
Total Int. Expense	100.0	135.4	187.3	154.4	115.7
Net Interest Margin	100.0	98.4	100.3	87.0	78.8
Loan Loss Provision	100.0	22.8	114.2	98.1	51.9
Net Interest Income	100.0	190.7	83.4	73.4	111.6
Non-Interest Revenue					
Fin. Ser. Fees	100.0	128.7	139.3	127.0	130.3
Trust Fees	100.0	102.9	113.2	111.8	107.4
Trad. Acct. Gain and Loss	100.0	250.0	400.0	−200.0	550.0
Invest. Gains and Losses	100.0	100.0	123.1	100.0	138.5
Other Non-Int. Revenue	100.0	136.9	230.0	148.1	108.1
Total Non-Int. Rev.	100.0	125.0	160.5	126.4	121.5
Non-Interest Expense					
Compensation	100.0	102.4	105.7	114.1	103.3
Occup. and Equip.	100.0	108.1	114.7	128.9	103.6
Other Non-Int. Expense	100.0	110.6	107.2	160.9	154.3
Total Non-Int. Exp.	100.0	106.0	107.8	131.3	119.2
Income before Taxes	100.0	−1,104.4	−264.4	857.8	177.8
Income Tax Expense	100.0	−269.2	−75.4	−80.0	70.8
Income before Ext. Items	100.0	1,610.0	350.0	−2,190.0	−170.0
Ext. Gains and Losses	ERR	ERR	ERR	ERR	ERR
Net Income	100.0	1,610.0	350.0	−1,970.0	−130.0
Preferred Dividends	100.0	107.7	107.7	107.7	100.0
Net Income to Common	100.0	4,400.0	800.0	−5,828.6	−557.1

Bank Name: Bankers Trust

Year (Most Recent, Last Col.)	1987	1988	1989	1990	1991
Period End Assets					
Interest-Bearing Deposits	$ 7,212	$ 8,717	$ 5,823	$ 4,593	$ 4,577
Resale Agreements	3,649	4,010	4,301	4,645	7,611
Domestic Loans	14,611	13,288	10,095	11,351	9,112
Foreign Loans	10,275	9,513	8,326	7,954	6,129
Trading Account Securities	5,747	6,585	12,202	17,228	23,580
Investment Securities	4,294	4,328	6,204	7,030	6,516
Total Earning Assets	$ 45,788	$ 46,441	$ 46,951	$ 52,801	$ 57,525
Other Assets	10,733	11,501	8,707	10,795	6,434
Total Assets	$ 56,521	$ 57,942	$ 55,658	$ 63,596	$ 63,959
Period End Equities					
Non-Int.-Bearing Deposits					
Domestic	$ 6,371	$ 7,506	$ 6,046	$ 6,189	$ 3,399
Foreign	297	181	216	896	643
Interest-Bearing Deposits					
Domestic	5,076	5,778	7,149	6,910	5,782
Foreign	18,477	19,025	12,809	14,593	13,010
Short-Term Borrowing	15,654	13,436	22,083	24,507	29,183
Long-Term Borrowing	2,571	2,450	2,435	2,650	3,081
Other Non-Int.-Bear. Liab.	5,186	6,067	2,534	4,827	5,449
Total Liabilities	$ 53,632	$ 54,443	$ 53,272	$ 60,572	$ 60,547
Preferred Stock	$ 0	$ 0	$ 250	$ 500	$ 500
Common Stock	2,889	3,499	2,136	2,524	2,912
Total Shareholders' Equity	$ 2,889	$ 3,499	$ 2,386	$ 3,024	$ 3,412
Total Equities	$ 56,521	$ 57,942	$ 55,658	$ 63,596	$ 63,959

Bank Name: Bankers Trust

Year (Most Recent, Last Col.)	1987	1988	1989	1990	1991
Average Assets					
Interest-Bearing Deposits	$ 8,813	$ 9,182	$ 7,949	$ 6,484	$ 4,485
Resale Agreements	5,092	5,819	10,691	6,848	7,667
Domestic Loans	15,390	13,887	11,763	10,345	9,800
Foreign Loans	9,854	9,925	9,330	8,390	7,274
Trading Account Securities	5,977	5,265	7,113	14,790	10,061
Investment Securities	3,429	3,819	4,194	7,940	5,520
Total Earning Assets	$ 48,555	$ 47,897	$ 51,040	$ 54,797	$ 50,807
Other Assets	9,373	9,722	9,466	9,313	10,448
Total Assets	$ 57,928	$ 57,619	$ 60,506	$ 64,110	$ 61,255
Average Equities					
Non-Int.-Bearing Deposits					
Domestic	$ 5,736	$ 5,642	$ 5,519	$ 4,002	$ 3,118
Foreign	224	261	234	398	580
Interest-Bearing Deposits					
Domestic	5,238	5,660	6,875	6,954	6,534
Foreign	18,369	17,612	17,438	16,411	13,620
Short-Term Borrowing	17,745	17,383	23,606	25,511	24,905
Long-Term Borrowing	2,564	2,533	2,529	2,546	2,725
Other Non-Int.-Bear. Liab.	5,376	5,332	1,095	5,529	6,483
Total Liabilities	$ 55,252	$ 54,423	$ 57,296	$ 61,351	$ 58,015
Preferred Stock	$ 0	$ 0	$ 84	$ 388	$ 500
Common Stock	2,676	3,196	3,126	2,371	2,740
Total Shareholders' Equity	$ 2,676	$ 3,196	$ 3,210	$ 2,759	$ 3,240
Total Equities	$ 57,928	$ 57,619	$ 60,506	$ 64,110	$ 61,255

Bank Name: Bankers Trust

Year (Most Recent, Last Col.)	1987	1988	1989	1990	1991
Income Statement					
Interest Revenues					
Deposits in Banks	$ 583	$ 634	$ 710	$ 646	$ 356
Resale Agreements	294	398	915	535	466
Domestic Loans	1,505	1,359	1,329	1,082	786
Foreign Loans	926	1,000	1,117	992	734
Trading Acct. Sec.	463	490	1,167	1,501	1,462
Investment Sec.	290	310	440	836	518
Total Int. Revenues	$ 4,061	$ 4,191	$ 5,678	$ 5,592	$ 4,322
Interest Expense					
Domestic Deposits	$ 366	$ 414	$ 579	$ 516	$ 380
Foreign Deposits	1,263	1,303	1,674	1,710	1,209
Other Int. Expense	1,425	1,548	2,522	2,573	1,996
Total Int. Expense	$ 3,054	$ 3,265	$ 4,775	$ 4,799	$ 3,585
Net Interest Margin	$ 1,007	$ 926	$ 903	$ 793	$ 737
Loan Loss Provision	−862	−50	−1,877	−194	−238
Net Interest Income	$ 145	$ 876	$ −974	$ 599	$ 499
Non-Interest Revenue					
Fin. Ser. Fees	$ 605	$ 694	$ 708	$ 559	$ 511
Trust Fees	293	322	381	468	567
Trad. Acct. Gain and Loss	202	221	313	601	957
Invest. Gains and Losses	11	11	1	20	46
Other Non-Int. Revenue	521	412	629	679	441
Total Non-Int. Rev.	$ 1,632	$ 1,660	$ 2,032	$ 2,327	$ 2,522
Non-Interest Expense					
Compensation	$ 961	$ 1,014	$ 1,103	$ 1,244	$ 1,236
Occup. and Equip.	205	239	257	285	303
Other Non-Int. Expense	315	369	513	582	648
Total Non-Int. Exp.	$ 1,481	$ 1,622	$ 1,873	$ 2,111	$ 2,187
Income before Taxes	$ 296	$ 914	$ −815	$ 815	$ 834
Income Tax Expense	−295	−267	−165	−150	−167
Income before Ext. Items	$ 1	$ 647	$ −980	$ 665	$ 667
Ext. Gains and Losses	0	0	0	0	0
Net Income	$ 1	$ 647	$ −980	$ 665	$ 667
Preferred Dividends	0	0	−5	−31	−34
Net Income to Common	$ 1	$ 647	$ −985	$ 634	$ 633
Other Data					
Loan Loss Reserve (EOP)	$ 1,298	$ 1,314	$ 2,732	$ 2,169	$ 1,806
Net Charge-Offs	$ 155	$ 34	$ 459	$ 757	$ 601
Nonperforming Loans	$ 1,156	$ 1,291	$ 1,397	$ 1,764	$ 1,750

Bank Name: Bankers Trust

Year (Most Recent, Last Col.)	1987	1988	1989	1990	1991
Overall Profitability Analysis					
Profit Margin for ROA	0.02%	11.06%	−12.71%	8.40%	9.75%
× Asset Turnover	0.10	0.10	0.13	0.12	0.11
= Return on Assets	0.00%	1.12%	−1.62%	1.04%	1.09%
Profit Margin for ROCE	0.02%	11.06%	−12.78%	8.01%	9.25%
× Asset Turnover	0.10	0.10	0.13	0.12	0.11
× Leverage Ratio	21.65	18.03	19.36	27.04	22.36
= Return On Common Equity	0.04%	20.24%	−31.51%	26.74%	23.10%
Operating Performance Analysis					
Gross Yield on Earn. Asset	8.36%	8.75%	11.12%	10.20%	8.51%
Rate Paid on Funds	6.29%	6.82%	9.36%	8.76%	7.06%
Net Interest Margin	2.07%	1.93%	1.77%	1.45%	1.45%
Non-Int. Rev. Percentage	28.67%	28.37%	26.36%	29.39%	36.85%
Non-Int. Exp. Percentage	32.66%	33.19%	28.17%	30.55%	37.89%
Loan Loss Prov. Percentage	21.23%	1.19%	33.06%	3.47%	5.51%
Segment Profitability Analysis					
Return from Bank Deposits	6.62%	6.90%	8.93%	9.96%	7.94%
Return from Resale Agrmnts	5.77%	6.84%	8.56%	7.81%	6.08%
Return from Domestic Loans	9.78%	9.79%	11.30%	10.46%	8.02%
Return from Foreign Loans	9.40%	10.08%	11.97%	11.82%	10.09%
Return from Trad. Acct. Sec.	11.13%	13.50%	20.81%	14.21%	15.06%
Return from Invest. Sec.	8.78%	8.41%	10.52%	10.78%	10.22%
Cost of Domestic Deposits	6.99%	7.31%	8.42%	7.42%	5.82%
Cost of Foreign Deposits	6.88%	7.40%	9.60%	10.42%	8.84%
Cost of Other Borrowing	7.02%	7.77%	9.65%	9.17%	7.22%
Risk Analysis					
Net Charge-Off Ratio	0.61%	0.14%	2.18%	4.04%	3.52%
Nonperform. Loans Perc.	4.65%	5.66%	7.58%	9.14%	11.48%
Loan Loss Reserve to Nonperform. Loans Ratio	112.9%	101.8%	195.6%	123.0%	103.2%
Loan Loss Reserve to Total Loans Ratio	5.22%	5.76%	14.83%	11.24%	11.85%
Long-Term Financing Ratio	48.93%	44.21%	44.07%	47.99%	45.68%
Capital Ratio	N/A	8.90%	8.08%	10.03%	10.86%

Bank Name: Bankers Trust

Year (Most Recent, Last Col.)	1987	1988	1989	1990	1991
Common Size Statement **Period End Assets**					
Interest-Bearing Deposits	12.76%	15.04%	10.46%	7.22%	7.16%
Resale Agreements	6.46	6.92	7.73	7.30	11.90
Domestic Loans	25.85	22.93	18.14	17.85	14.25
Foreign Loans	18.18	16.42	14.96	12.50	9.58
Trading Account Securities	10.17	11.36	21.92	27.09	36.87
Investment Securities	7.60	7.47	11.15	11.05	10.19
Total Earning Assets	81.01%	80.15%	84.36%	83.03%	89.94%
Other Assets	18.99	19.85	15.64	16.97	10.06
Total Assets	100.00%	100.00%	100.00%	100.00%	100.00%
Common Size Statement **Period End Equities**					
Non-Int.-Bearing Deposits					
Domestic	11.27%	12.95%	10.86%	9.73%	5.31%
Foreign	0.53	0.31	0.39	1.41	1.01
Interest-Bearing Deposits					
Domestic	8.98	9.97	12.84	10.87	9.04
Foreign	32.69	32.83	23.01	22.95	20.34
Short-Term Borrowing	27.70	23.19	39.68	38.54	45.63
Long-Term Borrowing	4.55	4.23	4.37	4.17	4.82
Other Non-Int.-Bear. Liab.	9.18	10.47	4.55	7.59	8.52
Total Liabilities	94.89%	93.96%	95.71%	95.24%	94.67%
Preferred Stock	0.00%	0.00%	0.45%	0.79%	0.78%
Common Stock	5.11	6.04	3.84	3.97	4.55
Total Shareholders' Equity	5.11%	6.04%	4.29%	4.76%	5.33%
Total Equities	100.00%	100.00%	100.00%	100.00%	100.00%

Bank Name: Bankers Trust

Year (Most Recent, Last Col.)	1987	1988	1989	1990	1991
Common Size Statement **Average Assets**					
Interest-Bearing Deposits	15.21%	15.94%	13.14%	10.11%	7.32%
Resale Agreements	8.79	10.10	17.67	10.68	12.52
Domestic Loans	26.57	24.10	19.44	16.14	16.00
Foreign Loans	17.01	17.23	15.42	13.09	11.87
Trading Account Securities	10.32	9.14	11.76	23.07	26.22
Investment Securities	5.92	6.63	6.93	12.38	9.01
Total Earning Assets	83.82%	83.13%	84.36%	85.47%	82.94%
Other Assets	16.18	16.87	15.64	14.53	17.06
Total Assets	100.00%	100.00%	100.00%	100.00%	100.00%
Common Size Statement **Average Equities**					
Non-Int.-Bearing Deposits					
Domestic	9.90%	9.79%	9.12%	6.24%	5.09%
Foreign	0.39	0.45	0.39	0.62	0.95
Interest-Bearing Deposits					
Domestic	9.04	9.82	11.36	10.85	10.67
Foreign	31.71	30.57	28.82	25.60	22.32
Short-Term Borrowing	30.63	30.17	39.01	39.79	40.66
Long-Term Borrowing	4.43	4.40	4.18	3.97	4.45
Other Non-Int.-Bear. Liab.	9.28	9.25	1.81	8.62	10.58
Total Liabilities	95.38%	94.45%	94.69%	95.70%	94.71%
Preferred Stock	0.00%	0.00%	0.14%	0.61%	0.82%
Common Stock	4.62	5.55	5.17	3.70	4.47
Total Shareholders' Equity	4.62%	5.55%	5.31%	4.30%	5.29%
Total Equities	100.00%	100.00%	100.00%	100.00%	100.00%

Bank Name: Bankers Trust

Year (Most Recent, Last Col.)	1987	1988	1989	1990	1991
Common Size Statement					
Income Statement					
Interest Revenues					
Deposits in Banks	10.24%	10.84%	9.21%	8.16%	5.20%
Resale Agreements	5.16	6.80	11.87	6.76	6.81
Domestic Loans	26.44	23.23	17.24	13.66	11.48
Foreign Loans	16.27	17.09	14.49	12.53	10.72
Trading Acct. Sec.	8.13	8.37	15.14	18.95	21.36
Investment Sec.	5.09	5.30	5.71	10.56	7.57
Total Int. Revenues	71.33%	71.63%	73.64%	70.61%	63.15%
Interest Expense					
Domestic Deposits	6.43%	7.08%	7.51%	6.52%	5.55%
Foreign Deposits	22.19	22.27	21.71	21.59	17.67
Other Int. Expense	25.03	26.46	32.71	32.49	29.16
Total Int. Expense	53.64%	55.80%	61.93%	60.60%	52.38%
Net Interest Margin	17.69%	15.83%	11.71%	10.01%	10.77%
Loan Loss Provision	−15.14	−0.85	−24.35	−2.45	−3.48
Net Interest Income	2.55%	14.97%	−12.63%	7.56%	7.29%
Non-Interest Revenue					
Fin. Ser. Fees	10.63%	11.86%	9.18%	7.06%	7.47%
Trust Fees	5.15	5.50	4.94	5.91	8.28
Trad. Acct. Gain and Loss	3.55	3.78	4.06	7.59	13.98
Invest. Gains and Losses	0.19	0.19	0.01	0.25	0.67
Other Non-Int. Revenue	9.15	7.04	8.16	8.57	6.44
Total Non-Int. Rev.	28.67%	28.37%	26.36%	29.39%	36.85%
Non-Interest Expense					
Compensation	16.88%	17.33%	14.31%	15.71%	18.06%
Occup. and Equip.	3.60	4.08	3.33	3.60	4.43
Other Non-Int. Expense	5.53	6.31	6.65	7.35	9.47
Total Non-Int. Exp.	26.01%	27.72%	24.29%	26.66%	31.95%
Income before Taxes	5.20%	15.62%	−10.57%	10.29%	12.19%
Income Tax Expense	−5.18	−4.56	−2.14	−1.89	−2.44
Income before Ext. Items	0.02%	11.06%	−12.71%	8.40%	9.75%
Ext. Gains and Losses	0.00	0.00	0.00	0.00	0.00
Net Income	0.02%	11.06%	−12.71%	8.40%	9.75%
Preferred Dividends	0.00	0.00	−0.06	−0.39	−0.50
Net Income to Common	0.02%	11.06%	−12.78%	8.01%	9.25%

Bank Name: Bankers Trust

Year (Most Recent, Last Col.)	1987	1988	1989	1990	1991
Trend Income Statement					
Interest Revenues					
Deposits in Banks	100.0	108.7	121.8	110.8	61.1
Resale Agreements	100.0	135.4	311.2	182.0	158.5
Domestic Loans	100.0	90.3	88.3	71.9	52.2
Foreign Loans	100.0	108.0	120.6	107.1	79.3
Trading Acct. Sec.	100.0	105.8	252.1	324.2	315.8
Investment Sec.	100.0	106.9	151.7	288.3	178.6
Total Int. Revenues	100.0	103.2	139.8	137.7	106.4
Interest Expense					
Domestic Deposits	100.0	113.1	158.2	141.0	103.8
Foreign Deposits	100.0	103.2	132.5	135.4	95.7
Other Int. Expense	100.0	108.6	177.0	180.6	140.1
Total Int. Expense	100.0	106.9	156.4	157.1	117.4
Net Interest Margin	100.0	92.0	89.7	78.7	73.2
Loan Loss Provision	100.0	5.8	217.7	22.5	27.6
Net Interest Income	100.0	604.1	−671.7	413.1	344.1
Non-Interest Revenue					
Fin. Ser. Fees	100.0	114.7	117.0	92.4	84.5
Trust Fees	100.0	109.9	130.0	159.7	193.5
Trad. Acct. Gain and Loss	100.0	109.4	155.0	297.5	473.8
Invest. Gains and Losses	100.0	100.0	9.1	181.8	418.2
Other Non-Int. Revenue	100.0	79.1	120.7	130.3	84.6
Total Non-Int. Rev.	100.0	101.7	124.5	142.6	154.5
Non-Interest Expense					
Compensation	100.0	105.5	114.8	129.4	128.6
Occup. and Equip.	100.0	116.6	125.4	139.0	147.8
Other Non-Int. Expense	100.0	117.1	162.9	184.8	205.7
Total Non-Int. Exp.	100.0	109.5	126.5	142.5	147.7
Income before Taxes	100.0	308.8	−275.3	275.3	281.8
Income Tax Expense	100.0	90.5	55.9	50.8	56.6
Income before Ext. Items	100.0	ERR	ERR	ERR	ERR
Ext. Gains and Losses	ERR	ERR	ERR	ERR	ERR
Net Income	100.0	ERR	ERR	ERR	ERR
Preferred Dividends	ERR	ERR	ERR	ERR	ERR
Net Income to Common	100.0	ERR	ERR	ERR	ERR

Bank Name: Citibank

Year (Most Recent, Last Col.)	1987	1988	1989	1990	1991
Period End Assets					
Interest-Bearing Deposits	$ 14,706	$ 10,706	$ 13,813	$ 7,546	$ 6,692
Resale Agreements	7,552	6,441	7,659	4,071	4,550
Domestic Loans	84,202	94,012	96,936	89,102	82,489
Foreign Loans	49,265	50,980	58,447	62,755	65,147
Trading Account Securities	5,594	3,924	9,018	7,518	12,064
Investment Securities	15,396	15,217	14,699	14,075	14,713
Total Earning Assets	$ 176,715	$ 181,280	$ 200,572	$ 185,067	$ 185,655
Other Assets	26,892	26,386	30,071	31,919	31,267
Total Assets	$ 203,607	$ 207,666	$ 230,643	$ 216,986	$ 216,922
Period End Equities					
Non-Int.-Bearing Deposits					
Domestic	$ 11,241	$ 12,190	$ 12,977	$ 11,482	$ 12,474
Foreign	4,004	4,065	4,760	4,642	4,829
Interest-Bearing Deposits					
Domestic	44,731	50,819	54,092	53,143	48,872
Foreign	59,585	56,998	66,093	73,185	80,300
Short-Term Borrowing	31,690	32,889	38,499	21,173	19,174
Long-Term Borrowing	24,364	23,998	23,990	23,226	23,382
Other Non-Int.-Bear. Liab.	19,182	16,843	20,156	20,405	18,402
Total Liabilities	$ 194,797	$ 197,802	$ 220,567	$ 207,256	$ 207,433
Preferred Stock	$ 1,590	$ 1,590	$ 1,840	$ 1,540	$ 2,140
Common Stock	7,220	8,274	8,236	8,190	7,349
Total Shareholders' Equity	$ 8,810	$ 9,864	$ 10,076	$ 9,730	$ 9,489
Total Equities	$ 203,607	$ 207,666	$ 230,643	$ 216,986	$ 216,922

Bank Name: Citibank

Year (Most Recent, Last Col.)	1987	1988	1989	1990	1991
Average Assets					
Interest-Bearing Deposits	$ 15,326	$ 13,604	$ 12,020	$ 12,685	$ 9,205
Resale Agreements	8,156	9,110	10,169	9,707	7,403
Domestic Loans	84,742	93,165	97,981	96,549	89,064
Foreign Loans	47,413	49,536	52,859	62,285	63,635
Trading Account Securities	7,215	6,146	10,090	10,233	12,760
Investment Securities	13,510	14,275	14,523	14,841	14,022
Total Earning Assets	$ 176,362	$ 185,836	$ 197,642	$ 206,300	$ 196,089
Other Assets	22,321	21,270	23,360	25,488	25,808
Total Assets	$ 198,683	$ 207,106	$ 221,002	$ 231,788	$ 221,897
Average Equities					
Non-Int.-Bearing Deposits					
Domestic	$ 10,076	$ 10,050	$ 10,154	$ 10,298	$ 10,263
Foreign	4,089	6,624	3,814	4,463	4,348
Interest-Bearing Deposits					
Domestic	41,767	47,488	52,482	54,387	51,120
Foreign	59,965	57,743	60,968	73,961	78,174
Short-Term Borrowing	32,334	36,064	40,767	33,761	25,433
Long-Term Borrowing	24,839	24,761	24,612	24,946	25,433
Other Non-Int.-Bear. Liab.	17,419	15,349	17,756	19,626	17,397
Total Liabilities	$ 190,489	$ 198,079	$ 210,553	$ 221,442	$ 211,704
Preferred Stock	$ 1,478	$ 1,590	$ 1,715	$ 1,715	$ 1,840
Common Stock	6,716	7,437	8,734	8,631	8,353
Total Shareholders' Equity	$ 8,194	$ 9,027	$ 10,449	$ 10,346	$ 10,193
Total Equities	$ 198,683	$ 207,106	$ 221,002	$ 231,788	$ 221,897

Bank Name: Citibank

Year (Most Recent, Last Col.)	1987	1988	1989	1990	1991
Income Statement					
Interest Revenues					
Deposits in Banks	$ 1,261	$ 1,362	$ 1,533	$ 1,474	$ 886
Resale Agreements	725	1,234	4,133	2,107	637
Domestic Loans	10,187	11,025	11,910	12,544	9,472
Foreign Loans	7,106	9,550	11,310	11,982	10,968
Trading Acct. Sec.	1,479	2,206	1,425	1,517	1,310
Investment Sec.	1,236	1,234	1,265	1,359	1,081
Total Int. Revenues	$ 21,994	$ 26,611	$ 31,576	$ 30,983	$ 24,354
Interest Expense					
Domestic Deposits	$ 2,920	$ 3,490	$ 4,481	$ 4,359	$ 3,396
Foreign Deposits	6,189	7,122	8,349	10,127	7,720
Other Int. Expense	6,419	8,394	11,388	9,312	5,973
Total Int. Expense	$ 15,528	$ 19,006	$ 24,218	$ 23,798	$ 17,089
Net Interest Margin	$ 6,466	$ 7,605	$ 7,358	$ 7,185	$ 7,265
Loan Loss Provision	–4,410	–1,330	–2,521	–2,662	–3,890
Net Interest Income	$ 2,056	$ 6,275	$ 4,837	$ 4,523	$ 3,375
Non-Interest Revenue					
Fin. Ser. Fees	$ 3,584	$ 3,887	$ 4,374	$ 5,024	$ 4,815
Trust Fees	0	0	0	0	0
Trad. Acct. Gain and Loss	177	277	256	271	457
Invest. Gains and Losses	195	108	180	52	330
Other Non-Int. Revenue	2,038	1,141	1,584	2,055	1,883
Total Non-Int. Rev.	$ 5,994	$ 5,413	$ 6,394	$ 7,402	$ 7,485
Non-Interest Expense					
Compensation	$ 3,922	$ 4,227	$ 4,457	$ 5,160	$ 4,811
Occup. and Equip.	1,466	1,641	1,760	1,864	1,807
Other Non-Int. Expense	2,902	3,113	3,481	4,075	4,479
Total Non-Int. Exp.	$ 8,290	$ 8,981	$ 9,698	$ 11,099	$ 11,097
Income before Taxes	$ –240	$ 2,707	$ 1,533	$ 826	$ –237
Income Tax Expense	–898	–1,009	–1,035	–508	–677
Income before Ext. Items	$ –1,138	$ 1,698	$ 498	$ 318	$ 914
Ext. Gains and Losses	0	160	0	140	457
Net Income	$ –1,138	$ 1,858	$ 498	$ 458	$ 457
Preferred Dividends	88	101	125	139	–179
Net Income to Common	$ –1,226	$ 1,757	$ 373	$ 319	$ –636
Other Data					
Loan Loss Reserve (EOP)	$ 4,618	$ 4,205	$ 4,729	$ 4,451	$ 3,308
Net Charge-Offs	$ 1,497	$ 1,752	$ 1,944	$ 2,863	$ 4,934
Nonperforming Loans	$ 7,593	$ 8,381	$ 10,221	$ 12,404	$ 12,094

Bank Name: Citibank

Year (Most Recent, Last Col.)	1987	1988	1989	1990	1991
Overall Profitability Analysis					
Profit Margin for ROA	−4.07%	5.80%	1.31%	1.19%	−1.44%
× Asset Turnover	0.14	0.15	0.17	0.17	0.14
= Return on Assets	−0.57%	0.90%	0.23%	0.20%	−.21%
Profit Margin For ROSE	−4.38%	5.49%	0.98%	0.83%	−2.00%
× Asset Turnover	0.14	0.15	0.17	0.17	0.14
× Leverage Ratio	29.58	27.85	25.30	26.86	26.56
= Return On Common Equity	−18.25%	23.63%	4.27%	3.70%	−7.61%
Operating Performance Analysis					
Gross Yield on Earn. Asset	12.47%	14.32%	15.98%	15.02%	12.42%
Rate Paid on Funds	8.80%	10.23%	12.25%	11.54%	8.71%
Net Interest Margin	3.67%	4.09%	3.72%	3.48%	3.70%
Non-Int. Rev. Percentage	21.42%	16.90%	16.84%	19.28%	23.51%
Non-Int. Exp. Percentage	34.81%	32.09%	28.59%	31.81%	39.37%
Loan Loss Prov. Percentage	20.05%	5.00%	7.98%	8.59%	15.97%
Segment Profitability Analysis					
Return from Bank Deposits	8.23%	10.01%	12.75%	11.62%	9.63%
Return from Resale Agrmnts	8.89%	13.55%	40.64%	21.71%	8.60%
Return from Domestic Loans	12.02%	11.83%	12.16%	12.99%	10.64%
Return from Foreign Loans	14.99%	19.28%	21.40%	19.24%	17.24%
Return from Trad. Acct. Sec.	22.95%	40.40%	16.66%	17.47%	13.85%
Return from Invest. Sec.	10.59%	9.40%	9.95%	9.51%	10.06%
Cost of Domestic Deposits	6.99%	7.35%	8.54%	8.01%	6.64%
Cost of Foreign Deposits	10.32%	12.33%	13.69%	13.69%	9.88%
Cost of Other Borrowing	11.23%	13.80%	17.42%	15.86%	11.85%
Risk Analysis					
Net Charge-Off Ratio	1.13%	1.23%	1.29%	1.80%	3.23%
Nonperform. Loans Perc.	5.69%	5.78%	6.58%	8.17%	8.19%
Loan Loss Reserve to Nonperform. Ratio	60.8%	50.2%	46.3%	35.9%	27.4%
Loan Loss Reserve for Total Loans Ratio	3.46%	2.90%	3.04%	2.93%	2.24%
Long-Term Financing Ratio	75.19%	73.28%	70.20%	70.68%	71.01%
Capital Ratio	N/A	N/A	6.44%	6.52%	7.46%

Bank Name: Citibank

Year (Most Recent, Last Col.)	1987	1988	1989	1990	1991
Common Size Statement **Period End Assets**					
Interest-Bearing Deposits	7.22%	5.16%	5.99%	3.48%	3.08%
Resale Agreements	3.71	3.10	3.32	1.88	2.10
Domestic Loans	41.36	45.27	42.03	41.06	38.03
Foreign Loans	24.20	24.55	25.34	28.92	30.03
Trading Account Securities	2.75	1.89	3.91	3.46	5.56
Investment Securities	7.56	7.33	6.37	6.49	6.78
Total Earning Assets	86.79%	87.29%	86.96%	85.29%	85.59%
Other Assets	13.21	12.71	13.04	14.71	14.41
Total Assets	100.00%	100.00%	100.00%	100.00%	100.00%
Common Size Statement **Period End Equities**					
Non-Int.-Bearing Deposits					
Domestic	5.52%	5.87%	5.63%	5.29%	5.75%
Foreign	1.97	1.96	2.06	2.14	2.23
Interest-Bearing Deposit					
Domestic	21.97	24.47	23.45	24.49%	22.53%
Foreign	29.26	27.45	28.66	33.73	37.02
Short-Term Borrowing	15.56	15.84	16.69	9.76	8.84
Long-Term Borrowing	11.97	11.56	10.40	10.70	10.78
Other Non-Int.-Bear. Liab.	9.42	8.11	8.74	9.40	8.48
Total Liabilities	95.67%	95.25%	95.63%	95.52%	95.63%
Preferred Stock	0.78%	0.77%	0.80%	0.71%	0.99%
Common Stock	3.55	3.98	3.57	3.77	3.39
Total Shareholders' Equity	4.33%	4.75%	4.37%	4.48%	4.37%
Total Equities	100.00%	100.00%	100.00%	100.00%	100.00%

Bank Name: Citibank

Year (Most Recent, Last Col.)	1987	1988	1989	1990	1991
Common Size Statement **Average Assets**					
Interest-Bearing Deposits	7.71%	6.57%	5.44%	5.47%	4.15%
Resale Agreements	4.11	4.40	4.60	4.19	3.34
Domestic Loans	42.65	44.98	44.33	41.65	40.14
Foreign Loans	23.86	23.92	23.92	26.87	28.68
Trading Account Securities	3.63	2.97	4.57	4.41	5.75
Investment Securities	6.80	6.89	6.57	6.40	6.32
Total Earning Assets	88.77%	89.73%	89.43%	89.00%	88.37%
Other Assets	11.23	10.27	10.57	11.00	11.63
Total Assets	100.00%	100.00%	100.00%	100.00%	100.00%
Common Size Statement **Average Equities**					
Non-Int.-Bearing Deposits					
Domestic	5.07%	4.85%	4.59%	4.44%	4.63%
Foreign	2.06	3.20	1.73	1.93	1.96
Interest-Bearing Deposits					
Domestic	21.02	22.93	23.75	23.46	23.04
Foreign	30.18	27.88	27.59	31.91	35.23
Short-Term Borrowing	16.27	17.41	18.45	14.57	11.46
Long-Term Borrowing	12.50	11.96	11.14	10.76	11.25
Other Non-Int.-Bear. Liab.	8.77	7.41	8.03	8.47	7.84
Total Liabilities	95.88%	95.64%	95.27%	95.54%	95.41%
Preferred Stock	0.74%	0.77%	0.78%	0.74%	0.83%
Common Stock	3.38	3.59	3.95	3.72	3.76
Total Shareholders' Equity	4.12%	4.36%	4.73%	4.46%	4.59%
Total Equities	100.00%	100.00%	100.00%	100.00%	100.00%

Bank Name: Citibank

Year (Most Recent, Last Col.)	1987	1988	1989	1990	1991
Common Size Statement **Income Statement**					
Interest Revenues					
Deposits in Banks	4.51%	4.25%	4.04%	3.84%	2.78%
Resale Agreements	2.59	3.85	10.88	5.49	2.00
Domestic Loans	36.40	34.43	31.37	32.68	29.75
Foreign Loans	25.39	29.82	29.79	31.22	34.45
Trading Acct. Sec.	5.28	6.89	3.75	3.95	4.11
Investment Sec.	4.42	3.85	3.33	3.54	3.40
Total Int. Revenues	78.58%	83.10%	83.16%	80.72%	76.49%
Interest Expense					
Domestic Deposits	10.43%	10.90%	11.80%	11.36%	10.67%
Foreign Deposits	22.11	22.24	21.99	26.38	24.25
Other Int. Expense	22.93	26.21	29.99	24.26	18.76
Total Int. Expense	55.48%	59.35%	63.78%	62.00%	53.67%
Net Interest Margin	23.10%	23.75%	19.38%	18.72%	22.82%
Loan Loss Provision	−15.76	−4.15	−6.64	−6.94	−12.22
Net Interest Income	7.35%	19.59%	12.74%	11.78%	10.60%
Non-Interest Revenue					
Fin. Ser. Fees	12.81%	12.14%	11.52%	13.09%	15.12%
Trust Fees	0.00	0.00	0.00	0.00	0.00
Trad. Acct. Gain and Loss	0.63	0.86	0.67	0.71	1.44
Invest. Gains and Losses	0.70	0.34	0.47	0.14	1.04
Other Non-Int. Revenue	7.28	3.56	4.17	5.35	5.91
Total Non-Int. Rev.	21.42%	16.90%	16.84%	19.28%	23.51%
Non-Interest Expense					
Compensation	14.01%	13.20%	11.74%	13.44%	15.11%
Occup. and Equip.	5.24	5.12	4.64	4.86	5.68
Other Non-Int. Expense	10.37	9.72	9.17	10.62	14.07
Total Non-Int. Exp.	29.62%	28.04%	25.54%	28.91%	34.85%
Income before Taxes	−0.86%	8.45%	4.04%	2.15%	−0.74%
Income Tax Expense	−3.21	−3.15	−2.73	−1.32	−2.13
Income before Ext. Items	−4.07%	5.30%	1.31%	0.83%	−2.87%
Ext. Gains and Losses	0.00	0.50	0.00	0.36	1.44
Net Income	−4.07%	5.80%	1.31%	1.19%	−1.44%
Preferred Dividends	−0.31	−0.32	−0.33	−0.36	−0.56
Net Income to Common	−4.38%	5.49%	0.98%	0.83%	−2.00%

Bank Name: Citibank

Year (Most Recent, Last Col.)	1987	1988	1989	1990	1991
Trend Income Statement					
Interest Revenues					
Deposits in Banks	100.0	108.0	121.6	116.9	70.3
Resale Agreements	100.0	170.2	570.1	290.6	87.9
Domestic Loans	100.0	108.2	116.9	123.1	93.0
Foreign Loans	100.0	134.4	159.2	168.6	154.3
Trading Acct. Sec.	100.0	149.2	96.3	102.6	88.6
Investment Sec.	100.0	99.8	102.3	110.0	87.5
Total Int. Revenues	100.0	121.0	143.6	140.9	110.7
Interest Expense					
Domestic Deposits	100.0	119.5	153.5	149.3	116.3
Foreign Deposits	100.0	115.1	134.9	163.6	124.7
Other Int. Expense	100.0	130.8	177.4	145.1	93.1
Total Int. Expense	100.0	122.4	156.0	153.3	110.1
Net Interest Margin	100.0	117.6	113.8	111.1	112.4
Loan Loss Provision	100.0	30.2	57.2	60.4	88.2
Net Interest Income	100.9	305.2	235.3	220.0	164.2
Non-Interest Revenue					
Fin. Ser. Fees	100.0	108.5	122.0	140.2	134.3
Trust Fees	ERR	ERR	ERR	ERR	ERR
Trad. Acct. Gain and Loss	100.0	156.5	144.6	153.1	258.2
Invest. Gains and Losses	100.0	55.4	92.3	26.7	169.2
Other Non-Int. Revenue	100.0	56.0	77.7	100.8	92.4
Total Non-Int. Rev.	100.0	90.3	106.7	123.5	124.9
Non-Interest Expense					
Compensation	100.0	107.8	113.6	131.6	122.7
Occup. and Equip.	100.0	111.9	120.1	127.1	123.3
Other Non-Int. Expense	100.0	107.3	120.0	140.4	154.3
Total Non-Int. Exp.	100.0	108.3	117.0	133.9	133.9
Income before Taxes	100.0	−1,127.9	−638.8	−344.2	98.8
Income Tax Expense	100.0	112.4	115.3	56.6	75.4
Income before Ext. Items	100.0	−149.2	−43.8	−27.9	80.3
Ext. Gains and Losses	ERR	ERR	ERR	ERR	ERR
Net Income	100.0	−163.3	−43.8	−40.2	40.2
Preferred Dividends	100.2	114.8	142.0	158.0	203.4
Net Income to Common	100.0	−143.3	−30.4	−26.0	51.9

Pharmaceutical Industry Analysis—Part A

Health care is a $750 billion business, making up approximately 12 percent of GNP. Annual health-care costs have increased at an average annual rate of close to 10 percent over the last decade, approximately three times larger than consumer prices in general. The increases in health-care expenditures result from inflation in the general economy, the enactment of Medicare and third-party reimbursement systems, the aging of the population, and the expanded use of more sophisticated, costly equipment. Pharmaceuticals, on the other hand, comprise a shrinking share of the health-care dollar, decreasing from 11 percent to 5 percent over the last decade. The reduction reflects a more competitive environment, expiration of patent protection for many leading drugs, and constraints imposed by the prospective payment system underlying Medicare and cost controls imposed by Medicaid. This case examines the strategies of three pharmaceutical firms (Bristol-Myers Squibb, Merck, and Mylan Laboratories) and the financial success of these strategies over the past several years.

OVERVIEW OF THE PHARMACEUTICAL INDUSTRY

Three main segments comprise the pharmaceutical industry: (1) ethical drugs, (2) generic drugs, and (3) proprietary drugs. Some firms also have a line of personal-care products.

Ethical Drugs   The ethical drug segment includes products that customers can obtain only by a physician's prescription. Ethical drugs comprise approximately 70 percent of pharmaceutical sales. The ethical drug segment tends to have the highest margins and rates of return of all segments of the industry because:

1. High levels of front-end research and development costs (approximately $230 million for a new product) create barriers to entry. R&D expenditures have historically averaged 11 percent of sales in this segment of the industry, with the percentage being closer to 16 percent in the last few years. Domestic pharmaceutical firms spend approximately one-fifth of their R&D budget abroad.

2. Patent protection creates near monopoly positions. However, the lengthy approval process by the Food and Drug Administration and increasing competition have effectively reduced patent life for new drugs from 17 to 7 years.

3. Relatively inelastic demand permits almost unbridled price increases, although competition from generic drugs and constraints imposed by the Medicare reimbursement system have dampened margins somewhat.

The high levels of fixed costs in the ethical drug segment (from both front-end R&D and capital-intensive manufacturing facilities) create both large risks and significant opportunities for economies of scale. To capitalize on these economies, most pharmaceutical firms have extensive foreign operations (comprising 40 to 50 percent of total sales). American pharmaceutical companies are responsible for more than half of total worldwide pharmaceutical shipments. Of the world's top 20 drug producers, 11 are U.S. firms. The degree of operating leverage in the industry also creates significant cash flow from operations, resulting in relatively little need for financial leverage.

Generic Drugs   The generic drug segment includes products that have chemical compositions similar to established ethical drugs but sell at prices that are approximately 50 percent less. The ability to charge the lower price reflects the absence of large front-end R&D costs that ethical drug companies need to cover. Nine out of ten of the most widely used prescription drugs are available generically. Generic drugs now account for approximately 30 percent of all prescriptions filled, up from 9.5 percent in 1975. Drug product selection laws enacted in many states that permit or compel pharmacists to substitute generic drugs for ethical drugs have enhanced growth in the generic business. Similar to ethical drugs, the manufacturing process for generic drugs is capital-intensive. With lower barriers to entry than for ethical drugs, many firms are now entering this market (including several established ethical drug companies). Ethical drugs with a combined sales value of $10 billion are expected to come off of patents in the next five years, providing the stimulus for continued rapid growth in the generic drug segment. Generic drugs could garner up to 40 percent of the domestic drug market in the 1990s.

Proprietary Drugs   The proprietary drug segment includes health-care products that consumers can purchase without a prescription. Proprietary drugs represent approximately 25 percent of pharmaceutical sales, growing at a rate almost as fast as ethical drug sales in recent years. The aging of the population, introduction of new proprietary drugs, switching of ethical drugs to proprietary status (ethical drugs cleared for nonprescription status receive three years of marketing exclusivity), and increased self-treatment to avoid the high cost of medical advice have aided this segment in recent years. The Commerce Department suggests that every dollar spent on nonprescription drugs saves an estimated $2 in health-care costs. Unlike ethical drugs prescribed by physicians, proprietary drug companies market their products directly to consumers. Advertising therefore plays a critical role. Advertising expenditures represent approximately 12 percent of sales for proprietary drugs.

Personal-Care Products   Several firms in the pharmaceutical industry have personal-care segments that market hair colorings, cosmetics, skin preparations, and similar products. The softening of prices and volumes in this segment (sales have grown only 4 percent annually in recent years, as compared to growth rates of 10 to 12 percent for pharmaceutical products) has led such firms to emphasize more heavily their ethical and proprietary drug segments. Some firms have recently sold their cosmetics and fragrance businesses, while others have continued their personal-care line of products, benefiting from their consumer marketing skills.

CURRENT ENVIRONMENT FOR THE PHARMACEUTICAL INDUSTRY

The following describes some of the principal factors currently affecting the industry.

Regulation The pharmaceutical industry is heavily regulated, requiring FDA approval before a firm markets domestically or exports a new drug. The time required for approval of a new drug has historically averaged 30 months. Late in 1984, the FDA made changes in the approval process that decreased the approval time to 24 months. In late 1986, Congress passed a law permitting pharmaceutical companies to export drugs still undergoing FDA approval as long as they cleared the importing country. Also in 1984, Congress passed the Drug Price Competition and Patent Restoration Act. This act permits firms to extend the patent life of ethical drugs by five years to compensate for delays in the FDA approval process. However, it also streamlined the FDA approval process for generic drugs. A discovery in 1989 that certain generic drug companies falsified documents submitted to the FDA for approval of new generic drugs has resulted in a slowdown in the approval process of such drugs.

A second major regulatory change affecting the pharmaceutical industry is the prospective payment system (PPS) under Medicare. Under PPS, the federal government reimburses hospitals a set amount for each of 470 diagnostic related groups (DRGs) of illnesses. If a hospital can operate at a cost less than the set reimbursement amount, it keeps the difference. If, on the other hand, the hospital's cost exceeds the set amount, the hospital absorbs the difference. Because of the incentive to control costs, hospitals have switched to generic drugs or forced ethical drug manufacturers to compete for business. The fixed reimbursement system also provides hospitals with incentives to reduce the length of stay in the hospital, which stimulates demand for home health care.

A third major regulatory change is a requirement that drug companies give state Medicaid programs the same discounts that they give other large-volume purchasers (such as the Veterans Administration). This legislation also pegs future price increases on drugs sold to Medicaid to changes in the consumer price index. This initial form of price control applies only to sales to Medicaid patients (which comprise 13 percent of pharmaceutical sales). Pressures may increase, however, to extend this pricing to Medicare patients (which comprise 30 percent of pharmaceutical sales).

Demographics Demographers expect the number of persons 65 years of age and older to increase 26 percent by the end of the century, twice the increase for the overall population. Individuals in the senior age group now average eleven prescriptions per year, versus seven for the general population. As a result, this group accounts for one-third of all ethical drug purchases. In addition, the number of physicians in the United States increased 30 percent in the decade of the 1980s. Family practice and internal medicine doctors, traditionally heavy prescribers of drugs, make up a significant proportion of the increase.

Competition   The domestic pharmaceutical industry is highly competitive, with no one firm accounting for more than 7 percent of industry sales, but 25 percent of the market is shared by four firms. To benefit from economies of scale, domestic pharmaceutical firms have extensive foreign operations. The U.S. firms have long enjoyed an advantage in international markets by providing a continuing stream of quality, sophisticated drug products. This advantage is beginning to erode, particularly in Japan and Western Europe, with competition from local pharmaceutical firms and easier foreign drug approval processes (particularly in Japan). A competitive problem for U.S. pharmaceutical firms, particularly in developing countries, is the abuse of product patents from weak patent infringement laws.

The weakening of the U.S. dollar has helped the profitability of most U.S. pharmaceutical firms in recent years. Volume increases in sales abroad are multiplied upward when translating sales in the foreign currency into U.S. dollars. FASB *Statement No. 52* has aided profitability somewhat in that unrealized translation losses under the all-current translation method need not flow through the income statement. However, most sales in less developed countries, because of their highly inflationary economies, are translated using the monetary/nonmonetary translation method, with unrealized translation gains and losses affecting net income.

Mergers and Alliances   Both domestic (Bristol-Myers and Squibb) and international mergers (Smith-Kline Beckman and Beecham Group) of major pharmaceutical firms have occurred in recent years. Firms are also entering into joint ventures or marketing alliances to an increasing extent, particularly with firms in Europe and Japan. These arrangements aim to expand product offerings, open new markets, and realize cost efficiencies in R&D and production.

AIDS Research.   Almost 50 U.S. companies are now conducting AIDS research, with the market for products to treat AIDS expected to reach $2 billion.

Other Factors.   Other factors impacting the reported profitability of pharmaceutical companies in recent years include:

1. Major cost-reduction programs aimed at improving manufacturing efficiencies, reducing employment, and eliminating low margin businesses.

2. Increased role of mail order distribution of drugs, with its share projected to increase from 4.3 percent in 1990 to 11.2 percent by 1995.

3. Reduced willingness of insurers to offer the levels of liability coverage desired by the pharmaceuticals, resulting in greater self-insurance.

4. Extensive stock repurchase programs, partially as a defense against hostile takeovers.

COMPANIES STUDIED

Bristol-Myers Squibb   Incorporated in 1933, Bristol-Myers held a traditional niche in proprietary drugs. Its corporate strategy now has it moving more heavily into ethical drugs. It merged with Squibb Corporation in 1989 in an effort to boost its involvement in ethical drugs. It has made significant leaps in anti-cancer drugs. Bristol-Myers Squibb is the most diversified of the three companies studied, with almost one-fifth of its sales in personal-care and household products. Richard Gelb, chairman, summarizes the firm's corporate strategy as follows: "We want to make people live longer, feel better, and look better."

Merck   Incorporated in New Jersey in 1934, Merck maintains its reputation as an "old-line" pharmaceutical. It has heavily invested in both basic and applied research and development and is currently the largest pharmaceutical firm in the world.

Mylan Laboratories   Incorporated in 1970, Mylan Laboratories is a leading manufacturer of generic drugs. Mylan markets its 30-plus generic drugs through other drug manufacturers, distributors, and directly to hospitals. It markets Maxzide, a prescription drug for high blood pressure, through American Cyanamid, and Eldepryl, a prescription drug for Parkinson's Disease, through a joint venture, Somerset Pharmaceuticals.

Exhibits 1, 2, and 3 present certain statistical data for Bristol-Myers Squibb, Merck, and Mylan Laboratories. Exhibit 4 breaks out the changes in sales for Bristol-Myers Squibb and Merck in volume, price, and exchange rate components.

REQUIRED

Financial statements for these companies appear at the end of the case (amounts in millions). Assess the relative profitability and risk of these three companies, evaluating the success of their corporate strategies and their current positioning.

Exhibit 1
Financial Data for Bristol-Myers Squibb

	1987	1988	1989	1990	1991
R&D/Sales..	7.4%	8.0%	8.6%	8.6%	8.9%
Advertising/Sales..............................	14.6%	13.9%	13.3%	12.9%	12.6%

Sales Mix

	1987	1988	1989	1990	1991
Pharmaceutical Products.................	44.8%	46.6%	48.3%	51.1%	52.9%
Medical Devices...............................	12.8	12.9	13.4	13.9	14.0
Nonprescription Health Products....	20.2	19.1	18.1	17.2	17.0
Personal and Household Products...	22.2	21.4	20.2	17.8	16.1
	100.0%	100.0%	100.0%	100.0%	100.0%
United States....................................	66.3%	63.5%	63.8%	61.3%	61.6%
Europe, Mideast and Africa..............	18.9	21.1	20.9	23.5	23.4
Other Western Hemisphere.............	7.1	7.1	7.6	7.9	7.2
Pacific..	7.7	8.3	7.7	7.3	7.8
	100.0%	100.0%	100.0%	100.0%	100.0%

Pretax Operating Income Mix

	1987	1988	1989	1990	1991
Pharmaceutical Products.................	49.5%	48.9%	54.8%*	59.3%	62.7%
Medical Devices...............................	11.0	12.7	13.6	13.3	12.1
Nonprescription Health Products....	23.2	22.8	16.9	14.9	14.8
Personal and Household Products...	16.3	15.6	14.7	12.5	10.4
	100.0%	100.0%	100.0%	100.0%	100.0%
United States....................................	75.8%	71.8%	91.8%*	65.7%	69.3%
Europe, Mideast and Africa..............	15.3	18.3	2.0	23.8	21.4
Other Western Hemisphere.............	6.6	6.4	6.3	7.5	5.8
Pacific..	2.3	3.5	(.1)	3.0	3.5
	100.0%	100.0%	100.0%	100.0%	100.0%

Asset Mix

	1987	1988	1989	1990	1991
Pharmaceutical Products.................	61.0%	60.2%	61.5%	63.1%	61.8%
Medical Devices...............................	13.3	14.2	14.4	14.4	15.2
Nonprescription Health Products....	11.5	11.9	11.5	11.6	12.1
Personal and Household Products...	14.2	13.7	12.6	10.9	10.9
	100.0%	100.0%	100.0%	100.0%	100.0%
United States....................................	61.8%	63.4%	65.2%	62.8%	59.9%
Europe, Mideast and Africa..............	23.4	21.4	21.0	23.5	25.1
Other Western Hemisphere.............	5.9	6.0	5.6	5.6	5.7
Pacific..	8.9	9.2	8.2	8.1	9.3
	100.0%	100.0%	100.0%	100.0%	100.0%

*Amounts exclude special charges related to the merger of Bristol-Myers and Squibb.

ROA Analysis

1987	Pharmaceutical Products	Medical Devices	Non-prescription	Personal and Household Prod.
Profit Margin	24.3%	19.1%	25.3%	16.1%
Asset Turnover	1.2	1.5	2.8	2.5
Return on Assets	28.7%	29.4%	71.3%	40.7%

1988

	Pharmaceutical Products	Medical Devices	Non-prescription	Personal and Household Prod.
Profit Margin	23.8%	22.3%	27.0%	16.5%
Asset Turnover	1.3	1.5	2.6	2.6
Return on Assets	30.3%	33.4%	71.5%	42.4%

1989 (Excluding Special Charges)

	Pharmaceutical Products	Medical Devices	Non-prescription	Personal and Household Prod.
Profit Margin	27.1%	24.3%	22.3%	17.4%
Asset Turnover	1.3	1.5	2.6	2.6
Return on Assets	34.6%	36.5%	57.0%	45.5%

1990

	Pharmaceutical Products	Medical Devices	Non-prescription	Personal and Household Prod.
Profit Margin	29.4%	24.1%	22.0%	17.8%
Asset Turnover	1.3	1.6	2.4	2.7
Return on Assets	39.0%	38.2%	53.7%	47.5%

1991

	Pharmaceutical Products	Medical Devices	Non-prescription	Personal and Household Prod.
Profit Margin	31.2%	22.7%	22.9%	17.1%
Asset Turnover	1.4	1.5	2.3	2.4
Return on Assets	43.7%	34.3%	52.6%	41.1%

1987	U.S.	Europe, Etc.	W. Hemisphere	Pacific
Profit Margin	23.7%	16.7%	19.2%	6.1%
Asset Turnover	1.8	1.4	2.0	1.5
Return on Assets	42.4%	22.6%	38.6%	8.9%

1988

	U.S.	Europe, Etc.	W. Hemisphere	Pacific
Profit Margin	24.3%	18.7%	19.3%	9.1%
Asset Turnover	1.7	1.7	2.0	1.5
Return on Assets	42.0%	31.7%	39.4%	14.1%

1989 (Excluding Special Charges)

	U.S.	Europe, Etc.	W. Hemisphere	Pacific
Profit Margin	24.8%	20.5%	21.6%	10.3%
Asset Turnover	1.6	1.7	2.3	1.6
Return on Assets	40.8%	34.3%	49.4%	16.3%

1990

	U.S.	Europe, Etc.	W. Hemisphere	Pacific
Profit Margin	24.9%	23.6%	21.9%	9.6%
Asset Turnover	1.7	1.7	2.4	1.5
Return on Assets	41.1%	39.8%	51.8%	14.6%

1991

	U.S.	Europe, Etc.	W. Hemisphere	Pacific
Profit Margin	27.3%	22.1%	19.7%	10.9%
Asset Turnover	1.7	1.6	2.1	1.4
Return on Assets	47.4%	34.8%	41.5%	15.4%

Exhibit 2
Financial Data for Merck

	1987	1988	1989	1990	1991
R&D/Sales	11.2%	11.3%	11.5%	11.1%	11.5%
Advertising/Sales	4.0%	4.1%	3.7%	3.3%	2.9%

Sales Mix

	1987	1988	1989	1990	1991
Human/Animal Care	91.5%	92.2%	92.5%	92.8%	93.2%
Spec. Chem./Environmental	8.5	7.8	7.5	7.2	6.8
	100.0%	100.0%	100.0%	100.0%	100.0%
United States	52.6%	50.4%	53.2%	52.7%	53.77%
OECD	42.7	46.7	44.3	45.0	44.3
Other	4.7	2.9	2.5	2.3	2.0
	100.0%	100.0%	100.0%	100.0%	100.0%

Pretax Operating Income Mix

	1987	1988	1989	1990	1991
Human/Animal Care	95.8%	96.7%	97.3%	97.4%	97.5%
Spec. Chem./Environmental	4.2	3.3	2.7	2.6	2.5
	100.0%	100.0%	100.0%	100.0%	100.0%
United States	59.9%	59.0%	68.7%	68.5%	73.1%
OECD	40.7	41.1	31.9	30.7	27.0
Other	(.6)	(.1)	(.6)	.8	(.1)
	100.0%	100.0%	100.0%	100.0%	100.0%

Identifiable Assets Mix

	1987	1988	1989	1990	1991
Human/Animal Care	90.0%	89.5%	90.0%	90.9%	91.4%
Spec. Chem./Environmental	10.0	10.5	10.0	9.1	8.6
	100.0%	100.0%	100.0%	100.0%	100.0%
United States	53.0%	58.2%	59.5%	59.5%	59.1%
OECD	42.7	38.6	38.3	37.8	39.1
Other	4.3	3.2	2.2	2.7	1.8
	100.0%	100.0%	100.0%	100.0%	100.0%

Segment Profitability

	1988		1989		1990		1991	
	U.S.	OECD	U.S.	OECD	U.S.	OECD	U.S.	OECD
Profit Margin	30.0%	26.4%	35.9%	24.0%	36.7%	23.1%	39.4%	21.1%
Asset Turnover	1.4	1.7	1.4	1.5	1.4	1.5	1.4	1.4
Return on Assets	41.7%	43.7%	49.8%	35.9%	52.5%	34.8%	53.8%	30.0%

Exhibit 3
Financial Data for Mylan

	1987	1988	1989	1990	1991
R&D/Sales	4.7%	4.7%	6.1%	6.4%	6.9%

Exhibit 4
Analysis of Changes in Sales

	1988–1989				1989–1990				1990–1991			
	Volume	Price	Exchange Rates	Total	Volume	Price	Exchange Rates	Total	Volume	Price	Exchange Rates	Total
Bristol-Myers Squibb												
Pharmaceutical	10%	4%	(3%)	11%	11%	4%	3%	18%	9%	4%	(1%)	12%
Medical Devices	9%	4%	(2%)	11%	11%	4%	2%	17%	3%	6%	—	9%
Nonprescription Health	—	1%	—	1%	3%	4%	—	7%	3%	5%	(1%)	7%
Personal and Household	(2%)	4%	(1%)	1%	(5%)	2%	1%	(2%)	(6%)	4%	—	(2%)
Total	6%	3%	(2%)	7%	6%	4%	2%	12%	5%	4%	(1%)	8%
Merck	10%	3%	(3%)	10%	12%	2%	3%	17%	10%	2%	—	12%

Bristol-Myers Squibb Company Balance Sheet

	1986	1987	1988	1989	1990	1991
Cash	$ 1,137	$ 1,101	$ 1,966	$ 510	$ 596	$ 1,435
Marketable Securities	730	1,246	546	1,772	1,362	148
Accts./Notes Receivable	1,139	1,349	1,467	1,578	1,776	1,971
Inventories	930	933	1,044	1,139	1,366	1,451
Other Current Assets	328	377	399	553	570	562
Current Assets	$ 4,264	$ 5,006	$ 5,422	$ 5,552	$ 5,670	$ 5,569
Investments	0	0	0	0	0	0
Property, Plant, and Equipment	2,609	2,950	3,346	3,804	4,271	4,718
Less Accum. Depreciation	893	1,023	1,158	1,454	1,640	1,782
Other Assets.....................	612	581	663	595	914	913
Total Assets	$ 6,592	$ 7,514	$ 8,273	$ 8,497	$ 9,215	$ 9,416
Accts. Payable—Trade	$ 352	$ 384	$ 476	$ 475	$ 530	$ 537
Notes Payable—Nontrade	290	415	679	281	397	553
Current Part L-T Debt	0	0	0	0	0	0
Other Current Liab.	1,124	1,330	1,458	1,903	1,894	1,662
Current Liabilities	$ 1,766	$ 2,129	$ 2,613	$ 2,659	$ 2,821	$ 2,752
Long-Term Debt	327	279	284	237	231	135
Deferred Tax (NCL)	54	142	165	60	150	112
Other Noncurrent Liab.	251	209	263	457	595	622
Minority Int. in Subs.	0	0	0	0	0	0
Total Liabilities	$ 2,398	$ 2,759	$ 3,325	$ 3,413	$ 3,797	$ 3,621
Preferred Stock	$ 0	$ 0	$ 0	$ 0	$ 0	$ 0
Common Stock	54	54	55	53	53	53
Additional Paid-in Cap.	503	455	487	396	504	485
Retained Earnings	4,052	4,594	5,207	4,796	5,428	6,235
Cum. Translation Adj.	–216	–116	–114	–149	–61	–90
Treasury Stock	–199	–232	–687	–12	–506	–888
Shareholders' Equity	$ 4,194	$ 4,755	$ 4,948	$ 5,084	$ 5,418	$ 5,795
Total Equities	$ 6,592	$ 7,514	$ 8,273	$ 8,497	$ 9,215	$ 9,416

Bristol-Myers Squibb Company Income Statement

	1987	1988	1989	1990	1991
Sales	$ 7,558	$ 8,558	$ 9,189	$ 10,300	$ 11,159
Other Revenues and Gains	213	192	257	192	177
Cost of Goods Sold	–2,302	–2,484	–2,656	–2,874	–2,930
Sell. and Admin. Expense	–3,226	–3,616	–3,806	–4,156	–4,470
Research and Development Expense	–563	–688	–789	–881	–993
EBIT	$ 1,680	$ 1,962	$ 2,195	$ 2,581	$ 2,943
Interest Expense	–52	–73	–63	–57	–56
Income Tax Expense	–560	–635	–692	–776	–831
Minority Int. in Earnings	0	0	0	0	0
Income from Contin. Ops.	$ 1,068	$ 1,254	$ 1,440	$ 1,748	$ 2,056
Income from Discont. Ops.	0	0	0	0	0
Extra. Gains (Losses)	0	0	0	0	0
Changes in Acct. Princ.	0	0	0	0	0
Preferred Stock Dividend	0	0	0	0	0
NI Avail. to Com.	$ 1,068	$ 1,254	$ 1,440	$ 1,748	$ 2,056

Bristol-Myers Squibb Company Statement of Cash Flows

	1987	1988	1989	1990	1991
Operations					
Net Income, Cont. Ops.	$ 1,068	$ 1,254	$ 747	$ 1,748	$ 2,056
Depreciation and Amort.	161	185	196	244	246
Other Addbacks	38	18	871	38	38
Other Subtractions	0	0	0	0	0
WC Provided by Ops.	$ 1,267	$ 1,457	$ 1,814	$ 2,030	$ 2,340
(Inc.)Decr. in Receivables	−169	−159	−211	−219	−269
(Inc.)Decr. in Inventories	30	−114	−123	−168	−114
(Inc.)Decr. in Other CA	−36	−22	−162	−8	4
Inc.(Decr.) Acct. Pay.—Trade	−35	109	38	72	40
Inc.(Decr.) in Other CL	233	218	−166	45	−166
Cash from Cont. Ops.	$ 1,290	$ 1,489	$ 1,190	$ 1,752	$ 1,835
Cash from Discont. Ops.	0	0	0	0	0
Cash from Extr. Gain/Loss	0	0	0	0	0
Net Cash Flow from Ops.	$ 1,290	$ 1,489	$ 1,190	$ 1,752	$ 1,835
Investing					
Fixed Assets Sold	$ 0	$ 0	$ 0	$ 0	$ 0
Investments Sold	8,341	5,083	7,639	1,733	4,090
Fixed Assets Acquired	−353	−468	−555	−513	−628
Investments Acquired	−8,836	−4,413	−8,679	−1,330	−2,865
Other Invest. Trans.	156	−29	−35	−54	−26
Net Cash Flow from Investing	$ −692	$ 173	$ −1,630	$ −164	$ 571
Financing					
Incr. S-T Borrowing	$ 96	$ 269	$ 0	$ 88	$ 169
Incr. L-T Borrowing	0	0	0	0	0
Issue of Cap. Stock	77	63	197	145	46
Decr. S-T Borrowing	0	0	−409	0	0
Decr. L-T Borrowing	−76	−3	−23	−49	−96
Acquisit. of Cap. Stock	−163	−487	−51	−562	−447
Dividends	−526	−641	−722	−1,116	−1,249
Other Financing Trans.	3	2	−8	−8	10
Net Cash Flow from Financing	$ −589	$ −797	$ −1,016	$ −1,502	$ −1,567
Net Change in Cash	$ 9	$ 865	$ −1,456	$ 86	$ 839

Merck & Co. Balance Sheet

	1986	1987	1988	1989	1990	1991
Cash	$ 381	$ 408	$ 854	$ 685	$ 806	$ 798
Marketable Securities	585	740	696	458	391	614
Accts./Notes Receivable	906	1,077	1,023	1,266	1,346	1,546
Inventories	580	660	658	780	893	991
Other Current Assets	59	122	159	221	331	362
Current Assets	$ 2,511	$ 3,007	$ 3,390	$ 3,410	$ 3,767	$ 4,311
Investments	392	459	403	737	1,012	1,044
Property, Plant, and Equipment	3,154	3,337	3,590	3,994	4,631	5,607
Less Accum. Depreciation	1,248	1,389	1,520	1,701	1,909	2,102
Other Assets	296	266	265	317	529	639
Total Assets	$ 5,105	$ 5,680	$ 6,128	$ 6,757	$ 8,030	$ 9,499
Accts. Payable—Trade	$ 773	$ 910	$ 833	$ 937	$ 1,138	$ 1,400
Notes Payable—Nontrade	373	851	459	327	793	338
Current Part L-T Debt	0	0	0	0	0	0
Other Current Liab.	271	448	617	643	896	1,076
Current Liabilities	$ 1,417	$ 2,209	$ 1,909	$ 1,907	$ 2,827	$ 2,814
Long-Term Debt	168	167	143	118	124	494
Deferred Tax (NCL)	439	429	336	311	256	291
Other Noncurrent Liab.	103	223	340	390	439	389
Minority Int. in Subs.	409	535	544	510	549	595
Total Liabilities	$ 2,536	$ 3,563	$ 3,272	$ 3,236	$ 4,195	$ 4,583
Preferred Stock	$ 0	$ 0	$ 0	$ 0	$ 0	$ 0
Common Stock	184	152	146	153	167	185
Additional Paid-in Cap.	0	0	0	0	0	0
Retained Earnings	3,378	3,920	4,580	5,394	6,387	7,589
Cum. Translation Adj.	0	0	0	0	0	0
Treasury Stock	−993	−1,955	−1,870	−2,026	−2,719	−2,858
Shareholders' Equity	$ 2,569	$ 2,117	$ 2,856	$ 3,521	$ 3,835	$ 4,916
Total Equities	$ 5,105	$ 5,680	$ 6,128	$ 6,757	$ 8,030	$ 9,499

Merck & Co. Income Statement

	1987	1988	1989	1990	1991
Sales	$ 5,061	$ 5,940	$ 6,550	$ 7,671	$ 8,603
Other Revenues and Gains	121	124	138	149	151
Cost of Goods Sold	−1,444	−1,526	−1,550	−1,778	−1,935
Sell. and Admin. Expense	−1,682	−1,878	−2,013	−2,388	−2,570
Research and Development Expense	−566	−669	−751	−854	−988
EBIT	$ 1,490	$ 1,991	$ 2,374	$ 2,800	$ 3,261
Interest Expense	−56	−76	−53	−70	−69
Income Tax Expense	−499	−664	−788	−918	−1,045
Minority Int. in Earnings	−29	−44	−38	−31	−25
Income from Contin. Ops.	$ 906	$ 1,207	$ 1,495	$ 1,781	$ 2,122
Income from Discont. Ops.	0	0	0	0	0
Extra. Gains (Losses)	0	0	0	0	0
Changes in Acct. Princ.	0	0	0	0	0
Preferred Stock Dividend	0	0	0	0	0
NI Avail. to Com.	$ 906	$ 1,207	$ 1,495	$ 1,781	$ 2,122

Merck & Co. Statement of Cash Flows

	1987	1988	1989	1990	1991
Operations					
Net Income, Cont. Ops.	$ 906	$ 1,207	$ 1,495	$ 1,781	$ 2,122
Depreciation and Amort.	210	205	222	254	264
Other Addbacks...........................	0	0	4	0	0
Other Subtractions......................	−91	−245	−66	−208	−12
WC Provided by Ops.	$ 1,025	$ 1,167	$ 1,655	$ 1,827	$ 2,374
(Inc.)Decr. in Receivables	−63	−106	−304	−52	−195
(Inc.)Decr. in Inventories	−80	−14	−122	−113	−99
(Inc.)Decr. in Other CA	0	0	0	0	0
Inc.(Decr.) Acct. Pay.—Trade	137	−77	104	201	226
Inc.(Decr.) in Other CL	129	417	48	193	128
Cash from Cont. Ops.	$ 1,148	$ 1,387	$ 1,381	$ 2,056	$ 2,434
Cash from Discont. Ops.	0	0	0	0	0
Cash from Extr. Gain/Loss	0	0	0	0	0
Net Cash Flow from Ops.	$ 1,148	$ 1,387	$ 1,381	$ 2,056	$ 2,434
Investing					
Fixed Assets Sold	$ 0	$ 0	$ 0	$ 0	$ 0
Investments Sold	4,938	2,678	8,659	8,228	8,519
Fixed Assets Acquired	−254	−373	−433	−671	−1,042
Investments Acquired..................	−5,004	−2,421	−8,848	−8,563	−8,801
Other Invest. Trans.	40	5	27	25	23
Net Cash Flow from Investing	$ −280	$ −111	$ −595	$ −981	$ −1,301
Financing					
Incr. S-T Borrowing	$ 478	$ 0	$ 123	$ 472	$ 0
Incr. L-T Borrowing	2,550	339	52	17	560
Issue of Cap. Stock	21	30	36	38	48
Decr. S-T Borrowing	0	−152	0	0	−591
Decr. L-T Borrowing	−2,563	−574	−329	−14	−94
Acquisit. of Cap. Stock	−1,000	0	−208	−745	−184
Dividends	−335	−505	−650	−750	−893
Other Financing Trans.	8	32	21	28	12
Net Cash Flow from Financing	$ −841	$ −830	$ −955	$ −954	$ −1,142
Net Change in Cash	$ 27	$ 446	$ −169	$ 121	$ −9

Mylan Laboratories Balance Sheet

	1986	1987	1988	1989	1990	1991
Cash	$ 14,970	$ 26,244	$ 36,751	$ 29,865	$ 21,919	$ 37,475
Marketable Securities	0	0	0	0	0	0
Accts./Notes Receivable	14,148	13,855	16,573	13,979	17,381	16,067
Inventories	14,569	16,565	19,974	22,949	23,167	29,098
Other Current Assets	818	990	990	996	421	740
Current Assets	$ 44,505	$ 57,654	$ 74,288	$ 67,789	$ 62,888	$ 83,380
Investments	0	0	0	1,500	24,072	18,045
Property, Plant, and Equipment	17,488	26,425	35,782	38,736	43,995	49,305
Less Accum. Depreciation	5,986	7,126	8,886	10,934	13,088	15,847
Other Assets	21	3,370	7,617	15,609	19,653	34,670
Total Assets	$ 56,028	$ 80,323	$ 108,801	$ 112,700	$ 137,520	$ 169,553
Accts. Payable—Trade	$ 2,137	$ 1,832	$ 2,949	$ 2,123	$ 3,388	$ 2,252
Notes Payable—Nontrade	0	0	0	0	0	0
Current Part L-T Debt	389	1,087	2,920	50	53	0
Other Current Liab.	3,058	3,610	5,639	4,431	3,782	9,682
Current Liabilities	$ 5,584	$ 6,529	$ 11,508	$ 6,604	$ 7,223	$ 11,934
Long-Term Debt	1,934	4,627	6,326	526	1,086	2,057
Deferred Tax (NCL)	967	1,185	1,305	1,292	1,978	2,288
Other Noncurrent Liab.	0	0	0	0	0	0
Minority Int. in Subs.	0	0	0	0	0	0
Total Liabilities	$ 8,485	$ 12,341	$ 19,139	$ 8,422	$ 10,287	$ 16,279
Preferred Stock	$ 0	$ 0	$ 0	$ 0	$ 0	$ 0
Common Stock	12,112	18,177	18,189	18,193	18,223	18,257
Additional Paid-in Cap.	49	11	134	159	597	1,115
Retained Earnings	35,835	50,174	71,719	86,306	108,793	134,274
Cum. Translation Adj.	0	0	0	0	0	0
Treasury Stock	–453	–380	–380	–380	–380	–372
Shareholders' Equity	$ 47,543	$ 67,982	$ 89,662	$ 104,278	$ 127,233	$ 153,274
Total Equities	$ 56,028	$ 80,323	$ 108,801	$ 112,700	$ 137,520	$ 169,533

Mylan Laboratories Income Statement

	1987	1988	1989	1990	1991
Sales	$ 95,135	$ 96,017	$ 87,930	$ 95,415	$ 91,082
Other Revenues and Gains	1,430	2,887	2,469	11,877	20,453
Cost of Goods Sold	–42,010	–46,921	–51,966	–58,460	–54,825
Sell. and Admin. Expense	–8,136	–9,679	–9,399	–10,586	–11,445
Research and Development Expense	–4,489	–4,513	–5,361	–6,070	–6,293
EBIT	$ 41,930	$ 37,791	$ 23,673	$ 32,176	$ 38,972
Interest Expense	–140	–384	–252	–12	–9
Income Tax Expense	–18,482	–12,199	–5,151	–5,954	–6,234
Minority Int. in Earnings	0	0	0	0	0
Income from Contin. Ops	$ 23,308	$ 25,208	$ 18,270	$ 26,210	$ 32,729
Income from Discont. Ops	0	0	0	0	0
Extra. Gains (Losses)	0	0	0	0	0
Changes in Acct. Princ.	0	0	0	0	0
Preferred Stock Dividend	0	0	0	0	0
NI Avail. to Com.	$ 23,308	$ 25,208	$ 18,270	$ 26,210	$ 32,729

Mylan Laboratories Statement of Cash Flows

	1987	1988	1989	1990	1991
Operations					
Net Income, Cont. Ops.	$ 23,308	$ 25,208	$ 18,270	$ 26,210	$ 32,729
Depreciation and Amort.	1,161	1,801	2,136	2,987	2,850
Other Addbacks	291	120	91	808	20,932
Other Subtractions	0	0	−13	−8,585	−16,544
WC Provided by Ops.	$ 24,760	$ 27,129	$ 20,484	$ 21,420	$ 39,967
(Inc.)Decr. in Receivables	293	−2,718	1,919	−3,421	1,424
(Inc.)Decr. in Inventories	−1,996	−3,409	−3,221	−173	−5,981
(Inc.)Decr. in Other CA	−172	0	−6	575	319
Inc.(Decr.) Acct. Pay.—Trade	−305	1,117	−826	1,265	−1,136
Inc.(Decr.) in Other CL	552	2,029	−1,207	−649	4,666
Cash from Cont. Ops.	$ 23,132	$ 24,148	$ 17,143	$ 19,017	$ 39,259
Cash from Discont. Ops.	0	0	0	0	0
Cash from Extr. Gain/Loss	0	0	0	0	0
Net Cash Flow from Ops.	$ 23,132	$ 24,148	$ 17,143	$ 19,017	$ 39,259
Investing					
Fixed Assets Sold	$ 0	$ 0	$ 0	$ 0	$ 0
Investments Sold	0	0	0	1,069	1,109
Fixed Assets Acquired	−8,937	−9,356	−2,954	−5,259	−5,310
Investments Acquired	0	0	−1,500	−15,800	0
Other Invest. Trans.	−3,370	−4,291	−7,251	−3,668	−14,566
Net Cash Flow from Investing	$ −12,307	$ −13,647	$ −11,705	$ −23,658	$ −18,767
Financing					
Incr. S-T Borrowing	$ 0	$ 0	$ 0	$ 0	$ 0
Incr. L-T Borrowing	4,981	4,066	0	0	0
Issue of Cap. Stock	63	135	29	468	552
Decr. S-T Borrowing	0	0	0	0	0
Decr. L-T Borrowing	−1,589	−532	−8,670	−50	−54
Acquisit. of Cap. Stock	0	0	0	0	0
Dividends	−3,006	−3,663	−3,683	−3,723	−5,434
Other Financing Trans.	0	0	0	0	0
Net Cash Flow from Financing	$ 449	$ 6	$ −12,324	$ −3,305	$ −4,936
Net Change in Cash	$ 11,274	$ 10,507	$ −6,886	$ −7,946	$ 15,556

Pharmaceutical Industry Analysis—Part B

The Pharmaceutical Industry (A) case describes the economics of the pharmaceutical industry and compares the strategies and financial performance of three U.S. firms: Bristol-Myers Squibb (ethical and proprietary drugs), Merck (ethical drugs), and Mylan Laboratories (generic and ethical drugs). This case examines the strategies and financial performance of three ethical drug companies headquartered in different countries: Merck (U.S.), Glaxo (U.K.) and Sankyo (Japan). The Pharmaceutical Industry (A) case contains relevant information on Merck.

Glaxo　Glaxo is the largest pharmaceutical company in the United Kingdom and the ninth largest worldwide. Five elements characterize its corporate strategy:

1. Nondiversification: Exclusive focus on the ethical drug segment of the pharmaceutical industry.

2. Concentration on all markets: Marketing of ethical drug products on a worldwide basis. Glaxo uses its own 7,000 member sales force as well as numerous marketing alliances with other pharmaceutical companies.

3. Organization that fits company objectives: Glaxo decentralizes its research and development, manufacturing, and marketing activities, giving local managers considerable freedom to manage their local operations.

4. Growth through internal resources: Glaxo has not engaged historically in acquisitions to obtain new technologies or enter new markets.

5. Commitment to research: Glaxo's research and development expenditures are similar to leading pharmaceutical companies in the United States.

Glaxo's product mix by therapeutic type appears below:

Sales Mix by Therapeutic Type	1987	1988	1989	1990	1991
Anti-ulcerants	47%	48%	50%	49%	47%
Respiratory	21	22	23	24	23
Systemic antibiotics	13	15	15	17	18
Cardiovascular	3	2	2	2	1
Dermatological	5	5	4	3	4
Other	11	8	6	5	7
	100%	100%	100%	100%	100%

Glaxo's anti-ulcer drug, Zantac, is the largest selling prescription drug worldwide. Although sales of Zantac have increased approximately 9 percent in recent years, industry analysts speculate that its sales may be near peak. Patent protection in the United States expires in 1995. To replace Zantac's contribution to revenues and profits, Glaxo recently introduced or will soon introduce drugs to treat chemotherapy nausea, migraine headaches, and asthma.

Glaxo's geographical sales mix appears on the next page:

Sales Mix by Geographical Location	1987	1988	1989	1990	1991
North America	38%	40%	45%	43%	40%
Europe	48	45	42	45	44
Rest of World	14	15	13	12	16
	100%	100%	100%	100%	100%

Glaxo has distinguished itself along two dimensions in recent years. First, it has developed a reputation within the pharmaceutical industry for its emphasis on marketing. It regularly ranks either number one or two (with Merck) on worldwide advertising expenditures. It pioneered the development of marketing alliances. Second, it has been a leader in using computerized information systems to manage research and development products and paper flow. A recent study by *The Economist* ranked Glaxo the second best-managed company in the United Kingdom.

Sankyo Sankyo is the second largest pharmaceutical firm in Japan and the twenty-fifth largest worldwide. It generates approximately 82 percent of its revenues from ethical drugs, with the remainder derived from medical devices (3 percent), agrichemicals (10 percent), and miscellaneous products (5 percent). Sankyo generated 98 percent of its revenue during fiscal 1991 from within Japan.

Sankyo's performance in recent years mirrors that of most Japanese pharmaceutical companies. Although Japan is the second largest market worldwide for pharmaceutical products, government restrictions limit the access to this market by non-Japanese firms. Government controls also limit the rate of price increases on drugs each year. Japanese companies control approximately 81 percent of the Japanese pharmaceutical market. Japanese companies act as licensees or distributors for most non-Japanese drugs (that is, the remaining 19 percent of Japanese pharmaceutical sales). This protected status has led Japanese pharmaceutical companies to rest on their laurels. With signs that the Japanese market is beginning to open to non-Japanese companies and the increasing worldwide consolidation of the pharmaceutical industry, Japanese companies have recently had to become more aggressive.

Sankyo has responded to this environment by placing greater emphasis on international expansion. It has granted licenses to European and American companies covering its anti-hyperlipemia drug, Mevalotin, and its antibiotic drug, Banan. It has also established subsidiaries in New York and Düsseldorf.

REQUIRED

a. The financial statements for Glaxo and Sankyo appear at the end of this case (amounts in millions). Glaxo does not disclose separately the amount for Cost of Goods Sold. The line titled "Selling and Administrative Expense" includes all operating expenses. Glaxo's data reflect a conversion from U.K. accounting principles to U.S. accounting principles. The line in Glaxo's balance sheet titled "Cumulative Translation Adjustment" is the amount necessary to convert the balance sheet to U.S. accounting principles. The line in Glaxo's income statement titled "Changes in Accounting Principles" is the amount necessary to convert net income to U.S. accounting principles. Sankyo's financial statements reflect Japanese accounting principles. The line titled "Changes in Accounting Principles" in Sankyo's income statement represents bonuses of directors and statutory auditors, which Japanese accounting principles treat as an adjustment of retained earnings but U.S. accounting principles treat as an expense. Japanese income tax law does not permit a deduction for these bonuses. Reconcile the amounts appearing in the attached financial statements for 1991 to the amounts appearing in the corporate annual report for that year.

b. Assess the relative profitability and risk of Merck, Glaxo, and Sankyo, identifying strategic or performance factors for the differences observed.

Glaxo Balance Sheet

	1986	1987	1988	1989	1990	1991
Cash	£ 35	£ 23	£ 40	£ 38	£ 20	£ 34
Marketable Securities	557	912	1,132	1,256	1,552	2,095
Accts./Notes Receivable	249	297	343	417	463	655
Inventories	276	288	310	351	392	494
Other Current Assets	76	94	107	146	224	223
Current Assets	£ 1,193	£ 1,614	£ 1,932	£ 2,208	£ 2,651	£ 3,501
Investments	46	51	53	63	56	28
Property, Plant, and Equipment	738	895	1,131	1,512	2,044	2,721
Less Accum. Depreciation	202	245	302	388	475	640
Other Assets	48	59	71	88	103	160
Total Assets	£ 1,823	£ 2,374	£ 2,885	£ 3,483	£ 4,379	£ 5,770
Accts. Payable—Trade	£ 57	£ 76	£ 95	£ 113	£ 123	£ 146
Notes Payable—Nontrade	106	197	252	142	383	871
Current Part L-T Debt	0	0	0	0	0	0
Other Current Liab.	322	334	389	422	605	718
Current Liabilities	£ 485	£ 607	£ 736	£ 677	£ 1,111	£ 1,735
Long-Term Debt	10	13	12	32	37	140
Deferred Tax (NCL)	85	138	153	179	249	340
Other Noncurrent Liab.	129	142	150	208	145	154
Minority Int. in Subs.	10	14	19	22	32	74
Total Liabilities	£ 719	£ 914	£ 1,070	£ 1,118	£ 1,574	£ 2,443
Preferred Stock	£ 0	£ 0	£ 0	£ 0	£ 0	£ 0
Common Stock	370	370	370	372	747	750
Additional Paid-in Cap.	0	1	1	37	9	39
Retained Earnings	720	1,079	1,413	1,882	1,976	2,419
Cum. Translation Adj.	14	10	31	74	73	119
Treasury Stock	0	0	0	0	0	0
Shareholders' Equity	£ 1,104	£ 1,460	£ 1,815	£ 2,365	£ 2,805	£ 3,327
Total Equities	£ 1,823	£ 2,374	£ 2,885	£ 3,483	£ 4,379	£ 5,770

Glaxo Income Statement

	1987	1988	1989	1990	1991
Sales	£ 1,741	£ 2,059	£ 2,570	£ 2,854	£ 3,397
Other Revenues and Gains	103	136	202	218	276
Cost of Goods Sold	0	0	0	0	0
Sell. and Admin. Expense	−938	−1,112	−1,417	−1,493	−1,840
Research and Development Expense	−149	−230	−323	−399	−475
EBIT	£ 757	£ 853	£ 1,032	£ 1,180	£ 1,358
Interest Expense	−11	−21	−26	−40	−75
Income Tax Expense	−245	−256	−316	−339	−359
Minority Int. in Earnings	−5	−5	−2	−8	−12
Income from Contin. Ops.	£ 496	£ 571	£ 688	£ 793	£ 912
Income from Discont. Ops.	0	0	0	0	0
Extra. Gains (Losses)	14	10	0	0	−31
Changes in Acct. Princ.	−15	−7	−54	−29	−71
Preferred Stock Dividend	0	0	0	0	0
NI Avail. to Com.	£ 495	£ 574	£ 634	£ 764	£ 810

Glaxo Statement of Cash Flows

	1987	1988	1989	1990	1991
Operations					
Net Income, Cont. Ops.	£ 496	£ 571	£ 688	£ 793	£ 912
Depreciation and Amort.	55	73	93	117	151
Other Addbacks	36	12	74	0	49
Other Subtractions	0	0	0	−26	−3
WC Provided by Ops.	£ 587	£ 656	£ 855	£ 884	£ 1,109
(Inc.)Decr. in Receivables	−48	−46	−74	−46	−128
(Inc.)Decr. in Inventories	−12	−22	−41	−41	−77
(Inc.)Decr. in Other CA	−19	−14	−40	−79	−7
Inc.(Decr.) Acct. Pay.—Trade	19	19	18	10	23
Inc.(Decr.) in Other CL	12	55	13	183	54
Cash from Cont. Ops.	£ 539	£ 648	£ 731	£ 911	£ 974
Cash from Discont. Ops.	0	0	0	0	0
Cash from Extr. Gain/Loss	14	10	0	0	0
Net Cash Flow from Ops.	£ 553	£ 658	£ 731	£ 911	£ 974
Investing					
Fixed Assets Sold	£ 25	£ 11	£ 9	£ 29	£ 32
Investments Sold	0	5	1	2	0
Fixed Assets Acquired	−193	−275	−373	−619	−621
Investments Acquired	−359	−227	−128	−301	−558
Other Invest. Trans.	−14	−9	−20	−14	0
Net Cash Flow from Investing	£ −541	£ −495	£ −511	£ −903	£ −1,147
Financing					
Incr. S-T Borrowing	£ 91	£ 55	£ 0	£ 241	£ 452
Incr. L-T Borrowing	3	0	20	5	90
Issue of Cap. Stock	1	0	38	21	33
Decr. S-T Borrowing	0	0	−110	0	0
Decr. L-T Borrowing	0	−1	0	0	0
Acquisit. of Cap. Stock	0	0	0	0	0
Dividends	−111	−156	−187	−291	−366
Other Financing Trans.	−8	−44	17	−2	−26
Net Cash Flow from Financing	£ −24	£ −146	£ −222	£ −26	£ 183
Net Change in Cash	£ −12	£ 17	£ −2	£ −18	£ 10

Sankyo Balance Sheet

	1986	1987	1988	1989	1990	1991
Cash	¥ 50,989	¥ 62,784	¥ 69,635	¥ 92,702	¥ 54,718	¥ 59,021
Marketable Securities	3,669	2,837	777	4,155	5,006	6,080
Accts./Notes Receivable	121,370	130,122	130,692	149,408	171,272	168,548
Inventories (EOP)	50,435	54,413	56,148	57,919	61,691	66,382
Other Current Assets	1,438	1,696	1,818	2,395	4,477	17,272
Current Assets	¥ 227,901	¥ 251,852	¥ 259,070	¥ 306,579	¥ 297,164	¥ 317,303
Investments	15,916	19,226	20,241	22,190	41,798	45,965
Property, Plant, and Equipment	122,810	134,107	144,469	157,631	168,983	181,790
Less Accum. Depreciation	61,816	67,585	74,319	82,730	91,473	99,173
Other Assets	5,545	4,804	4,196	3,389	5,335	6,115
Total Assets	¥ 310,356	¥ 342,404	¥ 353,657	¥ 407,059	¥ 421,807	¥ 452,000
Accts. Payable—Trade	¥ 80,159	¥ 87,879	¥ 86,007	¥ 95,662	¥ 93,431	¥ 87,815
Notes Payable—Nontrade	21,962	21,993	22,562	20,963	20,343	22,340
Current Part L-T Debt	0	0	0	0	0	0
Other Current Liab.	40,987	39,220	40,898	43,635	49,288	61,832
Current Liabilities	¥ 143,108	¥ 149,092	¥ 149,467	¥ 160,260	¥ 163,062	¥ 171,987
Long-Term Debt	5,080	19,092	9,077	35,393	28,779	23,462
Deferred Tax (NCL)	0	0	0	0	0	0
Other Noncurrent Liab.	25,359	27,142	29,696	31,216	33,011	34,484
Minority Int. in Subs.	2,988	3,208	3,454	3,695	4,735	5,953
Total Liabilities	¥ 176,535	¥ 198,534	¥ 191,694	¥ 230,564	¥ 229,587	¥ 235,886
Preferred Stock	¥ 0	¥ 0	¥ 0	¥ 0	¥ 0	¥ 0
Common Stock	21,313	21,315	25,768	27,704	30,496	33,073
Additional Paid-in Cap.	19,433	19,435	23,887	25,823	28,612	31,188
Retained Earnings	93,115	103,218	112,381	123,580	133,124	151,875
Cum. Translation Adj.	0	0	0	0	0	0
Treasury Stock	−40	−98	−73	−612	−12	−22
Shareholders' Equity	¥ 133,821	¥ 143,870	¥ 161,963	¥ 176,495	¥ 192,220	¥ 216,114
Total Equities	¥ 310,356	¥ 342,404	¥ 353,657	¥ 407,059	¥ 421,807	¥ 452,000

Sankyo Income Statement

	1987	1988	1989	1990	1991
Sales	¥ 387,902	¥ 400,150	¥ 426,041	¥ 425,634	¥ 453,140
Other Revenues and Gains	1,029	2,250	3,090	5,752	5,498
Cost of Goods Sold	−256,241	−263,154	−277,806	−268,614	−268,862
Sell. and Admin. Expense	−72,227	−75,628	−87,744	−95,750	−109,274
Research and Development Expense	−22,463	−25,133	−25,697	−27,077	−28,847
EBIT	¥ 38,000	¥ 38,485	¥ 37,884	¥ 39,945	¥ 51,655
Interest Expense	−2,570	−2,088	−1,977	−2,536	−3,890
Income Tax Expense	−24,457	−24,039	−21,443	−23,875	−25,696
Minority Int. in Earnings	−308	−339	−334	−517	−326
Income from Contin. Ops.	¥ 10,665	¥ 12,019	¥ 14,130	¥ 13,017	¥ 21,743
Income from Discont. Ops.	0	0	0	0	0
Extra. Gains (Losses)	0	0	0	0	0
Changes in Acct. Princ.	−279	−274	−291	−282	−305
Preferred Stock Dividend	0	0	0	0	0
NI Avail. to Com.	¥ 10,386	¥ 11,745	¥ 13,839	¥ 12,735	¥ 21,438

Sankyo Statement of Cash Flows

	1987	1988	1989	1990	1991
Operations					
Net Income, Cont. Ops.	¥ 10,665	¥ 12,019	¥ 14,130	¥ 13,017	¥ 21,743
Depreciation and Amort.	5,769	6,734	10,655	10,274	10,254
Other Addbacks	1,793	2,630	1,890	2,636	2,668
Other Subtractions	−369	−395	−1,010	−189	−1,541
WC Provided by Ops.	¥ 17,858	¥ 20,988	¥ 25,665	¥ 25,738	¥ 33,124
(Inc.) Decr. in Receivables	−7,520	−434	−17,375	−22,424	−5,396
(Inc.) Decr. in Inventories	−3,978	−1,735	−1,771	−3,772	−4,691
(Inc.) Decr. in Other CA	−1,490	−258	−1,918	−1,522	−4,675
Inc. (Decr.) Acct. Pay.—Trade	7,221	−2,323	10,712	−1,363	6,720
Inc. (Decr.) in Other CL	−1,268	2,129	2,992	4,121	−3,204
Cash from Cont. Ops.	¥ 10,823	¥ 18,367	¥ 18,305	¥ 778	¥ 21,878
Cash from Discont. Ops.	0	0	0	0	0
Cash from Extr. Gain/Loss	0	0	0	0	0
Net Cash Flow from Ops.	¥ 10,823	¥ 18,367	¥ 18,305	¥ 778	¥ 21,878
Investing					
Fixed Assets Sold	¥ 0	¥ 0	¥ 0	¥ 1,536	¥ 840
Investments Sold	832	2,060	1,232	882	1,926
Fixed Assets Acquired	−11,297	−10,362	−16,256	−14,896	−12,833
Investments Acquired	−355	−105	−6,163	−21,440	−6,654
Other Invest. Trans.	0	0	0	0	0
Net Cash Flow from Investing	¥ −10,820	¥ −8,407	¥ −21,187	¥ −33,918	¥ −16,721
Financing					
Incr. S-T Borrowing	¥ 31	¥ 569	¥ 0	¥ 0	¥ 2,219
Incr. L-T Borrowing	14,012	0	31,085	65	710
Issue of Cap. Stock	4	8,930	0	0	0
Decr. S-T Borrowing	0	0	−1,402	−819	0
Decr. L-T Borrowing	0	−10,015	−1,095	−898	−1,096
Acquisit. of Cap. Stock	−58	0	0	0	0
Dividends	−2,216	−2,582	−2,639	−3,192	−2,687
Other Financing Trans.	19	−8	0	0	0
Net Cash Flow from Financing	¥ 11,792	¥ −3,106	¥ 25,949	¥ −4,844	¥ −854
Net Change in Cash	¥ 11,795	¥ 6,854	¥ 23,067	¥ −37,984	¥ 4,303

Computer Industry Analysis*

The high growth rates and superior profitability enjoyed by the computer industry during the last four decades is now history. The computer industry as a whole is rapidly approaching maturity, with most products displaying commodity-like characteristics. New technological breakthroughs get quickly copied by competitors. Consolidation (through strategic alliances) and downsizing (through employee layoffs) appear the order of the day.

The workstation segment of the computer industry serves as one bright spot in an otherwise pessimistic picture. Workstations were originally developed in the early 1980s to serve the design and graphic needs of engineers and scientists and enjoyed growth rates of 40 percent per year throughout the 1980s. Industry analysts project growth rates in the low 20 percent per year in the early 1990s as workstation manufacturers begin targeting business users desiring to establish networked systems.

This case analyzes three leading firms in the workstation segment of the computer industry: Digital Equipment Corporation (DEC), Hewlett-Packard Corporation (HP), and Sun Microsystems (Sun).

OVERVIEW OF THE COMPUTER INDUSTRY

The computer industry during the last four decades has shifted its emphasis from the question, What can the machines do? (a technology-oriented question), to the question, What can the machines do for particular customers? (a user-oriented question).

The technology-driven phase witnessed the development of various computer types:

1. Mainframe computers—designed to satisfy data processing needs of large business and governmental entities.

2. Minicomputers—designed to provide more cost-effective computer power than the mainframes for medium-sized businesses and technical applications.

3. Microcomputers—designed to provide more cost-effective computer power than mainframes and minicomputers for individuals.

Technological innovations in all three computer types increased computing power at an improving value/cost ratio, ushering in supercomputers, superminicomputers, and supermicrocomputers.

The distinctions between computer types began losing significance in the 1980s as the technological differences between them dissipated and increased

---

*The author gratefully acknowledges the assistance of David Crowley in the preparation of this case.

competition forced the industry to turn its attention to satisfying particular users' needs. Certain companies, for example, targeted the engineering/scientific market (Apollo Computer, Sun Microsystems), while others focused on the education market (Apple Computer) or large-scale data processing market (Amdahl Computer, Cray Computer). Other companies maintained a presence in multiple markets (for example, IBM, Digital Equipment). Each company attempted to develop proprietary systems (hardware and software) to lock in customers and build monopoly power.

The rate of technological change and commodity nature of most computer hardware led customers, particularly business firms, to switch to competitors' products when they added to or replaced existing computers. These customers quickly learned that their old software would not run on their new hardware and that their old hardware would not interact with their new hardware. Efforts by the computer companies to offer proprietary products began backfiring on the industry. Customers clamored for standardized operating systems and software. Resistance to purchasing new computer hardware and software until the industry tackled the standardization problem coupled with U.S., and increasingly worldwide, recessions in the early 1990s dampened computer industry sales. The industry is currently engaged in a restructuring that will likely change significantly the players, their products, and their ways of serving customers' needs in the years ahead.

ECONOMICS OF THE COMPUTER INDUSTRY

The following discussion summarizes the more important economic characteristics of the computer industry:

1. Large fixed costs: High front-end research and development costs plus fixed costs from capital-intensive manufacturing processes provide for significant amounts of operating leverage.

2. High rate of technological change: Products often move from the growth stage to the maturity stage in two to three years, increasing the risk that firms will not realize the benefits of economies of scale possible with their operating leverage.

3. Relatively little product differentiation: The increased number of competitors in most industry segments coupled with blurred distinctions between hardware have caused customers to view hardware as a commodity, with relatively elastic demand. Suppliers are attempting to differentiate themselves on software, networking capabilities, service, installed base, and other dimensions.

4. Growth rates: The historical annual growth rate of over 20 percent for the overall computer industry has decreased to a growth rate of 10 percent during the last few years, with much of the continuing growth coming from abroad.

5. Cyclical sales: General business profitability, interest rates, anticipated tax law changes, and similar factors affect computer sales. With 24 percent of capital expenditures going into computers, discretionary changes that companies make in their capital budgets in response to economic conditions impact the revenue of computer firms.

6. Low financial leverage: Firms in the industry carry high operating leverage and product obsolescence risks and tend not to add financial risks as well.

7. Exchange rate changes: U.S. computer firms derive approximately 50 percent of their revenues from abroad. They source computer system components from various countries. Thus, exchange rate changes can significantly impact profitability.

COMPUTER WORKSTATION MARKET

Industry historians credit Digital Equipment Corporation for beginning the evolution of what popular parlance now calls the "workstation market." Digital introduced the first minicomputer in 1965 that, when coupled with appropriate software, satisfied the computation, design, and graphics needs of technical users (scientists, architects, engineers). Data General entered the market in 1971, Prime Computer in 1975, Apollo Computer in 1981 and Sun Microsystems in 1982.

Apollo Computer receives credit for creating the high-performance engineering workstation segment of this technical market in 1981. This segment caters to the design flexibility and high-quality graphics capabilities needed by engineers in computer-aided design (CAD), computer-aided manufacturing (CAM), and computer-aided engineering (CAE). The initial workstations used minicomputers, were single user, and relied on proprietary hardware and software. Apollo commanded a 50 percent market share in the mid-1980s, a period when engineering workstation sales doubled and sometimes tripled each year. Sun Microsystems targeted the low end of the engineering workstation market upon its entry in 1982 and commanded a market share of approximately 15 percent in the mid-1980s. Competition in this high growth market intensified in the mid-1980s when DEC introduced its Micro VAXII computer and IBM packaged a workstation around its PC-RT.

Two developments dramatically affected the proprietary strategies of these industry competitors in the second half of the 1980s. First, rapid technological change in the areas of processing speed and storage capability resulted in decreasing product life cycles of most products (less than two years). Customers often delayed purchasing workstations when they anticipated that new, innovative products would arrive on the market. Desiring to maintain an edge over their competitors, these customers often satisfied a portion of their workstation needs with the most technologically advanced products. As a consequence, firms often found that they had workstations manufactured by Apollo, Sun, DEC and other firms scattered among their engineers. The proprietary strategies of these firms meant that operating systems and applications software designed for one supplier's computer would not work on competitors' offerings. Customers demanded greater standardization. Sun Microsystems played an initial leadership role in striving toward standardization and, as a consequence, achieved the highest market share in the workstation market by the late 1980s. The UNIX operating system is now the accepted industry standard.

A second development in the late 1980s was the movement from single use/single user systems to multiple use/multiple user networked systems. The ability to access data bases, integrate design activities of several engineers or scientists, and communicate effectively became a priority. The lack of industry standards discussed above served as an impediment as networking developed.

Although competitors in the workstation market have not yet achieved full standardization, they have made considerable progress in a few short years. Four firms dominate the market in 1991: Sun Microsystems, Hewlett-Packard (which acquired Apollo Computer in 1989), Digital Equipment, and IBM.

Although the technical user market continues to grow, these firms are now targeting a wide range of business users. Many business firms find themselves with personal computers (PCs) sitting on office desks with little or no ability to interact with each other or to deal with large databases. In a word, networking has come of age in the office. Firms in the workstation market have recently tackled networking problems in the technical market and appear well positioned to move into the office market. The more advanced workstations have the capabilities of low-end mainframe computers and can serve as a central storage and processing center in such networks. Industry analysts expect the office networking market to grow at a rate greater than 20 percent a year in the 1990s and the competition to be fierce. Some of the factors affecting this new market are as follows:

1. Microsoft's DOS operating system dominates the PC market, whereas the UNIX operating system developed by AT&T is the standard in the workstation market. The vast inventory of applications software written for the PC runs for the most part on DOS.

2. The full benefits of networking occur when PCs, workstations, and mainframes link together. The four major workstation competitors enter this rapidly evolving market with different positionings. Sun Microsystems and Hewlett-Packard maintain positions in the market for mid-sized systems, with only a minor presence in PCs or mainframes. DEC's emphasis ranges from mid-sized systems to the lower end of mainframes, with little presence in the PC market. IBM is the dominant player in the PC and mainframe market but maintains a distant fourth position in the workstation market as of 1991. Given IBM's installed base in the two ends of the computer continuum, it should generate a greater presence in the mid-range as networking evolves.

3. Computer companies have traditionally marketed workstations through direct sales forces or value-added resellers, whereas computer dealers and retailers dominate the marketing of PCs. It is not yet clear what form the distribution network will take for networked office systems.

REQUIRED

The financial statements for these companies appear at the end of this case (amounts in millions). Assess the relative profitability and risk of Digital Equipment, Hewlett-Packard and Sun Microsystems, identifying strategic reasons for changes over time and differences between these firms. The present value of operating leases at 10 percent appear below (in millions):

	1986	1987	1988	1989	1990	1991
DEC	$573	$673	$912	$1,133	$1,223	$1,076
HP	$238	$243	$288	$ 455	$ 452	$ 452
Sun	$ 53	$ 92	$150	$ 182	$ 212	$ 255

Digital Equipment Corporation Balance Sheet

	1986	1987	1988	1989	1990	1991
Cash	$ 1,911	$ 2,118	$ 2,164	$ 1,655	$ 2,009	$ 1,924
Marketable Securities	0	0	0	0	0	0
Accts./Notes Receivable	1,903	2,312	2,592	2,966	3,207	3,317
Inventories	1,200	1,453	1,575	1,638	1,538	1,595
Other Current Assets	292	318	599	636	868	818
Current Assets	$ 5,306	$ 6,201	$ 6,930	$ 6,895	$ 7,622	$ 7,654
Investments	0	0	0	0	0	0
Property, Plant, and Equipment	3,263	3,859	5,210	6,249	7,027	7,429
Less Accum. Depreciation	1,396	1,732	2,115	2,603	3,159	3,651
Other Assets	0	79	87	127	165	443
Total Assets	$ 7,173	$ 8,407	$ 10,112	$ 10,668	$ 11,655	$ 11,875
Accts. Payable—Trade	$ 260	$ 431	$ 523	$ 554	$ 661	$ 773
Notes Payable—Nontrade	19	2	155	30	13	23
Current Part L-T Debt	3	2	0	0	0	0
Other Current Liab.	801	1,390	1,736	1,810	2,616	3,295
Current Liabilities	$ 1,083	$ 1,825	$ 2,414	$ 2,394	$ 3,290	$ 4,091
Long-Term Debt	333	269	124	136	150	150
Deferred Tax (NCL)	29	20	63	102	33	10
Other Noncurrent Liab.	0	0	0	0	0	0
Minority Int. in Subs.	0	0	0	0	0	0
Total Liabilities	$ 1,445	$ 2,114	$ 2,601	$ 2,632	$ 3,473	$ 4,251
Preferred Stock	$ 0	$ 0	$ 0	$ 0	$ 0	$ 0
Common Stock	129	130	130	130	130	130
Additional Paid-in Cap.	2,224	2,353	2,424	2,470	2,565	2,636
Retained Earnings	3,375	4,410	5,464	6,366	6,257	5,345
Cum. Translation Adj.	0	0	0	0	0	0
Treasury Stock	0	−600	−507	−930	−770	−487
Shareholders' Equity	$ 5,728	$ 6,293	$ 7,511	$ 8,036	$ 8,182	$ 7,624
Total Equities	$ 7,173	$ 8,407	$ 10,112	$ 10,668	$ 11,655	$ 11,875

Digital Equipment Corporation Income Statement

	1987	1988	1989	1990	1991
Sales	$ 9,389	$ 11,476	$ 12,742	$ 12,943	$ 13,911
Other Revenues and Gains	122	144	124	142	113
Cost of Goods Sold	−4,514	−5,468	−6,242	−6,795	−7,278
Sell. and Admin. Expense	−2,196	−3,066	−3,639	−4,521	−5,571
Research and Development Expense	−1,010	−1,307	−1,525	−1,614	−1,649
EBIT	$ 1,791	$ 1,779	$ 1,460	$ 155	$ −474
Interest Expense	−102	−38	−39	−31	−45
Income Tax Expense	−552	−435	−348	−50	−98
Minority Int. in Earnings	0	0	0	0	0
Income from Contin. Ops.	$ 1,137	$ 1,306	$ 1,073	$ 74	$ −617
Income from Discont. Ops.	0	0	0	0	0
Extra. Gains (Losses)	0	0	0	0	0
Changes in Acct. Princ.	0	0	0	0	0
Preferred Stock Dividend	0	0	0	0	0
NI Avail. to Com.	$ 1,137	$ 1,306	$ 1,073	$ 74	$ −617

Digital Equipment Corporation Statement of Cash Flows

	1987	1988	1989	1990	1991
Operations					
Net Income, Cont. Ops.	$ 1,137	$ 1,306	$ 1,073	$ 74	$ −617
Depreciation and Amort.	436	527	687	796	828
Other Addbacks	21	66	49	92	189
Other Subtractions	0	−83	0	0	0
WC Provided by Ops.	$ 1,594	$ 1,816	$ 1,809	$ 962	$ 400
(Inc.) Decr. in Receivables	−409	−280	−373	−241	106
(Inc.) Decr. in Inventories	−253	−122	−63	100	19
(Inc.) Decr. in Other CA	−34	−155	19	−91	−47
Inc. (Decr.) Acct. Pay.—Trade	171	93	31	107	−18
Inc. (Decr.) in Other CL	587	347	56	597	581
Cash from Cont. Ops.	$ 1,656	$ 1,699	$ 1,479	$ 1,434	$ 1,041
Cash from Discont. Ops.	0	0	0	0	0
Cash from Extr. Gain/Loss	0	0	0	0	0
Net Cash Flow from Ops.	$ 1,656	$ 1,699	$ 1,479	$ 1,434	$ 1,041
Investing					
Fixed Assets Sold	$ 53	$ 0	$ 0	$ 0	$ 0
Investments Sold	0	0	0	0	0
Fixed Assets Acquired	−748	−1,518	−1,223	−1,028	−738
Investments Acquired	0	0	0	0	0
Other Invest. Trans.	−80	−20	−67	−75	−289
Net Cash Flow from Investing	$ −775	$ −1,538	$ −1,290	$ −1,103	$ −1,027
Financing					
Incr. S-T Borrowing	$ 0	$ 150	$ 0	$ 0	$ 0
Incr. L-T Borrowing	0	5	40	18	14
Issue of Cap. Stock	189	243	231	296	240
Decr. S-T Borrowing	−17	0	0	0	0
Decr. L-T Borrowing	−64	−150	−153	−21	−112
Acquisit. of Cap. Stock	−782	−364	−815	−270	−241
Dividends	0	0	0	0	0
Other Financing Trans.	0	0	0	0	0
Net Cash Flow from Financing	$ −674	$ −116	$ −697	$ 23	$ −99
Net Change in Cash	$ 207	$ 45	$ −508	$ 354	$ −85

Hewlett-Packard Corporation Balance Sheet

	1986	1987	1988	1989	1990	1991
Cash	$ 1,372	$ 2,645	$ 800	$ 906	$ 1,077	$ 625
Marketable Securities	0	0	118	20	0	495
Accts./Notes Receivable	1,344	1,561	1,860	2,494	2,883	2,976
Inventories	981	1,117	1,478	1,947	2,092	2,273
Other Current Assets	117	167	164	364	458	347
Current Assets	$ 3,814	$ 5,490	$ 4,420	$ 5,731	$ 6,510	$ 6,716
Investments	0	0	0	0	0	0
Property, Plant, and Equipment	3,600	3,919	4,330	4,982	5,565	5,961
Less Accum. Depreciation	1,364	1,591	1,814	2,089	2,364	2,616
Other Assets	237	315	561	1,451	1,684	1,912
Total Assets	$ 6,287	$ 8,133	$ 7,497	$ 10,075	$ 11,395	$ 11,973
Accts. Payable—Trade	$ 285	$ 364	$ 486	$ 642	$ 660	$ 686
Notes Payable—Nontrade	229	979	507	1,341	1,896	1,201
Current Part L-T Debt	0	0	0	0	0	0
Other Current Liab.	1,004	1,392	1,577	1,760	1,887	2,176
Current Liabilities	$ 1,518	$ 2,735	$ 2,570	$ 3,743	$ 4,443	$ 4,063
Long-Term Debt	110	88	61	474	139	188
Deferred Tax (NCL)	151	154	176	248	261	243
Other Noncurrent Liab.	134	134	157	164	189	210
Minority Int. in Subs.	0	0	0	0	0	0
Total Liabilities	$ 1,913	$ 3,111	$ 2,964	$ 4,629	$ 5,032	$ 4,704
Preferred Stock	$ 0	$ 0	$ 0	$ 0	$ 0	$ 0
Common Stock	712	776	234	459	739	1,010
Additional Paid-in Cap.	0	0	0	0	0	0
Retained Earnings	3,662	4,246	4,299	4,987	5,624	6,259
Cum. Translation Adj.	0	0	0	0	0	0
Treasury Stock	0	0	0	0	0	0
Shareholders' Equity	$ 4,374	$ 5,022	$ 4,533	$ 5,446	$ 6,363	$ 7,269
Total Equities	$ 6,287	$ 8,133	$ 7,497	$ 10,075	$ 11,395	$ 11,973

Hewlett-Packard Corporation Income Statement

	1987	1988	1989	1990	1991
Sales	$ 8,090	$ 9,831	$ 11,899	$ 13,233	$ 14,494
Other Revenues and Gains	142	135	65	66	47
Cost of Goods Sold	–3,867	–4,832	–6,091	–6,993	–7,858
Sell. and Admin. Expense	–2,388	–2,859	–3,327	–3,711	–3,963
Research and Development Expense	–930	–1,056	–1,269	–1,367	–1,463
EBIT	$ 1,047	$ 1,219	$ 1,277	$ 1,228	$ 1,257
Interest Expense	–85	–77	–126	–172	–130
Income Tax Expense	–318	–326	–322	–317	–372
Minority Int. in Earnings	0	0	0	0	0
Income from Contin. Ops.	$ 644	$ 816	$ 829	$ 739	$ 755
Income from Discont. Ops.	0	0	0	0	0
Extra. Gains (Losses)	0	0	0	0	0
Changes in Acct. Princ.	0	0	0	0	0
Preferred Stock Dividend	0	0	0	0	0
NI Avail. to Com.	$ 644	$ 816	$ 829	$ 739	$ 755

Hewlett-Packard Corporation Statement of Cash Flows

	1987	1988	1989	1990	1991
Operations					
Net Income, Cont. Ops.	$ 644	$ 816	$ 829	$ 739	$ 755
Depreciation and Amort.	342	373	462	566	624
Other Addbacks	141	0	0	78	0
Other Subtractions	0	−189	−6	0	−41
WC Provided by Ops.	$ 1,127	$ 1,000	$ 1,285	$ 1,383	$ 1,338
(Inc.) Decr. in Receivables	−217	−319	−385	−409	−117
(Inc.) Decr. in Inventories	−136	−361	−324	−145	−181
(Inc.) Decr. in Other CA	−50	190	−130	−52	111
Inc. (Decr.) Acct. Pay.—Trade	306	122	134	18	26
Inc. (Decr.) in Other CL	65	238	−84	4	375
Cash from Cont. Ops.	$ 1,095	$ 870	$ 496	$ 799	$ 1,552
Cash from Discont. Ops.	0	0	0	0	0
Cash from Extr. Gain/Loss	0	0	0	0	0
Net Cash Flow from Ops.	$ 1,095	$ 870	$ 496	$ 799	$ 1,552
Investing					
Fixed Assets Sold	$ 0	$ 107	$ 120	$ 159	163
Investments Sold	0	439	174	59	191
Fixed Assets Acquired	−507	−648	−857	−955	−862
Investments Acquired	0	−57	−58	−199	−906
Other Invest. Trans.	0	−140	−531	−30	0
Net Cash Flow from Investing	$ −507	$ −299	$ −1,152	$ −966	$ −1,414
Financing					
Incr. S-T Borrowing	$ 0	$ 0	$ 799	$ 212	$ 0
Incr. L-T Borrowing	0	0	31	90	131
Issue of Cap. Stock	191	211	223	220	251
Decr. S-T Borrowing	0	−472	−95	0	−350
Decr. L-T Borrowing	0	0	0	−101	−428
Acquisit. of Cap. Stock	−220	−1,569	−140	0	−79
Dividends	−60	−69	−85	−102	−120
Other Financing Trans.	24	−17	15	19	5
Net Cash Flow from Financing	$ −65	$ −1,916	$ 748	$ 338	$ −590
Net Change in Cash	$ 523	$ −1,345	$ 92	$ 171	$ −452

Sun Microsystems Balance Sheet

	1986	1987	1988	1989	1990	1991
Cash	$ 50	$ 217	$ 128	$ 54	$ 394	$ 773
Marketable Securities	0	0	0	0	0	61
Accts./Notes Receivable	40	98	215	342	523	515
Inventories	39	66	143	309	205	224
Other Current Assets	4	16	46	175	175	228
Current Assets	$ 133	$ 397	$ 532	$ 880	$ 1,297	$ 1,801
Investments	0	0	0	0	0	0
Property, Plant, and Equipment	58	135	252	457	604	701
Less Accum. Depreciation	13	35	80	163	254	350
Other Assets	4	27	53	95	131	174
Total Assets	$ 182	$ 524	$ 757	$ 1,269	$ 1,778	$ 2,326
Accts. Payable—Trade	$ 30	$ 63	$ 120	$ 193	$ 166	$ 212
Notes Payable—Nontrade	15	36	31	124	20	73
Current Part L-T Debt	2	0	0	0	0	0
Other Current Liab.	20	56	108	146	307	428
Current Liabilities	$ 67	$ 155	$ 259	$ 463	$ 493	$ 713
Long-Term Debt	4	127	125	143	359	401
Deferred Tax (NCL)	0	0	0	0	0	0
Other Noncurrent Liab.	2	1	3	2	0	0
Minority Int. in Subs.	0	0	0	0	0	0
Total Liabilities	$ 73	$ 283	$ 387	$ 608	$ 852	$ 1,114
Preferred Stock	$ 0	$ 0	$ 0	$ 0	$ 0	$ 0
Common Stock	0	0	0	0	0	0
Additional Paid-in Cap.	85	182	244	476	629	905
Retained Earnings	24	59	126	186	297	486
Cum. Translation Adj.	0	0	0	0	0	2
Treasury Stock	0	0	0	−1	0	−181
Shareholders' Equity	$ 109	$ 241	$ 370	$ 661	$ 926	$ 1,212
Total Equities	$ 182	$ 524	$ 757	$ 1,269	$ 1,778	$ 2,326

Sun Microsystems Income Statement

	1987	1988	1989	1990	1991
Sales	$ 538	$ 1,051	$ 1,765	$ 2,466	$ 3,221
Other Revenues and Gains	7	12	4	14	39
Cost of Goods Sold	−273	−550	−1,010	−1,399	−1,758
Sell. and Admin. Expense	−122	−250	−433	−588	−812
Research and Development Expense	−70	−140	−234	−302	−357
EBIT	$ 80	$ 123	$ 92	$ 191	$ 333
Interest Expense	−11	−13	−14	−37	−49
Income Tax Expense	−33	−44	−17	−43	−94
Minority Int. in Earnings	0	0	0	0	0
Income from Contin. Ops.	$ 36	$ 66	$ 61	$ 111	$ 190
Income from Discont. Ops.	0	0	0	0	0
Extra. Gains (Losses)	0	0	0	0	0
Changes in Acct. Princ.	0	0	0	0	0
Preferred Stock Dividend	0	0	0	0	0
NI Avail. to Com.	$ 36	$ 66	$ 61	$ 111	$ 190

Sun Microsystems Statement of Cash Flows

	1987	1988	1989	1990	1991
Operations					
Net Income, Cont. Ops.	$ 36	$ 66	$ 61	$ 111	$ 190
Depreciation and Amort.	25	51	103	197	246
Other Addbacks	0	0	0	0	0
Other Subtractions	0	0	0	0	0
WC Provided by Ops.	$ 61	$ 117	$ 164	$ 308	$ 436
(Inc.) Decr. in Receivables	−58	−117	−127	−192	9
(Inc.) Decr. in Inventories	−32	−77	−165	104	−20
(Inc.) Decr. in Other CA	−31	−30	−79	−56	−53
Inc. (Decr.) Acct. Pay.—Trade	33	58	73	−1	46
Inc. (Decr.) in Other CL	35	52	37	135	120
Cash from Cont. Ops.	$ 8	$ 3	$ −97	$ 298	$ 538
Cash from Discont. Ops.	0	0	0	0	0
Cash from Extr. Gain/Loss	0	0	0	0	0
Net Cash Flow from Ops.	$ 8	$ 3	$ −97	$ 298	$ 538
Investing					
Fixed Assets Sold	$ 0	$ 0	$ 0	$ 0	$ 0
Investments Sold	0	0	0	0	0
Fixed Assets Acquired	−76	−117	−205	−213	−192
Investments Acquired	0	0	0	0	−61
Other Invest. Trans.	−23	−32	−35	−72	−27
Net Cash Flow from Investing	$ −99	$ −149	$ −240	$ −285	$ −280
Financing					
Incr. S-T Borrowing	$ 21	$ 0	$ 93	$ 0	$ 53
Incr. L-T Borrowing	121	0	16	313	0
Issue of Cap. Stock	96	63	153	118	261
Decr. S-T Borrowing	0	−6	0	−104	0
Decr. L-T Borrowing	0	0	0	0	−9
Acquisit. of Cap. Stock	0	0	0	0	−183
Dividends	0	0	0	0	0
Other Financing Trans.	0	0	0	0	0
Net Cash Flow from Financing	$ 238	$ 57	$ 262	$ 327	$ 122
Net Change in Cash	$ 147	$ −89	$ −75	$ 340	$ 380

Forest Products Industry Analysis*

The forest products industry includes firms involved in one or more links in the chain involving (1) timber growing, (2) building materials production, (3) pulp and paper production, and (4) converted paper manufacturing (writing and printing products, consumer tissue products, containers, bags, newsprint). Large, integrated firms that operated in all parts of the forest product chain traditionally dominated this industry. Many of these integrated firms have divested or scaled down their timber operations in recent years and focused their energies on higher value-added, downstream operations. A mature forest products market in the United States now requires firms to rethink their international strategies, a market where U.S. firms have a technological, wood fiber, and financial advantage. Environmental issues, including air and water pollution, wildlife preservation, and recycling create substantial uncertainties for the industry's future.

This case analyzes three companies that emphasize different parts of the forest products chain: (1) Georgia-Pacific Corporation (timber growing and building materials), (2) Boise Cascade Corporation (pulp and paper production), and (3) Scott Paper Company (consumer paper products).

AN OVERVIEW OF THE FOREST PRODUCTS INDUSTRY

Figure 1 depicts the forest products chain. Sawmills process harvested trees into either lumber and plywood or pulp. Primary construction and the repair and remodeling market are the principal users of lumber and plywood. Pulp is essentially ground up timber that serves as an input into the manufacture of paper and paperboard. Various types of timber create different qualities of pulp, which in turn convert after further processing into different qualities of paper and paperboard. The paper segment of the industry subdivides into various groups ranging from specialty papers (photography paper, sanitary paper products) to commodity papers (newsprint, bags). The paperboard segment similarly divides into specialty and commodity products.

The sections that follow discuss the economic characteristics and current conditions in the two main segments of the forest products industry: (1) lumber and building products, and (2) pulp and paper products.

LUMBER AND BUILDING PRODUCTS SEGMENT

Industry Economics

Life Cycle.   Sales of lumber and building products closely track conditions in the housing industry. Demographic studies indicate that the "baby boom" generation

*The author gratefully acknowledges the assistance of Robert Pik, Brian Reagan, and Maura Shaughnessey in the preparation of this case.

Figure 1
Overview of Forest Products Industry

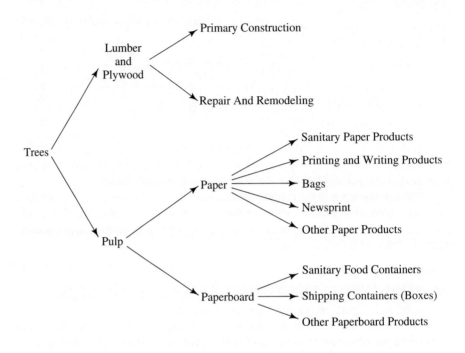

has already purchased housing and that the "baby bust" generation will likely demand fewer new housing units in the 1990s. The latter expectation results from both a smaller population base in the prime house-buying age bracket and a diminished ability to afford new housing. Analysts project sales in the lumber and building products segment in the United States to grow at about the growth rate in the general population, suggesting that this segment of the forest products industry is in the mature stage of its product life cycle. Some opportunities exist for expansion abroad, but the size and weight of most of the products in this segment limit the growth potential (unlike the pulp and paper segment discussed later).

Cyclicality.   The cyclicality of the housing market creates cyclicality risk for lumber and building products companies. The expected levels of interest rates, unemployment rates, and inflation in real estate values influence consumer demand for housing. The repair and remodeling market is somewhat countercyclical because consumers view repairing an existing house as an alternative to constructing a new one.

Capital Requirements.   Lumber and building products companies are relatively capital intensive as compared to most industries (although not as capital intensive as paper milling). One dollar of capital investment in the lumber and building products segment typically generates two dollars in sales (compared to an average of $2.30 for all industries combined). One reason for the level of capital intensity is the long growing period for trees. Trees grown in the Southeast take approximately 30 years to reach maturity, while trees grown in the Northwest take 60 to 70 years to mature. Timber processing plants are of moderate capital intensity. Companies in this segment reinvest 50 to 80 percent of their cash flow from operations each year. Of these capital expenditures, 10 to 15 percent goes toward the management of timber resources, while the remainder enhances harvesting techniques, remodels and maintains existing processing facilities, and builds or purchases new plant and equipment.

Competition. Because many of the previously integrated forest products companies retained a portion of their timber holdings when they placed greater emphasis on downstream operations, the lumber and building products segment has many competitors. However, a small number of resource giants (Georgia-Pacific, Champion International, International Paper, Weyerhauser, and Louisiana-Pacific) dominate the timber-harvesting activity and hold a large share of the total market. The capital intensity of timber processing plants requires firms to utilize operating capacity in order to benefit from economies of scale. The cyclicality of demand drives lumber and building products companies to compete aggressively for market share, particularly during recessionary periods.

In addition to competition between U.S. companies, Canadian companies maintain a major presence in U.S. markets. In recent years, Canadian companies have supplied one-third of all wood products consumed in the United States. The passage of the U.S.-Canada Free Trade Agreement should result in even greater competition as regulators in both countries remove remaining tariffs.

Central Role of Pulp Pricing. The market price of pulp affects both the revenues of timber-harvesting firms and the costs of paper manufacturing firms. Thus, it plays a major role in determining the profitability of the forest products industry. Worldwide supply and demand conditions set the market price for pulp. The driving force on the supply side is the amount of available pulp-making capacity, particularly new additions to that capacity in any year. The driving force on the demand side is the demand for paper, itself driven by the general level of economic activity. Pulp is an internationally traded commodity because countries without timber resources (for example, Japan) purchase pulp and process it through their own paper mills.

Technology. Technological change has impacted both timber growing and timber processing in recent years. Advances in biotechnology have produced hybrid trees that grow to maturity faster and provide higher quality, more disease-free wood. Advances in computer and laser technology permit the scanning of a log to identify the highest-value pieces of wood in the log. Computers then automatically program the saws to cut the log accordingly. The future potential of these and other technological innovations may significantly impact this segment of the industry, a segment not historically known for technological breakthroughs.

Current Environment

Residential Home Construction. After experiencing housing starts at an annual rate of 1.8 million units in the mid-1980s, housing starts declined continually in the late 1980s and early 1990s to a level of approximately 1 million units in 1991. High interest rates and satisfaction of the housing demand of the baby boomers started the downturn in 1987. The continuing slide results from a combination of factors:

1. Low levels of consumer confidence resulting from high levels of unemployment, expected future layoffs, and concerns about the competitiveness of U.S. industries relative to foreign competition.

2. Decreased rate of inflation in real estate values.

3. Tightened credit standards by financial institutions that experienced financial difficulties from past lending practices.

4. Decreased ability of the prime house-buying age group to afford new housing, related both to the absolute level of housing prices and to the level of outstanding consumer debt from automobile, clothes, and other purchases. A recent study by the U.S. Census Bureau found that 80 percent of potential home buyers under the age of 35 could not afford to buy the median priced home in their area.

5. Demographic shift in the proportion of the population in the prime house-buying age group.

The downward trends in the new single-family housing market should stimulate demand for multifamily rental units. However, favorable tax treatment of real estate development in the mid-1980s led to overbuilding in this market, resulting in a vacancy rate of 10 percent at the end of 1991. The longer-term outlook for multiple-family projects is more favorable, although such units consume one-third the amount of lumber of single-family dwellings.

Commercial Real Estate Construction. Commercial buildings tend to use other construction materials more than wood. However, the near-term outlook for commercial real estate construction does not bode well for the lumber and building products segment. The overbuilding that occurred in the mid-1980s has resulted in vacancy rates of 15 to 20 percent in most major urban areas. At current growth rates in the U.S. economy, demand will not appropriately match the available supply of commercial space until the mid-1990s.

Repair and Remodeling Market. The repair and remodeling market is less cyclical than new home construction. However, remodeling expenditures are discretionary to a large extent. During the recent economic downturn, consumers curtailed unnecessary remodeling expenditures, reducing the growth of sales in this market segment from the 6 percent growth rates experienced in the late

1980s. Nonetheless, remodeling expenditures have exceeded new home expenditures since 1987.

Environmental Concerns. Increasing concerns for the environment affect all segments of the forest products industry. Of particular concern to the lumber and building products segment are restrictions against the cutting of old-growth timber in the Northwest, home of the Northern Spotted Owl. These trees, hundreds of years old, are huge in size and provide wood for beams and other large cuts of lumber. The restrictions apply only to cutting on government-owned forests at the present time.

Excess Capacity. The projected lower growth rate for housing in the 1990s relative to the 1980s coupled with technological innovations that increase productivity in the processing of harvested timber suggest a likely downsizing in the lumber and building products segment during the next few years. One-fourth of the sawmills in the Pacific Northwest stood idle for part of 1990 and 1991 and some of these mills will not reopen.

PULP AND PAPER SEGMENT

Industry Economics

Life Cycle. The pulp and paper industry in the United States is mature, with future growth expected to track the general level of economic activity (2 to 3 percent annually). Some growth opportunities exist in particular market niches, such as packaging of microwave food products. More significant growth opportunities abroad appear on the horizon. Industry analysts project global paper sales to grow at a 5 percent annual rate throughout the 1990s, reflecting the anticipated economic growth in Western and Eastern Europe, East Asia, and less developed countries. U.S. paper companies now produce 30 percent of the world's paper and have a global market share of 33 percent. Exports, which represent 9 percent of sales, exceed imports. U.S. paper companies own the most technologically advanced, state-of-the-art paper mills in the world, with Canadian, Scandinavian, and European producers the nearest rivals. U.S. companies also own the world's largest and best-maintained wood fiber base and enjoy a strong financing position. Thus, U.S. companies appear well positioned to benefit from globalization.

Cyclicality. Because paper products serve a broad range of business and consumer needs, sales tend to track the general level of economic activity. For example, businesses ship many products in corrugated boxes, with demand rising and falling with industrial production. When the economy expands, businesses increase their advertising, use more newspaper and magazine space, and generally raise their demand for paper. As the number of business transactions increases, demand for computer paper rises.

Capital Requirements. The pulp and paper segment is highly capital intensive. New paper mills require $500 to $600 million of capital investment and three to four years to construct. One dollar of investment in plant and equipment generates $1.55 in annual sales, as compared to $2.30 for the manufacturing industry as a whole. The pulp and paper segment allocates 90 percent of capital expenditures to production-related investment and 10 percent to pollution control equipment. Long-term debt finances most new plant expenditures.

Achieving high capacity utilization of these capital-intensive plants is critical to success in the pulp and paper segment. The accepted guideline in the industry is that increasing the utilization of capacity from 91 to 95 percent permits selling prices to increase 25 percent. Even larger price effects occur when utilization climbs above 95 percent or falls below 91 percent. The increased prices from higher utilization occur because supply tightens as the pulp and paper producers near practical capacity. The declining prices at lower utilization levels occur because producers use lower prices to compete for the available demand in order to use their plants efficiently. These changes in prices and volumes directly affect bottom-line profitability because most operating costs (except pulp) are fixed.

Competition.   Twenty-nine predominantly pulp and paper firms appeared in the Fortune 500 listing in 1991 (as opposed to four predominantly lumber and building products companies). This large number is misleading, however, because most firms operate in only a few niche paper markets.

The more important characteristic than the number of competitors is the commodity versus specialty nature of the products that a particular firm offers. Pulp and commodity paper products such as newsprint, bags, boxes, and uncoated paper encounter highly competitive markets. The inherent difficulty in achieving product differentiation for these products dictates a low-cost, high-volume strategy. Producers achieve the low-cost objective by spreading their fixed capacity cost over as large a volume as possible. Prices in the short run respond quickly to the addition of new plant capacity (drives down prices) or the heavy utilization of existing capacity (drives up prices). These commodity products also actively trade in international markets. Decreases in the value of the U.S. dollar relative to other currencies stimulate sales of U.S. producers and vice versa.

Specialty papers include photographic film, glossy-coated paper for magazines and corporate annual reports, microwave packaging, and similar items. Because of the ability to product differentiate and target niche markets, specialty papers are somewhat less sensitive to the competitive forces discussed above for pulp and commodity papers.

Technology.   As in the lumber and building products segment, U.S. pulp and paper mills utilize computers to guide the production process. U.S. companies appear to have a worldwide technological edge at the present time, but new mill construction abroad will quickly dissipate this advantage.

Current Environment

Recessionary Conditions.   The U.S. economy reached the top of an economic cycle in 1989 and began a downward trend in 1990 and 1991. Sales and profits in the pulp and paper industry have followed a similar pattern.

Value of the U.S. Dollar.   The U.S. dollar generally declined in value relative to the currencies of most industrialized countries during 1989 and 1990. Its value increased in early 1991 following the war in the Middle East, but continued its slide later in the year.

Environmental Concerns.   Pulp and paper mills are a major source of pollution in the United States. These mills emit sulfur dioxide into the air, one of the biggest contributors to acid rain. These mills also use tremendous amounts of water in the processing of pulp and paper. Certain chemicals, particularly dioxin, get discharged into the water after processing. The papermaking process also produces solid waste in the form of sludge (small bits of fiber extracted from the water used in pulp and paper processing). With many landfills reaching capacity and contamination of local water supplies an increasing concern, disposal of this sludge presents a major problem for the industry. Industry analysts anticipate significant increases in pollution control expenditures in the years ahead.

Another important environmental issue is recycling. Approximately 40 percent of paper consumption currently ends up in landfills. Recycling offers the industry an opportunity both to conserve forest resources and deal with limited landfill space. In 1990, approximately 25 percent of the fiber used in paper manufacturing came from recycled materials. The American Paper Institute projects that percentage to increase to 30 percent by 1993. The percentages for certain paper products, such as newspapers and corrugated containers, are much higher.

There are practical limits to the benefits of recycling. A temporary constraint is the production capability of the paper industry to process the current volume of recycled paper. These firms must add new equipment that essentially returns paper to its original fiber state. Second, most fibers are susceptible to recycling only three to five times. At some point the fibers become sufficiently small that they do not bond with other fibers to form paper but get washed away as sludge. Third, there are limits to the proportion that recycled fibers bear to total fibers used to make paper. That proportion is currently around 60 percent.

SUMMARY OF FOREST PRODUCTS INDUSTRY

Exhibit 1 presents a summary of the economic characteristics and strategic alternatives for each of the main segments and product categories of the forest products industry.

Sensitivity to Value of U.S. Dollar.   Products commonly traded in international markets (pulp, linerboard, newsprint) are generally commodity-like in nature and easily transportable. In most cases, there is little new capacity worldwide, so active international markets exist. Changes in the value of the U.S. dollar significantly affect the attractiveness of exports by U.S. firms.

Sensitivity to Domestic Economic Cycles.   Products for which demand is likely to fluctuate over the economic cycle include lumber for construction, pulp

Exhibit 1
Paper Industry Economics and Strategic Alternatives

Segment Focus	Product Type and Use	Sensitivity to Value of U.S. Dollar	Sensitivity to Domestic Economic Cycles	Product Differentiation versus Low Cost Strategic
Lumber and Plywood	Construction	Low	High	Low Cost
	Repair and Remodeling	Low	Medium	Both
Paper and Paperboard	Pulp (input to paper manufacturing)	High	High	Low Cost
	Paperboard (food cartons)	Low	Medium	Both
	Linerboard (boxes)	High	High	Low Cost
	Newsprint (newspapers)	Medium	Medium	Low Cost
	Tissue (personal sanitary uses)	Low	Low	Both
	Uncoated (paper business forms, computer paper)	Low	Medium	Low Cost
	Coated Paper (annual reports, quality magazines)	Low	Medium	Both
	Specialty Paper (photographic, cigarettes)	Low	Low/Medium	Product Differentiation

used in paper and paperboard, and linerboard used in boxes for transporting goods. Economic cycles, on the other hand, do not affect specialty papers and tissues as much. Most paper products have some degree of sensitivity to the level of economic activity.

Strategic Focus. Products that are commodity-like in nature (lumber, pulp, newsprint) are subject to intense competition. Market prices respond quickly to the level of unused capacity. To compete in these markets, firms follow a low-cost strategy (minimize variable cost and operate plants as near as possible to capacity to minimize average unit fixed costs). The low-cost strategy permits these firms to generate a positive gross margin and force out marginal competitors. Firms with products that are unique or subject to strong consumer preferences (tissue, specialty papers) tend to follow product differentiation strategies. Competition is generally not as intense for these products and higher margins are achievable. Some products have both commodity and differentiation characteristics and offer opportunities for following either strategy.

COMPANIES STUDIED

Georgia-Pacific Georgia-Pacific manufactures and markets a comprehensive line of building products, and in many segments of that industry, it is the dominant player. Prior to 1990, Georgia-Pacific generated over 60 percent of its sales from building products and a majority of its profit from building products. The company has a well-developed distribution system, including an enormously successful do-it-yourself segment, that provides it with an effective marketing arm in an industry generally characterized as commodity oriented. The firm has targeted the repair and remodeling market as a major growth area and seeks acquisitions that could benefit from the strong distribution system.

Georgia-Pacific's vast timber holdings (the largest private-sector owner of timber in the United States) permit it to take advantage of attractive pricing situations in the pulp market. Market prices for pulp increased continually between 1987 and 1990. These price increases coupled with the relatively low value of the U.S. dollar provided an attractive environment for pulp sales. The proportion of the firm's sales and income from its pulp business increased significantly. A softening of pulp pricing began late in 1990 and continued during 1991.

Georgia-Pacific acquired Great Northern Nekoosa in 1990 and became the largest forest products company in the United States. Great Northern Nekoosa adds specialty papers to Georgia-Pacific's more commodity-natured paper products.

Boise Cascade   Paper and paper-related products comprise over approximately 80 percent of Boise Cascade's sales and profits. Boise has sighted its Office Products segment as a major growth vehicle. It views that market as one where value-oriented customer service can play an important role in building customer loyalty, thereby enhancing revenue stability and profitability. Consistent with its strategic focus in the paper segment, Boise has reduced its emphasis on its building products segment in recent years by divesting or shutting down marginal operations.

Scott Paper Company   Scott is primarily a manufacturer and marketer of consumer sanitary goods (paper towels, napkins, toilet tissue, and so on), which comprise over 70 percent of sales and 60 percent of profits. It also maintains a presence in the printing and publishing paper market. Scott's strategic focus centers on creating brand loyalty to enhance profitability and reduce sensitivity to business cycles experienced by other forest products companies. Scott also positions itself as a major player in international markets (approximately 30 percent of sales generated abroad in recent years). While consumer sanitary products are in the maturity stage in the United States, they are still a growth market abroad. Scott has positioned itself for significant growth in Europe once trade barriers are eliminated in 1992. Scott realized a pretax gain on the sale of Brunswick Pulp and Paper Company (net of special charges) of $185 million in 1988 and offset it against other expenses in the income statement. The income tax effect was $93 million.

Exhibits 2 to 5 present selected segment data for the three companies for the years 1987 to 1991. The financial statements for each company follow these exhibits (amounts in millions).

REQUIRED

Assess the profitability and risk of these three companies, identifying strategic reasons that might account for the changes over time and differences across firms.

Exhibit 2
Segment Data—Georgia-Pacific Corporation

Sales Mix	1987	1988	1989	1990	1991
Building Products.............	67%	63%	60%	47%	47%
Pulp and Paper..................	32	36	40	53	53
Other................................	1	1	—	—	—
	100%	100%	100%	100%	100%
Income Mix					
Building Products.............	58%	41%	36%	29%	50%
Pulp and Paper..................	41	58	63	67	48
Other................................	1	1	1	4	2
	100%	100%	100%	100%	100%
Asset Mix					
Building Products.............	45%	38%	31%	15%	16%
Pulp and Paper..................	54	58	47	68	68
Other................................	1	4	22	17	16
	100%	100%	100%	100%	100%
Return on Assets					
Building Products.............	25.0%	19.2%	25.5%	24.1%	20.5%
Pulp and Paper..................	15.0%	18.2%	27.3%	11.7%	5.0%
Profit Margin					
Building Products.............	8.8%	7.1%	9.1%	7.1%	6.4%
Pulp and Paper..................	13.2%	17.9%	22.7%	14.6%	5.9%
Assets Turnover					
Building Products.............	2.8	2.7	2.8	3.4	3.2
Pulp and Paper..................	1.1	1.0	1.2	0.8	0.8

Exhibit 3
Segment Data—Boise Cascade Corporation

Sales Mix	1987	1988	1989	1990	1991
Paper	54%	59%	55%	53%	50%
Office Products	19	20	22	24	26
Building Products	26	20	22	21	24
Other	1	1	1	2	—
	100%	100%	100%	100%	100%

Income Mix	1987	1988	1989	1990	1991
Paper	69%	81%	69%	63%	(178%)
Office Products	10	10	12	20	67
Building Products	20	8	18	14	201
Other	1	1	1	3	10
	100%	100%	100%	100%	100%

Asset Mix	1987	1988	1989	1990	1991
Paper	74%	75%	75%	78%	79%
Office Products	9	11	11	10	9
Building Products	13	11	11	9	9
Other	4	3	3	3	3
	100%	100%	100%	100%	100%

Return on Assets	1987	1988	1989	1990	1991
Paper	16.0%	22.9%	15.3%	5.8%	(2.8%)
Office Products	17.9%	18.4%	17.1%	14.1%	9.0%
Building Products	26.5%	16.3%	28.3%	11.1%	27.4%

Profit Margin	1987	1988	1989	1990	1991
Paper	15.1%	20.7%	16.3%	8.0%	(4.4%)
Office Products	6.5%	7.1%	6.6%	5.3%	3.3%
Building Products	9.3%	6.5%	10.8%	4.5%	10.4%

Assets Turnover	1987	1988	1989	1990	1991
Paper	1.1	1.1	.9	.7	.6
Office Products	2.8	2.6	2.6	2.6	2.7
Building Products	2.9	2.5	2.6	2.5	2.6

Exhibit 4
Segment Data—Scott Paper Company (Product Line)

Sales Mix	1987	1988	1989	1990	1991
Personal Care and Cleaning	73%	73%	75%	76%	82%
Printing and Publishing Papers ..	27	27	25	24	18
	100%	100%	100%	100%	100%
Income Mix					
Personal Care and Cleaning	63%	58%	56%	68%	98%
Printing and Publishing Papers ..	37	42	44	32	2
	100%	100%	100%	100%	100%
Asset Mix					
Personal Care and Cleaning	67%	67%	67%	67%	68%
Printing and Publishing Papers ..	33	33	33	33	32
	100%	100%	100%	100%	100%
Return on Assets					
Personal Care and Cleaning	11.9%	12.0%	8.5%	7.8%	5.8%
Printing and Publishing Papers ..	14.2%	17.6%	13.2%	7.0%	.3%
Profit Margin					
Personal Care and Cleaning	10.2%	9.7%	7.1%	7.8%	5.4%
Printing and Publishing Papers ..	16.5%	19.6%	16.5%	11.7%	.5%
Assets Turnover					
Personal Care and Cleaning	1.2	1.2	1.2	1.0	1.1
Printing and Publishing Papers ..	.9	.9	.8	.6	.5

Exhibit 5
Segment Data—Scott Paper Company (Geographical)

Sales Mix	1987	1988	1989	1990	1991
United States	75%	74%	74%	72%	66%
Europe	22	23	23	24	29
Pacific	3	3	3	4	5
	100%	100%	100%	100%	100%

Income Mix					
United States	80%	81%	85%	84%	55%
Europe	18	17	11	11	34
Pacific	2	2	4	5	11
	100%	100%	100%	100%	100%

Asset Mix					
United States	75%	75%	73%	67%	66%
Europe	23	22	23	29	30
Pacific	2	3	4	4	4
	100%	100%	100%	100%	100%

Return on Assets					
United States	13.5%	15.1%	12.1%	10.3%	3.3%
Europe	9.6%	10.6%	8.0%	2.9%	4.5%
Pacific	10.2%	13.0%	10.2%	10.6%	11.5%

Profit Margin					
United States	12.7%	13.6%	11.0%	10.3%	3.8%
Europe	9.3%	9.0%	8.0%	4.1%	5.2%
Pacific	10.9%	10.6%	10.2%	10.6%	10.6%

Assets Turnover					
United States	1.1	1.1	1.1	1.0	.9
Europe	1.0	1.2	1.0	.7	.9
Pacific	.9	1.2	1.0	1.0	1.0

Boise Cascade Corporation Balance Sheet

	1986	1987	1988	1989	1990	1991
Cash	$ 22	$ 11	$ 12	$ 20	$ 20	$ 15
Marketable Securities	13	11	11	5	6	7
Accts./Notes Receivable	360	359	394	422	413	367
Inventories	392	374	399	424	485	479
Other Current Assets	74	70	51	61	74	65
Current Assets	$ 861	$ 825	$ 867	$ 932	$ 998	$ 933
Investments	0	0	0	0	0	0
Property, Plant, and Equipment	3,800	3,721	4,038	4,600	5,274	5,465
Less Accum. Depreciation	1,318	1,357	1,473	1,583	1,727	1,913
Other Assets	191	186	178	194	240	244
Total Assets	$ 3,534	$ 3,375	$ 3,610	$ 4,143	$ 4,785	$ 4,729
Accts. Payable—Trade	$ 266	$ 254	$ 355	$ 392	$ 344	$ 292
Notes Payable—Nontrade	0	31	0	0	40	58
Current Part L-T Debt	51	47	73	30	137	41
Other Current Liab.	231	231	253	256	237	260
Current Liabilities	$ 548	$ 563	$ 681	$ 678	$ 758	$ 651
Long-Term Debt	1,155	938	925	1,498	1,935	2,191
Deferred Tax (NCL)	171	235	250	307	394	349
Other Noncurrent Liab.	85	79	77	84	122	90
Minority Int. in Subs.	0	0	0	0	0	0
Total Liabilities	$ 1,959	$ 1,815	$ 1,933	$ 2,567	$ 3,209	$ 3,281
Preferred Stock	$ 101	$ 97	$ 0	$ 12	$ 17	$ 25
Common Stock	73	113	112	95	95	95
Additional Paid-in Cap.	390	212	203	0	0	0
Retained Earnings	1,011	1,138	1,362	1,469	1,464	1,328
Cum. Translation Adj.	0	0	0	0	0	0
Treasury Stock	0	0	0	0	0	0
Shareholders' Equity	$ 1,575	$ 1,560	$ 1,677	$ 1,576	$ 1,576	$ 1,448
Total Equities	$ 3,534	$ 3,375	$ 3,610	$ 4,143	$ 4,785	$ 4,729

Boise Cascade Corporation Income Statement

	1987	1988	1989	1990	1991
Sales	$ 3,821	$ 4,095	$ 4,338	$ 4,186	$ 3,950
Other Revenues and Gains	9	8	21	3	98
Cost of Goods Sold	−3,067	−3,162	−3,420	−3,531	−3,590
Sell. and Admin. Expense	−340	−363	−406	−420	−411
Other Expenses and Losses	0	0	0	0	0
EBIT	$ 423	$ 578	$ 533	$ 238	$ 47
Interest Expense	−105	−100	−96	−117	−175
Income Tax Expense	−135	−189	−169	−46	49
Minority Int. in Earnings	0	0	0	0	0
Income from Contin. Ops.	$ 183	$ 289	$ 268	$ 75	$ −79
Income from Discont. Ops.	0	0	0	0	0
Extra. Gains (Losses)	0	0	0	0	0
Changes in Acct. Princ.	0	0	0	0	0
Preferred Stock Dividend	−7	−3	−11	−22	−22
NI Avail. to Com.	$ 176	$ 286	$ 257	$ 53	$ −101

Boise Cascade Corporation Statement of Cash Flows

	1987	1988	1989	1990	1991
Operations					
Net Income, Cont. Ops.	$ 183	$ 289	$ 268	$ 75	$ −79
Depreciation and Amort.	186	188	202	213	245
Other Addbacks	67	59	42	61	12
Other Subtractions	0	0	0	0	−142
WC Provided by Ops.	$ 436	$ 536	$ 512	$ 349	$ 36
(Inc.)Decr. in Receivables	−34	−34	−28	37	66
(Inc.)Decr. in Inventories	−40	−27	−44	−64	5
(Inc.)Decr. in Other CA	−1	−1	−10	−7	10
Inc.(Decr.) Acct. Pay.—Trade	−12	101	37	−48	−52
Inc.(Decr.) in Other CL	46	−4	28	−15	4
Cash from Cont. Ops.	$ 395	$ 571	$ 495	$ 252	$ 69
Cash from Discont. Ops.	0	0	0	0	0
Cash from Extr. Gain/Loss	0	0	0	0	0
Net Cash Flow from Ops.	$ 395	$ 571	$ 495	$ 252	$ 69
Investing					
Fixed Assets Sold	$ 221	$ 72	$ 66	$ 14	$ 143
Investments Sold	0	0	0	0	0
Fixed Assets Acquired	−238	−430	−699	−758	−299
Investments Acquired	0	0	0	0	0
Other Invest. Trans.	9	−13	−7	−26	−24
Net Cash Flow from Investing	$ −8	$ −371	$ −640	$ −770	$ −180
Financing					
Incr. S-T Borrowing	$ 31	$ 0	$ 0	$ 40	$ 18
Incr. L-T Borrowing	27	100	305	650	369
Issue of Cap. Stock	0	0	304	0	0
Decr. S-T Borrowing	0	−31	0	0	0
Decr. L-T Borrowing	−240	−196	−75	−92	−197
Acquisit. of Cap. Stock	−154	−13	−316	0	0
Dividends	−62	−58	−72	−80	−80
Other Financing Trans.	0	0	1	0	−3
Net Cash Flow from Financing	$ −398	$ −198	$ 147	$ 518	$ 107
Net Change in Cash	$ −11	$ 2	$ 2	$ 0	$ −4

Georgia-Pacific Corporation Balance Sheet

	1986	1987	1988	1989	1990	1991
Cash	$ 80	$ 70	$ 62	$ 23	$ 58	$ 48
Marketable Securities	0	0	0	0	0	0
Accts./Notes Receivable	618	771	905	890	409	228
Inventories	681	837	892	876	1,209	1,228
Other Current Assets	41	51	33	40	90	58
Current Assets	$ 1,420	$ 1,729	$ 1,892	$ 1,829	$ 1,766	$ 1,562
Investments	0	0	0	0	0	0
Property, Plant, and Equipment	5,896	6,617	7,973	8,241	11,678	11,152
Less Accum. Depreciation	2,361	2,654	2,961	3,304	3,707	4,208
Other Assets	159	178	211	290	2,323	2,116
Total Assets	$ 5,114	$ 5,870	$ 7,115	$ 7,056	$ 12,060	$ 10,622
Accts. Payable—Trade	$ 295	$ 355	$ 404	$ 394	$ 550	$ 488
Notes Payable—Nontrade	179	189	286	179	1,120	1,381
Current Part L-T Debt	134	153	32	31	324	346
Other Current Liab.	229	299	291	320	541	507
Current Liabilities	$ 837	$ 996	$ 1,013	$ 924	$ 2,535	$ 2,722
Long-Term Debt	893	1,298	2,514	2,336	5,218	3,743
Deferred Tax (NCL)	695	744	788	841	928	795
Other Noncurrent Liab.	124	152	165	238	404	626
Minority Int. in Subs.	0	0	0	0	0	0
Total Liabilities	$ 2,549	$ 3,190	$ 4,480	$ 4,339	$ 9,085	$ 7,886
Preferred Stock	$ 113	$ 0	$ 0	$ 0	$ 0	$ 0
Common Stock	86	89	76	69	69	70
Additional Paid-in Cap.	1,101	1,215	1,046	1,009	995	1,045
Retained Earnings	1,304	1,645	1,522	1,657	1,909	1,629
Cum. Translation Adj.	−20	−6	−5	−18	2	−8
Treasury Stock	−19	−263	−4	0	0	0
Shareholders' Equity	$ 2,565	$ 2,680	$ 2,635	$ 2,717	$ 2,975	$ 2,736
Total Equities	$ 5,114	$ 5,870	$ 7,115	$ 7,056	$ 12,060	$ 10,622

Georgia-Pacific Corporation Income Statement

	1987	1988	1989	1990	1991
Sales	$ 8,603	$ 9,509	$ 10,171	$ 12,665	$ 11,524
Other Revenues and Gains	66	0	0	48	344
Cost of Goods Sold	−7,164	−7,902	−8,135	−10,437	−9,942
Sell. and Admin. Expense	−583	−632	−689	−951	−1,083
Other Expenses and Losses	0	0	0	0	0
EBIT	$ 922	$ 975	$ 1,347	$ 1,325	$ 843
Interest Expense	−124	−197	−260	−606	−656
Income Tax Expense	−340	−311	−426	−354	−266
Minority Int. in Earnings	0	0	0	0	0
Income from Contin. Ops.	$ 458	$ 467	$ 661	$ 365	$ −79
Income from Discont. Ops.	0	0	0	0	0
Extra. Gains (Losses)	0	0	0	0	−63
Changes in Acct. Princ.	0	0	0	0	0
Preferred Stock Dividend	−2	0	0	0	0
NI Avail. to Com.	$ 456	$ 467	$ 661	$ 365	$ −142

Georgia-Pacific Corporation Statement of Cash Flows

	1987	1988	1989	1990	1991
Operations					
Net Income, Cont. Ops.	$ 458	$ 467	$ 661	$ 365	$ −79
Depreciation and Amort.	387	392	445	622	673
Other Addbacks	95	132	236	199	285
Other Subtractions	−70	−17	−27	−64	−477
WC Provided by Ops.	$ 870	$ 974	$ 1,315	$ 1,122	$ 402
(Inc.)Decr. in Receivables	−78	−102	15	929	92
(Inc.)Decr. in Inventories	−70	−38	16	34	−43
(Inc.)Decr. in Other CA	−10	20	−7	−6	13
Inc.(Decr.) Acct. Pay.—Trade	60	49	−10	156	−62
Inc.(Decr.) in Other CL	9	−38	29	−162	178
Cash from Cont. Ops.	$ 781	$ 865	$ 1,358	$ 2,073	$ 580
Cash from Discont. Ops.	0	0	0	0	0
Cash from Extr. Gain/Loss	0	0	0	0	0
Net Cash Flow from Ops.	$ 781	$ 865	$ 1,358	$ 2,073	$ 580
Investing					
Fixed Assets Sold	$ 11	$ 74	$ 66	$ 204	$ 1,251
Investments Sold	125	0	0	0	0
Fixed Assets Acquired	−699	−711	−493	−866	−528
Investments Acquired	−208	−468	−6	−8	0
Other Invest. Trans.	22	0	−67	−3,559	23
Net Cash Flow from Investing	$ −749	$ −1,105	$ −500	$ −4,229	$ 746
Financing					
Incr. S-T Borrowing	$ 0	$ 110	$ 0	$ 876	$ 253
Incr. L-T Borrowing	683	1,524	113	6,997	606
Issue of Cap. Stock	0	0	0	0	0
Decr. S-T Borrowing	−16	0	−107	0	0
Decr. L-T Borrowing	−339	−884	−305	−5,543	−2,055
Acquisit. of Cap. Stock	−255	−395	−468	0	0
Dividends	−115	−123	−130	−139	−140
Other Financing Trans.	0	0	0	0	0
Net Cash Flow from Financing	$ −42	$ 232	$ −897	$ 2,191	$ −1,336
Net Change in Cash	$ −10	$ −8	$ −39	$ 35	$ −10

Scott Paper Company Balance Sheet

	1986	1987	1988	1989	1990	1991
Cash	$ 26	$ 34	$ 374	$ 49	$ 114	$ 184
Marketable Securities	62	46	0	0	0	0
Accts./Notes Receivable	495	589	611	723	829	670
Inventories	342	440	522	581	735	571
Other Current Assets	41	83	108	54	54	56
Current Assets	$ 966	$ 1,192	$ 1,615	$ 1,407	$ 1,732	$ 1,481
Investments	176	224	254	375	322	333
Property, Plant, and Equipment...........................	4,299	4,809	5,272	5,969	7,079	7,172
Less Accum. Depreciation	1,691	1,934	2,160	2,392	2,698	2,977
Other Assets	189	189	175	387	465	484
Total Assets	$ 3,939	$ 4,480	$ 5,156	$ 5,746	$ 6,900	$ 6,493
Accts. Payable—Trade	$ 618	$ 796	$ 920	$ 992	$ 1,178	$ 1,314
Notes Payable—Nontrade	0	0	0	0	0	0
Current Part L-T Debt	79	94	129	221	334	158
Other Current Liab.	41	56	98	93	83	38
Current Liabilities	$ 738	$ 946	$ 1,147	$ 1,306	$ 1,595	$ 1,510
Long-Term Debt	1,412	1,382	1,450	1,678	2,455	2,333
Deferred Tax (NCL)	430	578	607	694	668	661
Other Noncurrent Liab.	0	0	0	0	0	0
Minority Int. in Subs.	0	0	0	0	0	0
Total Liabilities	$ 2,580	$ 2,906	$ 3,204	$ 3,678	$ 4,718	$ 4,504
Preferred Stock	$ 7	$ 7	$ 7	$ 7	$ 7	$ 7
Common Stock	564	569	463	428	432	439
Additional Paid-in Cap.	0	0	0	0	0	0
Retained Earnings	1,422	1,606	1,499	1,658	1,747	1,610
Cum. Translation Adj.	–36	–10	–2	–10	11	–53
Treasury Stock	–598	–598	–15	–15	–15	–14
Shareholders' Equity	$ 1,359	$ 1,574	$ 1,952	$ 2,068	$ 2,182	$ 1,989
Total Equities	$ 3,939	$ 4,480	$ 5,156	$ 5,746	$ 6,900	$ 6,493

Scott Paper Company Income Statement

	1987	1988	1989	1990	1991
Sales	$ 4,122	$ 4,726	$ 5,066	$ 5,356	$ 4,976
Other Revenues and Gains	47	54	65	61	90
Cost of Goods Sold	–2,713	–3,115	–3,493	–3,721	–3,388
Sell. and Admin. Expense	–966	–879	–939	–1,341	–1,547
Other Expenses and Losses......................	0	0	0	0	0
EBIT	$ 490	$ 786	$ 699	$ 355	$ 131
Interest Expense	–139	–147	–158	–199	–221
Income Tax Expense	–117	–238	–165	–8	20
Minority Int. in Earnings	0	0	0	0	0
Income from Contin. Ops.	$ 234	$ 401	$ 376	$ 148	$ –70
Income from Discont. Ops.	0	0	0	0	0
Extra. Gains (Losses)	0	0	0	0	0
Changes in Acct. Princ.	0	0	0	0	0
Preferred Stock Dividend	0	0	0	0	0
NI Avail. to Com.	$ 234	$ 401	$ 376	$ 148	$ –70

Scott Paper Company Statement of Cash Flows

	1987	1988	1989	1990	1991
Operations					
Net Income, Cont. Ops.	$ 234	$ 401	$ 376	$ 148	$ −70
Depreciation and Amort.	259	283	306	346	353
Other Addbacks	82	62	75	0	34
Other Subtractions	−36	−240	−250	−118	−91
WC Provided by Ops.	$ 539	$ 506	$ 507	$ 376	$ 226
(Inc.)Decr. in Receivables	−94	−14	−118	−2	110
(Inc.)Decr. in Inventories	−98	−65	−59	−72	119
(Inc.)Decr. in Other CA	−42	−18	56	1	−4
Inc.(Decr.) Acct. Pay.—Trade	178	112	115	97	174
Inc.(Decr.) in Other CL	14	49	−5	−10	−43
Cash from Cont. Ops.	$ 497	$ 570	$ 496	$ 390	$ 582
Cash from Discont. Ops.	0	0	0	0	0
Cash from Extr. Gain/Loss	0	0	0	0	0
Net Cash Flow from Ops.	$ 497	$ 570	$ 496	$ 390	$ 582
Investing					
Fixed Assets Sold	$ 0	$ 129	$ 19	$ 21	$ 71
Investments Sold	0	0	0	0	0
Fixed Assets Acquired	−380	−509	−791	−815	−315
Investments Acquired	0	0	0	0	0
Other Invest. Trans.	−82	60	−127	−48	20
Net Cash Flow from Investing	$ −462	$ −320	$ −899	$ −842	$ −224
Financing					
Incr. S-T Borrowing	$ 16	$ 0	$ 80	$ 72	$ 0
Incr. L-T Borrowing	540	303	448	890	387
Issue of Cap. Stock	0	0	0	0	0
Decr. S-T Borrowing	0	−36	0	0	−159
Decr. L-T Borrowing	−575	−156	−181	−340	−478
Acquisit. of Cap. Stock	0	0	−200	0	0
Dividends	−50	−56	−59	−59	−60
Other Financing Trans.	42	−4	−10	−46	22
Net Cash Flow from Financing	$ −27	$ 51	$ 78	$ 517	$ −288
Net Change in Cash	$ 8	$ 301	$ −325	$ 65	$ 70

Airline Industry Analysis

The airline industry has experienced more fundamental and dramatic changes in the last 15 years than any other U.S. industry. Moving from a regulated to a deregulated environment beginning in 1979, the industry went through a period of rapid growth in airlines of all sizes (national, regional, and commuter) and an equally rapid consolidation into a handful of megacarriers. These major carriers are currently pursuing international expansion at a rapid pace, using route extensions and cross ownership and marketing alliances with non-U.S. airlines. This case analyzes three airlines that began the 1980s as dominant players in particular regions of the U.S.: American Airlines in the Southwest, Delta Airlines in the East, and United Airlines in the Midwest. Through route extensions and acquisitions, however, these airlines now serve most U.S. markets as well as major growth markets abroad.

A HISTORICAL PERSPECTIVE

A historical perspective aids in understanding the current economics and conditions in the airline industry.

Prior to passage of the Airline Deregulation Act in October 1978, the Civil Aeronautics Board (CAB) regulated both routes and fare structures. Airlines often spent months or years justifying the need for new routes and proving that they would not hurt existing carriers. To obtain approval for desired routes, the CAB often required airlines to add service to less desired routes, such as small communities. The CAB essentially set fares on a cost-plus basis. These regulators permitted fare increases as long as the airline could prove that costs had increased. By aligning the number of airlines servicing any particular route to the number of passengers desiring that service, the CAB attempted to achieve optimal economies of scale in this capital-intensive industry. This regulatory system proved cumbersome, costly, and poorly responsive to changing environmental conditions. It also did not provide airlines with incentives to control costs, particularly labor.

The objectives of the Airline Deregulation Act were as follows:

1. To make available a variety of economic, efficient, and low-priced services.

2. To place maximum reliance on competitive forces to provide air transportation.

3. To prevent anticompetitive practices and conditions that would allow carriers to increase prices unreasonably, reduce services or exclude competition.

4. To maintain systems for small communities and isolated areas.

5. To encourage entry into new markets by existing and new carriers.

In short, the act permitted competitive forces to determine the amount and price of airline services. The following summarizes the effects of deregulation in the first half of the 1980s:

First, the major airlines abandoned many of the regional markets and small cities they were previously required to serve and concentrated their efforts on developing a limited number of "hub and spoke" networks. The hub is a major city and the spokes are connections to multiple smaller cities. The airlines arrange their flight times so that flights into the hubs from surrounding cities coordinate with flights leaving the hubs for other destinations (and vice versa). In this way, the airlines increase geometrically the number of cities served and retain passengers on their systems, thereby increasing revenues per passenger. Also, the airlines realize cost savings in reservation, passenger check-in, and baggage handling costs, as well as interairline record-keeping costs. The hub and spoke strategy not only permits airlines to increase revenues and decrease cost per passenger carried, but also permits them to gain a dominant market share in the area of the hub. American Airlines' initial hub was in Dallas/Ft. Worth, Delta's was in Atlanta, and United's was in Chicago. By the mid-1980s, most major airlines had three or more hubs. Some airports (Chicago, Dallas/Ft. Worth) are hubs for several airlines, resulting in intense competition for market share.

Second, the postderegulation period witnessed rapid growth in regional, commuter, and discount airlines. The regional and commuter airlines entered markets abandoned by the major carriers. Their competitive advantages included nonunionized workers, fuel-efficient planes better suited for shorter routes than the jets of the larger airlines, and near-monopoly positions in their market areas. Alaska Airlines, Midway Airlines, and America West Airlines were among the most successful of the regionals during the early 1980s. Discount airlines, such as People Express, also grew rapidly. Paying nonunion wages and offering no-frills service, these airlines followed a low-cost strategy to gain market share. They competed directly with the major carriers, forcing the latter to lower their prices through numerous discount and supersaver programs.

The airline industry entered a new phase in 1986—consolidation. Led by multiple airline acquisitions by Texas Airlines (Continental, Eastern), the major airlines realized that remaining a dominant player in a limited number of hub and spoke networks would not provide a successful strategy in the long run against a megacarrier like Texas Air. The major airlines therefore went on a buying spree of their own. Their objective was to build a national market serving virtually all major U.S. cities and to be one of the handful of megacarriers that would survive the consolidation. The acquisition targets tended to be the successful regional airlines (Republic, Frontier, Air Cal, Western). Such acquisitions permitted the major airlines to establish an immediate presence in new markets. The major airlines also established affiliation arrangements with the commuter airlines. Using the commuter airlines to feed flights in and out of major cities led to multiple small hub and spoke networks at lower cost to the majors than establishing the spokes themselves. The regional and commuter airlines, fearful of the competition from the megacarriers, quickly sold out or aligned themselves to avoid being left out of the consolidation.

The consolidation phase continues to evolve. Eastern Airlines and Pan Am have liquidated, while TWA, Texas Air, and Continental have filed for bankruptcy. Northwest and U.S. Air are experiencing operating problems. Meanwhile, the big-three carriers (American, Delta, and United) continue to increase their domestic market share. At the end of 1991, these three carriers commanded a 52 percent domestic market share, as compared to a 35 percent market share in 1985.

The early 1990s are witnessing the next phase—international route extension. The big-three carriers have acquired international routes from Eastern, Pan Am, and TWA in efforts to build global flight networks. These route extensions reflect the higher expected annual growth of international traffic (6.4 percent) versus domestic traffic (4.1 percent) during the 1990s. These U.S. airlines also anticipate heightened competition on international routes from non-U.S. airlines, particularly British Airways, Air France, Lufthansa, Swissair, and JAL in the years ahead.

ECONOMICS OF AIRLINES

The following economic attributes characterize the airline industry:

1. Airlines make heavy investments in fixed assets, representing 60 percent of total assets. Unused capacity (that is, unfilled seats on a flight) is lost forever. The average industry break-even point is 60 percent of available seats. Thus, significant economies and diseconomies of scale are possible.

2. Airlines acquire most of their equipment using either long-term debt financing or lease financing. Leasing permits the airlines to shift the tax benefits of ownership to some other entity that has taxable income, thereby reducing their cost of obtaining the equipment. Airlines have increasingly used leasing in the last several years as new planes have entered the market, debt levels have increased, and tax positions have deteriorated. Airlines classify some of these leases as capital leases and report them on both the assets and liabilities sides of the balance sheet. They treat many leases as operating leases, however, disclosing only the required lease payments in the notes.

3. Despite efforts to differentiate products in terms of service, on-time record, flight times, and other dimensions, airline flights are essentially commodity products. Intense competition on the basis of price causes airlines to operate near their breakeven points.

4. Air travel is sensitive to economic conditions. This is more true for personal than for business travel. Given the cost and speed advantages of air travel compared with other modes, however, the cyclicality dimension shows signs of lessening.

5. The rate of technological change in flight equipment is slow. New airplanes take many years to design, test, and build. The airline industry became painfully aware of this during the fuel crisis of the mid-1970s. New planes designed after the fuel shortages and price increases did not hit the market until the late 1980s.

6. Fuel cost represents a significant cost item for airlines. A one-cent change in the cost of fuel increases or decreases airline industry profits by $150 million. In the short run, fuel costs are noncontrollable by the airlines. Not only are fuel costs influenced by political forces, but airlines cannot shift their capacity to more fuel-efficient planes quickly.

7. The single most significant airline cost is salaries (representing approximately 35 percent of total costs). With a few exceptions, the major airlines are unionized. Prior to deregulation, the airlines were willing to grant concessions to the unions since the airlines could pass the increased costs to customers by way of higher fares. After deregulation, the airlines quickly realized that they could not compete with their existing cost structures, particularly against new, nonunionized regional, and discount airlines. After initial efforts failed to get the unions to accept concessions on wages, the airlines tried different approaches: (1) maintaining existing compensation arrangements with continuing employees but hiring new workers at lower rates (the two-tier or B-scale wage system), (2) decreasing compensation for all employees but granting such employees stock options or other incentives, and (3) filing for bankruptcy in an effort to negate labor agreements. In the early 1990s, the labor unions regained some of their negotiating power and exacted significant wage concessions, particularly from the big-three carriers. In addition to wage and benefit increases, the labor contracts reduced the required time for new employees to move from the B-scale wages to the A-scale wages.

CURRENT CONDITIONS

The following summarizes the more important current conditions in the industry:

1. The rapid growth in passengers carried (29 percent increase in the last five years) and number of flights has placed a severe strain on airport and flight-controller capacity. Recent bills introduced in Congress propose to reregulate at least the health and safety aspects of air travel.

2. Supersaver and frequent-flyer programs have replaced the fare wars, common during the first half of the 1980s. Evidence indicates that supersaver fares increase revenues because airlines use capacity that they would not otherwise use. The frequent-flyer program is a form of price discounting but requires multiple flights, rather than a single flight, to gain the discount. There are concerns as to whether the airlines adequately recognize the potential liability of frequent-flyer programs in their financial statements.

3. Computerized reservation systems have become a key to attracting passengers, as well as an important source of revenue for the airlines. Customers make 80 percent of all reservations through travel agents on one of these systems. Regional and commuter airlines have had to pay a fee to have their flights listed on these systems, increasing revenues for the major carriers. Responding to congressional concerns that the computerized reservation systems restricted competition in the industry, several airlines merged their systems, a move the Department of Transportation views as promoting competition.

4. Consumers and legislators are expressing increased concerns that the concentration in the industry is leading to lessened competition and almost insurmountable barriers to new entrants. Although the major airlines do have a dominant market share in their hub airports, competition is present in the overall system through various routing choices among the hubs. A recent Department of Transportation study concluded that average fares have decreased since deregulation and the hub and spoke networks have provided customers with more choice and convenience, with smaller cities receiving most of the benefit. The study also concludes, however, that markets dominated by a single carrier tend to have higher prices than more competitive markets.

FINANCIAL ANALYSIS OF AIRLINES

Analysts study the operating profitability of an airline by examining three critical elements:

1. Passenger revenues per revenue passenger mile: Revenue passenger miles equals total seats occupied by revenue-paying passengers on all planes flown multiplied by the number of miles flown.

2. Operating costs per available seat mile: The cost of compensation, fuel, and other operating costs divided by available seat miles. Available seat miles equal total seats available for revenue-paying passengers on all planes flown multiplied by the number of miles flown.

3. Load factor realized: Revenue passenger miles divided by available seat miles.

AIRLINES ANALYZED

American Airlines.   As judged by market share, American Airlines is the largest U.S. airline. It operates hub and spoke networks out of Dallas/Ft. Worth, Chicago, Raleigh/Durham, Nashville, San Jose, and San Juan. American Airlines' opening of the latter four hubs signalled its movement from primarily a southwest/midwest airline to one with a major eastern U.S. and Caribbean presence. In 1987, it acquired Air Cal, a successful airline servicing the western portion of the country, to complete its national market penetration. During 1988, American Airlines acquired most of its affiliated commuter airlines. During 1989, it acquired Eastern Airlines' Latin American routes. Since then it has more energetically established itself in Europe and Japan. Its SABRE reservation system, the world's largest, networks with Amadeus (a similar system in Europe).

Delta Airlines.   Delta ranks third, behind United Airlines, in market share. Its hub and spoke networks operate out of Atlanta, Cincinnati, and Dallas/Ft. Worth. To complete its national market penetration, it acquired Western Airlines in 1987.

Western was the ninth largest U.S. airline at the time and added new hubs for Delta in Los Angeles and Salt Lake City. Delta has cross ownership arrangements with Swissair and Singapore Airlines and has instituted cooperative programs with these airlines in areas such as promotions and employee training. It is a joint owner in WORLDSPAN, a computerized reservation system, with Northwest and TWA. Delta recently purchased transatlantic routes from Pan Am to add to its international route structure.

United Airlines.   United Airlines ranks a close second to American Airlines in market share. It operates hub and spoke networks out of Chicago, Denver, Washington, D.C., and San Francisco. In 1985 United acquired Pan Am's Pacific route system and now has the leading market share in that rapidly growing international market. It recently acquired Pan Am's London route in an effort to expand its European presence. United's Apollo computerized reservation system, the world's second largest, is a joint venture with U.S. Air and networks with Galileo, a partnership of primarily European carriers.

Exhibits 1 through 6 present various operating data for these airlines, followed by their financial statements (amounts in millions).

REQUIRED

Analyze the relative profitability and risk of American, Delta, and United, identifying strategic reasons for the differences observed.

Exhibit 1
Operating Statistics for American Airlines

	1987	1988	1989	1990	1991
Capacity Data					
Seat Miles Flown (000,000s)	56,794	64,770	73,503	77,085	83,335
Available Seat Miles (000,000s)	88,743	102,045	115,222	123,773	133,472
Load Factor Realized	64.0%	63.5%	63.8%	62.3%	61.7%
Break-Even Load Factor	58.5%	56.0%	57.9%	61.8%	61.6%
Operating Costs per Passenger Mile at Full Capacity					
Compensation	2.77c	2.88c	2.99c	3.14c	3.25c
Fuel	1.13	1.08	1.21	1.57	1.36
Other Operating Costs	3.69	3.90	4.25	4.66	5.04
Total	7.59c	7.86c	8.45c	9.37c	9.65c
Realized per Passenger Mile Data					
Passenger Revenues	10.83c	11.85c	12.39c	13.12c	13.52c
Other Revenues	1.84c	1.77c	1.87	2.08c	2.13
Compensation Cost	(4.32c)	(4.54c)	(4.69c)	(5.04c)	(5.27c)
Fuel Cost	(1.77c)	(1.70c)	(1.90c)	(2.51c)	(2.21c)
Other Costs	(5.77c)	(6.14c)	(6.66c)	(7.49c)	(7.11c)
Operating Profit	.81c	1.24c	1.01c	.16c	.01c
Present Value of Operating Leases at 10% (000,000s)	$2,067	$2,643	$3,116	$4,941	$7,002

Exhibit 2
Operating Statistics for Delta Airlines

	1987	1988	1989	1990	1991
Capacity Data					
Seat Miles Flown (000,000s)	38,415	49,009	55,904	58,987	62,086
Available Seat Miles (000,000s)	69,014	85,834	90,742	96,463	104,328
Load Factor Realized	55.7%	57.1%	61.6%	61.2%	59.5%
Break-Even Load Factor	51.1%	52.7%	56.1%	58.0%	62.6%
Operating Costs per Passenger Mile at Full Capacity					
Compensation	3.31c	3.15c	3.44c	3.55c	3.60c
Fuel	1.00	1.15	1.09	1.28	1.53
Other Operating Costs	2.99	3.18	3.64	3.63	4.09
Total	7.30c	7.48c	8.17c	8.46c	9.22c
Realized per Passenger Mile Data					
Passenger Revenues	12.81c	13.15c	13.56c	13.63c	13.80c
Other Revenues	1.03c	.96c	.91	.92	.97
Compensation Cost	(5.80c)	(5.52c)	(5.59)	(5.81)	(6.04)
Fuel Cost	(1.75c)	(2.01c)	(1.77)	(2.09)	(2.58)
Other Costs	(5.24c)	(5.57c)	(5.90)	(5.94)	(6.87)
Operating Profit	1.05c	1.01c	1.21c	.71c	(.72c)
Average Length of Passenger Flight (miles)	617	837	870	877	898
Present Value of Operating Leases at 10% (000,000s)	$2,860	$3,771	$3,738	$4,213	$6,018

Exhibit 3
Operating Statistics for United Airlines

	1987	1988	1989	1990	1991
Capacity Data					
Seat Miles Flown (000,000s)	66,348	69,101	69,639	76,137	82,290
Available Seat Miles (000,000s)	101,454	101,721	104,563	114,995	124,100
Load Factor Realized	65.4%	67.9%	66.6%	66.2%	66.3%
Break-Even Load Factor	63.0%	62.2%	63.0%	66.5%	69.5%
Operating Costs per Passenger Mile at Full Capacity					
Compensation	2.74c	2.79c	3.02c	3.09c	3.27c
Fuel	1.23	1.16	1.29	1.58	1.35
Other Operating Costs	3.98	4.22	4.61	4.96	5.18
Total	7.95c	8.17c	8.92c	9.63c	9.80c
Realized per Passenger Mile Data					
Passenger Revenues	10.33c	11.18c	12.26c	12.65c	12.51c
Other Revenues	2.17	1.81	1.81	1.84	1.66
Compensation	(4.19)	(4.11)	(4.54)	(4.66)	(4.93)
Fuel	(1.87)	(1.71)	(1.94)	(2.38)	(2.03)
Other Operating Costs	(6.09)	(6.21)	(6.92)	(7.50)	(7.81)
Operating Profit	.35c	.96c	.67c	(.05c)	(.60c)
Present Value of Operating Leases at 10% (000,000s)	$1,864	$2,680	$4,108	$5,664	$7,335

Exhibit 4
Airplane Fleet—American Airlines

	1987	1988	1989	1990	1991
Boeing 727	164	164	164	164	161
Boeing 737	31	24	11	18	5
Boeing 747	2	2	2	2	2
Boeing 757	—	—	8	26	49
Boeing 767	29	45	45	45	48
McDonnell Douglas DC-10	60	61	59	59	59
McDonnell Douglas MD80	118	153	180	213	250
McDonnell Douglas MD11	—	—	—	—	5
Airbus A300	—	13	25	25	30
Commuter Aircraft	26	134	172	183	240
Total	430	596	666	735	849

Exhibit 5
Airplane Fleet—Delta Airlines

	1987	1988	1989	1990	1991
Boeing 727	132	131	130	129	129
Boeing 737	86	74	74	72	72
Boeing 757	28	38	50	60	69
Boeing 767	22	30	30	33	45
McDonnell Douglas DC-8	12	7	2	—	—
McDonnell Douglas DC-9	36	36	36	36	32
McDonnell Douglas 11	—	—	—	—	2
McDonnell Douglas 82	8	22	—	—	—
McDonnell Douglas 88	—	—	40	63	83
McDonnell Douglas DC-10	9	6	—	—	—
Lockheed L-1011	35	39	40	40	43
Total	368	383	402	433	475

Exhibit 6
Airplane Fleet—United Airlines

	1987	1988	1989	1990	1991
Boeing 727	154	147	140	128	115
Boeing 737	92	127	149	179	196
Boeing 747	31	31	34	39	50
Boeing 757	—	—	5	24	47
Boeing 767	19	19	19	19	24
McDonnell Douglas DC8	29	29	27	19	—
McDonnell Douglas DC10	55	55	55	54	54
Lockheed L-1011	6	—	—	—	—
Total	386	408	429	462	486

American Airlines Balance Sheet

	1986	1987	1988	1989	1990	1991
Cash	$ 21	$ 45	$ 55	$ 120	$ 114	$ 94
Marketable Securities	1,062	968	1,232	481	836	1,155
Accts./Notes Receivable	690	729	833	886	951	803
Inventories	263	299	375	490	608	620
Other Current Assets	73	105	120	114	149	134
Current Assets	$ 2,109	$ 2,146	$ 2,615	$ 2,091	$ 2,658	$ 2,806
Investments	0	0	0	0	0	0
Property, Plant, and Equipment	7,016	7,952	9,381	11,489	13,117	15,584
Less Accum. Depreciation	2,274	2,364	3,109	3,670	3,971	4,537
Other Assets	677	689	835	967	1,548	2,355
Total Assets	$ 7,528	$ 8,423	$ 9,722	$ 10,877	$ 13,354	$ 16,208
Accts. Payable—Trade	$ 514	$ 560	$ 710	$ 929	$ 966	$ 1,001
Notes Payable—Nontrade	157	78	79	163	1,210	411
Current Part L-T Debt	122	123	135	270	109	625
Other Current Liab.	1,192	1,310	1,872	2,117	2,540	2,705
Current Liabilities	$ 1,985	$ 2,071	$ 2,796	$ 3,479	$ 4,825	$ 4,742
Long-Term Debt	2,412	2,782	2,749	2,306	3,272	5,879
Deferred Tax (NCL)	483	574	667	802	651	541
Other Noncurrent Liab.	139	165	212	524	879	1,252
Minority Int. in Subs.	0	0	0	0	0	0
Total Liabilities	$ 5,019	$ 5,592	$ 6,424	$ 7,111	$ 9,627	$ 12,414
Preferred Stock	$ 24	$ 150	$ 150	$ 0	$ 0	$ 0
Common Stock	59	59	59	62	62	68
Additional Paid-in Cap.	1,058	1,060	1,061	1,239	1,243	1,545
Retained Earnings	1,368	1,562	2,028	2,465	2,422	2,181
Cum. Translation Adj.	0	0	0	0	0	0
Treasury Stock	0	0	0	0	0	0
Shareholders' Equity	$ 2,509	$ 2,831	$ 3,298	$ 3,766	$ 3,727	$ 3,794
Total Equities	$ 7,528	$ 8,423	$ 9,722	$ 10,877	$ 13,354	$ 16,208

American Airlines Income Statement

	1987	1988	1989	1990	1991
Sales	$ 7,198	$ 8,824	$ 10,480	$ 11,719	$ 12,887
Other Revenues and Gains	48	144	148	64	4
Cost of Goods Sold	−6,737	−8,018	−9,735	−11,596	−12,882
Sell. and Admin. Expense	0	0	0	0	0
Other Expenses and Losses	0	0	0	0	0
EBIT	$ 509	$ 950	$ 893	$ 187	$ 9
Interest Expense	−187	−209	−174	−221	−349
Income Tax Expense	−124	−264	−264	−6	100
Minority Int. in Earnings	0	0	0	0	0
Income from Contin. Ops.	$ 198	$ 477	$ 455	$ −40	$ −240
Income from Discont. Ops.	0	0	0	0	0
Extra. Gains (Losses)	0	0	0	0	0
Changes in Acct. Princ.	0	0	0	0	0
Preferred Stock Dividend	−4	−10	−12	0	0
NI Avail. to Com.	$ 194	$ 467	$ 443	$ −40	$ −240

American Airlines Statement of Cash Flows

	1987	1988	1989	1990	1991
Operations					
Net Income, Cont. Ops.	$ 198	$ 477	$ 455	$ −40	$ −240
Depreciation and Amort.	486	553	613	723	883
Other Addbacks	120	94	135	32	77
Other Subtractions	0	0	−88	−152	−110
WC Provided by Ops.	$ 804	$ 1,124	$ 1,115	$ 563	$ 610
(Inc.)Decr. in Receivables	−17	−82	−47	−77	148
(Inc.)Decr. in Inventories	−37	−64	−90	−102	−55
(Inc.)Decr. in Other CA	−22	8	6	−35	15
Inc.(Decr.) Acct. Pay.—Trade	44	150	219	37	35
Inc.(Decr.) in Other CL	20	463	122	300	−9
Cash from Cont. Ops.	$ 792	$ 1,599	$ 1,325	$ 686	$ 744
Cash from Discont. Ops.	0	0	0	0	0
Cash from Extr. Gain/Loss	0	0	0	0	0
Net Cash Flow from Ops.	$ 792	$ 1,599	$ 1,325	$ 686	$ 744
Investing					
Fixed Assets Sold	$ 42	$ 14	$ 32	$ 0	$ 0
Investments Sold	0	0	0	0	0
Fixed Assets Acquired	−1,181	−1,186	−2,395	−2,901	−3,536
Investments Acquired	0	0	0	−355	−319
Other Invest. Trans.	−44	−491	647	−482	−716
Net Cash Flow from Investing	$ −1,183	$ −1,663	$ −1,716	$ −3,738	$ −4,571
Financing					
Incr. S-T Borrowing	$ 0	$ 1	$ 59	$ 1,175	$ 425
Incr. L-T Borrowing	532	178	672	2,265	4,379
Issue of Cap. Stock	148	0	5	0	300
Decr. S-T Borrowing	−79	0	0	−129	−246
Decr. L-T Borrowing	−230	−123	−133	−266	−1,096
Acquisit. of Cap. Stock	−24	0	−150	0	0
Dividends	−4	−10	−12	0	0
Other Financing Trans.	71	28	15	0	45
Net Cash Flow from Financing	$ 414	$ 74	$ 456	$ 3,045	$ 3,807
Net Change in Cash	$ 23	$ 10	$ 65	$ −7	$ −20

Delta Airlines Balance Sheet

	1986	1987	1988	1989	1990	1991
Cash	$ 61	$ 380	$ 823	$ 530	$ 68	$ 764
Marketable Securities	0	0	0	0	0	0
Accts./Notes Receivable	426	626	645	752	726	773
Inventories	36	42	52	57	68	70
Other Current Assets	60	131	131	136	155	285
Current Assets	$ 583	$ 1,179	$ 1,651	$ 1,475	$ 1,017	$ 1,892
Investments	38	55	63	67	412	419
Property, Plant, and Equipment......................	5,464	6,093	6,295	7,462	8,746	9,460
Less Accum. Depreciation	2,330	2,419	2,729	2,984	3,347	3,819
Other Assets	30	434	468	464	399	459
Total Assets	$ 3,785	$ 5,342	$ 5,748	$ 6,484	$ 7,227	$ 8,411
Accts. Payable—Trade	$ 270	$ 456	$ 559	$ 568	$ 582	$ 698
Notes Payable—Nontrade	50	25	16	0	65	56
Current Part L-T Debt	11	21	20	17	40	23
Other Current Liab.	415	679	797	1,178	1,146	1,378
Current Liabilities	$ 746	$ 1,181	$ 1,392	$ 1,763	$ 1,833	$ 2,155
Long-Term Debt	867	1,018	730	703	1,315	2,059
Deferred Tax (NCL)	578	689	619	567	533	392
Other Noncurrent Liab.	293	516	798	831	927	1,299
Minority Int. in Subs.	0	0	0	0	0	0
Total Liabilities	$ 2,484	$ 3,404	$ 3,539	$ 3,864	$ 4,608	$ 5,905
Preferred Stock	$ 0	$ 0	$ 0	$ 0	$ 23	$ 49
Common Stock	120	146	147	148	163	49
Additional Paid-in Cap.	93	484	506	514	163	163
Retained Earnings	1,088	1,308	1,556	1,958	880	884
Cum. Translation Adj.	0	0	0	0	2,144	1,748
Treasury Stock	0	0	0	0	0	0
Shareholders' Equity	$ 1,301	$ 1,938	$ 2,209	$ 2,620	-591	-338
Total Equities	$ 3,785	$ 5,342	$ 5,748	$ 6,484	$ 2,619	$ 2,506

Note: the original printing shows "Common Stock 120/146/147/148/163/49", "Additional Paid-in Cap. 93/484/506/514/163/163", "Retained Earnings 1,088/1,308/1,556/1,958/880/884", "Cum. Translation Adj. 0/0/0/0/2,144/1,748", "Treasury Stock 0/0/0/0/0/0", "Shareholders' Equity $1,301/$1,938/$2,209/$2,620/$2,619/$2,506".

Delta Airlines Income Statement

	1987	1988	1989	1990	1991
Sales	$ 5,318	$ 6,915	$ 8,089	$ 8,582	$ 9,171
Other Revenues and Gains	105	24	72	75	47
Cost of Goods Sold	−4,914	−6,418	−7,411	−8,162	−9,620
Sell. and Admin. Expense	0	0	0	0	0
Other Expenses and Losses....................	0	0	0	0	0
EBIT	$ 509	$ 521	$ 750	$ 495	$ −402
Interest Expense	−62	−65	−39	−27	−98
Income Tax Expense	−183	−149	−250	−165	176
Minority Int. in Earnings	0	0	0	0	0
Income from Contin. Ops.	$ 264	$ 307	$ 461	$ 303	$ −324
Income from Discont. Ops.	0	0	0	0	0
Extra. Gains (Losses)	0	0	0	0	0
Changes in Acct. Princ.	0	0	0	0	0
Preferred Stock Dividend	0	0	0	−18	−19
NI Avail. to Com.	$ 264	$ 307	$ 461	$ 285	$ −343

Delta Airlines Statement of Cash Flows

	1987	1988	1989	1990	1991
Operations					
Net Income, Cont. Ops.	$ 264	$ 307	$ 461	$ 303	$ −324
Depreciation and Amort.	278	354	393	459	521
Other Addbacks	200	44	11	106	50
Other Subtractions	−229	−158	−116	−81	−189
WC Provided by Ops.	$ 513	$ 547	$ 749	$ 787	$ 58
(Inc.)Decr. in Receivables	−95	−18	−108	26	−46
(Inc.)Decr. in Inventories	0	0	0	0	0
(Inc.)Decr. in Other CA	−2	−63	−9	−30	−133
Inc.(Decr.) Acct. Pay.—Trade	22	103	207	14	116
Inc.(Decr.) in Other CL	112	107	253	7	329
Cash from Cont. Ops.	$ 550	$ 676	$ 1,092	$ 804	$ 324
Cash from Discont. Ops.	0	0	0	0	0
Cash from Extr. Gain/Loss	0	0	0	0	0
Net Cash Flow from Ops.	$ 550	$ 676	$ 1,092	$ 804	$ 324
Investing					
Fixed Assets Sold	$ 44	$ 70	$ 93	$ 30	$ 25
Investments Sold	0	0	0	0	0
Fixed Assets Acquired	−1,225	−1,331	−1,481	−1,689	−2,145
Investments Acquired	−17	−6	0	−315	0
Other Invest. Trans.	−162	0	0	0	−52
Net Cash Flow from Investing	$ −1,360	$ −1,267	$ −1,388	$ −1,974	$ −2,172
Financing					
Incr. S-T Borrowing	$ 0	$ 0	$ 0	$ 65	$ 0
Incr. L-T Borrowing	1,810	1,399	80	1,117	2,702
Issue of Cap. Stock	1	1	1	376	477
Decr. S-T Borrowing	0	0	0	0	−9
Decr. L-T Borrowing	−638	−308	−19	−145	−322
Acquisit. of Cap. Stock	0	0	0	−591	−221
Dividends	−44	−58	−59	−113	−84
Other Financing Trans.	0	34	0	0	0
Net Cash Flow from Financing	$ 1,129	$ 1,034	$ 3	$ 709	$ 2,543
Net Change in Cash	$ 319	$ 443	$ −293	$ −461	$ 695

United Airlines Balance Sheet

	1986	1987	1988	1989	1990	1991
Cash	$ 102	$ 2,208	$ 1,087	$ 465	$ 221	$ 449
Marketable Securities	116	0	0	957	974	728
Accts./Notes Receivable	1,101	816	743	888	913	912
Inventories	215	222	175	249	323	336
Other Current Assets	1,615	181	166	179	209	457
Current Assets	$ 3,149	$ 3,427	$ 2,171	$ 2,738	$ 2,640	$ 2,882
Investments	0	0	0	0	0	0
Property, Plant, and Equipment..........................	8,339	7,857	7,782	7,704	8,587	10,184
Less Accum. Depreciation	3,651	3,851	3,841	3,806	3,838	4,189
Other Assets	880	793	589	571	605	999
Total Assets	$ 8,717	$ 8,226	$ 6,701	$ 7,207	$ 7,994	$ 9,876
Accts. Payable—Trade	$ 830	$ 496	$ 519	$ 596	$ 553	$ 580
Notes Payable—Nontrade	988	1,010	446	446	447	449
Current Part L-T Debt	147	47	85	84	89	108
Other Current Liab.	1,796	1,857	1,819	2,098	2,668	2,946
Current Liabilities	$ 3,761	$ 3,410	$ 2,869	$ 3,224	$ 3,757	$ 4,083
Long-Term Debt	2,066	1,427	2,060	1,334	1,249	2,423
Deferred Tax (NCL)	154	18	0	0	0	0
Other Noncurrent Liab.	440	446	546	1,083	1,315	1,772
Minority Int. in Subs.	0	0	0	0	0	0
Total Liabilities	$ 6,421	$ 5,301	$ 5,475	$ 5,641	$ 6,321	$ 8,278
Preferred Stock	$ 3	$ 3	$ 0	$ 2	$ 2	$ 1
Common Stock	251	292	117	117	117	126
Additional Paid-in Cap.	1,261	1,678	29	47	53	304
Retained Earnings	780	1,074	1,202	1,512	1,613	1,272
Cum. Translation Adj.	1	0	0	0	0	0
Treasury Stock	0	−122	−122	−112	−112	−105
Shareholders' Equity	$ 2,296	$ 2,925	$ 1,226	$ 1,566	$ 1,673	$ 1,598
Total Equities	$ 8,717	$ 8,226	$ 6,701	$ 7,207	$ 7,994	$ 9,876

United Airlines Income Statement

	1987	1988	1989	1990	1991
Sales	$ 8,293	$ 8,982	$ 9,793	$ 11,037	$ 11,663
Other Revenues and Gains	51	538	243	322	105
Cost of Goods Sold	−8,062	−8,317	−9,329	−11,074	−12,157
Sell. and Admin. Expense	0	0	0	0	0
Other Expenses and Losses......................	−67	0	−17	0	0
EBIT	$ 215	$ 1,203	$ 707	$ 285	$ −389
Interest Expense	−222	−214	−169	−121	−119
Income Tax Expense	3	−389	−214	−70	176
Minority Int. in Earnings	0	0	0	0	0
Income from Contin. Ops.	$ −4	$ 600	$ 324	$ 94	$ −332
Income from Discont. Ops.	339	524	0	0	0
Extra. Gains (Losses)	0	0	0	0	0
Changes in Acct. Princ.	0	0	0	0	0
Preferred Stock Dividend	0	0	0	0	0
NI Avail. to Com.	$ 335	$ 1,124	$ 324	$ 94	$ −332

United Airlines Statement of Cash Flows

	1987	1988	1989	1990	1991
Operations					
Net Income, Cont. Ops.	$ −4	$ 600	$ 324	$ 94	$ −332
Depreciation and Amort.	549	518	517	560	604
Other Addbacks	124	1	12	33	152
Other Subtractions	−30	−452	−268	−286	−134
WC Provided by Ops.	$ 639	$ 667	$ 585	$ 401	$ 290
(Inc.)Decr. in Receivables	−57	36	−147	−24	0
(Inc.)Decr. in Inventories	−59	46	−74	−74	−13
(Inc.)Decr. in Other CA	63	−11	−90	−65	−78
Inc.(Decr.) Acct. Pay.—Trade	21	46	80	−43	27
Inc.(Decr.) in Other CL	550	−12	304	521	112
Cash from Cont. Ops.	$ 1,157	$ 772	$ 658	$ 716	$ 338
Cash from Discont. Ops.	0	0	0	0	0
Cash from Extr. Gain/Loss	0	0	0	0	0
Net Cash Flow from Ops.	$ 1,157	$ 772	$ 658	$ 716	$ 338
Investing					
Fixed Assets Sold	$ 149	$ 1,012	$ 1,374	$ 1,738	$ 1,281
Investments Sold	1,157	1,441	0	0	248
Fixed Assets Acquired	−987	−1,372	−1,568	−2,576	−2,122
Investments Acquired	0	−10	−959	−11	0
Other Invest. Trans.	26	9	−23	−26	−358
Net Cash Flow from Investing	$ 345	$ 1,080	$ −1,176	$ −875	$ −951
Financing					
Incr. S-T Borrowing	$ 262	$ 0	$ 0	$ 1	$ 1
Incr. L-T Borrowing	337	1,843	1	0	687
Issue of Cap. Stock	304	0	0	0	247
Decr. S-T Borrowing	0	551	0	0	0
Decr. L-T Borrowing	−128	−1,445	−89	−91	−98
Acquisit. of Cap. Stock	−122	−2,841	0	0	0
Dividends	−42	0	0	0	0
Other Financing Trans.	−8	21	−16	5	4
Net Cash Flow from Financing	$ 604	$ −2,973	$ −104	$ −85	$ 841
Net Change in Cash	$ 2,106	$ −1,121	$ −622	$ −244	$ 228

APPENDIX A
Financial Statements for the Coca-Cola Company and Subsidiaries

A

The Coca-Cola Company and Subsidiaries Consolidated Statements of Income(Dollars in thousands except per share data)

Year Ended December 31,	Year 8	Year 7	Year 6
Net Operating Revenues	$10,236,350	$8,622,287	$8,065,424
Cost of goods sold	4,208,850	3,548,570	3,429,065
Gross Profit	6,027,500	5,073,717	4,636,359
Selling, administrative, and general expenses	4,075,936	3,347,932	3,038,058
Operating Income	1,951,564	1,725,785	1,598,301
Interest income	169,985	205,035	199,333
Interest expense	230,979	308,034	230,513
Equity income	110,139	75,490	92,542
Other income (deductions) — net	13,727	4,847	(33,243)
Gain on sale of Belmont Springs Water Co., Inc.	—	61,187	—
Income from Continuing Operations before Income Taxes	2,014,436	1,764,310	1,626,420
Income taxes	632,532	571,471	537,434
Income from Continuing Operations	1,381,904	1,192,839	1,088,986
Equity income (loss) from discontinued operation	—	21,537	(44,283)
Gain on sale of discontinued operation (net of income taxes of $421,021)	—	509,449	—
Net Income	1,381,904	1,723,825	1,044,703
Preferred Stock Dividends	18,158	21,392	6,426
Net Income Available to Common Shareholders	$ 1,363,746	$1,702,433	$1,038,277
Income (Loss) per Common Share			
Continuing operations	$ 2.04	$ 1.69	$ 1.48
Discontinued operation	—	.77	(.06)
Net Income per Common Share	$ 2.04	$ 2.46	$ 1.42
Average Common Shares Outstanding (in thousands)	668,570	691,962	729,225

See Notes to Consolidated Financial Statements.

The Coca-Cola Company and Subsidiaries
Consolidated Balance Sheets
(Dollars in thousands except per share data)

December 31,	Year 8	Year 7
Assets		
Current		
Cash and cash equivalents	$1,429,555	$1,096,020
Marketable securities, at cost (approximates market)	62,569	85,671
	1,492,124	1,181,691
Trade accounts receivable, less allowances of $29,510 in Year 8 and $14,347 in Year 7	913,541	768,335
Finance subsidiary—receivables	38,199	52,093
Inventories	982,313	789,077
Prepaid expenses and other assets	716,601	812,304
Total Current Assets	4,142,778	3,603,500
Investments and Other Assets		
Investments		
Coca-Cola Enterprises Inc.	666,847	695,195
Coca-Cola Amatil Limited	569,057	524,931
Other, principally bottling companies	788,718	710,297
Finance subsidiary—receivables	128,119	140,520
Long-Term receivables and other assets	321,977	354,881
	2,474,718	2,425,824
Property, Plant, and Equipment		
Land	147,057	146,482
Buildings and improvements	1,059,969	950,251
Machinery and equipment	2,204,188	1,890,960
Containers	374,526	307,012
	3,785,740	3,294,705
Less allowances for depreciation	1,400,175	1,273,486
	2,385,565	2,021,219
Goodwill and Other Intangible Assets	275,126	231,993
	$9,278,187	$8,282,536

December 31,	Year 8	Year 7
Liabilities and Shareholders' Equity		
Current		
Accounts payable and accrued expenses	$1,576,426	$1,386,516
Loans and notes payable		
Finance subsidiary	161,432	184,691
Other	1,742,179	1,234,617
Current maturities of long-term debt	97,272	12,858
Accrued taxes	719,182	839,248
Total Current Liabilities	4,296,491	3,657,930
Long-Term Debt	535,861	548,708
Other Liabilities	332,060	294,358
Deferred Income Taxes	264,611	296,055
Shareholders' Equity		
Preferred stock, $1 par value—		
Authorized: 100,000,000 shares; Issued: 3,000 shares of Cumulative Money Market Preferred Stock in Year 8 and Year 7; Outstanding: 750 shares in Year 8; 3,000 shares in Year 7, stated at aggregate liquidation preference	75,000	300,000
Common stock, $.50 par value—		
Authorized: 1,400,000,000 shares; Issued: 840,487,486 shares in Year 8; 837,819,578 shares in Year 7	420,244	418,910
Capital surplus	512,703	437,324
Reinvested earnings	6,447,576	5,618,312
Unearned compensation related to outstanding restricted stock..	(67,760)	(45,892)
Foreign currency translation adjustment	4,031	(7,206)
	7,391,794	6,721,448
Less treasury stock, at cost (172,248,315 common shares in Year 8; 163,789,772 common shares in Year 7)	3,542,630	3,235,963
	3,849,164	3,485,485
	$9,278,187	$8,282,536

See Notes to Consolidated Financial Statements.

The Coca-Cola Company and Subsidiaries
Consolidated Statements of Cash Flows

(Dollars in thousands)

Year Ended December 31,	Year 8	Year 7	Year 6
Operating Activities			
Net income	$1,381,904	$1,723,825	$1,044,703
Depreciation and amortization	243,888	183,765	169,768
Deferred income taxes	(30,254)	37,036	43,915
Equity income, net of dividends	(93,816)	(76,088)	(35,758)
Foreign currency adjustments	(77,068)	(31,043)	27,945
Gain on sale of businesses and investments before income taxes	(60,277)	(1,006,664)	—
Other noncash items (primarily nonrecurring charges in Year 8)	97,752	24,360	13,351
Net change in operating assets and liabilities (Year 8 reflects estimated tax payments of approximately $300,000 related to the Year 7 gain on the sale of Columbia Pictures Entertainment, Inc. stock)	(178,202)	279,382	(83,736)
Net cash provided by operating activities	1,283,927	1,134,573	1,180,188
Investing Activities			
Additions to finance subsidiary receivables	(31,551)	(57,006)	(172,866)
Collections of finance subsidiary receivables	58,243	188,810	145,358
Purchases of investments and other assets	(186,631)	(858,510)	(128,526)
Proceeds from disposals of investments and other assets	149,807	126,850	77,049
Proceeds from sale of businesses	—	1,680,073	—
Decrease (increase) in marketable securities	16,733	(3,889)	19,702
Purchases of property, plant, and equipment	(592,971)	(462,466)	(386,757)
Proceeds from disposals of property, plant, and equipment	19,208	60,665	43,332
Purchases of temporary investments and other	(113,875)	(145,009)	(258,481)
Proceeds from disposals of temporary investments	241,373	—	452,851
Collection of notes receivable—Columbia Pictures Entertainment, Inc.	—	—	544,889
Net cash provided by (used in) investing activities	(439,664)	529,518	336,551
Net cash provided by operations after reinvestment	844,263	1,664,091	1,516,739
Financing Activities			
Issuances of debt	592,417	336,370	140,929
Payments of debt	(81,594)	(410,690)	(992,527)
Preferred stock issued (redeemed)	(225,000)	—	300,000
Common stock issued	29,904	41,395	29,035
Purchases of common stock for treasury	(306,667)	(1,166,941)	(759,661)
Dividends (common and preferred)	(552,640)	(490,655)	(443,186)
Net cash used in financing activities	(543,580)	(1,690,521)	(1,725,410)
Effect of Exchange Rate Changes on Cash and Cash Equivalents	32,852	(22,896)	(29,543)
Cash and Cash Equivalents			
Net increase (decrease) during the year	333,535	(49,326)	(238,214)
Balance at beginning of year	1,096,020	1,145,346	1,383,560
Balance at end of year	$1,429,555	$1,096,020	$1,145,346

See Notes to Consolidated Financial Statements.

The Coca-Cola Company and Subsidiaries
Consolidated Statements of
Shareholders' Equity
(Dollars in thousands except per share data)

Three Years Ended December 31, Year 8	Preferred Stock	Common Stock	Capital Surplus	Reinvested Earnings	Unearned Restricted Stock	Foreign Currency Translation	Treasury Stock
Balance December 31, Year 5		$415,977	$338,594	$3,783,625	$(37,414)	$ (4,247)	$(1,309,361)
Sales to employees exercising stock options		906	18,880	—	—	—	(1,459)
Tax benefit from employees' stock option and restricted stock plans		—	5,491	—	—	—	—
Translation adjustments (net of income taxes of $19)		—	—	—	—	(12,763)	—
Stock issued under restricted stock plan, less amortization of $7,884		512	21,424	—	(14,053)	—	—
Purchases of common stock for treasury		—	—	—	—	—	(758,202)
Preferred stock issued	$300,000	—	(4,125)	—	—	—	—
Net Income		—	—	1,044,703	—	—	—
Dividends							
Preferred		—	—	(6,426)	—	—	—
Common (per share—$.60)		—	—	(436,760)	—	—	—
Balance December 31, Year 6	300,000	417,395	380,264	4,385,142	(51,467)	(17,010)	(2,069,022)
Sales to employees exercising stock options		1,481	39,914	—	—	—	(3,804)
Tax benefit from employees' stock option and restricted stock plans		—	14,811	—	—	—	—
Translation adjustments (net of income taxes of $900)		—	—	—	—	9,804	—

Three Years Ended December 31, Year 8

	Preferred Stock	Common Stock	Capital Surplus	Reinvested Earnings	Unearned Restricted Stock	Foreign Currency Translation	Treasury Stock
Stock issued under restricted stock plan, less amortization of $7,944	—	34	2,335	—	5,575	—	—
Purchases of common stock for treasury	—	—	—	—	—	—	(1,163,137)
Net income	—	—	—	1,723,825	—	—	—
Dividends							
Preferred	—	—	—	(21,392)	—	—	—
Common (per share—$.68)	—	—	—	(469,263)	—	—	—
Balance December 31, Year 7	300,000	418,910	437,324	5,618,312	(45,892)	(7,206)	(3,235,963)
Sales to employees exercising stock options	—	905	28,999	—	—	—	(2,762)
Tax benefit from employees' stock option and restricted stock plans	—	—	13,286	—	—	—	—
Translation adjustments (net of income taxes of $573)	—	—	—	—	—	11,237	—
Stock issued under restricted stock plan, less amortization of $11,655	—	429	33,094	—	(21,868)	—	—
Purchases of common stock for treasury	—	—	—	—	—	—	(303,905)
Redemption of preferred stock	(225,000)	—	—	—	—	—	—
Net income	—	—	—	1,381,904	—	—	—
Dividends							
Preferred	—	—	—	(18,158)	—	—	—
Common (per share—$.80)	—	—	—	(534,482)	—	—	—
Balance December 31, Year 8	$ 75,000	$420,244	$512,703	$6,447,576	$ (67,760)	$ 4,031	$ (3,542,630)

See Notes to Consolidated Financial Statements.

Notes to Consolidated Financial Statements

1. Accounting Policies

The major accounting policies and practices followed by The Coca-Cola Company and subsidiaries (the Company) are as follows:

Consolidation. The consolidated financial statements include the accounts of the Company and all subsidiaries where control is not temporary. The Company's investments in companies in which it has the ability to exercise significant influence over operating and financial policies, including some investments where there is a temporary majority interest, are accounted for by the equity method. Accordingly, the Company's share of the earnings of these companies is included in consolidated net income. The Company's investments in other companies are carried at cost. All significant intercompany accounts and transactions are eliminated in consolidation.

Certain amounts in the Year 7 and Year 6 financial statements have been reclassified to conform to the current year presentation.

Net Income per Common Share. Net income per common share is computed by dividing net income less dividends on preferred stock by the weighted average number of common shares outstanding.

Cash Equivalents. Marketable securities that are highly liquid and have maturities of three months or less at the date of purchase are classified as cash equivalents.

Inventories. Inventories are valued at the lower of cost or market. In general, inventories are valued on the basis of average cost or first-in, first-out methods. However, certain soft drink and citrus inventories are valued on the last-in, first-out (LIFO) method. The excess of current costs over LIFO stated values amounted to approximately $42 million and $34 million at December 31, Year 8 and Year 7, respectively.

Property, Plant, and Equipment. Property, plant, and equipment is stated at cost, less allowances for depreciation. Depreciation expense is determined principally by the straight-line method. The annual rates of depreciation are 2 percent to 10 percent for buildings and improvements and 7 percent to 34 percent for machinery, equipment, and containers.

Goodwill and Other Intangible Assets. Goodwill and other intangible assets are stated on the basis of cost and, if acquired subsequent to October 31, 1970, are being amortized, principally on a straight-line basis, over the estimated future periods to be benefited (not exceeding 40 years). Accumulated amortization was approximately $10 million and $3 million at December 31, Year 8 and 7, respectively.

Income Taxes. All income tax amounts and balances have been computed in accordance with APB Opinion No. 11, "Accounting for Income Taxes."

In December 1987, the Financial Accounting Standards Board (FASB) issued Statement of Financial Accounting Standards No. 96, "Accounting for Income Taxes" (SFAS 96). The FASB is considering certain amendments to this Statement, including a delay in the required adoption date to fiscal years beginning after December 15, 1992. Assuming no significant amendments, the adoption of SFAS 96 is not expected to have a material impact on the Company's financial position.

2. Inventories

Inventories consist of the following (in thousands):

December 31	Year 8	Year 7
Finished goods	$396,168	$304,150
Work in process	18,451	22,240
Raw materials and supplies	567,694	462,687
	$982,313	$789,077

3. Equity Investments

Coca-Cola Enterprises Inc. (CCE) is the largest bottler of Company products in the United States. The Company owns approximately 49 percent of the outstanding common stock of CCE and, accordingly, accounts for its investment by the equity method of accounting. A summary of financial information for CCE is as follows (in thousands):

	December 28, Year 8	December 29, Year 7
Current assets	$ 495,341	$ 493,387
Noncurrent assets	4,525,255	4,238,559
Total assets	$5,020,596	$4,731,946
Current liabilities	$1,054,791	$ 996,122
Noncurrent liabilities	2,339,326	2,055,687
Total liabilities	$3,394,117	$3,051,809
Net assets	$1,626,479	$1,680,137
Company equity investment	$ 666,847	$ 695,195

Year ended	December 28, Year 8	December 29, Year 7	December 30, Year 6
Net operating revenues	$4,034,043	$3,881,947	$3,874,445
Cost of goods sold.............................	2,359,267	2,313,032	2,268,038
Gross profit...	$1,674,776	$1,568,915	$1,606,407
Income before income taxes	$ 184,247	$ 137,931	$ 267,721
Net income available to common shareholders	$ 77,148	$ 53,507	$ 142,719
Company equity income	$ 34,429	$ 26,218	$ 63,757

Net syrup/concentrate sales to CCE were $602 million in Year 8, $569 million in Year 7 and $546 million in Year 6. CCE purchases sweeteners through the Company under a pass-through arrangement, and accordingly, related collections from CCE and payments to suppliers are not included in the Company's consolidated statements of income. These transactions amounted to $185 million in Year 8, $195 million in Year 7 and $168 million in Year 6. The Company also provides certain administrative and other services to CCE under negotiated fee arrangements.

The Company engages in a wide range of marketing programs, media advertising, and other similar arrangements to promote the sale of Company products in territories in which CCE operates. The Company's direct support for certain CCE marketing activities and participation with CCE in cooperative advertising and other marketing programs, net of fees charged for services provided, amounted to approximately $181 million, $178 million, and $163 million in Year 8, Year 7, and Year 6, respectively.

In June Year 8, the Company sold a temporary investment, Coca-Cola Holdings (Arkansas) Inc. (CCH Arkansas), to CCE for approximately $241 million and assumed indebtedness. Such amount approximates the Company's original investment made in Year 7, plus carrying costs.

In June Year 8, CCE recorded a pretax gain of approximately $56 million from the sale of two of its bottling subsidiaries. In December Year 6, CCE sold one of its bottling subsidiaries and recorded a pretax gain of approximately $104 million. The purchaser of these three former CCE bottling subsidiaries was Johnston Coca-Cola Bottling Group, Inc. (Johnston), a bottling company that is a 22 percent-owned equity investee of the Company.

Under a CCE share repurchase program, the Company sold 4 million shares and 3 million shares of CCE common stock for $60 million and $49 million in Year 8 and Year 7, respectively. The Company intends to maintain a 49 percent ownership interest in CCE.

If the Company's shares in CCE were valued at the December 31, Year 8, quoted closing price of the publicly traded CCE shares, the calculated value of the Company's investment in CCE would have exceeded the Company's carrying value by approximately $205 million.

Other Equity Investments. The Company owns approximately 51 percent of Coca-Cola Amatil Limited (CCA), an Australian-based bottler of Company products and manufacturer of snack foods. In August Year 7, the Company acquired 59.5 percent of CCA's common stock for approximately $491 million (including certain acquisition-related costs). In separate transactions during Year 8, CCA acquired an independent Australian bottler and the Company's 50 percent interest in a New Zealand bottling joint venture in exchange for consideration that included previously unissued common stock of CCA, resulting in a net reduction of the Company's ownership interest to its present level. The Company intends to reduce its ownership interest in CCA below 50 percent. Accordingly, the investment has been accounted for by the equity method of accounting. At December 31, Year 8, the excess of the Company's investment over its equity in the underlying net assets of CCA was approximately $317 million, which is being amortized primarily over 40 years.

In January Year 7, the Company received $2 million and 1.1 million shares of common stock of Coca-Cola Bottling Co. Consolidated (Consolidated) in exchange for 100 percent of the common stock of a bottling company which had been accounted for as a temporary investment. Such shares, with a carrying value of approximately $43 million at the transaction date, increased the Company's ownership interest in Consolidated from 20 percent to approximately 30 percent.

Operating results include the Company's proportionate share of income from equity investments since the respective dates of investment. A summary of financial information for the Company's equity investments, other than CCE, is as follows (in thousands):

December 31,	Year 8	Year 7
Current assets	$1,658,341	$1,504,051
Noncurrent assets	4,431,810	3,441,552
Total assets	$6,090,151	$4,945,603
Current liabilities	$1,696,796	$1,666,205
Noncurrent liabilities	2,518,902	1,947,918
Total liabilities	$4,215,698	$3,614,123
Net assets	$1,874,453	$1,331,480
Company equity investment	$1,310,209	$1,157,363

Year ended December 31,	Year 8	Year 7	Year 6
Net operating revenues	$7,312,904	$5,598,946	$3,673,640
Cost of goods sold	4,609,004	3,633,647	2,412,869
Gross profit	$2,703,900	$1,965,299	$1,260,771
Income before income taxes	$ 327,784	$ 199,255	$ 114,599
Net income	$ 205,436	$ 123,752	$ 66,445
Company equity income	$ 75,710	$ 49,272	$ 28,785

Net sales to equity investees, other than CCE, were $1.2 billion in Year 8. The Company participates in various marketing, promotional and other activities with these investees, the majority of which are located outside the United States.

If the Company's shares in publicly traded equity investees, excluding CCE, were valued at the December 31, Year 8, quoted closing price of each investee's publicly traded shares, the net calculated value would have been approximately $112 million less than the investment carrying value. Management believes carrying values are fully recoverable through future operations.

The balance sheet caption "Other, principally bottling companies" also includes various investments that are carried at cost.

4. Finance Subsidiary

Coca-Cola Financial Corporation (CCFC) provides loans and other forms of financing to Coca-Cola bottlers and customers for the acquisition of sales-related equipment and for other business purposes. The approximate contractual maturities of finance receivables for the five years succeeding December 31, Year 8, are as follows (in thousands):

Year 9	$38,199
Year 10	30,609
Year 11	20,156
Year 12	11,290
Year 13	7,111

These amounts do not reflect possible prepayments or renewals. Finance receivables include amounts due from Johnston of $56 million and $59 million at December 31, Year 8 and Year 7, respectively.

At December 31, Year 8, CCFC had outstanding interest rate swap agreements which effectively change CCFC's floating interest exposure on $60 million of commercial paper to a fixed rate of approximately 8.2 percent.

5. Short-Term Borrowings and Credit Arrangements

Loans and notes payable consist of commercial paper and notes payable to banks and other financial institutions.

Under lines of credit and other credit facilities for short-term debt with various financial institutions, the Company may borrow up to approximately $800 million. These lines of credit are subject to normal banking terms and conditions. At December 31, Year 8, the unused portion of the credit lines was approximately $600 million, of which approximately $500 million was available to support commercial paper borrowings. Some of the financial arrangements require compensating balances, none of which are presently significant to the Company.

6. Accrued Taxes

Accrued taxes are composed of the following amounts (in thousands):

December 31,	Year 8	Year 7
Income taxes	$618,590	$ 750,753
Sales, payroll, and miscellaneous taxes	100,592	88,495
	$719,182	$ 839,248

7. Long-Term Debt

Long-term debt consists of the following amounts (in thousands):

December 31,	Year 8	Year 7
11-3/8% notes due November 28, Year 9	$ 85,675	$ 85,675
9-7/8% series B notes due November 26, Year 10	59,667	31,034
5-3/4% notes due April 24, Year 14	222,977	212,623
5-3/4% notes due March 25, Year 16	166,953	148,854
Other	97,861	83,380
	633,133	561,566
Less current portion	97,272	12,858
	$535,861	$548,708

Notes outstanding at December 31, Year 8, were issued outside the United States and are redeemable at the Company's option under certain conditions related to U.S. and foreign tax laws. The 5-3/4 percent notes due April 24, Year 14, are denominated in Japanese yen and the 5-3/4 percent notes due March 25, Year 16, are denominated in German marks. Portions of such notes have been swapped for U.S. dollar, Swiss franc and Belgian franc denominated liabilities. The Company has designated such foreign currency borrowings as hedges against its net investments in those respective countries.

Other long-term debt consists of various mortgages and notes with maturity dates ranging from Year 9 to Year 31. Interest on a portion of this debt varies with the changes in the prime rate, and the weighted average interest rate applicable to the remainder is approximately 12.7 percent.

Maturities of long-term debt for the five years succeeding December 31, Year 8, are as follows (in thousands):

Year 9	$97,272
Year 10	78,353
Year 11	24,750
Year 12	14,103
Year 13	8,009

The above notes include various restrictions, none of which are presently significant to the Company.

At December 31, Year 8, the Company is contingently liable for guarantees of indebtedness owed by third parties of $139 million, of which $82 million is related to independent bottling licensees.

Interest paid was approximately $233 million, $319 million and $250 million in Year 8, Year 7 and Year 6, respectively.

8. Financial Instruments

The Company has various financial instruments with off-balance-sheet risk for the primary purpose of reducing its exposure to fluctuations in foreign currency exchange rates and interest rates. While these financial instruments are subject to the risk that market rates may change subsequent to the acquisition of the financial instrument, such changes would generally be offset by opposite effects on the items being hedged. The Company's financial instruments typically mature within one year of origination and are transacted at rates which reflect the market rate at the date of contract.

At December 31, Year 8, the Company had $1.3 billion of foreign currency financial instruments, substantially all of which were forward exchange contracts to purchase or sell foreign currency (primarily French francs, German marks and Japanese yen). These instruments were employed to hedge balance sheet and transactional exposure.

See Note 4 for discussion of interest rate swaps and Note 7 for discussion of foreign currency swaps and financial guarantees provided by the Company.

9. Preferred Stock

In the fourth quarter of Year 8, the Company redeemed 2,250 shares of its nonvoting Cumulative Money Market Preferred Stock (MMP) at the $225 million aggregate liquidation value plus an amount equal to accrued dividends. The remaining 750 shares of the MMP were redeemed after December 31, Year 8, at the $75 million aggregate liquidation value plus an amount equal to accrued dividends. During Year 8 and 7, weighted average dividend rates (per annum) for the MMP were approximately 6 percent and 7 percent, respectively.

10. Common Stock

On April 18, Year 8, the Company's shareholders approved an increase in the authorized common stock of the Company from 700 million shares to 1.4 billion shares, a two-for-one stock split and a change in the par value of common stock from $1.00 per share to $.50 per share. Accordingly, all share data has been restated for periods prior to the stock split. Common shares outstanding and related changes for the three years ended December 31, Year 8, are as follows (in thousands):

	Year 8	Year 7	Year 6
Stock outstanding at January 1	674,030	709,578	744,713
Stock issued to employees exercising stock options	1,810	2,962	1,811
Stock issued under restricted stock plans	858	68	1,023
Purchases of common stock for treasury	(8,459)	(38,578)	(37,969)
Stock outstanding at December 31	668,239	674,030	709,578

11. Restricted Stock, Stock Options and Other Stock Plans

The Company sponsors restricted stock award plans, stock option plans, Incentive Unit Agreements and Performance Unit Agreements.

Under the amended Year 7 Restricted Stock Award Plan and the amended Year 1 Restricted Stock Award Plan (the Plans), 10,000,000 and 6,000,000 shares of restricted common stock, respectively, may be granted to certain officers and key employees of the Company. 858,000 shares, 68,000 shares and 1,023,000 shares were granted in Year 8, Year 7, and Year 6, respectively. At December 31, Year 8, 9,944,000 shares were available for grant under the Plans. Shares issued under the Plans are subject to transfer restrictions and may be forfeited if the participant leaves the Company for reasons other than retirement (as defined by the Plans), disability or death or if a change in control of the Company occurs. The participant is entitled to vote and receive dividends on the shares, and, under the Year 1 Restricted Stock Award Plan, the participant is reimbursed by the Company for the personal income tax liability resulting from the stock award.

The Company's Year 6 Stock Option Plan (the SOP) covers 16,000,000 shares of the Company's common stock. The SOP provides for the granting of stock appreciation rights and/or stock options to certain officers and employees. The stock appreciation rights permit the holder, upon surrendering all or part of the related stock option, to receive cash, common stock, or a combination thereof, in an amount up to 100 percent of the difference between the market price and the option price. Options outstanding at December 31, Year 8, also include various options granted under previous plans.

Further information relating to options is as follows:

	Year 8	Year 7	Year 6
Options outstanding at January 1,	13,504,052	17,315,580	11,220,694
Options granted during the year	5,195,700	31,800	8,365,900
Options exercised during the year	(1,809,908)	(2,962,456)	(1,811,196)
Options canceled during the year	(357,392)	(880,872)	(459,818)
Options outstanding at December 31,	16,532,452	13,504,052	17,315,580
Options exercisable at December 31,	9,569,002	8,560,846	6,826,166
Shares available at December 31, for options which may be granted	1,558,616	6,642,616	6,516,902
Option prices per share			
Exercised during the year	$5–$39	$5–$23	$5–$19
Unexercised at December 31	$6–$48	$5–$24	$5–$23

In Year 6, the Company entered into Incentive Unit Agreements, whereby certain officers will be granted cash awards based on the market value of 600,000 shares of the Company's common stock at the measurement dates. The Incentive Unit Agreements provide that the officers be reimbursed by the Company for the personal income tax liability resulting from the awards.

In Year 3, the Company entered into Performance Unit Agreements, whereby certain officers will be granted cash awards based on the difference in the market value of 1,110,000 shares of the Company's common stock at the measurement dates and the base price of $10.31, the market value as of January 2, Year 3.

12. Pension Plans

In the United States, the Company sponsors and/or contributes to pension plans covering substantially all U.S. employees and certain employees in international locations. The benefits are primarily based on years of service and the employees' compensation for certain periods during the last years of employment. Pension costs are generally funded currently, subject to regulatory funding limitations. The Company also sponsors nonqualified, unfunded defined benefit plans for certain officers and other employees.

Outside the United States, the Company and its subsidiaries have various pension plans and other forms of postretirement arrangements. In Year 7, the Company adopted Statement of Financial Accounting Standards No. 87, "Employers' Accounting for Pensions" (SFAS 87), for international plans. The impact on Year 7 pension expense was insignificant.

Total pension expense amounted to approximately $30 million in Year 8, $23 million in Year 7 and $24 million in Year 6. Net periodic pension cost for the Company's defined benefit plans subject to SFAS 87 requirements in Year 8, Year 7 and Year 6 includes the following components (in thousands):

	U.S. Plans			International Plans	
Year Ended December 31,	**Year 8**	**Year 7**	**Year 6**	**Year 8**	**Year 7**
Service cost —benefits earned during the period..................	$10,684	$9,830	$11,762	$12,902	$12,133
Interest cost on projected benefit obligation..................	41,786	35,393	35,233	14,720	12,539
Actual return on plan assets.....	(9,121)	(95,254)	(62,357)	(3,811)	(16,108)
Net amortization and deferral..	(31,168)	56,548	25,785	(11,273)	2,240
Net periodic pension cost.........	$12,181	$6,517	$10,423	$12,538	$10,804

The table on the next page sets forth the funded status for the Company's defined benefit plans at December 31, Year 8 and Year 7 (in thousands):

December 31,	Assets Exceed Accumulated Benefits Year 8	Year 7	Accumulated Benefits Exceed Assets Year 8	Year 7	Assets Exceed Accumulated Benefits Year 8	Year 7	Accumulated Benefits Exceed Assets Year 8	Year 7
Actuarial present value of benefit obligations Vested benefit obligation	$340,598	$284,986	$(53,386)	$(40,985)	$ 84,890	$137,005	$(70,044)	$ 2,991
Accumulated benefit obligation	$362,724	$305,853	$ 57,372	$ 43,391	$ 89,263	$141,920	$ 72,938	$4,995
Projected benefit obligation	$424,118	$364,328	$ 65,703	$ 49,619	$129,435	$201,107	$113,842	$ 6,375
Plan assets at fair value (primarily listed stocks, bonds and government securities)	508,267	529,067	811	—	160,945	207,806	62,335	1,961
Plan assets in excess of (less than) projected benefit obligation	84,149	164,739	(64,892)[1]	(49,619)[1]	31,510	6,699	(51,507)	(4,414)
Unrecognized net (asset) liability at transition	(44,317)	(48,109)	23,416	23,089	(32,076)	8,361	38,121	1,064
Unrecognized prior service cost	28,302	5,810	1,175	580	2,017	1,588	—	—
Unrecognized net (gain) loss	(64,617)	(117,237)	5,647	(1,533)	5,171	(10,926)	58	540
Adjustment required to recognize minimum liability	—	—	(21,941)	(15,908)	—	—	(167)	(56)
Accrued pension asset (liability) included in the consolidated balance sheet	$ 3,517	$ 5,203	$(56,595)	$(43,391)	$ 6,622	$ 5,722	$(13,495)	$(2,866)

[1]Substantially all of this amount relates to nonqualified, unfunded defined benefit plans.

The assumptions used in computing the above information are presented below:

	U. S. Plans			International Plans (weighted average rates)	
	Year 8	Year 7	Year 6	Year 8	Year 7
Discount rates...	9%	9%	9%	8%	7%
Rates of increase in compensation levels........	6%	6%	6%	6%	4%
Expected long-term rates of return on assets.	9-1/2%	9%	8%	8%	8%

The Company also has plans that provide postretirement health care and life insurance benefits to substantially all U.S. employees and certain international employees who retire with a minimum of five years of service. The annual cash cost of these benefits is not significant. In 1990, the FASB issued Statement of Financial Accounting Standards No. 106, "Accounting for Postretirement Benefits Other than Pensions" (SFAS 106). The required adoption date for SFAS 106 for the Company is January 1, Year 11. SFAS 106 will require companies to accrue the cost of postretirement health care and life insurance benefits within employees' active service periods. Based on preliminary studies and evaluations, the adoption of SFAS 106 is not expected to have any significant impact on the Company's financial position.

13. Income Taxes

The components of income before income taxes for both continuing and discontinued operations consist of the following (in thousands):

Year Ended December 31,	Year 8	Year 7	Year 6
United States...	$ 494,544	$1,459,213	$ 439,149
Foreign..	1,519,892	1,257,104	1,142,988
	$2,014,436	$2,716,317	$1,582,137

Income taxes for continuing and discontinued operations consist of the following amounts (in thousands):

Year Ended December 31,	United States	State & Local	Foreign	Total
Year 8				
Current	$134,973	$ 26,515	$501,298	$662,786
Deferred	(49,387)	(2,596)	21,729	(30,254)
Year 7				
Current	$478,004	$ 84,072	$393,380	$955,456
Deferred	(8,025)	160	44,901	37,036
Year 6				
Current	$ 53,084	$ 14,329	$426,106	$493,519
Deferred	14,857	4,641	24,417	43,915

The Company made income tax payments of approximately $803 million, $537 million and $517 million in Year 8, Year 7, and Year 6, respectively.

A reconciliation of the statutory U.S. federal rates and effective rates for continuing operations is as follows:

Year Ended December 31,	Year 8	Year 7	Year 6
Statutory rate	34.0%	34.0%	34.0%
State income taxes—net of federal benefit	1.0	1.0	.8
Earnings in jurisdictions taxed at rates different from the U.S. federal rate	(2.6)	(1.6)	(.8)
Equity income	(1.8)	(1.5)	(2.0)
Other—net	.8	.5	1.0
	31.4%	32.4%	33.0

Deferred taxes are provided principally for depreciation, certain employee compensation-related expenses and certain capital transactions that are recognized in different years for financial statement and income tax purposes. The Company has manufacturing facilities in Puerto Rico that operate under a negotiated exemption grant that expires December 31, Year 27.

Appropriate U.S. and foreign taxes have been provided for earnings of subsidiary companies that are expected to be remitted to the parent company in the near future. Accumulated unremitted earnings of foreign subsidiaries that are expected to be required for use in the foreign operations were approximately $69 million at December 31, Year 8, exclusive of amounts that, if remitted, would result in little or no tax.

14. Acquisitions and Divestitures

The Company periodically engages in the acquisition and/or divestiture of bottling and other related companies. Generally, these transactions are not material to the financial position or results of operations of the Company, either individually or in the aggregate, and are therefore not separately identified herein.

In August, Year 7, the Company acquired all of the Coca-Cola bottling operations of Pernod Ricard for an aggregate purchase price of approximately $140 million. The fair values of assets acquired and liabilities assumed were $285 million and $145 million, respectively. Pernod Ricard operated the Coca-Cola bottling, canning, and distribution business in six major territories in France. The acquisition was accounted for by the purchase method. Operating results have been included in the consolidated statements of income from the date of acquisition and did not have a significant effect on consolidated operating results.

In August Year 7, the Company sold Belmont Springs Water Co., Inc., a bottled water operation, which resulted in a pretax gain of approximately $61 million.

See Note 3 for discussions of the equity investment in CCA, which was acquired in August Year 7, and the temporary investment in CCH Arkansas, which was acquired in July Year 8 and sold in June, Year 9.

15. Net Change in Operating Assets and Liabilities

The changes in operating assets and liabilities, net of effects of acquisitions and divestitures of businesses and unrealized exchange gains/losses, are as follows (in thousands):

Year Ended December 31,	Year 8	Year 7	Year 6
Decrease (increase) in trade accounts receivable	$ (87,749)	$(99,496)	$33,887
Increase in inventories	(169,442)	(34,709)	(25,744)
Increase in prepaid expenses and other assets...........	(65,758)	(204,222)	(35,496)
Increase (decrease) in accounts payable and accrued expenses	198,631	88,940	(36,139)
Increase (decrease) in accrued taxes	(111,014)	456,544	(17,618)
Increase (decrease) in other liabilities	57,130	72,325	(2,626)
	$(178,202)	$279,382	$(83,736)

16. Gain on Investment

In the third quarter of Year 8, the Company realized a pretax gain of $52 million on its investment in BCI Securities L.P. (BCI) resulting from BCI's sale of Beatrice Company stock. This gain is included in "Other income (deductions)–net" in the accompanying consolidated statements of income.

17. Nonrecurring Charges

In the third quarter of Year 8, the Company recorded nonrecurring, noncash pretax charges aggregating approximately $49 million related to its United States soft drink business. These charges reflect accelerated amortization of certain software costs due to management plans to upgrade and standardize information systems and adjustments to the carrying value of certain fountain equipment and marketing related items to amounts estimated to be recoverable in future periods. These charges are included in "Selling, administrative, and general expenses" in the accompanying consolidated statements of income.

18. Discontinued Operation

In November, Year 7, the Company sold its entire equity interest in Columbia Pictures Entertainment, Inc. (CPE) for approximately $1.55 billion in cash. The equity interest consisted of approximately 49 percent of the outstanding common shares of CPE and 1,000 shares of preferred stock. The sale resulted in a pretax gain of approximately $930 million. On an after-tax basis, the gain was approximately $509 million or $.74 per common share. The effective tax rate of 45 percent on the gain on the sale of CPE stock differs from the statutory U.S. federal rate of 34 percent due primarily to differences between the book basis and tax basis of the Company's investment in CPE.

CPE has been reported as a discontinued operation, and, accordingly, the gain from the sale of CPE stock and the company's equity income (loss) from CPE have been reported separately from continuing operations.

19. Lines of Business

The Company operates in two major lines of business: soft drinks and foods (principally juice-based beverages). Information concerning operations in these businesses at December 31, Year 8, Year 7, and Year 6, and for the years then ended, is presented below (in millions):

Soft Drinks

Year 8	United States	International	Foods	Corporate	Consolidated
Net operating revenues	$2,461.3	$6,125.4	$1,604.9	$ 44.8	$10,236.4
Operating income	358.1[1]	1,801.4	93.5	(301.4)	1,951.6
Identifiable operating assets	1,691.0	3,672.2	759.2	1,131.2[2]	7,253.6
Equity income				110.1	110.1
Investments				2,024.6	2,024.6[3]
Capital expenditures	138.4	321.4	68.2	65.0	593.0
Depreciation and amortization	88.5	94.4	28.3	32.7	243.9

Soft Drinks

Year 7	United States	International	Foods	Corporate	Consolidated
Net operating revenues	$2,222.2	$4,759.2	$1,583.3	$ 57.6	$8,622.3
Operating income	390.6	1,517.6	87.4	(269.8)	1,725.8
Identifiable operating assets	1,814.4	2,806.0	695.3	1,036.4[2]	6,352.1
Equity income				75.5	75.5
Investments				1,930.4[3]	1,930.4
Capital expenditures	136.3	215.6	61.6	49.0	462.5
Depreciation and amortization	73.9	48.4	30.7	30.8	183.8

Soft Drinks

Year 6	United States	International	Foods	Corporate	Consolidated
Net operating revenues	$2,012.0	$4,503.8	$1,512.1	$ 37.5	$8,065.4
Operating income	351.9	1,338.8	89.3	(181.7)	1,598.3
Identifiable operating assets	1,711.9	2,097.1	694.1	1,035.5[2]	5,538.6
Equity income				92.5	92.5
Investments				1,912.0[3]	1,912.0
Capital expenditures	80.2	159.2	82.0	65.4	386.8
Depreciation and amortization	66.9	42.8	32.0	28.1	169.8

Intercompany transfers between sectors are not material.
[1]Includes nonrecurring charges aggregating $49 million.
[2]General corporate identifiable operating assets are composed principally of marketable securities and fixed assets.
[3]Investments include investments in soft drink bottling companies and joint ventures for all periods and CPE for Year 6. The Company's investment in CPE, which was sold in November Year 7, approximated $598.1 million at December 31, Year 6.

20. Operations in Geographic Areas

Information about the Company's operations in different geographic areas at December 31, Year 8, Year 7, and Year 6, and for the years then ended, is presented on the next page (in millions):

Year 8

	United States	Latin America	European Community	Northeast Europe and Africa	Pacific and Canada	Corporate	Consolidated
Net operating revenues.............	$3,931.0	$813.0	$2,804.8	$562.8	$2,080.0	$ 44.8	$10,236.4
Operating income......................	440.4[1]	300.2	666.5	174.2	671.7	(301.4)	1,951.6
Identifiable operating assets	2,414.2	640.3	1,818.8	400.1	849.0	1,131.2[2]	7,253.6
Equity income						110.1	110.1
Investments						2,024.6[3]	2,024.6
Capital expenditures..................	204.0	59.7	203.5	38.8	22.0	65.0	593.0
Depreciation and amortization	115.6	18.0	54.5	7.6	15.5	32.7	243.9

Year 7

	United States	Latin America	European Community	Northeast Europe and Africa	Pacific and Canada	Corporate	Consolidated
Net operating revenues.............	$3,678.7	$646.2	$1,855.1	$425.2	$1,959.5	$ 57.6	$8,622.3
Operating income......................	468.2	226.7	540.6	147.3	612.8	(269.8)	1,725.8
Identifiable operating assets	2,476.0	515.4	1,342.8	328.8	652.7	1,036.4[2]	6,352.1
Equity income						75.5	75.5
Investments						1,930.4[3]	1,930.4
Capital expenditures..................	196.4	30.7	133.9	24.6	27.9	49.0	462.5
Depreciation and amortization	103.5	11.8	18.0	4.9	14.8	30.8	183.8

Year 6

	United States	Latin America	European Community	Northeast Europe and Africa	Pacific and Canada	Corporate	Consolidated
Net operating revenues.............	$3,411.2	$583.2	$1,618.3	$385.2	$2,030.0	$ 37.5	$8,065.4
Operating income......................	433.9	179.5	465.7	130.4	570.5	(181.7)	1,598.3
Identifiable operating assets	2,353.4	431.8	754.8	279.4	683.7	1,035.5[2]	5,538.6
Equity income						92.5	92.5
Investments						1,912.0[3]	1,912.0
Capital expenditures..................	159.2	65.6	55.5	13.8	27.3	65.4	386.8
Depreciation and amortization....	97.8	10.9	15.6	3.7	13.7	28.1	169.8

Intercompany transfers between geographic areas are not material.

Identifiable liabilities of operations outside the United States amounted to approximately $1,498.3 million, $1,082.8 million, and $946.2 million at December 31, Year 8, Year 7 and Year 6, respectively.

[1] Includes nonrecurring charges aggregating $49 million.

[2] General corporate identifiable operating assets are composed principally of marketable securities and fixed assets.

[3] Investments include investments in soft drink bottling companies and joint ventures for all periods and CPE for Year 6.

The Company's investment in CPE, which was sold in November Year 7, approximated $598.1 million at December 31, Year 6.

APPENDIX B
Financial Statements for PepsiCo, Inc. and Subsidiaries

B

PepsiCo, Inc. and Subsidiaries
Consolidated Statement of Income
(in millions except per share amounts)
Fifty-two weeks ended December 29, Year 8 and December 30, Year 7
and fifty-three weeks ended December 31, Year 6

	Year 8	Year 7	Year 6
Net Sales	$17,802.7	$15,242.4	$12,533.2
Costs and Expenses			
Cost of sales	8,609.9	7,467.7	5,957.4
Selling, administrative, and other expenses	6,948.1	5,841.4	5,154.3
Amortization of goodwill and other intangibles	189.1	150.4	72.3
Gain on joint venture stock offering	(118.2)	—	—
Interest expense	688.5	609.6	344.2
Interest income	(182.1)	(177.2)	(122.2)
	16,135.3	13,891.9	11,406.0
Income from Continuing Operations before Income Taxes	1,667.4	1,350.5	1,127.2
Provision for Income Taxes	576.8	449.1	365.0
Income from Continuing Operations	1,090.6	901.4	762.2
Discontinued Operation Charge (net of income tax benefit of $0.3)	(13.7)	—	—
Net Income	$ 1,076.9	$ 901.4	$ 762.2
Income (Charge) per Share			
Continuing operations	$ 1.37	$ 1.13	$ 0.97
Discontinued operation	(0.02)	—	—
Net Income per Share	$ 1.35	$ 1.13	$ 0.97
Average shares outstanding used to calculate income (charge) per share	798.7	796.0	790.4

See accompanying Notes to Consolidated Financial Statements.

PepsiCo, Inc. and Subsidiaries
Consolidated Balance Sheet
(in millions except per share amounts)
December 29, Year 8 and December 30, Year 7

	Year 8	Year 7
ASSETS		
Current Assets		
Cash and cash equivalents	$ 170.8	$ 76.2
Short-term investments, at cost which approximates market	1,644.9	1,457.7
	$1,815.7	1,533.9
Notes and accounts receivable, less allowance		
$90.8 in Year 8 and $57.7 in Year 7	1,414.7	1,239.7
Inventories	585.8	546.1
Prepaid expenses and other current assets	265.2	231.1
Total Current Assets	4,081.4	3,550.8
Investments in Affiliates and Other Assets	1,505.9	970.8
Property, Plant, and Equipment, net	5,710.9	5,130.2
Goodwill and Other Intangibles, net	5,845.2	5,474.9
Total Assets	$17,143.4	$15,126.7
LIABILITIES AND SHAREHOLDERS' EQUITY		
Current Liabilities		
Short-term borrowings	$ 1,626.5	$ 866.3
Accounts payable	1,116.3	1,054.5
Income taxes payable	443.7	313.7
Other current liabilities	1,584.0	1,457.3
Total Current Liabilities	4,770.5	3,691.8
Long-Term Debt	5,600.1	5,777.1
Nonrecourse Obligation	299.5	299.4
Other Liabilities and Deferred Credits	626.3	610.4
Deferred Income Taxes	942.8	856.9
Shareholders' Equity		
Capital stock, par value 1-2/3¢ per share		
authorized 1,800.0 shares, issued 863.1 shares	14.4	14.4
Capital in excess of par value	365.0	323.9
Retained earnings	4,753.0	3,978.4
Currency translation adjustment	383.2	66.2
	5,515.6	4,382.9
Less treasury stock, at cost		
74.7 shares in Year 8, 72.0 shares in Year 7	(611.4)	(491.8)
Total Shareholders' Equity	4,904.2	3,891.1
Total Liabilities and Shareholders' Equity	$17,143.4	$15,126.7

See accompanying Notes to Consolidated Financial Statements.

PepsiCo, Inc. and Subsidiaries
Consolidated Statement of Cash Flows
Fifty-two weeks ended December 29, Year 8 and December 30, Year 7 and fifty-three weeks ended December 31, Year 6 (in millions)

	Year 8	Year 7	Year 6
Cash Flows from Continuing Operations			
Income from continuing operations	$1,090.6	$ 901.4	$ 762.2
Adjustments to reconcile income from continuing operations to net cash generated by continuing operations			
Gain on joint venture stock offering	(118.2)	—	—
Depreciation and amortization	884.0	772.0	629.3
Deferred income taxes	106.1	71.2	20.1
Other noncash charges and credits—net	120.3	128.4	213.4
Changes in operating working capital, excluding effect of acquisition and sales of businesses			
Notes and accounts receivable	(124.8)	(149.9)	(50.1)
Inventories	(20.9)	(50.1)	13.8
Prepaid expenses and other current assets	(61.6)	6.5	37.8
Accounts payable	25.4	134.9	138.2
Income taxes payable	136.3	80.9	55.1
Other current liabilities	72.8	(9.4)	74.7
Net change in operating working capital	27.2	12.9	269.5
Net Cash Generated by Continuing Operations	2,110.0	1,885.9	1,894.5
Cash Flows from Investing Activities			
Acquisitions and investments in affiliates	(630.6)	(3,296.6)	(1,415.5)
Purchases of property, plant, and equipment	(1,180.1)	(943.8)	(725.8)
Proceeds from joint venture stock offering	129.6	—	—
Proceeds from sales of property, plant, and equipment	45.3	69.7	67.4
Proceeds from sales of businesses	—	—	283.2
Net sales (purchases) of short-term investments	(181.8)	12.3	(201.7)
Other, net	(119.7)	(97.9)	(58.7)
Net Cash Used for Investing Activities	(1,937.3)	(4,256.3)	(2,051.1)
Cash Flows from Financing Activities			
Proceeds from issuances of long-term debt	777.3	71.7	475.3
Payments of long-term debt	(298.0)	(405.4)	(190.0)
Net proceeds from (payments of) short-term borrowings	(86.2)	2,925.5	231.3
Cash dividends paid	(293.9)	(241.9)	(199.0)
Purchases of treasury stock	(147.7)	—	(71.8)
Other, net	(28.6)	(28.9)	(24.4)
Net Cash Generated by (Used for) Financing Activities	(77.1)	2,321.0	221.4
Effect of Exchange Rate Changes on Cash and Cash Equivalents	(1.0)	(17.1)	(1.4)
Net Increase (Decrease) in Cash and Cash Equivalents	94.6	(66.5)	63.4
Cash and Cash Equivalents—Beginning of Year	76.2	142.7	79.3
Cash and Cash Equivalents—End of Year	$ 170.8	$ 76.2	$ 142.7

Supplemental Cash Flow Information

Cash Flow Data

Interest paid	$ 656.9	$ 591.1	$ 286.5
Income taxes paid	$ 375.0	$ 239.7	$ 234.7

Schedule of Noncash Investing and Financing Activities

Issuance of treasury stock and debt for acquisitions	$ 105.1	$ 103.9	$ 328.2
Liabilities assumed/disposed of in connection with acquisitions/sales of businesses	$ 231.8	$ 446.8	$ 300.0
Issuance of treasury stock for compensation awards and conversion of debentures	$ 13.5	$ 9.3	$ 26.4
Additions of capital leases	$ 18.1	$ 15.7	$ 4.3

See accompanying Notes to Consolidated Financial Statements.

PepsiCo, Inc. and Subsidiaries
Consolidated Statement of Shareholders' Equity (shares in thousands, dollars in millions, except per share amounts)
Fifty-two weeks ended December 29, Year 8, and December 30, Year 7 and fifty-three weeks ended December 31, Year 6

| | Capital Stock | | | | Capital in Excess of Par Value | Retained Earnings | Currency Translation Adjustment | Total |
| | Issued | | Treasury | | | | | |
	Shares	Amount	Shares	Amount				
Shareholders' Equity, December 26, Year 5	863,083	$14.4	(81,844)	$(553.6)	$280.9	$2,776.7	$ (9.8)	$2,508.6
Year 6 net income						762.2		762.2
Cash dividends declared (per share—$0.27)						(209.2)		(209.2)
Shares reissued to Employee Stock Ownership Plan			365	2.5	1.6			4.1
Payment of compensation awards and exercise of stock options			972	6.6	0.5			7.1
Conversion of debentures			3,047	20.7	(2.6)			18.1
Translation adjustments							33.8	33.8
Purchase of treasury stock			(6,198)	(71.8)				(71.8)
Shares issued in connection with acquisitions			9,009	85.9	22.2			108.1
Shareholders' Equity, December 31, Year 6	863,083	$14.4	(74,649)	$(509.7)	$302.6	$3,329.7	$ 24.0	$3,161.0
Year 7 net income						901.4		901.4
Cash dividends declared (per share—$0.32)						(252.7)		(252.7)
Payment of compensation awards and exercise of stock options			901	6.2	2.6			8.8
Conversion of debentures			456	3.1	0.8			3.9
Translation adjustments							42.2	42.2
Shares issued in connection with an acquisition			1,266	8.6	17.9			26.5
Shareholders' Equity, December 30, Year 7	863,083	$14.4	(72,026)	$(491.8)	$323.9	$3,978.4	$ 66.2	$3,891.1
Year 8 net income						1,076.9		1,076.9
Cash dividends declared (per share—$0.38)						(302.3)		(302.3)
Shares reissued to Employee Stock Ownership Plan			8	0.1	0.2			0.3
Payment of compensation awards and exercise of stock options			1,072	7.8	9.1			16.9
Conversion of debentures			549	3.9	1.7			5.6
Translation adjustments							317.0	317.0
Purchase of treasury stock			(6,310)	(147.7)				(147.7)
Shares issued in connection with acquisitions			2,013	16.3	30.1			46.4
Shareholders' Equity, December 29, Year 8	863,083	$14.4	(74,694)	$(611.4)	$365.0	$4,753.0	$383.2	$4,904.2

Certain amounts above have been restated to reflect the Year 8 three-for-one stock split.

See accompanying Notes to Consolidated Financial Statements.

Notes to Consolidated Financial Statements (tabular dollars in millions except per share amounts)

1. Summary of Significant Accounting Policies

Principles of Consolidation.   The financial statements reflect the consolidated accounts of PepsiCo, Inc. and its wholly owned subsidiaries. All significant intercompany accounts and transactions have been eliminated. Investments in affiliates in which PepsiCo exercises significant influence but not control are accounted for by the equity method, and the equity in net income is included in the Consolidated Statement of Income under the caption "Selling, administrative, and other expenses." Certain reclassifications were made to Year 7 and Year 6 amounts to conform with the Year 8 presentation.

Stock Split.   On July 26, Year 8, PepsiCo's Board of Directors authorized a three-for-one stock split of PepsiCo's Capital Stock effective for shareholders of record at the close of business on August 10, Year 8. The number of authorized shares was also increased from 6 million to 1.8 billion. The Consolidated Financial Statements for Year 8, as well as all other share data in this report, reflect this stock split and the increase in authorized shares. Prior year amounts also have been restated for the stock split. The par value remained 1-2/3 cents per share, with capital in excess of par value reduced by the total par value of the additional shares.

Goodwill and Other Intangibles.   Goodwill and other intangibles arose from the allocation of purchase prices of businesses acquired, with the largest portion representing the value of Pepsi-Cola franchise rights reacquired in the acquisitions of franchised domestic soft drink bottling operations. Goodwill and other intangibles are amortized on a straight-line basis over appropriate periods generally ranging from 20 to 40 years. Accumulated amortization was $548 million and $359 million at year-end Year 8 and Year 7, respectively.

Marketing Costs.   Marketing costs are included in the Consolidated Statement of Income under the caption "Selling, administrative, and other expenses." Costs of materials in inventory and prepayments are deferred, and certain promotional discounts are expensed as incurred. All other costs of advertising and other marketing and promotional programs are charged to expense ratably over the year in which incurred, generally in relation to sales.

Classification of Restaurant Operating Expenses.   Operating expenses incurred at the restaurant unit level consist primarily of food and related packaging costs, labor associated with food preparation and customer service, and overhead expenses. For purposes of the Consolidated Statement of Income, food and packaging costs as well as all labor-related expenses are classified as "Cost of sales," and all other unit level expenses are classified as "Selling, administrative, and other expenses."

Cash Equivalents.   Cash equivalents are comprised of funds temporarily invested (with original maturities not exceeding three months) as part of PepsiCo's management of day-to-day operating cash receipts and disbursements. All other investment portfolios, primarily held offshore, are classified as short-term investments.

Net Income per Share.   Net income per share is computed by dividing net income by the weighted average number of shares and share equivalents outstanding during each year.

Research and Development Expenses.   Research and development expenses, which are expensed as incurred, were $101 million, $91 million, and $84 million in Year 8, Year 7, and Year 6, respectively.

2. Acquisitions and Investments in Affiliates

During Year 8 PepsiCo completed several acquisitions and affiliate investments in all three industry segments aggregating $736 million, comprised of $631 million in cash, $59 million in notes and $46 million in PepsiCo Capital Stock. The activity included acquisitions of a 54% equity interest in a Mexican cookie business, franchised soft drink bottlers in Canada, and franchised domestic restaurant operators.

During Year 7 PepsiCo completed a number of acquisitions with purchase prices aggregating $3.4 billion, principally for cash. The acquisitions included the franchised domestic soft drink bottling operations of General Cinema Corporation (GC Beverage), acquired on March 23, Year 7, for $1.77 billion, and Smiths Crisps Limited and Walkers Crisps Holdings Limited (the U.K. operations), two snack chips companies in the United Kingdom, acquired on July 1, Year 7, for $1.34 billion. The remaining activity consisted primarily of acquisitions of franchised domestic soft drink bottlers and restaurant operators.

Acquisition and affiliate investment activity in Year 6 aggregated $1.8 billion, principally comprised of over $1.4 billion in cash, $220 million in notes and $108 million in PepsiCo Capital Stock. The majority of these acquisitions were franchised domestic soft drink bottlers, the largest of which were the bottling operations of Grand Metropolitan Incorporated acquired on August 4, Year 6 for $705 million in cash. On December 31, Year 5 PepsiCo also acquired a 20% equity interest in Pepsi-Cola General Bottlers, Inc. (the remaining equity of which is owned by Whitman Corporation), contributing $177 million in cash and certain previously consolidated bottling operations with an aggregate carrying value of $17 million.

The acquisitions have been accounted for by the purchase method; accordingly, their results are included in the Consolidated Financial Statements from their respective dates of acquisition.

The following table presents the unaudited pro forma combined results of PepsiCo and the Year 7 acquisitions of GC Beverage and the U.K. operations as if they had occurred at the beginning of Year 7 and Year 6, and a substantial majority of the Year 6 acquisitions as if they had occurred at the beginning of Year 6. The aggregate impact of acquisitions in Year 8 and all other acquisitions for Year 7 and Year 6 was not material to PepsiCo's net sales, income or income per share; accordingly, no related pro forma information is provided. The pro forma information does not necessarily represent what the actual consolidated results would have been for these periods and is not intended to be indicative of future results.

	Year 7	Year 6
Net sales	$15,620.2	$13,930.9
Net income	$ 859.3	$ 649.3
Per share	$ 1.08	$ 0.82

3. Joint Venture Stock Offering

PepsiCo's Kentucky Fried Chicken joint venture in Japan (KFC-J) completed an initial public offering (IPO) to Japanese investors on August 21, Year 8. KFC-J is a joint venture whose principal shareholders are Mitsubishi Corporation and PepsiCo. The IPO consisted of 6.5 million shares of stock in KFC-J. Each principal shareholder sold 2.25 million shares and an additional 2 million new shares were sold by KFC-J. As a result of these transactions, each principal shareholder's interest declined from 48.7% to 30.5%.

PepsiCo's sale of 2.25 million shares generated pretax cash proceeds of $129.6 million. The resulting one-time gain from the IPO of $118.2 million ($53.0 after-tax or $0.07 per share) is comprised of a $94.3 million gain ($42.3 after-tax) from PepsiCo's sale of the 2.25 million shares and a $23.9 million ($10.7 after-tax) non-cash equity gain from the sale of the 2 million new shares by KFC-J.

4. Discontinued Operation Charge

The discontinued operation charge of $14.0 million ($13.7 after-tax or $0.02 per share) represents additional amounts provided in Year 8 for various pending lawsuits and claims relating to a business sold in a prior year. Substantially all of the charge is a capital loss for which PepsiCo derives no current tax benefit.

5. Inventories

Inventories are valued at the lower of cost (computed on the average, first-in, first-out or last-in, first-out methods) or net realizable value. Inventories computed on the last-in, first-out (LIFO) method comprised 54% and 56% of inventories at year-end Years 8 and 7, respectively.

	Year 8	Year 7
Raw materials, supplies and in-process	$315.4	$295.1
Finished goods...	285.3	266.5
Total (approximates current cost).......................	600.7	561.6
Excess of current cost over LIFO cost	(14.9)	(15.5)
	$585.8	$546.1

6. Property, Plant, and Equipment

Property, plant, and equipment are stated at cost. Depreciation is calculated principally on a straight-line basis over the estimated useful lives of the assets. Depreciation and amortization expense in Years 8, 7, and 6 was $686 million, $610 million, and $547 million, respectively.

	Year 8	Year 7
Land...	$ 785.4	$ 702.0
Buildings and improvements	3,173.7	2,815.6
Capital leases, primarily buildings	265.4	241.9
Machinery and equipment.....................................	4,753.2	4,058.9
	8,977.7	7,818.4
Accumulated depreciation and amortization........	(3,266.8)	(2,688.2)
	$5,710.9	$5,130.2

7. Leases

PepsiCo has noncancelable commitments under both capital and operating leases, primarily for restaurant units. Certain of these units have been subleased to restaurant franchisees. Lease commitments on capital and operating leases expire at various dates through Year 50.

Future minimum lease commitments and sublease receivables under noncancelable leases are as follows:

	Commitments		Sublease Receivables	
			Direct	
	Capital	Operating	Financing	Operating
Year 9	$ 39.2	$ 179.2	$11.5	$ 8.2
Year 10	35.1	160.9	10.9	7.8
Year 11	32.3	144.3	9.2	7.4
Year 12	30.6	130.4	9.0	6.9
Year 13	28.2	122.1	6.7	6.2
Later years.....................	175.3	582.8	22.1	29.1
	$340.7	$1,319.7	$69.4	$65.6

At year-end Year 8 the present value of minimum lease payments for capital leases was $194 million, after deducting $1 million for estimated executory costs (taxes, maintenance, and insurance) and $146 million representing imputed interest. The present value of minimum receivables under direct financing subleases was $46 million after deducting $23 million of unearned interest income.

Rental expense and income were as follows:

| | Rental | |
	Expense	Income
Year 8	$272.7	$10.5
Year 7	236.9	14.2
Year 6	219.7	13.2

Included in the above amounts were contingent rental expense of $21.4 million, $20.8 million and $16.8 million and contingent rental income of $4.9 million, $4.5 million, and $4.6 million in Year 8, Year 7, and Year 6, respectively. Contingent rentals are based on sales by restaurants in excess of levels stipulated in the lease agreements.

8. Short-Term Borrowings and Long-Term Debt

	Year 8	Year 7
Short-Term Borrowings		
Commercial paper (7.9% and 8.7% weighted average interest rate at year-end 8 and 7, respectively)	$ 3,168.8	$ 3,081.8
Current maturities of long-term debt issuances	1,085.0	316.8
Notes	624.8	594.8
Other borrowings	247.9	422.9
Amount reclassified to long-term debt (A)	$(3,500.0)	$(3,550.0)
	$ 1,626.5	$ 866.3
Long-Term Debt		
Short-term borrowings, reclassified (A)	$ 3,500.0	$ 3,550.0
Notes due Year 9 through Year 16 (7.9% weighted average interest rate at year-end 8 and 7) (B)	1,513.7	871.1
Zero coupon notes, $1.1 billion due Year 9-Year 30 (14.0% semi-annual weighted average yield to maturity at year-end 8 and 7)	348.1	308.7
Swiss franc perpetual Foreign Interest Payment bonds (C)	209.9	209.1
European Currency Units 7-5/8% and 7-3/8% notes due Year 8 and Year 10 (D)	135.2	239.3
Pound sterling 9-1/8% notes due Year 11 (D)	115.5	96.8
Swiss franc 5-1/4% bearer bonds due Year 13 (D)	104.7	86.9
Australian dollar notes due Year 8 (13.3% weighted average interest rate at year-end 7)	—	81.5
Italian lire 10-1/2% notes due Year 9 (D)	88.8	79.0
Canadian dollar 8-3/4% notes due Year 9 (B)	64.6	64.6
Capital lease obligations (See Note 7)	193.8	179.3
Other, due Year 9-Year 38 (8.9% and 9.0% weighted average interest rate at year-end 8 and 7, respectively)	410.8	327.6
	6,685.1	6,093.9
Less current maturities of long-term debt issuances	(1,085.0)	(316.8)
Total long-term debt	$ 5,600.1	$ 5,777.1

Long-term debt is carried net of any related discount or premium and un-amortized debt issuance costs. The debt agreements include various restrictions, none of which is presently significant to PepsiCo.

The annual maturities of long-term debt through Year 13, excluding capital lease obligations and the reclassified short-term borrowings, are: Year 9 $1.1 billion; Year 10 $531 million; Year 11 $474 million; Year 12 $120 million and Year 13 $134 million.

(A) At year-end Year 8 $3.5 billion of short-term borrowings were classified as long-term, reflecting PepsiCo's intent and ability to refinance these borrowings on a long-term basis, through either long-term debt issuances or rollover of existing short-term borrowings. At year-end Years 8 and 7, PepsiCo had revolving credit agreements aggregating $3.5 billion and $3.6 billion, respectively; with the current agreements covering potential borrowings through Years 12 and 13. These available credit facilities provide the ability to refinance short-term borrowings.

(B) PepsiCo has entered into interest rate swap agreements to effectively convert $679 million of fixed interest rate debt issuances to variable rate debt with a weighted average interest rate of 7.8% at year-end Year 8. The differential to be paid or received on interest rate swaps is accrued as interest rates change and is charged or credited to interest expense over the life of the agreements. Due to the frequency of interest payments and receipts, PepsiCo's credit risk related to interest rate swaps is not significant.

(C) The coupon rate of the Swiss franc 400 million perpetual Foreign Interest Payment bonds issued in Year 4 is 7-1/2% through Year 14. The interest payments are made in U.S. dollars at a fixed contractual exchange rate. The bonds have no stated maturity date. At the end of each 10-year period after the issuance of the bonds, PepsiCo and the bondholders each have the right to cause redemption of the bonds. If not redeemed, the coupon rate will be adjusted based on the prevailing yield of 10-year U.S. Treasury Securities. The principal of the bonds is denominated in Swiss francs. PepsiCo can and intends to limit the ultimate redemption amounts to the U.S. dollar proceeds at issuance, which is the basis of the carrying value in both years.

(D) PepsiCo has entered into currency exchange agreements to hedge its foreign currency exposure on these issues of non-U.S. dollar denominated debt. At year-end Year 8, the agreements effectively established U.S. dollar liabilities of $49 million with a weighted average fixed interest rate of 9.9% and $294 million with a weighted average variable interest rate of 7.5%. The carrying values of these agreements, which are based on current exchange rates, aggregated $101 million in receivables at year-end Year 8. Changes in these values resulting from exchange rate movements are offset by the changes in the carrying values of the underlying foreign currency denominated obligations, which are also based on current exchange rates.

The counterparties to PepsiCo's interest rate swaps and currency exchange agreements discussed above consist of a diversified group of financial institutions. PepsiCo is exposed to credit risk to the extent of nonperformance by these counterparties; however, PepsiCo regularly monitors its positions and the credit ratings of these counterparties and considers the risk of default to be remote.

9. Nonrecourse Obligation

In Year 5 PepsiCo entered into an agreement related to a nonrecourse obligation (the Obligation) under which it received net proceeds of $299 million. The Obligation and related interest are payable solely from future royalty payments from certain independent domestic franchisees of one of PepsiCo's restaurant chains for a period not to exceed 10 years. The Obligation carries a variable interest rate (8.4% as of December 29, Year 8) based upon a commercial paper rate. Under the terms of the agreement, principal repayments during the first five years can be readvanced; as it is PepsiCo's intent to elect this provision, the entire Obligation is considered noncurrent. Principal repayments, net of amounts readvanced, are estimated to be $244 million over the next five years.

10. Income Taxes

Provision for income taxes on income from continuing operations:

	Year 8	Year 7	Year 6
Current— Federal	$301.5	$221.7	$235.2
Foreign	126.6	89.5	52.8
State	62.3	38.0	40.6
	490.4	349.2	328.6
Deferred—Federal	66.0	95.7	37.4
Foreign	12.5	1.2	1.7
State	7.9	3.0	(2.7)
	86.4	99.9	36.4
	$576.8	$449.1	$365.0

The deferred income tax provision, which results from differences in the timing of recognition of revenue and expense for financial reporting and tax purposes, included amounts related to depreciation of property, plant, and equipment of $34.5 million, $36.3 million, and $44.0 million and amortization of intangibles of $46.0 million, $47.3 million, and $15.6 million in Years 8, 7, and 6, respectively.

U.S. and foreign income from continuing operations before income taxes is as follows:

	Year 8	Year 7	Year 6
U.S.	$ 915.5	$ 843.4	$ 773.4
Foreign	751.9	507.1	353.8
	$1,667.4	$1,350.5	$1,127.2

Consistent with the allocation of income for tax purposes, approximately 50% of the income arising from the sale of soft drink concentrates manufactured in Puerto Rico is included in Foreign in the above table. Under the terms of a Puerto

Rico tax incentive grant that was amended in Year 7 and expires in Year 24, the allocated soft drink concentrate manufacturing profits and all investment earnings in Puerto Rico were taxed at rates of approximately 7% and 4% in Years 8 and 7, respectively, with a nominal tax provided in Year 6. The 7% Puerto Rico tax is applicable through Year 24.

PepsiCo's soft drink concentrate manufacturing profits in Ireland were exempt from income tax through mid-Year 7, when a 20% tax, applicable through Year 28, became effective.

Deferred taxes were not provided on unremitted earnings of foreign subsidiaries that are intended to be indefinitely reinvested. These unremitted earnings aggregated approximately $605 million at Year 8 end, exclusive of amounts that if remitted in the future would result in little or no tax under current tax laws and the amended Puerto Rico tax incentive grant.

Reconciliation of the U.S. federal statutory tax rate to PepsiCo's effective tax rate on income from continuing operations:

	Year 8	Year 7	Year 6
U.S. federal statutory tax rate	34.0%	34.0%	34.0%
State income tax net of federal tax benefit	1.9	2.0	2.2
Earnings in jurisdictions taxed at lower rates (principally Puerto Rico and Ireland)	(3.9)	(3.9)	(3.7)
Nondeductible amortization of goodwill and other intangibles	1.6	2.0	1.4
Tax basis difference related to joint venture stock offering..	1.6	—	—
Other, net...	(0.6)	(0.8)	(1.5)
Effective tax rate...	34.6%	33.3%	32.4%

Deferred income taxes reflected in the Consolidated Balance Sheet under the caption "Deferred Income Taxes" included amounts related to timing differences of $741.9 million and $635.9 million and Safe Harbor leases of $200.9 million and $221.0 million in Years 8 and 7, respectively. Prepaid income taxes of $11.6 million in Year 8 are reflected under the Consolidated Balance Sheet caption "Prepaid expenses and other current assets." Current deferred income taxes of $8.2 million in Year 7 are reflected under the Consolidated Balance Sheet caption "Other current liabilities."

In prior years, PepsiCo invested in Safe Harbor leases (the Leases). These transactions, which do not impact the provision for income taxes, decrease income taxes payable over the initial years of the Leases and increase them over the later years. The deferred federal income taxes payable related to the Leases are based on the current U.S. federal statutory tax rate. Taxes payable related to the Leases are estimated to be $40 million over the next five years.

In December 1989 the Financial Accounting Standards Board (the FASB) amended Statement No. 96 on Accounting for Income Taxes to extend the required adoption date to 1992. As the FASB continues to review and evaluate possible amendments, including a further extension of the adoption date, PepsiCo is unable to predict the final FASB requirements and therefore cannot reasonably estimate the effects of adoption.

11. Retirement Plans

PepsiCo has noncontributory defined benefit pension plans covering substantially all full-time domestic employees as well as contributory and noncontributory defined benefit pension plans covering certain international employees. Benefits generally are based on years of service and compensation or stated amounts for each year of service. PepsiCo funds the domestic plans in amounts not less than minimum statutory funding requirements nor more than the maximum amount that can be deducted for federal income tax purposes. International plans are funded in amounts sufficient to comply with local statutory requirements. The plans' assets consist principally of equity securities, government and corporate debt securities and other fixed income obligations. Capital Stock of PepsiCo accounted for approximately 18.1% and 16.8% of the total market value of the plans' assets at the end of Years 8 and 7, respectively.

In Year 7, PepsiCo acquired Smiths Crisps Limited and Walkers Crisps Holdings Limited, two snack chips companies in the United Kingdom (the U.K. operations). The U.K. operations' employees are covered by various plans, including multi-employer plans. Pension expense and the required disclosures under SRFAS 87 were not determinable until completion in late Year 8 of a preliminary allocation of the assets of those plans, the transfer of relevant employees to separate plans and the appropriate actuarial valuations. Accordingly, the Year 8 information presented below includes both the domestic plans and the U.K. operations' plans, while the Year 7 and 6 information includes only the domestic plans.

Other international plans are not significant in the aggregate and therefore are not included in the disclosures below. None of these other international plans was significantly over or underfunded at the end of Year 8.

The net pension expense (credit) for company-sponsored plans (the Plans) included the following components:

	Year 8	Year 7	Year 6
Service cost of benefits earned	$ 48.1	32.0	$ 24.8
Interest cost on projected benefit obligations	63.3	47.1	40.0
Return on the Plans' assets			
Actual	(27.0)	(154.6)	(86.1)
Deferred gain (loss)	(55.9)	89.9	23.5
	(82.9)	(64.7)	(62.6)
Amortization of net transition gain	(19.0)	(19.0)	(19.0)
Pension expense (credit)	$ 9.5	$ (4.6)	$ (16.8)

For certain Plans accumulated benefits exceeded the assets, but the related amounts were not significant. Reconciliations of the funded status of the Plans to the prepaid pension liability included in the Consolidated Balance Sheet are as follows:

	Year 8	Year 7
Actuarial present value of benefit obligations		
Vested benefits	$ (549.9)	$ (449.0)
Nonvested benefits	(90.8)	(75.0)
Accumulated benefit obligation	(640.7)	(524.0)
Effect of projected compensation increases	(101.9)	(92.1)
Projected benefit obligation	(742.6)	(616.1)
Plan assets at fair value	985.7	869.8
Plan assets in excess of projected benefit obligation	243.1	253.7
Unrecognized prior service cost	42.4	26.2
Unrecognized net gain	(84.6)	(104.0)
Unrecognized net transition gain	(148.1)	(167.1)
Prepaid pension liability	$ 52.8	$ 8.8
Included in		
"Investments in Affiliates and Other Assets"	$ 85.3	$ 31.2
"Other Current Liabilities"	(17.0)	(14.3)
"Other Liabilities and Deferred Credits"	(15.5)	(8.1)
	$ 52.8	$ 8.8

The assumptions used in computing the information above were as follows:

	Year 8	Year 7	Year 6
Discount rate-pension expense credit	9.1%	10.1%	10.0%
Expected long-term rate of return on plan assets	10.2%	10.0%	10.0%
Discount rate-projected benefit obligation	9.5%	9.0%	10.1%
Future compensation growth rate	5.0%–7.0%	5.0%–7.0%	5.0%–7.0%

The Year 8 discount rates and rate of return represent weighted averages, reflecting the combined assumptions for domestic and the U.K. operations' plans in Year 8.

Full-time domestic employees not covered by the Plans generally are covered by multiemployer plans as part of collective-bargaining agreements. Pension expense for these multiemployer plans was not significant in the aggregate.

PepsiCo provides health care and life insurance benefits to certain retired nonunion employees, the costs of which are expensed as incurred. In December 1990, the FASB issued Statement of Financial Accounting Standards No. 106 (SFAS 106), "Employers' Accounting for Postretirement Benefits Other Than Pensions," which requires the recognition of postretirement benefit expenses on an accrual basis. PepsiCo has not yet determined the impact of accounting for these costs on an accrual basis; however, the Year 8 expense for health care claims incurred and life insurance premiums paid was $20.4 million. PepsiCo expects to implement SFAS 106 by its required adoption date in Year 11.

12. Employee Incentive Plans

In Year 7 PepsiCo established the PepsiCo SharePower Stock Option Plan. Under this plan, which was approved by the Board of Directors, all employees who meet eligibility requirements may be granted stock options. Executive officers, part-time and short-service employees principally comprise the non-eligible group. Executive officers may be granted similar benefits under the Year 5 Long-Term Incentive Plan. A stock option represents the right, exercisable in the future, to purchase one share of PepsiCo Capital Stock at the fair market value on the date of the grant. The number of options granted is based on a percentage of the employee's annual earnings. The grants may be made annually, have a term of 10 years from the grant date and generally become exercisable ratably over the five years after the grant date. SharePower options were granted to approximately 91,000 and 77,000 employees in Years 8 and 7, respectively.

The shareholder-approved Year 5 Long-Term Incentive Plan (the Plan), effective January 1, Year 6, provides long-term incentives to key employees through stock options, performance shares, stock appreciation rights (SARs) and incentive stock units (Units). The Plan authorizes up to a maximum of 54 million shares of PepsiCo Capital Stock to be purchased or paid pursuant to grants by the Compensation Committee of the Board of Directors (the Committee), which is composed of outside directors. There were 34 million and 43 million shares available for future grants at the end of Year 8 and 7, respectively. Payment of awards other than stock options is made in cash and/or PepsiCo Capital Stock as determined by the Committee.

Under the Plan, a stock option is exercisable for a specified period generally falling between 1 and 15 years from the date of grant. A performance share, equivalent to one share of PepsiCo Capital Stock, generally vests and is payable four years after the date of grant, contingent upon attainment of prescribed performance criteria. Employees may receive partial performance share awards if they become eligible for new or increased awards subsequent to a grant. A stock option is granted with each performance share. Beginning with the Year 6 award, a specific number of additional stock options are granted in lieu of a performance share. These additional stock options may be converted to a performance share at the employee's election within 60 days from the date of grant.

SARs, available to certain senior management employees holding stock options, may be granted in the year the related options become exercisable. They allow the employees to surrender an option for an amount equal to the appreciation between the option exercise price and the fair market value of PepsiCo Capital Stock on the date the SAR is exercised. SARs expire no later than the expiration date of the related options. The maximum number of stock options that can be surrendered for SARs is 30% of outstanding options that have been exercisable for more than one year. During Year 8, 147,570 SARs were granted. SARs outstanding at the end of Years 8 and 7 were 272,568 and 168,954, respectively.

Under the Plan, eligible middle management employees were granted Units, and beginning in Year 7, stock options are granted in lieu of the Units. A unit is equivalent in value to the fair market value of one share of PepsiCo Capital Stock at specified dates over a six-year vesting period from the date of grant. Units outstanding at the end of Years 8 and 7 were 585,149 and 671,902, respectively.

The combined estimated costs of performance shares, SARs and Units, expensed over the applicable vesting periods of the awards, were $13 million, $25 million and $16 million in Years 8, 7, and 6, respectively.

Award activity for Year 8 and Year 7 was as follows (in thousands):

	SharePower Plan	Long-Term Incentive Plan	
	Stock Options	Stock Options	Performance Options
Outstanding at December 31, Year 6	—	17,480	2,918
Granted	10,742	2,109	15
Exercised/Paid	—	(614)	—
Surrendered for performance shares	—	(49)	16
Surrendered for SARs	—	(29)	—
Canceled	(697)	(572)	(147)
Outstanding at December 30, Year 7	10,045	18,325	2,802
Granted	8,808	12,179	—
Exercised/Paid	(37)	(868)	(2,346)
Surrendered for performance shares	—	(1,228)	409
Surrendered for SARs	—	(44)	—
Canceled	(1,589)	(1,490)	(69)
Outstanding at December 29, Year 8	17,227	26,874	796
Exercisable at December 29, Year 8	1,840	4,139	
Option prices per share			
Exercised during Year 8	$17.58	$4.11 to $20.00	
Exercised during Year 7	—	$4.11 to $ 8.75	
Outstanding at year-end Year 8	$17.58 to $25.96	$4.11 to $26.44	

The above Long-Term Incentive Plan activity includes grants to middle management employees of 1,070,436 and 850,785 stock options in Years 8 and 7, respectively, 692,880 of which were exercisable at the end of Year 8.

13. Contingencies

PepsiCo is subject to various claims and legal contingencies. While the ultimate liability that could result from these matters cannot be determined presently, management believes such liability will not have a material adverse effect on PepsiCo's business or financial condition.

At the end of Year 8 PepsiCo was contingently liable under direct and indirect guarantees aggregating $97 million. The guarantees are primarily issued to support financial arrangements of certain restaurant and soft drink bottling franchisees and PepsiCo joint ventures. PepsiCo manages the risk associated with these guarantees by performing appropriate credit reviews in addition to retaining certain rights as a franchisor or joint venture partner.

14. Segment Data

Industry Segments		Net Sales			Operating Profits[a]			Identifiable Assets[b]		
		Year 8	Year 7	Year 6	Year 8	Year 7	Year 6	Year 8	Year 7	Year 6
Soft Drinks	Domestic	$ 5,034.5	$ 4,623.3	$ 3,667.0	$ 673.8	$ 577.6	$ 405.7			
	International	1,488.5	1,153.4	971.2	93.8	98.6	49.6			
		6,523.0	5,776.7	4,638.2	767.6	676.2	455.3	$ 6,465.2	$ 6,198.1	$ 3,994.1
Snack Foods	Domestic	3,471.5	3,211.3	2,933.3	732.3	667.8	587.0			
	International	1,582.5	1,003.7	581.0	202.1	137.4	45.2			
		5,054.0	4,215.0	3,514.3	934.4	805.2	632.2	3,892.4	3,310.0	1,608.0
Restaurants	Domestic	5,540.9	4,684.8	3,950.3	447.2	356.5	298.4			
	International	684.8	565.9	430.4	75.2	57.8	41.9			
		6,225.7	5,250.7	4,380.7	522.4	414.3	340.3	3,448.9	3,070.6	3,061.0
Total	Domestic	14,046.9	12,519.4	10,550.6	1,853.3	1,601.9	1,291.1			
	International	3,755.8	2,723.0	1,982.6	371.1	293.8	136.7			
		$ 17,802.7	$ 15,242.4	$ 12,533.2	$ 2,224.4	$ 1,895.7	$ 1,427.8	$ 13,806.5	$ 12,578.7	$ 8,663.1

Geographic Areas[a],[b]	Net Sales			Operating Profits[a]			Identifiable Assets[b]		
	Year 8	Year 7	Year 6	Year 8	Year 7	Year 6	Year 8	Year 7	Year 6
United States	$ 14,046.9	$ 12,519.4	$ 10,550.6	$ 1,853.3	$ 1,601.9	$ 1,291.1	$ 9,980.7	$ 9,593.4	$ 7,208.9
Europe	1,344.7	771.7	415.5	108.5	53.8	12.6	2,255.2	1,767.2	174.4
Canada and Mexico	1,089.2	899.0	726.3	164.2	117.1	52.5	689.5	409.5	324.4
Other	1,321.9	1,052.3	840.8	98.4	122.9	71.6	881.1	808.6	955.4
							13,806.5	12,578.7	8,663.1
Corporate Assets							3,336.9	2,548.0	2,472.2
Total	$ 17,802.7	$ 15,242.4	$ 12,533.2	2,224.4	1,895.7	1,427.8	$ 17,143.4	$ 15,126.7	$ 11,135.3
Interest and Other Corporate Expenses, Net[a]				(557.0)	(545.2)	(300.6)			
Income from Continuing Operations before Income Taxes				$ 1,667.4	$ 1,350.5	$ 1,127.2			

	Capital Spending			Depreciation and Amortization Expense		
	Year 8	Year 7	Year 6	Year 8	Year 7	Year 6
Soft Drinks	$ 334.1	$ 267.8	$ 198.4	$ 338.1	$306.3	$ 195.7
Snack Foods	381.6	257.9	172.6	232.5	189.3	156.8
Restaurants	460.6	424.6	344.2	306.5	269.9	271.3
Corporate	21.9	9.2	14.9	6.9	6.5	5.5
	$1,198.2	$ 959.5	$ 730.1	$ 884.0	$772.0	$ 629.3

Results by Restaurant Chain

	Net Sales			Operating Profits[a]		
Pizza Hut	$2,949.9	$2,453.5	$2,014.2	$ 245.9	$205.5	$ 149.7
Taco Bell	1,745.5	1,465.9	1,157.3	149.6	109.4	75.7
KFC	1,530.3	1,331.3	1,209.2	126.9	99.4	114.9
	$6,225.7	$5,250.7	$4,380.7	$ 522.4	$414.3	$ 340.3

[a]Unusual Items: Results for the years presented were affected by several unusual credits and charges, the impacts of which were a net credit of $35.2 million ($4.2 charge after-tax or $0.01 per shares) in Year 8, a net credit of $4.4 million ($1.8 after-tax) in Year 7 and a net charge of $23.9 million ($16.3 after-tax or $0.02 per share) in Year 6. The unusual items were as follows:

Soft Drinks: Year 8 included $10.5 million in charges for receivables exposures related to highly leveraged domestic retail customers. Year 7 included a $32.5 million credit resulting from a decision to retain a bottling operation in Japan previously held for sale and a $12.3 million reorganization charge to decentralize international operations. Year 6 included a $14.5 million reorganization charge to decentralize domestic operations and a $9.4 million loss resulting from the sale of a Spanish winery.

Snack Foods: Year 8 included $10.6 million in charges for receivables exposures related to highly leveraged domestic retail customers. Year 7 included a $6.6 million reorganization charge to decentralize domestic operations and a $4.3 million credit resulting from a decision to retain a domestic cookie production facility previously held for sale.

Restaurants: Year 8 included a $17.0 million domestic and a $0.6 million international charge for closures of certain under-performing restaurants as follows: $9.0 million at Pizza Hut, $4.0 million at Taco Bell and $4.6 million at KFC. Year 8 also included an $8.0 million charge to consolidate domestic Pizza Hut field operations and a $2.4 million charge to relocate international Pizza Hut headquarters. Year 7 included reorganization charges of $8.0 million at KFC and $5.5 million at Taco Bell to consolidate domestic field operations.

Corporate: Year 8 included a $118.2 million gain from an initial public stock offering by PepsiCo's KFC joint venture in Japan, an $18.0 million charge for accelerated contributions to the PepsiCo Foundation and a $15.9 million charge to reduce the carrying value of a Pizza Hut international joint venture investment.

[b]The identifiable assets at year-end Year 8 were not restated for certain previously consolidated KFC international joint ventures reported under the equity method since Year 7.

APPENDIX C
User Manual for
Financial Statement
Analysis Package

The Financial Statement Analysis Package (FSAP) performs certain analytical functions on financial statement data for a particular company and displays the resulting output in numerical and graphical formats. FSAP runs on an IBM personal computer or compatible equipment using Lotus 1-2-3 (version 2.01 or later) or on an Apple Macintosh computer using Microsoft Excel (version 2.2 or later). The IBM equipment needs 512K and the Macintosh needs 1 megabyte of memory. A printer for hard copy is desirable. The disks available with the text include the FSAP program files along with data files for the companies analyzed in the cases.

FSAP comprises three program files:

1A_FORM lets you input new company data or add to an existing data file for a company. You save the data file created by 1A_FORM under the name of the individual company. You then use the individual company data files with 1A_FSAP or 1A_GRAPH to perform the financial statement analyses.

1A_FSAP presents the following analyses for a particular company:

- Profitability and risk ratios.

- Common size balance sheets and income statements.

- Percentage changes in individual accounts in the balance sheet, income statement, and statement of cash flows, both annually and as compounded over the last five years.

1A_GRAPH presents graphs of certain financial statement data for up to three companies. Graphs available include:

- Bar graphs of net income and expenses relative to sales on both a dollar and percentage basis for individual companies.

- Line graphs of 16 financial statement ratios for up to three companies. (See the explanation for this program for a list of ratios available.)

This User Manual describes the use of the FSAP files with both Lotus 1-2-3 and Microsoft Excel.

Using FSAP Files with 1-2-3 Using FSAP Files with Excel	These two sections explain how to use the FSAP program files and menus with 1-2-3 and Excel.

Using 1A_FORM (in 1-2-3 & Excel) Using 1A_FSAP (in 1-2-3 & Excel) Using 1A_GRAPH (in 1-2-3 & Excel)	These three sections describe the features of each FSAP program file; each includes a table describing the main menu choices.

1A_FORM Data Input Form Guidelines for 1A_FORM Worksheet	These two sections show the structure for data entry into 1A_FORM and explain what you should enter on each line.

Copying FSAP Disks
1A_FSAP Output for Coke
1A_FSAP Output for PepsiCo

Using FSAP Files with 1-2-3

To run FSAP on an IBM or compatible personal computer, you need a computer with at least 512K memory and

1. MS-DOS operating system (or other operating system that works with Lotus 1-2-3).

2. A copy of Lotus 1-2-3 (version 2.01 or later).

3. The FSAP disk with data files.

If you will be using FSAP from a diskette, you should first make a copy to use and store the original in a safe place. Instructions for copying appear later in this User Manual.

Starting 1-2-3 and FSAP with a Hard-Disk Computer

If your computer has a hard disk, the operating system and 1-2-3 should be on the hard disk. You may use the FSAP files on a diskette in the A: drive or create a subdirectory for them on the hard disk. (Remember: if you will be using FSAP from a diskette, you should make a copy to use and store your original in a safe place.)

Creating a Subdirectory on a Hard Disk.

- At the C: prompt, create a new subdirectory by typing `md fsap`.

- Copy all files from the FSAP diskette to the new subdirectory by typing
`copy a:*.* c:\fsap`.

Loading the FSAP Files.

- At the C: prompt, start up 1-2-3 as you normally would by typing `123`.

- Use the /File Directory command (type `/fd`) to give location of FSAP files:

  `a:`   if you are using files on a diskette.
  `c:\fsap`   if you have stored the files in a hard-disk subdirectory called FSAP.

- Next use the /File Retrieve command (type `/fr`) to retrieve an FSAP file:
  1A_FORM   1A_FSAP   1A_GRAPH

- See instructions below for using the FSAP files in 1-2-3.

Starting 1-2-3 and FSAP with a Two-Diskette Computer

Start the computer with MS-DOS in the left-hand disk drive, then remove DOS and insert the Lotus 1-2-3 system disk in the left-hand drive (A:) and the FSAP disk with data files in the right-hand drive (B:). Next, load the FSAP files as follows:

- At the A: prompt, start up 1-2-3 as you normally would by typing `123`.

- Use the /File Directory command (type `/fd`) to give location of FSAP files:

  `b:`   for the right-hand diskette.

- Now use the /File Retrieve command (type `/fr`) to retrieve an FSAP file:
  1A_FORM   1A_FSAP   1A_GRAPH

- See instructions below for using the FSAP files in 1-2-3.

Using 1-2-3 and FSAP

The /File Retrieve command (see above) gives you a menu of files that includes 1A_FORM, 1A_FSAP, 1A_GRAPH, and company data files. Select one of these files by using the right or left arrow keys and then the Enter key, or by typing the file name and pressing the Enter key.

When you retrieve one of the three main FSAP files, you'll see a special FSAP menu rather than the regular 1-2-3 menu choices. Use these FSAP menus to carry out the specific operations for each FSAP file (later sections of this guide describe specific functions of the FSAP files).

Select menu choices	Do this just as you would in 1-2-3. Type the first letter of the menu choice or use the arrow keys to move the cursor to the desired choice and press the Enter key.
Remove the FSAP menu	To enter data or use the 1-2-3 menu, use the Exit menu choice, if available, or press the Escape key [Esc].
Return to the FSAP menu	Press Alt-m (use the Alt key as you would a shift key, holding it while you press 'm').
Get to the 1-2-3 menu	Press the Escape key [Esc] if necessary to remove the FSAP menu (you may need more than one Escape), and then press the / key for the regular 1-2-3 menu.
Cancel a menu choice	Use the Escape key [Esc].
Enter or change data in the worksheet cells	First remove any menus using the Escape key [Esc] or the Exit menu choice if available. You can then use the arrow keys to move to desired cells. Type the desired data (do not type commas or $ and % signs) and press the Enter key.
Print sections of the 1A_FSAP worksheet	Use the Print choice in the FSAP menu. Be sure that a printer is attached and turned on and that the paper is properly aligned.
Print graphs in 1A_GRAPH	Save the graph using the FSAP menu choice. This creates a .PIC file which you can print later using the PrintGraph function of Lotus 1-2-3. (If you have version 3.1 or later, refer to the manual for newer graph printing features.)
Recover from an error message	Press the Escape key [Esc]. You can then re-enter the menu system by pressing Alt-m. (A common error is the "protected cell" error which means you have tried to alter an area that is protected from user modification.)
Recover from a program malfunction	After a printer error, for example, you may have to enter a "break" to cancel the menu's automatic functions. On many computers you can do this by holding [Ctrl] and pressing [Scroll Lock]; on other computers, look for a key labelled [Break] or check the instructions for that computer. Following a break, press [Esc] to remove all the error messages. You can then return to the menu by pressing Alt-m.

For information on using each of the FSAP program files—1A_FORM, 1A_FSAP, and 1A_GRAPH—see the appropriate section below.

Using FSAP Files with Excel

To run FSAP on an Apple Macintosh computer, you will need a Macintosh with a hard-disk and at least 1 MB of memory and

1. The System Folder for the Macintosh.

2. A copy of Microsoft Excel (version 2.2 or later).

3. The FSAP Folder—all FSAP program files and data files must be in this folder.

You should have a Macintosh with a hard disk. The Excel application and the Macintosh System Folder do not leave sufficient space on a diskette for the necessary FSAP files; working with three diskettes is not practical because of the need to continually swap disks.

The FSAP Folder

You must keep all the FSAP files in the folder labeled "FSAP Folder," and the folder must have that name and must not be inside another folder. If you copy the files, copy the entire folder. If you copy the folder to a hard disk, do not put it inside another folder.

The main FSAP program files have names beginning with 1A_ and ending in .XLS. (Other files ending in .XLM, or .XLC within the Graph Folder, **must** be present for FSAP to work even though you will not use them directly.)

Data files have company names with no special endings. You must keep company files in the FSAP Folder, but you could omit them from copies you make if you need to save space.

Starting Excel and FSAP

Work on a Macintosh with Excel loaded on its hard disk. You may copy the FSAP Folder to the hard disk or work with the FSAP Folder on a diskette. If you work from a diskette, it is best to make a copy on a second disk and store the original copy in a safe place. You may get into the FSAP files in two ways:

Double-click on the Excel icon	Once the Excel application is active, use the File menu's Open choice to Open the FSAP Folder and select one of the FSAP program files. Use the files with names beginning with 1A_ and ending with .XLS: 1A_FORM.XLS 1A_FSAP.XLS 1A_GRAPH.XLS

or

Double-click on the desired Start Excel with an FSAP file by double-clicking
FSAP 1A_...XLS file on the desired file:

> 1A_FORM.XLS
> 1A_FSAP.XLS
> 1A_GRAPH.XLS

In case of error messages If you get a Macro Error or a message such as "Can't find TRANS123.XLM" when you are opening an FSAP file, the FSAP folder is probably not your "current folder." To correct this:

- Halt the macro or click OK to close the message box if necessary.

- Use the File menu to Close any Excel files that are open.

- Use File:Open to first open the FSAP Folder (which should not be inside another folder) and then open the appropriate 1A_...XLS file.

When you have successfully opened one of the 1A_...XLS files, a dialog box appears on the screen. Be patient, macro files must first be opened and hidden away.

Using Excel and FSAP

This is the main dialog box for 1A_FORM.XLS. Later sections of this manual explain the choices in this menu and for 1A_FSAP.XLS and 1A_GRAPH.XLS.

The rest of this section describes the use of the dialog box itself and basic Excel features.

Select a dialog box menu choice	Click the button beside your choice and then click the OK button. Alternatively, you can double-click on the button for the desired choice, or type the first letter of your choice and press the Return key.
Remove the dialog box	To enter data or use the regular Excel menu bar, click on the Cancel button.
Return to the dialog box	Press the appropriate option-Command key sequence. The Command key is the "pinwheel key" to the left of the space bar. (The Excel status bar at the bottom of the screen contains a reminder; if the bar is not showing you can activate it under Options:Worksheet... with Full Menus in effect):

option-Command-f   when using 1A_FORM.XLS
option-Command-a   when using 1A_FSAP.XLS
option-Command-g   when using 1A_GRAPH.XLS

Enter or change data in the worksheet cells	Cancel the dialog box if one is present. You can then use normal Excel features. Use the mouse, arrow keys, or Tab and Return to move to desired cells. Type the desired data (do not type commas or $ and % signs) and press Return or Enter. (Note: Some cells are protected or "locked" and can't be changed.)
Print sections of 1A_FSAP worksheet	The easiest method is to use the "Print selected range" choice in the FSAP dialog box. If you are familiar with Excel, you may use the normal Excel Print features.
Print 1A_GRAPH graphs	When a graph first appears, you are given dialog box choices to save and print the graph. Or you can cancel the box and use normal Excel features, including Print Preview and Page Setup.
Macro errors	Halt the Macro and use Excel's File:Open command to make sure that FSAP Folder is the "current folder." If that is OK, try quitting Excel and restarting FSAP. Be sure all files are in a folder called FSAP Folder.
Graph errors	(Such as "Can't Find .....FSAP Folder" or a graph with no data plotted.) Be sure that FSAP Folder is not stored inside another folder, and that FSAP Folder contains the Graph Folder. Restart FSAP if necessary.

When done, select the "Quit Excel" option in the dialog box for whichever FSAP file you are using. Always use Shutdown in the Special menu to eject disks before turning off a Macintosh.

Using 1A_FORM (in 1-2-3 and Excel)

Use 1A_FORM to create a new data file or change an existing data file. You save the data file created by 1A_FORM under a company name and then use it with 1A_FSAP or 1A_GRAPH. This section describes how to use the features of 1A_FORM in both the 1-2-3 and Excel versions. If you need help using menus in 1-2-3 or Excel, refer back to the appropriate section.

Create a new data file	Start 1A_FORM and then exit the FORM menu so that you can enter data into the cells of the worksheet. There are columns for six years of data with the most recent year in the last column; all cells should have a number or a zero. This User Manual includes a skeleton data input form and guidelines explaining each line on the input form.
Update an existing data file	Start the 1A_FORM program and then use the FORM menu choice to Load the appropriate data file.
	Change individual entries. Exit the FORM menu (Cancel in Excel) so that you can enter or change data in the spreadsheet cells.
	Add data for a new year. Use the Move choice in the FORM menu to move the data left one column. This removes data from the earliest year and leaves the last column blank so that you may enter a new year's data. Exit the FORM menu to enter the new year's data.
Check for mathematical accuracy	Return to the FORM menu and select Check or Verify Data Integrity. All numbers in the Financial Data Checks area should be zero indicating that data is correct mathematically (assets equal equities, and so on). N/A appears in the last column if you have moved the data.
Save the data	DO NOT USE the normal 1-2-3 or Excel Save commands! Return to the FORM menu if necessary and use the Save choice in that menu. This ensures that you assign a new name to your data file rather than accidentally replace the 1A_FORM file itself.

1A_FORM Menu Choices

1-2-3	Excel	Explanation
Load	Load existing data file.	Loads an existing data file to be updated.
Move	Move data left one column.	Moves data left one column so you can add a new year of data.
Check	Verify data integrity.	Displays data check area. All numbers should be zero for mathematical accuracy. (The last column will be N/A if data has been moved.)
Exit	(No equivalent in Excel; click the Cancel box.)	Leaves the menu so you can work on the data in the worksheet.
	Clear current data.	In Excel only, erases current data in worksheet.
Save	Save current data.	Lets you save the data under a company name.
Retrieve	Transfer to another program.	Closes existing file and lets you open another component of FSAP.
Quit	Quit Excel.	Closes existing file and quits 1-2-3 or Excel.

Using 1A_FSAP (in 1-2-3 and Excel)

Use 1A_FSAP to analyze data in an existing company data file as created by 1A_FORM. This section describes how to use the features of 1A_FSAP in both the 1-2-3 and Excel versions. If you need help using menus in 1-2-3 or Excel refer back to the appropriate section.

Use Load in the FSAP menu to select an existing company file and merge its data into the 1A_FSAP program. Once you load the data, you can use the Analyze menu to view various types of analysis of the data. The Print menu lets you print any of these analyses if your computer is attached to a printer. The analyses available in the Analysis and Print menus are organized and numbered as follows:

Cash Flow Analysis	1.1	Changes in Cash Flow
	1.2	Change in % (Interperiod % Changes)
Financial Ratio Analysis	2.1	Profitability Factors
	2.2	Risk Factors
Income Statement Analysis	3.1	As % of Sales
	3.2	Changes in % (Interperiod % Changes)
Balance Sheet Analysis	4.1	Common Size Statement
	4.2	Changes in % (Interperiod % Changes)
Profitability Analysis	5.1	Profitability Analysis ("the rack")

Additional menu choices let you erase or save the current data in the 1A_FSAP format. If you wish to analyze data from another company, use the Load choice again; this erases existing data in 1A_FSAP (but not the company data file) when the next company is loaded.

1A_FSAP Menu Choices

1-2-3	Excel	Explanation
Load	Load existing data file.	Loads data from company file into FSAP.
Analyze	Analyze current data.	Analyzes current company data. (See above for list of analysis types.)
Test	Data sensitivity test.	Lets you change data used by FSAP without affecting the data saved in the company file; you may change any data cells in this area.
Delete	Clear current data.	Erases current data from FSAP to save disk space.
Save	Save current data.	Saves 1A_FSAP worksheet with current data for later analysis. (Use Delete or Clear current data if you later want to remove data from the worksheet.)
Print	Print selected range.	Prints selected data analysis. (See above for list of analysis types.)
Retrieve	Transfer to another program.	Closes existing file and lets you open another component of FSAP.
Quit	Quit Excel.	Closes existing file and quits 1-2-3 or Excel.

Using 1A_GRAPH (in 1-2-3 and Excel)

Use 1A_GRAPH to graph various financial statement items. This section describes how to use the features of 1A_GRAPH in both the 1-2-3 and Excel versions. If you need help using menus in 1-2-3 or Excel refer back to the appropriate section.

Begin by Loading data. You can load either one, two, or three companies into 1A_GRAPH. Once you have loaded one, two, or three files, use the GRAPH menu to prepare income graphs or graphs of financial ratios. The choices are spelled out in submenus and listed below.

Saving and printing graphs in 1-2-3   Graphs appear on the full screen. Press any key to return to the worksheet; you may then choose to "Save a graph for later printing." If yes, you are asked for a name — a .PIC extension is added automatically. You can print PIC graphs later using the Lotus PrintGraph feature. (Users of newer versions of 1-2-3 can Escape the GRAPH menu and use the 1-2-3 /Print Graph command.)

Saving and printing graphs in Excel   Graphs initially appear with a dialog box which you can use to save and print the graph. You may also Cancel the box and print the graph using the regular Excel menu features including Print Preview and Page Setup. You could also use Excel to save the graph but BE SURE TO RENAME IT before you save it.

1A_GRAPH Menu Choices

1-2-3	Excel	Explanation
Load	Load company data.	Loads stored data for company 1, 2, or 3.
Inc-Graph	Inc. Stmt. Graph.	Graphs income statement for one company; gives you a choice of $ or % basis.
1-Graph	1st Group Graph.	Each lets you choose one of eight ratios (see below); displays data for all companies loaded.
2-Graph	2nd Group Graph.	
Delete	Clear data.	Erases data for one or more companies.
Save	Save file with data.	Saves the 1A_GRAPH file with data but does not save graphs; see above to save graphs (use Delete or Clear data if you later wish to remove the data).
Retrieve	Transfer to another program.	Closes existing file and lets you open another component of FSAP.
Quit	Quit Excel.	Closes existing file and quits 1-2-3 or Excel.

	1st Group Graphs		2nd Group Graphs
ROTA	Return on Total Assets	R/AAR	Sales / Average Accounts Receivable
ROE	Return on Common Equity	COGS/AI	COGS / Average Inventory
NI/R	Net Income / Revenues	R/AWC	Sales / Average Working Capital
R/ATA	Revenues / Average Total Assets	R/AFA	Sales / Average Fixed Assets
LTD/TA	Long-Term Debt / Total Assets	CFFO/CL	Cash Flow from Operations / Current Liabilities
Lev	Capital Structure Leverage	CFFO/TL	Cash Flow from Operations / Total Liabilities
PM (ROA)	Profit Margin for ROA	CR	Current Ratio (Current Assets / Current Liabilities)
GM/R	Gross Margin / Sales	TIE	Times Interest Earned

1A_FORM Data Input Form

Line No.

1.	Company Name/Tax Rate						
2.	Year (Most Recent, Last Col.)						
3.	Cash						
4.	Marketable Securities						
5.	Accts./Notes Receivable						
6.	Inventories (EOP)						
7.	Other Current Assets						
8.	Current Assets	0	0	0	0	0	0
9.	Investments						
10.	Property, Plant, and Equip.						
11.	Less: Accum. Depreciation						
12.	Other Assets						
13.	Total Assets	0	0	0	0	0	0
15.	Accts. Payable—Trade						
16.	Notes Payable—Nontrade						
17.	Current Part L-T Debt						
18.	Other Current Liab.						
19.	Current Liabilities	0	0	0	0	0	0
20.	Long-Term Debt						
21.	Deferred Tax (NCL)						
22.	Other Noncurrent Liab.						
23.	Minority Int. in Subs.						
24.	Total Liabilities	0	0	0	0	0	0
25.	Preferred Stock						
26.	Common Stock						
27.	Additional Paid-in Cap.						
28.	Retained Earnings						
29.	Cum. Translation Adj.						
30.	Treasury Stock						
31.	Shareholders' Equity	0	0	0	0	0	0
	Total Equities	0	0	0	0	0	0
34.	Sales						
35.	Other Revenue and Gains						
36.	Cost of Goods Sold						
37.	Sell. and Admin. Expense						
38.	Other Expenses and Losses						
39.	EBIT	0	0	0	0	0	0
40.	Interest Expense						
41.	Income Tax Expense						
42.	Minority Int. in Earnings						
43.	Income from Contin. Ops.						
44.	Income from Discont. Ops.						
45.	Extra. Gains (Losses)						
46.	Changes in Acct. Princ.						
47.	Preferred Stock Dividend						
48.	NI Avail. to Com.	0	0	0	0	0	0

50.	Net Income, Cont. Ops.						
51.	Depreciation and Amort.						
52.	Other Addbacks						
53.	Other Subtractions						
54.	WC Provided by Ops	0	0	0	0	0	0
55.	(Inc.) Decr. in Receivables						
56.	(Inc.) Decr. in Inventories						
57.	(Inc.) Decr. in Other CA						
58.	Inc. (Decr.) Acct. Pay.—Trade						
59.	Inc. (Decr.) in Other CL						
60.	Cash from Cont. Ops.	0	0	0	0	0	0
61.	Cash from Discont. Ops.						
62.	Cash from Extr. Gain/Loss						
63.	Net Cash Flow from Ops.	0	0	0	0	0	0
64.	Fixed Assets Sold						
65.	Investments Sold						
66.	Fixed Assets Acquired						
67.	Investments Acquired						
68.	Other Invest. Transact.						
69.	Net Cash Flow from Investing	0	0	0	0	0	0
71.	Incr. S-T Borrowing						
72.	Incr. L-T Borrowing						
73.	Issue of Cap. Stock						
74.	Decr. S-T Borrowing						
75.	Decr. L-T Borrowing						
76.	Acquisit. of Cap. Stock						
77.	Dividends						
78.	Other Financing Trans.						
79.	Net Cash Flow from Financing	0	0	0	0	0	0
81.	Net Change in Cash						

Guidelines for 1A_FORM Worksheet

Line No.

1. Company Name/Tax Rate: Put the name of the company whose data you are entering in the first available column. Enter the marginal tax rate for the five most recent years in the remaining five columns, with the most recent year in the last column.

2. Year: Enter the most recent year in the last column to the right. The worksheet should have six years of balance sheet data (for example, December 31, 1987 through 1992) and five years of income statement and statement of cash flows data (for example, for the years 1988 through 1992). Put zeros in the first column (for example, 1987) for the income statement and statement of cash flows.

3. Cash: Amount as shown on the balance sheet. Prior to the issuance of FASB *Statement No. 95*, some firms combined cash and marketable securities on the balance sheet. If the notes to the financial statement do not give sufficient information to disaggregate cash and marketable securities, enter the combined amount on line 3.

4. Marketable Securities: Amount as shown on balance sheet. (See instructions for line 3.)

5. Accounts/Notes Receivable: Include amounts receivable from customers net of allowance for uncollectible accounts.

6. Inventories: Include raw materials, work in process, finished goods, and supplies.

7. Other Current Assets: Include all current assets not included in the lines above.

9. Investments: Include investments in securities that are not part of current assets. Some firms merge this item with "other assets." If so, enter zero on "investments" line.

10. Property, Plant, and Equipment: Enter the acquisition cost, or gross amount, of this item.

11. Accumulated Depreciation: Enter as a positive amount.

12. Other Assets: Enter any remaining assets not included in one of the above asset categories.

15. Accounts Payable—Trade: Enter here the amount shown as "Accounts Payable." Exclude Notes Payable unless they are specifically labeled as "trade notes." Some firms include "other current liabilities" with accounts payable. If so, place the total on the accounts payable line.

16. Notes Payable—Nontrade: Enter short-term borrowings, such as bank loans, on this line.

17. Current Portion of Long-Term Debt: Enter the amount if this item is separately disclosed among current liabilities on the firm's balance sheet. Some firms combine notes payable and current portion of long-term debt. If so, enter the combined amount on one line or the other.

18. Other Current Liabilities: Combine all remaining current liabilities shown on the balance sheet.

20. Long-Term Debt: Include conventional long-term debt, capitalized leases, convertible bonds, and so on.

21. Deferred Taxes: Include deferred taxes shown on the balance sheet among noncurrent liabilities. Include deferred investment credits on this line if reported.

22. Other Noncurrent Liabilities: Include all other noncurrent liabilities.

23. Minority Interest in Subsidiaries: Very few large companies disclose this item separately. Enter zeros if you have no data for this.

25. Preferred Stock: Include all preferred stock at its book value.

26. Common Stock: Amount equals the par or stated value of outstanding shares.

27. Additional Paid-in Capital: As reported.

28. Retained Earnings: As reported.

29. Cumulative Translation Adjustment: As reported. Enter as a positive or negative amount as appropriate.

30. Treasury Stock: Cost of treasury shares held is entered as a positive amount.

34. Sales: Include revenues from sales of goods and services. This is generally the amount labeled as "sales" on the income statement.

35. Other Revenues and Gains: Includes equity in earnings of subsidiaries, interest revenue, and other similar revenues.

36. Cost of Goods Sold: As reported.

37. Selling and Administrative Expenses: As reported.

38. Other Expenses and Losses: Include all other expenses and losses except interest and income taxes.

40. Interest Expense: Include interest expense net of any amount capitalized. This is usually the amount shown on the income statement.

41. Income Tax Expense: Include total tax expense for the period (current, deferred, and so on).

42. Minority Interest in Earnings: As reported, if disclosed. Enter zeros if not disclosed.

43. Income from Continuing Operations: As reported.

44. Income from Discontinued Operations: As reported (watch sign).

45. Extraordinary Gains (Losses): As reported (watch sign).

46. Changes in Accounting Principles: As reported (watch sign).

47. Preferred Stock Dividend: Firms may report this item in the income statement or in a separate statement of changes in retained earnings. Enter as a positive amount.

50. Net Income from Continuing Operations: As reported on first line of statement of cash flows (SCF).

51. Depreciation and Amortization: As reported on SCF.

52. Other Addbacks: As reported in deriving working capital from operations.

53. Other Subtractions: As reported in deriving working capital from operations. Enter as a negative amount.

55. (Increase) Decrease in Receivables: Use the amount as shown in SCF rather than on the comparative balance sheet if possible. Enter debit changes in accounts receivable (increases) as negative amounts; enter credit changes (decreases) as positive amounts.

56. (Increase) Decrease in Inventories: Same as for receivables.

57. (Increase) Decrease in Other Current Assets: Same as for receivables.

58. Increase (Decrease) in Accounts Payable-Trade: Be very careful with the sign of the change. Compare the direction of the change with that shown on the comparative balance sheet if you are unsure. Enter credit changes in accounts payable as positive amounts; enter debit changes as negative amounts.

59. Increase (Decrease) in Other Current Liabilities: Exclude changes in Notes Payable—Nontrade and Current Portion of Long-Term Debt.

61. Cash from Discontinued Operations: As reported.

62. Cash from Extraordinary Gains/Losses: As reported.

64. Fixed Assets Sold: As reported, if disclosed. Enter zeros if not disclosed.

65. Investments Sold: As reported, if disclosed. Enter zeros if not disclosed.

66. Fixed Assets Acquired: As reported. Enter as a positive amount.

67. Investments Acquired: As reported. Enter as a positive amount.

68. Other Investing Transactions: The net of all other transactions classified in the "investing" section of the SCF. Prior to the adoption of FASB *Statement No. 95*, many firms used a sources and uses format rather than an operating, investing, and financing format. Thus, for earlier years, it may not be clear whether you should classify a particular item as investing or financing. You must exercise judgment in these cases. Enter the amount as positive or negative depending on its effect on cash flows.

71. Increase in Short-Term Borrowing: As reported. Prior to the adoption of FASB *Statement No. 95*, firms often included this item in the change in working capital accounts, net of any decreases in short-term borrowing. If so, enter the net amount either on line 71 (net increase) or line 74 (net decrease).

72. Increase in Long-Term Borrowing: As reported.

73. Issue of Capital Stock: As reported.

74. Decrease in Short-Term Borrowing: As reported. (See explanation for line 71.) Enter as a positive amount.

75. Decrease in Long-Term Borrowing: As reported. Enter as a positive amount.

76. Acquisition of Capital Stock: As reported. Enter as a positive amount.

77. Dividends: As reported. Enter as a positive amount.

78. Other Financing Transactions: Enter net amount as a positive or negative as appropriate. (See explanation for line 68.)

81. Net Change in Cash: Use the amount as shown on the SCF rather than on the comparative balance sheet. Enter as a positive or negative amount as appropriate.

Copying FSAP Disks

It is safest to work from a copy of the FSAP files and store your original disk in a safe place. This section describes methods for copying your diskette and FSAP files on both IBM compatible and Macintosh computers.

Copying a Diskette on IBM or Compatible Computers

To copy your entire FSAP diskette, you need a new unused diskette to copy to; this procedure formats the target disk and erases any information previously on the disk. Start the computer [on a two-diskette system, start with DOS in the left-hand drive (A:) and then remove it] and copy the FSAP diskette as follows:

On a hard-disk computer   Type `diskcopy a: a:` Follow the instructions the computer gives you. When asked to insert the source disk, insert your original FSAP diskette; when asked for the target disk, insert the new diskette you are copying to.

On a two-diskette drive computer   Put the original FSAP diskette (the source) in the left-hand (A:) drive and the new diskette you are copying to (the target) in the right-hand (B:) drive. Type `diskcopy a: b:`

Copying Files between Disks on IBM or Compatible Computers

Instead of copying the entire diskette, you can copy all of the files from one disk to another. For this purpose, use the Copy command and specify first the source and then the destination disk:

`copy a:*.* b:`   Copies all the files from disk in A: drive to disk in B: drive.

`copy a:*.* c:\fsap`   Copies all the files from disk in A: drive to subdirectory called FSAP on the hard disk.

Copying the FSAP Folder between Disks on a Macintosh Computer

To make a copy of the FSAP folder on another disk, simply drag the icon for the FSAP Folder to the second disk. The original copy is left behind on the first disk and the folder with its contents copied onto the second disk. Remember that the FSAP Folder must not be inside any other folder when you use it.

1A_FSAP Output for Coke

1.1 CFA—CHANGES IN CASH FLOW

OPERATING:	Year 4	Year 5	Year 6	Year 7	Year 8
Income from Cont. Opns.	934	916	1045	1724	1382
Depreciation and Amort.	430	152	170	184	244
Other Addbacks	279	39	72	37	98
Other Subtractions	-375	-148	-36	-1114	-261
Decr(Incr) in Rec'bles	-221	0	34	-100	-88
Decr(Incr) in Inventory	3	-81	-26	-35	-169
Decr(Incr) in Other CA	-97	48	-36	-204	-66
Inc(Decr) A&N Pay.-Trade	125	195	-36	89	199
Inc(Decr) in Other CL	231	110	-20	529	-55
CASH FROM CONT OPNS	1309	1231	1167	1110	1284
+Cash fr. Disc.& Extra.	0	0	0	0	0
TOTAL CASH FROM OPNS	1309	1231	1167	1110	1284
INVESTING:					
Fixed Assets Acquired (Sold)	206	175	344	402	574
Investments Acquired (Sold)	-950	-751	694	956	-37
Other Investing Transactions	0	0	0	0	172
CASH BEFORE DIV. AND					
EXTERNAL FINANCING	153	305	1517	1664	845
Less Dividends:	402	422	443	490	552
CASH BEFORE EXT. FIN.	-249	-117	1074	1174	293
FINANCING:					
Inc(Dec) ST Borrowing	310	988	-789	165	472
Inc(Dec) LT Borrowing	125	104	-63	-240	38
Inc(Dec) Cap. Stock	-59	-564	-431	-1126	-502
Other Financing Transactions	0	0	-29	-22	33
CHANGE IN CASH	127	411	-238	-49	334

1.2 CASH FLOW ANALYSIS - INTERPERIOD % CHANGES

OPERATING:	COMPOUND GROWTH RATE	INTERPERIOD % CHANGES			
		Year 5	Year 6	Year 7	Year 8
Income from Cont. Opns.	10.3%	-1.9%	14.1%	65.0%	-19.8%
Depreciation and Amort.	-13.2%	-64.7%	11.8%	8.2%	32.6%
Other Addbacks	-23.0%	-86.0%	84.6%	-48.6%	164.9%
Other Subtractions	-8.7%	-60.5%	-75.7%	2994.4%	-76.6%
Decr(Incr) in Rec'bles	-20.6%	-100.0%	n/a	-394.1%	-12.0%
Decr(Incr) in Inventory	n/a	-2800.0%	-67.9%	34.6%	382.9%
Decr(Incr) in Other CA	-9.2%	-149.5%	-175.0%	466.7%	-67.6%
Inc(Decr) A&N Pay.-Trade	12.3%	56.0%	-118.5%	-347.2%	123.6%
Inc(Decr) in Other CL	n/a	-52.4%	-118.2%	-2745.0%	-110.4%
CASH FROM CONT. OPNS	-0.5%	-6.0%	-5.2%	-4.9%	15.7%
+Cash fr. Disc. & Extra.	n/a	n/a	n/a	n/a	n/a
TOTAL CASH FROM OPNS	-0.5%	-6.0%	-5.2%	-4.9%	15.7%
INVESTING:					
PP&E Acquired/Sold	29.2%	-15.0%	96.6%	16.9%	42.8%
Inc(Decr) in Investments	-55.6%	-20.9%	-192.4%	37.8%	-103.9%
Other NC Opr'g Assets Acquired	n/a	n/a	n/a	n/a	n/a
CASH BEFORE DIV. AND EXTERNAL FINANCING	53.3%	99.3%	397.4%	9.7%	-49.2%
Less Dividends:	8.3%	5.0%	5.0%	10.6%	12.7%
CASH BEFORE EXT. FIN.	n/a	-53.0%	-1017.9%	9.3%	-75.0%
FINANCING:					
Inc(Dec) ST Borrowing	11.1%	218.7%	-179.9%	-120.9%	186.1%
Inc(Dec) LT Borrowing	-25.7%	-16.8%	-160.6%	281.0%	-115.8%
Inc(Dec) Capital Stock	70.8%	855.9%	-23.6%	161.3%	-55.4%
CHANGE IN CASH	27.3%	223.6%	-157.9%	-79.4%	-781.6%

2.1 PROFITABILITY FACTORS

	Year 4	Year 5	Year 6	Year 7	Year 8
RETURN ON ASSETS:					
Profit Margin	11.9%	14.1%	14.4%	21.5%	15.0%
x Asset Turnover	1.1	0.9	1.1	1.1	1.2
= Return On Assets	13.5%	13.0%	15.2%	24.5%	17.5%
RETURN ON COMMON EQUITY:					
Return On Assets	13.5%	13.0%	15.2%	24.5%	17.5%
x Common Earnings Leverage	90.3%	84.5%	86.8%	88.3%	88.9%
x Capital Structure Leverage	2.4	2.5	2.5	2.5	2.5
= Return On Com. Equity	28.8%	27.2%	33.1%	54.6%	39.2%
OPERATING PERFORMANCE:					
Gross Margin/Sales	46.4%	52.6%	55.6%	56.6%	58.9%
Oper. Profit Before Tax/Rev.	18.4%	21.1%	21.2%	22.3%	21.3%
Net Income-Cont. Ops./Revenues	10.1%	11.4%	12.2%	18.5%	13.1%
ASSET TURNOVER:					
Sales/Aver. Accts Rec.	8.8	8.7	11.5	11.2	11.5
COGS/Average Inventory	5.0	4.2	4.8	5.0	4.8
Sales/Aver. Fixed Assets	4.8	4.6	5.0	4.7	4.6

2.2 RISK FACTORS

	Year 4	Year 5	Year 6	Year 7	Year 8
LIQUIDITY:					
Current	1.36	1.00	1.13	0.99	0.96
Quick Ratio	0.71	0.52	0.70	0.55	0.57
Days Payables Held	96	145	124	115	123
Days Receivable Held	42	42	32	33	32
Days Inventory Held	73	86	77	74	77
Operating Cash Flow to Current Liabilities	55.0%	35.8%	33.4%	34.0%	32.3%
SOLVENCY:					
Total Liabilities/Total Assets	58.0%	61.4%	55.1%	57.9%	58.5%
LT Debt/Total Assets	16.3%	9.6%	10.2%	6.6%	5.8%
LT Debt/Owner's Equity	38.8%	24.9%	22.8%	15.7%	13.9%
Operating Cash Flow to Total Liabilities	29.8%	24.6%	25.3%	24.9%	25.1%
Interest Coverage Ratio	9.12	6.05	7.85	6.73	9.76
Operating Cash Flow to Cap. Exp.	3.51	4.10	3.02	2.40	2.17

3.1 INCOME STATEMENT ITEMS AS % OF SALES

	Year 4	Year 5	Year 6	Year 7	Year 8
Sales	100.0%	100.0%	100.0%	100.0%	100.0%
Cost of Goods Sold	-53.6%	-47.4%	-44.4%	-43.4%	-41.1%
GROSS MARGIN	46.4%	52.6%	55.6%	56.6%	58.9%
Other Revenue	6.4%	4.8%	2.6%	3.9%	2.9%
Sell., Gen'l., & Admin. Exp.	-31.1%	-34.8%	-36.4%	-37.3%	-39.8%
Other Expenses & Losses	-2.1%	-0.5%	0.0%	0.0%	0.0%
Income Tax Expense on Oper.	-7.6%	-7.9%	-7.4%	-7.5%	-6.9%
OPERATING MARGIN	11.9%	14.1%	14.4%	15.6%	15.0%
Interest Expense	-2.1%	-3.6%	-2.8%	-3.4%	-2.2%
Income Tax Savings on Interest	1.0%	1.5%	0.9%	1.2%	0.8%
Minor. Int. in Earnings	0.0%	0.0%	0.0%	0.0%	0.0%
INCOME--CONTIN. OPS	10.8%	12.0%	12.5%	13.3%	13.5%
Income From Discont. Ops	0.0%	0.0%	0.0%	5.9%	0.0%
Extra. Gains & Losses	0.0%	0.0%	0.0%	0.0%	0.0%
Changes in Acct. Princ.	0.0%	0.0%	0.0%	0.0%	0.0%
NET INCOME	10.8%	12.0%	12.5%	19.2%	13.5%
Preferred Stock Dividend	0.0%	0.0%	0.1%	0.2%	0.2%
NET INCOME AVAILABLE TO					
COMMON SHAREHOLDERS	10.8%	12.0%	12.5%	19.0%	13.3%

3.2 INCOME STATEMENT ITEMS--INTERPERIOD % CHANGES

	COMPOUND GROWTH RATE	INTERPERIOD % CHANGES			
		Year 5	Year 6	Year 7	Year 8
Sales	4.2%	-11.6%	8.9%	7.5%	14.2%
Cost of Goods Sold	-2.4%	-21.8%	1.9%	5.2%	8.1%
GROSS MARGIN	10.6%	0.0%	15.2%	9.4%	18.8%
Selling & Admin Expense	10.9%	-1.3%	14.0%	10.2%	21.7%
Income Tax Exp on Oper	1.8%	-8.6%	1.6%	9.9%	5.1%
OPERATING MARGIN	10.3%	4.7%	10.5%	16.6%	9.8%
Interest Expense	5.5%	50.0%	-17.2%	33.3%	-25.3%
Inc Tax Savings on Int	28.1%	30.4%	-29.6%	33.3%	-25.3%
Minor. Int. in Earnings	n/a	n/a	n/a	n/a	n/a
INCOME—CONTIN. OPS	10.3%	-1.9%	14.1%	14.2%	15.8%
Income From Discont. Ops	n/a	n/a	n/a	n/a	-100.0%
Extra. Gains & Losses	n/a	n/a	n/a	n/a	n/a
Changes in Acct. Princ.	n/a	n/a	n/a	n/a	n/a
NET INCOME	10.3%	-1.9%	14.1%	65.0%	-19.8%
Preferred Stock Dividend	n/a	n/a	n/a	266.7%	-18.2%
NET INCOME AVAILABLE TO					
COMMON SHAREHOLDERS	9.9%	-1.9%	13.4%	63.8%	-19.9%

4.1 BALANCE SHEET COMMON SIZE STATEMENT

	Year 4	Year 5	Year 6	Year 7	Year 8
ASSETS:					
Cash and Mkt. Securities	10.6%	17.6%	16.5%	14.3%	16.1%
Accts/Notes Receivable	12.9%	8.0%	10.5%	9.9%	10.3%
Inventories	11.1%	9.3%	10.5%	9.5%	10.6%
Other Current Assets	10.0%	14.6%	6.1%	9.8%	7.7%
CURRENT ASSETS	44.7%	49.5%	43.6%	43.5%	44.7%
Investments	26.4%	30.5%	32.1%	29.3%	26.7%
Property, Plant, & Equip.	33.3%	31.6%	39.0%	39.8%	40.8%
Less Accum. Depreciation	12.3%	12.5%	15.4%	15.4%	15.1%
Other Assets	7.9%	0.9%	0.8%	2.8%	3.0%
TOTAL ASSETS	100.0%	100.0%	100.0%	100.0%	100.0%
LIABILITIES:					
Accts. Payable-Trade	15.9%	17.1%	14.5%	16.7%	17.0%
Notes Payable—Nontrade	8.7%	22.7%	18.3%	17.3%	20.5%
Current Part LT Debt	0.0%	0.0%	0.0%	0.0%	1.0%
Other Current Liabilities	8.3%	9.4%	5.7%	10.1%	7.7%
CURRENT LIABILITIES	32.9%	49.3%	38.5%	44.2%	46.3%
Long-Term Debt	16.3%	9.6%	10.2%	6.6%	5.8%
Deferred Tax (NCL)	4.6%	2.5%	3.6%	3.6%	2.9%
Other NCL	4.3%	0.0%	2.8%	3.5%	3.6%
Minority Int. in Subs.	0.0%	0.0%	0.0%	0.0%	0.0%
NONCURRENT LIAB.	25.1%	12.1%	16.6%	13.8%	12.2%
TOTAL LIABILITIES	58.0%	61.4%	55.1%	57.9%	58.5%
STOCKHOLDERS' EQUITY:					
Preferred Stock	0.0%	0.0%	4.0%	3.6%	0.8%
Common Stock	5.0%	5.0%	5.6%	5.1%	4.5%
Additional Paid-in Cap.	3.6%	4.1%	4.4%	4.7%	4.8%
Retained Earnings	43.3%	45.3%	58.9%	67.8%	69.5%
Treasury Stock	8.4%	15.7%	27.8%	39.1%	38.2%
Cum. Translation Adj.	-1.4%	-0.1%	-0.2%	-0.1%	0.0%
STOCKHOLDERS' EQUITY	42.0%	38.6%	44.9%	42.1%	41.5%
TOTAL EQUITY & LIAB.	100.0%	100.0%	100.0%	100.0%	100.0%

4.2 BALANCE SHEET—INTERPERIOD % CHANGES

	COMPOUND GROWTH RATE	Year 4	Year 5	INTERPERIOD % CHANGES Year 6	Year 7	Year 8
ASSETS:						
Cash and Mkt Securities	11.5%	2.7%	65.3%	-16.1%	-4.0%	26.3%
Accts/Notes Receivable	1.2%	20.5%	-37.8%	16.7%	4.7%	16.0%
Inventories	1.5%	2.2%	-16.7%	0.3%	1.3%	24.5%
Other Current Assets	19.4%	183.7%	45.6%	-63.0%	80.0%	-11.8%
CURRENT ASSETS	6.9%	25.9%	10.6%	-21.5%	11.1%	15.0%
Investments	12.5%	61.3%	15.2%	-6.2%	1.5%	2.0%
Property, Plant, & Equip.	4.7%	-7.3%	-5.4%	10.2%	13.3%	14.9%
Less Accum. Depreciation	4.4%	-9.0%	1.6%	10.4%	10.8%	9.9%
Other Assets	-16.4%	-2.1%	-88.8%	-23.0%	307.0%	18.5%
TOTAL ASSETS	6.1%	21.4%	-0.2%	-10.8%	11.2%	12.0%
LIABILITIES:						
Accts./Notes Pay.-Trade	7.3%	20.2%	7.3%	-24.4%	28.3%	13.6%
Notes Payable:Nontrade	34.9%	70.2%	161.9%	-28.2%	5.1%	33.0%
Current Part LT Debt	n/a	n/a	n/a	n/a	n/a	n/a
Other Current Liabil.	8.9%	48.6%	13.2%	-46.1%	97.4%	-14.3%
CURRENT LIAB.	16.5%	37.5%	49.5%	-30.3%	27.5%	17.4%
Long-Term Debt	-14.3%	17.7%	-41.2%	-5.2%	-27.9%	-2.4%
Deferred Tax (NCL)	-3.8%	18.7%	-44.9%	28.6%	9.6%	-10.5%
Other NCL	-5.2%	-17.7%	-100.0%	n/a	42.7%	12.9%
Minority Int. in Subs.	n/a	n/a	n/a	n/a	n/a	n/a
NONCURRENT LIAB.	-10.0%	9.8%	-51.8%	22.1%	-7.9%	-0.5%
TOTAL LIABILITIES	6.7%	24.0%	5.6%	-20.0%	16.8%	13.2%
STOCKHOLDERS' EQUITY:						
Preferred Stock	n/a	n/a	n/a	n/a	0.0%	-75.0%
Common Stock	43.5%	501.4%	0.2%	0.2%	0.5%	0.2%
Additional Paid-in Cap.	-5.9%	-50.4%	13.4%	-2.9%	19.1%	13.5%
Retained Earnings	15.8%	17.2%	4.4%	15.9%	28.1%	14.8%
Treasury Stock	42.5%	16.7%	85.7%	58.1%	56.4%	9.5%
Cum. Translation Adj.	n/a	-34.8%	-95.8%	240.0%	-58.8%	-157.1%
STOCKHOLDERS' EQUITY	5.3%	18.0%	-8.3%	3.7%	4.2%	10.4%
TOTAL EQUITY & LIAB.	6.1%	21.4%	-0.2%	-10.8%	11.2%	12.0%

5.1 PROFITABILITY ANALYSIS

	Return on Assets		
Level 1	Year 6	Year 7	Year 8
	15.2%	24.5%	17.5%

	Profit Margin				Asset Turnover		
Level 2	Year 6	Year 7	Year 8		Year 6	Year 7	Year 8
	14.4%	21.5%	15.0%		1.1	1.1	1.2

Level 3	Year 6	Year 7	Year 8		Year 6	Year 7	Year 8
Sales	100.0%	100.0%	100.0%	Receivable			
COG Sold	(44.4)	(43.4)	(41.1)	Turnover	11.5	11.2	11.5
Sell & Ad	(36.4)	(37.3)	(39.8)	Inventory			
Other (net)	2.6	3.9	2.9	Turnover	4.8	5.0	4.8
Inc. Taxes	(7.4)	(7.5)	(6.9)	Fixed Asset			
Oper. Inc.	14.4%	15.6%	15.0%	Turnover	5.0	4.7	4.6

1A_FSAP Output for Pepsico

1.1 CFA—CHANGES IN CASH FLOW

OPERATING:	Year 4	Year 5	Year 6	Year 7	Year 8
Income from Cont. Opns.	458	605	762	901	1091
Depreciation and Amort.	401	563	629	772	884
Other Addbacks	138	180	233	200	226
Other Subtractions	0	0	0	0	-118
Decr(Incr) in Rec'bles	-49	-60	-50	-150	-125
Decr(Incr) in Inventory	24	2	14	-50	-21
Decr(Incr) in Other CA	28	44	38	7	-62
Inc(Decr) A&N Pay.-Trade	126	-97	138	135	26
Inc(Decr) in Other CL	105	142	130	71	209
CASH FROM CONT OPNS	1231	1379	1894	1886	2110
+Cash fr. Disc. & Extra.	0	0	0	0	0
TOTAL CASH FROM OPNS	1231	1379	1894	1886	2110
INVESTING:					
Fixed Assets Acquired (Sold)	840	673	659	874	1135
Investments Acquired (Sold)	-1275	-611	-1334	-3284	-682
Other Investing Transactions	-1	-124	-58	-98	-120
CASH BEFORE DIV. AND					
EXTERNAL FINANCING	-885	-29	-157	-2370	173
Less Dividends:	163	175	199	242	294
CASH BEFORE EXT. FIN.	-1048	-204	-356	-2612	-121
FINANCING:					
Inc(Decr) ST Borrowing	1211	413	231	2925	-86
Inc(Decr) LT Borrowing	-78	-140	285	-334	479
Inc(Decr) Cap. Stock	-75	0	-69	0	-148
Other Financing Transactions	-1	-24	-28	-46	-29
CHANGE IN CASH	9	45	63	-67	95

1.2 CASH FLOW ANALYSIS - INTERPERIOD % CHANGES

	COMPOUND	INTERPERIOD % CHANGES			
OPERATING:	GROWTH RATE	Year 5	Year 6	Year 7	Year 8
Income from Cont. Opns.	24.2%	32.1%	26.0%	18.2%	21.1%
Depreciation and Amort.	21.9%	40.4%	11.7%	22.7%	14.5%
Other Addbacks	13.1%	30.4%	29.4%	-14.2%	13.0%
Other Subtractions	n/a	n/a	n/a	n/a	n/a
Decr(Incr) in Rec'bles	26.4%	22.4%	-16.7%	200.0%	-16.7%
Decr(Incr) in Inventory	n/a	-91.7%	600.0%	-457.1%	-58.0%
Decr(Incr) in Other CA	n/a	57.1%	-13.6%	-81.6%	-985.7%
Inc(Decr) A&N Pay.-Trade	-32.6%	-177.0%	-242.3%	-2.2%	-80.7%
Inc(Decr) in Other CL	18.8%	35.2%	-8.5%	-45.4%	194.4%
CASH FROM CONT. OPNS	14.4%	12.0%	37.3%	-0.4%	11.9%
+Cash fr. Disc. & Extra.	n/a	n/a	n/a	n/a	n/a
TOTAL CASH FROM OPNS	14.4%	12.0%	37.3%	-0.4%	11.9%
INVESTING:					
PP&E Acquired/Sold	7.8%	-19.9%	-2.1%	32.6%	29.9%
Inc(Decr) in Investments	-14.5%	-52.1%	118.3%	146.2%	-79.2%
Other NC Opr'g Assets					
Acquired	231.0%	12300.0%	-53.2%	69.0%	22.4%
CASH BEFORE DIV. AND					
EXTERNAL FINANCING	n/a	-96.7%	441.4%	1409.6%	-107.3%
Less Dividends:	15.9%	7.4%	13.7%	21.6%	21.5%
CASH BEFORE EXT. FIN.	-41.7%	-80.5%	74.5%	633.7%	-95.4%
FINANCING:					
Inc(Decr) ST Borrowing	n/a	-65.9%	-44.1%	1166.2%	-102.9%
Inc(Decr) LT Borrowing	n/a	79.5%	-303.6%	-217.2%	-243.4%
Inc(Decr) Capital Stock	18.5%	-100.0%	n/a	-100.0%	n/a
CHANGE IN CASH	80.2%	400.0%	40.0%	-206.3%	-241.8%

2.1 PROFITABILITY FACTORS

	Year 4	Year 5	Year 6	Year 7	Year 8
RETURN ON ASSETS:					
Profit Margin	6.5%	6.7%	7.6%	8.6%	8.6%
x Asset Turnover	1.3	1.3	1.3	1.2	1.1
= Return On Assets	8.7%	9.1%	9.8%	9.9%	9.5%
RETURN ON COMMON EQUITY:					
Return On Assets	8.7%	9.1%	9.8%	9.9%	9.5%
x Common Earnings Leverage	76.4%	77.0%	77.0%	69.1%	70.3%
x Capital Structure Leverage	3.6	3.7	3.6	3.7	3.7
= Return On Com. Equity	23.6%	26.1%	26.9%	25.6%	24.5%
OPERATING PERFORMANCE:					
Gross Margin/Sales	59.8%	61.2%	51.9%	51.0%	51.6%
Oper. Profit before Tax/Rev.	10.0%	10.8%	11.3%	12.7%	13.1%
Net Income-Cont. Ops./Revenues	4.9%	5.2%	5.8%	5.8%	6.1%
ASSET TURNOVER:					
Sales/Aver. Accts. Rec.	12.6	13.5	13.9	13.7	13.4
COGS/Average Inventory	9.2	10.3	14.3	15.1	15.2
Sales/Aver. Fixed Assets	2.9	2.9	3.0	3.2	3.3

2.2 RISK FACTORS

	Year 4	Year 5	Year 6	Year 7	Year 8
LIQUIDITY:					
Current	1.13	1.08	0.84	0.96	0.86
Quick Ratio	0.78	0.82	0.67	0.75	0.68
Days Payables Held	71	65	47	47	46
Days Receivable Held	29	27	26	27	27
Days Inventory Held	40	35	26	24	24
Operating Cash Flow to Current Liabilities	60.7%	55.8%	57.4%	49.9%	49.9%
SOLVENCY:					
Total Liabilities/Total Assets	74.4%	72.2%	71.6%	74.3%	71.4%
LT Debt/Total Assets	32.8%	28.6%	23.9%	40.2%	32.7%
LT Debt/Owner's Equity	127.9%	102.8%	84.0%	156.2%	114.2%
Operating Cash Flow to Total Liabilities	24.6%	22.1%	26.1%	19.6%	18.0%
Interest Coverage Ratio	3.59	4.23	4.30	3.21	3.42
Operating Cash Flow to Cap. Exp.	1.39	1.78	2.61	2.00	1.79

3.1 INCOME STATEMENT ITEMS AS % OF SALES

	Year 4	Year 5	Year 6	Year 7	Year 8
Sales	100.0%	100.0%	100.0%	100.0%	100.0%
Cost of Goods Sold	-40.2%	-38.8%	-48.1%	-49.0%	-48.4%
GROSS MARGIN	59.8%	61.2%	51.9%	51.0%	51.6%
Other Revenue	1.3%	1.0%	0.9%	1.2%	1.0%
Sell., Gen'l., & Admin. Exp.	-51.0%	-51.2%	-41.4%	-39.3%	-39.0%
Other Expenses & Losses	0.0%	0.0%	0.0%	0.0%	-0.4%
Income Tax Expense on Oper.	-3.7%	-4.1%	-3.8%	-4.3%	-4.6%
OPERATING MARGIN	6.5%	6.8%	7.6%	8.6%	8.7%
Interest Expense	-2.8%	-2.6%	-2.7%	-4.0%	-3.9%
Income Tax Savings on Interest	1.3%	1.0%	0.9%	1.4%	1.3%
Minor. Int. in Earnings	0.0%	0.0%	0.0%	0.0%	0.0%
INCOME--CONTIN. OPS	4.9%	5.3%	5.9%	5.9%	6.1%
Income From Discont. Ops	0.0%	-0.1%	0.0%	0.0%	-0.1%
Extra. Gains & Losses	0.0%	0.0%	0.0%	0.0%	0.0%
Changes in Acct. Princ.	0.0%	0.0%	0.0%	0.0%	0.0%
NET INCOME	4.9%	5.2%	5.9%	5.9%	6.0%
Preferred Stock Dividend	0.0%	0.0%	0.0%	0.0%	0.0%
NET INCOME AVAILABLE TO COMMON SHAREHOLDERS	4.9%	5.2%	5.9%	5.9%	6.0%

3.2 INCOME STATEMENT ITEMS—INTERPERIOD % CHANGES

	GROWTH RATE	Year 5	Year 6	Year 7	Year 8
Sales	17.7%	23.6%	13.3%	17.2%	16.8%
Cost of Goods Sold	23.2%	19.5%	40.3%	19.4%	15.3%
GROSS MARGIN	13.4%	26.4%	-3.9%	15.2%	18.2%
Selling & Admin Expense	10.0%	24.2%	-8.4%	11.1%	16.0%
Income Tax Exp on Oper	24.0%	38.1%	3.9%	33.3%	23.6%
OPERATING MARGIN	26.6%	30.3%	26.4%	31.7%	18.6%
Interest Expense	27.2%	12.9%	16.2%	76.8%	13.0%
Inc Tax Savings on Int	54.5%	-1.8%	-1.3%	76.8%	13.0%
Minor. Int. in Earnings	n/a	n/a	n/a	n/a	n/a
INCOME—CONTIN. OPS	24.2%	31.8%	26.0%	18.2%	21.1%
Income From Discont. Ops	n/a	n/a	-100.0%	n/a	n/a
Extra. Gains & Losses	n/a	n/a	n/a	n/a	n/a
Changes in Acct. Princ.	n/a	n/a	n/a	n/a	n/a
NET INCOME	23.8%	29.6%	28.1%	18.2%	19.5%
Preferred Stock Dividend	n/a	n/a	n/a	n/a	n/a
NET INCOME AVAILABLE TO COMMON SHAREHOLDERS	23.8%	29.6%	28.1%	18.2%	19.5%

4.1 BALANCE SHEET COMMON SIZE STATEMENT

ASSETS:	Year 4	Year 5	Year 6	Year 7	Year 8
Cash and Mkt. Securities	11.5%	15.0%	14.5%	10.1%	10.6%
Accts/Notes Receivable	10.2%	9.8%	8.8%	8.2%	8.3%
Inventories	5.4%	4.8%	4.0%	3.6%	3.4%
Other Current Assets	4.1%	3.0%	2.0%	1.5%	1.5%
CURRENT ASSETS	31.2%	32.6%	29.3%	23.5%	23.8%
Investments	5.0%	6.4%	7.4%	6.4%	8.8%
Property, Plant, & Equip.	67.1%	66.5%	59.8%	51.7%	52.4%
Less Accum. Depreciation	19.3%	20.9%	19.7%	17.8%	19.1%
Other Assets	16.0%	15.3%	23.2%	36.2%	34.1%
TOTAL ASSETS	100.0%	100.0%	100.0%	100.0%	100.0%
LIABILITIES:					
Accts. Payable-Trade	10.7%	8.0%	7.9%	7.0%	6.5%
Notes Payable—Nontrade	2.9%	7.2%	13.0%	5.7%	9.5%
Current Part LT Debt	0.0%	0.0%	0.0%	0.0%	0.0%
Other Current Liabilities	14.1%	15.0%	13.8%	11.7%	11.8%
CURRENT LIABILITIES	27.7%	30.2%	34.8%	24.4%	27.8%
Long-Term Debt	32.8%	28.6%	23.9%	40.2%	32.7%
Deferred Tax (NCL)	9.7%	8.9%	7.2%	5.7%	5.5%
Other NCL	4.2%	4.5%	5.8%	4.0%	3.7%
Minority Int. in Subs.	0.0%	0.0%	0.0%	0.0%	1.7%
NONCURRENT LIAB.	46.7%	42.0%	36.8%	49.9%	43.6%
TOTAL LIABILITIES	74.4%	72.2%	71.6%	74.3%	71.4%
STOCKHOLDERS' EQUITY:					
Preferred Stock	0.0%	0.0%	0.0%	0.0%	0.0%
Common Stock	0.1%	0.1%	0.0%	0.0%	0.1%
Additional Paid-in Cap.	3.6%	3.2%	2.8%	2.2%	2.1%
Retained Earnings	29.3%	30.8%	29.9%	26.3%	27.7%
Treasury Stock	6.8%	6.1%	4.6%	3.3%	3.6%
Cum. Translation Adj.	-0.5%	-0.1%	0.2%	0.4%	2.2%
STOCKHOLDERS' EQUITY	25.6%	27.8%	28.4%	25.7%	28.6%
TOTAL EQUITY & LIAB.	100.0%	100.0%	100.0%	100.0%	100.0%

4.2 BALANCE SHEET—INTERPERIOD % CHANGES

	COMPOUND GROWTH RATE	Year 4	Year 5	INTERPERIOD % CHANGES Year 6	Year 7	Year 8
ASSETS:						
Cash and Mkt Securities	14.7%	0.9%	46.9%	19.6%	-5.2%	18.4%
Accts/Notes Receivable	16.9%	26.3%	8.0%	10.5%	26.7%	14.1%
Inventories	9.0%	13.4%	0.5%	2.3%	23.3%	7.3%
Other Current Assets	-20.8%	-61.1%	-19.3%	-16.0%	2.7%	14.7%
CURRENT ASSETS	7.9%	-10.4%	17.4%	11.1%	8.8%	15.0%
Investments	45.4%	72.4%	45.3%	42.2%	17.6%	55.1%
Property, Plant, & Equip.	18.6%	40.9%	11.4%	10.9%	17.4%	14.8%
Less Accum. Depreciation	21.1%	23.7%	21.6%	16.6%	22.4%	21.5%
Other Assets	86.1%	390.5%	7.7%	86.6%	112.0%	6.8%
TOTAL ASSETS	23.9%	37.0%	12.4%	23.4%	35.9%	13.3%
LIABILITIES:						
Accts./Notes Pay.-Trade	12.4%	38.1%	-15.6%	21.5%	19.8%	5.8%
Notes Payable:Nontrade	36.4%	-32.3%	177.3%	124.6%	-40.3%	87.9%
Current Part LT Debt	n/a	n/a	n/a	n/a	n/a	n/a
Other Current Liab.	18.4%	30.0%	19.5%	14.0%	14.9%	14.5%
CURRENT LIAB.	21.0%	21.1%	22.5%	42.2%	-4.7%	29.2%
Long-Term Debt	37.0%	126.6%	-2.1%	3.0%	128.8%	-7.8%
Deferred Tax (NCL)	3.0%	-4.4%	3.5%	-0.5%	7.0%	10.0%
Other NCL	24.3%	59.2%	21.4%	57.8%	-5.3%	2.6%
Minority Int. in Subs.	n/a	n/a	n/a	n/a	n/a	n/a
NONCURRENT LIAB.	27.8%	71.3%	1.2%	8.1%	84.0%	-1.0%
TOTAL LIABILITIES	24.9%	48.4%	9.1%	22.4%	40.9%	8.9%
STOCKHOLDERS' EQUITY:						
Preferred Stock	n/a	n/a	n/a	n/a	n/a	n/a
Common Stock	22.9%	0.0%	0.0%	0.0%	0.0%	180.0%
Additional Paid-in Cap.	5.3%	1.8%	1.0%	7.6%	7.1%	9.3%
Retained Earnings	18.2%	14.3%	17.9%	19.9%	19.5%	19.5%
Treasury Stock	5.4%	16.8%	0.9%	-7.9%	-3.5%	24.2%
Cum. Translation Adj.	n/a	-2.4%	-75.0%	-340.0%	175.0%	480.3%
STOCKHOLDERS' EQUITY	21.7%	12.0%	21.8%	26.0%	23.1%	26.0%
TOTAL EQUITY & LIAB.	23.9%	37.0%	12.4%	23.4%	35.9%	13.3%

5.1 PROFITABILITY ANALYSIS

		Return on Assets		
Level 1		**Year 6**	**Year 7**	**Year 8**
		9.8%	9.9%	9.5%

	Profit Margin					Asset Turnover		
Level 2	**Year 6**	**Year 7**	**Year 8**			**Year 6**	**Year 7**	**Year 8**
	7.6%	8.6%	8.6%			1.3	1.2	1.1

Level 3	**Year 6**	**Year 7**	**Year 8**			**Year 6**	**Year 7**	**Year 8**
Sales	100.0%	100.0%	100.0%	Receivable				
COG Sold	(48.1)	(49.0)	(48.4)	Turnover		13.9	13.7	13.4
Sell & Ad	(41.4)	(39.3)	(39.0)	Inventory				
Other (net)	0.9	1.2	0.6	Turnover		14.3	15.1	15.2
Inc. Taxes	(3.8)	(4.3)	(4.6)	Fixed Asset				
Oper. Inc.	7.6%	8.6%	8.7%	Turnover		3.0	3.2	3.3

Index